Commodore

War, Peace, and Big Ships

By

Sir James Bisset

The 3rd Book of the Sail Ho! Trilogy

K.B., C.B.E., R.D., R.N.R., LL.D. (Cantab.)

Commander of the Legion of Merit (U.S.A.) Commodore (retd) of the Cunard White Star Line Wartime Captain of *Queen Mary* and *Queen Elizabeth*

Second Edition edited by
Kyle Vernon

Other books by Kyle Vernon

Digby the Church Mouse: Saving Home

A Davis Mountains Ghost Story

Edited by Kyle Vernon

Sail Ho! 2nd Edition by Sir James Bisset

Tramps and Ladies 2nd Edition by Sir James Bisset

In some cases wording was altered to align with cultural norms and/or spelling conventions, however, some spelling, particularly in speech mannerisms and accent simulation, was not altered to preserve the integrity and feel of the text. In the original text hyphens were used frequently for compound adjectives, but with this redrafted edition many of those were either compounded, separated, or converted to commas. A few sensitive racial references in the series that were used during the time have also been altered. Due to size of this printing Imperial Units were not converted.

By Kyle Vernon

Some stories are just too good to be allowed to fade away. This is one of those stories.

By the time Sir James Bisset sat down to pen his trilogy of memoirs, chronicling a lifetime at sea and a career unlike any other, the world was turning its attention elsewhere. The 1950s and early 1960s, when his books were released, were years of breathtaking technological progress, as the space race ignited imaginations, jet engines shrank the globe, and the shadow of the Cold War loomed over everything. Against this backdrop, the harrowing tales of the Second World War and the quieter days of seafaring in its aftermath began to fade in the public's consciousness. It was a time of looking forward, not backward.

This context is essential in understanding why Bisset's trilogy, Sail *Ho!*, *Tramps and Ladies*, and this final volume, *Commodore: War, Peace, and Big Ships*—did not initially receive the attention it so richly deserved. In particular, the Australian market, where memoirs often struggled to find their footing amid other literary trends, proved an uphill battle for Bisset's work. Sir James was in the right place at the right time to live one of the most extraordinary careers in maritime history, but when it came to writing about it, his timing was less fortunate.

And yet, in revisiting these volumes today, one finds something timeless: the extraordinary tale of a man who not only bore witness to history but played an integral part in shaping it. Among his countless achievements, Sir James Bisset stands alone as the only man to have commanded both the *R.M.S. Queen Mary* and the *R.M.S. Queen Elizabeth* during the Second World War. These legendary liners became essential instruments of war under his command. Bisset's strategic acumen and extraordinary bravery ensured their survival and success in a theatre of war dominated by the relentless menace of German U-boats.

The Atlantic during the war was a vast graveyard of ships, its cold waters patrolled by an invisible enemy. For Allied convoys, the U-boats were a terror without equal, sending thousands of men and millions of tons of materiel to the bottom. The *Queen Mary* and *Queen Elizabeth*, however, were different. Capable of unprecedented speeds for ships of their size, up to 30 knots, they became immune to the submarine threat, outrunning U-boats driven by maniacal Captains that would relish the opportunity to sink anything Bisset commanded. It was Sir James Bisset who had the audacity to lean into this speed, defying conventional convoys and constant zig-zagging across the ocean caution to use speed to keep his passengers and crew safe.

Under his command, these vessels became more than transport ships; they were vital to the Allied war effort. The *Queen Mary* alone could carry up to 16,000 troops in a single voyage, her enormous capacity making her equivalent to several troopships combined. Similarly, the *Queen Elizabeth*, launched at the cusp of war and transformed into a troopship before ever embarking on her intended life as a luxury liner, played a pivotal role in ferrying soldiers across the Atlantic. These ships, which might have been reduced to wreckage in less capable hands, instead became icons of Allied ingenuity and determination.

Bisset's wartime command was not without peril. Steering two of the world's largest ships in waters teeming with U-boats required an uncanny mix of intellect, instinct, and nerve. His memoir recounts moments of tension with vivid detail, from zigzagging through the Atlantic to minimize the risk of torpedo attack to enduring gruelling voyages through rough seas and worsening weather. Yet, despite these challenges, Bisset never allowed complacency or despair to cloud his leadership. His steadfastness saved not only the ships but also the lives of thousands of servicemen and women who depended on their safe passage.

Yet for all his accomplishments and extraordinary experiences, Sir James Bisset's memoirs were not met with the acclaim they deserved when first published. This was not due to any shortcoming in the writing itself—his prose is clear, evocative, and deeply human, but rather because of the context in which they emerged. The horrors of the 1940s, from the blitz to the Holocaust to the Battle of the Atlantic, had receded into the background of public consciousness. A new generation, shaped by the atomic age and the tensions of the Cold War, was more interested in the future than in the Past The niche Interest in seafaring memoirs struggled against a tide of public indifference, particularly in Australia, where the market for such works was notably small.

Time, however, has a way of reshuffling priorities. Today, we are fortunate to revisit *Commodore* with fresh eyes, recognizing its value not only as a historical document but also as a testament to human courage and adaptability. Bisset's trilogy allows us to glimpse a world that is gone but not forgotten, a time when the seas were both pathways and battlefields, and when the men who sailed them carried the weight of empires on their shoulders.

This third volume, in particular, is a masterful conclusion to his life story. It captures the transition from the immediacy of war to the complexities of peace, reflecting on how global conflict reshaped the maritime world and how one man found his place within it. There is an understated poetry to Bisset's reflections, a sense of wonder and humility that belies his extraordinary achievements. His voice is that of a mariner, shaped by years of listening to the ocean's rhythms, and his insights resonate deeply with those who understand that the sea is as much a teacher as it is a challenge.

Sir James Bisset's story reminds us that history is not merely the sum of battles and treaties but also the lived experiences of individuals whose choices and actions ripple outward in ways they may never fully grasp. To command the *Queen Mary* and *Queen Elizabeth* in wartime was an honour and a responsibility of the highest order. To live to tell the tale, and to tell it so well, is a gift to us all.

In reading *Commodore: War, Peace, and Big Ships*, we find ourselves transported to the bridge of these great liners, feeling the spray of salt air and the tension of navigating hostile waters. We gain not only an understanding of Bisset's world but also an appreciation for the qualities that made him such an extraordinary leader: courage, intellect, and an unshakeable sense of duty.

As you turn these pages, take a moment to reflect on the man behind the words. Sir James Bisset was not just a sailor or a commodore; he was a witness to history, a participant in its unfolding, and a storyteller who ensured that its lessons would not be lost His memoirs may not have found their audience in the 20th century, but they endure as a testament to a life lived with purpose and conviction.

It is an honour to introduce this work to you. May it inspire, enlighten, and transport you, just as Sir James Bisset himself once carried thousands across the seas—through war, peace, and the uncharted waters of a remarkable life.

ABOUT THE COVER

Cover art for all three volumes of the Second Edition of the Sail Ho! trilogy was generated using AI. On this edition the *R.M.S. Queen Mary* pushes through a storm at sea enroute to being converted into a troopship for World War Two. Grey was selected as the background colour representing Bisset's advancing years.

James Gordon Partridge Bisset

(15 July 1883 – 28 March 1967)

HONORS AND AWARDS

- Decoration for Officers of the Royal Naval Reserve(RD) – 28 March 1923
- Commander of the Order of the British Empire (CBE) –1942 Birthday Honours
- **Knight Bachelor, 10 July 1945**
- Honorary Doctor of Laws (LL.D.)(Cambridge), 1946
- British War Medal, 1914-1918
- Mercantile Marine Medal, 1914-1918
- Victory Medal, 1914-1919 (U.K.)
- 1939-1945 Star
- Pacific Star
- Atlantic Star
- War Medal, 1939-1945
- Legion of Merit, Commander (U.S.A.)

British Knight Bachelor

The Knight Bachelor is an award given to men by the monarch of the United Kingdom. It is the oldest form of knighthood in the British honours system.

Editor Notes about this Second Edition.

Because of their rarity, it took me nearly a decade to find and collect all three of the books in the series. A quick check of the Internet reveals that original copies of the trilogy are available, but mostly at collectors and rare book prices. Since I feel the message is more important that the value, I decided to redo the trilogy in hopes others may enjoy it as much as I have. I also sincerely hope that I can do the series a favour through enhancing it.

I must acknowledge that others have reprinted the series, but the attempts I have seen seem to be unprofessional and lacking. With AI and access to Public Domain materials I feel the works of Bisset can be improved than when they originally went to press in the last century.

Even though the AI pictures may be lacking in detail it is my goal to give the reader something visual to ponder over – by filling in those missing details the reader can be transported back to THAT scene and image the world Bisset experienced. I hope you enjoy my edition, but I hope you enjoy Bisset's personal story more.

Kyle Vernon
Summer 2025

About the Editor

Originally from Midland, Texas and now living in Lubbock, Texas, Kyle Vernon has taught assorted topics for thirty-three years across four nations spanning two continents, including working in a combat zone as a civilian contract instructor for Central Texas College and the US Army.

As a senior in High School in 1983, he created a boardgame about his hometown. Called "Midland Millions," it went on to break state and national sales records. Vernon graduated from Midland College in 1986 and Texas Tech University in 1990.

Married since 1988 to Teri, it was her service in the US Army that transported their young family to England 1999-2003. This allowed Kyle to collect books 1 and 3 of the Sail Ho! trilogy. Book 2 would be purchased via eBay auction after returning to the USA.

Vernon presently teaches Astronomy to High School students at Frenship High School in Wolfforth, Texas.

This second edition of this trilogy is dedicated to my wife Teri

Table of Contents

My Training in the Royal Naval Reserve— Engaged to be Married —
The Royal Navy and the Merchant Navy — I Learn Naval Drill and
Gunnery — Torpedoes a New Weapon — Training Ashore and Afloat-
H.M.S. "Suffolk" — How Nautical Tonnages are Calculated — The
Rear-Admiral's Goat — Naval Routines at Sea — The Firth of Forth —
A Garland on the Masthead — A Sailor's Wife- H.M.S. "Princess Royal"
— A "Crack" Battlecruiser — Be Prepared — "There Will Never be a
War!" — A Cruise to Spain — "Der Tag!"

ON 1st January 1913, I stepped ashore from the Cunard liner *S.S. Carpathia*, at Liverpool, with twelve months' leave, to undergo training as an officer in the Royal Naval Reserve. I was twenty-nine years of age and had been at sea for fourteen years. I had served in sailing vessels and in tramp steamers and had been for six years in the Cunard service, on the transatlantic and Mediterranean routes. I had passed the examinations for Master Mariner and Extra Master before entering the Cunard service as Fourth Officer in the *S.S. Caronia* in 1907, and had slowly won promotion, to the rank of Second Officer in the *Carpathia* in February 1912. In that liner, which was on the Mediterranean run, from the Adriatic ports to New York, I had been away from England for eleven months. It was good to be home again.

Hastening to London, I became engaged to be married. May and I had been sweethearts for two years, but mostly by letter writing, as I was seldom in London where she lived, but absence had made our hearts grow fonder, as seems to be usually the case when sailors fall in love, or when lasses fall in love with sailors.

On this occasion, I had only ten days' leave in London before beginning my naval training; so we decided to get married when I would have my next shore leave.

All too soon came the day, 11th January 1913, when I had to leave London, and go by train to Devonport (near Plymouth) to join *H.M.S. Vivid.* She was a ship that didn't float, for that was the name of the Royal Naval Barracks at Devonport — a shore establishment.

Two years previously, I had learned something of the ways of the Royal Navy, during one month's probationary training in an old cruiser, *H.M.S. Hogue,* moored off Sheerness at the mouth of the Thames. I had then been commissioned as a Sub-Lieutenant in the Royal Naval Reserve; but of guns, ammunition, torpedoes, and suchlike naval necessities I had everything yet to learn — and now the time had come for me to begin to learn it.

The Royal Naval Reserve consisted of volunteer officers and seamen of other ranks of the British Merchant Service, who knew how to handle seagoing vessels, carrying cargo and passengers, but required additional training in the routines, disciplines, customs, and techniques of the combat navy, to enable them to serve, if need be, in warships in time of war.

The Merchant Service, or Mercantile Marine, consisting of privately-owned trading vessels, is older than the Royal Navy. Long before King Henry VIII had established a fleet of "King's Ships," armed to protect seaborne commerce, British merchant vessels- known as "merchantmen" — had carried guns to protect themselves. With the introduction of steam propulsion and ironclad arma-ment, the Royal Navy became specialized as the Fighting Service, while vessels of the Mercantile Marine ceased to carry guns, and were recognized, by international conventions, as "noncombatant." The "King's Navy," which was the "Queen's Navy" during the long reign of Queen Victoria, eventually became known as the "Royal Navy" — to avoid the need of making changes of name to suit the sex of sovereigns of the realm — and was entitled to use the prefix "H.M.S." before the names of its vessels. This abbreviation could conveniently refer either to His or Her Majesty's Ships, in accordance with the sex of the occupant of the throne for the time being.

H.M. Ships, having royal prestige and authority, took precedence over privately owned vessels. They had a pride and a discipline much stricter than that of the Merchant Service. Their officers, in general, had higher social status and were better educated than most of the officers of the Merchant Service, who had usually gone to sea as boys, to earn a living by hard work in rough living conditions.

Many merchant seamen were rough and gruff in their manners and attire; but it was recognized that, in time of war, the Merchant Service could supply a great reserve of both officers and men skilled in seamanship. For this purpose, the Royal Naval Reserve was officially established in 1861, to give merchant seamen some naval training, which would enable them to serve in warships if required. It was not until 1922, as a recognition of the work performed and heavy casualties suffered by merchant seamen during the 1914-18 war, that King George V announced that the Merchant Service would thereafter be known as "the Merchant Navy," and so it is known to this day.

But, before the 1914-18 war, there was a more clearly marked class distinction between officers of the Royal Navy and those of the Royal Naval Reserve than there is today.

Usually, officers of the R.N.R. were of older age groups, and more experienced in seamanship than officers of the Royal Navy of equal or sometimes higher ranks than themselves. There was some friction, but not much, if junior officers of the R.N. attempted to adopt a patronizing attitude to the R.N.R. officers. That kind of class distinction disappeared under wartime stresses and strains, when officers and men of the R.N. and the R.N.R. served together in warships and in armed merchant vessels, sharing dangers and discomforts in common.

Some mercantile shipowners in peacetime did not view the R.N.R. favourably. Putting profits before patriotism, they begrudged giving officers in their employ leave to undergo the basic naval training, which required a year's absence from an officer's normal occupation. But the Cunard Steamship Company was one which encouraged its officers to join the R.N.R. It was obvious that some Cunard liners would be requisitioned by the Admiralty in wartime for use as troop transports or hospital ships, and some would be armed with guns and converted into armed merchant cruisers for auxiliary naval service. Therefore, it was recognized, by the Cunard and other British steamship companies which owned large liners, that the naval training of key personnel in the companies' service would facilitate the taking over of companies' ships by the Royal Navy during war emergencies.

There was prestige in being allowed to fly the Blue Ensign of the R.N.R. on passenger liners in peacetime. This was permitted by the Admiralty when a liner was under command of an officer of the Royal Naval Reserve and carried at least seven other officers and ratings of the R.N.R.

I have certainly never had reason to regret my decision to volunteer for training in the R.N.R. It stood me in good stead during the wars of 1914-18 and 1939-45, when I was given command of armed vessels.

But, in 1911, when I had first joined the R.N.R., war had seemed only a remote possibility. The British Navy was more than twice as large as any other navy. Very few people thought that Germany would ever challenge Britain's sea supremacy; and, even in 1913, some of my friends considered that I was only wasting my time to gain naval knowledge which would probably never be of any practical use.

I was one of a batch of ten officers of the Merchant Service called up for R.N.R. training in *H.M.S. Vivid* in January 1913. We were quartered in the naval barracks at Devonport, formed into a class for instruction chiefly by naval petty officers, and put through our paces at squad drill, musketry, ceremonial drill, route marches, and a gunnery course lasting for two months. The experience was enjoyable, and the course of instruction not difficult. We gained a smattering of gunnery, and all passed at the end of the course, without any trouble.

Then we were transferred to *H.M.S. Defiance* for a torpedo course. She was one of the old "wooden walls" — a sailing ship of the Crimean War period — moored in the upper reaches of Devonport Harbour, and used as a torpedo training establishment for the R.N. and R.N.R.

We lived on board and spent our days taking torpedoes to pieces and putting them together again and learning how they behave. Occasionally we were taken in a torpedo boat for a short cruise outside Plymouth Harbour, fired torpedoes, and recovered them when they surfaced. A good time was had by all, and, at the end of two months, we again all passed.

The dirigible torpedo[1] was viewed at that time by some experts as potentially the most destructive of all naval weapons, since in its nature it was designed to strike and explode against enemy vessels below the waterline and sink them. Invented. and patented by an Australian, Louis Brennan, in 1874, it was originally intended as a device for protecting harbours, to be fired from shore stations. Brennan sold his invention to the British War Office, and in 1887 was appointed manager of the Brennan torpedo factory.

The Royal Navy had quickly realized that torpedoes could be fired also from vessels at sea, and for this purpose had begun building a large number of torpedo boats. These were small craft of about 250 tons, capable of developing a speed of up to 25 knots, equipped with two tubes on deck to launch torpedoes. These were mounted on swivels amidships. The tactical idea was that torpedo boats, being small and travelling at high speeds, would be difficult to hit by enemy gunfire. Under cover of darkness, or in the heat of a general naval engagement, they would sneak or dash up to enemy battleships or cruisers and sink them.

Foreign nations, especially Germany, also developed the naval use of torpedoes and torpedo boats. The logical defence against torpedo boats was a screen of torpedo boat destroyers, intended to accompany battleships or cruisers into action. The T.B.Ds were vessels of about 300 tons, with speeds of up to 30 knots, armed with deck guns, and with torpedoes, launched from tubes mounted on the decks. Britain and Germany both had large flotillas of torpedo boats and of torpedo boat destroyers.

But the most sinister development was the installation of torpedoes in submarines, or undersea vessels, known in Germany as "U-boats." These horrible things had not been used in warfare prior to 1914, and few people had any idea that submarines, using torpedoes, would attack and sink unarmed merchant ships.

Torpedoes in surface vessels had been used only once in actual battle, and that was by the Japanese Navy, under command of the British trained Admiral Togo, in the destruction of the Russian Fleet, outside Port Arthur, during the battle of the Yellow Sea in 1904. In that battle, high explosive shells also were used for the first time in naval gunnery under actual war conditions.

When the results of the battle of the Yellow Sea were fully known, European navies intensified the building of torpedo boats, torpedo boat destroyers, and submarines, and equipped battleships and cruisers with torpedo tubes, in addition to deck guns. But despite the intense rivalry in naval construction, no one had the slightest conception of the terrible destruction of merchant shipping that would ensue from the use of naval torpedoes in a modern style war between Britain and Germany as the chief protagonists, which all except a few prophets considered would be extremely unlikely to occur.

After qualifying in the gunnery and torpedo courses at Devonport, I was promoted to Lieutenant, R.N.R., in May 1913, and appointed to *H.M.S. Suffolk*, flagship of the Ninth Cruiser Squadron, for training afloat. I was ordered to join

HMS Suffolk 1904 (Public Domain)

her at Lamlash, on the Isle of Arran, in the Firth of Clyde.

H.M.S. Suffolk was a coal burning cruiser, built in 1903, with a speed of 24 knots, and a crew (or "complement") of 678, commanded by Captain Phillip Franklin, R.N. As flagship of her squadron, she flew the flag of Rear Admiral Craddock, R.N. She had fourteen 6-inch guns, nine 12-pounders, and two torpedo tubes. She was of 9800 tons displacement.

The tonnage of naval vessels is calculated in a different way from that of merchant vessels. For non-nautical readers, I should explain this technical point, if only in a general way, without too many details.

In merchant vessels, the tonnage does not refer to the weight of the vessel, but to the cubic capacity of her permanently enclosed spaces. The method of measuring that capacity is a matter of traditional usage, said to have originated with the number of casks or "tuns" of wine that the earliest English merchant vessels could carry across the Channel from France. The carrying capacity of a vessel in tuns was an indication of her size. A tun was considered to occupy 100 cubic feet of space. When barrels or casks are stacked, they have air spaces around them.

In the course of centuries, a convention became established that a volumetric measurement of 100 cubic feet is a "tonnage unit," and that prevails today. A merchant vessel, described as, say, "1000 tons gross," has a total of 100,000 cubic feet of permanently enclosed spaces. This capacity is arrived at by measuring the spaces in her cargo holds, crew and passenger accommodation, storerooms, engine and boiler rooms, forecastle, wheelhouse, chartroom, and every other place in her that is not open to the weather when she is at sea.

But, though that description indicates her overall size, it does not indicate her carrying or earning capacity. This is known as "net tonnage," or "registered tonnage," and it is on that basis that vessels have to pay harbour dues, pilotage dues, and other extortions. The net tonnage is a measurement of her cargo carrying and passenger carrying space, expressed in units of 100 cubic feet. It is computed by deducting from her gross tonnage all her "propelling space" and "navigating space" — that is, the space occupied by her boilers, engine rooms, coalbunkers, water tanks, shaft tunnels, and auxiliary machinery, besides crew quarters, storerooms, chartroom, wheelhouse and any other enclosed spaces used in connection with the navigation, handling, and propulsion of the vessel.

To reduce costs of harbour dues, pilotage, and other expenses, it is to the financial advantage of the shipowner to reduce the registered tonnage or net tonnage of his vessel to the utmost by careful measurements of all propelling space and navigating space in her, and this is invariably done with very great care.

On the other hand, "displacement tonnage" is the actual weight of a vessel in tons. That name for this method of measurement is used because a vessel floating in water displaces, or pushes aside, its own weight in water. It is the usual method of describing the tonnage of naval vessels, which are not concerned with passengers or cargo.

For some purposes, the displacement tonnage of merchant vessels is stated. It varies according to whether a vessel is "light" or "loaded, "that is, whether she has on board cargo, fuel, stores, fresh water, ballast, or any other weight than that of her structure. This method of measurement is necessary to determine the Plimsoll mark, which indicates when she is fully loaded for going safely to sea.

The various methods of measuring the size of seagoing vessels may appear complicated; but sailors understand them easily enough. It is not the weight in tons of a warship that counts in battle, but her type or class, armament, weapons, speed, and striking power. Therefore, the tonnage of a fighting vessel is seldom mentioned in short descriptions of her. It is enough to say that she is "a 30-knot cruiser," or "destroyer," or whatever she may be, with the number and calibre of the bigger guns that she carries, and that is enough to identify her, for friend or foe.

H.M.S. *Suffolk* was moored in Lamlash Bay, in company with three other cruisers of the "County" class and a flotilla of a dozen destroyers. The squadron was getting ready to put to sea for manoeuvres when I joined her. As I stepped on board and saluted the quarter-deck, the first thing that attracted my attention was a goat, advancing along the deck towards me in a menacing manner.

I discovered later that this animal was owned by Rear Admiral Craddock, who was an animal lover, and he also kept two handsome dogs on board his flagship. It was the Admiral's habit every morning in port, before breakfast, to get into a dinghy, with his two dogs sitting in the stern sheets, and go for several pulls around the ship. This was his daily exercise. At other times, the dogs and the goat roamed freely around the decks.

The goat, a large "Billy" with curving horns, was anything but a favourite with the officers and ratings. He amused himself by coming up behind anyone who was not on the alert for that danger and butting him playfully behind the knees. The sailors, when cleaning guns or other metalwork, tempted Billy's appetite with wads of emery cloth soaked in colza oil and stained with verdigris. These the goat ate with relish, and, contrary to the hopes of the sailors, seemed to thrive on the diet!

I was the sole R.N.R. officer on board *H.M.S. Suffolk*, but I was made welcome and being now a fully-fledged Lieutenant with a certificate in gunnery, I was put in charge of the forward gun turret, which mounted twin 6-inch guns. I was assigned also for duties on the Watch and Station Bill — watchkeeping on the bridge or on stations entering or leaving port — with no feeling that I was an outsider.

The squadron put to sea for gunnery and other exercises and fleet manoeuvres. Although much that is done in a warship in peacetime appears to be only a waste of time and money, it is necessary "in time of peace to prepare for war" — and the watchword of the Royal Navy was, "Be prepared!"

Life on board *H.M.S. Suffolk* was easier going than in some other warships. The manoeuvres took us around the north of Scotland, and we put into the great naval base at Scapa Flow in the Orkney Islands, where a hundred or more British warships of various fleet units lay at anchor, or were constantly arriving and departing in purposeful activity.

After a few days at Scapa Flow, we proceeded again to sea, for further exercises, and, a week later, put into the Firth of Forth, at the approach to Edinburgh. We passed under the Forth Bridge, considered at that time one of the engineering marvels of the world, its two spans, each of 1,710 feet long, supported on three cantilevers, one of these on Inch Garvie islet in midstream, carrying railway lines on girders 157 feet above water level.

Upstream from the bridge, we anchored at the naval base at Rosyth. As the Suffolk was to remain there for some weeks for refit, I applied for two weeks' shore leave, for the purpose of getting married, and this was granted.

On my way to London, after sending a telegram to my bride-to- be to give her due warning in time to fix the wedding day, I had some hours to wait in Edinburgh for a train and took the opportunity of visiting Edinburgh Castle — a sight to thrill anyone of Scottish descent, as the symbol of Scotland's ancient independence. We were married in London on the 28th of June 1913. On that day, in accordance with the custom of the Royal Navy, a garland of green leaves was hoisted to the masthead of *H.M.S. Suffolk* at Rosyth. We received also a handsome wedding gift of plate from the captain and officers.

Our honeymoon was spent in North Wales. We returned to London, where my wife was to continue to live until such time as we could decide where to make our home. I would be re-entering the Cunard service at the end of my naval training. Like other officers in that service, I would have short leave ashore at the end of each voyage, and occasional periods of longer leave. A sailor is more often away from home than at home, but such is life, and it cannot be helped, and the wives of sailors know what to expect, and they face the situation without worrying too much. After all, hundreds of thousands of women are married to sailors; and there are many other occupations beside seafaring which take the breadwinner away from home.

To a sailor the home port means not only where his vessel begins and ends her round voyage, but also where he makes his home. In England the excellent railway services enabled sailors to make their homes anywhere within convenient reach of their home ports.

Being now a married man, I had to think seriously of such problems, but, in the course of years, with wars disturbing all normal expectations of a settled life, the problems of finding a fixed abode were never easy to solve.

In the meantime, at the end of my wedding leave, I returned to Rosyth and rejoined *H.M.S. Suffolk*. She put to sea again for more exercises and then put into the naval base at Plymouth for an extended stay. At this, my wife moved to Plymouth, where the married officers and ratings of H.M. Ships were usually given shore leave at weekends.

After I had served four months in *H.M.S. Suffolk*, she was ordered to the West Indies Station (Bermuda), where she would remain for one year. This did not suit me, being newly married. Also, I needed only eight months to complete my R.N.R. training. I therefore applied to the Admiralty for transfer to a ship in home waters. This was granted, and I was ordered to proceed to Portland to join *H.M.S. Princess Royal*. I did so with elation, as she was a "crack" ship. I joined her on 27th September 1913.

The *Princess Royal* was a 31-knot battlecruiser, and one of the most modern and powerful Dreadnoughts in the British Fleet. She was completed in 1912, and carried eight 13-inch guns, besides sixteen 4-inch guns and three torpedo tubes. She was much bigger than the Suffolk, having a displacement of 26,350 tons, a length of 700 feet, and a beam of 86 feet. With three funnels, she was a coalburner but also used oil as a supplementary fuel. She had 4 propellers, and 42 boilers, and carried a complement of 1000 souls.

Under the command of Captain Brock, the *Princess Royal* was noted for very strict discipline. The pace in her was much livelier than in the leisurely old *Suffolk*. I should explain that in a big warship the ranks of Captain and Commander are different. The Captain is in command, but the Commander is his Chief Officer .and has authority in everything, under the Captain's orders. This responsibility in the *Princess Royal* was placed on Commander Alister Beale, who kept everyone on

HMS Princess Royal 1913 (Public Domain)

board bang up to the mark.

We went out into the North Sea on manoeuvres with the Grand Fleet, and I found it an inspiring show of Britain's naval power.

On three evenings a week, Captain Brock invited three or four officers to dine with him, in rotation. I was invited several times and found that the Captain always steered the conversation to sailing ships. He had served in sail as a boy and knew much more about sailing vessels and their rigs than most of the officers invited to his table. He encouraged me to speak of my own experiences in sail, which now seemed very remote from the immense mechanical power and complexity of the *Princess Royal*.

Captain Brock had unbounded faith in the superiority of the Royal Navy over all other navies and was convinced that for this reason there would never be a war. He considered that the *Princess Royal*, with her 13-inch guns, was invincible, and was inclined to scoff at the idea that submarines could ever become dangerous. He regarded them as a newfangled idea to waste time and money.

One day when we were on manoeuvres in the North Sea, a British submarine of the theoretical "enemy" force surfaced, .and signalled that a direct hit had been scored on the *Princess Royal.* "Nonsense!" roared Captain Brock. "It's impossible!" He signalled accordingly, but the commander of the submarine firmly insisted that the *Princess Royal* was "sunk." The flag wagging dispute continued, until the dummy torpedo was salvaged, with its practice head badly crumpled as undeniable proof of the direct hit. Even then, Brock continued to assert that the hit was of no real importance. Many other senior officers of the Royal Navy viewed submarines with derision.

In November 1913, the *Princess Royal* put in to Scapa Flow to refuel. That was nine months before the outbreak of the European war of 1914-18. Many other warships, great and small, lay at anchor in the basin, when an order came from the Commander-in-Chief that an exercise was to be carried through on the assumption that enemy submarines had penetrated the harbour defences, and were about to attack the ships at anchor. This order made Captain Brock snort. In the middle of a sleety winter's night, the signal came through to begin the exercise.

"Action stations!"

"Out torpedo nets!"

This was a big manoeuvre and was carried out in quick time. In the middle of it all, Captain Brock ordered the "Still" to be sounded on the bugle. From the bridge deck, he questioned Commander Deale on the correctness of an order that had just been given.

Beale, who had a high pitched voice and a short temper, began his answer by saying, "In time of war, Sir — " but he got no further. With the utmost scorn in his voice, Brock roared, "War? War?

There will NEVER be any WAR!"

There could be no comment on that opinion — at that time — even though it made all our smartness on manoeuvres seem rather futile! In February 1914, the *Princess Royal,* along with other ships, was ordered on a cruise to Spain, to "show the flag" in that friendly country — one of the normal peacetime tasks of the Royal Navy. We put into the port of Pontevedra, in north-western Spain, near Cape Finisterre, and anchored — not entirely by accident — alongside German cruiser which was already paying a courtesy visit to that port.

As a matter of courtesy, also, the officers of the German cruiser were invited on board *H.M.S. Princess Royal* for dinner in the wardroom mess. It was a convivial occasion, and the liquor flowed freely. Under the stimulus of grog, witty speeches were made, as the usual toasts were proposed, drunk with enthusiasm, and responded to.

All were merry and bright when, late in the evening, as a final toast, one of the German officers rose to his feet, raised his glass, and said, solemnly, "I give you this toast, gentlemen — Der Tag!" The day, the great day, the long awaited day, when they would die fighting us! German and British officers, guests and hosts, sprang to their feet and drank the toast with enthusiasm.

Little did they know, and little did we know, that Der Tag was near — only six months ahead of us — and what it would mean, to them and to us, in losses of ships and men.

"Three cheers for Der Tag!"

Well, so be it.

CHAPTER ENDNOTES:

(1) A dirigible torpedo is a propeller driven torpedo that is launched from a shore based platform and guided by wires.

Send-off from the "Princess Royal" — A Passage in H.M.S. "New Zealand" — Lionel Halsey and Lieutenant Battenberg — My Training in Destroyers — H.M.T.B.D. "Syren" — The Attractions of Portsmouth — Advantages and Disadvantages of Service in Destroyers — Their Uses in Naval Tactics — A Training Cruise — Night "Attack" on Portsmouth Harbour — Blown to Pieces in Theory — I Rejoin the Cunard Service — First Officer in the "Caronia" — Keen Competition on the Atlantic Routes — British and German Rivalry in Big Ships — The Outbreak of War.

WHILE I was training in the battlecruiser, *H.M.S. Princess Royal*, at Pontevedra, Spain, I received a signal from the Admiralty, ordering me to return to England, for destroyer training. How to get there was a problem left for me to solve.

Fortunately, a battlecruiser, *H.M.S. New Zealand*, which was in our company at Pontevedra, had orders to proceed to Bantry Bay, in south-western Ireland, for gunnery trials. I was told to transfer to her for passage to Ireland, and from there to go to London for orders.

I had then served five months in the *Princess Royal* and had got on well with her wardroom and gunroom officers, who decided to give me a sendoff. At dinner on the evening of 5th March 1914, when I was to leave her and go on board the *New Zealand*, I realized that there was a subtle scheme to get me tight. Drinks were being lavished on me by all and sundry, and I was scarcely in a position to refuse them. But, before I was too far gone, I had a premonition That it would be unwise to present myself on board the *New Zealand* in a state of alcoholic collapse. My orders were to be on board before 11 p.m. I had to use tactics which in ordinary circumstances might have been deplorable.

There were some large flower vases dotted about the wardroom. With careful manoeuvring and much regret I managed to pour several whiskies into the flower vases instead of into my gullet and so gained an undeserved reputation of being well able to hold my liquor. Even with this subterfuge, I was decidedly merry. The picket boat which took me to the *New Zealand* was manned by officers of the *Princess Royal*. This was an honour, and I duly appreciated it. Even though they were all well-lit up with grog, as I was, they handled the boat smartly alongside.

On board *New Zealand*, the Officer of the Watch summed up the situation at a glance. He showed me to my cabin without delay, and in a few minutes, I had turned into my bunk and was sleeping off the effects.

H.M.S. New Zealand was a new battlecruiser, completed in 1912. She had a speed of 29 knots and mounted eight 12-inch guns and twenty 4-inch guns, with three torpedo tubes. She had a displacement of 18,750 tons and carried a complement of 800. This Dreadnought had been presented to the Royal Navy by the New Zealand Government, at a cost of 1.5 million pounds.

When I awoke next morning, and looked out of the porthole, I saw that the *New Zealand* was at sea and belting along to the northward at an economical cruising speed of about 18 knots. Being only on passage in her for the short run of approximately 500 miles to Bantry Bay — which would be covered in less than two days — I was not on the Watch and Stations Bill, and had no other duties assigned to me.

Going below for breakfast, I found several mouldy-looking officers there, who scarcely acknowledged my presence. They looked the worse for wear and tear, and I soon discovered the reason. The *New Zealand* had been on a cruise around the world, "showing the flag" in many ports, and her officers had had more than their due share of entertaining and being entertained.

H.M.S. New Zealand was commanded by Captain Lionel Halsey, R.N., who in courtesy invited me to his quarters for a chat. Like other senior officers of the Royal Navy, he was interested in the lore of sail and immediately began questioning me about my experiences on the Cape Horn route in my younger days. Such questions always surprised me a little in the ultra-mechanical surroundings of a powerful dreadnought, as also in big passenger liners, until I realized that all men who serve in mechanical contraptions at sea have a yearning for the beauty of sailing vessels — in the ideal, if not in the reality.

In the wardroom of the *New Zealand*, the only lively officer I found was young Battenberg, a Lieutenant, R.N., whose father, Prince Louis Battenberg, was the First Sea Lord. Before lunch and dinner, he would come up to me and say, "I'll shake the sticks with you, Bisset!" — and we would gamble for a solitary drink. He always won, I noticed. Plenty of experience at the game?

When we arrived at Bantry Bay (Berehaven), I was sent ashore in a picket boat and caught the train for Cork. Having a few hours to spare before going aboard the packet boat bound for Fishguard in Wales, I called on some distant relatives who lived in Cork. I had never seen them previously, and, when I announced my identity, they couldn't have been more surprised if I had said that I had just landed from Mars.

They made me all the more welcome at that. I was beginning to think that a R.N.R. officer's training fits him to absorb more grog than he is used to in the Merchant Service. When at sea in Cunarders, I was abstemious, and almost a teetotaller. Irish whiskey is powerful and served in big nips. However, my cousins escorted me in good time to the packet boat, and our farewells were in a merry mood.

The name "packet boat" — applied to the well-found steamers on passenger runs across the North Sea, the Channel, and the Irish Sea — is technically a misnomer, as a "boat" is an undecked vessel. But what of that? There are people who would call even the *Queen Mary* a boat.

Arrived at Fishguard, I took the train to London, and had a joyful reunion with my wife, who by that time was beginning to realize some of the drawbacks of being married to a sailor! After a few days, I presented myself at the Admiralty and was ordered to proceed to Portsmouth to join *His Majesty's Torpedo Boat Destroyer Syren* for training. She was one of a dozen destroyers, lying moored to buoys, side by side, with only nucleus crews on board. This is known in naval parlance as "lying in trot."

H.M.T.B.D. Syren was a four funnelled "old" 30-knot coal burning destroyer, built in 1896. At the time when I joined her, I doubt whether she could have done more than 24 knots for any length of time. She was of 300 tons displacement, 210 feet long by 21 feet beam long, low, and sleek. When fully manned, she would have a complement of ninety, in uncomfortably crowded quarters. She had bunkers for 80 tons of coal, which would give her a steaming radius of not more than six hours, at full speed. Like others of her class, she was designed to operate out of ports on special missions at short radius, rather than to remain at sea for any lengthy patrols.

In command of the *Syren* was Commander W. H. Williams, R.N., and I was designated as the First Lieutenant; but we were the only two navigating officers on board. There were also on board an engineer officer, a gunner, and half a dozen naval ratings, including seamen and stokers. She went to sea only occasionally, for exercises to keep her and her crew in seagoing trim, but, between whiles, for long intervals, she lay idle.

It was in mid-March 1914, that I joined the *Syren* for three months' destroyer training. That was only five months before the outbreak of the great European war of 1914-18, but no one had any inkling that Der Tag was so near.

Commander Williams explained that my training would consist chiefly of getting used to the feeling of being in a destroyer, and that perhaps later on we would be ordered to sea for practice in handling her. I would have shore leave every night and at most weekends. My work on board as watchkeeper during the daytime would consist mainly of inspecting and supervising the war against rust — furbishing, cleaning and painting ship, to keep her spick and span. "A restful holiday," he said.

Portsmouth, the biggest British naval base, was known to sailors as "Pompey." It had extensive naval shore establishments, repair shops, naval dry docks, and shipbuilding yards. It was the supreme "leave port" of the Royal Navy.

Warships were arriving and departing daily, on the various naval occasions of peacetime. The commercial life of Pompey practically depended on naval pay, and harpies thrived there. Dozens of hotels, boarding houses, and apartment houses catered for naval men and their wives; and thousands of married sailors had their homes permanently there, viewing Pompey as a home port.

When it became evident that my R.N.R. destroyer training course would consist of three months' rest cure at Portsmouth, my wife came to stay with me. We found comfortable "diggings" near the dockyard and had a quiet restful spell together.

It did not take me very long to grasp the essentials of routine in a destroyer lying in trot. One walk around in *H.M.T.B.D. Syren*, on deck and below, was enough to indicate all that it was necessary to know that she would be damned uncomfortable at sea. She was a long steel box containing practically all machinery — nearly all propelling space, and very little navigating space or living quarters. The original idea of torpedo boat destroyers was to destroy torpedo boats. That meant coming to grips with enemy torpedo boats before they could discharge their torpedoes at our bigger ships. For this purpose, destroyers were powered with steam engines out of all proportion to the size of their hulls. They could be driven at from 25 to 30 knots, so that they could keep up with battleships and cruisers a hundred times bigger than themselves, or overtake and engage enemy torpedo boats, which were difficult targets for the guns in big ships under their sneaking attack.

For this purpose, destroyers mounted guns, though not many, and these were of light calibre, as necessitated by the small size of the vessels themselves. The Syren mounted only one gun. It was a 4-inch gun, forward, in an open turret which was known as the "conning tower" and served also as the navigating bridge.

The conning tower was almost on the forecastle head — that is, placed 40 feet from the bows, which, in relation to her overall length of 210 feet, meant that her four funnels and propelling machinery were amidships, and in the four-fifths of her space abaft the conning tower.

Naval designers had quickly realized that torpedo boat destroyers could also themselves act as torpedo boats — that is, they could be equipped with torpedoes to attack enemy big ships. The Syren had two 18-inch torpedo tubes, on swivels amidships. Her forecastle head had a turtle back steel decking.

When destroyers carried torpedoes — and this had quickly become the general rule — they were potentially destroyers not only of old style torpedo boats, but also of big ships. The romantic name "destroyer," like "Dreadnought" for big ships, made an appeal to the imagination of the taxpaying public, who had to foot the bill for naval building programmes.

The original designation of "T.B.D." was officially retained, even though destroyers were now intended to destroy more than torpedo boats. With the development of submarines, they had another function, namely to seek out and destroy the enemy's lurking undersea torpedo firing vessels either by shell fire or by ramming them when they were on the surface or partly submerged. For this purpose, destroyers required not only great speed, but also extreme manoeuvrability, and were designed with steering gear to give a flexibility in altering course which enabled them to turn on their heel at full speed.

A further use of destroyers was as scouts, and also as escorts of convoys of merchant vessels or troopships within their limited steaming radius from their shore bases.

In the early months of 1914, when I was undergoing destroyer training, the tactical uses of destroyers had not been tested in actual battle and were still a matter of theory. The same applied to submarines, and, to some extent, to minefields. The war then looming would test all those theories to the utmost Many other comparatively new devices in naval warfare, including the use of aircraft, and even of wireless, were still to be tested under war conditions.

Britain had held undisputed naval supremacy for more than a hundred years since the battle of Trafalgar in 1805, and the Royal Navy had not been seriously challenged since then. Nothing had been neglected to maintain both technical and numerical superiority over any possible enemy, or combination of enemies, at sea. There would be many surprises in store; but the policy of building large numbers of destroyers, in addition to the big ships, would be proved soon enough, in actual wartime conditions, to have been a wise precaution.

Officers and men who had to serve in destroyers had a mentality of their own, in keeping with the romantic idea that they were "sea wolves" and, to a certain extent, free roamers — or, as officers in bigger ships called them, "pirates." The commander of a destroyer was an all-rounder, not a specialist He was his own navigator — in so far as navigation was sometimes necessary — signaller, gunner, and perhaps everything else, except engineer.

Discipline in the small vessels was much more free-and-easy than in big battleships and cruisers, where most, if not all, the officers were specialists.

Officers in big ships called destroyer officers "salt horses" — meaning nonspecialists, a term of disdain. As destroyers spent most of their time in port being incapable of long cruises the service attracted married men. It also gave opportunities to officers of not very high rank to attain command, if only of a small vessel, with some extra pay and allowances for command.

Against these advantages, was the decided disadvantage that destroyers, when at sea in heavy weather, are the most uncomfortable vessels that the diabolical ingenuity of naval architects has ever devised. They "roll their guts out" and have extremely cramped living quarters.

Professional naval officers regarded destroyers as "bad service" as far as prospects of promotion were concerned. An officer in command of a destroyer was likely to be left there for years. His good qualities were not immediately under the observation of Admirals, as were those of officers in big ships. As for sociable or wardroom life in a destroyer, it scarcely existed, compared with the service in big ships.

Any scorn that might have been felt for destroyers in peacetime soon evaporated in wartime, when they quickly made their usefulness felt, and became the hardest worked units of the Royal Navy, being given tasks of endurance, difficulty, and danger, which could scarcely have been envisaged during the easy going days in port in peacetime.

During my three months' training in H.M.T.B.D. *Syren* she put to sea only once, and that was on a training cruise from Portsmouth to Dover and back. We left Portsmouth in a dense fog, which meant proceeding at quarter speed, or less, but, although there was no breeze, there was a heavy swell, which showed me how she could roll. This was the smallest ocean going vessel in which I had ever voyaged.

My station was with the Commander on the conning tower, and we navigated by compass and by guess, fully exposed to the weather, with several frights as we avoided collisions in the traffic crowded waters of the English Channel and Strait of Dover. At last we crawled into Dover Harbour, and there lay at anchor in a heavy ground swell for twenty-four hours. And she rolled, and she rolled.

A Petty Officer growled, "She'd roll even in dry dock!"

Then we got orders to carry out a night exercise. We were to return to Portsmouth and make a sneak attack, in simulated war conditions, on the harbour defences.

All lights on the navigational aids into the harbour would be dowsed for the purposes of the exercise. If we could creep into harbour without being spotted, the attack would be deemed successful.

It was a dark night, with no moon, and no fog, when we arrived off Portsmouth in a stiff gale with high running seas which stood the *Syren* on end and really showed me what it means to be on the bridge of a destroyer when she "thrusts into it" with seas washing over her decks from stem to stern. The powerful but old engines had made her vibrate, shaking us like dice in a box, on the passage from Dover.

Now we crept into harbour at dead slow, hoping for the best, in the total darkness. Standing beside me on the bridge of the conning tower was Commander Williams, tense and anxious. Our 4-inch gun was loaded with blank. Gunner Yandall was standing by the gun.

Suddenly, as we were passing a quarter of a mile from one of the outlying island forts, our steering gear jammed!

We were heading for the dimly discerned fort, and had to go full speed astern to avoid running aground!

The wash of our propellers gave us away. The fort opened fire on us with 6-inch guns at almost point blank range. It was a terrifying experience. If the guns had been firing high explosive shells instead of blanks, we would have been blown to Kingdom Come in a few seconds. As things were, our faces were blackened with smut and wads from the gunpowder used in the blank charges.

I sprang to help Gunner Yandall, and we fired three rounds of blank from our 4-inch gun. Then we switched on our navigation lights as a signal of surrender.

At this, the navigation lights of the port entrance were also switched on, and the "attack" was over. We scurried to the mooring buoys in disgrace, and made fast It took a few stiff nips of Nelson's Blood to restore our shattered nerves, and to give us the feeling that it was not altogether our fault that the steering gear had jammed at such a critical moment.

So ended my training in destroyers, and my training, for the time being, in the Royal Naval Reserve.

On 2nd June 1914, I rejoined the Cunard service on the active list, with promotion to the rank of First Officer in R.M.S. *Caronia*, on the run from Liverpool to New York.

My wife came to live at Liverpool, which would be my home port, I expected, for many a year to come; for who would have thought that war was so near?

I knew the *Caronia* well, having served in her as Fourth Officer seven years previously, when I had first joined the Cunard service. Now she was commanded by Captain Charles Appleton Smith, a jovial old style sailor man, with a large Roman nose. I had served under him for a year as Fourth Officer in the Cunard liner *S.S. Ultonia* in 1908 on the Mediterranean trade from Trieste and Fiume to New York.

The *Caronia*, a twin screw steamer of 19,000 tons, launched in 1904, was becoming a veteran of the transatlantic run. With her sistership, the triple screw *Carmania*, she was one of the "pretty sisters," typical "ocean greyhounds," which, at their launch, had been the biggest vessels in the world. They had a speed of 18 knots,• and took seven days for the crossing. This meant, allowing for a week in port at each end, that I would be home every three weeks. I looked forward to settling down comfortably into married life and regular routines.

The *Caronia* and *Carmania* had long since ceased to be the biggest ships in the world. The Cunard fleet had been augmented since their day with the two "crack" liners, *Mauretania* and *Lusitania*, each of 31,000 tons, launched in 1907, with speeds of 25 knots. Now, in 1914, the gigantic *Aquitania*, 45,646 tons, had been brought into service, as an upholder of Britain's prestige.

In addition to these, four new medium sized liners, *Franconia*, *Laconia*, *Alaunia*, and *Andania*, had been added to the Cunard fleet between 1911 and 1913.

But competition on the transatlantic passenger routes was keen.

R.M. S. Caronia (Public Domain)

The White Star Line, American owned but under the British flag, had in service a number of comfortable liners of about 20,000 tons, and two gigantic liners, the *Olympic* (launched in 1911) and the *Britannic* (completed in 1914), each of 46,000 tons. These were sisterships of the *Titanic*, which had sunk after colliding with an iceberg in mid-Atlantic in April 1912.

The *Olympic* remained for two years the biggest ship in the world; but the *Mauretania* continued to hold the Blue Riband of the Atlantic for the speediest crossing of the Atlantic, and in 1910 set a record which stood for nineteen years thereafter. This record was made on a westbound crossing, from Daunt's Rock (off Queenstown in Ireland) to Sandy Hook (at the entrance to New York

Harbour), a distance of 2780 miles, which she did in 4 days 10 hours 41 minutes, at an average speed of 26.06 knots.

The two big German companies, Nord Deutscher Lloyd and the Hamburg-Amerika Line, had for many years been engaged in keen rivalry with British liners on the transatlantic route.

Nord Deutscher Lloyd had several well-appointed liners in service of from 17,000 to 19,000 tons, and in 1909 had put the *George Washington* (25,000 tons) on the route from Bremen to New York, calling at Southampton. Then, in 1913, they put into service a vessel of 34,000 tons, the *Columbus*, slightly bigger than our *Lusitania* and *Mauretania*.

The Hamburg-Amerika Line also had a fleet of comfortable and beautiful liners of from 17,000 to 24,000 tons; but in 1913 they launched for service on the New York run three superliners of 52,000 tons — *Imperator*, *Vaterland*, and *Bismarck*, which there- upon became, and for a long time remained, the biggest ships ever built.

They were considerably bigger than the two newest British vessels, Britannic and Aquitania, which were both ready to go into service in June or July 1914. In this mercantile field, the rivalry between Britain and Germany was direct and obvious; but in the overall picture the British Mercantile Marine was much larger, in total tonnage and number of vessels and seamen, than the German Mercantile Marine.

Germany was Britain's nearest rival for maritime supremacy, both in naval and mercantile building programmes. That was not in itself any good cause for a war between the two nations, if political and other factors had not disrupted peaceful relationships.

How that antagonism arose and flared into an armed struggle on a scale of intensity, ferocity, and long duration that was terrible in its effects on both nations, is a matter of history beyond my scope as a seaman to attempt to analyse. The issue was decided not only on land, but also at sea.

Perhaps chiefly at sea. Britain's naval might, and long sustained total sea blockade of Germany, eventually brought the Kaiser down, as it had brought Napoleon down a century previously, and would bring Hitler down in course of time.

That statement does not minimize the struggles of the other fighting services, on land and in the air, against Germany's armed might; but it emphasises that warfare at sea was vital in contributing to the final result. The story that I have to tell is only of my own experiences during two wars at sea between Britain and her allies, and Germany and her allies, with an interlude of peace between those wars. My experiences were similar to those of hundreds of thousands of other British merchant seamen, in one way or another. What I have to record is more or less typical, and it is only for that reason that I put the details into print, to throw some light on events which, for younger generations, may already be fading into the fabulous or nebulous regions of a bygone era. My training in the Royal Naval Reserve had been timely. I had finished it only three months before war was declared, with a suddenness — as far as I and millions of others were concerned — of a thunderclap from a clear sky.

I made only two voyages from Liverpool to New York and return as First Officer in the *Caronia*, in June and July, 1914. When she arrived at Liverpool on 22nd July, she was put into dock for refit and therefore taken off her regular run for the time being. I could look forward to a few weeks' living at home until she was ready to go into service again.

Even then, the political preliminaries to the war were in full swing in Central Europe. Britain declared war on Germany on 4th August, 1914, and, from that day, a life-and-death struggle had begun, which would throw the whole world into convulsions, introducing the Modern Era of long continued turmoil and profound changes in techniques, and also in ideas of right and wrong.

The old days and old ways had come to a sudden end. This was Der Tag — at last.

3

*From Peace to War — "Caronia" Converted to a Merchant Cruiser —
"Gutting" Her for War Service — Guns Mounted — Under the White
Ensign — Ship's People Signed On Under Articles of War — Naval
Discipline and Routine — A Shake-up All Round — Gunnery Exercise —
Smartening up the "Black Squad" — On Patrol in the Chops of the
Channel — We Capture a German Barque — The Big Blockade of
Germany — The Game of Life and Death.*

W**HEN** the *R.M.S. Caronia* had been put into dock for refit, at
Liverpool, on 22nd July, 1914, her crew, including the officers, had
been paid off. This was the usual procedure at the end of each
voyage in British merchant vessels. The crew signed articles at the beginning of
each voyage and were paid off when the vessel returned to her home port. Under
this system most of the crew received no pay while they were ashore in their home
port and were signed on again — if they applied for re-employment — when the
next voyage was ready to begin.

It was a practice carried over from sailing ship days, when vessels remained in
their home ports for lengthy periods, sometimes for months, awaiting cargoes or
charters for a new voyage. The "articles" were a contract between the shipowner
and the crew, defining the conditions of employment for a voyage outwards and
homewards, terminating at the home port. Men who were paid off from sailing
vessels could not afford to remain on shore unemployed for months and usually
signed on in some other vessel after a week or two. This meant that sailing vessels
seldom had the same crews for more than one voyage.

But in transatlantic liners, which "turned around" in their home ports within a week or so, to begin a new voyage, the same crew usually signed on again, after a week ashore without pay. So there was, in a sense, continuity of employment for the crews, throughout the year, but with one week in every four of unemployment for most of them. (Officers were given "shore pay," and a few of the crew were retained on board, at daily wage rates while the ship was in port.)

Liners were usually laid up once a year in their home port for refit, for a period of three weeks, with consequent unemployment for the crews for that period. That was the situation when the crew of the *Caronia* were paid off at Liverpool a fortnight before the outbreak of the Great European War. Like everyone else of the "ship's people," I expected to be signed on again in my former position (First Officer) when her refit was completed.

The *Caronia* had a complement of 500 ship's people, made up of 60 in the Deck Department (officers, seamen, and others con-cerned with navigation of the liner): 160 in the Engine Department (engineer officers, stokers, and trimmers), and 200 men and 80 women in the Catering Department (pursers, cooks, stewards, and stewardesses). Most of these were out of work for three weeks on shore. On the day that war was declared, my wife and I were at the Royal Agricultural Show at Wavertree on ·the outskirts of Liverpool.

Without waiting to be sent for, I hastened to the Cunard office and was told to go immediately on board the *Caronia*, as she had been commandeered by the Admiralty, and was to be converted to an armed merchant cruiser.

Captain Smith and some of the officers and others of the crew were already on board. More men kept arriving, on their own initiative, or were hastily rounded up by messages sent to their homes. A few hours after the declaration of war, practically the whole of her crew were at work on board; and, supplemented by big gangs of shore labourers, were stripping everything movable from the passenger quarters.

Arrangements to convert selected merchant vessels to armed mer-chant cruisers, troop transports, or hospital ships in the event of war had been made long previously. The changeover of these vessels from a peacetime to a wartime footing was carried out in accordance with carefully prepared Admiralty plans; but those plans had been drawn up necessarily on a theoretical basis. There had to be some "muddling through" — not surprising in view of the vast scale of naval mobilization and fleet dispositions which had to be done at top speed in all British naval bases and other ports, to conform with the strategic plans of blockading Germany and "bottling up" the German Navy.

Britain had not been caught napping. The War Book had been put into operation, in its preliminary stages of precautionary measures, several days perhaps several weeks, before the outbreak of war. It may have been no coincidence that the *Caronia* had been laid up at Liverpool on 22nd July. She was one of four Cunarders designated for immediate conversion to strictly combatant service on the outbreak of war. The other three were the *Aquitania*, the *Carmania*, and the *Laconia*.

The Cunard Company had a fleet of twenty-five ocean going vessels, of which sixteen were passenger liners on the transatlantic run, and nine were smaller cargo steamers working from Liverpool to Mediterranean ports. The total number of navigating officers in Cunard employ was 163. Of these, the very high proportion of 139 had received naval training, and had been commissioned as officers in the Royal Naval Reserve.

U.S.S. Mahomet showing "Dazzle Camouflage" of the type used in WW1 to throw off U-Boats. Dazzle paint cold distort size and angle of the bow under the right conditions.
(Public Domain, U.S. National Archives)

Berthed next to the *Caronia* in the Mersey Dock was the 46,000-ton *Aquitania*, being stripped for her conversion to an armed merchant cruiser. This was a pathetic mistake, as she was too big to handle on naval manoeuvres as a unit in an auxiliary cruiser squadron. Her bulk would make her a target much too easy for enemy guns to hit. She was not only the biggest, but also the newest vessel in the Cunard Service, having made only three voyages to New York before she was commandeered by the Admiralty.

She had taken three years to build and had accommodation for 3200 pas-sengers and 1000 crew. Her cruising speed of 23 knots did not put her into the record breaking class, but no expense had been spared to make her passenger quarters luxurious, in furniture and fittings. All this material, in a brand new condition, had to be hastily taken out of her and stored in warehouses on shore. A total of 5000 men were engaged in "gutting" her and the *Caronia*. More than 2000 wagonloads of material were removed from the two liners within forty-eight hours.

On board the *Caronia* were hundreds of men milling around on deck and below in the alleyways, carrying furniture, beds, bedding, crockery, glassware, silverware, carpets, curtains, and everything else that would be of no use on war service, and slinging it overside to be loaded into horse drawn wagons in the wharf. Simultaneously, gangs of painters were painting her hull and superstructure grey, and her funnels black.

Below decks, carpenters, joiners, plumbers, and electricians were dismantling the passenger cabins, removing all wooden panelling and partitions, washbasins, electric light fittings, and almost ever thing else that was not part of her basic structure. The crew's quarters were left intact, and also the first-class smoke room, which was to be used as a wardroom for officers. With those exceptions, the once luxurious "floating hotel" soon looked an empty steel shell, her decks and 'tween decks bare and desolate.

An even speedier transformation was performed in the *Aquitania*. In four days she was not only gutted and repainted into dazzle, she also had eight 6-inch guns mounted (in gun positions which had been built into her structure before she was launched). On 8th August, wearing the White Ensign, and under command of a Captain of the Royal Navy — with a complement of R.N. and R.N.R. officers and ratings, Royal Marines, and a "Black Squad" of her usual engineers, stokers and trimmers signed on under wartime articles — she moved away from her berth into the Mersey stream and headed out to sea to begin her patrol duties as an auxiliary cruiser.

In the meantime, on 7th August, the *Caronia*'s sistership, *Carmania*, had arrived from New York and berthed at the Liverpool Landing Stage, on her normal schedule. She had left New York on 1st August, with 2600 passengers, including 2000 in the third class — of whom many were Germans or Austrians, who were mak-ing a bid to get home before hostilities began. These people had taken a chance, hoping or expecting that Britain would remain neutral in a dispute which at first had seemed to concern only Austria and Serbia.

Hundreds of police were waiting on the Landing Stage, to scrutinize the passports of the *Carmania*'s passengers as they disembarked, and to take the Germans and Austrians into custody for internment. This caused delay, but on the next day, as soon as *H.M.S. Aquitania* had moved out of her berth, the *Carmania* moved into it, to be stripped and converted.

Quick and lively, the two famed "pretty sisters" became "ugly sisters." The *Caronia* was now under command of Captain Shirley Litchfield, of the Royal Navy, with Lieutenant Aubrey Peebles, R.N., as his First Lieutenant. They came on board accompanied by a Gunner (that is, Gunnery Officer), with twenty R.N. ratings (including armourers and seamen gunners) and a detachment of twenty Royal Marines in charge of a sergeant. She was commissioned by Captain Litchfield as a King's Ship on 8th August and thereby was taken over from Cunard control on that date.

Her peacetime Master, Captain C. A. Smith, together with six of her officers, including myself, who held commissions in the R.N.R., had received orders to proceed to Portsmouth to be drafted for naval duties. We had each been given a uniform allowance of fifty golden sovereigns, for the purpose of outfitting ourselves in R.N.R. uniforms. As far as I was concerned, it was a windfall, and I put the money into the Post Office Savings Bank. My R.N.R. uniform was fully serviceable.

Captain Litchfield took one look at the *Caronia* and instantly decided that it would be an advantage to retain the services of some of the Cunard officers who were used to handling her. He had never been in command of any vessel bigger than a light cruiser of 3000 tons displacement. A passenger liner of 19,000 tons volumetric measurement is as bulky in her external measurements as a battlecruiser of the heaviest class, and her superstructure stands much higher than that of a battlecruiser.

On grasping this obvious fact, Captain Litchfield urgently applied to the Admiralty to appoint the *Caronia*'s former master (Captain Smith), Chief Officer (Henry McConkey), First Officer (myself), and Second and Third Officers in our R.N.R. rankings, as navigating officers under his command. An order was issued cancelling our orders to proceed to Portsmouth — much to our disappointment, as we had hoped to see active service in regular fighting ships rather than in a thin-skinned, lightly gunned, converted liner. During the next two days, ten other R.N.R. officers from various steamship companies joined up, and also several R.N. midship- men, and sixty R.N.R. ratings from Scotland. These were men from the fishing fleet who had undergone R.N.R. training, and, on the outbreak of war, had gone into barracks at Rosyth, on the Firth of Forth.

One of the R.N.R. officers, who had been retired for several years, arrived on board in a uniform coat that could not be buttoned by several inches. He was unable to see his own boots, but he scented battle like an old warhorse. "The exercise will do me good," he said. "It will take some of the fat off me."

Captain Litchfield interviewed all officers, and, according to their seniority and previous experience, appointed them to various specialist duties as watchkeepers, gun officers, fire control, signals, or navigating officers. I was made a navigating officer. The First Lieutenant and Gunner prepared a Watch and Stations Bill, and instituted naval routine.

While the ship was being gutted, gangs of shipwrights and metal- workers had been making preparations to receive the eight 4.7-inch guns. The wooden deck planking was removed from the gun positions, and the steel deck underneath strengthened by means of stanchions, girders, and beams, to withstand the shock of gunnery discharge and recoil. The bulwarks were cut out fore and aft on any Deck to allow the training to a wide angle of guns to be placed there in broadside. On all the gun positions, steel gun rings were then bolted down, ready for the gun pedestals.

Unfortunately, the wrong gun rings had been supplied! When the guns arrived and were hoisted on board, it was found that the bolt holes in their pedestals would not align with the gun rings. This discovery caused a commotion. Numerous officers from the naval supply depot on shore appeared on the scene and discussed the mistake with astonishment and vituperation. A gang was set to work with acetylene burners to remove the wrong rings. After some hours' delay, the right ones were found and fitted. The guns were then securely mounted, and the ship took on her warlike appearance. These were quick firing guns, with a range of 1,000 yards.

A large amount of ammunition was taken in, to magazine platforms built in the holds. A rangefinder was fitted, together with two semaphores, and searchlights were mounted on the wings of the bridge.

Armoured plates were riveted into position over vulnerable parts of the ship. Other parts were reinforced with coal, bags of sand, and rope screens (as protection against flying splinters). Speaking tubes were fitted from the bridge into the aft steering- room, and control telephones were installed from one end of the ship to the other, in naval fashion.

Bunker coal, fresh water, provisions and stores were loaded, sufficient to enable her to remain three weeks at sea. To complete the seagoing complement, Captain Litchfield retained the services of the ship's surgeon, who was given R.N.R. rank. The ship's carpenter, blacksmith, plumber, and painter were given the rank of Petty Officers, R.N.R., and retained. The chief steward and fifty others of the Cunard catering department were signed on as cooks, waiters, und officers' servants, under what was known as "T. 124 Articles" — combining certain features of Merchant Service Articles and the Naval Discipline Act.

Hundreds of stewards from the *Aquitania*, *Caronia*, and *Carmania* — and also from the *Laconia*, which was likewise being fitted out as an A.M.C. at another berth in the Mersey — were superfluous after the ships had been stripped. Most of them drifted into the Army or found other occupations on shore.

Captain Litchfield next turned his attention to the Engine Department. He interviewed the engineers, and this gave them an opportunity to ventilate a long standing grievance. For years the Admiralty had been granting commissions in the Royal Naval Reserve to suitable deck officers, but the number of engineers so admitted had been very limited: a shortsighted policy. The *Caronia* carried twenty engineers of great experience, not one of them holding a commission. They volunteered for service ·in her under naval discipline — it was either that or lose their jobs — but they put the case strongly before the Captain, requesting that they should be admitted to R.N.R. status.

Admiralty approval was obtained, and each engineer was enrolled in the R.N.R. with a temporary commission. The Chief became a Commander, the Second a Lieutenant-Commander, and the other Lieutenants and Sub-Lieutenants, according to their ages and experience. (These were the only four ranks in the R.N.R. at that time.) They were given a uniform allowance of twenty pounds each and came under the R.N.R. pension scheme.

The final problem was to sign on the firemen and trimmers — 140 of them, nearly all "Liverpool Irish" — who had been working in Cunarders for years. As conscription had not then been introduced, they could be brought under naval discipline only by signing the T. 124 Articles as volunteers. There was some jibbing at this. These men had a natural horror of naval or any other kind of discipline. They had been used to doing their work in their own way, and being left to their own devices when off watch. A few of them walked off the ship, refusing to sign, but most of them signed, though with a surly demeanour.

All this drastic transformation of the ship was completed within six days after the declaration of war. On 10th August, being fully commissioned, manned, coaled, stored, watered and ammunitioned, *H.M.S. Caronia* put to sea under sealed orders.

As we proceeded down the Mersey, the difference between Naval and Merchant Service routines was apparent. Under peacetime routine, the *Caronia* usually had eight people stationed on the bridge when she was entering or leaving port. These were: the Captain, the Pilot, the Second Officer, the Fourth Officer, a quartermaster (helmsman) and standby quartermaster, and two bridge boys (messengers).

But now, under naval routine, as she made her way slowly down the Mersey, there were seventeen people on her bridge — Captain Litchfield, R.N., in command; Cunard Captain Smith, Commander, R.N.R., acting as navigator; a Mersey pilot; First Lieutenant Peebles, R.N.; two watchkeeping officers; two midshipmen; a helmsman and a standby helmsman (quartermasters); four A.B. seamen, namely the Captain's messenger, the First Lieutenant's messenger, and two other ratings standing by as additional messengers if required; two signalmen; and a wireless operator.

Things went fairly smoothly until the tugs were cast off and she was steaming quietly down channel, making for the harbour mouth. It was then that Captain

Litchfield, having taken stock, decided that, as there was a war on, he had better shake the R.N.R. people up a bit and let them know that they were now in His Majesty's Navy. He was a tall, alert man of forty-five, and a strict disciplinarian.

The quartermaster at the wheel had been in the *Caronia* for years. He knew the harbour channels perfectly, and what wheel orders to expect when steering in them. But he had an unfortunate habit, when he was under the stress of excitement, of drawing in his breath and sucking his teeth with a clicking noise. This in no way interfered with his efficiency as a helmsman, and was probably an aid to mental concentration on his task.

Captain Litchfield stood it for awhile, then, fixing him with a piercing eye, rapped out, "Stop sucking your teeth, man!" The Q.M. was so humiliated and astonished at this interference with his private affairs that he let the ship wander slightly off her course. "Relieve the wheel!" roared the Captain. The standby quartermaster took over the steering, while the dismissed Q.M. stood by him, and, in his agitation, sucked his teeth more loudly than before.

The Captain ordered him off the bridge. "Go below," he said, "and, next time you are in port, visit a dentist!"

A midshipman who rashly indulged in a smile at this incident was the next to come under the lash. "What is your name?" the Captain thundered.

"Richards, sir."

"Do you find anything to laugh at?" "No, sir."

"Then stop it instantly, or you will be laughing on the other side of your face before I've finished with you!"

Next, the Captain noticed that there was a fault in the electric equipment on the "clear view screen" which was not working smoothly. Turning to the officers of the watch (Henry McConkey and myself), he asked, "Gentlemen, was this inspected and tested before the ship unmoored?"

"I inspected it, sir," said Mcconkey, promptly. "It appeared to be in order."

"Well, it was not in order! Have it attended to immediately!"

An electrician was sent for. He had been in the ship for years, and had now the temporary status of Petty Officer, R.N.R. He came running up to the bridge, wearing his naval uniform, and carrying his toolkit. One button of his jacket was undone. He saluted the Captain.

"You're not properly dressed!"

The electrician looked thunderstruck at this reprimand. "What's wrong with me, sir?" he asked, in bewilderment.

"Do up your buttons!"

During the next hour, until the pilot left her at Lynus Bay Pilot Station, everyone on the bridge got a heave about something. The course was then set for open water. The Captain, having definitely established himself, left the bridge. We breathed freely again and went off stations onto sea routine.

Opening his sealed orders, the Captain found that his instructions were to proceed to a defined position in the Irish Sea for gunnery practice, and to test the calibration of the guns. After that, he was to join the Third Cruiser Squadron, patrolling in the Chops of the Channel (the western approaches) between south-western Ireland and Ushant in France, to intercept any enemy vessels, whether armed or unarmed, that might be found there.

Three days were spent in the gunnery exercises. The two after guns were manned by the Royal Marines, who were thoroughly trained and skilful. The other six guns were manned by R.N.R. officers and ratings, including the Scotch fishermen, who had received some training, but needed more practice. A target was dropped overboard, and each gun was tested in turn at 6000 yards range.

There was a "dummy loader" on board, enabling each gun crew to practice loading. A loading competition was held daily, timed by stopwatches, and bets were laid freely on the results. Some of the stewards and cooks asked to be allowed to form a gun's crew, to practice loading. To this the Captain agreed, styling them "Emergency Gun's Crew," a title of which they were very proud. They practiced assiduously, and, later in our cruise, actually succeeded one day in winning the loading competition!

And that wasn't a story to tell to the Marines.

At intervals during the gunnery exercises, the Captain ordered boat drill and boat training, which included recovering targets after gun practice. In peacetime, the *Caronia* carried twenty-eight lifeboats under davits. These had all been removed, except two, which were retained as sea boats for war service. To provide floatage for her wartime complement of 350 people, if it were necessary to abandon ship, she had these two lifeboats and eighteen Maclean Patent Collapsible Boats, which were a kind of raft with sides which could be pulled up. They were stacked on deck, occupying very little space.

The Scotch fishermen, as was only to be expected, proved smart at boat handling; but all members of the deck crew were put through their paces at handling the boats in naval fashion. The collapsible boats were put overside and tested, and the method of handling them demonstrated.

Having built up the fighting efficiency of his ship in the Deck Department, Captain Litchfield set course southwards in the Irish Sea, making for our rendezvous with the cruiser squadron, to begin our patrol duties. We steamed there at half speed (9 knots) to economize coal. Like all the other transatlantic Royal Mail Steamers, the *Caronia* was designed with coalbunkers and freshwater tanks of sufficient capacity for only a week or ten days at sea at full speed. This period could be protracted to three weeks by reducing the speed of the vessel, which required less coal in her furnaces, and consequently made the work of the firemen and trimmers down below somewhat easier than the hard labour to which they were accustomed.

Captain Litchfield now decided that the time had come to smarten up the Engine Department.

The stokers and trimmers worked in three watches — four hours on and eight off — forty-five men in each watch. This meant that there were at any time ninety of them off duty, sleeping or otherwise taking it easy in their quarters, where, under peacetime conditions, they made their own rules, lived rough, gambled and fought among themselves, and remained apart from the passengers and from everyone else on board. When they were off duty, they were seldom interfered with, either by their own officers or by the Captain. They dressed as they pleased, usually in dirty moleskin pants and sweat grimed singlets, with grimy sweat rags knotted around their necks, and, wearing blucher boots, clumped along the deck to and from their quarters and the engine room companionway, at the changes of the watch, but were otherwise seldom seen. There was no love lost between them and the seamen, including the deck officers, who viewed the grimy stokehold toilers as being little better than animals.

To be fair, though that description was aptly applied to many of them, they belonged to a class of men who had never had much chance in life to be anything except rough and tough. In the slums of Dublin, Glasgow, or Liverpool, where most of them had been born and reared, the children of desperately poverty stricken parents had few opportunities of acquiring education or social polish. Obtaining employment at first as dockside labourers, those who had more brawn than brains signed on as firemen or trimmers in ocean going steamers. (The firemen shovelled coal into the furnaces, and the trimmers wheeled the coal to them in barrows from the bunkers.) Working down below in scorching heat, they developed a permanent thirst, which they assuaged in drunken orgies ashore when they were paid off at the end of each voyage.

The work of the Black Squad was essential in the coal burning steamers. Big liners, such as the *Lusitania* and *Mauretania*, had a hundred men down below in the stokehold in each watch and that meant 300 or more firemen and trimmers in the ship's complement. While the ship was at sea, their time was divided between the grilling racket of the stokehold and their squalid living quarters. The engineer officers knew how to handle them, but of discipline in the ordinary sense there was none. They knew no fine words- only raucous yells for more coal, more steam, more speed, delivered in a jargon which was a mixture of Scotch, Irish and Lancashire dialects, with hoarse profanities which no one except themselves could understand.

As long as they did their work, without shirking it, or causing too much trouble, no notice was taken of their crude behaviour or slovenly garb, provided that they kept themselves out of sight and out of mind of the passengers, away from the passenger quarters and promenade decks. Any shirkers or troublemakers among them were noted by the engineers and told at the end of the voyage not to apply again to be signed on. (The conversion of all big liners from coal burning to oil burning in the 1920s put an end to the employment of numerically large Black Squads.)

In the Royal Navy, the big coal burning battleships and cruisers also had to carry a large number of stokehold ratings, who were considered a necessary evil, if not simply a damn nuisance, greatly increasing the number of people for whom quarters and food had to be provided. But naval stokers were not signed on and off casu-ally at the beginning and end of each voyage. They were signed on, like the naval seamen, for long service. They wore uniforms and were under naval discipline, with Petty Officers (Leading Stokers) to control them. They received training in barracks before going on board, and had to keep themselves clean, clean shaved, and neat, and to obey orders properly given.

Captain Litchfield was disgusted by what seemed to him the horrible slackness of discipline among the *Caronia*'s stokehold hands, and their slovenly appearance and habits. One fine afternoon, as we were steaming southwards through st George's Channel, the Captain ordered that all stokehold ratings off watch should be mustered for inspection.

The ninety men concerned turned out on deck in a shambling mob, grumbling and muttering. Some were garbed in trousers and singlets only, others in overalls. They were mostly unshaven, and grimy with sweat and coal dust A guard of Marines stood by, as the Gunner's Mate and R.N. Petty Officers marshalled the Black Squad, with much noise and jostling, into some sort of line, in two rows, for inspection.

The Captain, the First Lieutenant, the Chief Engineer, and other officers now descended from the bridge, and, before inspecting the men themselves, inspected their quarters. These were in a filthy condition. The Captain emerged with a grim look on his face, and inspected the men, walking slowly up and down the lines, staring at each man with obvious disgust Some of them were overawed, some were sullen, and a few stared back at him defiantly.

The inspection was finished in silence. The Captain then stood away a few paces and delivered an address that was short if not sweet. "You are in the Royal Navy now," he began, "and don't forget it. You have signed up for six months, under articles of war. You are in a King's Ship, under my command. In future you are going to keep yourselves and your quarters clean or take the consequences. I'll smarten you up, my lads, make no mistake about that. From now on, you'll wear the King's Uniform, and I'll see that you don't disgrace it. Your quarters are filthy, and you'll clean them, and keep them clean, for daily inspection. Each watch will have an hour's drill each day, to smarten you up, and you need it. Remember, this ship may be under the enemy's fire at any moment. You have volunteered for service, knowing that risk. All bunks will be taken out of your quarters, and hammocks slung instead. What's good enough for the Navy is good enough for you. Every man must shave daily, keep himself and his clothes and boots neat and clean, obey orders promptly, move smartly, keep his eyes and ears open and his mouth shut, and behave decently at all times, afloat or ashore. That will do you now. Dismiss!"

The Black Squad were astounded at being spoken to in such a firm manner for the first time in their lives. They shuffled off to their quarters, muttering and grumbling, and no doubt there was mutinous talk among them, when they were safe in what had formerly been their stronghold; but they had to knuckle under, and they knew it.

Next day they were given uniforms, which had an effect of subtly transforming their mental outlook. Their living quarters were stripped and cleaned, hammocks slung instead of the bunks, and fodder, vehicles, and other material which could be converted to the use of the enemy's fighting forces).

The blockade rules were tightened by an Order-in-Council of 20th August 1914, enabling not only absolute contraband but also conditional contraband to be seized in vessels under neutral flags, bound for ports in neutral countries — such as Holland, Denmark, Norway, or Sweden from which they might be transhipped to Germany.

This caused much argument when neutral ships were held up and taken into port, for the ultimate destination of their cargoes to be determined. It was impossible for the Germans to enforce a counter blockade of Britain under International Law, as without naval supremacy they could not escort captured British or neutral vessels from the Atlantic or North Sea into their own ports.

It was this strategic disadvantage which eventually induced the Germans to attempt a counter blockade of Britain by the indiscriminate sinking of merchant vessels in the waters surrounding the British Isles. They made their own Rules of War to suit themselves, thereby stirring up intense hatred, which eventually brought the U.S.A. into the war against them. But, in the early stages of the war, the ferocity of "total war" had not yet been put into practice. War was still a game to be played according to the rules, and there was very little hatred in it. It was not yet the dirty game that it became later, when hundreds of British merchant vessels (including a large number of sailing vessels) were sunk by German submarines, many without any warning whatever.

The capture of the barque Odessa by *H.M.S. Caronia* was a feather in our cap on our first short cruise, but as our coal was now nearly all used up, we had to return to Liverpool to refuel.

By this time, at the end of nearly three weeks, Captain Litchfield had fully instituted naval discipline and smartness on board. It had been a very good idea to leave the first-class smokeroom intact, to serve as a wardroom in which all officers in the ship could meet on a friendly footing. In peacetime there was no messroom in Cunarders, in which deck officers and engineer officers could meet and relax together when off watch. Each department had its own messroom in different parts of the ship, and these were only small rooms, skimpily furnished, in which meals were served. Deck officers and engineers were often complete strangers to one another. This estrangement had given rise to the saying, "Oil and water won't mix."

But they mixed all right in wartime. In the comfortable big wardroom of *H.M.S. Caronia*, navigators, gunners, signallers, and engineers, of both R.N. and R.N.R. rankings, were a happy and friendly crowd.

As for the ratings, constant drills and exercises had worked wonders, and even the Black Squad now took a pride in looking smart.

On the way home to Liverpool, Captain Litchfield mustered the ship's company and made a short speech of congratulation. He said: "The ship is now a highly efficient fighting machine, and we are ready to give a good account of ourselves if we come in contact with the enemy. On arrival in port, the crew will be given three days' leave."

This was greeted with loud cheers, and the verdict was that we deserved it.

The transition from peace to war had been no joke; but we were not the only men who had been smartened up. Millions of others, on sea and land, in all the combat forces, were being condi-tioned for a struggle that would be much longer and more deadly than we could imagine at that time.

Optimists were saying, "The war will be over by Christmas." That was true enough, but they didn't mention which Christmas. There would be four Christmases before the world would again enjoy a peaceful merry Christmas.

When *H.M.S. Caronia* berthed at Liverpool, on 4th September 1914, to take in coal and stores for another cruise, one month after the outbreak of war, it seemed that war was only an interesting game. We did not know that it would become a dirty and cunning game before it could be fought to a finish.

"Caronia" on the North American Station — "Carmania's" Victory in a Gallant Sea Fight — Our Patrol Outside American Ports — German Liners Tied Up in New York — The German Counter Blockade of Britain — U-Boat Campaign Begins — The Tragedy of the "Lusitania" — Warnings Disregarded — We Wish Her "Bon Voyage" — My Friend Percy Hefford — The Appalling Death roll — Hatred Unleashed.

AFTER refuelling at Liverpool, *H.M.S. Caronia* was loaded with naval stores, provisions, and ammunition, and sent across the Atlantic, in mid-September, 1914, to join the cruiser squadron on the North American Station, which had its base at Halifax in Nova Scotia.

We did not know when, if ever, we would see Liverpool again. My wife remained at Liverpool, and, like the wives of all other naval officers and ratings on active service in wartime, could only wait for whatever news, good or bad, might come to her at any time.

Soon after we arrived at Halifax, we received thrilling news. The *Caronia's* sistership, *Carmania*, equipped as an armed merchant cruiser on the West Indies Station, had been sent to examine the waters near Trinidad, to see if any enemy vessels were sheltering there. On 14th September she had encountered the German liner *Cap Trafalgar*, a vessel of 18,500 tons with a speed of 18 knots, carrying a cargo of coal, intended for refuelling German warships in the South Atlantic.

The *Cap Trafalgar*, approximately the same size and speed as the *Carmania*, had left Buenos Aires on 15th August, and had been converted, at sea, into an armed merchant cruiser, under the German war flag. The two vessels were evenly matched in gun power. They met in single combat off Trinidad.

Both ships were heavily damaged by gunfire, and the *Cap Trafalgar* was sunk. The *Carmania* limped into Pernambuco for repairs. Nine of her crew were killed and twenty-six wounded in this duel Which was unique in modern naval annals as the only action fought, in modern times, between two armed merchantmen in the traditions of olden times, ship to ship, slugging it out — no thought of running away — and cheers from the winners for the gallantry of the losers as their ship went down with colours flying.

The British cruiser squadron based on Halifax consisted of *H.M.S. Bristol*, *H.M.S. Essex*, and a few other armoured warships of the Royal Navy, now supplemented by *H.M.S. Caronia*. Our task was to maintain a patrol in the sea lanes leading to and from New York, Boston, and other American ports in that vicinity.

To do that, we would have to seek out and destroy any armed German or other enemy vessels that might prowl there. We would also have the duty of arresting any enemy merchant vessels on the high seas, to bring them into a British port (Halifax or Bermuda) for adjudication. Further, we would have the right, under inter-national agreements, to inspect any vessel at sea flying the flag of neutral nation, and to escort her at our discretion into a British port to inspect her cargo for contraband goods intended to be delivered to our enemies.

The U.S.A., like the Scandinavian countries and Holland, was neutral, and entitled to trade with both sides engaged in the war. But, as Britain had proclaimed a blockade of Germany, the British Navy had the right to prevent contraband from reaching Germany in neutral ships. This right was undeniable, but the Masters of ships under the neutral flags did not like it any the more for that and usually protested volubly when they were held up and their papers demanded, or if they were escorted into Halifax for inspection of their cargoes. They protested all the more loudly if they knew that their cargoes were in fact destined for delivery to Germany.

The German Navy was powerless in the early months of the war to send any substantial force to sea to interfere with British shipping, or with neutral vessels bound for British or French ports. Our armed patrol outside New York and Boston was never challenged by German warships.

The presence of a British naval squadron there was a deterrent to the few German surface raiders who were at large in the Atlantic when the war began. The Germans had no bases for refuelling in the Western Atlantic. That was in itself enough to keep them away, but we had to be on guard against the possibility of sneak raids by German cruisers which might be refuelled at sea from tramp steamers, or might succeed in creeping out of the North Sea, into the Atlantic, around the north of Scotland, through the British Grand Fleet's cordons.

A large number of British merchant vessels continued to trade to and from American ports under the protection of the British Navy on the high seas. Among them the big Cunarders, *Lusitania* and *Mauretania*, together with other Cunarders, ran on their normal schedules between Liverpool and New York, carrying passengers, mails, and cargoes (including war material) without interruption from the enemy.

German merchant traffic had come to a standstill on the North Atlantic routes within a few days after the outbreak of war. In New York Harbour there were a dozen or more liners of the Nord Deutscher Lloyd and the Hamburg-Amerika Line tied up and unwilling to venture out to be captured — as would be almost a certainty by the British naval patrols. Among them was the mammoth new liner *Vaterland* (52,282 tons), the biggest ship in commission in the world, put into service by the Hamburg-Amerika Line only a few months before the war. She had entered New York Harbour, on her regular schedule, on the day that war was declared. Her sistership, *Imperator* (52,022 tons) was at Hamburg when war was declared, and was laid up there, out of service during the war. The third German mammoth liner *Bismarck* (56,551 tons) was launched but not quite completed and lay in the shipbuilding dock of Blohm & Voss, Hamburg, during the war.

The *Caronia's* patrol cruises from Halifax to the approaches to New York (keeping strictly outside U.S.A. territorial waters) and return to base, occupied three weeks. The distance was only 600 miles each way. For most of the time we cruised at four knots, to conserve fuel. Usually there were two or three cruisers in company — either within sight or at close call by radio. Most of the work of boarding and inspecting vessels under neutral flags was done by the armoured cruisers, which could make a much greater show of force than the *Caronia*. We spent most of our time hanging about off New York, watching the comings and goings of the busy traffic ng that great port, including the regular arrivals and departures the *Mauretania* and *Lusitania* and other Cunarders and White Star Liners.

At the end of three weeks, relieved by another cruiser on the station, we would return to Halifax for refuelling, and for a week's rest in port for the crew, before going out again on patrol. Winter set in, and the patrol work was monotonous and uneventful, but tiring, as constant vigilance had to be maintained. Often there were false alarms, as reports came from our intelligence services In New York that one or another of the German liners laid up there was getting steam up, ready to put to sea. Probably the Germans amused themselves by making a black smoke occasionally from their funnels to hoax us.

We kept close watch on the harbour exits, especially at nighttime, but none of the enemy owned liners came out. Often, we hailed the *Lusitania* or *Mauretania*, when they were homeward bound from New York, and sent a boat to them with our mailbags, including dispatches for the Admiralty. Those two big and beautiful liners — the speediest merchant ships in the world — had been originally designed for quick conversion into armed merchant cruisers, but they had not been commandeered by the Admiralty immediately on the outbreak of war, as the *Aquitania* was. Their regular arrival at, and departure from, New York, on their normal schedules, while the German liners skulked in harbour, was a demonstration to Americans of Britain's naval supremacy, if such a demonstration were needed.

The *Aquitania*, after becoming involved in a collision, had limped back into Liverpool in September 1914, for repairs, and then was laid up for many months in idleness, until a decision was made to refit her as a troopship.

Halifax in winter is not a cheerful place as a leave port. The war was not "over by Christmas," and nobody now knew how long it would last Towards the end of January 1915, my wife, in company with the wives of other officers on the North American Station, I brought over to Halifax in a small passenger steamer, *S.S. Missanabe*. This appeared to be an indication from the Admiralty it was intended to keep the *Caronia* on the North American Station for a long time, perhaps for the duration of the war. that being so, May and I got an apartment on shore, and made a home of it, even though I could be at home only one week in four.

A few days after the *Missanabe* had left Liverpool, a German U-boat appeared in the Irish Sea on 30th January 1915, and sank three small British cargo steamers by gunfire, off the entrance to the Mersey. These ships were sunk after their crews had been given a warning to take to the boats. That was the first effective indication that the German Navy intended to attempt to establish a counter-blockade of Britain by U-boat operations On 4th February 1915 — six months after the outbreak of war — the Germans officially declared that all the waters surrounding Great Britain and Ireland were considered by the German Navy to be a war zone.

The German declaration added: "On and after 18th February 1915, every enemy merchant vessel found in the said war zone will be destroyed, without its being always possible to avert the dangers threatening the crews and passengers on that account ... Neutral powers are accordingly forewarned not to continue to entrust their crews, passengers, or merchandise to such vessels . . . In view of the misuse of neutral flags ordered by the British Government and the accidents of naval war, it cannot always be avoided to strike even neutral ships in attacks that are directed at enemy ships."

This declaration was to some extent, but not entirely, a bluff. It was not within the power of German naval surface vessels to establish or maintain a blockade of Britain under international agreements for the conduct of blockades. The only chance which the Germans might have of counter blockading Britain would be by the use of U-boats, which could not capture merchant ships and escort them into German ports as prizes of war but could only destroy them.

The British Admiralty had already declared the whole North Sea to be a "seat of war" and had laid minefields on the northern side of Dover Strait, and along the coast of Holland, across the mouth of Heligoland Bight, and in waters between Scotland and Norway, to prevent sorties by the German Navy and access to German ports by neutral merchant ships.

Now, by means of their U-boats, including submarine minelayers, the Germans intended to extend that war zone to Britain's Western Ocean approaches. This was a bluff only to the extent that, when their proclamation was issued in February, 1915, the German Navy had only twenty-three U-boats in service; but at that time, as they alone knew, their shipyards were hard at work building a fleet of 200 bigger and better U-boats, and crews were being trained to man them, for the unrestricted U-boat campaign to be developed later. In prewar days, and at the beginning of the war, the U-boats had a slow speed (five knots under water), and a limited cruising range. They were propelled, when submerged, by electric motors powered by storage batteries. These batteries had to be frequently recharged, by oil driven motors carried on board for that purpose. U-boats had to come to the surface frequently to recharge their batteries and to renew their air supply. They were then visible and vulnerable. They surfaced mainly at nighttime, or cautiously In the daytime if the horizon, as revealed in their periscopes, was clear. The periscope could operate when the U-boat was submerged to a depth of six fathoms (30 feet) or less. It was an arrangement of mirrors in a telescopic tube, which could be pushed up by hydraulic power to five or six feet above the surface when the U-boat's hull was submerged. The utmost depths to which U-boats could submerge was fifty fathoms.

U-boats, even when surfaced, presented a difficult target for gunfire. They were almost awash and had no silhouette against the sky. Countermeasures including sinking them by gunfire when they could be sighted or ramming them when they were surfaced or partly submerged. Minefields were laid to trap them, and steel nets to entangle them were stretched across Dover Strait and other channels. But the nets were ineffective. U-boats could dive under them or navigate over them on the surface at certain conditions of the tide. Depth charges had not been thought of, in that early stage of the war. The answer that is always found to every new weapon of war had not yet been found.

The sinking by a U-boat of the three small cargo steamers in the Irish Sea, at the approaches to Liverpool, on 30th January 1915, had demonstrated the enemy's ability to develop long range cruising submarines which could menace all Britain's Western Ocean approaches. Probably because of this threat, followed by the German official declaration of counter blockade four days later, the champion

Cunarder *Mauretania* was withdrawn from the New York run about that time, and was kept in port at Liverpool pending a decision as to her further use.

So it happened that both the *Aquitania* and *Mauretania* were laid up for several months; but that precaution was not applied to the *Lusitania* — known familiarly as the "Lucy" — which continued in service as an unarmed merchant vessel on the Liverpool to New York run, as though everything were peaceful and serene. The result of that carefree decision to carry on regardless of risks, when a disaster that shocked British complacency into a terrible awakening to the real extent of the U-boat menace.

On Saturday, 1st May 1915, the *R.M.S. Lusitania* (32,000 tons, average speed 25 knots) left New York on her normal schedule, Without the slightest secrecy. On the contrary, the date and time of her departure had been regularly advertised for weeks previously

In American newspapers. She had on board 1257 passengers and crew of 702 total, 1959 souls. Among the passengers were 159 Americans. Some of these were international celebrities, such as Arthur Vanderbilt, multimillionaire; Charles Frohmann, the most famous and well liked American theatrical producer; and Elbert Hubbard, popular philosopher and sage, author of the bestselling book, Message to Garcia.

The *Lusitania*'s cargo consisted of a large quantity of foodstuffs and sheet metal — which could properly be regarded by the Germans as conditional contraband — and some absolute contraband, including 4200 cases of small arms ammunition and 100 cases of shrapnel shells (not loaded). These items were all declared in her manifest lodged with the New York Port authorities.

On the morning when the *Lusitania* was due to depart, an advertisement appeared in the shipping columns of the principal New York newspapers: In some of the newspapers, it was placed alongside the Cunard advertisement:

> NOTICE!
> TRAVELLERS intending to embark on the Atlantic voyage are reminded that a state of war exists between Germany and her allies and Great Britain and her allies: that the zone of war includes the waters adjacent to the British Isles: that, in accordance with formal notice given by the Imperial German Government, vessels flying the flag of Great Britain, or of any of her allies, are liable to destruction in those waters and that travellers sailing in the war zone on ships of Great Britain or her allies do so at their own risk.
> IMPERIAL GERMAN EMBASSY
> Washington, D.C., April 22, 1915

There was nothing new in this reminder, and no one was bluffed by it into cancelling a passage in the *Lusitania*. The German counter blockade of Britain had been proclaimed nearly three months previously. In that time the *Lusitania* had made several crossings of the Atlantic. It was considered by naval experts and by the public that with her great speed she could easily outrun any submarine that might attempt to challenge her.

But in that theory, there were some inconsistencies, to which not much thought had been given. To economize fuel, some of the *Lusitania*'s boilers were not fired. This reduced her speed to 21 knots and increased her time on the passage from five days to six. Even at that, no submarine could catch up with her

R.M.S. Lusitania in port.
(Public Domain, United States Library of Congress's Prints and Photographs division under the digital ID cph.3g13287)

in mid-ocean. But, if she reduced speed in the narrow waters of the British Isles, when nearing her destination, she would be vulnerable.

It was 12.30 p.m. on 1st May when the Lucy moved her great bulk away from the Cunard Pier into the Hudson River, and headed down the harbour, past Battery Point and the Statue of Liberty, homeward bound, as so often before.

Three hours later, outside U.S.A. territorial waters, she slowed down for a rendezvous with three ships of our cruiser squadron. *H.M.S. Bristol*, *H.M.S. Essex*, and *H.M.S. Caronia* were there in company, waiting to deliver our mailbags on board.

All four ships were stopped and drifting on the long swell. There was scarcely a breeze to ruffle the surface of the ocean, as the cruisers sent off boats to deliver the mailbags. A light mist clung around the ships, like a shroud. The cruisers had been maneuverer to within a cable's length of the big Cunarder — the Armoured cruisers on one side, the *Caronia* on the other.

On the bridge of the *Lusitania* I could see her Master, Captain Will Turner, and his Staff Captain "Jock" Anderson. I knew them both well, having served under them as Junior Third Officer in the old champion transatlantic liner, *S.S. Umbria*, seven years previously. Since then Captain Turner had commanded the *Caronia* in, the *Carmania*, the *Mauretania*, and the *Aquitania*. He had only recently taken command of the Lucy, relieving Captain Daniel Dow, who had commanded her in the early months of the war. He and .Jock Anderson both came briefly to the port wing of the bridge, to wave their greetings to former shipmates who were in the *Caronia*.

Then, through the swirling mist veils, I saw the Lucy's Second Officer, Percy Hefford. He was a special friend of mine, as we had served together as First and Second Mates in an old rattletrap trump, *S.S. Nether Holme*, before either of us had joined the Cunard service. That had been in 1906, the year the *Lusitania* was launched on the Clyde. It had been Percy Hefford's dream of ambition then to serve some day in the *Lusitania*. Now, there he was.

We semaphored to one another with our arms "Cheerio!" "Good-bye!" "Good voyage!" "Good luck!"

In a few minutes the mailbags were delivered. The four propellers of the *Lusitania* began turning, churning a wake of foam, as she was gathering speed and with three long blasts of her foghorn — the sailors' Farewell — she made off eastwards, and was soon lost to our view in the mist

A week later we learned the terrible news that stunned the world and, in a sense, altered the course of the war and of human history. It was the sinking of the *Lusitania* by a torpedo fired without warning from a German U-boat, a manmade disaster more horrifying for that reason than the wreck of the *Titanic* three years previously — that aroused the intense indignation and hatred against Germany which eventually brought the U.S.A. into the war. That was the turning point in American public opinion, which, until then, had been "isolationist" and neutral.

At 2.10 p.m., on Friday, 7th May, the *Lusitania* was steaming eastwards along the southern shore of Ireland. She was ten miles offshore, abeam of the Old Head of Kinsale. Her speed had been reduced to 18 knots, so that she would arrive off the Mersey Bar, at her home port, only 270 miles away, at full tide. She was held on a straight course for forty minutes, so that a four-point bearing could be taken on the Old Head of Kinsale, as a precise navigational "fix."

The weather was clear and the sea smooth. There was no other vessel in sight. No one would have thought that there was a war on. No warship of any kind had come out from Queenstown Harbour, or from anywhere else, to escort the big Cunarder, which was at that time the only "gigantic" liner on the transatlantic service.

The neglect to provide naval escort for her in the narrow waters as she approached her destination was all the more remarkable as no less than twenty-three British merchant vessels had been tor-pedoed and sunk by German U-boats near the coasts of Britain and Ireland in the preceding seven days.

This information had not been published, and Captain Turner did not know it. The German counter blockade of Britain had begun in earnest! It was not a bluff, but a grim reality!

The Admiralty apparently had no plans to deal promptly with the submarine menace, of which there had been ample warning. One explanation of that neglect is that the Admiralty was preoccupied with the serious situation in the Eastern Mediterranean, where a major strategic operation was in progress. A large military force had been landed on Gallipoli Peninsula on 25th April, with heavy casualties, in an attempt to force the Dardanelles and open sea communications with Russia, to strengthen the Eastern Front and draw off German forces from the Western Front. The naval support of that operation had weakened British naval forces in home waters. Most of the ships of the Home Fleet had to be concentrated in the North Sea and on guarding the transport of troops across the Channel from Britain to France.

This disposition of naval units had left the Western Ocean approaches to the British Isles only lightly guarded for the time being. Yet on that fine afternoon there were some warships of the Irish Coast Patrol — including a few old cruisers, and some torpedo boats and armed trawlers and yachts — at anchor in the naval stations at Queenstown and Bantry Bay, and none of them at sea on patrol. There seems to have been no good reason why they were sheltering in harbour, except sheer complacency and unrealism.

Lurking undisturbed and surfaced, only ten miles offshore and twenty miles from Queenstown harbour, on the main route of shipping, was the German U-20, commanded by Captain Walther Schweiger. This was Schweiger's first patrol in a U-boat. In one week out from Emden, he had sunk three British merchant vessels — a schooner and two steamers — in the waters off Queenstown. He had only two torpedoes left, and just enough oil fuel to enable him to get back to his base.

Through his binoculars, Schweiger saw a large steamer approaching from the westward. He ordered "Diving stations," and the U-boat slid beneath the surface, to level out at six fathoms, going ahead on a course to converge with that of the steamer.

According to his log, Schweiger did not at first recognize the *Lusitania*, and had no special orders to wait for her and destroy her. From his point of view, it was merely a chance that she came within the focus of his periscope vision, holding a straight course, It then reduced speed, in perfect conditions of clear visibility and a smooth sea.

When the *Lusitania* was "crossing the T" of his course, at 2000 yards range, Schweiger launched a torpedo at her in these perfect conditions for a hit. Percy Hefford on her bridge saw the wake of the torpedo too late to alter course. It struck the liner amidships fill her starboard side and exploded. A second detonation followed immediately from the explosion of something inside her hull, destroying the bulkheads of her watertight compartments.

Within twenty minutes, the *Lusitania* had plunged to the bottom. The death toll was appalling — 785 of her passengers and 413 of her crew perished — a total of 1198 souls of the 1959 who were on board. Among those who perished were my friends Staff Captain Jock Anderson and Second Officer Percy Hefford. Captain Will Turner went down with his ship but was picked up from the water in a half-drowned and dazed condition and survived.

As soon as the torpedo struck the *Lusitania*, her wireless operator had sent out the S.O.S. with her position. This brought to the rescue a dozen or more light naval craft, tugs, trawlers and other small seagoing vessels from Queenstown. They picked up 761 survivors and a great number of dead bodies. Only a few lifeboats had been successfully launched in the short time before the liner sank. Others had capsized when the liner took a heavy list, as they were being launched.

Of 159 Americans on board, 124 had perished. Among them were Arthur Vanderbilt, Charles Frohmann, and Elbert Parker Hubbard.

If it is any use expressing an opinion a long time after the event, part of the blame for the tragedy of the *Lusitania* must rest on the Admiralty for neglecting to provide an escort for a ship of her size and importance on that main route of shipping where German submarines had sunk vessels only a few days previously.

Captain Turner could not be blamed for reducing speed. If he had arrived at the Mersey Bar too soon to cross it at high tide, and had to wait there, he might have been a sitting duck shot for submarines lurking at that entrance. He could perhaps be blamed for keeping his ship on a straight course for forty minutes, while taking a four point bearing on the Old Head of Kinsale, instead of zigzagging; but taking bearings was a matter of routine in navigation. Antisubmarine tactics, such as zigzagging, had not yet been fully developed.

As to why the *Lusitania* sank so rapidly, making it impossible either to beach her or to launch her boats effectively with the ensuing frightful death toll, the explanation may be in the second explosion that shook her, and split her open, after the torpedo struck. This may have been caused by ammunition carried in her cargo, or by a boiler explosion. There was no legal reason why ammunition should not have been carried in her, and there seemed no practical reason not to carry it, as no one seriously expected that the *Lusitania* would be torpedoed without warning.

That was the essence of the tragedy. Nine months after the war had begun, people were not yet mentally adjusted to the ruthlessness of war. Even in high places, men in positions of the utmost responsibility were still thinking of war as a game to be played in accordance with old fashioned rules.

It was the sinking of the *Lusitania* that first indicated to millions of people that in this war not only men in uniform, but also civilians, would suffer, and that all old fashioned ideas of chivalry and decency would go into the discard, in a fight to the finish.

From then on, the "Great" War became a "Hate" War, with no holds barred. An old proverb took on a new and sinister meaning — "All's fair in love and war."

Old days and old ways had at last ended on that day when the giant Lucy plunged to the deeps. Complacency was at an end, and the Modern Age had begun, with few moral scruples remaining, and every ruse allowable in a dirty fight.

I N May, 1915, *H.M.S. Caronia* was ordered to return from the North American Station to Liverpool, to be equipped with 6-inch guns. These would have a much greater range and hitting power from the 4.7-inch guns mounted in her at the beginning of the war. The essence of naval tactics in gunnery is to outrange the enemy — to stand off and pound him to pieces while his guns of smaller calibre and shorter range cannot reach their mark. The *Caronia* was now commanded by Captain A. Norton, R.N., who had relieved Captain Litchfield, R.N., in April.

One fine afternoon, at 3 p.m., while we were steaming homewards across the Atlantic, the crew were taking it easy, as usual at that time of day. Suddenly the bugle sounded "Action stations." We all rushed to our stations, buckling on our lifebelts and other battle gear, and wondering what was coming next.

Soon enough we knew, as in the distance to the eastwards we sighted a large battleship steaming towards us, making smoke from four funnels, and bristling with big guns She was flying the White Ensign, but what of that? The flying of false colours was a well-known ruse of war at sea, though probably not in regular warships. Why then had Captain Norton ordered us to battle stations? If the stranger was a British ship, he would have had code signals from her by wireless before she hove in sight. Evidently, he thought that she might be an enemy battleship which had got out into the Atlantic.

Instead of turning tail and trying to run away from her obviously greater gunpower and range than ours, he altered course to close the range. If there was a man in the *Caronia* who didn't have a sinking feeling at the pit of his stomach at that moment, he must have had nerves of iron, or no imagination. It was obvious that the battleship, with her 10-inch or possibly 13-inch guns, would be able to blow us to smithereens long before the range was closed to 9000 yards for our puny 4.7-inch guns, which in any case could not do much damage to the battleship's heavily armoured decks and sides.

The manoeuvre was suicidal, and it seemed obvious that we had only a few minutes to live. My battle station was on the bridge as a navigating officer. The bridge would be the first target for the enemy's gun layers.

The range closed to five miles, and still the battleship did not open fire on us. Our guns would be useless until the range closed to a little under two miles. Our gun crews were tense. This was more than the Nelson Touch. It was madness.

Suddenly the battleship altered course. Was she running away from us? Incredible! More likely she was getting into position to give us a broadside. Not that this manoeuvre was necessary. Her big guns in her forward turrets would have been more than enough to blow us out of the water, with one hit.

When the range had closed to three miles, Captain Norton suddenly smiled and gave the order, "Off stations!"

The "enemy" was one of our own ships, flying her true colours. Captain Norton had known this all the time, but he wanted to test the behaviour of the *Caronia*'s people under stress, and to see what our reactions would be in such an emergency. We watched the battleship bearing away from us, until she was out of sight. Captain Norton mustered all hands on deck and informed us that his order for battle stations had been an exercise. He congratulated us on our coolness and efficiency.

But that was not all. Several of the R.N. and R.N.R. officers had noticed some peculiarities in the battleship that we had met, and no one had been able to identify her positively from her silhouette and signals. There were all kinds of naval secrets and mysteries, and this was one of them. What was an unaccompanied British battleship doing in mid-Atlantic, cruising at a speed of only eight knots?

Later, some of us were told the answers. She was a "dummy" battleship! Some genius at the Admiralty had had the bright idea of camouflaging old 6000-ton cargo steamers with false wooden hull frames and superstructures, mounting wooden guns in sheet iron turrets in them, and adding dummy funnels and other fitments, to make them look like Dreadnoughts. They were then sent on patrol into the North Atlantic, to fool German Naval Intelligence on the dispositions of our Grand Fleet!

No doubt there were German spies in some of the American, Norwegian, Swedish, Danish, Dutch and other neutral steamers, or oven in British passenger liners on the Atlantic routes. The dummy battleships appeared on the horizons of such vessels, at a sufficient distance to be mistaken for the real thing but avoided coming in near enough for the hoax to be detected.

Whether the reports of mighty British capital ships cruising in the North Atlantic ever reached Germany, or not, is impossible to say; but the war at sea had become a battle of wits, and all sorts of ruses were employed. The dummy battleships were the reverse of the "Q" ships (or Mystery Ships) which were later used to trap submarines.

In the "Q" ships, cargo steamers, and even sailing vessels, were manned by naval personnel (not in uniform), carried concealed guns, and sailed under the false colours of mercantile ensigns, either British or neutral. If a U-boat surfaced and ordered a "Q" Ship to stop for inspection of her papers or cargo, the "Q" ship would pretend to surrender, and then, when the submarine came nearer, would open fire on her at almost point blank range.

The "Q" ships were warships disguised as merchant vessels; but the dummy battleships were merchant vessels disguised as warships. In the end there were so many ruses of war that almost every old fashioned rule for the honourable conduct of war at sea went by the board.

This was the immediate result of the German tactics of sinking British merchant ships at sight, without any warnings or formalities, by means of torpedoes fired from submerged submarines, as demonstrated so dramatically in the sinking of the *Lusitania*; but in the early stages of the U-boat campaign, the Germans had orders to respect neutral flags, and for a while did so.

The Germans on their side claimed that the British blockade of German and neutral coasts in the North Sea by means of minefields was unethical and could lead to the sinking of ships without warning, since there is little difference between the effects of a concealed mine and a torpedo. They claimed also that British merchant ships had improperly used neutral flags.

The *Lusitania*, when commanded by Captain Dow, in February 1915, had hoisted the American flag, on the instructions of the Admiralty, while she was in the Irish Sea, making for the entrance to the Mersey. This was not contrary to internationally agreed rules, but it suited the Germans to claim that it was so, in what they had declared to be a war zone.

So the modern age technique of a "war of words," to accompany the shooting war, was developed to an extent unprecedented in history, and it could fairly be said that, in modern wars, "truth is the first casualty."

There had always been ruses of war, since the use of the wooden horse filled with soldiers at the siege of Troy, and probably before then; but never until the 1914-18 war had there been such a widespread use of propaganda and counter propaganda, espionage and counter espionage; so much secrecy, so much censorship, and so much mystification, concealment, deceit and camouflage as in that war which was optimistically described as "the War to end War."

The *Caronia* docked safely at Liverpool, and there I was paid off and demobilized from the Royal Naval Reserve, to become once again a merchant service officer.

I was appointed as First Officer in the renowned *S.S. Mauretania*, which, under the command of Captain Daniel Dow, Commodore of the Cunard Line, was now in service as a troopship. As such, she was a merchant vessel under charter to the War Office, manned by officers and crew rated as civilians, and she wore the Red Ensign of the Merchant Service.

She was not armed for combat, except that she carried one 6-inch gun mounted at the stern, manned by naval ratings. It was the duty of the Royal Navy to escort and protect troopships.

Most if not all the *Mauretania*'s officers held commissions in the Royal Naval Reserve but were officially demobilized and were now in the employ of the Cunard Line as merchant seamen, carrying paybooks and wearing uniforms as such. This point would become of importance chiefly if we were taken prisoner by the enemy, when we would be viewed as civilians, that is, as "noncombatants" for purposes of compensation, or of internment.

As civilians, we signed on under Merchant Service Articles, and not under Articles of War. The routine and disciplines were those. of the Cunard Line, and not of the Royal Navy.

The *Mauretania* had been stripped of her luxurious peacetime fittings and hastily converted into a troopship early in May 1915, to convey troops from Britain to the "new" theatre of war in the Eastern Mediterranean. That campaign had been opened by the landing of troops on Gallipoli Peninsula on 25th April, in an attempt to force the Dardanelles Straits, capture Constantinople, and clear a sea route to Russia.

Heavy casualties and been inflicted on the landing forces, which consisted of British, French, Australian, New Zealand and Indian troops, and a naval division. Reinforcements had been urgently called for. On 21st May 1915, the *Mauretania*, under command of Captain James Barr, had left Liverpool, bound for Mudros Harbour on Lemnos Island in the Aegean Sea — the British advanced naval and military base for the land operations on Gallipoli — carrying 3400 troops of three Scottish regiments. She had safely delivered them to their destination and returned to Liverpool for more. When I joined her, on 2nd July 1915, she was coaling for a second trooping voyage, under command of Captain Dow.

My wife, who had been left at Halifax in Nova Scotia, took passage home across the Atlantic in the United States liner *New York*, a passenger vessel of 10,500 tons, which, being under the American flag, was not likely at that time to be torpedoed by a German U-boat. Yet the immunity of a neutral flag was by no means a certainty, and I was greatly relieved when the *New York* arrived safely and berthed in the Mersey. We then made our home again at Liverpool, which I hoped would be my home port for a long time, if I continued in the Cunard service throughout the war, and afterwards. But what seaman can make plans for home lire in wartime? He must go wherever he is sent and make his home as opportunities permit.

Coaling the *Mauretania* was a big operation. She had been de-signed and built to make the Atlantic passage in five days, burning 1000 tons of coal a day when travelling at full speed. Allowing for reserves, she had a total bunker capacity of 7000 tons, in the compartments of the "double skin" along her sides, which had been designed in that way for protection against shell fire if she should be converted to an armed merchant cruiser.

For a similar reason, her twenty-five boilers, heated by 192 furnaces, were placed deep in the ship, below the waterline; but when she was launched in 1906, little if any thought had been given by her designers to the possibility that she, or her sistership, *Lusitania* would be vulnerable to a strike by a torpedo, below her waterline, amidships, exploding in the boiler rooms.

Having been designed for the "express" service between Liverpool and New York — a distance of 3036 nautical miles — each of these two beautiful superliners, covering that distance at full speed, averaging 25 knots, or 600 miles a day, consumed 5000 tons of coal on each passage from port to port. They had to be refuelled both at Liverpool and New York.

Their extreme steaming range, at full speed, would be, say, 4200 miles, sufficient for the passage of approximately 2000 miles from Liverpool to the Dardanelles. But even on that passage, the *Mauretania* could not carry enough coal for a return voyage. The wartime routes included detours and zigzags which considerably added to her coal consumption at sea.

Even when lying in port with banked fires, she burned 140 tons of coal daily. With all her fires out, except in the furnaces of two boilers for powering winches and the lighting and heating systems, her coal consumption in port could be reduced to 40 tons a day. To bring her from that condition to "steam up and ready for sea" required 400 tons of coal, just to lay the fires.

On her first voyage as a troopship, before I joined her, the *Mauretania* was seven days on the passage from Liverpool to Mudros, where she arrived on 29th May. She had steered zigzag courses under Admiralty directions which had greatly added to the length of the passage. When she anchored in Mudros Harbour, the usual delays had occurred in getting the troops transhipped from her into smaller steamers to be landed on Gallipoli Peninsula, seventy miles away. There was much muddle in the Dardanelles campaign, and this was some of it. The navy signalled that, when she was cleared of troops, she was to return to Liverpool.

Captain Barr had replied, requesting 7000 tons of coal, and 3000 tons of fresh

Keeping the boilers fired on the R.M.S. Mauretania. The ship could use up to 1000 tons of coal each day depending on speed requirements. On a coal-fired steamship, the primary positions responsible for keeping the boilers working were "firemen" (also called "stokers") who shoveled coal into the furnaces to create steam, and "coal trimmers" who broke down and distributed coal from the bunkers to the firemen, all overseen by engineering officers who monitored the boiler pressure and water levels; collectively, these workers were often referred to as the "Black Gang."

(Public Domain)

water. In the circumstances, this request caused a great sensation. There were some naval colliers and water tankers in the harbour, but the Commander-in-Chief, Rear-Admiral Wemyss, was taken by surprise at what seemed to him an unreasonable demand, of which he had had no forewarning.

After some hesitation, he agreed to supply the *Mauretania* with enough coal and fresh water to get her to Malta. A naval collier lay alongside her, but coaling proceeded so slowly that the intake was scarcely enough to feed the big Cunarder's banked fires. Further signals passed, and next day two colliers came alongside, with 500 bluejackets to do the heavy manual work of loading. Finally, on 10th June, after lying for twelve days at Mudros, she had accumulated 2500 tons of coal in her bunkers and left for Malta.

Arrived there, Captain Barr met with similar naval incomprehension of his needs. He was ordered to anchor in a small bay at the eastern end of the island. Coaling began immediately from a small collier but went so slowly that Captain Barr decided to take her on to Naples while she had enough coal to reach there. She had arrived at Naples on 14th June. The Cunard Company had an office there, and agents who knew something about coaling large liners. Within an hour, she was surrounded at her moorings a dozen barges, holding 200 tons of coal each. Long planks were slid from the barges to her side ports. These were apertures two feet six inches square, with iron plates bolted over them. The plates were hinged at the bottom, and, when unbolted, could be pulled t to an angle of forty-five degrees, forming chutes into which e coal was poured. There were twenty of these ports on each side. When the ship was fully loaded, the ports were five feet above the waterline.

It was imperative to tighten the nuts on the bolts of the plates when they were shut to, so that they would be watertight when the ship was at sea. The tightening was done with special spanners, three feet long, to give extra leverage as the bolts were forced home.

One thousand Italian labourers were engaged at Naples to run up and down the planks, from the coal barges to the side ports, with baskets of coal. By this primitive but effective method, she took in six thousand tons of bunker coal in two days, and cleared out of Naples, to arrive at Liverpool on 22nd June, after a voyage that had lasted twenty-four days.

At Liverpool there were facilities for coaling her in the dock, with cranes and slings, but at neap tide she and the late lamented *Lusitania*, and also the *Aquitania*, could not berth in the dock, and sometimes had to be coaled from barges while lying at the Cunard buoys in the Sloyne, a stretch of water out of the mainstream of traffic.

Though as a Liverpool-born man I hate to admit it, the Mersey was not big enough to accommodate the biggest new Cunarders comfortably. In the Sloyne, the ebb tide sometimes races at four or five knots. The moorings at the Cunard Buoys had to be strengthened to hold the gigantic liners, which, with their massive superstructures, put an immense strain on mooring cables if a breeze was blowing. For this and other reasons, it appeared possible that Liverpool would eventually cease to be the terminal port of the largest Cunard and White Star liners — a prospect that was viewed with horror by Liverpudlians, who had inaugurated and had thrived the transatlantic steamship traffic for more than a hundred years.

Southampton is nearer to London by rail, and much more convenient than Liverpool for a call at Cherbourg to serve American passengers going to and from France. The *Aquitania* (46,000 tons) and the White Star *Olympic* (46,400 tons) were both in service now at troopships carrying troops from Britain to the Eastern Mediterranean and based on Southampton. The newest big White Star liner, *Britannic* (48,000 tons), which at the outbreak of the war had not been put into service on the Atlantic mail run, was being equipped at Belfast for use as a hospital ship.

To be appointed as Senior First Officer in the *Mauretania* was one of the greatest satisfactions of my life. I was then nearly thirty- two years of age. She was not the biggest ship in the world, but she was the Champion liner and had held the Blue Riband of the Atlantic for eight years since she first went into service in 1907; and she was something more than the world's speediest liner: she was "a lady."

She was a thoroughbred. Exactly what gave her that quality was difficult to define, but it was unmistakable in her. She was a personality, and everyone who served or voyaged as a passenger in her was aware of that feeling of distinctiveness that belonged to her. Having been built at Newcastle-upon-Tyne, she was sometimes described as "the biggest Geordie" and was in fact the biggest ship ever built in England — all the other big British ships having been built, subsequently, in Scotland on the Clyde, or in Northern Ireland at Belfast

Accommodation for the crew, including the Black Squad, was not concentrated forward and aft, as in small steamers, but dispersed along the passenger decks, chiefly on inside cabins or compartments which had no light or air except from alleyways. There were six passenger decks, identified by the letters A to F. A was the boat deck, B the promenade deck, C the shelter deck, and the other three, being within the steel hull, were known technically as the "upper," "main," and "lower" decks.

The expensive first-class staterooms, library, and lounge were " on A Deck and B Deck, but there were first-class cabins all the way down to E Deck. The first-class dining room was on D Deck. Second- and third-class dining rooms, smoking rooms and general rooms were on various decks from B to E. On F Deck was the cheapest third-class accommodation, for emigrants. A grand staircase, or companionway deluxe, spiralled from deck to deck amid ships. The woodwork panelling in the first-class rooms was especially beautiful, and elaborately carved. Everything in her was in the best of taste and style, according to the ideas of her period, as could be fitted to the lady that she undoubtedly was.

But it was neither the luxury and comfort of her furnishings and fittings; nor the compact but adequate disposition of her living accommodation; and not even her great speed, power, and comparative freedom from vibration that made her a favourite, and beloved. It was that rare phenomenon, a "happy ship," or, as some called her, a "lucky ship," in which everything seemed to be as it should. Very great care had been taken in her design, building, and testing, Though her general specifications were the same as those of the *Lusitania*, the "Geordies" of Newcastle-upon-Tyne had put all their skill and pride into building her, and in service she surpassed her sister.

Coaling was in progress when I joined her. This was a noisy and messy job, which the stewards and cleaners specially hated. Though all of the portholes and doors of the passenger quarters were closed, and the ventilators sealed, it was impossible to prevent fine particles of coaldust from penetrating everywhere. This had to be washed and brushed off before the passengers came on board.

Most of her luxurious furniture and fittings had been removed and stored on shore when she was converted into a troopship. hammocks had been slung and bunks installed in some of the larger public rooms and suites, increasing her carrying capacity from 2200 civilian passengers to nearly 4000 troops if required.

Military officers were on board, inspecting the ship in consultation with the Staff Captain, to arrange for the quartering of the troops we were to carry reinforcements for two Irish regiments, the Leinsters (infantry) and the Munsters (infantry), going out to Gallipoli under the command of General Sir Bryan Mahon. When these dispositions were made, the troops came plodding up the gangways, carrying their kits. They were mostly weedy looking youths, who, according to their officers, were only half-trained. Conscription had just been introduced, and Britain was called on to make a far greater contrition of troops for operations on land than had ever been anticipated when war was first declared.

While the troops were being embarked, a party of sixty army nurses came on board unexpectedly. A hasty readjustment of accommodation had to be made, to give them suitable cabins and other compartments.

On 9th July 1915 — after a stay of seventeen days in port at Liverpool the *S.S. Mauretania* began her second trooping voyage to Mudros. She had on board 3644 troops, 60 nurses, and 850 crew — a total of 4554 souls. Her troop carrying capacity was equal to three troopships of ordinary size.

In her crew of 850, only sixty or seventy were seamen concerned the navigation of the ship. We considered ourselves the top seemingly carefree bridge officers, resplendent in gold braid, carry a weight of responsibility that sometimes makes them feel anything but jolly? But what makes a ship's officer seem so cheerful when he is off duty, or ashore, or retired from the sea, is the very fact that at those times he is off duty! That same man on watch on the bridge, secluded from the passengers in his care, is usually grim, severe, and intensely concentrated. He is two personalities in one skin — off watch and on watch. It could scarcely be otherwise.

All the watchkeeping officers in the *Mauretania* held Master Mariner's Certificates, and most of us Extra Master's Certificates. We had been trained to take responsibility, and we took it.

But the final responsibility was the Captain's. He was the All Seeing Eye, on watch twenty-four hours a day, sleeping or waking, whether he was on the bridge or not. He was held responsible for everything that happened in the ship, at sea or in port, even for what might happen in his ship while he was ashore in a port. That being so, his task was to organize the work of his subordinates in such a way that they were responsible to him. Every one of the ship's people had defined tasks and was skilled in doing them.

If anything went wrong, blame could be fixed on somebody's neglect of duty, but that did not apply to the hazards of war, except in so far as these could be avoided by intelligent anticipation, or by the countermeasures of practicable defence.

At the Mersey Bar, the *Mauretania* was met by an escort of destroyers, which kept with her, as a "screen" against submarine attack, for sixty miles on her course. Then a stiff southerly breeze sprang up, raising a choppy sea head on, which merely threw a little spray across the *Mauretania*'s bows; but at our speed of 25 knots it had the destroyers plunging bows under, and they had to give up the attempt to keep up with us.

We received a wireless message, stating that the sixty nurses we had on board should not have been there, but should have embarked in another vessel that was bound for Malta.

More muddle! Someone had blundered. But, as we were under Admiralty orders to proceed to Mudros nonstop, steaming past the entrances to all intermediate harbours (where U-boats might have been lurking) at full speed, it was out of the question for us to disembark the nurses either at Gibraltar or Malta, and they would have to go on with us to Mudros.

Two months previously, in May, 1915, the first German U-boat had appeared in the Mediterranean. This U-boat had left Wilhelmshaven in Germany on 25th April and had been navigated by her commander (Hersing) around the north of the Shetland Islands. into the Atlantic Ocean, then southwards to the Strait of Gibraltar, through that Strait, and then eastwards the entire length of the Mediterranean to the Dardanelles — a passage of some 4000 miles, which would have been impossible for any German surface vessel at that time.

Off the Dardanelles, on 25th and 27th May, Hersing had torpedoed and sunk two British battleships, *H.M.S. Triumph* and *H.M.S. Majestic*, and also a "dummy" battleship, disguised to look like *H.M.S. Tiger*. He had then navigated his U-boat through the minefields of the Dardanelles, and arrived at Constantinople on 5th June. He was hailed there as a hero, which, from the nautical point of view, it must be admitted that he undoubtedly was.

Hersing's remarkable feat had caused a general and understandable scare in the Mediterranean. What he could do, other German U-boat commanders could perhaps do. There were, in fact, other U-boats in the Mediterranean — smaller craft that had been sent overland by rail from Germany to the Austrian ports in the Adriatic Sea, and there assembled and put into service. In these circumstances, the British and French navies were on the alert for a danger to which no effective countermeasures had been evolved defence against an invisible and sneaking foe.

All naval and mercantile shipping in the Mediterranean including the large number of vessels supplying the Allied military operations at the Dardanelles navigated at night without lights, and many collisions occurred.

On 16th July 1915, the *Mauretania* arrived off Mudros, and was admitted without delay through the boom of mined nets protecting the entrance to the harbour against U-boat attack.

The troops we carried were disembarked to encampments on shore, to await passage to the peninsula. Many of the military officers had a fatalistic outlook, believing that they would never return from the peninsula — and that premonition was only too true, Gallipoli was a shambles. The strategic plan had failed when the invasion of the peninsula was held by resolute and well prepared defence, and the element of surprise had been lost No amount of heroism — and there was great heroism by the rank-and-file of the assault troops — could alter that tragic truth.

All that the British and French Higher Commands could do was to fling more and more troops into the beachheads, which were reinforced and supplied only by sea communications, while the well-entrenched and resolute defenders of the Peninsula were reinforced and supplied by land communications The odds against our side were hopeless, but to withdraw might have been even more disastrous than to hold on to the positions so gallantly won. A withdrawal could only be made by sea, in a region where at least one U-boat had struck, and more might lurk.

Lemnos Island, the advanced operational base, which included Mudros Harbour, was a barren place, with no trees or other vegetation, or natural supply of fresh water. The hillsides around the harbour were dotted with camps and store dumps. A water distilling plant was being constructed, to obtain drinking water from sea water. In the meantime, water was brought to the island in tank steamers, some of these coming out all the way from England. Muddle prevailed. Much of the transport of troops, supplies, and even the evacuation of sick and wounded, was done in the "Black Carriers." These were small cargo steamers, painted black in the belief that they would thereby become invisible at night, even if that colour silhouetted them more clearly against sea and sky in the daytime. The use of neutral grey paintwork was restricted to naval vessels. Though rated as belligerent vessels, the Black Carriers at times were used for transporting sick and wounded from the Peninsula, without hospital ship markings.

On shore at Mudros the arrangements for the reception of troops were chaotic. Within a few hours after disembarking from the *Mauretania*, on a scorching day, General Mahon sent a message to Captain Dow, asking for a large tent, presumably to be used as his orderly room. One was hastily put together from tarpaulins and sent off to him with the Captain's compliments.

There were dozens of naval and mercantile ships of many kinds in the harbour. Among them the *Mauretania* rode at her anchor like a graceful giantess. Fortunately for us, the use of aircraft as bombers had not been introduced into the tactics of war at that stage in the game, or we would have been a sitting target.

Our sixty nurses caused a flutter of excitement among the naval and military personnel at Mudros, as they were the first womenfolk seen in that outlandish place since the war operations had begun. They were quickly transferred to a Black Carrier, and left immediately for Malta.

The *Mauretania* was viewed as a godsend. She had brought out large quantities of urgently needed stores for the naval and military messes, and also mails and parcels from home.

Not only that, but Captain Dow permitted her bars and dining rooms to be thrown open to all who cared to use them, with iced drinks and expertly cooked meals provided at nominal prices.

To men who had spent three months grilling and sweating in that benighted area, she offered the comforts temporarily of a miraculously appeared floating first-class hotel.

Naval arrangements for coaling her were on this occasion completed fairly quickly. On 23rd July 1915, after a stay of only one week in the harbour, we hove up the anchor and put to sea, with enough coal to make for Naples to get some more.

U-boats permitting.

6

*"Mauretania" Attacked By a U-boat — Captain Dow's Quick Thinking
— Night navigation in the Greek Archipelago — The Cliffs of Andros —
A Secretive Engineer — No Lights in the Graveyard Watch — The
Green) the Red) and the White — A Collision! — Heavily Damaged
Tramp — "We'll Take Her into Port!" — Courage of Modest Heroes.*

IT was 4 p.m. when we cleared out of Mudros Harbour and set course
southwards in the Aegean Sea. As usual on leaving port, the Captain was
on the bridge, and all officers were on stations. We were met outside the
heads by two French and two British destroyers, which formed an escort and
steamed with us, as the *Mauretania* quickly worked up to full speed of 25 knots,
with frequent zigzags on a predetermined plan.

It was beautiful to see how quickly the Maurrie, for a vessel of her size,
answered her helm. This had been first noticed on her trial runs, over the
"measured mile" in the Firth of Clyde, in November,1907. While she was running
at 26 knots, the helm had been put hard down. With all four propellers at full
speed ahead, she had turned so sharply, with her rudder only, that the official
report stated: "The diameter of the turning circle was only three and three- quarter
lengths — a very good result."

The result was not so good for a plodding tramp steamer that she had passed
just before turning. Her sudden alteration of course had raised a wash which
nearly capsized the tramp.

Everyone who served on the bridge of the *Mauretania* was aware of her
marvellous responses to movements of her rudder. As we zig-zagged, it was

noticeable that she could alter course almost as easily as the destroyers of her escort. That was indeed phenomenal, all destroyers are built to "turn on their heel." It was suspected that U-boats would lurk outside Mudros. The destroyers remained in company with us for fifty miles from the harbour mouth.

Chief Officer Dolphin was O.O.W.(Officer on Watch) from 4 p.m. to 8 p.m., but Captain Dow remained on the bridge with him while we were in the danger zone. I went to my cabin in the "flat" abaft the bridge when we were clear of the land. I had nearly eight hours to wait before I would go on watch at midnight.

In the feeling of tension that prevailed, I did not lie down for a nap. I kept my uniform and boots on. All our boats were swung out in their davits. We had very few troops on board — only a few dozen naval and military personnel returning for various reasons to England; but there were 850 ship's people to be thought of.

Towards 6 p.m., in the dusk, and after the destroyers had left us, I heard the lookout in the crow's nest sound his bell and sing out urgently, "Periscope on the starboard bow!" This cry was instantly repeated by an extra lookout on the starboard wing of the bridge. I sprang onto the bridge, in time to witness a fine feat of seamanship and quick thinking by Captain Dow. He was verifying the lookout's report in a split second before taking action. Having done so, he thundered an order:

"HARD A-PORT!"

The helmsman spun the wheel as ordered. In the nautical practice of that time, the order to port the helm referred to the tiller orders of olden days. That is, by putting the wheel to starboard, the tiller was put to port, but the rudder went to starboard, and the ship's head paid off to starboard.

This was a brilliant manoeuvre, which took the U-boat commander by surprise. He had launched twin torpedoes, which travelled at 35 knots below the surface of the water, aimed to strike the *Lusitania* broadside on, according to his estimate of her speed, which, at that time, was 25 knots.

Captain Dow's order threw the enemy's calculations out of gear.

His order to port the helm was given when the U-boat was 60 degrees on our starboard bow, at half a mile range, a few seconds later the torpedoes had been launched. So sharply did the Maurrie answer her helm, that, as the torpedoes raced towards her — their wake clearly visible from the bridge — they passed under her stern, one missing her by five feet, the other by thirty feet.

The U-boat's periscope vanished from sight. Her commander had decided to get out of the way, either because he had no more torpedoes, or because he feared that the *Mauretania* was attempting to ram him. It's hard to say who had the bigger fright; but ramming him was no part of Captain Dow's tactics, which were solely to evade the torpedoes. If he had turned the ship to port, that is, away from the

U-boat instead of towards it, one of the torpedoes would probably have struck her.

We had no time to loiter and consider the situation. As soon as the torpedoes had passed under our stern, the Captain again altered course, to bring the ship stern-on to the presumed position of the U-boat, thus offering the minimum target for any further torpedoes that might be launched, and at the same time bringing our one and only gun at the stern to bear on the enemy's position. The rapid changes of our course, amounting to a double slewing within two minutes, had been done at 25 knots, but the Captain now sang out through the speaking tube to the engineer in charge below to increase speed. Within a few minutes more we were travelling at 26½ or 27 knots into the dusk, thereby putting a safe distance rapidly between us and the hidden U-boat.

On first sighting the torpedoes streaking towards us, the Captain had ordered the alarm to be sounded for "Boat stations." All except the deck crew on watch, the gunners at the stern, and the engine room crew down below, had assembled at boat stations, wearing lifebelts, and remained closed up there for half an hour, until we were clear of that region, and the order was given to "disperse." Darkness set in, and tension eased. The chief danger now would be of collision, as the *Mauretania*, like all other vessels, naval and mercantile, did not show her lights at nighttime in a war zone.

I went to my cabin and turned in for a nap.

At 10 p.m., an explosion shook the ship. I leaped out of my bunk, and hastened to the bridge. The Captain was already there. The Junior First Officer was O.O.W. (Officer on Watch)

People were tumbling up from down below, wearing lifebelts, and assembling at their boat stations, thinking that we had been hit. But a happier explanation was forthcoming. The gunner at the stern had sighted an object which he took to be a U-boat. He had let fly at it, with his 6-inch gun, which made quite a bang.

Fortunately he had missed. The "object" switched on steaming lights and searchlights and was identified as a French destroyer which had not previously made contact with us by wireless. We did not loiter to explain but sped on.

At midnight I took over the watch on the bridge, in the darkest hours of the night. We were then approaching Doro Channel, a strait six miles wide between the Greek Islands of Euboea and Andros. This could be a lurking place for U-boats. The Captain me onto the bridge for the navigation of the channel, and set course at a speed of 18 knots, hugging the cliffy Andros side of the strait. We could see the dark mass of the land two miles away on our port side.

When I came on watch, I noticed one of the Junior Engineers on the bridge, with his toolkit, inspecting the steering gear, or tinkering with it. This was not unusual, and I took little notice of him as he continued hanging about unobtrusively, watching the helmsman and presumably making a routine check of that part of the steering gear. He did not say anything to me, or to the Captain.

Though the night was moonless, the sky was clear, and there was enough starlight to enable the land on our port beam to be clearly enough discerned.

Captain Dow was standing alongside the helmsman and giving him steering orders to keep the ship's course parallel with the shore. He increased speed to 22 knots, to get out of the strait quickly in case a U-boat was lurking there.

Halfway through, when he ordered a slight alteration of the course, the helmsman moved the wheel accordingly, then at once said, "There's something wrong, sir!"

The ship's head was paying off rapidly to port. The Captain himself took the wheel and spun it in an attempt to bring her back on course but instantly recognized that the gear had broken down.

He rang the engines to **STOP**, at the same time shaking the telegraphs violently to indicate urgency. That order was promptly obeyed, but by this time the ship was headed at an alarming speed, ' Under her mighty momentum, towards the towering cliffs.

For the second time on that day, Captain Dow acted decisively to save his ship in a serious emergency. It is no light matter to under **FULL ASTERN** immediately after the engines have been running from **FULL AHEAD** to **STOP**, in a ship displacing 40,000 tons of water, surging along under momentum at a speed of perhaps knots. That momentum would have carried her onto the rocky shore in a few minutes.

To order **FULL ASTERN** with all four propellers might have ripped the blades out of the turbines, or at least would have used such violent vibration that some damage to the ship would be been inevitable. The Captain therefore took a cool and seamanlike decision. Leaving the port engines stopped, he ordered the starboard engines full astern.

There was not time to man the emergency steering gear on the after bridge (at the stern). The rudder was presumably swinging free. The effect of the Captain's order was to cause the ship's head to pay off to starboard, while still having headway on. After what seemed an age, she began to sheer off, when she was a little less than half a mile from the shore. It was a mercy that she had not grounded, but Captain Dow's decision had been taken in the knowledge that there was deep water almost to the edge of the cliffs. When she was stern-on to the shore, he ordered **SLOW AHEAD** on all four propellers and was just going to order the emergency steering gear on the after bridge to be manned, when the young engineer officer, who had been lurking on the bridge, stepped forward and said, "I can fix it, sir!"

"What's wrong with it?" asked the Captain.

"It's all my fault, sir. I was changing over from one gear to another at midnight, and I'd no sooner pulled the pin out when the quartermaster moved the wheel, and I haven't been able to put the pin in again! If you put the wheel amidships now, I'll have it in in a few seconds!"

"Do so, then," said the Captain, grimly.

It was done, and we resumed the voyage; but that young engineer, who had tried to do a job, as it were, secretly, at the change of the watch, without notifying the O.O.W. what he was doing, had nearly wrecked the ship.

The Captain and the Chief Engineer conferred briefly and demoted the culprit, who was also given some unpleasant duties, to do down below, in which he could do no great harm.

As the coast was now clear, the Captain, after writing his "Night orders," retired to his cabin for a nap, leaving me in charge on the bridge. At 3.30 a.m., in the darkest hour before the dawn, we were belting along at 25 knots, in open water after passing through the Zea Channel. Suddenly, I sighted a faint green light ahead.

No red light was visible. From this I was entitled to infer that a vessel was crossing our bows, proceeding in a westerly direction athwart our southerly course.

The *Mauretania* was herself blacked out, showing no navigation lights. As the green light ahead had appeared so suddenly, it was a logical inference that the officer in charge of the vessel crossing our bows had taken the cover off his starboard light for our information.

The faintness of the green gleam indicated an oil lamp, possibly on a small steamer. The wartime practice was to cover the navigation lights, on both wings of the bridge, with sacks which could be whipped off in an emergency.

I therefore gave the order, "Hard a-starboard!" and the *Mauretania*'s head began to pay off to port, to clear, as I supposed, the stern of the vessel ahead, with plenty to spare.

At that moment, I got one of the biggest frights of my life. A red light suddenly became visible, and then a white light. I then realized that the steamer was headed towards us, fine on our starboard bow, and very near, so that a collision was inevitable. She was heading for a position below our bridge.

I at once gave the helm order, "Hard a-port!" hoping thereby to swing the *Mauretania*'s stern away from the bow of the oncoming steamer, and to waltz around her, or at least to reduce the force of the impact.

The manoeuvre was effective to a limited extent, in the short time available, but the other vessel, now glimpsed as a tramp steamer, struck the *Mauretania*'s starboard side, bows on, abreast of our Number Four funnel, with a sickening crash.

Instantly I rang our engines to **STOP**, and a moment later to **FULL ASTERN STARBOARD**, while giving the helm order, "Hard a-port!" The *Mauretania* swung around on her heel, and came to rest in the darkness a quarter of a mile from the stricken tramp.

Captain Dow hurried onto the bridge, in no pleasant mood, it could only be expected in the circumstances. My own thoughts were anything but cheerful, as the O.O.W. has to take responsibility for any such mishap. Briefly I reported to the Captain what had happened. I knew that I would later have to clear my yardarm, if possible, and to seek some explanation of the eccentric showing of green and red lights in the steamer that had bumped into us.

"Find out if she's in need of help," the Captain ordered. "We must st and by, but this is no place to linger in. It will be daylight In half an hour!"

With the Morse lamp I signalled, "What ship is that? Are you In need of help?"

The answer came winking back: "*S.S. Cardiff Hall*. Bows heavily damaged. We are down by the head. Number One hold already full. May have to abandon ship. Two men badly injured. Send a boat."

Captain Dow said to me, "Obviously we cannot leave her to sink. Lower the sea boat, and go over to her, but make haste, and turn as quickly as you can."

Within a few minutes I had our emergency boat manned, with eight seamen, and took my place in the stern sheets, as, with a rattle of well-oiled blocks, the boat was lowered and, at the orders, "Out oars! Give way together!" my crew bent their backs to their task.

As we approached the *Cardiff Hall* on the lee side, I saw that her bows were stove in for twenty feet from her stem, and she was badly down by the head. It seemed that at any moment she would "take a dive." Her two boats on the lee side were swung out under davits and partly lowered, but not into the water. Most of her crew were already in the boats, with their hastily gathered bags of belongings piled up around them.

"Way enough," I ordered. "Hold water both." (Oars on both port and starboard sides of the boat to be held in the water and backed to bring her to a standstill.)

On the deck of the tramp, I could see her Captain, First and Second Mates, and carpenter moving about with hurricane lanterns and sounding rods, sounding the wells and holds to ascertain if she was making more water. I hailed the Captain. "Have you decided if you are going to abandon her? We cannot stand by too long. It will be daylight soon, and there are U-boats about. My orders are to return to my ship as quickly as possible."

The Captain leaned over the lee rail and sang out, "I'm not going to leave her. I think that I can take her into Syros for repairs. Number Two hold is dry, and its forrard bulkhead is holding. Take off my injured men and leave us to it."

Hearing this, the crew of the tramp passed the two injured men from one of their boats into mine, then climbed on deck and stood by their Captain. From the bridge of the *Mauretania*, the Morse lamp was winking, signalling to me to return without delay.

I asked the Captain of the tramp, "Why did you show your green light only at first, and then your red light afterwards?"

He answered sarcastically, "The famous Floating Hotel *Mauretania* was showing no lights at all, belting along at 25 knots in the dark!"

"True enough, Captain," I admitted. "No steaming lights by Admiralty orders. I'm very sorry this has happened, but will you tell me why you uncovered your green light first?"

"Easily explained," said the Captain, a little less grumpily. "It's nobody's fault. I'm sorry we bumped you, but it couldn't be helped. My Second Mate was alone on the bridge, except for the helmsman. He's no chicken. He's nigh on seventy and he has gout. He uncovered the starboard light first, and then rushed across the bridge to uncover the port light, see? He couldn't have uncovered both lights at the same time!"

"It's nobody's fault, then, Captain," I said. "There's a war on. I hope you make port safely."

Inwardly, I was greatly relieved at having discovered a reasonable explanation of the cause of the collision.

"We'll make it," said the Captain. "No need for you to stand by any longer."

"Thanks. Goodbye. Good voyage!"

I ordered my boat's crew to "Give way," and we pulled back to the *Mauretania*, where the boat falls were dangling as we had left them. Within a few minutes our boat was hoisted and stowed, and our voyage was resumed as daylight began to come in.

The wallowing *Cardiff Hall* was already under way, on a course set for the Greek port of Syros. Black smoke was pouring from her one funnel; her single screw was almost out of the water, and her battered bow submerged.

Courage and seamanship never failed among the shipmasters, officers, seamen, and engineers, in many a tramp steamer of that humble kind under attack by the enemy or damaged in collisions during the war. They limped into port with no thought of abandoning a ship while she could float, make way, and steer. They had no expectation of rewards, or even of public acclaim, for doing their duty. They were the unsung heroes of the Great War of 1914-18, in which sixteen thousand men of the British Merchant service lost their lives, and 3400 ocean going British merchant ships were sunk.

There was little or no spectacular glory attached to that sacrifice of so many men, and so many ships, of our Mercantile Marine — the "Navy of Supply" — but that sacrifice was, in many more ways than one, essential to the ultimate victory of the Allied forces in the life-and-death struggle between nations, which was fought, on both sides, with ferocity and desperation, to the bitter end.

The *Mauretania* had not been seriously damaged in her collision with the Cardiff Hall. Examination showed that only one of her side bunkers, at the point of collision, was admitting water. These compartments had watertight bulkheads, isolating them from the any other compartments within the hull, and the leak was one which could be kept in check by pumping.

Captain Dow decided to make for Malta for repairs and set course accordingly. On hearing my report in detail, and taking statements also from others who were on the bridge and on look-out at the time of the collision, he informed me that in his opinion had given the correct orders, and had done everything that I could have done in the circumstances, and added that he would commend me for having handled the ship in such a way that she'd suffered only minor damage.

That relieved my anxiety. So ended an eventful day. When I went off watch at 4 a.m., I felt that we had been in the thick of things since leaving Mudros only twelve hours previously. We had been attacked by a U-boat; we had fired on a friendly warship; we had narrowly avoided running aground; and we had collided with another steamer at sea. All that in twelve hours was setting a hot pace that couldn't be kept up. Yet the *Mauretania* had lived up to her reputation as a "lucky ship." Any one of those incidents could have ended disastrously!

Arrived at Malta, 540 miles away, we were directed to anchor in a bay at the eastern end of the island. A diver went down and discovered three cracks in the *Mauretania*'s steel hull plates, below the waterline. He hammered sheet lead into the cracks, thus sealing the leaks. It was remarkable that we had not suffered greater damage than this, considering that the *Cardiff Hall*'s bows had been crumpled by the impact.

We went on to Naples for coal, and arrived at Liverpool on 3rd August 1915, after an absence from home of twenty-four days.

The first year of the Great War had ended. The situation on all fronts was grim, and would become grimmer.

The *Mauretania* was put into dry dock at Liverpool for replacement of her fractured hull plates. We heard that the *Cardiff Hall* had safely made the port of Syros, proceeding stern first After repairs there, she went on to Malta to be fitted with a new bow.

Nearly three years later, the case of *Mauretania* v. Cardiff Hall came before the Admiralty Court in London. The verdict was: "No blame on either side. Ships not showing proper navigation lights owing to wartime conditions."

7

Troopship Camouflage — "Dazzle" — Painting the "Mauretania" — U-boat Campaign Intensified — The "Arabic" Torpedoed — An Infernal Machine in the Mails — U-boat Jitters — Attacked by a Grampus — A Lookout's Mishap — "Mauretania" Converted to a Hospital Ship — Captain Rostron reads Articles of War — Three Voyages under the Red Cross — Burials at Sea — The Road to Berlin — Good Diet for Frost bitten Soldiers — Hospital Ship Service Ends — A Combatant Again.

O N 25th August, 1915, the *Mauretania* again left Liverpool on a trooping voyage to Mudros. This time she carried 3347 troops, chiefly reinforcements for various British army units which had suffered heavy casualties during the battle of Sari Bair on Gallipoli peninsula a few weeks previously.

During her service as a troopship, the Grand Old Lady was "dazzle-painted" in an extraordinary manner. In a strange attempt to disguise her identity, or to make her more difficult to sight at sea, some genius of camouflage had recommended that her sides and funnels should be painted in large diamond shaped patterns in black, white, and grey, and this recommendation had been put to effect. The result looked like a harlequin's costume, or perhaps chessboard. Whether it would confuse a U-boat commander, not, is impossible to say. It was one of those theories that bright people sometimes have to baffle the foe, or to win a war. Probably in choppy seas the diamond patterns made her, if not "invisible," then at least hard to focus in a periscope when she was travelling at full speed under grey skies; but, in the bright sunlight and blue waters of the Mediterranean, especially in calm weather, or when she was travelling slowly, or at a standstill in harbour, the camouflage seemed to make her exceptionally conspicuous!

The U-boat campaign was becoming more lively. On 19th August, a U-boat had torpedoed and sunk the *S.S. Arabic*, a White Star liner of 15,000 tons, off the south coast of Ireland, with the loss of forty-four lives, including several American citizens.

On that same day, a British "Q" ship (warship disguised as a merchant steamer), the *S.S. Baralong*, in the same region, had engaged and sunk a U-boat. The *Baralong* had been wearing American colours until the enemy was well within range, then had lowered them and hoisted the White Ensign, opening fire from guns previously concealed.

These German U-boats had been lurking in the Chops of the Channel, after having cruised from the North Sea, around the north of Scotland, and then southwards through the Irish Sea.

The *Mauretania* was accompanied from Liverpool by a screen of destroyers in the Irish Sea and St. George's Channel, but we usually left them astern, unable to keep up with us, when we reached the open Atlantic, and headed south-westerly on a wide circuitous course that took us far out to sea before we headed easterly for the Strait of Gibraltar.

Apart from our escort of destroyers, our 6-inch gun, our dazzle camouflage, and our zigzag course, we had what was hoped would be a defence of a sort: fifty soldiers with rifles were stationed at the bows and stern. The idea was, that if we came across a U-boat on the surface, the snipers would "pick off" the U-boat's crew. Apparently, the Army authorities, who had issued this order, were unaware that Fritz would be unlikely to show himself in that way during an attack on the *Mauretania* — but "orders are orders," and our guard was solemnly mounted, and changed with routine reliefs, by day and by night, throughout the voyage!

Our best defence was the Maurrie's speed and manoeuvrability on zigzag courses, which gave submerged U-boats very little chance of taking effective aim at her with torpedoes. That, and destroyer escort in narrow waters, enabled her to get through the danger zones unscathed.

We carried thousands of bags of mail, including letters and parcels for the troops at Lemnos and on Gallipoli, and a large cargo of naval and military stores.

The mails were in charge of the Second Officer. A few hours and parcels for the troops at Lemnos and on Gallipoli, and a large cargo of naval and military stores.

The mails were in charge of the Second Officer. A few hours after he had left Liverpool, while this officer was checking the mailbags, heard an ominous ticking sound, which he traced to a registered bag. Was it an infernal machine — a time bomb? Quick thinking was necessary. Grabbing the bag and taking mental note of its entification number, the officer dashed up on deck and threw the bag overboard.

It was the wisest thing to do in the circumstances. The lives of 4,200 people on board would have been endangered by the explosion of a timebomb in the mail room down below.

The Second Officer reported to the Captain what he had done, and in due course the information was conveyed to the Post Office authorities in Britain and to the counter espionage service.

After inquiries, it was established that one of the packets in that had contained a gift from a fond mother in Liverpool to her dear son. The gift was an alarm clock, which she had wound up fore putting it into the post only a few hours before the ship had left port.

On 3rd September, we anchored in Mudros Harbour, and disembarked the troops. Our arrival was joyously greeted, not only cause the reinforcements were urgently needed, but also because the large amount of mails and stores that we had brought.

We remained at Mudros only six days, and cleared out from there on 9th September, with some troops, including "walking wounded," bound for home. We carried also mails from the troops, — a sad burden — many bags of letters and parcels to be returned their senders. The men to whom they had been addressed had been killed in action or had died of wounds or illness.

Bound for Naples to refuel, we were nearing that port when received a marconigram from the Cunard agent, informing us that there was a labour strike at Naples, and instructing us to on northwards to Spezzia, in the Gulf of Genoa, to refuel.

Arrived at Spezzia, we found that the facilities for coaling in port were inadequate for our needs. After labouring for five days we had taken in only 2500 tons. The Captain decided, after conferring with the naval authorities and the Cunard agents, to proceed to Gibraltar for more.

On 17th December we left Spezzia. Next day the Captain received a naval wireless signal, directing him to make for the French port Toulon. The signal stated that there was "exceptional submarine activity."

At that time we were only 200 miles from Toulon. Our course altered accordingly to make for that port. I came on watch midnight. It was a very dark night, and flat calm, but the surface of the water was shimmering with phosphorescent marine organisms. As the *Mauretania* ploughed on at 25 knots, she threw up a bow wave which broke into millions of glowing gems of light — a beautiful sight.

In addition to the usual lookouts in the crow's nest and at the bows, there were lookouts stationed on the wings of the bridge. All lookouts had been warned to be especially alert for periscopes or the wake of torpedoes.

Soon after 1 a.m., I heard a gurgling, strangled cry of horror from the lookout on the starboard wing, who was spluttering, gesticulating and jumping up and down in excitement as he pointed overside amidships, and almost incoherently sang out, "TORPEDO!"

I ordered the helm hard a-port, then rushed to the wing of the bridge to verify the situation. The *Mauretania* was answering her helm swiftly, as usual, when I saw the "torpedo" — it was a great gleaming fish, probably a grampus, which, as I sighted it, altered course with a flick of the tail, and bore away to pass under our stern.

I glanced at the lookout man and found that he was spluttering and groaning with his hand to his mouth. This puzzled me. I ordered the helmsmen to bring the ship back onto her original course. By the time that this was done, the lookout man was lurching and staggering towards me on the darkened bridge, as though ' he were drunk, but he was groaning in agony. I took him by the arm and found that his jacket was sticky with blood! By the dim light of the compass lamp — the only light on the bridge — I peered at him, saying rather sharply, "What's wrong with you?"

His only answer was to continue his agonized groaning. On looking more closely at him, I could see that he was bleeding heavily at the mouth. Presently he slumped to the deck. I ordered the stand-by quartermaster and a bridge boy to carry him down to the ship's hospital, and to awaken the doctor.

In the meantime I posted a new lookout on the starboard wing of the bridge. It was not until sometime later that I discovered what had happened. Seeing the grampus making for the ship, and mistaking it for a torpedo, the lookout had become so excited that he had bitten off the tip of his tongue! This was the cause of the bleeding, and of his incoherent cries. The poor fellow nearly died of loss of blood before the doctor staunched the flow.

Next morning the *Mauretania* passed into the security of Toulon Harbour, and moored with her anchors down and her stern fast to the breakwater. She was the biggest vessel that had ever entered this important French Naval Base until that time. Her almost unannounced arrival, immense size, weird dazzle painting, and tremendous requirements of coal created a sensation among the local inhabitants.

As no arrangements had been made for coaling her there, the French Naval Authorities had to refer the matter to some higher authority for instructions. When it became apparent that no information could be obtained as to our probable length of stay, Captain Dow instructed the Chief Engineer to let the fires die out, to save coal.

The Captain cabled to Liverpool for instructions; but this message was delayed by censorship, or the problem of coaling her was tossed to and fro between French and British naval and civilian authorities in Toulon, Paris, Gibraltar, London, Liverpool, and goodness knows where else.

R.M.S. Mauretania arriving at the undersized Toulon Harbor.
(AI generated image)

Day after day went by, with our coal, water, and stores beginning to run low, and it looked as if we were forgotten. On the tenth day a signal came, "Proceed to Gibraltar for coal." There was no mention of taking in coal or water at Toulon. The Chief Engineer calculated that we would just make Gibraltar, with luck, if we cleared out immediately.

A head of steam was raised, and we put to sea on 29th September. By dint of sweeping out the last remaining dust from the bunkers, and steaming at only 15 knots, we managed to crawl into Gibraltar two days later. All that delay and added risk had been caused by some jittery naval person who had ordered us into Toulon — probably on sighting a grampus!

The *Mauretania* would be such a big "bag" for a U-boat, especially while she was in service as a troopship, that every precaution for her safety was justifiable. Her effectiveness was chiefly in her great carrying capacity and speed; but these qualities were counteracted by the lengthy deviations of route, and by unduly long delays in ports.

At Gibraltar there was no undue delay. The navy coaled her in thirty-six hours, with enough to take her on to Liverpool.. and there we arrived on 5th October, after an absence of forty-one days, which was certainly no record of speed for a voyage to Mudros and return.

On her three trooping voyages from Liverpool to Mudros, be-tween May and October 1915, the *Mauretania* had taken out 10,391 troops for the Dardanelles campaign: a substantial achievement for one vessel, despite the delays in port.

The military situation on Gallipoli Peninsula had become a stalemate, and already in October the Higher ups were making secret preparations to withdraw the Allied forces and call off the campaign there, to cut the losses.

Dysentery was raging among the Allied troops on Gallipoli, and also at Lemnos Island. This was one of the factors in the decision to give up the Dardanelles campaign.

Soon after the *Mauretania* had berthed at Liverpool, we were informed that she was to be transformed into a hospital ship. Colonel G. R. Brown, of the Royal Army Medical Corps, arrived on board to superintend the arrangements.

Lounges, smoke rooms, and some of the dining rooms were stripped bare of furniture and converted into wards. Great numbers of cots were installed, side by side. These cots were shallow wooden boxes, secured to the deck with four short legs, with mattresses and other bedding inside the boxes. The promenade deck was completely closed in by glass windows and fitted with 200 cots on each side. Accommodation was provided in the ship for 2500 patients, 350 medical staff, and 850 crew.

The outside of the hull and superstructure was now painted white, and — in accordance with international conventions — the ship had a green band, marked with red crosses, running completely around her. This band, three feet wide, was twenty-five feet above the waterline. There were three vivid red crosses painted on each side — one amidships, one forward, and one aft. The funnels were painted a buff colour. For nighttime, a row of green electric lights was fitted above the green painted band, and the red crosses were picked out with red lights.

Big gangs of painters were employed. One of their tasks was to scrape off the thick black paint which had covered the glass in every porthole and external window in the ship while she had been in troop carrying service, so that not a gleam of light would show outboard and give her away to Fritz. Now, too, the long disused deck lights were fitted with new and powerful lights. It was intended that she should be a blaze of lights at sea, leaving Fritz no excuse for sinking her in error.

The command of the ship was transferred to Captain Arthur Rostron, under whom I had served previously in two other Cunarders, the *S.S. Brescia* and the *S.S. Carpathia*. I had been with him as Second Officer in the *Carpathia* when she had rescued the survivors of the *Titanic* in 1912.

Captain Rostron, at forty-six years of age, was one of the most respected shipmasters in the Cunard Service. He was not the conventional "jolly sea dog," but a great seaman for all that slightly built, but wiry, and with sharp, keen features, piercing blue eyes and agile movements, which had caused him to be nicknamed the "Electric Spark."

He was an idealist, a total abstainer from strong drink, a nonsmoker, and a non-swearer. He believed in the "Power of Prayer," as he phrased it, but did not attempt to convert anybody to his beliefs. Yet he was a strict disciplinarian, and a man who could take quick decisions correctly, and stick to them.

During the alterations to the ship, which took a fortnight, most of the crew had some shore leave, or were paid off, and stood by to be signed on again, under Title. 124 Articles.

On the day before we were to leave Liverpool, the crew of 850 presented themselves to be signed on a lengthy procedure which was supervised by the Purser and his clerks. Captain Rostron, being an extremely conscientious man, decided that no man should sign without understanding what he was signing. He therefore gave instructions that the crew should be mustered in the third-class dining room, where he would read the Articles of War aloud, for all who wished to hear them read.

The third-class dining room was down below on D Deck, forward. It had not been converted into a hospital ward. About 650 of the crew assembled there, standing packed together, in a stifling atmosphere, on a hot afternoon. There was scarcely room to move, as the Captain stood on a dais, and, adopting his severest expression and sternest tone of voice, began to read.

There was intense silence in the crowd as he read through the preamble and then passed on to the various crimes and their punishments. He came to the first crime to incur the death penalty and read out in ringing tones: "Whosoever commits this crime shall suffer DEATH, or such other punishment as is hereinafter amended."

At this point, a cook, who had been standing in the front row, became so overcome with emotion that he swooned away, and had to carried out. Whether it was the stifling atmosphere, or the solemnity of the occasion, or the contagion of example, several more swooned before the Captain had finished reading all the penalties.

The Captain concluded, "Now, men, that will give you something to think about! Sign on, or not, as you please, but never let me hear any complaint that you didn't know what you are invited to sign!"

It says much for the British character in wartime that, even after severe warning, the whole of the crew, including those who had swooned, signed the Articles without any further demur.

Included in the medical equipment of the ship were elaborate operating theatres, X-ray rooms, pharmacies, and special stores of many kinds, including extra supplies of frozen poultry and ' other delicacies for invalid cookery.

The medical staff, in charge of Colonel Brown, comprised thirty doctors, seventy nurses, and 183 orderlies. The Cunard staff attended to catering and cleaning, as previously when the Maurrie was in troopship service. But, on this occasion, there was no gun at her stern, and she carried no weapons of defence or offence whatever. On 22nd October 1915, we left the Mersey and headed south- wards in the Irish Sea, without destroyer escort, and without steering a zigzag course. Compared with trooping voyages, this was a joyride. At nighttime we were a blaze of lights.

Sensible new arrangements had been made for us to call at Naples, on both the outward and homeward trips, to avoid the need of coaling at Mudros.

When we put in to Naples, the consuls of Switzerland, Sweden, the United States, and other neutral countries, were invited to inspect the ship, to satisfy themselves that she was simply and solely a hospital ship, and not carrying troops, weapons, ammunition, or war stores. They did so, and their reports were transmitted to their governments, and thence to the governments of Germany and Germany's allies.

We arrived at Mudros on 31st October. The work of embarking the sick and wounded began immediately. As there was no wharf there at which such a big ship could berth, we lay at anchor out in the bay, half a mile offshore. Many of the patients were brought off from the hospital camps in small motor barges. It was impossible for the stretcher bearers to carry them aboard from these, as they were so far below the gangway doors.

To deal with that problem, a flat oblong wooden box, fitted with a wire sling at each corner, was lowered by an electric crane which was part of the equipment of the ship, used normally for hoisting mails, cargo, or luggage to the foredeck. One stretcher at a time, with a patient strapped to it, was lashed into the box, and the crane then hoisted the box, patient and all.

The crane had been designed for swift loading. It had only two movements — full speed and stop. Some of the patients said afterwards that the sensation of being wounded in battle was much more pleasant than shooting up seventy feet into the air, hoisted by that crane!

However, they all arrived on deck safely and quickly.

But most of our patients were embarked from small hospital ships which had come directly from Gallipoli and lay at anchor in Mudros Harbour. These ranged alongside, and their sick and wounded were carried by stretcher bearers from their decks through a door in the *Mauretania*'s side.

A small naval hospital ship lay at anchor a quarter of a mile away. Her commander sent a signal to the *Mauretania*: "Please come alongside for wounded." That was in the right tradition of naval seniority; but, in this instance, like the mountain going to Mahomet, it just didn't happen.

In four days we had embarked 2312 wounded and sick, most of the sick being sufferers from dysentery. It was good to see those men, who had suffered so much, settled at last into comfortable surroundings, with every expert care and attention to their needs.

We cleared out from Mudros on 4th November, and made a speedy passage to Naples for coal, and for a further consular inspec-tion, and then home.

Considering the numbers of seriously wounded and sick on board — all cot cases — it said much for the medical care they re-ceived that only ten men died on the passage home. They were buried at sea. Army chaplains attended to the funerals.

All those who died were dysentery cases. The boatswain and the lamp trimmer — old Cape Horn sailors both — were given the job of sewing up the bodies in canvas, with a furnace bar at the feet to make them sink.

This was done in a small room on the orlop deck, appointed as a morgue. I was instructed by the Captain to keep an eye on the work and see that it was done properly. Captain Rostron knew that I, like himself, had been in sail, and that I had experience of the procedures of burial at sea.

Going aft to the morgue, on the first day when bodies had been placed there, I found the boatswain and "Lampy," with two corpses stretched on a table, busily sewing the canvas shroud around the bodies. They were both smoking pipes and also chewing tobacco as they sewed.

"What's this?" I said, sharply. "Do you think it's respectful to the dead to be smoking here?"

"Well, sir," said the bosun, "it's like this. We ain't disrespectful, by no manner o' means, but these here sojers might have died of some catching disease. You know yourself, sir, that tobacco smoke kills germs. What's more, if we pricks our fingers with the needle, a quid of chewed tobacco stops the bleeding, and also stops germs from getting in. So we hopes, Mister, as how you won't mind if we 1mokes and chews at this job what has to be done by somebody. And we knows, Mister, that the dead sojers won't mind if we smokes and chews while we sews 'em up. It will be the last kind thing that we can do for them!"

That line of reasoning was so complete that I had to agree at once. "Very well then, Bosun," I said. "Carry on with what you're doing, but keep the door closed, so that people won't see you smoking and chewing baccy and think wrongly of you!"

With that I left them to their gruesome task. I had the duty of making a similar inspection each day.

Including our call at Naples, we made a smart passage home from Mudros in seven days, but on this occasion, we were directed to make for Southampton instead of Liverpool.

We berthed at Southampton Docks on 11th November. This was the first time that I had entered that spacious haven, which in later years I would enter and leave many times, in vessels much bigger than the *Mauretania*; but at that time I had no inkling of such a possibility.

On arrival, we were informed that Southampton would be the home port for the *Mauretania*'s further service as a hospital ship. It was more convenient than Liverpool for ships voyaging to the Mediterranean, saving almost a day's steaming on each passage. It was also nearer than Liverpool to the many big military hospitals in the south of England, which were receiving tens of thousands of sick and wounded soldiers from the battlefields of France and Flanders.

I sent a telegram to my wife, and she came to Southampton, to set up yet another new home for us, in a new home port.

After a stay in port of only twelve days, the *Mauretania* left Southampton on 23rd November 1915, on her second voyage to Mudros as a hospital ship.

There were strong rumours that she would be stopped in the Mediterranean by a U-boat and searched for war materials. There was positively nothing of that kind on board, but Captain Rostron decided, on our first day out, to make a special inspection, in case there might be something accidentally on board which might justify a German search party in declaring the ship to be a belligerent vessel.

The Captain and the Colonel, accompanied by several officers — including myself — and a party of the doctors, went through the ship, with the zeal of a mother with a fine tooth comb looking for lice. Nothing missed the scrutiny of the Captain's eagle eye. In one of the wards, he noticed a cardboard box, brightly lettered with the words, THE ROAD TO BERLIN.

"What's this?" he asked. The box was opened. Inside it was a "Silver Bullet" game. It was made in the form of a miniature battlefield. The silver bullet had to be rolled from London, across the map, and past numerous obstacles, to Berlin, which was represented by the Kaiser with his mouth wide open, to receive the bullet.

The inspection party gathered around to discuss this war winning weapon. "Germans have no sense of humour," the Captain decided. "A U-boat commander might not see the joke!"

Medical orderlies and stewards were dispatched to make a thorough search of all the wards, cabins, and storerooms for games and pastimes. Within a short time, 112 "Roads to Berlin" were found and solemnly thrown overboard.

The U-boat didn't materialize after all. It was just another of those rumours that fly around in wartime.

On this second voyage, the *Mauretania* brought home 2021 patients and arrived in Southampton on 15th December 1915. Home for Christmas!

That was the second Christmas of the war, and there was less "peace on earth, goodwill to all men" among the Christian nations than ever before.

At that time, though there was no hint of it in the newspapers, the huge operation of withdrawing the Allied military forces from Gallipoli Peninsula was in full swing.

Between 8th and 20th December, a total of 80,000 men, 5000 horses, and 200 guns were withdrawn from the Suvla Bay and Anzac Cove beachheads, without casualties. The Turks were completely "deceived, as small rearguards in the frontline trenches kept up a vigorous fire while the main body withdrew under cover of darkness, embarking in boats and barges to ships standing offshore. Only a token force remained at Cape Hellas, and these were finally withdrawn early in January. Large quantities of stores were left behind, partly destroyed by the rearguards.

On 7th January 1916, the *Mauretania* again left Southampton a hospital ship, bound for Mudros. On this voyage we brought 1974 patients, including hundreds of men with frostbitten toes, In the last days of the evacuation from Gallipoli, there had n torrential rain, followed by a sharp frost Men standing in water in the flooded trenches had become frostbitten before they realized it. They suffered agony, but bore up bravely, and were seriously overjoyed to be in the *Mauretania*, away from the pestilential shambles of the Gallipoli Peninsula. The thirty doctors in the ship were mostly middle aged men, who had been in general practice in civilian life, and had volunteered for this service. The R.A.M.C. Colonel had to handle them tactfully, for they resented interference.

One doctor had a ward of one hundred patients, all with frostbitten feet, but otherwise in pretty good shape. His diet sheets, every day, for the evening meal, read: "One hundred chicken diets, and 100 bottles of stout."

When checking these sheets, the Colonel ventured a remark: "Are you devoting enough time and thought, Doctor, to the individual diets of your patients?"

The doctor, a Canadian, replied, "Yes, Colonel, I have given the matter very serious thought. My diets will do my patients better than all the slops in Christendom!"

And how right he was! — as his patients all agreed.

On 25th January 1916, the *Mauretania* berthed again at Southampton. At that time the evacuation of Gallipoli Peninsula had been completed. It was obvious that the *Mauretania*'s services would not be required again as a hospital ship voyaging to the Mediterranean.

She was too big and valuable to be risked on the short voyages of hospital ships to and from France. Her cruising range was not sufficient for troopship voyages to South Africa, India, or Australia. It would have been folly to put her back again into commercial service on the run to New York. U-boat attacks on merchant shipping had increased. Among many others, two small Cunard steamers, the *S.S. Caria* and the *S.S. Veria*, had been sunk by U-boats in November and December 1915.

While the various authorities deliberated on her future, the *Mauretania* was laid up at Southampton for a month. That suited my personal interests well enough, as I could have some shore leave and home life for a while.

Towards the end of February 1916, a decision was taken to send her to Liverpool, and to terminate her charter as a hospital ship. Her medical staff and most of the catering staff were paid off at Southampton. With a nucleus crew, we took her to Liverpool, to be dismantled.

There, I was paid off and left her.

On 14th March 1916, I was mobilized again into the Royal Naval Reserve and ordered to proceed to the R.N. barracks *H.M.S. Vivid*, at Devonport, to be drafted for service in destroyers.

I had become a combatant again.

My Service in Destroyers — "Maids of All Work" — Coal burners and
Oil burners — H.M.T.B.D. "Alarm" — The Battle of Jutland — My First
Command — H.M.T.B.D. "Roebuck" — The Plymouth Extended
Defence Flotilla — "Engineburg" — The Senior Officer of the Port
Flotilla — A Beastly Nuisance — Hunting Subs — The Lance Bombs —
Patrol Programme — A Capful of Wind — A Bit of a Bump.

MANY other officers of the Royal Naval Reserve, some of whom had experience in handling big ships, were drafted, as I was, for war service in destroyers, which were almost the smallest combat vessels in the Royal Navy. Our special experience in big ships was disregarded, and we had to adjust ourselves to techniques of seamanship to which we were unaccustomed.

I had done two months training in destroyers two years previously, but now I had to go through the course again, as though I were a novice. That was under an Admiralty rule whereby all R.N.R. officers called up for combat service were required to do a refresher course, on the assumption that they might have forgotten what they had previously learned.

It was necessary to "requalify." That, too, may have been reasonable enough in some cases, as far as I was concerned, the requalifying course put no great strain on me. I was able to relax for two months at Devonport. My wife came down, and we established a new home at Plymouth, nearby. Like other married officers in the Royal Navy.

At the outbreak of the war, the Royal Navy had 243 destroyers in commission. An additional 303 were completed and put into service during the war. Of the total of 546 British destroyers on war service, eighty were lost by enemy action or other wartime hazards, such as collisions.

The destroyers were described as "ubiquitous," and as "maids-of-all-work." They were chiefly patrol and escort vessels, based on. harbours all-round the coast, and usually unable to remain more than a few days at sea without having to put back into port for refuelling. They operated in flotillas, of three or more in company, but sometimes alone. Their commanders had much more freedom of action and initiative than was possible in the squadrons of heavier warships at sea.

Being posted to the destroyer service, I soon became reconciled to its disadvantages. These were compensated by advantages which officers in bigger

H.M.T.B.D. Alarm (Public Domain, Imperial War Museum and Wikimedia)

warships could only envy — short cruises, easy going discipline, scope for initiative, and some home life.

On 10th May 1916, I joined H.M.T.B.D. Alarm, at Plymouth, as First Lieutenant, under Captain Hellier, R.N., to complete my training in active service conditions. Captain Hellier was an elderly man, who had retired from the Royal Navy several years previously, and had been managing a cattle ranch in Argentina. He had returned to England when war was declared, and had rejoined the active list

The *Alarm* was one of the larger and more modern destroyers. Completed in 1911, she used oil fuel and therefore could remain at sea much longer than coal burning destroyers, and required only a small number of engine room ratings down below. With a displacement of 780 tons, she had a speed of 27 knots and mounted two 4-inch and two 12-pounder guns, besides two 21-inch torpedo-tubes. She had a high forecastle, on which one of her 4-inch guns was mounted, forward of the conning tower, the other being at the stern, and the two 12-pounders amidships.

She had a complement of seventy. There was a cabin for the Captain, and a wardroom of sorts for the officers (First Lieutenant, Sub-Lieutenant, Midshipman, Gunners and Engineers), but the living quarters were cramped, as in all other destroyers, though much less so than in the older and smaller coal burning vessels.

Putting to sea from Plymouth on 10th May, we had a rendezvous, off the Scilly Isles, to escort some merchant steamers to Belfast and Londonderry, in the north of Ireland. At that time the "convoy system" had not been developed fully but was in the experimental stage. On our return from Londonderry, we escorted steamers to Holyhead in North Wales, and others from there to Plymouth. Captain Hellier left a good deal of the work to me, and I gained valuable experience in handling a small ship and in the routine of destroyers and in coastal navigation.

We met with no U-boats or other enemy vessels and returned to Plymouth on 28th May. There, Captain Hellier informed me that he intended to recommend me for command of a destroyer, gratifying news, as there was extra pay for command, besides the satisfactions of being entrusted with responsibility.

Two days after our return, the electrifying news was flashed around that the German High Seas Fleet had emerged and was being engaged by the British Grand Fleet in the North Sea, at the battle of Jutland. That was Der Tag! How we wished that we could have been there! What happened in that engagement has been a matter of argument among experts ever since.

In a running action that lasted for two days, the British Fleet lost three battleships, two heavy cruisers, and eight destroyers. The Germans lost two battleships, four light cruisers, and five destroyers. Other ships on both sides were damaged. The Royal Navy lost approximately 6000 officers and ratings killed.

With. the German casualties added, not less than 10,000 seamen ad lost their lives, and many more than that were wounded, in the most tremendous sea battle of all time; yet neither side could claim an outright victory. The action was not fought to a finish, it was broken off, by orders of the Commanders-in-Chief on both sides, to keep the main strength of their respective fleets in being.

This apparently inconclusive result was a disappointment to griping critics in Britain, especially to armchair critics of the tactics adopted by the British Commander-in-Chief, Admiral of the fleet Jellicoe; but when the full story was told, it was obvious that he had taken the correct decision. A pursuit of the retiring German Fleet might have led him into minefields, or to nests of U-boats and destroyers waiting to attack in conditions of low visibility or at nighttime.

The undeniable fact was that the German High Seas Fleet had retired to its harbours. It never emerged again in full strength to challenge Britain's command of the seas — at least with surface vessels. To that extent the battle of Jutland, despite the British Navy's heavier losses, was a British victory. This was clear enough to any — except the critics who had a political axe to grind. On the man side it could fairly be said, after wartime prejudices were med, that their High Seas Fleet had fought well and bravely against forces greatly superior in numbers and fire power.

That battle was the only largescale head on clash of the rival surface navies during the war. Britannia still "ruled the waves," but from that time onwards the Germans made a long sustained, fierce, and determined effort to rule beneath the waves — with an unrestricted U-boat campaign that very nearly brought Britain to starvation.

On 1st June 1916, I was appointed to command a destroyer of the Plymouth Extended Defence Flotilla. She was *H.M.T.B.D. Roebuck*. So, at the age of thirty-three years, after having served for eighteen years at sea, I was given my first command of a seagoing vessel. She was no mammoth or monster, but just a little "maid-of-all-work," and, with all her faults, she was beautiful to me.

H.M.T.B.D. Roebuck was an old, coal burning, 30-knot, twin screw destroyer, built in 1897, and had thus been nineteen years in service when I took command of her. In fact, she had been at sea a year longer than I had! She was one of thirty-five "C" class destroyers still in service when the war began. They were almost obsolete, but too useful to be scrapped when there was a war on. The war had reprieved her from the shipbreakers, and there was plenty of life in the old girl yet, as she showed whenever we took her to sea in heavy weather. She could roll and buck better than a prairie broncho, but her speed of 30 knots was theoretical. I fancy that she would have shaken herself to pieces at anything over 25 knots; but for all that she had a great heart.

Of 335 tons displacement, she had three funnels, a straight stem, a turtle back bow — which was sometimes called a "shovel nose" — and a "big" bridge — that is, a superstructure athwartships, of oblong shape, in contrast with the smaller rounded or turret shaped armoured conning towers of later built destroyers.

She carried a 4-inch gun on the bridge, another in the after "band- stand," and two 9-pounders amidships, besides two swivel mounted 18-inch torpedo tubes on deck amidships.

Her bunkers held 80 tons of coal, enough for only twelve hours' steaming at full speed; but with careful nursing and a reduction of cruising speed to four or five knots, she could remain at sea, on patrol, for forty-eight hours. She had a normal complement of sixty, which was increased to a total of seventy-three in wartime. The living quarters were extremely cramped, but this could be endured on the patrol routine of forty-eight hours at sea and twenty-four hours in port for refuelling, rest, and recreation.

My First Lieutenant was a youthful officer of the R.N.R. We had also a midshipman, R.N., a Gunner, R.N., and a Chief Engineer, R.N. The Midshipman was a lad of seventeen, who had qualified at Dartmouth Naval College. The Gunner and the Chief Engineer were Warrant Officers. There would be very little, if any, sleep for any of us, and least of all for me, while we were at sea. I would have to stand watch, in alternation with the First Lieutenant, for navigational purposes, but both of us would be on the bridge if anything of interest was in the offing. I had a tiny cabin to myself right aft. The other officers shared a wardroom, and could snatch a little rest, when circumstances permitted, on its settees.

The Chief Engineer was a picturesque figure. He was a large, portly man, who sported a "Hindenburg" moustache, of which he took great care. When he was in bed, he wore an elastic gadget on it, to keep it trained and pressed close to his face. He was well known in Devonport ships and dockyard, under the nickname of "Engineburg!" He proved to be a good man and shipmate and was as well versed in "the laws of the Navy" as any man afloat.

I took over the *Roebuck* in the forenoon while she was lying at the coal wharf in Devonport, getting ready to go to sea on a routine patrol. The officer from whom I was taking over the command was a jolly fellow with a red nose. He said, "You can have her, and good luck to you. She rolls her guts out, but she's all right. I'm going to a shore station for a rest cure."

After I had put my dunnage on board, met the officers, and had a quick look around, my first job was to go and receive instructions from the Senior Officer of the Port Flotilla, Commander Howard, R.N., who had his headquarters in a torpedo boat (T.B. 99), berthed a short distance from the coal wharf. (Torpedo boats, being considered obsolete, seldom put to sea, and were used chiefly for port defences.)

Commander Howard received me cordially in his compact little cabin. "It's a beastly nuisance," he Drawled, "and extremely tiresome that you'll be leaving harbour at rather short notice after taking over. You are to leave the coal wharf at 1 p.m., that is, in only one and a half hours from now, so that you'll scarcely have time to get used to your new command. I'm sorry, old chap, but the fact of the matter is that the commander you are relieving has been hitting the bottle rather hard lately. It was decided only this morning to transfer him to a shore station, to keep him out of temptation, don't you know?"

Despite this seemingly affected manner of speaking, the S.O.P.F. was a highly efficient officer. His pleasant, languid style of conversation was a mask for his careful attention to detail. He found practically everything "extremely tiresome," or "a beastly nuisance," but It had to be done well, as I quickly realized when he went on to give me some practical hints on running a destroyer, and on my general responsibility to himself as Senior Officer.

The Plymouth Extended Defence Flotilla, consisting of three destroyers and a torpedo boat, based on Plymouth, patrolled a stretch of the coast for seventy miles to the eastward of Plymouth, between Eddystone Lighthouse and Lyme Regis Bay. The patrol would take us eastwards around Prawle Point and Start Point, and past the harbours of Dartmouth, Tor Bay, Teignmouth, Exmouth, Sidmouth, and Lyme Regis, almost to Portland Bill.

"Extremely boring," explained Commander Howard. "Your job will be to escort merchant vessels, hunt subs, and discover and survey any minefields laid by Fritz in his new campaign that has just started with long range minelaying subs. Beastly nuisance, eh, what?"

I agreed that it would indeed be extremely boring if I bumped into one of Fritz's mines or failed to avoid a torpedo from a U-boat. "There's not much chance," I said, gloomily, "of sinking a sub that's submerged and out of sight, is there?"

"They're a beastly nuisance," said the S.O.P.F., languidly. "But use your own discretion, old chap. You can ram 'em if the periscope is showing, or shell 'em if they're on the surface, or lay alongside 'em, and throw a 'lance bomb' on 'em!"

We both laughed cynically. Lance bombs were the Admiralty's latest brilliant idea for counteracting the U-boat menace. They resembled a harpoon with a grenade attached to its head. Each destroyer was provided with a supply of these weird weapons. The idea was that the destroyer should creep alongside a U-boat closely enough to enable a lance bomb to be hurled by hand from the destroyer's decks, so that it would explode against the U-boat's side. Absurd though that idea was, it was the precursor of the "depth charges" which later proved effective against U-boats, but the primitive lance bombs were likely to be more dangerous to their users than to the enemy.

"Have a gin, old chap," suggested the S.O.P.F., pouring out two drinks. "Best o' luck. Here's to the skin off your nose. Cheerio. Chin chin!"

So I was launched on my new career as a Destroyer Commander. • I felt like Drake finishing his game of bowls at Plymouth Hoe before going out to demolish the Dons.

Going on board my ship again at noon, I got her ready to put to sea.

The three destroyers in the Plymouth Extended Defence Flotilla where the *Roebuck*, the *Sunfish*, and the *Bittern*. They were of about the same age, size, speed, and armament. Under the patrol programme, there were at any time two vessels of the flotilla at sea, and one in port.

Each vessel remained for forty-eight hours at sea and then turned to port for twenty-four hours. This was done in rotation.

When one vessel came off patrol, and entered port, she was met by the relief vessel going out.

Once a month, also in rotation, each destroyer was laid up in port one week, for boiler cleaning and general mechanical overhaul. While that was being done, her place in the patrol was taken by a torpedo boat (T.B. 107).

It was a "chummy" service. The crews of the four vessels in the flotilla knew one another well. When a destroyer was laid up for her cleaning, her crews went aboard the other vessels of the flotilla.

When they came into port off patrol and went ashore together for a few convivial drinks. At sea, two of the vessels were always in company — if not in sight of one another all the time, at least in radio contact, and working over prescribed areas in accordance with a hm, so that one could instantly call the other in any emergency.

I was to take the *Roebuck* out that day to relieve the *Bittern* patrol. It was necessary for me to get away smartly from the coal wharf at the prearranged time, to meet the *Bittern* at the entrance to Plymouth Sound.

The Captain of the *Bittern*, Lieutenant-Commander B. Irving, R.N.R., was a special pal of mine. He was in peacetime an officer the White Star Line. I had met him many years previously in Liverpool, when we were both apprentices in sailing ships, and on various occasions subsequently, when we had happened to be in port together. We had more recently renewed acquaintance during a refresher course at Devonport. He was a stocky, sturdy man, inclined to be hard with his crews, relying on Cape Horn methods enforcing discipline rather than on the Book of Rules, but crews had the utmost respect for him as a sterling seaman, chock full of "guts."

I had no intention of keeping Bill Irving waiting outside. At 1 p.m. precisely, I stepped onto the bridge of the *Roebuck*, and gave orders, "All hands to stations for leaving harbour," "Stand by engines," "Let go fore and aft," "Bear off."

The procedure when a destroyer left a wharf was old fashioned. Handy on deck were half a dozen "bearing out spars." These were wooden poles, twenty-five feet long, which were used by hand to her away from the wharf before her propellers were started.

Unfortunately for me on this first occasion in my life when I was putting to sea in command, I met with a mishap. Whether it was my fault, or not, it was my responsibility!

A fresh breeze was blowing us onto the wharf, and this made the bearing off spars almost useless. Two or three men were pushing on each pole, grunting as they pushed, with little effect. No sooner had they moved her away from the wharf a few feet, than the wind blew her back again hard alongside.

After five minutes of this, I tried to help them, by ordering the starboard engine (on the weather side) slow astern, and the port engine slow ahead, with the helm hard a-port, to swing her head out into the stream.

In ordinary circumstances, this manoeuvre should have been effective, but at that moment a capful of wind pressed her abeam in a strong gust To my dismay, I felt a bump, as the port propeller fouled some stone steps at the end of the wharf.

"Blast those steps!" I groaned.

Despite that, the ship's head was paying off to starboard, and she had a little headway on, while the men at the stern continued to fend her off vigorously with their spars. I therefore rang the engines to half speed ahead and astern, and, as she drew away from the wharf, I rang for half speed ahead both, with the wheel amidships, until she was well out into the stream.

Even then, with the strong cross harbour breeze blowing, I was unwilling to stop and let go the anchor for inspection of possible damage. I wondered if the port propeller would presently drop off, or if I would have to make for the mooring buoys for an inspection before proceeding to sea.

A fine thing to happen at the outset of my first voyage in command! Hoping for the best, I rang the engines to slow ahead both and set course down harbour. Then, through the speaking tube, I asked Engineburg to come up to the bridge. From what I could see of the port propeller's wake and could judge from the manner in which the ship was steering, it seemed that the propeller was functioning normally, but I feared that the bump might have done some damage down below to the propeller shaft or gears, or to the engines. "Nothing serious, sir!" said Engineburg with a grin. "We felt a bit of a bump, but it's had no effect on the engines, as yet. I think that you could carry on! She was built on the Clyde, like myself, sir, and she can take hard knocks. I reckon that she'll see this patrol through, and I'll inspect the propeller when we return to port."

With that assurance, I kept on going down the harbour, at 10 knots, as though nothing unusual had happened, as far as any observers on shore or on other ships might remark. I entered the occurrence in the logbook, with the Chief Engineer's report, and met the *Bittern* at our rendezvous dead on time.

Carrying out the patrol, in company on the first day with the *Sunfish*, according to instructions, and on the second day with the *Bittern*, I kept the speed down to four knots, not only to economize coal, but also to avoid any strain on the damaged propeller. We sighted no U-boats or mines, met with no heavy weather, and had no occasion to put on any burst of speed.

When we returned to port, relieved by the *Sunfish*, and berthed again at the coal wharf, Engineburg went down over the stern, and discovered that a small piece had been broken off the tip of one of the wings of the port propeller.

This did not prevent us from putting to sea again for another patrol; but, when that was finished, she was laid up for a week for her turn at boiler cleaning; and then a new propeller was fitted. "It's a beastly nuisance," said the S.O.P.F., when I reported the situation to him. "Extremely tiresome, but these things do happen, old chap — so don't worry too much about it. You can't be blamed for every breeze that blows. The *Roebuck* isn't the *Mauretania*, you know! In destroyers we can't afford to pay tugs to get us away. When it's time to shove off, we have to shove off. Join me in a gin and bitters? Here's to better luck next time. Cheerio, Bisset, old boy! Are we down hearted? No!"

The Destroyer Patrols — Groping in the Dark — Minelaying Submarines — The Minesweepers — We Sight a Derelict — A Lucky Charm — The Unrestricted U-boat Campaign — Appalling Losses of Merchant Ships — U.S.A. Enters the War— Primitive Hydrophone — "Roebuck" to the Rescue — A Japanese Castaway — Spirit of the Merchant Service.

FOR two and a half years, from June, 1916, until the Armistice in November, 1918, and for a few months after that, I served in the Plymouth Extended Defence Flotilla, mostly in command of H.M.T.B.D. *Roebuck*, and for a short time in command of H.M.T.B.D. *Sunfish*. For the whole of that period, I was patrolling off the coast of Devon, between Plymouth and Lyme Regis.

That was my little contribution to the ultimate result achieved. I was like the hundreds of thousands of others at sea, and the millions on land, who "did their bit" for the common cause, suffered some hardships, took some risks, and did whatever the call of duty required, without complaining too much, or expecting any praise or reward.

Those were wasted years, as all war years are but, until the world's problems can be solved without war, all old sailors, old soldiers, and old airmen, and any other old battlers, will have tales to tell, sometimes true, sometimes not, of their personal shares in war's excitements. The truer the tale, the more improbable it sometimes seems. Any man who managed to survive the risks of war was to some extent lucky. Of the total of 35,000 seamen who served in British destroyers during the 1914-18 war, nearly 5000 perished on active service. In the flotilla of four vessels in which I served, one vessel was sunk, with the loss of seventy-three lives. Those of us who survived were favoured by the fortunes of war.

My experiences in destroyers were typical of the experiences of thousands of other men in that service, on the routine patrols of the British coasts. At any moment when a destroyer was at sea, she was exposed to the risks of being torpedoed by a U-boat, or of striking an enemy mine, or at nighttime of being in collision with an unlit vessel — risks difficult to guard against, which were products only of wartime conditions.

The stretch of coast along which our flotilla patrolled, between Eddystone Light and Lyme Regis, is sheltered to some extent from the westerlies, and out of the mainstream of traffic in the channel, but handy to it. It was frequented by coastal steamers and fishing trawlers, and sometimes by trans-ocean steamers hugging the coast to shelter from the weather or conforming with Admiralty orders to make detours from the main traffic lanes, to avoid U-boats or minefields.

But that bight on the English shore of the Channel was also a place of shelter for German U-boats and for "UC-boats"[1] — their submarine minelayers. Several British cargo steamers were sunk by torpedoes or mines in this vicinity, as happened also in each of the other patrol areas (twenty-one numbered zones of coastal waters), around the shores of Britain and Ireland.

Destroyers had been designed originally for attacking enemy surface vessels. Their torpedoes and guns were useless against vessels which were submerged and invisible! In two and a half years I never had occasion to fire a torpedo. On a few occasions we blazed away with our guns at the almost impossible target of a distant periscope, In the vague hope that a high explosive shell might wreck a U-boat lurking below the surface; but, at the first ranging shot, the periscope would be withdrawn beneath the surface, and the enemy had become invisible.

What to do then, in the days before depth charges were perfected, was always a problem. There was a romantic idea that destroyers should charge the presumed situation of the submerged enemy at 10 knots in the hope of ramming him. In the early stages of the war such tactics had succeeded a few times, but the operation as almost as dangerous to the ramming vessel as to the U-boat. in some cases the forefoot of the ramming vessel was so seriously damaged that she had to limp into port for repairs. In some other cases, when ships simply blew up without trace or survivors, it was possible that a U-boat had been rammed, and its torpedoes exploded by the impact.

The only practical chance of destroying a U-boat was to find it on the surface and hit it by shellfire before it could dive. The U-boats surfaced chiefly at nighttime, to recharge their batteries. Destroyers carried searchlights on the bridge, but these gave warning of their approach to the enemy. All that could be said was that the destroyer patrols, by day and by night, made the U-boats wary of surfacing. To that extent the patrols were a deterrent to U-boat activity; but the terrible toll taken by U-boats showed that the countermeasures against them were ineffectual, until depth charges were brought into use.

On patrol, the *Roebuck* usually cruised at four knots, with at least ten men on lookout — some on the bridge, and others on deck forward and aft, sweeping the sea with binoculars for any sign of a periscope, or perhaps of a floating mine, or of wreckage, or anything else unusual. We also had the duty of escorting merchant vessels through our patrol area, and of identifying and reporting to our shore base by radio any vessels sighted. This required much visual signalling, with flags and Morse lamps, since many of the coastal cargo steamers were not equipped with radio.

In addition to two wireless operators, we had two signalmen, of long training and service in the Royal Navy, who, like most men of their rating, were wondrously expert at sending and receiving with flags, semaphore, and Morse lamps. A signalman was always stationed on the bridge, with the Officer of the Watch and the helmsman.

Some merchant service officers were not remarkably clever at reading hand flag signals sent by our naval signallers. On one occasion we received a wireless message, instructing us to order all steamers in the vicinity to proceed at full speed into Plymouth, as U-boats were reported in the vicinity. We passed on this order by hand flag signals to the only steamer in sight, an ancient tramp. The request came several times to repeat the message, and in the meantime the tramp altered course to come nearer to us, and stopped, while her Master, a burly, grizzled greybeard, leaned out from the wing of her bridge, and sang out through his megaphone, "DO YOU MEAN THAT WE HAVE TO GO BACK TO PLYMOUTH?"

"That's correct," I told him. "Make full speed for Plymouth. There's a German sub around here."

"Damn the Navy," the greybeard sang out. "Too many orders.
Why can't they leave us alone?"

"Orders are orders," I reminded him. "Get going at full speed for Plymouth, and don't argue, Captain, or the sub might get you while you're lying there stopped."

"He might get me going back to Plymouth, and miss me if I hold on my course."

"Complain to the Admiralty, Captain, but you've got to go back. Please move on, quickly!"

"To hell with the Admiralty, and don't send your flag signals so quickly next time, young fellow!"

With that, the sturdy veteran rang his engines to full ahead, turned around, and set course for Plymouth, doing all of a rollicking seven knots.

He reached port safely and was allowed to resume his voyage next day. He had all my sympathy, but he had to learn, like many others of his stout breed, that the Navy knows best ... sometimes.

I got to know my leading signalman well and had a genuine respect for his skill at his work. He was a middle aged man, the father of a large family. He had his home in Plymouth and had been in destroyers for many years.

One dark night, when we were feeling our way along, with all lights out, I heard the signalman on the bridge groaning in pain. "Ooh! Oogh!" he was grunting at intervals.

"What's wrong?" I asked him. "Have you got the stomach-ache or the toothache?"

"Excuse me, sir, I can't help it!" he replied, evasively. "Oogh! Oogh!"

"But what's your trouble?"

"Well, sir, it's like this. My wife is in labour pains at this moment. I know it well, sir, from experience. We have so much sympathy between us that I feel the labour pains myself. It helps her if I groan and go through the pain with her."

We were forty miles from Plymouth at that time; but I had too much respect for his feelings to laugh at his obviously serious belief. "Do you want to be relieved on watch?" I asked. "Do you want to go below and groan?"

"No, sir, I can groan quite well on watch, if you don't mind my groaning, sir."

"Carry on, then," I said.

"Oogh! Oogh!" he groaned, at intervals.

After a while I asked, "Are you sure that it's started at home?" "Quite sure, sir. Oogh! My wife and I can send messages to one another by thoughts."

This, I thought, was a new development of naval signalling. After a while, he stopped groaning, and said, "The pain's eased and the baby is born!" I looked at my watch. It was 3 a.m.

Next day, when we returned to port, he hurried ashore, with twenty-four hours' leave. He came back on board an hour later, all smiles, before I had left the ship. "A fine bouncing baby boy," he told me. "Born at three o'clock last night!"

I congratulated him and gave him a golden sovereign for luck. Anyone who can explain this incident satisfactorily is entitled to do so. I merely state the facts.

On patrol at nighttime, all vessels in our area proceeded without steaming lights. The hazards of collision were acute. We were groping in the dark, playing a ghostly game of hide-and-seek, in which friend or foe could at any moment materialize in the blackness, but only as darker shapes. This game of Blindman's Buff was played also sometimes by day, in the fogs which, especially in the winter months, blanket the Channel. After a few months on this service, we developed "cats' eyes" — but some men are born with that ability of night vision more highly developed than the average, even without practice.

After months of tension and constant lookout for danger, real or imaginary, we became case hardened and able to keep lookout as a matter of routine, without fraying our nerves overmuch. This was not indifference to danger but rather a mental adjustment, and acceptance of an abnormal situation as normal.

Soon after I took over command of the *Roebuck*, we had the luck to discover an enemy minefield. This had evidently been laid by a UC-boat. Each of these underwater minelayers carried fifteen or twenty mines, which they could lay like horrible eggs. The mines were anchored to the seabed, by cables which allowed them to lie buoyant six feet below the surface of the water at low tide. They were laid in a pattern.

Each mine had a number of "horns" on it, which, on being pressed in by contact with the bow or side of a ship, caused the cordite inside the mine to explode. Under international agreements, mines were fitted with a plug of soft metal, which corroded in salt water, so that, after a predetermined period of time, the mine filled with salt water, became harmless, and sank to the seabed.

The British Navy had some minelaying surface vessels, which had laid many minefields off the German coast, and in other areas of the North Sea. The Germans had countered with minelaying submarines. As a defence, Britain put into service a large number of minesweeping trawlers, and built, launched, and commissioned one hundred minesweeping sloops which were vessels of the Royal Navy, many of them commanded by officers of the Royal Naval Reserve, and of the Royal Naval Volunteer Reserve, (R.N.V.R.).

The minesweepers usually worked in pairs, steaming parallel courses, with a long wire cable suspended between them, supported by an underwater "kite" in such a way that the cable was dragged in a bight ten feet below the surface, abaft of the two minesweeping vessels. This "sweeping cable" picked up the anchor cables of the mines, and by its friction rubbed the horns of the mines, causing them to explode, or cutting them adrift, so that they came to the surface, and could then be destroyed by gunfire.

In that technique, the minesweepers themselves were likely to strike mines, and many of them were sunk in that way, with heavy loss of life.

While patrolling close inshore, in the direction of Portland Bill, I happened to sight an object awash in choppy seas. We identified it as a mine which had been anchored, by the enemy's miscalculation, with too much cable, so that it was partly exposed to sight at low tide. I realized then that I was either on the edge of a minefield, or in the midst of one, so I rang the engines to stop, not knowing in which direction I could safely proceed. I sent a wireless signal to the minesweepers which presently came speeding toward us and began the difficult and dangerous specialist task of surveying the minefield, sweeping up the mines, and destroying them.

While this was being done, I succeeded in steering clear. My job then was to stand by, in company with the *Bittern*, to warn merchant vessels to alter their course and go clear of the field. This required much scurrying around for several hours, and much lollygagging, while from time to time explosions indicated that the mines were being destroyed. We also had some target practice at mines that were cut loose and floating adrift.

The operation went off without any mishap. A terse report was made through the proper channels to the Admiralty. The report was then pigeonholed and was of no further interest to anyone. It was only another little job done: an incident in the lives of the men on that destroyer patrol and in the minesweepers: scarcely worth mentioning, except those tens of thousands of little incidents like that — at sea, on land, and in the air — unrewarded and almost unrecorded — eventually added up to winning the war.

Sometimes there were more dramatic incidents. One afternoon we had reached the eastern limit of our patrol area when we sighted a steamer stopped and rolling about in the rough seas whipped by a strong westerly breeze.

Going nearer to investigate, we could get no signals from her and could not see anyone on board. She had a heavy list to port, which was her weather side. We ranged up on that side, and saw that she had a gaping hole amidships, in the vicinity of the engine room. Obviously, she had been torpedoed, or had struck a mine, and had been abandoned. Her boats were gone. It was astonishing that she had remained afloat. The hole in her side was big enough to drive a horse and cart through. It extended below the waterline. I could see the water racing in and out of it as she rolled to windward and leeward, beam on to the seas.

A derelict is always dangerous to shipping, especially in busy traffic lanes. This one would have to be either salvaged or sunk. With considerable difficulty I managed to get one of our boats away, and the First Lieutenant scrambled aboard the derelict. On his return he reported that she had been completely and hurriedly abandoned. Her confidential books had been taken away, but the steel box for holding them was in the Captain's cabin, with a few papers in it. The Lieutenant brought this box back with him.

The afternoon was well advanced. I reported the situation by wireless code to our base at Plymouth and was ordered to stand by until a tug arrived. Towards dusk the tug hove in sight, and we again launched our boat, with the First Lieutenant and eight ratings, to go aboard the derelict and assist the tugmaster to make his towline fast The wind and the seas were rising, and the derelict was now wallowing deeply, as the tug took her in tow and headed for Portland. I was glad to have our men off her, as she didn't look as if she could last much longer.

Soon after the tow began, the derelict rolled over and foundered. The tugmaster slipped his wire, and one more British freighter had gone to Davy Jones's locker.

We resumed our patrol, and I examined the box which the First Lieutenant had brought off. It contained some unimportant documents, but among them was an envelope containing a piece of what looked like dried parchment. On the envelope were the mystifying words: OUR LITILE DARLING'S CAUL.

I couldn't make sense of this, nor could the First Lieutenant; but our Chief Engineer (Engineburg) quickly enlightened us. He explained that some infants are born with a membrane over the head, which is known as a "caul."

A child born with a caul is lucky. More than that, the caul itself is a lucky charm, especially against drowning!

So it had proved on this occasion. I heard later that the Master and the entire crew of the damaged tramp steamer, some twenty men in all, had landed safely on the coast of Dorset. No doubt the Master had thought that his ship would sink almost immediately when he had given the order to abandon her; but in his haste he had left his Lucky Caul on board — and his ship had remained afloat until that caul was taken off her!

I hope that he got his little darling's caul back, for I handed it over to the proper authorities to be forwarded to him.

Towards the end of 1916, the U-boat campaign was intensified. On an average at least one hundred merchant vessels were being sunk every month, mostly in the waters around the western coasts of Britain and France. Among these, two Cunarders, the *Franconia* (18,000 tons) and the *Alaunia* (13,000 tons) were sunk in October 1916; and, on 21st November 1916, the gigantic White Star *Britannic* (46,000 tons), in service as a hospital ship, struck a mine in the Zea Channel in the Aegean Sea, and sank with a loss of twenty-one lives. The minefield had been laid there only one hour previously by a German UC-boat which had been navigated from Cuxhaven in Western Germany to the Mediterranean.

In December 1916, the appalling total of 167 merchant vessels were sunk by U-boat action. This could be described as the beginning of the unrestricted submarine warfare campaign, although the Germans did not officially declare that campaign until 1st February 1917. What it meant was that all shipping bound for the ports of Britain or her allies, and whether under belligerent or neutral flags, would be liable to be sunk by U-boats without warning.

From the beginning of the war, in August 1914, until the end of December 1916, a total of 519 British merchant vessels, and 420 merchant vessels of nations allied with Britain, had been sunk by U-boat action, either with torpedoes or by mines. In that time 49 U-boats had been destroyed.

Even though, in the total of 939 British and Allied vessels sunk, many were sailing vessels or small steamers, it was only too obvious that the U-boats were a fearsome weapon of destruction, and that they could do their deadly work almost, if not quite, with impunity. But when they intensified their campaign, to include sinking at sight the vessels of neutral as well as belligerent nations, the situation became extremely serious, and Britain was brought to the verge of starvation. For fifty or more years previously, British agriculture had been allowed to fall into a relative decline, so that seaborne imported foodstuffs were required to feed the majority of the population. At the height of the unrestricted U-boat campaign, early in 1917, supplies of food in Britain were enough to last only another six weeks, with strict rationing.

In those circumstances the German counter blockade by U-boats had very nearly succeeded. In January 1917, a total of 180 merchant vessels were sunk; in February, 260 vessels; in March, 338 vessels; in April, 430 vessels.

In that total of 1208 vessels sunk in four months, 339 were owned by neutral nations, including the U.S.A.

On 6th April 1917, the U.S.A. declared war on Germany and the other powers of the Central European Alliance. That declaration was a direct consequence of the unrestricted U-boat campaign. The Germans had played for high stakes and had lost the game.

Among British merchant vessels sunk in 1917 were nine Cunarders. Six of these were small cargo steamers, but three of them were passenger liners the *Ivernia* (14,000 tons), the *Laconia* (18,000 tons), and the *Ultonia* (10,400 tons).

I had served in peacetime in both the *Ivernia* and the *Ultonia*. I was hopping mad at the news that they were sunk — not that it was any use feeling so irate; but it made the war seem all the more real and worth winning. Probably some similar feeling had brought the Americans into the war. The sinking of merchant ships by U-boats seemed a dastardly and uncivilized thing to do.

Every new weapon in warfare has brought a similar reaction of indignation from its victims, until the appropriate defence is devised.

The Plymouth Extended Defence Flotilla on several occasions picked up survivors from steamers that had been sent to the bottom by U-boat action.

One night, in midwinter, when I was on patrol in the *Roebuck*, shortly after nightfall, the weather shut down on us in a dense fog. The sea was dead calm, and there was no breeze. In these circumstances — in those days before wireless direction finding, radar, and other aids to navigation in fog had been invented — we cruised along in our patrol area at dead slow, or stopped, listening all the while intently for any sound of ships' foghorns, or even of propellers. My chief concern was to avoid being accidentally rammed by a merchant steamer.

Twice during the First Watch, large merchant vessels passed. very close to us, going full speed, with no lights showing or fog-horn blowing, their master's just taking a chance, and probably hoping that "Jerry" would not be trying to torpedo anyone under such blind conditions.

In peacetime, in such thick fog at nighttime, steamers would have proceeded at dead slow, advertising their whereabouts with 'lights and foghorn; but to have done that while Jerry was lurking around and would have been extremely foolish.

The alternative, to drive on into the darkness and fog, was also dangerous, and contrary to all the peacetime principles of sound seamanship, and of the Board of Trade Regulations for preventing collisions at sea, but it was better than offering Jerry a shot at a sitting duck.

In the *Roebuck*, I felt that we were in less danger from U-boats than from being run down by a merchant steamer. By listening keenly, we might be able to get out of the way of the ships we were supposed to be protecting.

During one of our stop periods, my Chief Engineer, the redoubtable Engineburg, came up to the bridge. He reported that, while he was sitting in the wardroom aft, with everything very quiet, he had heard the dull thud of a distant underwater explosion. We had not heard it on the bridge.

Leaving the First Lieutenant on the bridge, I went down with Engineburg to the wardroom, and we sat in silence there, listening intently. After half an hour, I heard the unmistakable sound of a distant, muffled, explosion. "That sounded louder than the first one!" remarked Engineburg. On the bridge, the First Lieutenant, and the midshipman and signalman with him, had heard nothing at all.

By accident, and in a primitive way, Engineburg had applied the principle of the "Hydrophone," an underwater listening gear which was later used extensively in hunting U-boats. Sounds originating under water travel a surprisingly long distance through water. In the wardroom aft, which was below the *Roebuck*'s waterline, we had heard distant explosions caused by torpedoes or mines striking a ship, or two ships.

The sound had come from the seaward, not the landward side of our position. I set course in the general direction from which, as it seemed to me, the sound had come. We proceeded at dead slow, groping along, on a wide zigzag track, peering into the darkness and fog, looking and listening· for boats or wreckage or anything that might explain the explosions that we had heard. After several hours, I began to think that we were on a hopeless quest; but I kept on with the search.

"It was just as well that I did so. At 2 a.m., when I was on the bridge with the Gunner, we both heard a faint wailing cry, in a high pitched voice, on our starboard bow, which sounded as though were being hailed by a disembodied spirit.

Was it a U-boat trick to decoy us? All hands were ordered to on stations, as the wailing cry was repeated, and continued at intervals, and we crept towards it at dead slow.

The fog and darkness were so thick that visibility was practically nil. Suddenly, only a few feet away from our side amidships, we saw a dinghy. It was drifting, and damaged. Three men were in it: two of them, apparently dead, were lying on the thwarts, and the third was standing up, gesticulating, and wailing in a high pitched voice, in some foreign language.

This man sprang up to our deck by grabbing the rails, with the agility of a monkey. He was a Japanese, who could speak some English. He was blue with cold, for he was lightly clad and barefooted, and wet through, in the temperature almost at freezing point; but he was a man of iron. He insisted on helping our crew to lift the other two men out of the dinghy onto the *Roebuck*'s deck.

They were white men unconscious from shock and cold, wearing only pyjamas, and barefooted. We took them and the Japanese down to the galley, to thaw out. When we got there, the Japanese fainted. Bending over him, to force some grog between his teeth and to loosen his clothing, I found that he had a money belt around his waist, with a good number of golden coins in it. This was one of those times when it is no use being surprised at anything. After much attention and dosing, one of the other men came to.

He told me that he was Mate of a British cargo steamer bound from Leith to Plymouth with cement. "I was in my bunk asleep," he said, "and then, as if by magic, I found myself swimming in the sea!" Presently the Japanese and the other man also came to.

They had both been deckhands in the tramp. They had been off watch, sleeping in their bunks under the forecastle, when there was a big explosion, and they found themselves in the water in total darkness, without knowing how they had got there. Japan was Britain's ally in the war. The Japanese seaman was serving in an English ship to learn English.

"I lucky!" he grinned. "I wear my money belt in bed. I have fifty gold sovereigns. Salt water no hurt."

He was a good swimmer, he said. He had found a boat floating and had got into it. He had dragged the Mate and the other seaman out of the water into the boat. The ship had gone down, and all hands with her, except those three. They saw no other swimmers and heard no cries. They did not use the oars, for they did not know where they were, or in which direction to steer. The boat was the ship's dinghy, which had been lashed on the afterdeck. Apparently, the explosion, caused by a torpedo or mine, had broken the lashings and had set the dinghy adrift.

There were no provisions in the dinghy. All three men were dazed. "I heard you and sang out," said the Japanese.

"What did you sing out?"

"Sheep ahoy!" His voice was high treble, almost falsetto.

"Well, we heard you, anyway."

I headed the *Roebuck* for the nearest port, Dartmouth, and at daylight landed the three castaways there, to be taken to hospital. That was the last that we saw of them, for our base was at Plymouth, but we heard that they recovered after treatment for shock and immersion, and that all three, including the Japanese, signed on again immediately in another coaster.

That was what thousands of other merchant seamen did after being torpedoed and reaching shore — went to sea again, undaunted.

CHAPTER ENDNOTES

(1) The Type UC I coastal submarines were a class of small minelaying U-boats built in Germany during the early part of World War I.

An undated/uncredited photo of Capt. James Bisset displayed on the back cover of the first two books. (Bisset)

THE United States entered the war after the gigantic struggle had been raging in Europe for two years and eight months. At that time the war situation was a stalemate, but Britain, France, and Russia had suffered heavy casualties and had borne the full brunt of the enemy's attack and had taken its edge off.

The intervention of America was decisive, but it was not true that "America won the war." Nor could it be fairly claimed that the Americans had entered the war tardily. The traditional policy of the U.S.A. was to remain aloof from European conflicts. Millions of American citizens were of German, Austrian, and Hungarian birth, and to that extent sympathetic with the Central European Powers. It was no easy matter for the American Government to unify American public opinion in favour of armed intervention in Europe, either on one side or the other.

Many Americans, even those of British descent, held anti-British opinions as a legacy of "the ancient grudge" — of the American War of Independence. There were also millions of Americans of Irish descent, who considered the English to be oppressors of their old country. In this complicated situation, the chief factor that influenced American public opinion in favour of active intervention the German policy of unrestricted submarine warfare. The Americans claimed, "freedom of the seas." When the Germans began sinking American ships, the Americans got their dander up and decided to hit back.

Great though their contribution to victory was, it was not more a reinforcement of Britain, France, Russia, and their allies a critical time when both sides in the European conflict were exhausted and almost "bled white." The help that the Americans I was all the more welcome as it was timely; but the enemy they to meet was almost as exhausted as the friends they went to help.

"The Yanks are coming!" was the popular song. "We're coming over, we're coming over, and it will soon be over when we're over, over there!"

But it was not so soon over. Another nineteen months of horrible destruction, at sea, on land, and in that new region of fighting, the air had to be endured before peace, of a kind, could be restored among the wounded nations.

American help could not have been quickly effective without Britain's command of the seas, both naval and mercantile.

Of a total of 2,027,914 U.S. troops brought across the Atlantic to Europe, 1,075,333 were carried in British ships; 557,788 by the American Naval Overseas Transportation Service; in vessels, formerly of German ownership, which had been sheltering in American ports and were commandeered by the U.S. Navy; and the remainder, 394,798 troops, in American owned and American built vessels.

As an example of the contribution made by the British Merchant Service at this time, it is enough to mention that the *S.S. Mauretania*, fitted as a troop transport, in seven months carried 60,000 American pa across the Atlantic. She was making the round voyage in a fortnight, carrying on an average nearly 4000 troops on each east-bound passage.

With their immense energy and industrial resources, the Americans began a huge shipbuilding programme of both naval and mercantile vessels. The total American naval personnel were expanded in nineteen months from 95,000 to 535,000, many of them necessarily hastily trained; and the U.S. Naval ship building programme expanded and rapidly completed in a like proportion.

Many American warships, heavy and light, crossed the Atlantic to help the British and French navies in countermeasures against U-Boats. These included eighty-five destroyers, and 120 submarine chasers equipped with depth charges.

The British Admiralty was also taking energetic and realistic measures to destroy U-boats. Towards the end of 1917, and early in 1918, the methods of offence and defence against these dangerous pests were at last becoming effective. Thousands of craft of all sorts and sizes were pressed into the Auxiliary Patrol and fitted to carry depth charges.

The depth charges were bombs, 300 pounds in weight, intended at first to be dropped over the stern of a destroyer or other anti-submarine vessel going at full speed, and timed to explode at twenty, thirty, or forty fathoms below the surface in the vicinity, or presumed vicinity of a submerged U-boat. Later, this method was supplemented by "throwers," which were a kind of catapult capable of throwing a pattern of three or four depth charges several hundred yards.

Depth charges were carried on board yachts, tugs, trawlers, drifters, coastal steamers, ferry boats, and motorboats operating out of all ports around the British coasts. In addition, naval aircraft, both British and American, were constantly patrolling and dropping depth charges on anything that even faintly resembled a periscope.

The convoy system had now become highly developed. Large numbers of merchant vessels, loaded with desperately needed cargoes, and escorted by cruisers and destroyers, were able to approach our coasts and make port in comparative safety.

The German U-boat commanders, despite their undoubted bravery, were being harried to such an extent that they began to feel the "breeze vertical." As with every other new weapon of war in history, an answer had been found to the U-boat weapon. And, with that, Germany's defeat became only a matter of time.

The Plymouth Extended Defence Flotilla continued its operations as formerly, but now we were equipped with depth charges and supported in our patrol area by many small auxiliary vessels which scurried hither and thither dropping depth charges lavishly, and no doubt killing millions of fish, and probably some U-boats. Early in 1918, to economize coal and save a few hours at sea, our flotilla began operating out of Dartmouth and Torquay as bases. At Dartmouth we refuelled from coal hulks.

I was still in command of *H.M.T.B.D. Roebuck*. During one of her boiler cleaning periods, I went into the Naval Hospital at Stonehouse (near Plymouth) with a bad attack of tonsillitis. At the same time, by coincidence, my wife was taken to hospital suffering from German measles — a tragic thing to happen, for she was expecting a baby.

Our son Barry was born soon afterwards, but to our deep grief, which endures to this day, he lived only five weeks. In his little way he was a victim of wartime conditions, which included shortages of hospital facilities and drugs; but then, as now, the effects of German measles on childbirth are often fatal.

On service again in the *Roebuck*, in the spring of 1918, I had another saddening experience. At this time the flotilla was based on Torquay. My friend Bill Irving was still in command of the *Bittern*. We were both reconciled to serving for the remaining duration of the war in destroyers. The Admiralty seldom promoted destroyer commanders, being satisfied to leave them in routines with which they were thoroughly familiar.

The *Bittern* went to Plymouth for ten days, for boiler cleaning and refit. After this, she resumed her place in the patrol programme, by taking forty-eight hours on duty, and I was due to relieve her lt 8 a.m. outside Dartmouth.

The *Roebuck* was moored alongside a coal hulk in Dartmouth. I had slept on board, as the weather was thick. I had spent a restless night, listening to heavy rain pattering on the deck above my head, and to the creaking of the moorings as we surged to and fro, and up and down, alongside the hulk in the strong S.E. breeze. At 7.15 a.m., I was called with a cup of tea, and turned out of my bunk reluctantly, looking forward to an uncomfortable day lit sea. At 7.50 the First Lieutenant reported, "All ready for leaving harbour." A few moments later I went onto the bridge, gave the order, "Cast off," and the men on deck having fended

The H.M.S. Bittern was a C-Class Destroyer and a duplicate to the other sister ships in her class such as the H.H.S. Chamois shown here.
(Public Domain and this photo Q 38460 comes from the collections of the Imperial War Museums (collection no. 2107-01)

her off from the hulk with the bearing out spars, I rang the engines to full ahead and we proceeded to sea.

It was usual for the incoming vessel to wait somewhere near the harbour entrance, ready to enter as soon as her relief hove in 1lght. On this occasion, there was no sign of the *Bittern*, so I stood off the land for a few miles, expecting at any moment to get a radio Crom Irving, giving his position.

It was a clear morning, with a heavy leaden sky, and bright patches here and there as the sun strove to break through. The wind had fallen light, but a tumbling "jobble" of a sea remained: the result of the dirty weather during the night.

Where was the *Bittern*? I steamed along the coast slowly for an hour, frequently calling her by radio, but without getting any reply. Surmising that she may have been detached for some special duty, I sent a radio to the Commander-in-Chief, asking for information. It sometimes happened that a destroyer was detached from the flotilla temporarily for escort or rescue work, but when On service again in the *Roebuck*, in the spring of 1918, I had another saddening experience. At this time the flotilla was based on Torquay. My friend Bill Irving was still in command of the *Bittern*. We were both reconciled to serving for the remaining duration of the war in destroyers. The Admiralty seldom promoted destroyer commanders, being satisfied to leave them in routines with which they were thoroughly familiar.

What sometimes happened that a destroyer was detached from the flotilla temporarily for escort or rescue work, but when this was done the other vessels of the flotilla were always notified. The absence of any such signal on this occasion had me worried. Another hour passed, during which I went down to the ward- room for breakfast I was just swallowing my last cup of coffee when the signalman came down and handed me a coded radio- gram. Getting out the secret code, I deciphered a startling message:

"*Bittern* missing. Search area HYK."

Hurriedly taking some bearings of the land, I laid off a course on the chart to take us to the centre of that area, and we set off at full speed. Presently another signal came; "Sending twelve motor launches to assist you in search."

Obviously something serious had happened, but what? Had the *Bittern* been torpedoed, or struck a mine, or rammed a U-boat and sunk herself in the process, or collided during the dark and stormy night with a steamer or some other vessel? Was she perhaps still afloat, but with her radio out of action? Thinking of Bill Irving and the other seventy-two men of her complement, I crammed on all possible speed, until we were doing 28 knots and being thrown about violently in the head-on choppy seas. My thoughts were racing with the engines. I hoped desperately to be in time to effect a rescue.

It took just under an hour to reach area HYK, but there was no sign of the *Bittern*. I at once began a systematic "triangular pattern" search, with all available hands on deck keeping a sharp lookout for anything in the nature of wreckage.

By now the breeze had died, and the sea was flattening out into a calm, so that it was possible to see small objects in the water at a distance of half a mile or more.

After a while, the twelve naval motor launches came chugging out in single line ahead. Using flag signals, I got them spread out abreast at distances of half a mile, and sent them off on a three mile search from the base of my triangle.

No sooner had they started than another message came through from the C.-in-C." Steamer reports having rammed unidentified vessel at 3 a.m. in area HYJ. May have been enemy submarine. Heard cries and remained in vicinity for one hour but found nothing. Search HYJ closely."

This area was five miles to the eastward of the one we were searching. I was puzzled that either *Bittern* or a steamer should have been there during the night, as it was off the prescribed track for shipping, which was close to the coastline.

I recalled the launches, and we set off for the new search area. Almost immediately after arriving there, we found an oar in the water, and, picking it up, saw that it was branded *Bittern*. A few minutes later, one of the launches picked up an officer's cap. Then we found the remains of a badly broken boat, and several other objects, some of them branded *Bittern*.

It had become only too obvious that the steamer had rammed *Bittern* during the heavy rain and darkness. The destroyer with her displacement of 400 tons would have been badly smashed by a steamer of several thousand tons probably belting along at full speed with all lights out.

Gloom spread over us as we continued the search. Every small piece of wreckage we found made it appear more certain that the *Bittern* had sunk with all hands. It was just another tragedy of the war — seventy-three good men gone, leaving widows, orphans, and others bereaved to mourn them.

My thoughts went out particularly to her Captain. He was my best friend. It was hard to think that I would never see Bill Irving again. He was so virile, so "alive," and always so cheerful. I could Imagine that he would die fighting, with a grim smile on his face- and now he'd gone under — probably without being able to raise a hand to save himself, or his crew, or his ship — the victim of a ghastly error.

We cruised around until dark, informing the C.-in-C. at intervals of our finds. Then orders came for the motor launches to return to base, and for the *Roebuck* to abandon the search and resume patrol. I hated having to leave that area. Even seventeen hours after the collision, we might have found some ·survivor, or bodies supported by lifebelts; but our search had been thorough, and at last hope had to be abandoned. It was evident that the *Bittern* had gone to the bottom suddenly, taking all her complement with her. The next thirty-six hours on patrol hung heavily. We were given no further information by radio. At last our turn on duty came to an end. At 8 a.m., I was waiting outside Dartmouth for my relief, the *Sunfish*. She appeared punctually, and in half an hour I was tied up alongside the coal hulk.

After breakfast, I jumped into the dinghy to go ashore and make my report. As we approached the landing steps, I saw an officer standing at the head of the steps to welcome me. The shock almost unnerved me. It was Lieutenant-Commander "Bill" Irving, Captain of the *Bittern*!

I thought that my brain had gone phut[1], or that I was seeing a ghost But when the dinghy bumped alongside, and Irving's brawny hand gripped mine, I knew that he was no spook. Relief surged through me, as I began to think that by some miraculous means he and his crew had been saved.

"What happened?" I gasped, excitedly.

"I'm the luckiest man alive," Irving said, grimly. 'I'm a man with a poisoned thumb."

This scarcely made sense until he explained further. A few hours before he was due to go out on patrol, he had attended the Naval Hospital for treatment of a poisoned thumb. The doctors had decided that he was unfit for duty. At the last moment, his second-in-command had been ordered to take over command of the *Bittern* temporarily, and Irving had stayed on shore for further medical treatment.

"Yes," he repeated, glumly, 'I'm the luckiest man alive, one of the luckiest men in this war — the only survivor of my ship, for the simple reason that I wasn't in her when she went down!"

Later that day, Irving and I read the report of the incident that had been made by the steamer's Master. Knowing the habits of the patrol, we felt able to make a correct surmise of what had happened.

In the heavy weather, with rough seas, rain squalls, and darkness, the First Lieutenant of *Bittern* had almost certainly decided that U-boats would not attempt to work that night. Accordingly, he had put his ship head-on to the wind and seas, so that she would not roll and wallow too violently, and had stood away slowly to the south-eastward, intending to return to the patrol area when the weather fined up, or at daylight.

In these circumstances she would be steaming without lights, as was customary, and the crew — except those actually on watch — would be below, trying to get some sleep.

The Captain of the cargo steamer, according to his own report, had decided to cut across the bight, instead of hugging the coast on the prescribed track, in conditions of wind and sea that would have been dangerous for him on a lee shore. At 2 a.m., when the steamer was headed into seas twelve feet high from trough to crest, the lookout had sighted a small black object under her bows. Before any action could be taken to alter course, there was a collision.

At the moment of impact, the steamer's bows had lifted up on a high sea. The men on the bridge felt a second impact immediately under the bridge, indicating that they had passed over the as yet unidentified object.

They had heard some cries, which several of the crew imagined were in the German tongue. All the circumstances seemed to indicate that they had rammed a U-boat lying on the surface in the hours of darkness to recharge batteries.

The Captain of the steamer stated that he had stood by but had been unable to see any survivors. So perished *H.M.T.B.D. Bittern* and all her gallant crew, except her Captain, Lieutenant-Commander B. Irving, R.N.R., who then, and for many years afterwards, had every reason to reiterate the claim that he was one of the luckiest men alive.

Shortly after this incident, the *Roebuck* was taken off the patrol and sent on a special mission under another commander. I was transferred to command of *H.M.T.B.D. Sunfish*, and served in her for the last few months of the war. The other two vessels in the flotilla were torpedo boats.

A little while after the Armistice of 11th November, 1918, the epidemic of Spanish influenza swept through Europe. It was said that this epidemic — one of the "Four Horsemen of the Apocalypse" — killed more people than had died in battle.

To guard against the virus infection — communicated by breathing— millions of people walked about wearing gauze masks over their noses and mouths. Death and desolation stalked the cities of Britain, us elsewhere, at the end of a war in which populations had been reduced by starvation, worries, and ordeals to a low level of physical resistance.

The flu affected many men in destroyer patrols, who spent one day out of three in ports, coming in contact with people on shore. So many men went down to it in our little flotilla that one vessel was laid up, and the crews were so reduced in the others that we were shorthanded. The war was over, but we had to carry on until further orders.

I was congratulating myself on having escaped the 'flu, when I went down like a ton of bricks. We put in to Torquay, and landed several of the crew who had also gone down to it.

Doctors were working overtime. A naval surgeon came on board lo see me. He said, "The hospitals and hotels are all full, and I have nowhere to put you. You have a cabin to yourself here. I suggest that you lay up on board, dose yourself with aspirin and whiskey, and perhaps you'll recover!"

I followed this advice for a few days, but got steadily worse, and felt that my end was near! As I had become utterly useless in command, I was carried ashore in Dartmouth and put into a boarding house that had been taken over as a hospital. There my good wife nursed me back to health.

On returning to the *Sunfish*, I found that, a few hours previously, the First Lieutenant, who had been acting for me in command, had got foul of a buoy in the harbour and had stripped all the blades off the starboard propeller.

She was ordered to Plymouth to lay up; but she was never repaired. She went to the shipbreakers. It did not matter then. The war was over. Victory was ours, and at what a price!

The immense procedure of demobilizing millions of fighting men could not be done in less than several months. I was transferred to command of T.B. 108 of the Plymouth Port Flotilla, with very little work to do; but I remained on duty.

Yes, the war was over; but what would the peace be like? My profession as a merchant seaman, I knew, would be over crowded for a long time, until merchant fleets could be built up again to replace the frightful losses of 3400 British merchant vessels sunk during the war.

The Cunard Line alone had lost twenty steamers by enemy action. Among them, in the last year of the war, were the liners *Andania* (13,000 tons), the *Aurania* (13,900 tons) and the *Carpathia* (13,600 tons) — the last name of special sentimental interest to me, as I had served in her as Second Officer under Captain Rostron, when we had picked up the survivors of the *Titanic* in 1912. And now she was gone, too.

On 19th February 1919, my dear mother died at Liverpool, aged sixty-three. I had been given leave to go there, and soon afterwards I was demobilized from the Royal Naval Reserve and rejoined the Cunard Line.

We had won the war; and how could we "win the peace"?

CHAPTER ENDNOTES

(1) "phut" is an informal British term that means to stop working or to come to grief. It can also be used as a noun to describe the sound of distant or muffled explosive sound.

O N March 1919, I was demobilized from the Royal Naval Reserve; and rejoined the Cunard Line. I was appointed as Chief Officer of R.M.S. *Carmania*, which left Liverpool on 8th March, bound for New York.

At that time thousands of officers and men were being demobilized from the R.N.R., and facing an uncertain future of employment In Britain's war depleted mercantile marine. To make good the loss of 3400 British merchant vessels sunk during the war, the shipping companies were desperately building and buying vessels to cope with peacetime trading and to reabsorb into civilian employment the seamen now being discharged in immense numbers after combatant service.

The Cunard Line had lost twenty steamers during the war. Only four big and speedy passenger liners of prewar days remained in service — the *Aquitania*, *Mauretania*, *Caronia*, and *Carmania*. There were also two medium sized slower passenger liners surviving, the *Saxonia* and the *Pannonia*; and five small cargo steamers of prewar completed in Germany after the war, handed over to the White Star Line, and renamed *Majestic*.

These three gigantic liners remained throughout the 1920s, and until the mid-1930s, the biggest ships in the world.

To compete with them, France, Italy, Germany, and Britain all entered the "big" shipbuilding race.

In 1921, the Compagnie Generale Transatlantique (French Line) launched the *Paris* (34,569 tons); and in 1927 the *Ile de France* (43,153 tons).

The Nord Deutscher Lloyd (German), even after Germany's defeat, launched in 1922 the *Columbus* (32,567 tons); in 1928 the *Europa* (49,746 tons); and in 1929 the *Bremen* (51,731 tons).

The Italian Line ("Italia" Company) in 1932 launched two beautiful, speedy, big liners — the *Rex* (51,062 tons) and the *Conte Di Savoia* (48,502 tons).

Then, in 1935, the French Line put into service their superb superliner, *Normandie* (82,000 tons).

It was to meet that competition that the Cunard Line laid down the *Queen Mary* (81,237 tons) in 1930, launched her in 1934, and put her into service in 1936. She was not quite as big in tonnage as the *Normandie*, but had a greater speed, and took the Blue Riband.

Cunard had the last word when the *Queen Elizabeth* (83,673 tons) was laid down in 1936, launched in 1938, and made her first voyage in 1940. She was, and to this day (1960) is, and may remain for all time, the biggest passenger liner ever built.[1]

Such was the nature of the international competition that developed on the Atlantic routes during the twenty years of peace that followed the defeat of Germany in the 1914-18 war. It was an era of renewed rivalry in "big" shipbuilding, on a scale which may perhaps never be repeated so extensively.

Coal fuel was succeeded by oil fuel, which enabled bigger and bigger ships to be worked without unmanageable numbers of firemen and trimmers down below, and without the need for immense coal storage in bunkers.

What the future may hold, with atomic energy for fuel, no one can confidently predict; but there are some reasons which make it seem unlikely that passenger ships of 80,000 tons and upwards will again be built. The chief reason is that transatlantic air services are carrying passengers and mails in ever increasing competition with ships; another reason is that 50,000 tons is probably the optimum size for conveniently handling vessels into and out of ports, and for staffing of passenger services.

My experiences at sea — chiefly in the North Atlantic — during the twenty years of peace, 1919-39, were developed against a background with special features in maritime history. These were: (i) the extensive rebuilding of merchant fleets to replace war losses; (ii) the transition from coal burning to oil burning steamers; (iii) the virtual disappearance of sailing vessels from the ocean routes; (iv) an intense international and inter-Company competition for passenger and mail traffic; (v) the building of bigger and bigger passenger liners, to "mammoth" size; (vi) the pioneering of long distance trans-ocean flying; (vii) the rapid development of radio, and of mechanical aids to navigation.

Changes such as these occur almost imperceptibly or are taken for granted as they occur. When I compare, in memory, my way of life and work as a seaman in 1939, with what it was in 1919, the great changes that had occurred in seamanship during that interim stand out more clearly than they did while they were occurring; besides, I was gradually being given more responsibility, and the cares that go with it. When the war of 1914-18 ended, I was thirty-five years of age and had been twenty years at sea. I had no thought of taking up any other profession; nor had I any hankering to settle on land After I had made two voyages in the *Carmania*, my post as Chief officer in her was given to Tom Pooley, who was a senior officer in the Cunard service, ahead of me in rank and length of service. That kept me "on the beach," like many others, waiting for vacancies to occur.

May and I decided to take a holiday. We went to Shepperton-on-Thames (upriver from London), and, of all the things that we could have done, we hired a "camping out boat," and I became a freshwater sailor, for four weeks.

Then we took a flat in London, and I waited, a little anxiously, forward of my appointment to a ship. At last, after I had been nearly four months ashore, I was appointed First Officer in *S.S. Verbania* and joined her in Glasgow on 1st August 1919.

She was a new vessel, a single screw coal burning steamer of 5021 tons, with a speed of 11 knots, built at Glasgow during the war, and completed in 1918. Like the other "V" ships, she was a freighter, and to all intents and purposes a tramp under the Cunard house flag — that is — she did not work out of Liverpool on regular schedules but went wherever there were cargoes to be picked up or delivered. Our first voyage was from Glasgow to Montreal with a cargo of scotch whiskey. The master of the Verbania was Captain Peel, a worried looking man, and no wonder, for, as he informed us, he had six daughters! There were only three deck officers, four engineers, cook, steward, carpenter, boatswain, and a small crew of seamen and stokers. As far as watchkeeping was concerned, I was back to my freighting days, but it was all in good cause, as the "V" ships were only stopgaps while new Cunarders were being built.

Wallowing along at 11 knots, the *Verbania* took eleven days to cross the Atlantic from Glasgow to Montreal, a passage of 2693 miles. This was my first visit to the River st Lawrence, a grand waterway when it is ice free, as it was when we arrived there in mid-August and steamed on past Quebec to Montreal.

As First Officer I was in charge of the Graveyard Watch, 12 midnight to 4 a.m. One night, in mid-Atlantic, I noticed the Captain come out of his cabin in his pyjamas at 3 a.m. and walk about barefoot on deck. I watched him carefully for a while, wondering what he was up to.

Then I became worried, and, approaching him carefully, found that he was walking with his eyes shut — in his sleep. Believing that it is unwise to awaken a sleepwalker, I stood by to guard him against any mishap; and presently he went back to his cabin and turned in. He is the only sleepwalker I have ever known at sea. It was uncanny to see the master of a vessel with that habit.

Being second-in-command, I thought it advisable to speak to him about it tactfully next day. He admitted at once that he knew that he was a sleepwalker. "When my feet get cold, I go back to bed," he said.

"Why not barricade yourself in your cabin, and lock the door?" I suggested.

"It would be useless. I have tried doing that, but no matter how carefully and laboriously I do it, I get up in my sleep and take it all away and walk out without any trouble!"

After that, on several occasions, I saw the Captain walking the deck in his sleep. Always I eyed him carefully. There can be scarcely any more unsuitable place for the night wanderings of a sleepwalker than on the deck of a cargo steamer in mid-ocean. The hazards are many companionways, hatches, winches and other deck gear, and the possibility of going overside if the vessel suddenly rolls, but Captain Peel calmly negotiated them all with his eyes closed. This seems to throw some light on the "sixth sense" which enables a walker's feet to "see" or feel obstacles not perceived by the eyes. I merely record the facts.

In this case the Captain's usual order to the Officer of the Watch on retiring, "Call me if you sight anything unusual," required a special interpretation. No sight could have been more disturbing to him the Captain inspecting the decks in his sleep; but I never called him. I only watched him, as a sort of guardian angel, and heaved a big sigh of relief when he dreamed his way back to his bunk.

After discharging our cargo of whiskey at Montreal — some if not all of it probably intended for overland transport to the U.S.A. — we proceeded to New York to pick up a general cargo, including pigs of lead and copper for London. We lay at a drab wharf downtown. One of the big changes noticeable in New York, in comparison with, say, ten years previously, was the almost total motorization of traffic in the streets. The horse had practically disappeared. This was the first big city in the world to become motorized.

Loaded down to the Plimsoll after a fortnight's stay in New York, the *Verbania* cleared out, homeward bound for the Port of London. There we arrived on 17th September 1919.

Though I had been twenty-one years at sea, this was the first time that I had entered the Port of London from seaward. My station, First Officer, was at the bows, in charge of the anchors and the mooring lines forward. It is a great experience for a seaman to enter the River Thames for the first time. The navigation of thirty miles upriver from the Nore to the Pool of London, with a Thames pilot on the bridge, is filled with interest Apart from the main streams of traffic up and down river, there are miles of docks on both sides of the stream, as the river, in its upper reaches — Gallions Reach, Woolwich Reach, Bugsby's Reach, Blackwall Reach, Greenwich Reach, Limehouse Reach — winds past the Isle of Dogs to London Pool: all those names evocative of a thousand years of seafaring history.

I had been in some great rivers — the Mersey, the Clyde, the st Lawrence, the Hudson, the Mississippi, the Plate among them — but none so traffic crowded and imagination stimulating as the London river, the main artery of an empire. Whenever I think of it, I recall H. S. Merriman's words, in The Sowers: "Men travel far to see a city, but few seem curious about a river. Every river has, nevertheless, its individuality, its great silent interest Every river has its influence over the people who pass their lives within sight of her waters."

The Cunard Line "belonged" to the Mersey. Now we were venturing into the Thames, which, for us, was off the beaten track. The war had changed everything. Old days and old ways were ended.

Would London now be my home port? May was waiting for me there. We had a flat in Kensington. After three weeks in port, the Verbania cleared out of London on 8th October 1919, with a cargo of general merchandise for New York. Captain Peel on his own request had now been relieved of his command, to take a rest cure. Probably he was worried by his sleepwalking habits. Like all other masters of merchant vessels during the war, he had been under great nervous strain and was feeling the aftereffects.

The new master of the *Verbania*, Captain Stafford, was also, as I soon discovered, in a state of nervous tension and inclined to worry, but he was a decent and kindly man and good seaman for all that. I suppose that all shipmasters at that time were on edge after their war ordeals.

We had a slow trip of thirteen days to New York and lay there for six weeks before completing our return cargo. This delay was not due to mismanagement, but simply to the commercial problem of obtaining goods at that time awaiting shipment from New York to London.

At last we cleared out, early in December, and arrived back in London on 18th December. Home for Christmas ... the Sailor's Dream. Service in a tramp, even a Cunard tramp, was slow and frustrating after war's excitements. As First Officer I had the responsibility for the paintwork and other deck gear. No one who has been a Mate in a sailing vessel can bear the sight of anything in a ship not spick and span. I kept the deckhands at work, and made various improvements round the bridge, and on deck, and in the crew's quarters, that brought the *Verbania* a little nearer to Cunard "class"; but nothing could make her more than what she was: just a tramp; and I felt that I was in a dead end job.

Early in the New Year of 1920, we began loading a cargo of China clay for Philadelphia. We cleared out of London on 10th January, in bitterly cold weather. That was a especially severe winter in the North Atlantic.

No sooner were we headed westwards in the Channel, than we encountered westerly gales, which continued for day after day, as we drove on into very high seas, thirty feet from trough to crest, which frequently broke over the bows and surged along the decks, throwing icy spray over the bridge. Our rate of progress was slowed to five knots, and at last we had to heave to — keeping the ship head — on to the seas, with the propeller barely turning over at slow ahead; to give steering way.

Next day, when we took sights at noon, we found that our position was thirty-nine miles astern of what it had been on the previous day. Hove to, we had drifted that distance.

The Chief Engineer reported that bunker coal was running low and would probably not be sufficient to enable us to make Philadelphia if the westerly weather continued. On this, the Captain decided to alter course and to put into Halifax for bunkers. It was a difficult decision to take, as this diversion would take us north-westerly into colder weather, out of the Gulf Stream, and possibly into fogs off the Newfoundland Banks; yet it would certainly be better than running out of coal and having to be towed into port! The westerly gales abated as we neared the land; but then we ran into fog, and had to crawl along, feeling our way, in weather that was now icily cold, and consistently below freezing point, with Icicles in the rigging and on the decks. At last, three weeks out of London, we crept into Halifax Bay, and found the inner harbour frozen over, and the air temperature at 16 degrees below freezing point.

We were unable to go under the coal cranes but anchored at the edge of the ice. A coal lighter came alongside, and we began to fill our bunkers, using her donkey engine to hoist the coal on hoard.

During that day, the seamen attending to various jobs on deck kept getting frostbitten fingers, ears, noses and cheeks. The Second Officer and I were kept busy rubbing the affected parts with snow and giving each sufferer a dose of medicinal comforts brandy. After three bottles had gone, I had to announce, "There is no more brandy."

This proved to be the most effective cure of all. After that announcement, all complaints of frostbite ceased.

But the cold was intense. When we had 150 tons of coal hoisted In from the lighter, her donkey engine stopped. It had frozen. The Captain consulted the Chief Engineer and decided that he had now enough coal to take us to Philadelphia.

At 3 p.m., we hove up the anchor, and, with a pilot on board, steamed out of the bay in a drizzle of sleet. Soon after the pilot had left us, we ran into thick fog.

The Captain set a course to the southward to take us well clear of the coast When I had finished my work on station at the bows, I went up to the bridge. We were proceeding at slow speed ahead. The fog was so thick that visibility was practically nil. Our steam whistle was hooting at half-minute intervals.

"'Strange thing," the Captain remarked. "Since we dropped the pilot, the wind has shifted right around!"

That was puzzling indeed. It was only a light breeze that had been blowing from dead ahead, but now it was blowing from dead aft. "I've never seen a breeze veer as quickly as that before," said the Captain. "Have you?"

"No," I said. "It's uncanny."

We were on the wing of the bridge, peering into the murk. At that moment, the helmsman sang out from the wheelhouse. "I think there's something wrong with the compass!"

"WHAT?" The Captain and I jumped as if we were shot and hurried into the wheelhouse to investigate.

"I haven't moved the wheel for ten minutes," said the helmsman, "and she's stuck on her course."

The Captain's face was white with anxiety, as he rang the engine to stop, and then slow astern. The spirit compass in the wheelhouse had frozen solid. I jumped up to Monkey Island the observation point above the bridge, where there was a Dry Standard Compass, used for taking bearings.

"We're headed due north," I reported.

On a quick calculation, we reckoned that we were less than half a mile from the shore, and nearer than that to some outlying rocks shown on the chart. On our port beam we could hear surf breaking at a distance impossible to estimate in the fog. All hands available were posted on lookout, as, with infinite care, and going dead slow, we put the helm hard over and turned her head south again by the Dry Standard Compass.

An hour later the weather cleared. By bearings off the land we calculated that when we had put her about, we had been not more than a few hundred yards from the rocks.

It was bitterly cold all the way from Halifax to Delaware Bay, a passage of some 800 miles, which took us four days of navigation among fishing fleets and across the tracks of steamers bound to or from New York, Boston, and the other ports of the north-eastern and middle eastern states.

At last we rounded Cape May into Delaware Bay, and, taking on a pilot, began the passage of eighty miles up the Delaware River to Philadelphia. As we got into the upper reaches, nearing the port, the temperature dropped several degrees below freezing- point, and we saw that the river was frozen for some distance out from the banks, though with open water in the centre.

As we went on stations for entering port, we met fog, and the pilot decided to anchor. I was standing by the anchors. The engines were stopped, and, at the critical moment, the order came from the bridge, "LET GO!"

I released the brake. The anchor dropped onto the ice ... and stayed there!

We hove up the anchor off the ice, the engine was put astern for a few revolutions until we had backed clear of the ice, and then the anchor was let go again, and plunged to the bottom.

When the fog cleared, we hove up the anchor, proceeded up channel, and moored safely at Philadelphia, a friendly and beautiful city, in which snow lay deep on the streets and rooftops.

For three weeks we lay there, discharging our cargo of China clay, and loading grain and cotton. Then we cleared out for home, bound this time for Liverpool, the port of Lancashire's cotton mills. We arrived home on 8th March 1920. As the *Verbania* was then to be laid up for a while, I was paid off, and given shore leave, to wait for another ship. I was not really sorry to leave her. Three voyages in seven months, including that last very severe winter Voyage, had not been enjoyable. I was wondering what fate the Marine Superintendent might have in pickle for me. "Just wait awhile," he said, mysteriously, "and you might be in a bigger ship, soon!"

With that half promise, I had to be content. At this time my brother Douglas had decided to emigrate to Australia. I saw him off, wondering if I would ever see him again.

For two months I was on the beach. May and I lived in London, not knowing where our future home might be. At last the call came. I was to join the *R.M.S. Mauretania*, at Southampton, on 8th May 1920 As Senior First Officer!

The Grand Old Lady, still under command of Captain Rostron, had finished her troopship service and was decked out again in her regalia of peacetime service, comfort and luxury. She still held the Blue Ribbon of the Atlantic, but was now operating from Southampton as a base, making a call at Cherbourg, on the regular Scheduled run to New York.

May and I moved to Southampton, which would be my home port, I hoped, for many a day.

And the *Mauretania* would be my ship, too, for many a day, I hoped, and confidently expected. I could not have wanted one better. She was the most beautiful steamship ever built, I believed then, and sometimes still believe.

CHAPTER ENDNOTES

(1) Weighing 248,663 gross tonnes and measuring 365 metres (1,1967 feet), the *Icon of the Sea* is the largest cruise ship in the world. Christened on 23 January 2024, the Icon has a maximum capacity of 7,600 passengers and 2,350 crew across 20 decks.

*In the "Mauretania" Again— Peacetime Passenger Schedules—
Celebrities at Sea— The Ordeal of Coaling— The "Boat Train"— A
Common Misnomer— Calling at Cherbourg— Passengers from Paris—
Heaving the Lead— Obsolete Routine — French Accents— A Wind-
jammer's Call for Help— Brotherhood of the Sea— I Stand Again on the
Deck of a Barque— Farewell to the Soul of a Sailor.*

BETWEEN 8th May, 1920, and 22nd July, 1922, I made eleven
voyages as Senior First Officer in *R.M.S. Mauretania* from
Southampton via Cherbourg to New York and return.

Usually a voyage lasted twenty-eight days— that is, five days on the passage
in each direction, and nine days in port at each end. The long stay in port
amounted to a slow "turn around." This was due to the schedules of the passenger
and mail service, with departures on a fixed day in each week (Wednesday) both
from Southampton and New York. The service was maintained by four steamers,
the *Aquitania, Mauretania, Caronia,* and *Carmania* — the two last named until new
vessels became available.

The *Aquitania* and *Mauretania* could make the crossing in five days, the other
two in six days; but this did not give enough margin of time for the *Aquitania* and
Mauretania to unload and load cargo, and refuel, to maintain the weekly schedules
without the help of the others in rotation. For this reason the two big liners lay at
their berths, usually from Monday in one week until Wednesday in the following
week, while a smaller liner took the mails and passengers on the intervening
Wednesday departure.

The long stay in port at the end of each passage was uneconomic, but unavoidable for the purpose of maintaining the advertised schedules. Even with that arrangement, the *Mauretania* made only eleven voyages during the fourteen months that I served in her on this occasion. For part of the time she was laid up at Southampton for boiler cleaning and general refit to bring her appointments up to post-war standard.

I was now well contented, as I had some home life for eight or nine days in every four weeks. Apart from that, the living and working conditions, including food of the highest quality, and congenial company, on board the Grand Old Lady, were as near perfection as any seafaring man could ever hope to enjoy. The

R.M.S. Mauretania (Public Domain)

Maurrie was a favourite with Atlantic travellers, despite the fact that she was becoming old fashioned in her fittings and arrangements. A specialty on her menu was roast beef. It was Scottish beef- announced as "the Roast Beef of Old England"— served in big sirloin joints, both hot and cold, and always of the best quality.

She had accommodation in peacetime service for 2335 passengers — 560 first-class, 475 second-class, and 1300 third-class and carried a crew of 812, making a total of 3147 souls on board when she was fully booked out, as she usually was.

The mailrooms held thousands of bags of mails on each passage. in relation to her size, she had small cargo holds, with hatches in the welldecks forward and aft of her long midships superstructure.

Yet we did carry a few thousand tons of cargo, mostly general merchandise from England, and grain and frozen meat and poultry from New York. Part of the cargo space was refrigerated. On almost every westbound passage we carried gold bars as cargo, carefully checked into and out of the strong rooms, under heavy guard. There was at that time a one way flow of gold from almost all countries to the U.S.A., in part payment of war debts and trade balances.

The passengers were a cosmopolitan lot. In the first-class there were on every passage some celebrities, American, British, and from Continental European countries.

Cunard officers had opportunities of meeting and, chatting affably, In the course of years, with almost all the famous or notorious people in the world-Sovereigns, Princes and Princesses, aristocrats Of many nations, millionaires, statesmen, artists, writers, musicians, theatrical people, sportsmen— all making pilgrimages in one direction or another across the Atlantic, and a little relaxed while at sea, yet expecting to be taken notice of by ships' officers off duty, if only for a few minutes' chat about the weather and the ship's speed.

We became used to celebrities; it was always necessary to study the passenger lists in advance carefully, so that we would know "Who was Who, and What was What." during the five days that such precious human cargo was in our care.

An officer usually has neither time nor inclination to be anything more than correctly polite to all paying passengers, regardless of their fame or notoriety, or obscurity, on shore. When the ship departed or arrived, dozens of reporters swarmed on board, to "get the story." They were usually handled by the Purser's Department.

Very few celebrities are shy of reporters. That is one reason why they are celebrities. We could read about them in the papers. It was some satisfaction that they liked it to be known that they had crossed in the *Mauretania*. That was a feather in their cap, or in ours.

As First Officer I was responsible for the cleanliness of decks and paintwork on all open decks. Coaling ship was my bugbear. At Southampton, and at New York, she needed to take in 5000 tons of coal through her forty side ports — twenty on each side. After discharging passengers, baggage, mails, and cargo, she would be "boomed off" twenty feet from the quay, and before long would be surrounded by coal barges, each in its own little cloud of coaldust

This was a long and dirty job for the carpenter and his mates, who were lowered in stages over the side, to open or close the ports as required. The ports were covered with heavy steel plates, secured by nut headed, screw bolts, and made watertight with gaskets of buckram and red lead.

When these were removed, the plates fell open on hinges at the bottom, forming scoops into which the coal was dumped from the barges — a slow and dusty. process. Sometimes she was not finished coaling until three or four hours before passengers were due to embark. Tremendous activity was then required to remove the fine coating of black dust which penetrated to every part of the ship. All the open decks and paintwork had to be washed down with hoses, and the teakwood rails wiped down clean. I had to walk miles around the deck!! to supervise this work. We could not risk complaints from passengers that their clothing had been soiled on a dirty rail or bulkhead. That was the greatest disadvantage of coal burning passenger liners— they had to be coaled.

Passengers were brought to Southampton from London by a special train, which pulled onto the quay alongside the ship. From that moment there was tremendous bustle and excitement. The '*Mauretania*, like other Cunarders, departed from, and arrived at, 'Southampton so punctually, according to advertised schedules, that ' local people had a saying: "You can set your watch by her."

Railroad transit, between London and Southampton, and Paris and Cherbourg, was included in the steamer fare. The trains were luxuriously equipped, and, in a sense, "belonged" to the trans-Atlantic travel service and schedules.

While the passengers streamed up the gangways, and were sorted out to their cabins, and as the luggage and mail were hoisted on board and stowed, the navigating officers were usually handy on deck, in case any complications should arise.

A charming lady, just embarked on her first voyage, after taking a quick look around, saw the Junior Third Officer standing by on the boat deck, waiting to go on stations for leaving port. She went up to him, and said, excitedly, "Oh, officer, isn't this a beautiful boat!"

"You mean the *Mauretania*?" asked the Junior Third banteringly. "Sure, she's a beautiful boat!"

"Pardon me, madam, this isn't a boat — it's a ship."

"My! My!" retorted the fair one. "At Waterloo Station in London this morning there was a big notice board at the end of the platform, reading THIS WAY TO THE BOAT TRAIN. How do you account for that? I suggest, young man, that you take steps to have it altered to THIS WAY TO THE SHIP TRAIN!"

Later, the lady pursued the point by consulting a dictionary. She discovered that a boat is "a small ship," and a ship is "any large seagoing vessel."

She announced her decision: "It's O.K. to call a boat a ship, but it's all wrong to call a ship a boat. I'll write to the station master at Waterloo and tell him of his mistake!"

This kind of thing can go on forever. Let go the moorings fore and aft, and we'll make for the calmer waters of the mighty ocean.

Cherbourg in Normandy, France, is 83 miles by water from Southampton, almost due south across the Channel from the mouth of the Solent. The passage there in the *Mauretania* took a little under four hours from berth to berth. The express train from Paris was usually waiting at the quay when we anchored. To get the passengers, mails, and baggage on board, from five or six large steam tenders, and to clear out, took only an hour or so.

Old customs die hard, and the heaving of the hand lead is one of them. Entering Cherbourg, a few miles off the entrance, Captain Rostron gave the order "On stations."

This routine required the placing of two A.B. seamen "in the chains" — on a platform overside under the bridge on each side — as "leadsmen." Their duty was to keep on taking soundings of the depth of water in the channel by means of a handline weighted with lead and marked in fathoms and to sing out the soundings to the bridge as the ship moved to her anchorage.

With a pilot on board, such a procedure was obsolete and unnecessary, but old time shipmasters would have felt uncomfortable if the ritual had been neglected. The leadsmen's soundings were usually inaccurate. The chains were twenty feet above water, and the vessel's rate of progress made a vertical sounding difficult. The *Mauretania* had a draught of 36 feet. It was by no means unusual for the leadsman to sing out, "By the mark five" — meaning that she was floating in five fathoms (30 feet) of water! No one would believe him. Probably the Captain would say calmly, "Get someone in the chains next time who knows how to heave the lead!" — and then would proceed to his anchorage unperturbed by the fact that, according to the leadsman's report, he was fast aground.

One of our passengers, who had embarked at Southampton, was a bright looking lass, intent in finding out about everything. As we entered Cherbourg, the bright lass leaned over the rail at the fore end of the promenade deck and gazed at one of the leadsmen engaged in this futile task. After a few moments she sang out to him, "What are you doing?"

"Taking soundings, miss." "What for?" she demanded. "To find out how deep it is."

"Good gracious, you've been here often enough before. You surely ought to know it by now!" And she walked away, quite unaware that she had hit the nail squarely on the head.

Just then the Second Officer, as a matter of routine, sang out from the bridge, "What water have you got?"

The seaman, who had not yet got bottom on account of the speed, lied cheerfully, "No bottom at twelve fathoms, sir!" The harbour charts showed that there was a depth of nine fathoms in that position. Presently, when the ship had almost lost her way, he managed to get two "up-and-down" casts showing nine fathoms, which was duly entered in the logbook. Then the wash of the propellers going astern drew the lead forward under the stem.

Nowadays, with echo sounding gear, the old fashioned hand lead has been discarded, except in emergencies. It served a useful purpose in sailing vessels, especially in unfamiliar or poorly charted harbours; but was futile in big steamers regularly using well-known ports. Its best use was in rivers, such as the Mississippi or the Plate, in which floodwaters brought down silt, forming uncharted mudbanks.

There was much excitement when the passengers from Paris came on board and met friends or relatives who had joined the ship at Southampton. I overheard one fond mamma asking her son "Did you have any trouble with your French?"

"No, Mom," he replied, "but the Frenchmen did!"

One afternoon, in Autumn, 1920, when the *Mauretania* was making an eastward passage, homeward bound, I came on watch at noon, and sights were taken, as usual. We were in Lat. 48 deg. RO min. N., Long. 21 deg. 50 min. W., and nicely on schedule.

It was clear weather, with a gentle southerly breeze, and slight seas running. The bugle had sounded for lunch, the passengers were making their way to the dining rooms, and the Captain had gone off the bridge. I was on watch assisted by the Junior Third Officer. There was no other vessel in sight. The way was clear to the ever receding horizon, ten miles ahead, as the Maurrie belted along, in her usual supreme way, at a speed of 25 knots.

Just another uneventful watch, I was thinking, but who knows what is below the horizon? At 1 p.m., the lookout man in the crow's nest st ruck his bell three times and confirmed through the "navy phone" telephone to the bridge, "Object dead ahead, sir."

I used a telescope, and soon discerned royals, and presently the lop gallants, and then the upper topsails and gaff topsail of a three-masted barque, headed northwards across our bows, with her sails nicely filled and the yards squared in the fair breeze.

She was ten miles away when I sighted her. There was no need to alter our course. She would be comfortably clear, and we would pass astern of her, with a few miles to spare, in another twenty or twenty-five minutes.

"Let the Captain know," I said to the Junior Third Officer. "He always likes to see an old windjammer. There are not so many of them now!"

That last remark was only too true. More than 300 square rigged sailing vessels, chiefly British, had been sunk by U-boats at the approaches to the British Isles during the war. They had been "sitting ducks," and there were now scarcely any full rigged ships remaining under the British flag.

The Junior Third went below to the first-class dining room; and, five minutes later, Captain Rostron came onto the bridge, all smiles. He had excused himself from the celebrities who had the privilege of being seated at his table. By this time, as the *Mauretania* was eating up the miles, the barque's lower topsails were in sight, and presently we could see all her sails, and her hull.

"A trim little barque," said Captain Rostron. "And she has some flags up, too." He studied her through the long glass with keen interest "A Norwegian," he remarked. "Doesn't she make you feel envious, Bisset?"

"Not exactly," I smiled. "But I wouldn't mind being in her for a while, and wouldn't you, Captain?"

"We'd all like to be young again!" Captain Rostron had been Mate of a famous clipper, Cedric the Saxon, twenty-five years previously. He was well aware, too, that I had served my time in sail. "What's that signal she's flying?" he asked the Junior Third Officer. "Perhaps she wants to verify her position?"

The Junior Third rested the telescope firmly against a stanchion and looked long and earnestly at the three small flags that hung limply in the breeze on the barque's gaff. Then slowly he announced: "F-G-L."

Instantly I turned up the signal book and read out the international code meaning: "I am in need of a doctor."

"Answer him," the Captain ordered crisply. "Tell him to heave to and we'll send a boat."

The Blue Ensign fluttered up to our gaff peak, and the Answering Pennant was also hoisted, meaning, "I understand your signal," and then the flags of the international code: "We are sending a boat and a doctor."

"Stand by engines," the Captain ordered. "Man the starboard sea boat and warn the doctor to be ready." Then he said to me, "You go in the boat, Bisset, and give them every help you can." He added, "And take with you a hundredweight of fresh beef, some potatoes, onions and cabbages, and a case of oranges with my compliments. She's probably a hundred days out from the West Coast — you know what that means, Bisset!"

"I do, only too well," I answered, and sent orders to the Chief Steward accordingly.

Now, as the *Mauretania* rapidly closed the distance, we could see the barque expertly handled as she was put about, with her head pointed almost into the wind, and her main yards backed, to bring her to a standstill. My heart went out to her. She was almost a replica of the County of Pembroke, in which I had served my apprentice ship, on three voyages around the world, finishing seventeen years previously.

"Half speed," the Captain ordered. Then, "Hard down the helm," then, at intervals, "Stop" .and "Full astern" and "Stop." The *Mauretania* had made a graceful turn around the barque and came to a standstill three hundred yards from her weather quarter.

"Man the boat and lower away!"

The news had circulated through the liner, and passengers and crew crowded the rails, anxious to witness this drama of mid-ocean. The sea boat was hanging in the davits, level with the boat deck. My crew of eight took their places and I stepped into the stern sheets, followed by the doctor, who, grasping his little black bag, and looking nervous at the prospect of an unusual experience of being lowered a long way to the water, took his seat alongside me.

"Lower away," I ordered. "Hold on to the lifelines."

The boatswain repeated, "Lower away!" and, with a rattle of heaves, the boat was lowered down the ship's side and hit the water with a smack.

"Shove off. Give way together!" My crew bent their backs to the oars. The boat, rising and falling in the ocean swell and the slight seas, moved smartly towards the barque on our errand of mercy. We passed under her stern, where a line was thrown to us, and we ranged alongside her amidships on her lee side. A Jacob's ladder was already let down there. The doctor and I clambered up the few rungs, and over the bulwarks to stand on the deck of the barque, while the Norwegian sailors, leaning over the rail, conversed eagerly.

In their accented English with the men in the boat. They were astounded: the mighty *Mauretania* to the rescue! but why not? In the brotherhood of the sea, no ship is haughty. The provisions were handed up overside and accepted with joy by the Norwegian sailors.

The doctor looked around him in astonishment at the tiny proportions of everything, in comparison with the huge liner we had just left and stared overhead at the maze of cordage and sails. As for me, I was overwhelmed with emotion. It all came back to me.

I knew that, even in the dark, I could have put my hand on every rope and line. My brass bound uniform, gold braid and buttons, seemed out of place. I wished that I were in dungarees. The First Mate of the barque met us, and said, "The Second Mate is seriously ill in his bunk under the poop. I'll lead the way there."

"Mister," I said, "I could find my way there blindfold."

He smiled. "Old Cape Horner, eh?"

"You've said it," I answered. "I'm at home here."

It was a strange feeling. We walked aft. The Master of the barque was waiting for us at the break of the poop. He had on his brus-bound uniform and cap. I saluted him with respect. "Very good of you to come," he said, with dignity, in good English.

He escorted us to the saloon, a wondrously neat and clean little apartment, with bare deck planks, holystoned as white as a hound's tooth. At the after end were crimson plush cushions on the transom lockers, and, at the fore end, a sideboard with a marble top and a brass rail around it. The bulkheads were panelled with bird's eye maple, polished to perfection. The barometer was exactly where I looked for it. In the centre of the saloon, over the polished table, hung a swinging tray, suspended by brass chains from the deckhead, and holding red Venetian wineglasses. I felt like a boy apprentice again, allowed into the Old Man's holy of holies.

The Captain opened a door, and admitted the doctor into a small cabin, where a tall, blond haired young man lay stretched out, unconscious, in the bunk. "My Second Mate," said the Captain. "He has been sick for a month, and unconscious now for two days. He does not speak, or eat, or drink. I do not know what to do anymore."

The doctor asked a few questions, then began an examination of his patient. In a few minutes he stepped out into the saloon, where the Captain, the First Mate, and I had been waiting in silence.

"I am sorry," said the doctor, gravely. "He is beyond our aid.

You have done everything possible, I assure you."

"What is the trouble?" asked the Captain, his voice shaking with emotion.

"Pneumonia. He is no longer breathing. He died perhaps half an hour ago. Nothing could have been done for him. The poor fellow. A fine young man, too."

"Frostbite around Cape Horn," said the Captain, forlornly. "We must bury him at sea. His father and mother will be heart-broken. We sighted no steamer for many days. Then came your big steamer and so kindly stopped."

"It was our duty to stop," I said. "I am only sorry that we came too late!"

"Thanks! Thanks!" said the Captain, brokenly, his blue eyes filling with tears. "I must not delay you anymore. You have such an important big ship ... "

"Not more important than yours," I said, and meant it.

We shook hands and got back silently and sorrowfully into our boat. "Shove off. Give way together," I ordered.

"Goodbye! Goodbye! Good luck to you all!" the Norwegians sang out, as we pulled away. "Thanks, thanks!"

"Goodbye, goodbye! Good luck!"

As I steered towards the *Mauretania*, I could hear the Captain and the Mate of the barque singing out orders to square away the yards and set sail. Glancing over my shoulder, I saw the seamen hauling around the mainyard, and others swarming aloft to shake out sail.

The *Mauretania* was immense, silhouetted against the sky. To see her there in mid-ocean, stopped, with smoke pouring from her four funnels and spreading away in the breeze, and her deck rails crowded with three thousand people, was a great contrast with the little barque we had left, so lonely and bereaved. The passengers did not yet know the result of our mission, but Captain Rostron and the other seamen in the liner knew. The barque's Norwegian ensign was lowered to half-mast

The passengers raised a cheer as our boat ranged alongside. "Hook on — hoist away," came the orders from the boat deck, and in a few moments the boat was lifted slowly from the sea and swung inboard to rest in her chocks.

The doctor and I went to the bridge to make our reports. "Resume the voyage," said the Captain to me. I rang the engines to full ahead and set course. As the liner gathered way, passing astern of the barque, both vessels dipped their ensigns in salute, and then brought them to half-mast

Captain Rostron stepped over to the switch and blew three long blasts on our hoarse throated, far resonant, steam whistle. It was the Sailors' Farewell, but this time also a solemn requiem for the soul of a brother seaman

"Fire Down Below!" — The "Mauretania" in Danger — A Conflagration in Port — Five Hours' Ordeal — Much Damage by Flames and Water — She Takes a List To Starboard- — Nearly Rolls Over — A Diving Job on the Main Deck — Hard Work with Spanners- Extensive Damage — We Take Her Back to the Tyne — A Rousing Welcome from the "Geordies" — I Wait for Another Ship — A Requalifying Course in the R.N.R. — Seasick Gunners — Keeping Awake in Lectures — Promotion

ON 22nd July 1921, the *Mauretania* docked at Southampton, as usual. The passengers disembarked, the mails and cargo unloaded, and most of the crew were given shore leave. Captain Rostron went to his home in Liverpool for a few days. The fires were banked in the furnaces, except under one or two of the boilers, to keep up a head of steam for use in the cargo winches, the electric light plant, and for the hot water services, ventilation, and fire pumps.

A few of the crew remained on board, in each of the various departments. The deck officers, as usual, were on duty in rotation, to exercise a general supervision of the routines in port. Gangs of cleaners were on board. They were workers from on shore, among them some carpet cleaners, who, on this occasion were cleaning the carpets on E Deck, in the first-class cabins, which were below the first-class dining room on D Deck. Contrary to rules, one of these cleaners had been using petrol to clean greasespots on a carpet, and struck a match, perhaps to light his pipe. However it happened, a fire started down below on that deck.

At 1.30 p.m., after having had lunch on shore, I was returning to the ship to go on afternoon duty. I was strolling at my leisure along the wharf, when suddenly I heard a commotion as I neared The gangway, and a hoarse shout of "Fire!"

Sprinting up the gangway to the promenade deck, I saw the Marine Superintendent, Captain McNeil, running along that deck at full speed, making for the Chief Engineer's office. He sighted me, and gasped out, "There's a fire down below on E Deck. Tell the Chief there's no pressure in the firehoses!"

He dashed away. I raced to the Chief Engineer's office, found him, and informed him of the situation. He sprang out of his chair us though something

Style and opulence came with the cost of flammability as seen here in this photo of the Mauretania's Verandah Café (Public Domain)

had stung him, and rushed out through the door, to disappear down below.

The alarm on board was now general; but at that time of the clay there were not more than twenty or thirty of the crew all told available. I hurried along to the Grand Staircase and met thick smoke rising. When I got down to E Deck, in a choking condition, I found several stewards and others of the crew standing within twenty feet of the flames, which had now ignited the wooden panelling of the passenger cabins below the dining room. The heat was scorching, and the smoke billowing thickly. They looked at me helplessly. In their hands they held firehoses, from which only a trickle of water was oozing.

The thick black smoke was coming from burning carpets, but flames were flickering in red tongues on the woodwork panelling. At sea there would have been full pressure in the pumps, to spurt salt water through the firehoses which were connected to mains on every deck; but in port there would be no pressure until the pumps were started. No one would know that better than the Chief Engineer; but would he have enough head of steam in the reserve boilers to work the pumps?

The *Mauretania* had cost £1,500,000 to build, fourteen years previously. She had survived all the war's dangers, and now was going to go up in smoke in peacetime, lying at her berth, through the carelessness of a fool? The beautiful woodwork, which was one of her main features, had become the greatest danger to her life. It was old, seasoned, varnished wood, dry and highly flammable.

Suddenly water spurted strongly from the jets of the firehoses, great work, Chief! The men holding the hoses directed the streams of water at the seat of the fire. Dense clouds of steam billowed along the alleyway, mingling with the pungent, acrid smoke of the burning carpets and furniture.

This was too much for the few of us down below there to endure. We were choking and gasping. One of the men holding a hose collapsed. The others were staggering, and on the verge of collapse. They dropped the hoses, which writhed, flooding along the alleyway. We had to give up, and make for fresh air, dragging the collapsed steward with us.

At that moment two seamen came plodding down the Grand Staircase, wearing smoke helmets. They picked up the abandoned hoses and directed the jets of water again at the flames, which were now spreading rapidly along the alleyway panelling.

The smoke helmets they wore were of an old fashioned kind, something like divers' helmets, supplied with fresh air pumped into them by bellows through a flexible pipe fifty feet long. I helped to operate the bellows, which rested on the staircase at the level of D Deck. Within a few minutes, the smoke was so dense everywhere that the bellows were pumping smoke instead of air into the helmets. Both men down below collapsed. Half a dozen of us, nearly choking ourselves, went down and with much difficulty dragged them up the stairs. The flames were now roaring along the alleyway on E Deck. The two abandoned hoses were still spurting water jerkily and raising clouds of steam. We had to drag ourselves up to C Deck, gasping for air.

But now the Southampton Fire Brigade had arrived, and the firemen were pouring water from the city mains, through broken portholes in the ship's side. They brought up-to-date smoke helmets, but, being unfamiliar with the interior of the ship, and having to drag great lengths of hose with them, they had difficulty in getting to the seat of the fire.

Ventilation for the section on fire was through large steel uptakes, passing through several decks to the big ventilators on A Deck. These uptakes passed up through the first-class dining room, and on through other parts of the first-class accommodation, including the beautifully decorated main lounge, with its glorious woodwork and silk curtains. The uptake shafts were encased in exquisite, carved panelled wood, with mirrors and filigree work. These were now smouldering, bulging, and cracking with the heat, as also was the fine parquet flooring round about.

As Marine Superintendent, Captain McNeil was in command in the absence of Captain Rostron. He conferred with the Fire Brigade Chiefs. All efforts were now directed to confining the fire to the lower midships sections and preventing it from spreading fore and aft. Gangs with hoses were placed on decks A to D, to play water on any woodwork or ironwork that got hot, while the firemen on E Deck, in their smoke helmets, closed in from both ends on the seat of the fire, and gradually reduced the intensity of the flames.

The ship was lying moored with her port side against the wharf. The steel side doors had been open on that side on D and E Decks, for the use of the firefighters, but not on the starboard side. Hundreds of tons of water, from the city mains and from the ship's pumps, were washing about on these two decks, which, being inside the hull, were, from a shipwright's point of view, the upper and main decks of the vessel. (The three decks of the superstructure amidships were the top decks, viewed as added on to the vessel's hull.)

Water sloshing around on D and E Decks would in ordinary circumstances drain out through scuppers into the bilges at a lower level, and at first did so; but gradually the scuppers became blocked with debris. Some water poured out through the side doors on the port side, but there was no outlet for water accumulating on the starboard side.

At 5.30 p.m., after four hours of firefighting, the flames had been subdued, but water was still being poured in great quantities onto smouldering woodwork and carpets, and the smoke was still thick in the alleyways. There had been a tremendous damage to the ship's fittings and furnishings by water as well as by fire. On E Deck, the water was ankle deep, and steadily getting deeper on the starboard side, as the scuppers there became blocked.

Suddenly one of the big mooring wires forward on the port side snapped, and the ship took a list to starboard of about fifteen degrees. This caused all the water on E Deck to flow over to the starboard side, where it lay to a depth of six feet or more, with no outlet. As this water was rapidly accumulating from the many hoses still in play, I realized that there was a danger that the stern mooring lines would also soon snap, and that the vessel might actually roll over on her side and founder, less something could be done quickly to bring her back to an even keel, by letting the water away on the starboard side.

Easier thought of than done, as the side door on E Deck was secured from the inside by two heavy vertical bars — "strong backs" — and four large bolts, with nuts. This door, which weighed half a ton, was hinged to open outwards. When the ship took her list to starboard, the surface of the water on that side lapped a few inches above the top of the closed door. Something like panic spread 1! 1among the firefighters down below when they realized that the ship was likely to roll over and drown them like rats in a trap; but they manfully stuck to their work of playing jets on the smouldering wood panels. There was horror too among the big crowd on the wharf as the ship leaned away from the wharf.

I got hold of the carpenter and one of his mates, and a seaman, and devised a plan to open that starboard side door. We fastened lifelines around our waists, so that we could be hauled out if necessary. Then we waded and swam to the door, carrying the special large spanner to fit the nuts.

We found that the top bolts were too far below the surface to be reached with our heads above water. The carpenter ducked under, and, by skill and good luck, got the spanner into position on one of the nuts. Then he had to come up for air. Our lungs were filling with smoke, which lay on top of the water like a fog.

We took it in turns to duck down and give a couple of heaves on the spanner; but, quickly we realized that the door could not be opened unless all four nuts were slackened off together. Getting to the two lower nuts was a problem, as they were three or four feet beneath the surface. Our eyes, ears, and noses were clogged with charred wood and other debris, but we continued our efforts, and, after half an hour of hard work, we had all four nuts loosened. The door opened very slightly, and some water began gushing out around the edges.

From then on, every turn of the nuts increased the outflow of water, until presently we had all four nuts off their threads, and the door swung open. The water now gushed out in a cascade, and, but for the lifelines around our waists, would have carried us with it. The surface level of the water on E Deck quickly lowered, and, as it did so, the ship gradually came upright. Within ten minutes, all the water had drained away except a few inches on the deck to the level of the doorsill.

Smoke poured out through the opened door, and we gasped at the fresh air. But we were utterly exhausted; I could scarcely drag one leg after another as I went topside for a hot bath and dry clothing, and a stiff nip of grog.

By this time the fire was under control, and the ship saved, but the horrible stench of smoke and burnt fabrics and paint permeated everywhere. It was obvious that a very great deal of damage had been done to the passenger compartments, and that the liner would be in no shape to make her scheduled departure for New York a few days later.

In all the excitement, no one had thought to send a telegram to Captain Rostron at Liverpool, to inform him that his ship was on fire. He had a shock when he read of it in the newspapers next morning. He took the first available train to Southampton, and arrived on board in the afternoon, in company with several members of the Board of Directors of the Cunard Line and various officials, including engineers, marine surveyors, and insurance assessors.

The "Heads" were aboard in full force, glumly inspecting the damage. The fire could scarcely have occurred at a more inconvenient time. The passenger accommodation was fully booked for the next voyage, on both westbound and eastbound passages. There was no ship to replace the *Mauretania* immediately if she were withdrawn from service for repairs. She had suffered no serious damage to her hull, superstructure, or engines. A proposal was made to board off the gutted section on E Deck, and to make quick renovations of the scorched dining room on D Deck and other minor repairs, so that she could leave for New York at the scheduled time.

On further consideration, the management decided to cancel that voyage. This was, from the commercial point of view, a courageous decision, requiring hasty notifications to three or four thousand booked passengers, the refunding of many thousands of pounds in fares, and the loss of mail contract money for the time being hut questions of prestige and publicity were involved. The reporters in New York would be sure to swarm on board, to inspect the boarded-up section, and to ask questions. Many people might become nervous of sea travel, on reading of a fire having occurred in the Champion Cunarder.

For this reason the Directors decided to lay up the Maurrie for a refit, and, while they were about it, to have her converted into an oil burner. That would give her a new lease of life. The cost would be a quarter of a million pounds, and she would be out of service for seven or eight months, at a time when there was an acute shortage of shipping and exceptionally heavy passenger traffic on the North Atlantic routes; but the decision was taken, and it was a good decision in the circumstances.

Most of the ship's people were paid off, except the navigating and engine room crews, required to take her from Southampton to Newcastle-upon-Tyne, where she was to be renovated and converted to oil fuel in the yards of her original builders, Swan Hunter I Wigham Richardson.

For this passage, I was retained as First Officer. What's more, the Cunard management gave me special thanks for my part in saving the ship, with a handsome cash bonus, and also paid the cost of a new uniform to replace the one that had been ruined when I was helping to fight the fire. Others who had taken part in fighting the fire were also given cash bonus rewards

A few days later, after being partly coaled — and that would be the last time that she would ever be coaled — the Maurrie steamed out of Southampton Water, without any passengers, and headed for the Strait of Dover, and into the North Sea.

We arrived off the mouth of the Tyne on a Sunday at dawn and waited for high water. At 11 a.m. we proceeded into the river, with an escort of tugs, to berth at the dock in Swan Hunter's yard at Wallsend, from which she had started on her seagoing career nearly fifteen years previously. This was her first and only return to the Tyne.

The riverbanks were lined with tens of thousands of "Geordies" who turned out on that fine summer morning to see and cheer "their" ship: the biggest ship ever built in England. It was a great day, and they were as proud of her as a dog with two tails.

I stayed by her for ten days, clearing decks, boats, ropes and other gear to be stowed on shore during her refit. Then I was paid off, and went to Liverpool, wondering how long I might have to wait for another ship.

In the prevailing shortage of shipping, many officers were ashore, and I would have to wait my turn. I was promised a job in the new *S.S. Albania*, then nearing completion at Greenock on the Clyde. She was expected to be ready for service in November — four months to wait!

Like many others, I would have to be laid on shore for that time, and it was no use grumbling. May and I made our home again at Liverpool, so that I would be handy at short call if some sudden opportunity arose; but I had learned to be patient.

On 3rd October 1921, I was called up for a requalifying course of one month's training in the Royal Naval Reserve, at Devonport. There was now no war in the offing, but the Admiralty intended to keep R.N.R. officers up to the mark.

I had been demobilized from the R.N.R. two years and seven months previously, with the rank of Lieutenant, R.N.R. Now, by undergoing a requalifying course, I would become eligible, if I passed, for promotion to the rank of Lieutenant-Commander, R.N.R., with the slightly higher emoluments of that rank: not that I expected or wished ever again to be called up for combatant service in a war. The League of Nations was propounding the ideal of permanent peace. There was much talk of disarmament, especially of naval disarmament, but nobody really believed in it; and Britain's motto was still, "Be prepared!" — even though there was nobody in sight at that time to be prepared against

The requalifying course — a fortnight in gunnery and a fortnight in torpedoes — was little more than a pleasant holiday, in the good company of a few dozen other R.N.R. officers, waiting for ships, who hadn't forgotten much of what they had learned on war service so recently.

The day we looked forward to in the gunnery course was when we had to go to sea in an old fashioned gunboat of little more than 100 tons displacement, to fire off some 4.7-inch shells at a towed target. This, we thought, would be much more in our line than sitting indoors listening to dry lectures on the theory of gunnery.

We joined the gunboat after a hearty breakfast, and took along a large hamper of ham sandwiches, bread and cheese, and bottled beer, supplied by the mess caterer, who gave R.N.R. officers — all seasoned seamen in their thirties and forties — credit for hearty appetites.

All were in good spirits as the little old gunboat churned her way down harbour and into the open water of the Channel, making for the target area near Eddystone Lighthouse, eleven miles offshore. A fresh south-westerly breeze was blowing, with a choppy sea and swell, in which the gunboat began bucketing about in a most alarming manner.

For some reason probably connected with their heavy breakfasts, all but two of the R.N.R. officers became seasick! The exceptions happened to be an officer named Rupert Whalley, and myself. Even the Lieutenant-Commander, R.N., who was in charge of our training, became seasick.

It was a deplorable sight; but Whalley and I never felt better in our lives. About 11.30 a.m., we had clawed off the land ten miles and picked up the target in the appointed place. The R.N. officer in charge pulled himself together wanly and announced the details of the exercise. We were to carry out firing exercise for an hour, then have lunch. (Loud groans from the seasick "seamen.") Then we would fire again until 3 p.m., and return to harbour. (More groans.)

However, we closed up around one of the "four-point-sevens," determined to show the R.N. that the R.N.R. could rise to any and every occasion. We set the sights for range and deflection, loaded the gun, and waited for the order, "Fire when your sights come on!"

The violent motion of the gunboat made this almost impossible. These little vessels had never been intended for going to sea, but only for harbour defence: they were hopelessly obsolete, thirty or forty years of age: museum pieces. But we fired away as best we could, realizing that the ammunition had to be got rid of somehow, and had probably been already written off in the naval stores as "expended."

No more unsuitable weather or vessel could have been chosen for the exercise. From my observation of about forty splashes, it seemed certain that, if the target had been as big as a battlecruiser, we wouldn't have hit her.

Whalley and I were the only ones to take lunch. The others lay around in the small messroom and tried not to listen to our heartily exaggerated conversations about the appetizing qualities of fat ham sandwiches and bottled ale.

After lunch, according to plan, we fired at the target again for another hour or so, and, when all the ammunition was expended, headed for port.

A signal was sent to the Commander-in-Chief, Plymouth: "Firing exercise satisfactorily completed. Request permission to enter harbour."

We landed at 4 p.m. Over tea, all except Whalley and myself agreed that it had been a most uncomfortable day. However, at the end of the fortnight's training, all passed in gunnery.

We then proceeded to *H.M.S. Defiance* at her moorings up harbour, for the torpedo course. A feature of this course was a series of lectures on "electricity." Twice a week, at 2 p.m., immediately after lunch, Chief Petty Officer Woods tried to teach us the rudiments of this branch of science. Having had a good lunch, followed by a couple of glasses of port, we were a sleepy class, and all liable to doze off at any moment.

Woods was placid and good tempered about this; but he always concluded his lecture by saying, "That is all for today, gentlemen. I hope that I haven't kept you awake!"

At the end of the course we all passed. In due time I was notified of my promotion to Lieutenant Commander, R.N.R.

On 24th November 1921, I joined the new Cunarder, *R.M.S. Albania*, as First Officer. After completing her trials in the Firth of Clyde, she had just been delivered to her owners at Liverpool, which would be my home port again for a while.

14

*The "Albania" — The "A" Ships — Cargo carrying to Montreal — Four
Voyages in the "Saxonia" — The Oldest Cunarder — Hamburg My
Temporary Home Port — Inflation of the Mark — A Lively Christmas
Party — The Captain's Medicine — Prohibition in New York — A
Musical Shipmaster — Two Voyages in the "Scythia" — A Smart New
Liner — Refresher Training in H.M.S. "Malaya" — Chief Officer in the
"Caronia" — Conversion from Coal to Oil fuel — My Father's Death*

THE *S.S. Albania* was one of a series of seven cargo and passenger
liners, averaging between 12,000 and 14,000 tons, built hastily for the
Cunard Line, at the end of the 1914-18 war, with the intention of
opening up a trade chiefly with Canada. Their names all began with the letter "A."

Among these, the *Albania* was the ugly duckling. Changes were made in her
design, which made her an oddity among the "A" ships. Intended to be used
chiefly in the wheat carrying trade from Montreal during the seasons when the st
Lawrence River was ice free, and at other times from New York, she had large
cargo holds, with four masts, a small superstructure, and accommodation for only
eighty cabin passengers. She was a twin screw coal burning steamer of 12,767
tons, with a speed of 15 knots.

I served in her for eleven months, making two winter voyages to New York,
followed by four to Montreal — all from Liverpool as a home port. On the first
voyage, under Captain F. G. Brown and Chief Officer Edkins, I was Senior First

Officer in her. Then Edkins went sick with 'flu, and I was Chief Officer on the other five voyages.

There were six watchkeeping officers in the *Albania*. Among them, my junior assistant on watch was Harry Grattidge. I passed on to him the knowledge that senior officers had passed on to me when I was a junior watchkeeping officer. That was in accordance with the traditions of the Merchant Navy. The ladder of promotion was a long one and had to be climbed the hard way. Seniors did all that they could to help juniors: and so the lore of practical seamanship was kept alive, as it will be, I expect, in perpetuity.

We loaded wheat both at New York and Montreal. It was poured as bulk grain into the holds by means of suction pipes and chutes from trains of freight cars. On each of our eastbound passages, we carried 10,000 tons of the golden grain. Bulk wheat in a ship's hold tends to "settle" and become more compact under the ship's motion at sea, thus leaving an airspace under the deckheads of the holds, with a tendency to instability in the cargo. To counteract this, there was a hopper or "feeder" filled with grain, on the orlop deck, from which grain trickled into the holds, keeping them filled to the deckheads, without need of opening the hatches at sea.

Loading and unloading the *Albania* took three weeks. This gave me opportunities of becoming acquainted with life on shore in New York and Montreal, and of spending more time at home, in Liverpool, than service in the bigger passenger liners allowed. It was surprising how many tens of thousands of cases of Scotch whiskey, Irish stout, and English ale and gin, could be loaded into the *Albania*'s holds on the voyages to Montreal. It seemed unlikely that the Canadians would have such a thirst in their cold country. We had only to deliver the grog to the consignees at the wharf. In all probability they sold it at a steep profit to agents of bootleggers, who had their own methods of getting it across the border into the "dry" U.S.A.

The route from Liverpool to Montreal in the summer months was through the iceberg strewn zones of the North Atlantic; but now the international Ice Patrol was in full operation. The position of every drifting berg was sent out by radio daily to warn shipping. We seldom needed to slacken speed, except on overcast or foggy nights, when we were in the thick of the bergs. We travelled on the Cape Race route, passing along the southern and western shores of Newfoundland and Anticosti Island, into the Gulf of st Lawrence and the st Lawrence River, and not going too close inshore, where bergs lurked. The saying was, "Plenty of open water to the southward." This track from Liverpool, 2880 miles, took us nine or ten days.

As the *Albania* made only six voyages in eleven months, we spent much more time ashore than at sea. It was a placid existence. The passenger accommodation was not swanky. She was a one-class ship, for people of moderate means, mainly

Canadian tourists going to and from Britain and Europe, in good tourist-class style: an innovation that was becoming increasingly popular. She also carried mails to and from Montreal and therefore wore the Royal Mail pennant at her signal yard.

On 30th October 1922, I was paid off from the *Albania*, at Liverpool; and ten days later joined the old *Saxonia*, at Southampton, as Chief Officer.

The *Saxonia* was a veteran of twenty-two years' service. Built on the Clyde, and completed in 1900, she was a twin screw, coal burning steamer of 14,280 tons, with a speed of 15 knots, and old fashioned "quadruple expansion" engines. Despite or because of her age, she was a real Cunarder, and one of the best, with accommodation for 2000 passengers, in three classes, and a crew of 500. She, and her sistership *Ivernia*, had the reputation of being the steadiest ships on the Atlantic run. A remarkable feature of their design was a tall single funnel amidships, stretching up 106 feet above the waterline. I had served in the *Ivernia*, as Third Officer, away back in 1908, on the Liverpool to Boston run.

The two "steady sisters" had been on troopship service during the war, but the *Ivernia* had been sunk on 1st January 1917, by a U-boat in the Mediterranean. The *Saxonia* in 1922 was the oldest Cunarder still in service. She was to be used now, rather strangely, to open up a passenger and cargo service between Hamburg and New York. At that time the German post-war oil burning, turbine driven ships, of the most up-to-date design, were still on the stocks, and not yet in service.

The Master of the *Saxonia* was Captain Malin, under whom I had not previously served. He proved to be a fine seaman and good shipmate. We went first to New York, under the terms of the charter, and then started in the Hamburg-New York trade. We arrived at Hamburg on 14th December 1922.

As Hallberg would be my home port while the charter lasted, May came over from England, and we got lodgings at a large pension owned by an Austrian, Herr Prem, in a district known as "An der Alster," on the banks of a lake.

The people of Germany were desperately poor, as attempts were being made to make them pay for the war. The mark was being rapidly devalued. In the end the printing presses went mad, and marks became valueless. Millions of Germans lost their life savings or sold their possessions dirt cheap to foreign speculators who held "hard" currency or gold.

On our first arriving at Hamburg, when marks were 9000 to the pound, we felt like millionaires, for the first and only time in our lives — but the feeling didn't last long. The American syndicate which had chartered the *Saxonia* and other vessels for the trade between German ports and New York was buying German goods cheaply and could get them even more cheaply by waiting a little longer. Fortunes were being made by speculators who had foreign money. They swarmed into Germany like vultures at the scent of carrion.

The *Saxonia* remained for six weeks in Hamburg, waiting for a full cargo in these chaotic conditions. May and I spent Christmas in Germany. The boarders at Prem's house, An der Alster, were a cosmopolitan clot Russians, Poles, Dutch, and even Chiliano merchants, and some Austrians and Germans. We had our meals at one long table, all very friendly: the others helping May and me with our halting German and getting some amusement from our efforts to express ourselves in that hard speech.

May and I decided to give a Christmas party. Herr Prem and his wife were all for it. We hired a band of three musicians and had electricians in to arrange fancy lighting. Herr and Frau Prem did the catering, and we supplied whiskey, beer, schnapps, and liqueurs — all costing us very little when paid for with our English money.

Forty guests turned up, in almost equal numbers of men and women. There was much eating, drinking, singing, and dancing. The fun grew fast and furious, and everybody had a grand time- thanks to the "bloody Englanders" who belonged to the nation which had stopped Germany from winning the war. But even the Germans in the party didn't bear us any grudge for that.

At midnight, the Consul for Chile, who was present with his family, announced that they had enjoyed themselves so much that the party would be continued on the following evening, at his expense, and everyone there was cordially invited. (Loud applause.) At 3 a.m., things still going strong, the pianist fell off his piano stool, and we had to get a substitute. At 4 a.m., the party wound up, and we all went to bed for twelve hours, except Herr and Frau Prem and the staff, who had to clear up the wreck.

At 8 p.m. we started all over again. I was young enough then to dance every dance, including several with Frau Prem. She weighed sixteen stone. She waltzed and polka'd like a circular battering ram and carried me along with her. The song hit in Germany at that time was:

"Komm, mein Mädchen,
und trinken
ein Liqueurchen..."

meaning, "Come, my lass, and drink a little liqueur..."

There were more big parties at New Year. The *Saxonia* cleared out of Hamburg for New York on 29th January 1923. She now had a new Master, Captain F. E. Storey, who had relieved Captain Malin. He suffered from diabetes. His doctor had ordered him to drink three fluid ounces of whiskey per day, as a medicine.

When we neared New York, the Captain suddenly realized that all hard liquor would have to be placed under Customs seal while we were in port. How would he be able to take his medicine, as the doctor ordered, in a "dry" ship?

He asked me to stow three bottles of whiskey away in some secret hiding place, so that it would be available in port for him when he needed it. This was a request, not an order. A shipmaster has great power, but no right to order anyone to do an illegal act. However, 1 tried to oblige him. I took the three bottles of whiskey down to Number Two hold, and stowed them away on some overhead beams, where I thought that no one would think of looking for them.

A few days after we had berthed in New York, Captain Storey, with a conspiratorial wink, remarked to me, "My supply of medicine is getting low."

Choosing a quiet hour, I went down into the hold. To my dismay, I found that the three bottles of whiskey had disappeared! Whether they had been removed by the Customs searchers, or by someone of our own crew, or by stevedores, there was no means of guessing. When I told the Captain the sad news, he almost collapsed. Up to that moment, he had had great faith in me.

"It may be a matter of life or death!" he lamented.

Next day he went to a doctor on shore and got a prescription for three ounces a day — supplied by a pharmacist at an exorbitant price. That was one of the most expensive ways of beating the prohibition laws.

Americans had started to drink seriously when prohibition arrived. Before then, when hard liquor had been easily obtainable, people had not bothered much about it. But when they were told that they couldn't have it, they decided that they must have it. Bootleg liquor, mostly of very poor quality, was sold in immense Portland Roads, under command of Captain Backhouse, R.N. As she would not be putting to sea for exercises, my training in her was only a matter of getting in my time and keeping in touch with "the ways of the Navy."

May came down to stay at Weymouth, nearby. As a married officer in a ship in port, I was entitled to shore leave daily and spent fifty per cent of my time ashore. It was a pleasant break, and some home life; but where was our home? A sailor's home can be only where his heart is, and that is in his ship's home port: at many different places, from time to time, if he serves in many ships.

Having completed that phase of my naval training, I rejoined the *Scythia* as Chief Officer. She left Southampton on 15th December 1923, for New York. I spent Christmas Day in New York, far from home. We cleared out soon afterwards, on schedule, and arrived in Southampton on 6th January 1924. I was looking forward then to a fairly long term of service in the *Scythia*, with our home at Southampton; but it was not to be.

On arrival, I was paid off, and instructed to proceed to Barrow-In-Furness, to join the *Caronia* as Chief Officer. She was being converted there, after twenty years of service as a coal burner, for a new lease of life as an oil burner. The conversion would take four months, but it was necessary to retain a few officers and seamen in her, as a nucleus crew, while she was in the shipyard, virtually as caretakers and night watchmen: not a strenuous life.

May joined me at Barrow, and we took "diggings" near the shipyard. I was on board for eight hours daily, but there were two other officers (Bateman and John Wood) to relieve me on watch in rotation; and in fact we had nothing much to do: it was a restful holiday. The Chief Engineer, Fred Allen, had most of the worry and responsibility, as gangs of shipyard engineers and shipwrights came on board and went down below daily. The hull resounded to the clang of steel, as the bunkers were converted to oil tanks, and the other necessary alterations were made, to do away with the work of the Black Squad.

The conversion of passenger liners from coal burning to oil burning was becoming general in the 1920s. Apart from the fact that oil fuel was much cleaner to handle than coal and required very much less labour and time in refuelling the ship, and in feeding the furnaces, this great change was a matter of economics, with far reaching implications.

For example, the *Mauretania* burned 1000 tons of coal a day when she was at sea. After being converted to an oil burner, she burned 750 tons of oil a day. But the price of a ton of oil was three times that of a ton of coal. Therefore, the cost of running the *Mauretania* on oil fuel was more than double the cost of running her with coal. Against this, there was the great saving of wages for refuelling her and feeding her furnaces operations now performed not by heavy manual labour of large gangs of men, but simply by turning on cocks.

The overall result was a substantial economy in the running costs of a large vessel. Against that, from Britain's national point of view, was the extremely serious disadvantage that Britain had no flow oil supply at home. For a century, since the invention of the steam engine, Britain's prosperity had been built largely on her great natural supplies of high quality steaming coal. Now the extensive conversion of both naval and mercantile vessels to oil burning was causing widespread unemployment in the coal mining industry and was throwing onto the labour market also thousands of men who had formerly worked in ships as firemen and trimmers. This was one of the main causes though few realized it at the time — of the industrial troubles which culminated in the General Strike of 1926. For several years before then, there had been many strikes of coalminers. The unions were attempting to obtain higher wages and shorter hours of work, at a time when mine owners were finding it increasingly difficult to sell coal to British and foreign shipowners, and to the Royal Navy.

Many colliers were being scrapped, or converted to oil tankers, to supply what had formerly been British coaling stations at Gibraltar, Malta, Suez, and elsewhere; or to bring tank oil from far distant places to Britain. Like many other great changes in techniques, this one came on gradually but steadily, scarcely comprehended by people accustomed to thinking in terms of earlier techniques. Instead of being a supplier of coal to many foreign countries, Britain was becoming a buyer of oil in ever increasing quantities. That affected the general economic situation, and contributed to the worldwide Depression which came at the end of the 1920s.

In the meantime there was a boom in shipbuilding, as all British yards were working full time and overtime, to replace the appalling losses of merchant vessels during the war. Yet the horizon of the years ahead was clouded. Other nations also, including the Dutch, the Germans, the French, the Italians, and the Americans, were busily building ships. The competition on the Atlantic routes would be intense. The U.S.A.'s policy of restricting immigration had killed the almost unlimited trade in migrants that had flourished for many years before the war.

As against this, hundreds of thousands of Americans had suddenly felt a keen desire to visit Europe as tourists. The development of the "tourist" trade, and of "tourist class" accommodation in liners, and eventually of "luxury cruise" tours, offered new scope to the enterprise of ship owning companies. That was a new phase in the 1920s, when so many old ways were going into the discard.

While I was at Barrow, my father died at his home at Wallasey, Cheshire, near Liverpool. He had long become reconciled to the fact that my seagoing career suited me. "You would never have made a good accountant, anyway, Gordon," he would say. "Going to sea suits you, so make the best of it, and don't be lazy if you want to gain promotion."

I went down to his funeral. I have served under many shipmasters — always known to the crews as "the Old Man" — but my "Old Man" on shore was the best "Old Man" of them all, for keeping me up to the mark, in accord with his character as "a guid Scot."

At the end of April 1924, the *Caronia* was ready to go into service again. Under command of Captain Diggle, with myself as Chief Officer, she went through her trials satisfactorily as an oil burner, and we took her to Liverpool to open up a new service from there to Quebec.

I had every reason to feel an affection for the *Caronia*. She was the first Cunarder in which I had gone to sea, seventeen years previously, as her Fourth Officer, with everything to learn of Cunard routines. Now, as her Chief Officer, on her first voyage as an oil burner, after I had served in her also as First Officer while she was an armed merchant cruiser during the war, I felt that she was an old friend of mine.

Her sister the *Carmania*, had also been reconditioned, and converted into an oil burner (in 1921). Like many other ships and people in Britain, the two famous "pretty sisters" had lived through the war, and were carrying on, with a new lease of life and vigour, even though they were older now, to "win the peace."

FOR a year, from May, 1924, until May, 1925, I had stability of employment as Chief Officer in the Caronia, voyaging on regular schedules from Liverpool, which was now once again my home port, where my wife and I could, for the time being, settle down.

The Caronia made six voyages to Quebec between 1st May and 11th October 1924. As winter drew in, the trade with Quebec was proving unprofitable. Not much cargo, and few passengers, were offering, to support regular scheduled calls of a liner of 20,000 tons. The Caronia was transferred to the New York run, from Liverpool.

After six voyages on that run, I had a month's holiday ashore.

Then came a step up in my nautical career, as far as swank was concerned, when, on 20th June 1925, I joined the *R.M.S. Franconia*, at Liverpool, as Chief Officer. Built after the war at Clydebank, she was the second of that name in the Cunard lineage. Her predecessor, built on the Tyne and completed in 1910, had only a short career, having been sunk by a U-boat in October 1916.

The new *Franconia* was an oil burning, twin screw, turbine driven steamer of 20,341 tons gross, with a speed of 16 knots. She had a straight stem, a "cutaway" stern, a single funnel, and two masts. She had accommodation for 253 first-class and 600 tourist- class passengers and carried a crew of 434. She and her sister, Carinthia (built on the Tyne and completed in 1925), were designed for the Atlantic passenger and mail service, and for special service as "luxury cruise" tourist steamers. There was no third-class accommodation in them: a realistic recognition of the fact that the pre-war emigrant trade across the Atlantic had come to an end. In every way the *Franconia* was one of the smartest new Cunarders of medium size — if 20,000 tons can be called medium size, as it was in comparison with the giant ships then in service and being built.

The Master of the *Franconia* was Captain George Washington Melson, O.B.E., R.N.R. I had served as a junior officer under his command fifteen years previously, in the little Cunard cargo steamer *Brescia*, when he was known as "the Silver King," because of his habit of touching up aluminium paintwork to make his ship spick and span: a harmless hobby for a shipmaster. During the war, he had been awarded the Order of the British Empire (O.B.E.) for gallant service in the Royal Naval Reserve. Now, in command of the *Franconia*, he was in his glory, as she was one of the smartest liners afloat.

To capture the luxury cruise tourist trade, her hull and super- structure had been painted white all over, except for the Cunard colours of her funnel — red with a black top and two thin black rings. The "boot topping," near and below water level on the hull, instead of being black, was sea green. She looked and was a beautiful ship in all her appointments.

We crossed to New York with passengers, mails, and cargo from Liverpool, and then embarked a full passenger list of tourists for a summer cruise to the Arctic Sea. The cruise was to be of one month's duration. All the passengers were Americans.

Among them was a bright boy named Bruce Cheever, twelve years of age, travelling with his mother and his brother Martin. Within an hour after coming on board, Bruce found out that I was the Chief Officer, and began asking me questions about running the ship, and offering to help.

Being a systematic lad, Bruce had decided to keep a diary of the tour, which he called his "Logbook." He asked me each day to help him with the entries. After the cruise, Bruce's parents had his logbook typed and presented me with a copy of it.

We left New York on Tuesday, 30th June 1925. Outside Sandy Hook, the ship stopped, and Bruce asked me why. "To drop the pilot," I told him.

"Gosh," said Bruce, "he'll make a big splash. Will you drop him from the bridge?" He was disappointed when the pilot, a fat man, climbed down a rope ladder into a dinghy. "That's not dropping him!" Bruce complained.

So it went on, throughout the cruise. On Friday, 10th July, the *Franconia* called at Reykjavik, in Iceland. The passengers went ashore to see the town and were taken in motor buses to the hot springs (geysers), a few miles inland. Bruce recorded: "We entered the harbour amid icebergs thousands of feet high and saw a whale 450 feet long. Then we drove to the hot springs in bobsleighs drawn by striped reindeer. The beautiful Icelandic music and the smell of codfish drying in the sun will linger in my mind too long."

Two days later, bound for the North Cape in Norway, we crossed the Arctic Circle in open water. Bruce, being disappointed at seeing nothing much, wrote in his log: "What a sight! Snow and polar bears as far as the eye could see. We cut through a gap made by the kindly Esquimaux, who threw us pieces of blubber in exchange for chewing gum and ice cream... It's daylight all night tonight. Strafe it."

On Tuesday, 14th July, the *Franconia* anchored at Hammerfest, the most northerly port in Norway. The tourists went ashore for a few hours to take photographs and buy souvenirs at this small fishing port. Bruce bought a pocketknife there, as he did also at every other port at which we called.

Then in the afternoon came the highlight of the cruise — its most advertised attraction — a visit to the North Cape to see the Midnight Sun. We anchored the ship, in clear weather and a calm sea, half a mile from the shore. The cruise directors (the Raymond Whitcomb Co., of New York) had arranged for local boatmen to take all the passengers ashore. I went with them, keen to see the great sight. We landed at the foot of a cliff, and climbed the precipitous atone steps to the summit of the headland. From there we had a walk of half a mile, across a bare and stony plateau, to the northern edge of the Cape.

It was 11.30 p.m., but the sun was still shining in a clear sky, with a clear horizon. It was sinking slowly. When it had nearly touched the horizon, it began slowly to rise again. A truly magnificent, and, to a sailor who had so often "shot" the sun at noon, an awe inspiring sight!

The wondrous spectacle was not visible from the bridge of the *Franconia*, but the Officer of the Watch greeted it with a series of long blasts on the ship's deep-toned steam whistle — as a signal also for the passengers to return on board.

All sorts of jokes were being bandied around: "It's been a fine morning all night, hasn't it?" — "This country is no good for romance. Too much daylight!" "Yes, but what about wintertime, when it's nighttime for six months: a good time and place for a honeymoon!" There was a small Norwegian post office at the North Cape, which did a roaring business in postcards. These would be date stamped there. The postmaster also sold trinkets and souvenirs as a sideline.

Bruce bought a pocketknife.

Parties of ship's stewards waited along the track with thermos flasks of coffee, and sandwiches, to cheer the travellers onwards. All were embarked again by 1 a.m., in the bright morning sunlight. Bruce remarked in his log: "The descent of the dizzy cliff was dangerous. I was fortunate in going in front and being able to catch 3 or 4 old ladies as they went plunging into space."

We hove up the anchor and headed southwards along the rugged coast of Norway. Next day we entered Lyngen Fjord, a deep and narrow indentation which has its mouth almost in 70 deg. N. Lat., well to the north of the Arctic Circle (which is the parallel of 66 deg. 32 mins. N.).

We let go the anchor near a Lapp village, and the passengers went ashore, to take photographs and buy curios from these primitive people. As Bruce remarked: "They live in mud houses and are very deLAPPidated. Ha. Ha."

On 7th July, the *Franconia* entered Trondheim Fjord and berthed at the beautiful Norwegian city there. The passengers went ashore and returned laden with purchases. Bruce remarked in his diary: "I asked the Chief Officer what would happen if a man fell overboard. He said that he would throw a boy overboard ... I suppose he means a buoy. I asked him why they said, 'All hands on deck', when they mean all feet on deck, and he couldn't tell me ... We have encountered mountainous seas, which threatened to swamp our frail barque ... My mother bought me a sailor's hat at Trondheim, as I have decided to become a sailor."

For four days after leaving Trondheim, the *Franconia* cruised along the coast southwards, putting into several of the fjords, and on 22nd July berthed at Bergen, the second largest city of Norway. Bruce noted: "I bought a Viking boat. Paid twelve bucks for it.

The Chief Officer is having a box made for me to take it home in. He thinks it's a fine boat. He ought to know. He's been going to sea for twenty-seven years and probably knew a couple of Vikings when he was a kid. But they don't use Viking boats any more now.

They use motorboats that break down. So I'll use mine on the lake in Chicago and make everybody envious."

On 23rd July, we entered Oslo Fjord and remained there two days. Bruce remarked: "We rode miles in a one-horse cab named a Stokejerry. In another ten years, when I become a millionaire, I shall return to Oslo, buy up all the Stokejerries, and build a bon- fire of them, and so rid the country of a pestilential nuisance. Bought a knife in Oslo."

The *Franconia*'s next call was at Gothenburg, in Sweden. There Bruce's mother bought a cuckoo clock. Many other passengers also bought cuckoo clocks, and, bringing them on board, insisted on winding them up to see if they worked properly. Wrote Bruce: "The whole ship is full of cuckoos ... I have now collected a bag of money, 200 coins of different countries, weighing three pounds, and worth at least one dollar. I carry them in my righthand trouser pocket for safety. Mr Bisset says it gives me a list to starboard."

The next call was at Copenhagen, where we stayed two days. Tours by autos and buses were arranged to see the sights of the Danish capital, including the Royal Palace, with its fine pictures. At most of the ports of call, I managed to get a few hours ashore. The ship's people enjoy these tours, and have their minds broadened by travel, almost as much as the passengers and get paid for doing it!

Our last port of call was at Amsterdam, where the passengers had a busy and tiring day ashore, rushing around to art galleries, cathedrals, and shops, with a visit to a typical Dutch village on the Zuider Zee crammed in for good measure. They returned on board laden with souvenirs.

A Hansom Cab is a close match to a Stokejerry Cab (Library of Congress)

Next day, 30th July, the cruise ended at Boulogne, exactly one month after our departure from New York. The passengers, and their now greatly increased amount of baggage, were landed at Boulogne, so that some could go to Paris, and some by channel ferry to Folkestone, and thence to London: to be returned as individual passengers by Cunard liners to New York, from either Southampton or Cherbourg, at their choice. All the friendly people whom we had got to know so pleasantly streamed ashore, and we never saw any of them again. For such was life in a Cunarder: meeting thousands and thousands of people every year, and getting to know them a little, and then farewell at the gangway and they were gone. The *Franconia* returned to Liverpool, an empty ship. From there, between August and November 1925, I made five voyages in her to New York on the scheduled run.

During this time I received notification that I had been awarded the Royal Decoration of the Royal Naval Reserve (R.D., R.N.R.). This was an award for fifteen years' service in the R.N.R. My commission as Sub-Lieutenant had been gazetted on 1st June 1910.

Time was passing! I was now forty-two years of age and had been going to sea for twenty-seven years. I had become a senior officer in the Cunard service, as Chief Officer in the swanky *Franconia*, with three gold stripes on my sleeve; and my next step up the ladder of promotion, if I could earn it, would be an appointment to Captain in the Company's service, with command of a liner; but, on the law of averages, I might have to wait several years yet for that: there were many officers ahead of me on the roster of seniority.

As far as it had gone, my sea career had been successful: not more so than that of hundreds of other officers in the transatlantic passenger and mail services, whose experiences had been similar to mine; but a little more than that of thousands of other officers of the Merchant Navy who had not had the good luck to join such a big company as Cunard, and consequently had had fewer opportunities of advancement.

We learned now that the *Franconia* had been engaged by Thomas Cook & Son for an Around-the-World cruise of 30,000 miles, to last four and a half months, beginning in January 1926, from New York.

An officer in a cruise ship is expected to be more sociable than could be expected of him in a short run of a week or so across the Atlantic on the scheduled services. There would be much more organized entertainment on board. The navigating officers, when not on duty on the bridge, were required to be part of "the show," and would have little time to themselves for the time honoured "horizontal exercise" which keeps officers of the watch fit when they take naps in their hours off duty. Nor would there be much leisure in ports. It was usual for one or more of the navigating officers to go with the sightseeing parties on the "conducted tours" on shore, as representatives of the ship, unobtrusively, in case of any untoward incidents.

Was this what I had dreamed of when I had first gone to sea as an apprentice in the little Cape Horn barque, County of Pembroke, twenty-seven years previously? No, it had been beyond my wildest dreams then! I might have been happier if I had remained in sail, or perhaps if I had become master of a tramp, with no pretensions to sociability or swank! Only a seaman.

But what's the use of quarrelling with what fate throws us into? Officers in luxury cruise liners were selected not only for their navigational ability, but also for their tact and sociability in helping to make the paying customers feel happy. I had to admit that I enjoyed talking to passengers and answering their questions.

I was now cast in the role of a luxury cruise officer, and I would have to play up to that part, to the best of my ability.

During the Midnight Sun cruise of the *Franconia*, in the summer of 1925, I had the idea of writing a book, which would answer, in handy printed form, some of the questions that passengers in liners ask ships' officers. Therefore, in my spare time, I began compiling a manuscript of a book to be entitled *Ship Ahoy! Nautical Notes for Ocean Travellers*.

I was already, to some extent, a successful author. Several years previously, after the Titanic disaster of 1912, the powers that be had decided that every member of a ship's crew in passenger liners should know something about handling a lifeboat.

The Board of Trade had instituted an examination and granted a Lifeboatman's Certificate to all who passed it. Lifeboat Schools were set up in several ports in Britain. The shipping companies expected the officers of their ships to hold classes for seamen, engineers, and stewards, and to prepare them for the examination. A difficulty was that some officers were themselves in need of Instruction in handling boats! Others, who were excellent seamen, were unable to instruct a class of men. I had therefore concluded that there was need for a handy booklet, giving systematic details of the construction of lifeboats, their gear and sails and how to use them, and how to lower the boats and handle them properly. This could be used as a textbook for the Lifeboatman's Certificate examination.

Having gathered a mass of information, I got a brother Cunard Officer, D. W. Sorrell, who was a good draughtsman, to prepare the diagrams, on a profit sharing basis; and, when everything was ready, we went to see the firm of Birchall & Sons, printers, of Liverpool, to ask for an estimate of the costs of printing and publishing the booklet. So chary were we that we ordered only 1000 copies to be printed.

That first edition, a booklet of 32 pages, with the title of *Lifeboat Efficiency*, was published in November 1924, while I was serving as the Chief Officer in the *Caronia*. At the price of sixpence, it was rapidly sold out and reprinted again and again. Within a few years 30,000 copies had been sold. It became the standard textbook on its subject and remained so for many years. (I revised and slightly enlarged the booklet in 1933, and again in 1935, 1939, 1940, and 1944. By that time it was in its twenty-fifth edition. A more up-to-date book, by another author, then came on to the market, and mine went out of print, after being the best-seller, and the only seller, in its field for twenty years.)

It was the early success of Lifeboat Efficiency that encouraged me to write *Ship Ahoy!* I wrote the book rapidly while serving as Chief Officer in the *Franconia* on the run between Liverpool and New York, in August and September 1925. The Foreword indicated my intention:

> *The author's idea in placing this book before the seagoing public is to try to give them an explanation of some of the everyday sights, sounds, gadgets, and occurrences that they will be seeing and hearing round the decks of a modern liner on a voyage across the ocean. During thirty-six years' experience at sea, in all types of vessels, I have been asked thousands of questions by passengers about all the subjects touched on in this book. It is borne in upon me that the average passenger looks upon the ship as something more than a floating hotel and is interested in knowing a little of the working and navi-gating of a great liner from port to port, and also about the numerous lifesaving and navigational appliances with which she is equipped.*

With that in mind, I wrote chapters on the crew and organization of a liner; on icebergs; the Gulf Stream; ships' lights; the "nautical mile"; time, and the alteration of the clock; the steam whistle; ships' bells; lifeboats; lifebuoys; seasickness; "stargazing"; ocean waves; the observation of the sun's altitude for latitude; the crow's nest; the hand log and the patent log; anchors and cables; the Gyro compass; propellers; judging distance at sea; the wireless direction finder; flags; ships' freshwater supply; charts; the North Atlantic tracks: and I put in the Rules of Deck Tennis for extra measure, together with a glossary of nautical terms and phrases.

All this, I hoped, would be of fascinating interest to the tens of thousands of passengers who crossed the Atlantic annually: there was no other book on the market attempting to explain the techniques of navigation in a nontechnical but nevertheless authentic way. I got my friend D. W. Sorrell to do some illustrations and, when the *Franconia* berthed in New York in September, I went along with the manuscript and drawings to show them to the well-known American publisher, Mr. Doran.

He received me courteously, listened carefully to my persuasive arguments, and promised to read the manuscript himself. When the *Franconia* returned to New York three weeks later, I hastened to Mr. Doran's office to learn his decision.

"A very interesting book," he told me, "but, unfortunately not many people would want to buy it! I don't suppose that we could sell even one thousand copies of it."

He handed the manuscript and drawings back to me, and I returned to the ship feeling considerably deflated. On returning to Liverpool, I asked Birchalls to quote a price for printing 1000 copies. I had decided to have it published at my own expense and risk.

The manuscript was being set in type when the *Franconia* left Liverpool on 31st December 1925, for New York, to begin the Around-the-World cruise. Mr.

Birchall promised me that proofs would be awaiting me when the ship called at Naples at the end of January. If I corrected them and returned them punctually, completed copies of the book would be waiting for me at the Cunard office in New York at the end of the cruise, in May 1926.

All that was done, and, in course of time, 15,000 copies of *Ship Ahoy!* were sold, in edition after edition, until it went out of print during the 1939-45 war.

16

"Franconia's" Around-the-World Cruise — A Cook's Tour in a Luxury Liner — Handling Passengers Tactfully — Ports of Call — Madeira — How to Bargain — Gibraltar, Monaco and the French Riviera — Naples — Athens — Alexandria and a Trip to Cairo — The Suez Canal — Bombay — Colombo.

O N 14th January, 1926, the *Franconia* was ready to depart from New York on her Around-the-World cruise. There were 373 passengers booked. The accommodation had been rearranged so that there was only one class-first, but some cabins, or staterooms, were more expensive than others.

The fare was many thousands of dollars, including, as it did, nearly five months afloat, with quarters and meals equivalent to those of a first-class hotel, plus a sea passage of nearly 30,000 miles, with calls at thirty ports in many different countries. The passengers were mainly citizens of the U.S.A., but there were also some from Britain, and some from Latin American countries. They were all wealthy people, with "money to burn" and leisure to enjoy a long holiday, almost regardless of expense. A large proportion of them were elderly or middle aged couples, who had perhaps worked hard at professions or in business to accumulate wealth. They were now prepared to spend some of their hard earned money on a sea cruise which would be not only a holiday, but also an education. Some of them had young people, their sons and daughters, with them, but these were a minority.

All, young or old, had the self-confidence of wealthy people, which in some cases amounted to an arrogant attitude — the belief that money can buy anything. On the day before the ship was due to leave New York, there was intense activity. Gangs of cleaners were hard at work, to make everything spotless. Joiners were scurrying around, moving furniture, and preparing the cabins to suit the imperious ideas of individual passengers. One would want a bunk removed, another a settee, another a wardrobe, and so on: the main idea being to make room for a great quantity of luggage in each cabin or stateroom — not unreasonably, as the passengers had to bring clothes with them for five months in all sorts of weather and varied climates.

Big gangs of stewards were busy, hoisting in twenty times the quantity of stores usually carried on a mere transatlantic voyage. Frozen meat, poultry, fish, butter, cheese, eggs, fruit, vegetables, and other perishables were being stowed away in the ship's refrigerated cargo space, after the Catering Department's refrigerators had been filled. The engineers were busy down below, taking in 2860 tons of oil fuel. The carpenter and his mates were filling the freshwater tanks, which held 2400 tons.

The seamen too were busy; but, instead of washing down the decks with hoses, they were hard at work shovelling ice and snow overside. New York was in the grip of a blizzard, and the temperature below freezing point. We would be glad to get away to warmer climes.

The ship was due to leave at 12 noon. Our passengers began coming on board at 9.30 a.m. It seemed that each passenger was accompanied by at least half a dozen friends, for fond farewells. By 11 a.m., the ship was packed. What with stewards trucking heavy trunks along to the staterooms, and bellhops delivering mail, parcels and flowers, and everyone talking at once, and all excited, too, pandemonium was let loose.

The departure of the ship was delayed for an hour, to allow everything to be sorted out. At 12.30 the steam whistle blew, and gongs were sounded up and down the alleyways and on the decks with the cry, "All visitors ashore, please!"

There were no tearful goodbyes. Everybody was happy. A thousand or more paper streamers were thrown from the wharf to passengers lining the rails on A, B, and C Decks. They hung in great festoons as if loath to let us be gone. Then the real moorings were taken in, and the paper moorings stretched and snapped as we parted from the shore, at 1 p.m.

The sun was shining, in the crisp, cold winter air. The skyscrapers of New York and the Statue of Liberty stood out crystal clear as we proceeded downriver. Lunch was served immediately. There was a scramble for places until people had found their hooked tables, with the aid of the Second Steward.

At 2.30 p.m., we dropped the pilot, off Sandy Hook. An hour later, when we were outside the twelve-mile limit of U.S.A. jurisdiction — the bar opened! There was such a rush that it almost seemed that this was one of the main attractions of the cruise. At 4 p.m. we held a Passengers' Boat Muster. It was poorly attended, perhaps because the weather was cold, with a biting wind offshore; perhaps because some passengers suffered from seasickness. One lady, when asked by the cabin steward to put on her lifebelt and go to her boat station, said, "Let her sink!" and turned her face to the bulkhead. Our passengers were more used to giving orders than to being ordered what to do. They could only be "requested."

Next day we were well out to sea, steering on a Great Circle course, trending E. by S., for our first port of call, Funchal, in the Madeira Isles, a passage of 2750 miles, scheduled to take us eight days. It was one of the longest st retches of open water in the programme of the tour and would give the passengers a chance to settle down into shipboard routine.

As we got into the beneficent influence of the Gulf Stream, the temperature rose, from 28 deg. F. at noon in New York, to 48 deg. at noon on the next day at sea. The remainder of the snow and ice on the superstructure and rigging thawed and dripped all over the decks. The passengers also were thawing out a little and getting to know one another. A dance held in the lounge that evening was well attended: a good augury.

The ship's crew consisted of some 500 people, under command of Captain G. W. Melson, with Staff Captain J. Chatworth Musters as his assistant, and myself as Chief Officer, and six watchkeeping officers. On the payroll also were the Chief Engineer and his staff, two surgeons, the Purser and his staff, and the Chief Steward and his staff.

The handling of the passengers was a matter for the Cruise Director, Mr Ross Skinner, representing Thomas Cook & Son. He had two Associate Directors and a staff of nine other assistants, besides a "hostess," three chaplains, and a dentist!

Cook's office, on B Deck, aft, was open daily from 10 a.m. to 4 p.m. at sea, and always in ports. It provided banking facilities and foreign money exchange; organized lectures and recreational features on board; received complaints; and organized sightseeing tours ashore in the ports that we were to visit. This took much of the pressure off our Purser and his assistants, who normally had to cope with passengers' problems and complaints.

My watch on the bridge was from 4 a.m. to 8 a.m., and from 4 p.m. to 8 p.m., assisted by Junior Second Officer Parry. When we were three days out at sea, Parry received a wireless message, stating that his mother was dying. What could one do? Another message came next day that she had died: he was grief stricken, but stood watch as usual, and, when off duty, chatted politely to the pleasure-seeking passengers on board, who had no idea of his bereavement.

In the dining room, the watchkeeping officers had a table to ourselves. That was necessary so that we could take our meals, or leave the table, as required, without having to make excuses. Everyone wore evening dress at dinner: the officers in mess jackets. At all times we had to be smartly dressed, and sociable, making friends impartially with the passengers, but not favouring any. Under Cunard rules, it was forbidden for officers to drink with passengers, or to visit them in their staterooms, or to invite them into our cabins. We could chat with them on deck or in the public rooms, and were expected to attend dances when we were off watch, or not in need of sleep; and, if possible, to attend lectures, concerts, divine service, and to take part in deck games — playing with the passengers, and not among ourselves — in short, our task was to be "good mixers," without becoming too personally friendly with anyone.

Lantern slide lectures were being given by Cook's lecturers, describing Madeira and the Mediterranean ports that we were to visit. At each of these lectures, the Cruise Director tactfully read out a list of "Don'ts":

"Requested not to waste fresh water, or to run the showers in the swimming bath for more than a few seconds at a time. There is no shortage of fresh water, but there is none to waste.

"Requested not to throw lighted cigars or cigarettes over the side, as they may blow into an open port and cause a fire. "Requested not to open portholes if they have been shut by the steward. They will never be shut without very good reason. "Requested, when walking the decks for exercise, to walk aft on the port side, and forward on the starboard side, to obviate confusion.

"If you have a complaint or difficulty, don't nurse it; but report it to the proper authority, and every effort will be made to cope with it."

There were many organized recreations on board, and some unorganized among them the time honoured game of "Ask the Officer."

Within one hour I was asked, by three different passengers: (1) What is the sun's declination at noon? (2) What are railway trains like in India? (3) What is the Evening Star now?

The favourite question was, "Where are we now?" To answer it we exhibited charts of the North Atlantic, with the ship's position marked on them each day at noon, and the day's run. Another big question was, "What's the time?" Going eastward, the clocks had to be advanced about twenty-five minutes a day, at our average speed of 15 knots. Big indicator boards were put up, showing the amount of the alteration of the clock to be made. Passengers crowded around these and regarded the whole thing as an unmitigated nuisance. Which it is especially to anyone trying to explain it to passengers who had seemingly never in their lives given thought to the measurement of time by the sun and the stars and the earth's rotation. "I thought time was the same everywhere," said one sweet young thing. How could I begin to explain to her that it's not?

At 7 a.m. on Friday, 22nd January, we dropped anchor in the harbour of Funchal, Madeira. The inhabitants of this Portuguese colony had been well forewarned of our arrival. Dozens of boats were putting off from the shore. The first to arrive were the diving boys, ready to dive for coins thrown to them.

Soon other boats arrived, with baskets of canaries and parrots, and wicker chairs and tables and embroidery for sale. These bum boatmen were not allowed on board, but they did a brisk trade, shouting and gesticulating to passengers who leaned over the rails and lowered lines to haul up the purchased articles. The passengers had been warned by the Cruise Director in a lecture: "Never pay the price asked for anything, in any port that we visit. On hearing the price of any article you wish to buy, walk away from it as if it were the last thing in the world you desire. Carry this procedure out several times, until the price has dropped about 500 per cent. Then offer half that, and it will be thrust upon you."

At 8 a.m., the passengers began landing, by means of motor launches. The ship was due to leave at 6 p.m. I was not able to go ashore, as I was busy replenishing our fresh water. This was brought off in lighters holding 150 tons each and fitted with pumps. We managed to get in 850 tons at an average rate of 90 tons an hour. Between 4 p.m. and 5.30 p.m. our passengers returned, tired and laden with purchases: some of them sleepy from too much Madeira wine. At 6 p.m. prompt we hove up the anchor and put to sea.

Our next port of call was Gibraltar, where we arrived in the morning, two days later. At 9 a.m., the passengers went ashore in a large tender, which held them all. They were met by guides with carriages, and were shown around Gibraltar, returning on board for lunch at 1 p.m. In the meantime we took in 1200 tons of oil fuel, and also filled up our freshwater tanks, and got supplies of fresh fish, vegetables and fruit.

We also embarked seven new passengers — all Spaniards — at Gibraltar, including a man 6 feet 7 inches high. We had to knock the end out of his bunk for him. He moved about the ship with a perpetual stoop.

At 3.30 p.m., we hove up the anchor. Our passengers had now become aware of the fact that we had anchors. Many of them crowded forward to see the anchor hove up. They leaned over the rail, watching the chain come in, link by link, as if they expected something curious to come out of the water. When at last the anchor appeared, they photographed it!

Our next port of call, Monaco, two days later, was to be one of the highlights of the cruise. We anchored at 1.30 p.m., and most of the passengers went ashore for the afternoon and evening, to gamble at the Casino. Next day, Cook's had arranged a motor tour to Nice, by the "Corniche drive." Four of the ship's officers, including myself, were invited. We changed into civilian garb and went ashore with the 380 passengers. Cook's had ninety-six automobiles lined up, each with a number placard, to which tickets given to us corresponded, enabling the allotted vehicles to be easily found. Four passengers to each car, with French chauffeurs, and away we went for a magnificent day's outing, visiting Mentone,

Beaulieu, and Nice (for lunch at the Negresco Hotel), and then to the Casino at Monte Carlo, for a few hours watching the cosmopolitan crowd of gamblers at the roulette and trente-et-quarante tables[1].

At 5 p.m. we officers returned to the ship, but many of the passengers remained playing at the Casino until after midnight. All being reported on board at 1.30 a.m. we hove up the anchor at 2 a.m. We arrived at Naples at 1 a.m. on 29th January and were due to leave there at 2 p.m. on the following day. That would give our passengers ample time to enjoy the sights, sounds, and smells of Naples, and for some of them to make excursions to Vesuvius and the ruins of Pompeii.

I received notice of a registered package awaiting me at the post office and knew what would be in it: proofs of my book, *Ship Ahoy!* Accompanied by the Cunard interpreter, Carlo, who wore a splendid frockcoat with large brass buttons, and a monumental peaked cap, I went to the post office, a large building with a dirty courtyard, and there, after much argument, and inspection of my parcel by the Customs officials, I received my proofs, and was glad to get back on board the clean ship, to open them with all the trepidation of a novice author. I decided to post them back to the printers from our next port of call, Athens.

Naples at this time was a squalid city, despite its beautiful surroundings. Our passengers, as usual, accumulated some interesting memories and many curios and objects of art. We cleared out next day at 2 p.m.

On 1st February we arrived outside Athens at 7.30 a.m. That was in the Morning Watch, when I was on the bridge with Second Officer Parry. The Captain came onto the bridge later as we bore up for the anchorage off the port. The morning was fine and clear. Captain Melson was a man who liked to do things himself. He had acquired that habit in sailing ships and small cargo steamers and could never quite lose it in big liners. The usual procedure on entering port was to call all officers on stations — some on the bridge, some at the bows and some at the stern-to attend to anchoring or mooring or to deal with any other emergency that might arise in narrow waters. But on this occasion the Captain said to me, "Don't call the officers for stations. We'll take her in with the watch on deck. You go forrard and stand by the anchors."

I went to the bows with the carpenter and an A.B. seaman, and got ready to "let go" when we would arrive at our anchorage in Phaleron Bay. No pilot had come out to meet us. This bay with its wide open mouth presents no special difficulties. I could see Captain Melson and Parry on the bridge. In his usual energetic manner, the Captain was running up and down to Monkey Island to take bearings, laying her off on the chart, handling the engine- room telegraphs, supervising the leadsman in the chains, and doing everything else himself.

Apparently, with all these jobs that he had given himself, he forgot to reduce speed in time as we neared the shore. Suddenly the anchor telegraph rang forward: "Let go."

She appeared to me to have too much speed, but the telegraph was supplemented by a great yell from Melson: "LET GO BOTH ANCHORS!" I gave the carpenter the order to unscrew the brakes, and both anchors hit the water and plunged to the bottom, while the cables ran out with a tremendous clatter through the hawse pipes, and stretched aft along the sides as the mud hooks sank into the mud bottom and got a good hold.

By now the wash of the propellers going full astern came surging forward. The cables soon slackened off, and I realized that she was ashore. She had gone aground very gently, for I had felt no jar. Soundings over the bow showed that she was almost afloat. The Captain was keeping the engines going full astern, as I hove on the windlass. He used the helm hard over each way, which caused her stern to swing to port and starboard. So she gouged out a channel for herself, and, to our great relief, she started to move astern.

Backing her until she reached seven fathoms, we anchored again. the people on board realized that we had been on the mud. A thorough examination, by sounding all the double bottom tanks and bilges, revealed that no damage had been done.

At 9 a.m., wretched little tenders came alongside, to take the passengers ashore in relays. There had been a lecture on the preceding evening, and all were eager to go ashore and see the ruins of antiquity. Dozens of vendors were allowed on board at our anchorage. But our passengers were becoming expert buyers. They beat the vendors down unmercifully. It was a case of "Greek meet Greek." Then came the shock, as officials announced that there was a special "Museum and Antiquities" tax, of one pound sterling a head for every tourist landing at Athens. This came as a surprise to Thomas Cook & Son, who had not budgeted for that item. So once again Greek met Greek — and the Greeks won the argument:

Thomas Cook had to pay!

Everyone waited on shore to see the moon rise over the Parthenon — something to write home about. I had now finished correcting my proofs and sent them off by mail to Liverpool. All our tourists were safely on board by 1 a.m., and we cleared out half an hour later.

At 8 a.m. on 3rd February, the *Franconia* berthed alongside the Quai de Mahamede, at Alexandria in Egypt. There were special trains to convey our passengers to Cairo and Luxor. All got away that afternoon, and the ship was strangely quiet and peaceful. Next morning after breakfast, I mustered the ship's crew for boat drill. That was something which could not be neglected, even if we were on a "world cruise" — or, as some of the facetious Yanks were now calling it, a "world booze."

The Purser (T. H. Cullum) and I caught the noon train, in company with the Cruise Director, Ross Skinner, for a trip to Cairo, 130 miles by a comfortable train. We joined the excursion organized for the Passengers, on camelback (yes!) to the Pyramids and the Sphinx. My ride on a camel, a "ship of the desert," nearly made me landsick. My dragoman said, "She lady camel four years old name Moses very good camel me poor man you give me tip now" — and in one breath.

I gave him a quarter-dollar, and he said, "Police man not let me have tip if police man speak you satisfied you speak yes no speak about tips!"

All this at the foot of the mighty Pyramids and of the mysterious Sphinx somewhat spoiled the mystical effect. Wherever we went we were besieged by beggars howling for baksheesh. They were driven away by our guides with whips and harsh Arabic curses. Despite its glories of antiquity, modern Egypt seemed a place of dreadful poverty and dirt, disease, and millions of flies. I returned on board ship on the third day, and we took her on to Port Said, where the remainder of our passengers were to join her, after their excursion to Luxor.

Next came the passage of the Suez Canal. It took us sixteen hours to pass through, partly at nighttime, with a searchlight at our bows, the ship piloted in turn by two Canal pilots.

Then we were into the Red Sea, on the long passage of 2690 miles from Suez to Bombay, scheduled to take eight days. "Whites" were now worn by passengers and by the crew. We felt natty in our white uniforms and were much complimented by the passengers on our cool, spick and span appearance. An extra (canvas) swimming pool was rigged up on the foredeck, and much patronized. People in some parts of the ship, especially the lower decks, were complaining of the heat, but there was little that could be done. Fans and forced draughts were circulating air, but it was hot air! There was relief after we had passed out of the Gulf of Aden into the open waters of the Arabian Sea. Lectures were held on India, and everyone was busy arranging details of the tours to be organized on shore in that ancient, colourful, land. Looking ahead to our Crossing the Line ceremony, a Ladies Sewing Committee was formed to prepare costumes and wigs for the "Father Neptune" show, which everyone was anticipating keenly, except myself. It had been decided (as a closely guarded secret) that I was to be Father Neptune. But that was a long way ahead. India and Ceylon were yet to come.

For eight days the *Franconia* lay at anchor in Bombay Harbour, while our passengers went on long excursions inland in India. They travelled in four special trains, visiting Benares, Delhi, and Agra. All bought solar topees[2] and sunglasses from vendors who came on board as soon as the ship anchored.

During their absence, we refuelled from a large oil tanker, filled the freshwater tanks, and had an easy time. Our passengers returned from their excursions, laden with purchases. On 26th February, we hove up the anchor and shaped our course for Colombo.

Two days later, we moored to buoys, fore and aft, in Colombo Harbour, and remained there for four days, while our paying guests went ashore for excursions to Kandy and other places in picturesque Ceylon, spending money liberally on buying local treasures, as usual.

At sea again on 3rd March, we set course for Padang in Sumatra. All were expectant of the ceremony of Crossing the Line. Those who, like myself, had parts to play in this sea pageant, were busily learning their parts, and rehearsing. Being cast in the star role of Neptune, I was becoming a little anxious; but gradually it was being borne in on me that I had missed my vocation by going to sea.

I should have been an actor.

One day, I went up to Monkey Island, above the wheelhouse, to rehearse my lines. I thought that it might be helpful to get a critical opinion from the quartermaster and the standby quarter- master, who were at the wheel below me. Down the voice pipe I said to them, "Listen in, while I speak King Neptune's part."

After declaiming my whole speech, I called down the voicepipe,

"How was that?"

I heard a hoarse whisper, "Tell him it was bloody awful!" followed immediately by the enthusiastic comment, "Very good, Indeed, sir!"

CHAPTER ENDNOTES

(1) Trente et Quarante, ("Red and Black"), French card game played at Monte Carlo and French and Italian gambling casinos. It is not popular in North America. The name Trente et Quarante is derived from the fact that the winning point always lies between thirty and forty

(2) A solar topee is another name for a pith helmet, a lightweight hat that protects the head from the sun. It's also known as a safari helmet, topi, sun helmet, or salacot.

17

"Crossing the Line" — An Elaborate Neptune Pageant — The Script — Cast of Characters — Prologue — Musical Effects — Bombastic Bilge — My Histrionic Efforts — Alleged Funny Business — Certificates for Everybody — Neptune Dinner — Padang — Java — Singapore — Peking the "Forbidden City" — Ructions on Board — Manila Hong Kong — Shanghai — Korea — Japan — The Hawaiian Islands — San Francisco — My Brother Jack — Los Angeles — Panama Canal — Havana — Home to New York — The World Circumnavigated.

WHEN we left Colombo, on 3rd March, 1926, bound for Padang in Sumatra, the preparations for Crossing the Line proceeded apace. The script for the show was compiled by one of the passengers, Mr J. E. S. Heath, in collaboration with the ship's surgeon, Dr T. Gwynne Maitland, and myself. It was all bilge, but what of that? The idea was to have fun.

The producer was Dr. Maitland. The cast of characters, selected and rehearsed for weeks previously, was:

King Neptune The Chief Officer (myself)
Queen Amphytrite Miss Connolly (a passenger)
Polyphemus The Boatswain
Davy Jones The Chief Steward
Davy Jones' Clerk The Assistant Purser
Barber The Second Officer
Mermaids The Stewards' Writer

Sea UrchinsTwo Bellboys
ExecutionerAn Engineer
ManicuristA nurse
PolicemenFour Male Passengers
BearsFour Male Passengers
Old Men of the SeaSix Sailors
DoctorAn Engineer
Doctor's AssistantAn Engineer
TritonsSix Bandsmen
Sea HorseTwo Electricians
HeraldA Steward
Effervescent WesternerHead Waiter

Elaborate costumes for all these thirty-nine players had been prepared by the Ladies' Sewing Committee. All the necessary properties had been made by the carpenter and sailors. Ropeyard wigs and beards, and incidental effects of all kinds, had been manufactured with care. The seahorse, a frightful monstrosity, was built and operated by two electricians — one the forelegs, the other the hindlegs. The music for the pageant was to be performed by the ship's orchestra of ten musicians.

The "stage" was the forecastle head. The ducking ceremony was to take place in the canvas swimming pool, size fifteen feet square and five feet deep, rigged on the foredeck.

The prologue of the show took place at 9.30 p.m. on 5th March, the eve of our Crossing the Line. It represented the arrival of King Neptune's emissaries on board, hailing the ship, and announcing that Neptune would hold his court on board on the morrow.

A group was posed during darkness on the starboard side of the forecastle head, just abaft the windlass. It consisted of POLYPHEMUS, standing; FOUR MERMAIDS, lying on deck at his feet; FOUR BEARS, on the awning spars overhead; and TWO SEA URCHINS, standing. The HERALD posed on top of the rail around the stem, grasping the jackstaff with his left hand. With a property trumpet in the other hand, he struck the attitude of sounding a fanfare.

A powerful spotlight was trained on the HERALD, with an electrician standing by, to switch it on and off as required. A floodlight was trained on the group, with an electrician attending. Two hoses with spraying nozzles were fixed so as to play jets of water into the air, sailors standing by the hydrants. Two sailors stood by with red pyrotechnic lights, and buckets of water for dousing them. The orchestra was concealed in the passenger entrance to the lower deck. The cornetist crouched behind the windlass, ready to blow the fanfare.

The boatswain (playing Polyphemus) had developed stage fright. It was therefore hastily arranged that he would open his mouth and pretend to hail the ship, while I, hidden behind the windlass, would sing out his lines for him.

When everything was assembled, I informed the Officer On Watch (O.O.W.) on the bridge, by telephone. He in turn, by telephone, ordered the lookout in the crow's nest to strike one bell and report in a loud voice, "An object on the starboard bow, sir."

The spectators were crowded at the forward rails of A, B, and C Decks. There was a prolonged blast on the steam whistle. The orchestra struck up "Fingal's Cave" and stopped in the middle of a double forte passage. The spotlight was then switched onto the HERALD, while the hidden cornet player blew a prolonged note.

While POLYPHEMUS cupped his hands and pretended to be hailing, I sang out, from behind the windlass, "SHIP AHOY!" (The title of my book!)

O.O.W.:(on the bridge): Hello.

POLYPHEMUS (fake): What ship is that? (Hoses turned on.)

O.O.W.: *R.M.S. Franconia.* Who is that hailing? (Floodlights switched onto group, and red flares ignited.)

POLYPHEMUS: We, the envoys of mighty King Neptune, demand that ye shall show cause why thus by your presence ye pollute our equatorial waters.

O.O.W.:We await His Majesty's pleasure.

POLYPHEMUS: Only on sufferance of my liege lord do ye cross the Line.

O.O.W We crave His Most Potent Majesty's permission.

POLYPHEMUS: Tomorrow, two hours before sunset, prepare royally for his reception and render him homage. Deliver to our nimble messengers your papers. (SEA URCHINS rush along to bridge, receive documents, and rejoin group on forecastle head. Lights switched off and hoses turned off. HERALD resumes position on rail at stem.)

POLYPHEMUS: Until tomorrow. (Cornet player blows a prolonged note. Spotlight on HERALD, who bends over as though descending into the ocean. As note finishes, out spot. Band resumes playing "Fingal's Cave." As they finish, a long blast is blown on the steam whistle.)

The following afternoon, all was in readiness for the big show. KING NEPTUNE'S COURT assembled on the forecastle head and at the fore end of the canvas swimming tank. The orchestra (concealed) struck up "Entry of the Gladiators," by Fucik, while the whole Court paraded around on the forecastle head, the MERMAIDS dragged along the deck by the OLD MEN OF THE SEA. (They were inside nets, with mats underneath them.)

CHORUS: all singing:

NEPTUNE'S SONG

Blow, blow the trumpet,
Beat, beat the drum:
See Old Father Neptune come!
Hail with all your might and main
Great Poseidon and his train.

On reaching the platform rigged at the fore end of the tank, the Court mounted the steps. The OLD MEN OF THE SEA carried the MERMAIDS up the steps, and deposited them at the foot of the throne whereon NEPTUNE and AMPHYTRITE sat.

Neptune then rose and got rid of the following bilge:

NEPTUNE: Behold us, Neptune, Ruler of the seas! A King — aye, more than a King — a God. We hold dominion absolute over all this boundless and eternal Ocean.

CHORUS OF THE COURT: Hail, Neptunus Rex!

NEPTUNE: Ye puny mortals, who infest the land, delving, destroying, scarring her fair face, scratching on her lovely cliffs your ephemeral names, your truthless tales and comic semblances, stand awed and powerless at the marge of our vast realm. For, since first savage man trembling crept to taste my bitter waters, none has tamed, nor ever shall tame, nor harness, our stallions, nor mar nor change this our halidom.

CHORUS: The sea, the sea, the sea!

NEPTUNE: Now, who be these that rashly dare to cross our sacred Line? Disturbing us in the deep silences, till, in majestic wrath, with our Queen and our Court, we leave our coral palaces, our cool and oozy crystal caves, and cry you halt, demanding tribute and allegiance?

So far, so good. At this stage, the Head Waiter, planted among the spectators, was supposed, in the guise of an EFFERVESCENT WESTERNER, to interrupt me by singing out, "Say, Neptune, step on the gas!"

Unfortunately the fathead missed his cue. I gave it to him again:

..."tribute and allegiance." But, as there was no interjection, I continued:

NEPTUNE: Cease, mortal, cease thy flippant speech. Are we to be thus familiarly addressed we, whose august presence none dare approach save with bowed head and bended knee? Hark ye, rouse not our wrath, lest shrieking horrors fly and seas gigantic leap, engulf, and lick their frothy lips.

THE EFFERVESCENT WESTERNER (late on his cue): Say Nep., step on the gas.

NEPTUNE: (unperturbed): And yet, methinks, ye meant us no dis- courtesy. We also can be gracious when so it suits our mood, to soothe our coursing seas and smooth them, that the changeling halcyon may rest thereon. Besides, 'tis much too hot for choler, and we must away to our green caverns.

CHORUS: Away, away, to our green caverns. (They sing again "The Neptune Sanft'.)
NEPTUNE: (taking a deep draught from his beaker, after blowing off a cottonwool froth, breaks forth into a solo so called song or recitative):

> I live in the deep, mid the whales and the fishes,
> With shoals of young mermaids to tend to my wishes;
> My Queen Amphitrite presides o'er my cave,
> 'Twas she who invented the Permanent Wave:
> And if they should my laws defy-

CHORUS:

> Down among the dead men,
> Down among the dead men,
> Down, down, down, down,
> Down among the dead men
> let them lie.

After several verses of this, I mustered my court.
NEPTUNE: Where is my handsome young son, Polyphemus?
POLYPHEMUS: Here, your Majesty. (NEPTUNE pats him on head.)
NEPTUNE: Where are my Tritons?
(TRITONS line up before throne and emit a bloodcurdling blast on their property trumpets.)
Ha, ha. Such music doth enchant mine ear. Where are my sea urchins? (URCHINS approach throne, and, with knees knocking together, utter in weak, piping voices, a sage remark.)
URCHINS: Here we are, Your Majesty. (NEPTUNE gives them a clout on the ear.)
NEPTUNE: Where are my leeches?
DOCTOR AND ASSISTANT (stepping forward, deliver themselves of unbearable claptrap): We are your learned and bland Court Physicians; 'Tis by our great learning we hold our positions
NEPTUNE: (wrathfully): Avaunt, ye quacks and bloodletters, and quit me sight. (They quit, muttering in their beards.) Where are my barbers? (BARBERS trip mincingly up to throne, brandish their implements, and utter some unutterable balderdash.)
BARBERS: Here we are, ready and willing To give a shingle or shave for a shilling.
NEPTUNE: Where is the Queen's Handmaiden?
(MANICURIST kneels before QUEEN, who shoots out a huge false foot, studded with corns and bunions, to be pedicured.) Display not your charms to

the vulgar herd, madam. Wait until we reach the privacy of our coral caverns. (QUEEN, with coy look at NEPTUNE, withdraws her foot from sight.) Where are my policemen and bears?

POLICEMEN (brandishing truncheons): We are the ones who go out to catch 'em —

BEARS (growling): and we are the ones who duck 'em and splash 'em.

NEPTUNE: (chanting): Where is my stallion who rides through the foam, All sleek and shining by curry and comb?

(Alleged comic business by prancing SEA HORSE.) And where is my Executioner?

(EXECUTIONER brandishes huge axe, and takes position by block, endeavouring to assume a grim expression.)

NEPTUNE (continues): And, last but not least, where is my great Rhadamanthus, my old friend, Davy Jones?

DAVY JONES (steps forward, and with a magnificent gesture intones some intolerable tripe): Your majesty, the Court is here assembled.

NEPTUNE: (grandiloquently, if possible): Then, on with the ritual!

After this ridiculous rhetoric, the bears jumped into the pool, and the police dashed among the spectators to seize the first victim, who, already in a bathing suit, made a show of being unwilling. The doctors, barbers, executioner, and manicurist prepared their instruments. The horse created consternation by squatting on his hindquarters (clever business by the two electricians inside him). The Old Men of the Sea, the Mermaids, the Tritons, and other odds and ends ranged themselves alongside the pool.

The victim was dragged before the throne, where Davy Jones read out a preposterous charge. King Neptune pronounced sentence. The prisoner was manicured, examined by the doctors, lathered by barbers, executed by the executioner, and then tipped into the pool, where the bears ducked him.

After some fourteen victims had been ducked, the farce having lasted long enough, if not too long, the Court made a more or less graceful exit, by parading around on the forecastle head, to the tune of "The Neptune Song," and disappeared, as unobtrusively as possible, into the depths of the ship by the forward companionway to E Deck, while the orchestra played Verdi's Aida march. The ceremony had lasted an hour and a half. As all the passengers were to get Certificates of Crossing the Line, signed by the Captain, whether they had been ducked or not, most of them were satisfied to get the certificates without the ducking.

That evening there was a Neptune Dinner, with a specially printed menu card, offering such courses as sea serpent, flotsam and jetsam, grilled dolphins, walrus cutlets, sirloin of seahorse, roast pelicans, driftwood, beachcombers' salad, dandy funk, mermaids' whispers, hokey pokey, hard tack, cracker hash, and Adam's ale.

After that, there was a Neptune Dance, and by that time we were undoubtedly in the southern hemisphere. Next day we anchored in Emma Haven, the little port of Padang, approximately one degree south of the Equator, on the western side of the large island of Sumatra. Most of the passengers set off in tenders and ship's lifeboats for the shore and went on a train journey into the highlands to see a native village, an exhibition of native arts and crafts, and native dances. They returned to the ship seven hours later, after a hot and tiring day, but laden, as usual, with purchases.

From there we went on to Batavia in Java, where there were excursions to Borobadoer and Djockya — and then to Singapore, where we were again in the northern hemisphere. Almost everyone bought Malacca canes at Singapore, and also rattan basket chairs ' to use on deck. Most of our passengers visited Raffles Hotel, sampled the famous "million dollar" cocktail, and had rides in rickshaws.

Next we were bound for Manila, in the Philippine Islands, but a sort of mutinous situation was developing among the passengers. Thomas Cook & Son had regretfully announced that, owing to the civil war in China, it would not be possible for our tourists to visit Peking. The railway line was in the hands of bandits or rebels. Vigorously the malcontents among the passengers protested at this change in the advertised itinerary. They practically blamed Thomas Cook & Son for the civil war in China. It appeared from what they said that ninety per cent of our world trippers had joined the cruise solely for the purpose of visiting Peking.

Never before, or since, have I seen such arrogance and petulance of wealthy people, enraged at being frustrated. One elderly female plutocrat bailed me up on deck. "You knew very well," she said, "before we left New York, that we would not be going to Peking, but of course your lips were sealed."

The old buzzard! It was useless to argue with her, and impossible to mollify her. "I demand to be taken to Peking!" she said. She was one of many who had this idea in their heads, and I did not envy the Cruise Director's attempts to appease them. But Ross Skinner was a model of tact and patience.

On 18th March, we anchored off Manila breakwater. A tug circled the liner, with a band playing American airs. Doctors boarded the ship; but fifteen of our sulky passengers refused to be examined. This held everything up for an hour and a half, while the band on the tug continued playing a welcome. At last, the medical inspection was completed. We hove up the anchor and proceeded to berth at a wharf in the inner harbour. Here another band of fifty musicians stood on the pier, loudly playing "Marching Through Georgia," so that it was almost impossible for our seamen to hear the mooring orders.

However, we made fast, and our passengers streamed ashore, eager to set foot on American soil again. We remained there two days, while the tourists made excursions to the interior, by auto, and also by river canoe.

On 22nd March we arrived at Hong Kong, and remained there for four days. Our passengers bought a tremendous amount of curios, wearing apparel, and anything and everything else offered. Every cabin in the ship was now stacked to overflowing with all kinds of curios and junk. There were hundreds of canary birds whistling, and caged parrots screeching, on all the decks. Several of the passengers had tried to bring monkeys aboard at Singapore. They were annoyed at the Captain's order: No animals. Nothing could please them.

Our next port of call was Woosung, forty miles up the Yangtze Kiang, where the passengers disembarked into two steam tenders for a further passage of fifteen miles up the Wangpoo River, to Shanghai. Some stayed in Shanghai overnight, others returned to the ship and made a further excursion next day. It was interesting to see the look of relief on their faces as they stepped on board the *Franconia*, each one loaded down with parcels, and tired out. Following them came many crates and packing cases full of furniture, rugs, silks, Chinese idols, curios, and other junk, labelled with the names of the purchasers. Many of our passengers spent thousands of dollars each on purchases around the world. They could have bought the same things in New York, perhaps a little more expensively; but they couldn't resist a bargain.

On 31st March, we cleared out of the Yangtze Kiang, and set course for Dairen (Port Arthur). The cruise had now lasted two and a half months. There were still some grumblers because we were bypassing Peking; but the facts had to be faced, at last

On 1st April, we arrived at Dairen. The passengers went ashore for a day's sightseeing, shopping, and grumbling. Next day we went on to Chemulpo, from where the trippers had an excursion to Seoul, the capital of Korea. This was a fairly good substitute for Peking, and, after that, the Peking Agitation on board gradually subsided, and everyone was happy again.

We went to Japan, calling at Beppu, then through the beautiful Inland Sea to Kobe, and on to Yokohama. We remained in Japanese ports and waters for a fortnight, during which our passengers had excursions to Kyoto, Tokyo, and most of the other places of interest, and, as usual, returned laden with purchases.

On 29th April, we arrived at Honolulu, and from there went on to Hilo, for a trip to the volcanic craters.

On 6th May, we entered the Golden Gate of San Francisco. I had two pleasant surprises here. One was the arrival of two copies of *Ship Ahoy!*, thoughtfully sent on to me there by Birchalls. The other surprise was the arrival on board of my brother Jack. I had not seen him for fourteen years. He was doing well in the States, working for a firm of electrical engineers in Los Angeles. He had come up to San Francisco in his automobile to greet me. I found him almost completely Americanized, in dress and speech. Captain Melson allowed me liberal shore leave, and Jack showed me the sights of the city.

On 9th May, we anchored at San Pedro, the port for Los Angeles, and Jack was again waiting to show me the "sights" of the Movie Capital. When the time came at last for parting, Jack was upset, as I was also, but partings had been a routine of my existence for twenty-eight years of seafaring, and I had learned to bear them with equanimity.

The *Franconia* went on, and, on 19th May, anchored in Balboa Roads, at the entrance of the Panama Canal. The passage of the Canal was a memorable experience for everyone on board, as we rose through the locks to Gautum (freshwater) Lake and then descended to sea level again, on the Atlantic side.

Now we had circumnavigated the globe. We went on to Havana, where we arrived on 22nd May. A short way inside the harbour we made a "running moor" — that is, we let go the port anchor and paid out ninety fathoms of cable as the ship ran ahead; then we let go the starboard anchor, and hove the ship astern between the two, leaving us moored with forty-five fathoms on each.

Our passengers were now thoroughly satisfied with the entertainment and education they had experienced on the cruise.

The Cruise Director had been taking orders for Ship Ahoy! — an advance copy of which was on display in the Cruise Office — and had 200 orders in hand. Very satisfactory! On 25th May — the day before we were due in New York — everybody was busy packing and exchanging addresses and issuing invitations to each other to "be sure and call if you're ever out our way." (I wonder if such reunions ever materialize?)

On the forenoon of 26th May, we were steaming gaily up to Quarantine, with all our flags a-flying: the ship "dressed," rainbow fashion. At last we reached pier 56, and slid alongside the knuckle with the tide, then slewed her quietly into berth, and got the gangways out at 1.45. The pier was thronged with excited people, milling around in affectionate reunions, among all the trunks, boxes, and crates of curios.

A quantity of *Ship Ahoy!* had been delivered on board. I went on the dock and said goodbye to as many of our Cookites as possible, at the same time delivering the books to those, who had ordered them, during the delay while baggage was being cleared through the Customs.

By 4 p.m., the last of our passengers had left the dock. It remained only for Ross Skinner and his staff to heave a sigh of relief, and to clear up the paperwork of a highly successful World Cruise.

In four months and twelve days we had steamed 28,008 nautical miles; visited thirty ports; consumed 19,800 tons of fresh water, and 12,000 tons of oil fuel.

More Naval Training — Promoted to Com-mander, R.N.R. — A Christmas Cruise to the West Indies — Yuletide at Sea — Elaborate Festivities — Captain Santa Claus — A Treat for the Kiddies — Boar's Head and Plum Pudding — Keeping Watch Above and Below — The Unceasing Vigil of the Ship's People — Porto Rico in Sight — A Mishap Entering San Juan Harbour — Fast on a Sandbank — Getting Her Off.

RETURNED to Liverpool, in June, 1926, after an absence of six months, I had a week's leave on shore. Then May and I went together to stay at Devonport, where I was to do a requalifying course of training in the R.N.R. This course included gunnery, torpedoes, and anti-gas training.

The anti-gas course, held at the Royal Naval Barracks at Devonport, was, at times, amusing. From the moment the classes started, at 10 a.m. each day, until they finished at 3 p.m., we had to carry our gasmasks, and to put them on whenever we were ordered to do so. In the lecture room, while the instructor was droning on about the various kinds of poison gases, a Petty Officer outside, without warning, would hurl a stink bomb through a window into the room. The instructor would sing out, at the top of his voice, "GAS!" and we would have to get our masks out of their cases and pull them over our heads in two seconds, or less.

Over the top of the lecturer's platform was a large, printed notice:
THERE ARE TWO KINDS OF PEOPLE IN THE GAS SCHOOL — THE QUICK AND THE DEAD.

After doing this course, and requalifying in gunnery and torpedo — in all, a month's training — I was promoted to Commander, R.N.R., the highest rank at that time in that service. I was then forty-three years of age. While I was undergoing R.N.R. training at Devonport, I received a letter which, to some extent, settled an argument.

During the *Franconia*'s World Cruise, one of our lady passengers had asked me a poser: "Which are the 'Seven Seas' referred to by Kipling?" She had a volume of Kipling's verse, entitled The Seven Seas, and quoted from a poem in it:

> Far and Far our homes are set
> Round the Seven Seas;
> Woe for us if we forget,
> We who hold by these!
> Unto each his mother-beach,
> Bloom and bird and land-
> Masters of the Seven Seas,
> Oh, love and understand.

Much shipboard debate, and hurried research in the ship's library, had followed. One expert, after consulting an encyclopaedia, learnedly contended. "The term 'Seven Seas' is used in the Mercantile Marine to refer to the seas that wash the shores of Eastern Asia — namely, the Yellow Sea, Sea of Japan, Java Sea, Banda Sea, Flores Sea, Celebes Sea, and Molucca Sea."

Someone else, after studying an atlas, remarked, "Add the Sea of Okhotsk, Behring Sea, Sulu Sea, Arafura Sea, and Timor Sea — that makes twelve, not seven!"

Feeling that Kipling could not be limited even to those twelve seas, I also studied the atlas and compiled a list of all the seas in the world, in alphabetical order, beginning with the Adriatic Sea, and ending with the Zuider Zee. There were forty-nine of them — seven times seven, and I afterwards discovered a few more. Admirers of Kipling came to his defence by insisting that the poet must have referred, not to "seas," but to the seven oceans that wash the shores of the British Empire.

To check on this proposition, I proved, from the atlas, that there are not seven, but eight oceans, as follows: the North Atlantic Ocean, South Atlantic Ocean, Arctic Ocean, North Pacific Ocean, South Pacific Ocean, Antarctic Ocean, Indian Ocean, and Southern Ocean.

As this left the main problem unresolved, I decided to seek an answer from the fountainhead. Therefore, on returning to Liverpool, I wrote a letter addressed to Rudyard Kipling at his home address, as follows:

8th June 1926

Dear Sir,

I have just returned from a world cruise in the R.M.S. *Franconia* of the Cunard Line, during which we carried tourists to the places mentioned on the enclosed slip. During the cruise I held the position of Chief Officer, and every day was called upon to answer numerous questions, foolish and otherwise.

I thought that it might interest you to know that a very frequent question was, "What are the seven seas referred to in the title of Rudyard Kipling's volume of verse, The Seven Seas?"

Being a sailor of twenty-eight years' experience, I reckoned that I ought to know, so, with the aid of an atlas, I picked out all the oceans and seas of the world, as per enclosed list; but, as far as answering the question went, I am still in doubt. I have lately had a book printed, entitled *Ship Ahoy!*, in which I have attempted to answer, from a sailor's point of view, a lot of questions that are usually asked on board ship. If it runs to a second edition, I intend including this list in it, and would also like to be able to supply the answer to the question referring to the title of your poems.

Will you be kind enough to tell me? If you will accept a copy of my book, *Ship Ahoy!*, I shall be very pleased to send you one,

I am, Sir,

Yours faithfully,
J. G. P. BISSET,
Lieut.-Comdr, R.N.R.

To this, after a few days delay, I received the following reply, with the great poet's autograph signature:

Bateman's, Burwash,
Sussex, 11th June 1926
Dear Captain Bisset,
Very many thanks for your letter and the wonderful list of seas which you send with it. The expression "seven seas" is a very old one and means of course all the seas in the world. But the seven which I think about as the Seven Seas are the North and South Atlantic; North and South Pacific; Mediterranean; Indian Ocean; and Arctic and Antarctic Seas. It's not scientific, of course, but it will do for passengers.

I shall be very grateful indeed for a copy of Ship Ahoy!
Yours sincerely,
RUDYARD KIPLING.

The poet's letter left the confusion worse confounded. Apart from promoting me to Captain, and using the words "of course" twice, Kipling had given me a list of seven seas that added up to eight! Five of his seven seas are oceans, and of the other three he described two oceans as "seas."

After Kipling's death, the controversy boiled up several times, in the London Times and other newspapers, but, as far as I'm aware, I have the only authentic definition from the poet himself. The Concise Oxford Dictionary attempts to

R.M.S. Franconia early in her Cunard career. (Public Domain)

settle the argument by defining the Seven Seas as: "The Arctic, Antarctic, North and South Pacific, North and South Atlantic, and Indian Oceans." This definition omits the Southern Ocean (to the south of Australia). The only way to put an end to the argument is to assume that Kipling used the term "the Seven Seas" in a mystical sense, or with poetic licence, or for the sake of alliteration,' or because, as he stated in his letter to me, it is an old expression. Everyone can't be logical all the time.

Rejoining the *Franconia* as Chief Officer under Captain Melson, on 17th July 1926, at Liverpool, I made five voyages in her to New York on the normal passenger run. On the sixth voyage, we arrived in New York on 19th December 1926 and got her ready for service again as a cruise ship.

She was booked out for two cruises — the first, a short one of fourteen days to the Caribbean; and after that for a "Southern Hemisphere Around-the-World Cruise" — to last nearly six months.

The cruise to the Caribbean was to be a "Christmas Cruise," advertised also as a "Winter Cruise to the Sunshine."

On 20th December we left New York in a blizzard, with a full ship of 853 passengers, including many families with schoolchildren on vacation. There were not less than 150 children on board. One of the advertised features of the cruise was to be "Christmas at Sea."

Our first port of call was to be San Juan, on Porto Rico Island, the former Spanish possession ceded to the U.S.A. in 1898. The distance from New York to San Juan is 1400 miles. We cruised at a reduced speed of only 12 knots, so that our passengers could spend Christmas Day at sea, and arrive at San Juan on 26th December. Active preparations were being made for Christmas Day celebrations in grand style. Everything had been planned for weeks beforehand. The seafarer, whether in a windjammer, a rusty old tramp, a warship, or a lordly liner, can be depended upon to celebrate Christmas to the best of his ability; but always with the feeling that he is making the best of a bad job, for his thoughts are far away, and he knows that "there's no place like home" — at Christmas time.

Even in windjammers, there was plum duff and an extra tot of grog for all hands, and thoughts of home. But in a cruise liner crowded with holidaymakers and a large number of children, with everything organized, at lavish expense, on a bright, clear, sunny day in tropical waters, Christmas is "really something."

The organized programme began at 11 a.m., with a Church Service held in the Main Lounge, which had been specially decor-ated during the night and early morning hours. It was impossible to provide seating for all the passengers and crew. An overflow attendance thronged the decks, looking in through the wide open windows. The sea fortunately was smooth, with only a slight ocean swell; the sun was shining brightly, and everybody happy and excited.

At eleven o'clock, the Captain and the officers (except those on watch), resplendent in whites and gold braid, filed in, and the service began. The Captain conducted the service, and the Purser read the lessons. After the service, the choir sang carols. The Captain and the officers and other ship's people filed out of the lounge for the change of the watch at noon.

Lunch was served at one o'clock. Then the dining room was cleared, and a big Christmas tree erected there for the children's party at three. All the children thronged in. The stewards had charge of the party, and made it go with a swing. The tables were loaded with good things to eat and drink. When these were demolished, there were romping games to be played.

In the middle of it all, Santa Claus arrived and presented each child with a stunning gift from the tree. It had been intended that the Chief Steward should be Santa Claus; but Captain Melson, who liked to do everything himself, decided to play that role, and played it well. There was no reason why he should not do so; but, as he made his exit, dozens of the adult passengers crowded around him on deck to take his picture in his Father Christmas rigout and beard. At this, he suddenly felt embarrassed, and disappeared into his quarters to resume his rightful role as Master, resplendent in whites, gold braid, and brass hat.

The children's party was over at five o'clock, and preparations began for Christmas dinner. At 8 p.m. the bugles sounded, and the two dining rooms were quickly filled. The orchestra played "The March of the Gladiators," the kitchen doors were thrown open, and a file of cooks in their white uniforms and tall white caps marched in, each bearing a dish: There were roast turkeys, rounds of beef, boars' heads, salmon, and the usual variety of jellies, blancmanges, fruit, and mince pies; and, last of all, two chefs bearing aloft an enormous plum pudding ablaze with brandy flames.

Streamers were flung about in such profusion that the table wards could scarcely fight their way through the entanglements. Above the din of rattles and squeakers, the popping of champagne corks indicated that the wine stewards were being kept hard at work. Afterwards the orchestra and the passengers moved out to the lounge, where dancing went on till long after midnight: everyone delighted and happy.

Having cleared up the "wreck" — as they termed it — in the dining rooms, the Senior Stewards sat down to their Christmas dinner, waited on by the Junior Stewards. An hour later the Juniors and theirs, waited on by the Seniors.

Likewise the seamen and the engineers, in their messrooms, had their Christmas dinners, in rotation before and after the 8 p.m. change of the watch. Towards midnight, all except the officers on watch, and those standing by for the change of the watch at midnight, were enjoying a slap-up Christmas spree with jolly singsongs. The responsibility of watchkeeping makes it impossible for the crews of vessels at sea to enjoy the Christmas Spirit too much! No officer would dare to take a drink, even a wee drop, during two hours or more before he goes on watch, especially on the bridge. His mind must be clear, his vision sharp, his wits unmuddled. Too much may depend at any moment on his correct reactions to an emergency.

So, throughout the festivities, the work of running the ship went on undisturbed. The officers and quartermasters on the bridge kept their vigil; bells were struck at each half-hour, repeated from the crow's nest, with the cry of "A-a-all's well and lights burning brightly" from the lookout men; the Captain occasionally excused himself from the company of the revellers below, and went onto the bridge, to see for himself that all was indeed well: he was pleased that his passengers were enjoying themselves, but even more pleased, in his heart, to be away from them, in that part of the ship which was specially his. A Captain can never really relax at sea. The safety of his vessel is always uppermost in his thoughts: his is the ultimate responsibility, ingrained in him in years of training for command.

Down below in the engine rooms and boiler rooms, the engineers, greasers, and firemen were calmly and stolidly going about their duties among a maze of intricate, thudding machinery. It was Christmas up above; but, down there in the heat and glare, men's thoughts were on pressure gauges, revolutions per minute, and the need for instantaneous reaction to a signal that could at any moment come with a clang of the telegraph — to reduce speed, stop, or go astern — perhaps to avert a collision or other disaster.

Only when their watch ended could these men relax a little and think about Christmas; but their next watch would come, and they would be back to the old grind again. They did not complain of that and had no wish to change their way of life. It was their choice, and they liked it. Men who "go down to the sea in ships and do business in the great waters" grow to love their ships and engines and have a fine sense of achievement in getting the best out of them in all conditions.

Whether they belong to the Deck Department, the Engine Department, or the Catering Department, all the ship's people are ready and willing to "do their bit" in fair weather or foul, in war or peace, winter or summer, day or night, come Christmas or any other season. A ship at sea is a living thing, and she imperiously demands attention at all times: she must not be neglected even for an instant: everyone who belongs to her is her servant, her slave, with a task and a responsibility.

My watch on the bridge, from 4 a.m. to 8 a.m., and from 4 p.m. to 8 p.m., allowed me to join conveniently in the festivities. I was able to sit undisturbed at the Christmas dinner, and afterwards to join in the dancing until midnight, when I turned in for a few hours' shuteye.

I was called with a cup of tea at 3.45 a.m. When I went on the bridge, the island of Porto Rico was only twenty miles to the southward. We were steaming at five knots, to arrive off the entrance to San Juan harbour at 8 a.m. Presently, in the glowing tropical dawn, the lookout man sang out "L-a-and Ho!" and we sighted the shore ahead, a dim blue line on the horizon, which gradually took clearer shape.

A few minutes before the change of the watch at 8 a.m., I rang the engines to stop, and we lay at rest in the gentle swell off the entrance, as a pilot boat came out to meet us.

The Captain came on the bridge, and, with the pilot on board, all officers and seamen were ordered to stations for entering port: my station being, as usual, in charge of anchors and mooring lines at the bow.

With a leadsman in the chains, chanting the soundings, the ship was steered into the entrance. The *Franconia* was the largest vessel that had entered San Juan harbour until that time. The approach is difficult. Captain Melson was attending to everything that required his attention, but in the circumstances could only be guided by the pilot's advice. It appeared that the pilot, a Latin American, may have had a hangover from his Christmas celebrations.

Whatever the reason, he failed to bring us to our anchorage. He piled the ship up on a sandbank. I felt her bows gliding into the sand, and sticking there, as the Captain telegraphed and sang out, "LET GO BOTH ANCHORS" and rang the engines to **STOP** and **FULL ASTERN**.

The anchors plunged to the bottom, but the ship had already lost way and was fast in the sandbank. It was impossible to use the anchors for heaving her astern. Their cables were vertical. Despite the churning of the propellers at full astern, with the rudder alternately a-port and a-starboard, she refused to back off the bank.

Soundings inside forward and amidships showed that her hull was undamaged: she was not leaking; but she was fast in gluey mud and sand, into which she had grounded deeply. Luckily there were no rocks or coral in the sandbank. The ship was on an even keel; but not so the pilot, as the Captain in no uncertain terms expressed opinions of his ability and ancestry.

We had grounded not far from our intended anchorage. Launches were already approaching, to take the tourists ashore. Captain Melson allowed the passengers to disembark there and then. The arrangements for sightseeing ashore could proceed normally. He hoped to be able to refloat the ship quickly, so that the tour to other ports in the West Indies could continue, as scheduled, next day.

A nice mishap to occur on Boxing Day, after our Christmas festivities! The officers and seamen in the Deck Department now had to turn to for long hours of work, trying to get her off the bank before she settled too deeply into it.

Two tugs came out, made their hawsers fast to the bitts at the stern, and took the strain. She refused to budge. With the aid of the tugs, we laid out both anchors with heavy wire cables astern, then hove on them while at the same time the tugs strained to tow her off, and the ship's propellers revolved at full speed astern.

Among the dangerous maze of taut wires and cables that stretched across the afterdeck, half deafened by the rattle and clatter of winches and capstans, blinded by clouds of escaping steam and tugboats' grimy smoke, harassed and anxious for the safety of his ship, with the pitiless tropic sun beating down on his bald head, stood the Captain, directing operations.

At the critical moment, unobserved by the sweating, toiling sailors who would have chased her unceremoniously from that dangerous spot, a dainty, little old lady, clutching a small camera, crept up to the Captain's side. "Captain, dear," she said, "would you be so kind as to dress up as Santa Claus again, so that I may take your photograph?"

Unable to think of an appropriate polite comment, the Captain beckoned to two sailors, and said brusquely, "Escort this lady to a place of safety!"

They took her by the arms and urgently hustled her out of the danger zone. She never got her picture of Santa Claus.

Despite all our efforts the ship remained fast aground. All day, and until late at night, we laboured to get her off. We were almost dropping from lack of sleep, but could not relax the efforts, renewed at intervals, to prevent her from settling more deeply into the mud. The supreme effort came at high tide, when everything was kept going at full pressure, for half an hour, to get her off the bank — without success!

The Captain now decided to lighten the ship by discharging the fresh water and oil fuel from her double bottom tanks. This was done but had little effect at low and half tide. It seemed, however, that she had moved a little; perhaps only a few feet, but every inch was something gained.

Next afternoon, on the full tide, with the tug hawsers and the anchor cables strained to their utmost, and the twin propellers racing madly astern, she moved! Almost imperceptibly at first, and then she went with a run and slid off the bank.

We anchored in deep water. The carpenter's soundings reported that there were no leaks in her bottom. Now it was necessary to refill the freshwater tanks, and also to take in oil fuel from tankers that had been standing by to come alongside. The wireless had been running hot with a sequence of signals to and from New York. After conferring with the cruise organizers, the owners decided to abandon the remainder of the cruise, and to recall the ship to New York.

This was announced by the Cruise Director to the passengers. Fifty per cent of their passage — money would be refunded. That was fair enough, in fact handsome. They had had Christmas at sea and had visited at least one port in the West Indies. By the time we got back to New York, the cruise would have lasted ten days, instead of fourteen. Everyone was satisfied.

We were back at New York on New Year's Day, 1927. The *Franconia* was put into dry dock for examination, but no damage had occurred. Her bottom was given a coat of paint, and she was floated out into the river, to be berthed and got ready for the "Southern Hemisphere Around-the-World Cruise," scheduled to begin ten days later.

19

Southern Hemisphere Cruise — Around World in 140 Days — Playboys and Girls in Luxury — Thirty-two Ports in Many Lands and Climes — South Sea Isles — New Zealand and Australia — My Brother Douglas at Sydney — A Stowaway's Mistake — New Guinea, Indonesia, and Ceylon — East African Ports — South Africa — A Raft For Tristan da Cunha — We Pass "The Lonely Island" — South American Ports — Martinique — Back to York

AT five minutes before midnight, on 12th January, 1927, *Franconia* left her berth in New York, to begin her second cruise around the world. So, with five minutes to spare, she avoided "sailing" on the thirteenth of the month! Old superstitions die " hard. We had 254 passengers on board, and were to pick up another 50 in Jamaica, and 26 in California — a total of 330, and roost of them in the "million dollar" class, or near it.

The night was bitterly cold, the temperature 16 degrees below freezing point, the water in the dock covered with ice. At the orders from the bridge, "Let go moorings," down dropped our two remaining 8-inch manila hauling lines onto the ice; a few shivering men of the shore gang threw them off the posts, and we backed into the river.

A puffing tug came under the port bow, and, putting her blunt, nose against us, pushed us around, headed downriver. This done, a short blast from our steam whistle dismissed Mister Tug, and we were well under way down harbour at five minutes after twelve on the thirteenth. The river was full of ice. From my station at the bows, I could hear it cracking away under our stern with dull metallic thuds.

Captain Melson was in command; the Staff Captain was W. A. Hawkes, R.D., R.N.R.; and I was Chief Officer, as formerly.

Thomas Cook & Son had organized the cruise. The Cruise Director, Ross Skinner (who, as some people said, had begun his career as a World Cruise Director with Noah in the Ark), had a staff of fourteen assistants on board, in addition to two lecturers, two chaplains, a dentist, a bookseller, a photographer, a cineroatograph[1] operator, and male and female hairdressers — all on Cook's staff.

Our passengers were mainly elderly people — retired businessmen, professors, doctors — some of them of world fame — and their wives, with a few younger dependants. Three of our passengers were booked only as far as our first port of call, Kingston, Jamaica. They were smart looking men, in fact a gang of cardsharpers. On the short passage of four days to Kingston, they relieved one of our millionaires' of 2400 dollars and another of 600 dollars. But they were not quite clever enough. The victims complained to Ross Skinner, who, by radio inquiries to New York, established the gang's identity. He gave the sharpers an alternative, too: refund the money they had "won" or to be arrested by the Captain's orders and to be handed over to the police at Kingston. They refunded the money and left the ship at Kingston.

Our passengers went ashore for a day's motor touring in Jamaica. Here fifty British passengers joined the ship. They had come out from England in the Elder Fyffe liner *Cavena* — one of the stylish so called "banana boats" — which have luxurious first-class passenger accommodation and so had avoided New York's icy weather.

From Jamaica we went on southwards across the Caribbean Sea, passed through the Panama Canal, and called at San Pedro, the port of Los Angeles, to pick up our twenty-six Californian and other Western American passengers. Here I again saw my brother Jack, and spent a day with him ashore.

We cleared out of San Pedro on 28th June, and the cruise proper had begun, as we set course for Honolulu.

The special advertised attraction of this cruise was its itinerary to many ports of call in the southern hemisphere which, for most Europeans and North Americans, are "down under" and far away and strange. Eighty of our passengers were old friends, who had been with us on the northern hemisphere cruise a year previously.

Departing from Honolulu on 4th February, we headed south- wards for the Samoan Islands. Now we would be entering the southern hemisphere and were due to "Cross the Line" on 8th February. Ever since leaving San Pedro, I had been busy rehearsing the "Neptune Show". On this occasion, I was not only to be King Neptune, but producer of the show as well. Fortunately I was well experienced, from the previous year, and everything went well, with vim, vigour and gusto. Ross Skinner declared that it was the most spectacular Neptune Pageant he had ever seen; and that was high praise.

Our voyage continued, with many varied scenes and experiences of many lands and peoples, on the scheduled route, as follows:

APIA, Samoa: (11th Feb.): In a lumpy N.W. swell off the open roadstead, we anchored at a safe distance from the reef and sent 200 passengers ashore in motorboats to land through surf on the beach, most of them getting wet. They saw native dances, bought curios, and visited R. L. Stevenson's tomb.

SUVA, Fiji: (14th Feb.): Berthed at the Government wharf in comfort. All passengers ashore to buy curios and see a native war dance.

AUCKLAND, New Zealand: (18th-21st Feb.): Berthed at Queen's Wharf. 180 of our passengers went in automobiles on overland tour, via Rotorua, to rejoin the ship at Wellington.

WELLINGTON, New Zealand: (23rd Feb.): Everyone well pleased with the sights of New Zealand. The tourists described Rotorua as "a mixture of steam, stinks, and scenery, all good.."

MILFORD SOUND, New Zealand (25th Feb.): We steamed four miles into the Sound, a scene of stupendous grandeur, and afterwards entered the adjoining Bligh Sound and George Sound, similarly grand. A party of our English passengers played deck tennis throughout the passage of the Sounds — not in the slightest interested in the wonderful views.

HOBART, Tasmania: (28th Feb.): Anchored in the Derwent, and our passengers went for a trip to the old convict settlement at Port Arthur, finding it "morbid." Thirty-five of them left the ship for overland tours of Tasmania, Victoria, and New South Wales, to rejoin the ship at Sydney. We embarked a Tasmanian Devil for the New York Zoo.

MELBOURNE, Victoria: (2nd-3rd March): Berthed at Prince's Pier. Passengers attended an exhibition of boomerang throwing at the Melbourne Cricket Ground, and also Nellie Melba's "farewell concert" in her hometown, and the Flemington races. A Melbourne newspaper, The Morning Post, reported: "The tourists wear clothes of a cut and style not usually seen here outside of the movies... Their blasé outlook upon the affairs of the world coincides with their general appearance of contentment and self-importance."

SYDNEY, New South Wales: (5th-8th March): Berthed at Circular Quay, in the world's best harbour. Our passengers went for drives around the city, and to the Blue Mountains and Jenolan Caves. For me, the highlight of the visit was a reunion with my brother Douglas, who strolled on board unconcernedly soon after we berthed. I had not seen him for seven years, since he had emigrated to Australia in 1920, after being demobilized from the Royal Marine Light Infantry. He liked Australia, was married (with two children), and was doing well as Chief Accountant in a big department store. I found him, as ever, quiet and undemonstrative. I visited him and his wife, Gwen, at their home at Lindfield. At that time the Sydney Harbour Bridge was not built, and we crossed the harbour by ferry. We went for a Sunday picnic to Manly and enjoyed a dip in the surf — a grand experience! I made up my mind that, when I retired from the sea, Sydney would be the place for me. After leaving Sydney, we found a stowaway on board. His excuse was that he wanted to cross the harbour and had thought that the *Franconia* was a ferry!

PORT MORESBY, Papua: (13th March): Anchored one mile from the pier, and took our passengers ashore in lifeboats, to visit the native village of Hanaubada, and to see a native' war dance at the cricket ground. Despite the steamy heat, the squalor of the native village, and the dinginess of the white town (as it was then), our passengers considered that Port Moresby was one of the most interesting places that we had visited — probably because there were so many natives on view, naked, or nearly so!

BATAVIA, Java: (20th-21st March): Berthed at Tandjong Priok. Passengers visited Batavia, Buitenzorg, and Bandoeng. Saw native dances and bought many curios.

SINGAPORE: (23rd-24th March): Passengers visited a rubber factory, a Chinese temple, and Raffles Hotel; rode in rickshaws and bought curios.

COLOMBO, Ceylon: (28th-30th March): Visits ashore to Galle Face, Mount Lavinia, Kandy, and Anuradhapura. Many curios brought aboard, here, as at all other ports.

MOMBASA, East Africa: (6th April): Native dances at the sports ground.

ZANZIBAR, East Africa: (7th April): Visit to Bubububu and the Sultan's Palace.

DAR-ES-SALAAM, East Africa: (8th April): Visits to the bazaars, and rickshaw rides.

DELAGOA BAY, Mozambique: (12th-13th April): Taken by a pilot up the difficult channel to Louren o Marques port, where 105 of our passengers boarded a comfortable modern train for a railroad trip through the Big Game Reserve (Kruger National Park), to rejoin the ship at Durban.

DURBAN, South Africa: (14th-20th April): Most of our passengers went from here on a twelve days' inland tour, to visit Victoria Falls, Kimberley, and Johannesburg, and to rejoin the ship at Cape Town. At this port I bought materials, and began construction of a raft, intended to deliver gifts to the inhabitants of Tristan da Cunha, the "lonely island" in the South Atlantic.

PORT ELIZABETH, South Africa: (22nd April): I had been here (in Algoa Bay) twenty-seven years previously, as a boy in the barque County of Pembroke, and remembered the open bay, exposed to S.E. swell and seas, only too well. Our few remaining passengers went ashore to see a snake farm. Travel broadens the mind.

CAPE TOWN, South Africa: (24th-29th April): Excursions ashore to Table Mountain, the Cape of Good Hope, and Stellenbosch. My preoccupation was with my Tristan da Cunha raft, as I may call it, since it was built to my design by the carpenter and joiners. We put it overside in Table Bay for a trial, and it floated with good stability.

The Island of Tristan da Cunha was not scheduled for a call on the *Franconia*'s cruise, but, as we would pass close to it on our passage across the South Atlantic from Cape Town to Buenos Aires, our passengers had requested the Captain to call there, and he had agreed to do so, if the weather permitted.

It was a lady passenger who had originated this idea, soon after we had left Sydney. She had been studying maps and reading books in the ship's library. Her heart was full of sympathy for the unfortunate inhabitants of Tristan da Cunha, the loneliest place in the world. Soon she had persuaded everybody in the ship that it would be our duty to call there, to present the inhabitants with gifts.

Studying the available information, we ascertained that Tristan da Cunha is 1400 miles from Cape Town, and 2500 miles from Buenos Aires. We would have to make a very slight detour from our course to call there.

During the war between Britain and the U.S.A., 1812-15, American privateers used Tristan da Cunha as a base from which to raid British shipping, even into the bays of South Africa. To remedy this state of affairs, the British Government, in 1816, annexed Tristan da Cunha, and stationed a garrison there for several years. With the opening of the Suez Canal in 1869, and the increasing disuse of the Cape of Good Hope route for sailing vessels to India, China, and Australia, the "lonely island" lost its former strategic importance.

In 1927, as far as we could ascertain, there were only a· few dozen people there, chiefly descendants of Dutch and British settlers from South Africa, who preferred isolation. They lived by fishing and agriculture. As there was very little direct trade between Argentina and Cape Town, few steamers ever passed that way. The people were lucky if a vessel called once in two years.

Captain Melson's intention was to anchor the *Franconia* off the island, and put my raft overboard, with provisions and gifts. The inhabitants, skilful boatmen, would be able to tow the raft ashore. That raft, if I may say so, was a work of art. Its overall length was twelve feet long by nine feet wide. The scantlings were of three-inch by three-inch timber, to which were lashed for buoyancy two forty-four gallon casks, one at each end, and four forty-gallon drums, two at each side.

Mortised into one another and into the scantlings were four stout side planks of twelve-inch by three-inch timber, stood on edge. This left an opening in the centre, seven feet long by five feet wide and twelve inches deep. The opening was decked in underneath with planks, twelve inches by three inches by five feet, caulked and pitched.

To fit into that opening, we had built a watertight wooden box, of tongue-and-grooved pine, three feet high, stiffened with corner pieces inside. The box was painted, then covered with canvas, tacked and tarred twice, then fitted into the raft, caulked around the sides and secured with scantlings and buckram. A lid was made to be fitted to the box, secured and tarred, and lashings placed around the whole, so that, if the raft capsized, the box would not fall out. The final touch was a flagstaff at each of the four corners, to carry two British and two American flags.

Everything was going according to plan. When we arrived at Cape Town, Thomas Cook & Son informed the newspapers of the *Franconia*'s intended call at Tristan da Cunha (weather permitting) and suggested that anyone who wished to send gifts or comforts to the islanders should address parcels to Captain Melson on board.

The result was overwhelming. Hundreds of parcels arrived, including fishhooks, rattraps, flannel, tobacco, groceries, medicines, gardening tools, soap, candy and dried fruits, books and magazines, toys, sporting gear, mouth organs, boots and shoes, clothing of all sorts — and even some solid old pieces of Dutch furniture — obviously too much to go into the box on my raft! However, we took it all on. If the weather were calm, it might have been possible to deliver it all into the islanders' boats alongside.

The strangest gift was a basket of nonvenomous snakes! Someone, hearing that the islanders were troubled by a plague of rats, decided that snakes would keep the rats down: and this view had support from scientists in Cape Town, so we took the basket of snakes also. We carried four bags of mail for the islanders, including letters that had been waiting at Cape Town for many months for an opportunity of a mail delivery.

When we cleared out of Cape Town on 29th April, and headed westwards into the Atlantic, an exhibition of all the gifts for the Lonely Islanders was held in the lounge, and attracted much admiration. It was my responsibility to fit as much of it as possible into the box on my raft. Aided by some of the lady passengers, I got a surprising quantity into the box. The leftover articles, including the snakes, would have to take their chance.

Next day the barometer began to fall, a strong N.W. gale blew up, the sea rose rapidly, with frequent heavy squalls, and the ship was labouring into the teeth of the Roaring Forties — a full gale.

On 1st May, the gale reached hurricane force. The wind shifted to due west, and at 2 a.m. a particularly heavy sea struck on the starboard side. It smashed eight windows on B Deck, five on C Deck, carried our accommodation ladder clean away, and broke a chunk out of the teakwood rail.

We had expected to reach Tristan da Cunha in the forenoon of Tuesday, 3rd May; but, because of the head-on weather, the ship's speed had been reduced.

Captain Melson now calculated that we would be abeam of the island at 9.30 p.m. on that day. He added, "After dark, I wouldn't go within a hundred miles of it!" and informed the Cruise Director accordingly.

If we hung about, waiting for daylight on Wednesday, in order to stand in towards the island and launch the raft, that would mean a late arrival at Montevideo, and curtailment of our stay at that port, in order to keep up with the tour programme at Buenos Aires.

The gale had abated slightly, but big seas were still running. The Cruise Director convened a general meeting of passengers in the main lounge, to take a show of hands on whether they wished the call at Tristan to be abandoned.

Having explained the position, he found himself on a hornet's nest The working party of the Tristan fund and all their friends, plus the folks who didn't care a damn for the bright lights of Buenos Aires — "the Paris of the South" — and wanted to see something unusual and primitive, were about equally matched by the tougher guys and dolls who wanted to have a whale of a time in the Big City.

Emotional speeches were made on both sides. Several shows of hands produced an inconclusive result. The question was finally settled by the intervention of a cattle rancher from Texas, who was also an oil millionaire. He had spoken scarcely a word throughout the entire voyage. Now he rose to his full height of six feet six inches, and bellowed, "To hell with the Lonely Island!"

There was nothing more said. The Captain shaped course for Montevideo.

Our basket of snakes was thrown overboard. The raft and all its contents, and the surplus gifts, were stowed on the 'tween deck. We eventually took them on to Liverpool, where the box was opened for Customs inspection, all perishable goods removed, and the others repacked. It lay in storage at Liverpool for three years, until an opportunity came, and it was at last delivered to its destination.

After this our cruise continued:

MONTEVIDEO, Uruguay: (9th May): Passengers ashore for a drive, and lunch of roast partridge.

BUENOS AIRES, Argentina: (10th-12th May): Everyone pleased with the gay nightlife.

SANTOS, Brazil: (15th May): Train excursion' to Sao Paulo, in the mountains, 2400 feet above sea level. Visit to a snake farm (where antivenom for snakebite is obtained).

RIO DE JANEIRO, Brazil: (16th-19th May): Second-best harbour in the world, but surrounding scenery much more picturesque than Sydney. Excursions to summit of Corcorada Peak by funicular railway, and to Sugarloaf Rock by aerial cable car. Gambling at Casino de Copacabana. Passengers all declared Rio the most beautiful city that we had visited.

MARTINIQUE, Leeward Islands, Antilles: (28th May): Anchored at Fort de France, landed passengers for a drive, and picked them up same afternoon at Saint Pierre.

NEW YORK, U.S.A.: (2nd June): Back in civilization! And everyone talking of Lindbergh's flight across the Atlantic, from New York to Paris non-stop — a portent of air transits of ocean distances, which might make sea travel obsolete. Landed our passengers, their trunks and crates of curios; and dozens of cages of parrots — and the Tasmanian Devil — all in good condition.

Summary of the cruise: Total distance steamed, 35,467 miles; oil fuel consumed, 14,000 tons; fresh water consumed, 20,000 tons; bar sales, total £7250.

CHAPTER ENDNOTES

(1) A cinematograph was an early motion picture device that combined a camera, film processing, and projection. The term was used for cameras, projectors, and even complete systems that could print film

*I Turn Down a Shore Job — Appointed Staff Captain in the "Berengaria"
— "Berry Pie" — Senior Training in the R.N.R. — H.M.S. "Victory" —
The Competition of "Big" Ships — "Bremen" Takes the Blue Riband —
Mammoth Liners on the Stocks — I Become a Cunard Captain — My
First Voyage in Command — "Tiny" Ford and Harry Grattidge — The
"Captain's Tiger" — Some Strange Requests — A Christening at Sea —
Captain Rostron Retires — A Yacht on Deck — My Service in the
"Aquitania" — "World's Champion Stowaway."*

WHILE I had been away from home for seven months, "cruising" in the *Franconia*, May had gone, at my suggestion, to Switzerland, to enjoy also a change of scenery and climate. She was waiting for me at Liverpool when the *Franconia* returned there on 13th June 1927. I was paid off, and due for a month's shore leave, but fate intervened.

The Marine Superintendent of the Cunard Line, Captain Luke Ward, invited me into his office for a chat, and then popped a surprise on me. He offered me a shore· job, as Cunard Wharfinger at Liverpool! If I accepted it, there would be no more going to sea for a long time, perhaps forever. I would be able to make a home in Liverpool and would have a responsible and well paid position in charge of all Cunard wharfage in the Mersey.

"May I have time to think about it?" I asked.

"Certainly; let me know tomorrow," said the M.S. "The present Wharfinger is due to retire in a year's time. You would be his assistant for that time, to learn the ropes, and then take over in full charge."

The only difficulty that I could foresee was that, by taking this shore job, I would miss promotion to Captain in the Cunard service, which would be within my reach after a few more years at sea. I went home and told my wife about the offer. I gave her a glowing account of what it would mean: home life and no more going to sea.

She asked me a great many questions. Then she announced, "If you take my advice, you'll refuse the job! You are cut out for a sailor, and you won't really enjoy spending the rest of your life stuck on a dock at Liverpool!"

Not entirely convinced, I went down to the docks next morning and looked the job over. It was raining. The wharf sheds were cold and draughty. There was mud underfoot. I looked inside the Wharfinger's Office. It was a dim, dirty, smelly caboose, reeking of stale tobacco smoke. Suddenly I had a vision of world cruising and sunny skies, the clean orderliness of shipboard life, music, good food, gaiety and the ever changing scenes of voyaging, and the old allure of the open ocean, in fair weather or foul: never monotonous. I went to Captain Ward's office and told him of my decision. I

Thanked him for his offer and declined the job.

He smiled and sprang another surprise. "Very well then, you prefer going to sea?"

"That's it," I said.

"Then here's another offer. Staff Captain Edkins, of the *Berengaria* is due for shore leave. Join her the day after tomorrow, as Acting Staff Captain under Captain Rostron."

Staff Captain of Cunard's biggest liner! I was thunderstruck but managed to collect my wits. "Thanks for the opportunity, Captain," I said. "I'll take the position and do my best "

"It means," he said, "that you'll have to forgo your shore leave for the time being. Further, you'll be Staff Captain for only one voyage to New York, and then you'll have to step back to Chief Officer of the *Berengaria* when Edkins returns to duty."

"That will suit me," I told him. I was thinking that an appointment as Chief Officer in the *Berengaria* would be well worth for- going shore leave. "I'll go down to join her at Southampton tomorrow."

"Then, that's that," he said, and shook hands with me cordially. "You've earned it!"

That evening, my wife and I dined out and went to a theatre to celebrate my escape from a shore job — thanks to her common sense and good advice. Next morning I took train to Southampton. I have never ceased to admire the unselfishness of her advice to me at that critical moment in my career. My old friend, superior, and shipmate, Captain Sir Arthur Rostron, now Commodore of the Cunard Line, welcomed me on board the gigantic *Berengaria* at Southampton. "Hello, Staff Captain Bisset," he said with a grin. "Here we are again!"

Captain! Well, it was only temporary. I would have to get an extra ring sewn on my sleeve, if only for one voyage. The *S.S. Berengaria* (formerly the German *Imperator*) was a vessel of 52,000 tons, with four propellers and an average speed of 22 knots. Designed before the war as a coal burner, she had been converted to oil fuel after she had been handed over to Britain in part-payment of war reparations. In effect, she was the compensation to the Cunard Line for the loss of the Lusitania. She had three funnels, a straight stem, a cutaway stern, eight

Former German ship Imperator given to England after WW1 converted to oil and named R.M.S. Berengaria (US Navy Archives, Public Domain)

decks, a high midships superstructure, flush foredeck and a slightly raised poopdeck. She was 909 feet long and 98 feet beam, with powerful turbine engines.

Originally, she had accommodation for 4000 passengers, including 2000 emigrants deep down below. But, when the emigrant trade to the U.S.A. stopped in 1921, the so called "steerage" accommodation had been remodelled to cabin accommodation. She could then carry 2723 passengers and had a crew of 1053-making a total of 3776 souls when she was a full ship, as she usually was, for she was a favourite with Atlantic travellers. In every way she was a well-built, well found "gigantic" steamer, with excellent seagoing qualities and comfortable accommodation. Her decorations and furnishings were of a somewhat heavy Teutonic style, but solid and good.

The main lounge on the promenade deck was the biggest public room in any vessel of that time. The impression of great size was accentuated by the fact that the high deckhead, containing a very large skylight, was supported by cantilever girders, which did away with all supporting pillars and stanchions inside.

When the *Berengaria* was in port, visitors were allowed on board for a small fee, which went to local hospitals. Stewards were told off to take the visitors around in gangs of about twenty. On my own first exploration of the ship at Southampton, I happened to be in the main lounge when one of these gangs came through, all starry eyed at the scenes of splendour. The steward in charge stopped them in the centre of the lounge and announced, "'Ere y'are, ladies and gents, the biggest public room in any ship afloat — and you will notice that the roof is entirely supported by NO pillars!"

My work as Acting Staff Captain was not concerned with navigation, but with control of the staff, discipline, boat and fire drills, bulkhead door drills, and assisting the Captain generally. I had to act instead of the Captain in the daily inspection of every part of the ship, to ensure that she was spick and span and shipshape, and to listen to any complaints from passengers or crew. This procedure occupied two or three hours every morning and required a promenade of several miles fore and aft along all decks and alleyways, during which I inspected all the compartments, and received reports on every detail of administration, referring anything of importance to the Captain for decision.

On my first inspection, going along one of the decks deep in the bowels of the ship, I ran my finger along the top of a crossbeam overhead, and found the beam covered in dust I reminded the steward in that section that it was his duty to clean everything, top and bottom. When he wasn't looking, I took a penny from my pocket and placed it on top of one of the beams in his section. If it was still there next morning, that would indicate that he was dodging work.

When I came around next morning, and put my hand up to find the penny, there were two halfpennies there. After that I took more direct methods of discipline and got along much better.

If I had any conceit as a temporary Staff Captain, it was taken out of me on the first day when the passengers came aboard. Feeling somewhat self-conscious with the four rings on my sleeve, I was standing on deck near the head of the gangway watching the passengers arrive and doing my best to look serene and resplendent as the Captain's deputy and second-in-command of this great and stylish vessel.

I was aloof but observant, I thought. A young lady who had just come on board bustled up to me aggressively. "Say," she asked, "are you the Deck

Stooard?" With what was left of my self-esteem, I had to explain gently that I was not.

After one voyage, Staff Captain Edkins took over my job, and I stepped back to Chief Officer, taking the place of the former Chief Officer (Kenyon) who was transferred to another ship. As Chief Officer in the *Berengaria*, I now stood watches on the bridge of a liner considerably bigger than any other vessel in which I had served. She was one of the three biggest liners then afloat — the other two being her sisters *Majestic* (ex-*Bismarck*), and *Leviathan* (ex- *Vaterland*); the next biggest after these three being our Aquitania — all of them on the passenger and-mail run from Southampton to New York, via Cherbourg, as also was the Mauretania (which still held the Blue Riband, having set a new speed record in 1924, with a crossing at an average speed of 26.25· knots).

My way of life had now become settled, serene, and secure. May and I made our home at Southampton. For nearly four years June 1927 to May 1931), I served in the *Berengaria* as Chief Officer, and later on several voyages as Staff Captain. I made forty crossings of the Atlantic in her, thirty-three of them under Captain Rostron, six under Captain Protheroe, and one under Captain Charles.

Passengers came and went, but the ship's people were constantly in her. The smooth handling of a staff of nearly one thousand men and women, to make a "happy ship," required not only supervision of their work, but attention to their welfare and contentment. The ship was, for three weeks in every four, their place of abode: their home.

The crew had their own Social and Athletic Club and maintained cricket and football teams which played a "points" competition on sports grounds ashore when the ship was in port; they had also a Concert Party, which entertained the passengers at least once on each crossing with talent that constantly improved with practice. Another activity was a ship's magazine, named Berry Pie, printed on board under the editorship of the Ship's Librarian. One issue was produced on each passage, and copies of it eagerly bought by the passengers as souvenirs. Most of the literary contributions came from members of the crew. One day the Editor asked me if I would write a short article for it. I had not thought of doing such a thing, but, after much cogitation and head scratching, I produced some-thing about going to sea in sail. After all, I had a reputation of a sort as an author. Lifeboat Efficiency was now in its tenth edition, and *Ship Ahoy!* in its third edition. These sales had been made chiefly on board ship. The bookshop in the *Berengaria* carried a good display of *Ship Ahoy!* and usually sold a couple of dozen copies on each passage.

I had no reason to be conceited at this success. One day, on the deck outside my cabin window, I heard two pert young lady passengers discussing *Ship Ahoy!* Said one, "Have you seen the Staff Captain's last book?"

"I hope so!" answered the other, fervently.

Despite that, my article in Berry Pie was effective. On the day after it appeared, a passenger approached me and told me that he was the proprietor of a magazine published in New York under the name of Sea Stories. "I've seen your article in Berry Pie," he said. "Would you write something of the same kind, but more fully for me? We pay one cent per word, on publication."

We had a drink together, and I promised to do my best That evening I got some sheets of foolscap and a lead pencil, and began work on an article entitled, "My First Voyage." With visions of one cent a word, I padded it out until it was bursting at the seams. At a rough calculation, my effort extended to nearly 14,000 words. I thought so little of its chances, that I did not even bother to have it typed but sent it off with a covering note: "If this is not acceptable, throw it away."

When next the *Berengaria* arrived in New York, there was a letter for me from the editor of Sea Stories, with a cheque for 137 dollars, and a copy of the magazine containing my article. Some months later, the magazine "folded." No wonder!

But this success had started me off on a career of nautical journalism, which became a hobby for me. For many years thereafter, I sent off a large number of articles on shipping matters to magazines and newspapers in Britain and the U.S.A. Many of these were accepted, and paid for, but seldom at the high rate of my first effort.

While I was posted in the *Berengaria*, I was called up for further training in the Royal Naval Reserve. For six weeks (October- December 1928), I attended a Senior Officers' Technical Course on board *H.M.S. Victory*, at Portsmouth.

Nelson's flagship of the battle of Trafalgar, bedded in concrete in a dock alongside the Royal Naval Barracks, gave its name also to the shore station. All the officers attending the course of training held the rank of Commander, R.N.R., and several of them were masters of ships in the Merchant Navy. The training placed emphasis on the responsibilities of command, under the routines of the Royal Navy. This proved of great value to me in the years ahead.

During the years that I was posted in the *Berengaria*, I occasionally made a voyage to New York as a relieving officer in other liners — sometimes as Staff Captain in the *Aquitania*, once as Chief Officer in the *Samaria*, and once as Chief Officer in the *Alaunia* (to Montreal).

The *Aquitania*, 45,600 tons, with four screws and a speed of 23 knots, had accommodation for 3230 passengers and a crew of 1000. Of pre-war design (completed in 1914), she had been intended to cater partly for the emigrant trade, having accommodation for nearly 2000 passengers in the third class. She was a comfortable big ship and eventually had an exceptionally long seagoing life of thirty-six years, from 1914 to 1950. In that sense she was one of the greatest Cunarders of her period and became "the Grand Old Lady" in her old age. My service in her as Relieving Staff Captain added to the knowledge that I was acquiring of the handling of big ships and helped to equip me for responsibilities that would come later.

With the *Berengaria*, *Aquitania*, and *Mauretania* as "big" ships, and the *Samaria*, *Laconia*, *Franconia*, and *Carinthia* as "medium- sized" liners (20,000 tons) of post-war design, all on the run to New York in the 1920s, the Cunard Line was maintaining its high standards of service, but against a competition that was again becoming severe.

The White Star Line had in service the *Majestic* (56,000 tons), the *Olympic* (46,000 tons), the *Homeric* (34,000 tons), besides a number of medium-sized ships. The United States Line had the *Leviathan* (59,000 tons, biggest ship afloat at that time), besides some medium-sized liners.

The *Leviathan*, *Majestic*, *Berengaria*, and *Homeric* had all been confiscated from Germany as war reparations; but the Germans were coming up again. In 1922, they put into service the *Columbus* (32,000 tons); in 1928, the *Europa* (49,000 tons); and in 1929 the *Bremen* (51,700 tons). There was much excitement when the *Europa* and the *Bremen* appeared. They were both owned by Nord Deutscher Lloyd, and had many new features of design and equipment, with every comfort and luxury for passengers.

In 1929 the *Bremen* took the Blue Riband of the Atlantic, with a westbound passage at a speed of 27.83 knots. On her return (east-bound) passage she attained an average speed of 27.91 knots. Thus she gained the acclaim of being the speediest merchant vessel in the world, taking the mythical trophy from our *Mauretania*, which had held it for twenty-two years. Her sistership, *Europa*, also developed an average speed of 27 knots on Atlantic passages. These two big and smart liners were making the Atlantic crossing (between Cherbourg and New York) in four and a half days, compared with five days taken by their rivals. The few hours gained were not in themselves as important as the prestige they carried; but prestige is important.

British, French, and Italian companies made plans to meet the German challenge.

Towards the end of the 1920s, the Italian Line began building the *Rex* (51,000 tons) and the *Conte di Savoia* (48,000 tons), both designed for a speed of 28 knots.

The French Line had put into service in 1926 a "big" ship, the *Ile de France* (43,000 tons), but she developed a speed of only 23 knots, and, although a beautiful vessel, was no record breaker. Then it was announced in 1929 that the French had laid down, and were building, a mammoth superliner, the *Normandie*, of 80,000 tons, which would be not only the greatest vessel in the world, but also the speediest, with a designed speed of 30 knots!

It was to meet that challenge that the Cunard Line made preparations to build two "wonder ships" of 80,000 tons. The first of these (later to be named the *Queen Mary*) was laid down in Brown's yard at Clydebank in December 1930 and was then known as "Number 534" — this being the 534th vessel built in those yards. At that time the worldwide Trade Depression began to make itself felt. The financial stringency retarded, for a while, the progress of building both these mammoth ships.

It was in the midst of that depression that I attained the summit of my ambition. On 13th May 1931, the Directors of the Cunard Line appointed me Captain in the Company's service.

I was then nearly forty-eight years of age and had been going to sea for thirty-three years. I had been in the Cunard Service (including war service) for twenty-four years. I had served as an officer in seventeen different Cunarders, small and great. That was a typical probation of a Cunard Captain. Appointment to that

Postcard image of the R.M.S. Aurania (author collection)

rank was rightly considered one of the highest honours in the Merchant Service, and one of the hardest to win.

I felt proud of it, but not boastful; for I knew only too well that the Master of a Cunarder has responsibilities and worries that can be shared with no one: he must take them, and take the consequences of any error, great or small; for there is no one to blame, except him, if anything goes wrong. So in the hard school of the sea a man may learn to command others, but only if he first learns to command himself.

My first command in the Cunard service — or of any merchant vessel — was of the R.M.S. Aurania, on a voyage from Liverpool to Montreal, May-June 1931. I was to make only one voyage in the Aurania, relieving her Master, who was due for his annual leave. After that, I was to return to the *Berengaria* as Staff Captain, until an opportunity would arise for me to be given command of another vessel in the Cunard fleet.

The *Aurania* was a well found, twin screw, oil burning steamer of 14,000 tons, launched in 1924. She had a speed of 15 knots and carried 484 cabin-class and 1222 third-class passengers, with a crew of 270. She was one of seven "A" vessels, built after the war for the Canadian trade to Montreal and Quebec. I was familiar with these vessels and that route, having made voyages to Montreal previously in the Albania and recently in the *Alaunia*, and to Quebec in the Caronia.

On this, my first voyage in command of a Cunarder, I had as Chief Officer Charles Ford, a man who stood six feet four inches in his socks and consequently was nicknamed "Tiny." He was a huge bulk of a man, with a keen sense of humour, and a conscientious officer. The First Officer was Harry Grattidge, who had been a junior officer with me when I was Chief Officer in the *Albania* ten years previously on voyages to Montreal and New York. As an officer, Grattidge was tactful yet firm. I always enjoyed his company, as he had a good sense of humour, was generous, fond of music, and had a fund of amusing stories.

I could not have had better men than Ford and Grattidge with me on my first voyage in command. Little did we know it then, but, in order of seniority, myself, Ford, and Grattidge were all destined to become, in that order of succession, Commodores of the Cunard Line! None of us could have imagined such a thing at that time.

Now, for the first time in my seagoing career, I had a "Captain's Tiger" — in other words, a steward specially attending to the shipmaster's cabin, bringing him meals, making the bed, cleaning the cabin, valeting uniforms, and so on. The name, "Captain's Tiger," is supposed to have originated in the days of the old East-Indiamen, when shipmasters engaged native Asian "boys" as their personal attendants, and garbed them in gorgeous Oriental dress, vying with other captains in ostentatious display. The Oriental dress was often of striped silk, which caused these stewards to be known as "tigers." The competition in fantastic garb grew so keen that shipowners put a ban on the practice. Yet the old name, "Captain's Tiger," persisted, and remains to the present day. It is the theme of many a jest on shipboard. Passengers hear that the Captain has a tame "Tiger" on board, and are always curious to see it, if possible.

I had to conduct Divine Service, for the first time in my life, and insisted on doing it, even though there were some clergymen on board; for the ship is "the Captain's parish." After breakfast on that Sunday morning, a lady asked to see me, stating that she had a request to make. Her request was that we should not sing the hymn, "Eternal Father, strong to save."

"Why not?" I asked her. "It frightens me!" she said.

That being so, I complied with her request

We had a full ship of passengers; for, although immigration to the U.S.A. had been stopped, the portals of Canada were still open, and large numbers of British and Continental European migrants were voyaging third-class in the Cunard "A" ships to Montreal: more than ever as the Trade Depression worsened.

Off Cape Race we ran into fog. I reduced speed to dead slow and kept the steam whistle going at 1½-minute intervals. It was a deep, booming note, which would certainly worry some people. A lady sent a letter up to me: "Dear Sir, will you kindly stop blowing the foghorn, as my son, aged six, is unable to get any sleep!"

I got the Purser to move her and her child temporarily to a cabin away down below, where they could scarcely hear the noise; and with that she was satisfied.

A few hours before we left Montreal, a man brought two boys, aged ten and eleven, on board. They were his sons, travelling to England to live with their grandparents. Their mother had died in Canada. The boys were placed in charge of a motherly stewardess. Their father then asked to see me and made an unusual request The boys, he said, had with them an urn containing the ashes of their mother. She had requested that her ashes be scattered from a ship in mid-ocean. Would I see that this was done with due solemnity?

There was no reason why I should not. On a day of calm weather, far out at sea, I had the stewardess bring the two boys and the urn up to the bridge, and there, from the port wing on the leeward side, in the presence of the two wide-eyed boys, I performed the sad ritual of scattering their mother's ashes to the winds and waters.

On this passage, too, I performed my first christening. In olden days of sailing ships, when voyages lasted many months, shipmasters were often required to baptize infants born on board ship. They were authorized, also, to perform marriages as well as funerals at sea. But on steamship passages of the North Atlantic, which seldom last more than ten days, even in the slowest liners, a shipmaster would not perform marriages or christenings except in circumstances of extreme urgency; and even funerals are avoided, if the relatives, informed by radio, agree that the body should be brought ashore for burial.

Embarked at Montreal in the *Aurania* was a young Swedish woman in an advanced stage of pregnancy, travelling with her husband. They expected to arrive in Sweden before the child was born. After clearing the land, we ran into a bit of heavy weather, and suddenly a girl baby was born. The ship's surgeon, who was a young man, and the nurse, were highly excited. The child was premature, and feeble. The doctor thought it possible that the baby would not survive. He suggested, after conferring with the parents, that I should christen it "just in case ..."

After studying the law and practice of such occasions and making myself familiar with the procedures and prayers laid down in the Church of England

Book of Common Prayer, I performed the ceremony in the passengers' cabin, in the presence of the Purser, the doctor, the nurse, the parents, and a steward and stewardess, with a few others standing by in the alleyway near the open cabin door. Strangely enough, from that moment the child began to grow strong and healthy.

On returning to Liverpool, I handed over my temporary command, and rejoined the *Berengaria* at Southampton, as Staff Captain. I remained in that post for eighteen months, until the end of the year 1932. On 13th May 1932, my old friend and mentor, Captain Sir Arthur Rostron, K.B.E., R.D., R.N.R.,

Bisset takes control of the R.M.S. Berengaria from retiring Cunard Commodore Sir Arthur Roston, who was in command of the R.M.S. Carpathia when it responded to the R.M.S. Titanic SOS.

(Public Domain, Wikimedia)

Commodore of the Cunard Line, retired on reaching the age limit. In a ceremony held on board, I had the privilege of presenting him, on behalf of the crew, with an illuminated address. His was a record of service at sea that few have equalled or excelled. I had served with him in four ships — the *Brescia*, the *Carpathia*, the *Mauretania*, and the *Berengaria* — and never saw him make any serious mistake of judgment or seamanship.

On one westbound voyage in the *Berengaria*, leaving Southampton on 4th September 1931, we had an unusual piece of deck cargo. It was the yacht Amberjack II, a Bermuda rigged schooner which had finished third in the transatlantic yacht race earlier that year. She had left Newport, Rhode Island, on 4th July, and crossed the finishing line at Plymouth Sound on 26th July — great sailing for a craft of only forty-six feet length overall, with a beam of thirteen feet, and a crew of seven.

We hoisted the yacht on board, to a cradle on the foredeck of the *Berengaria*, using the ship's own "jumbo" derrick, strengthened with extra topping lifts and a preventer stay. The hydraulic weight gauge showed that the weight was eighteen and a half tons. Four of the yacht's crew were with us as first-class passengers — her Skipper and owner, Paul Rust; Second Mate, "Surm" Lane; Boat- swain, "Hank" Hill; and Engineer, Emmet Hart. (Her auxiliary engine had been sealed during the race, except for the electric lighting plant.)

We lashed the yacht down securely on deck with wire cables and covered her with tarpaulins. After we had left Cherbourg, soon after midnight, the Master-at-arms reported to me that there was a light showing under the tarpaulin covers of the yacht. I went with him to investigate and found three of the crew members asleep in their own bunks in the yacht's cabin! They explained that, with all due deference to the luxury and comfort of the *Berengaria*'s staterooms, they had grown so used to roughing it that they couldn't sleep in comfortable beds.

As they were doing no harm there, I left them to it. They continued to live in this way in a ship-within-a-ship, and so were able to claim, if they wanted to win a bet, that they had crossed the Atlantic both ways in the yacht. Each day, when the weather was fine, the tarpaulins were removed. I sat several times with them in their cabin, drinking rum — a Staff Captain is not a watchkeeping officer! — and heard the story of their adventures.

There were some people who asked me what good I thought could come of young men risking their lives in such a hazardous voyage as they had made. My answer could only be, "They have guts. If that qualification is not 'good', both for now and for posterity, I'll be willing to swallow the anchor and seventy-five fathoms of cable."

On one of my voyages in the *Aquitania*, as relieving Staff Captain, soon after we had left Cherbourg, westward bound, the Master-at-Arms came up to me and announced, "We have found a stowaway."

"Where is he?" I asked.

"It's not a he, it's a she," he told me, and continued, "I was walking through the third-class passenger quarters, and found a small crowd of people surrounding a girl who was selling postcards at sixpence each. I took one, and here it is."

He handed me the postcard. It bore the picture of the girl. Printed underneath it were the words, THE WORLD'S CHAMPION STOWAWAY, with a list of the ships that she had stowed away in, and the punishments she had endured.

"What have you done with her?" I asked.

"She admitted being a stowaway, and she is now locked up."

I went along to see the World's Champion Stowaway, and found her impudent and defiant, and altogether a bit of a nuisance, and silly as well. "Now I'll add the *Aquitania* to my list of ships!" she boasted.

We kept her in the lockup, and, on arrival in New York, handed her over to the dock police, as required by law. They returned her on board just before the ship left. When we arrived at Southampton, she was again handed over to the police and given a month's hard labour. I don't know if that cured her. It's surprising what some people will do to become World's Champions.

21

Captain of the "Ascania" — Five Years Trading to Canada — London my Home Port — Winter and Summer Tracks in the North Atlantic — Evolution of Aids to Navigation — The Gyrocompass — The Fathometer — Wireless Direction Finder — Sable Island and Fog — The Captain's "Fog Chair" — A Narrow Shave — Navigation of the Bay of Fundy — The "Blue Nose" Seamen of Olden Times — A Welcome at St. John — The Need for "Magic Binoculars."

O N 15th December, 1932, I joined R.M.S. *Ascania*, in command, and remained in command of her for five years.

In that period, I made forty-five voyages in her across the North Atlantic Ocean, trading from London to Montreal in the eight months of each year when the River St. Lawrence was ice free, and to Halifax, St. John, and New York in the winter months — returning on each voyage to London as a home port.

This was the most settled occupation that I have ever had in my seafaring career. On an average I made nine voyages a year. The average time of a passage each way, depending on seasonal conditions and ports visited, was between nine and thirteen days. The round voyage was usually completed in a few days under a month. She would then be berthed at the Surrey Commercial Docks in the Thames for ten days, before beginning a new voyage.

May and I at last had a home, or fixed abode, in London. It was in a "mews" flat off Baker Street. I was able to get home from the Surrey Dock in an hour. Once a year my ship was laid off for one voyage, for her annual refit, and I had three weeks' home leave. On these occasions I would usually be put to work painting and decorating our flat, a task I undertook with all the joy of a home lover.

In five years of this settled existence, I had as much home life and regularity of fixed employment as any seaman on ocean voyages could ever hope for. It was a welcome change after so many years of voyaging as a subordinate officer in many different vessels, on many and varied routes, from many home ports. The *Ascania* was my ship, and I was well settled in as her Master. This was the summit of a seaman's ambition, to be in command of a well found ship, and to stay with her for years.

R.M.S. Ascania in 1927 (Public Domain)

The *Ascania* was a twin screw, oil burning steamer of 14,440 tons gross, 8143 tons net, and 20,760 tons displacement. She had a speed of 14½ knots. Built by Armstrongs on the Tyne and completed in 1925, she had been seven years in service when I was given command of her. She had a single funnel, a straight stem, a cut-away stern, and was 538 feet in length overall and 65 feet beam. Her midships superstructure was 290 feet long. Her "moulded depth" was 43 feet, and draft 31 feet 7 inches when fully loaded. Her navigational and mechanical equipment were thoroughly up-to-date. She had geared turbine engines and carried 2245 tons of oil fuel. She was a typical passenger liner of her period, in design a smaller version of the *Franconia*. She was a comfortable ship, without luxury, a favourite especially with Canadian travellers, and a very steady ship in a sea way.

She carried 198 first-class and 498 tourist-class passengers, and a crew of 367; total 1072 souls. The capacity of her cargo holds was 298,600 cubic feet. There were four passenger decks besides the boat deck. On A Deck, which was glassed in, was a lounge, drawing room, smoking room, children's playroom, and a veranda cafe. The bridgehouse, with the Captain's cabin and navigating officers' quarters, were as usual at the fore end of the boat deck. She had two masts, and flush decks fore and aft of the midships superstructure.

She was one of seven "A" ships — the *Albania, Andania, Antonia, Ausonia, Aurania, Alaunia,* and *Ascania* — completed between 1921 and 1925 and specially designed for the Canadian trade. They were all about the same size, but not exactly alike. They provided a regular once-a-week service between London and various railhead ports in Eastern Canada.

On my first voyage in the *Ascania,* leaving London in wintertime, on 16th December 1932, I had orders to make for Halifax in Nova Scotia. In that season the St. Lawrence River was blocked by ice, but Halifax, as a rail terminal at an ice free ocean port, provided ingress and egress for the Canadian trade, and as such had a busy life in winter.

My orders were to proceed from Halifax to St. John, New Brunswick, in the Bay of Fundy, where steamers of the Canadian Pacific Railway Line ("C.P.R.") had held a monopoly of the Atlantic trade for many years. My voyage would inaugurate a weekly Cunard service to that port.

The C.P.R. steamer services across the Atlantic had begun in 1903. They carried mails, passengers, and cargo from Montreal and Quebec in the ice free months and St. John as their "ocean door" in the winter months, trading chiefly to Belfast, Glasgow, and Liverpool. The Cunard "A" ships had provided competition for them after the war, in the st Lawrence ports, and now intended to do the same at St. John. The winter track westward to Halifax, as laid down in 1913 by international agreement — to reduce risks of collisions on the busy North Atlantic "lanes" — follows the Great Circle course from Fastnet to Lat. 45 deg. 55 min. N., Long. 50 deg. W., and from there westwards by rhumb line to Halifax, passing sixty miles north of Sable Island. (Rhumb line is a course cutting all meridians of longitude at the same angle; or it could be defined nontechnically as a set compass course in a straight line, disregarding the earth's curvature.)

The ocean surrounding Sable Island, and eastwards to the Banks, is the most hazardous region of the North Atlantic. It often has fogs in winter. There are hundreds of fishing trawlers, in sail or with engines, working on the Newfoundland Banks, besides the trans-ocean steamer traffic to and from Canadian ports.

In summer, when icebergs are drifting southwards in the thaw from Labrador and Newfoundland, the trans-ocean steamer tracks pass sixty miles south of Sable Island, to avoid the bergs. There is a shorter track to the St. Lawrence, via the Strait of Belle Isle (between Newfoundland and Labrador), used in some summer months when that Strait is ice free; but this track is beset by icebergs.

I had vivid memories of being nearly wrecked on Sable Island twenty-six years previously, in the old rattletrap tramp steamer, *Nether Holme*, and I was well content now to give it a wide berth. But, during those twenty-five years, there had been wonderful improvements in aids to navigation. In the old *Nether Holme* we had no gyrocompass, gyro pilot ("Iron-Mike"), fathometer (echo sounding machine), or wireless direction finding gear. We had to feel our way in fog, darkness, blizzards, or gales, ascertaining our position by the use of chronometers, sextant, magnetic and spirit compasses, the patent log, and the hand worked "sea lead" for soundings.

Now, in the *Ascania*, as a dense fog set in when we were abeam of Sable Island, I was able to get cross bearings, by means of the wireless direction finder, from wireless beacons on Sable Island, Cape Race, and other points on shore, to fix our position accurately at any given moment. The gyrocompass kept us true on course; the fathometer gave us the soundings of the seabed (a help in fixing positions of the ship) continuously.

There was still one great invention not yet introduced: radar. In fog or the vicinity of icebergs, land, or other ships, it was necessary to proceed at dead slow, with the steam whistle going at 1½-minute intervals. Our range of vision with the naked eye was limited in dense fog to fifty yards, or less. Binoculars were of no use in piercing the fog shroud. The naked ear, if that term may aptly be used, was as important as the naked eye. The officers on watch and the lookout men had to strain their hearing as well as their eyesight, listening for the steam whistles of other vessels or foghorns of trawlers; but those signals were muffled in the fog, and capricious. Even when an invisible vessel's steam whistle or foghorn was heard, it was usually impossible to judge its distance, or 'position, or course. In fog, before the introduction of "the magic binoculars" of radar, seamen were partly blind and deaf, if not dumb.

In dense fog, a shipmaster seldom leaves the bridge. He dares not relax vigilance. All others — the officers of the watch, the helmsmen, the lookout men — stand their watches in rotation, and then go below for a sleep in their bunks. The Captain sees them come and go, but he remains on the bridge — an "all seeing eye" and "all hearing ear," as far as is humanly possible. On this occasion we were in dense fog for thirty-eight hours. I remained on the bridge throughout every watch. As my weariness increased, I took occasional catnaps in the fog chair.

All steamers on the "foggy trades" have a fog chair on the bridge — for the use of the Master only. Woe betides any officer of the watch who would presume to sit in it. An officer must "stand his watch" — literally standing on his feet — for four hours, and that is endurable. But no man, even a super Captain, could stand on the bridge for the entire duration of the passage through a dense fog, which may sometimes last for two or three days and nights.

We were proceeding on course at dead slow, with the steam whistle blowing, and frequently taking wireless bearings and reading the fathometer graph. An officer and a lookout man were on each wing of the bridge, in addition to two lookouts in the crow's nest and two extra lookouts on the forecastle head. The fog had closed in on us at midnight, when we were six days out from London.

Since then, I had been twenty-seven hours on the bridge, with only a few catnaps in the fog chair. This had a cushioned seat high enough for me to be able to see ahead over the bridge dodgers or through an opened window of the wheelhouse. It also had armrests and a footrest I would relax in the chair· for only a few minutes at a time — not to sleep, but to ease my aching feet.

At 3 a.m., in the Graveyard Watch, I suddenly leaped from my chair and leaned out through the wheelhouse window. During an interval between the blasts of our steam whistle, I had heard a faint sound ahead, above the humming of our slow moving engines. "Stop her," I ordered. Then I sang out to the officers, "Did you hear anything?"

"No, sir," they answered. "Well, keep your ears open!"

At that moment there came the hoarse sound of a steam whistle fine on our starboard bow. "Full astern!" I ordered. A vibration shook the ship as the twin screws churned astern, and I blew three short blasts on our whistle.

In less than a minute, we sighted the lights of a small tramp steamer, which suddenly altered her course to sheer off, and slithered along our starboard side with not more than fifty feet clearance. Then she disappeared in the murk astern. "A close shave," I remarked, to the worried looking officers and lookout men. They could not understand how I had heard the stranger's whistle, when they had all been unable to hear it.

I had good hearing and eyesight, but probably not better than those faculties in the eight other men who were on lookout. The explanation is in the mental equipment of command, which gives a shipmaster a "sixth sense" — of full responsibility and sharpened alertness. Besides that, a man who has been keyed up by a long vigil becomes more mentally alert, no matter how weary he may be physically, than men who have been enjoying normal sleep and rest

At last the fog lifted. We made the port of Halifax safely, and I was able to catch up on my arrears of sleep. After a few days, having landed most of our passengers and discharged and loaded cargo, we cleared out of Halifax, making for St. John.

This was my first navigation into the Bay of Fundy, and it caused me some anxiety, which I was careful not to show. The passage from Halifax to St. John is only 262 miles, all coastwise, in water traditionally beset with hazards of fog, blizzards, capricious gales, variable tidal currents, and shoals. This was the sea district of some of the greatest seamen of sailing ship days, renowned under the name of "Blue Noses" — in obvious reference to the icy winter temperatures.

I had served under a "Blue Nose Skipper," Captain Raymond Parker, in the *S.S.* Jura, twenty-seven years previously, and he had made my blood run cold with some of his yarns of the dangers of navigation in the Bay of Fundy in his younger days under sail. I remembered those stories now, of the "iron men in wooden ships," fighting their way into and out of that dreaded bay in fogs, blizzards and gales, and the hazards of uncharted currents, amid rocky islands and shoals, many of which at that time were unlit.

Those old time Blue Nose seamen had no aids to navigation except a wobbly compass; a chronometer; a quadrant or sextant for "shooting the sun"; a deep sea lead; a handline log; and their well-thumbed charts, supplemented by their expert local knowledge. There were few lighthouses, no fog signals, no buoyed channels, and certainly no wireless direction finder stations. My thoughts harked back to those old time sailors. I could see them in my mind's eye — the crew of a full rigged ship, homeward bound and bearing up for St. John, after many months at sea, perhaps after weathering Cape Horn, and now in a howling blizzard in their home waters, head reaching under lower topsails; wet through, chilled to the marrow of their bones, blinded by driving icy spray and sleet, with no shelter on the poop deck except a rag of canvas stretched in the mizzen rigging: all hands on deck, wading in water waist deep, with the lee rail under, hauling around the yards, or going aloft to make or take in sail, with numbed fingers — and blue noses.

The ship drifting onto a rockbound lee shore; her Master peering into the murk, dreading to hear the breakers pounding on a hidden reef — casting the deep sea lead, twenty-eight pounds in weight, and the sagging line stretching out to windward as the ship drifted away from it — then fifty fathoms to pull in by hand through a block on the backstay — "Hand over hand, my hearties!" — fingers frozen stiff and white, so that strong men cried out in agony and desperation, but continued at their work, watch after watch on deck — What a life!

Such were my grim thoughts as I stood on the bridge of my ship, a modern steamer, rounding Cape Sable, the southern point of Nova Scotia. We had been in fog all the way for a hundred sea miles since leaving Halifax. I had been twenty four hours without sleep; but, fog or no fog, I intended to stay on the bridge until we berthed. I had no intention of taking horizontal exercise in my cabin while my ship was in the Bay of Fundy. Catnaps in the fog chair would be my only rest

Thinking of the old time Blue Noses, I had no reason to feel sorry for myself or for my crew. My officers and men on watch were warmly clad in dry clothes and boots, on dry decks high above the ship's waterline, and, to some extent, in shelter. The helmsman, in a steam heated wheelhouse, was steering an exact course by a gyro compass that was independent of the vagaries of the earth's magnetism. Did I want a sounding? Turn a switch on the echo- & sounding machine, and immediately a red light stabbed the edge of its dial, marked in fathoms, indicating, every three seconds, the exact depth of water under the keel.

Having rounded Cape Sable, we were standing to the north-westward, to make Lurcher Shoal Light Vessel, at the S.E. entrance to the Bay of Fundy. The Lurcher has a powerful light, visible fifteen miles in clear weather; now it was shrouded in fog. "Take a wireless bearing on the Lurcher," I ordered. The Officer of the Watch went to the direction finder, put on the earphones, moved the loop aerial slowly to and fro by means of a handwheel fitted over a gyro compass repeater, and in a few seconds reported, "Lurcher bearing North 35 degrees West "

Away to starboard, the diaphone fog signal on Cape Fourchu was blaring out its half-minute snort, audible fifteen miles. My charts showed the set and drift of the currents in the Bay of Fundy for every hour of the twenty-four and in all localities. Presently the fog cleared. From every headland or dangerous reef the friendly beams from lighthouses, light vessels, or light buoys, shone forth to guide us.

In the year 1833, as records show, there were only eight "lights" in the Bay of Fundy region, and no fog signals. In 1933, there were thirty-four first-class lights, 120 second-class lights, sixty marking buoys, forty diaphone fog signals, and three wireless direction finding stations in that same region, all maintained by the Canadian Department of Marine.

Thanks to science, and modern emphasis on safety at sea, the Bay of Fundy had lost its old time terrors, and the race of Blue Nose seamen had become only a legend. I made the port of St. John without any difficulty.

The chief problem of berthing in this harbour is caused by the phenomenal rise and fall of the tide in the Bay of Fundy, with a difference of fifty or sixty feet between high water and low water levels. This interfered, to some extent, with the discharging and loading of cargo. The moorings and the gangway had to be constantly watched as the ship rode up and down alongside the quay. As soon as we berthed, a welcoming party of citizens, headed by the Mayor and the Harbour Commissioners, came on board. After a short· tour of inspection of the ship, they forgathered in my cabin — about fifteen of them — and, as it was a very cold morning, they enjoyed a few good slugs of Scotch whiskey. Then they began making speeches, and almost every one of them said the same thing: it was a great day for St. John when the Cunard Line began making regular calls there; it would bring much extra business to the port.

As the request of the editor of the local newspaper, I wrote an article, extolling the excellent navigational aids in the approaches to the port. This brought me next day a visit from an irate old skipper of a coastal steamer — a stout and sturdy Scot — who said to me, "Mon, ye hae ruined all my good work! For thirty years I've been navigating in this district, and I've never failed to complain that the approaches to the por-r-t are terr-r-ible, mon, aye, TERR-R- IBLE! In fact, I have impressed on the Harbour Commissioners that it is only by dint of extraordinary skill that I hae managed to avoid disaster. And now ye hae ruined everything and made me oot a liar!"

I mollified him with a wee dram, or two, and then showed him the navigational aids on the bridge of the *Ascania*. "Mon," he said, "your ship's foolproof!" With that backhanded compliment I had to be content, and we parted good friends. His parting shot was, "But you can't see through a fog, and you never will!"

His pessimistic prediction was not to be proved wrong until radar was installed in ships, ten years later as a "war secret."

Many a time in the *Ascania*, when I was fogbound, I developed a longing for magic binoculars which would see through fog; so much so that I intensively studied all the data that I could find on the causes of fog. I wrote an article on it, which was published in the Daily Telegraph, London, on 3rd January 1934. This article concluded with the words: "The mariner envisages the invention of a magic pair of television binoculars, through which he may peer into the thickest of fogs and see everything clearly within a mile radius."

I could not have believed then that my hope or prediction would ever come true. I was hoping for a miracle, but in due time I had the joy of seeing that miracle happen.

22

Trading to Canada — Navigation of the St Lawrence — The Cape Race Route — Terminal at Montreal — The Belle Isle Route — Ice- bergs in Season — My Fiftieth Birthday — The Italian Superliner "Rex" — Merger of the Cunard and White Star Lines — Docking in London River — The Pilot and the "Mud Pilot" — The Launching and Naming of the "Queen Mary" — A Wild Atlantic Gale — Tragedy of the "Millpool"

DURING the four winter months, from December, 1932, to March, 1933, I made three voyages in the *Ascania* from London to Halifax and St. John. It was a hard trade for cold, fog, and ice. On one voyage to Halifax, I found the harbour covered in thin ice — not enough to close the port, but the temperature at noon was sixteen degrees below freezing point. The decks were usually under snow and ice while we lay in port. To touch ironwork with bare hands would mean a severe "frost burn. "

It was at this time that new steering orders were introduced in British ships, making a drastic break with tradition. Until then, when it was intended to turn the ship's head to star- board, the order was, "Port the helm." Likewise, when it was intended to turn the ship's head to port, the order was, "Starboard the helm."

These orders were a legacy of olden times, when ships were steered by means of a tiller on the poop, which levered the rudder to the opposite side from that to which the tiller was moved. When the tiller was put to port, then the rudder moved to star- board, and the ship's head "paid off" to starboard. Similarly, when the tiller was put to starboard, then the ship's head paid off to port. Helm orders referred not to the rudder, but to the tiller. The Captain, Officer of the Watch, or Pilot, would direct the steersman's movements of the tiller.

When the steering wheel was introduced on the poopdeck of sailing vessels, it operated a tiller placed below the deck, out of sight. The tiller was worked by a vertical chain gear from the wheel. When the wheel was moved to port, the tiller went to starboard, and vice versa. But as steering wheels were introduced only gradually, the old time "helm orders" continued to be used, referring to the movements of the invisible tiller, and all seamen understood that fact perfectly.

When steam propulsion was introduced as an auxiliary to sail, and later when sail was discarded, the steering wheel was transferred from the poop to a bridge amidships (in order to give better visibility ahead). Then the tiller was not only out of sight of the bridge, but also at a considerable distance abaft the steering wheel. It was connected to the wheel by rods and chains riding aft from the bridge along the bulwarks, leading around a horizontal quadrant on the poop.

Later, a "steering engine," operated by steam power, was installed amidships, connected to the steering wheel on the bridge. This enabled the steering gear to be operated with very little manual exertion, in response to the slightest movements of the geared steering wheel on the bridge.

A further development occurred when the connecting gear from the steering engine was removed from its exposed position on the bulwarks and carried aft inside the hull below decks. There it could be inspected and kept in order without difficulty, even when seas were breaking on deck.

Despite this gradual mechanical improvement, the original and ancient "helm orders," referring to the tiller, were retained. The helmsman was usually an older A.B. seaman, who had gone to sea as a boy, and was used to the old time orders.

But, in some countries, which had less ancient sea traditions than Britain, helm orders in steamers referred not to the movements of the invisible tiller, but to the wheel which was in the steersman's hands. The order, "Port the helm" — or its equivalent in a foreign language — then meant putting the wheel to port. This turned the rudder to port, and made the ship's head pay off to port. It was a more logical and direct order than that of the British tradition.

Sometimes it caused confusion when British ships were entering or leaving foreign ports with local pilots.

At an international Conference for the Safety of Life at Sea, held in London in 1927, it was decided that the antiquated steering- orders, referring to the tiller, should be discarded in the ocean going ships of all nations. The date of this drastic change was fixed, with ample notice, to occur on 1st January, 1933.

On and after that date, steering orders would have the same meaning in ships of all nations, referring directly to movements of the wheel, instead of to the tiller.

Despite the forebodings of the nautical conservatives, the change of steering orders was affected without any serious mishaps. But, as a precaution, and to make the change easier, ships' officers and pilots, for many months after the change, gave the orders as "Wheel to port" or "Wheel to starboard."

Later, during the 1939-45 war, even the old words "port" and "starboard" were discarded as wheel orders in some ships, and "left" and "right" substituted. But this was unnecessary. There never yet was a seaman of any nationality who did not know that, on board ship, looking towards the bows — as the man at the wheel does — the lefthand side of the ship is the port side, and the righthand side the starboard.

When I returned to London in March 1933, after my third voyage to Halifax and St. John, my ship was laid up for a month for her annual refit. I then began trading in her to Montreal, clearing out of London on 20th April. The River St. Lawrence is free of ice from the middle of April until the end of November.

The westbound track, from April until mid-July each year, is on the Great Circle course from Fastnet Light (off the S.W. of Ireland) to a point ten or twenty miles south of Cape Race (the S.E. extremity of Newfoundland); thence by way of Cabot Strait, on the south of Newfoundland, into the Gulf of St. Lawrence; thence north-westerly across that Gulf to enter the mouth of the St. Lawrence River, which is eighty miles wide at its debouchure into the Gulf near Anticosti Island.

Ships are navigated, without need of a pilot, for 290 miles up the wide estuary from Anticosti Light to Father Point, a village on the southern shore, where the river is twenty-five miles wide. Here a pilot is taken on board.

From Father Point we proceeded upriver 158 miles to Quebec, the river gradually narrowing to ten miles wide at Goose Island, then suddenly to a channel one mile wide between the Isle of Orleans and the northern shore, at the approaches to Quebec. Usually the *Ascania* did not call at Quebec but proceeded with a new pilot on board for another 139 miles upstream to Montreal. The St. Lawrence River, never less than a mile wide in the reaches between Quebec and Montreal, is a superb waterway, receiving as it does the spillover of the Great Lakes, and the drainage of a vast snowmelt in Upper Canada. In the season of the thaw it has a strong freshwater current or flood. Montreal was the head of navigation, because of the rapids, including, among others upstream from that city, Niagara Falls.

The distances on the Cape Race route from London to Montreal are approximately as follows:

At an average speed of 14½ knots, the *Ascania.* in perfect conditions could make that passage in nine days; but, when she was slowed down by fogs, the proximity of icebergs, and river caution, as she usually was, she would take ten days or more from port to port.

From the middle of July until the middle of November in each year, the ocean passage was shortened by 130 miles. We then entered the St Lawrence estuary by

	Nautical Miles	Aprox Kilometers
London to Fastnet	516	955
Fastnet to Cape Race	1708	3163
Cape Race to Anticosti	392	726
Anticosti to Father Point	290	537
Father Point to Quebec	158	293
Quebec to Montreal	139	257
TOTAL	3203	5931

way of the Strait of Belle Isle, between the northern side of Newfoundland and the Labrador shore. The "iceberg season" begins in April, when the bergs drift offshore in the thaw, going southwards to melt in the Gulf Stream. Until they are all melted in August, they are a cause of anxiety to shipmasters, especially at nighttime, or in fogs.

As a direct consequence of the Titanic disaster of 1912, the International Ice Patrol was established. The patrol vessels charted and broadcast the position, course, and rate of drift of all wandering icefields and isolated bergs on the North Atlantic tracks of shipping. This information enabled shipmasters to proceed confidently at full speed in clear weather.

It was another matter entirely when fog closed in, as it some- times did for three or four days, when we were in the vicinity of ice. Then we would crawl along at dead slow, with the steam whistle blowing, listening intently for echoes from bergs, and keeping a sharp lookout for small pieces of ice ("growlers") that might indicate a disintegrating berg nearby. Frequently also we took readings of the temperature of the air and of the seawater and watched for flights of birds which sometimes made their operational bases on bergs drifting far out at sea.

But in fog (before the invention of radar) there was no reliable indication of a berg's position. The "growlers" floated chiefly to leeward of a berg's line of drift; a lowering of water temperature would occur to windward; but the line of drift could be caused by currents rather than by winds, since seven-eighths of a berg's bulk is submerged; and seabirds could range a great distance in any direction from a berg which had been their temporary resting place.

In fog we were "blind. "I would frequently stop the ship's engines, and let her run her way off, while we intently watched and listened. During dark hours, I would stop her completely when I knew that ice was near; and I would post extra lookouts on both sides of the ship, to detect if she were drifting onto a berg, sideways on. With these precautions, there was no danger of colliding with an iceberg. In five years in the *Ascania*, I sighted thousands of them and managed to give them all a wide berth; but keen and constant watchfulness was essential. Nor was there much real danger of colliding with other vessels of large tonnage. We were in constant touch by wireless with ships at varying distances, telling each other our positions, courses, and speeds, and reporting on bergs sighted and the conditions of visibility. But sometimes the Master of an old tramp, or of a fishing trawler, perhaps with only one wireless operator, would not be cooperating in this exchange of information, and would be relying on his perhaps not very efficient steam whistle to make his presence known.

Like most other shipmasters on this route, I felt that it was better to arrive late in port than not to arrive at all. Many a time, my ship was stopped, or proceeding at dead slow, in dense fog for two or three days near the Newfoundland Banks, until the fog lifted, and I felt that we could press on safely. On these passages I would sometimes take thirteen days to get to Montreal — but what of that? — we got there.

On 15th July 1933, on my sixth voyage in command of the *Ascania*, when she was berthed at Montreal after my first passage of the Strait of Belle Isle, I had my fiftieth birthday.

Fifty years of age! I didn't feel like it. The passing of the years was brought home to me when I received a notice that I was placed on the Retired List of the R.N.R., with the rank of Captain, R.N.R. This was routine, but it offended my sense of the fitness of things. I had never felt more fit for active service in my life. I had been going to sea thirty-five years and had held my commission in the Royal Naval Reserve for twenty-three years — and now I was "retired" — well, it was only one of the "ways of the navy" in peacetime. I would be put on the active list again if war broke out, I supposed. Meanwhile, I could look forward to another thirteen years' service in the Cunard Line. Cunard Captains were usually pensioned off at or near sixty-three years of age. Who could know what the future would hold? I was now becoming one of the senior Cunard Captains ... enough of such morbid thoughts!

There were more opportunities of getting to know passengers on this Canadian route than in the bigger, speedier, more crowded, more luxurious liners on the New York run. I had many friends ashore in Halifax and Montreal, and opportunities of relaxation while the ship was berthed in those ports and in London.

The trade of St. John proved unprofitable and was dropped after one winter season. We then called at Halifax in the winter months and went on to New York for additional cargo and passengers, returning to London eastbound by the busy traffic lane from the Nantucket Light Vessel to the "Corner" in Lat. 42 deg. N. Long. 50 deg. W., and thence by Great Circle course to Fastnet. On this route I often sighted at sea, or visited, in port at New York, the gigantic superliners of the luxury passenger trade. Among them was now the new Italian liner *Rex* (51,000 tons) which in 1933 took the Blue Riband of the Atlantic from the Bremen, with a westbound passage, from Gibraltar to Ambrose Light Vessel, at an average speed of 28.92 knots. And now shipping circles were all agog with rumours of the two mammoth 80,000-ton liners, one French and one British, which were actively under construction, as the Depression lifted. Most sea experts thought that they would both be too big to handle. How wrong can experts be?

Also in the offing was a merger of the Cunard and White Star Lines. The gigantic Cunarder, known as "Job Number 534" of Brown's shipyards on the Clyde, had been laid down in 1930, but work had been suspended on her for twenty-eight months during the Depression. Then the British Government had made a substantial loan to the Cunard Company, to enable her to be completed. One of the conditions of this loan was a merger of the Cunard and White Star Lines, and this merger was effected in March 1934, with Cunard holding two-thirds of the shares.

The merged Company, now known as Cunard White Star Limited, took over nine White Star passenger liners. They were the *Majestic* (56,000 tons), *Olympic* (46,000 tons), *Homeric* (34,000 tons), the *Britannic* and *Georgie* (each of 27,000 tons), the *Adriatic* (24,000 tons), the *Albertic* and *Laurentic* (each of 19,000 tons), and the *Doric* (16,000 tons). The merger of Cunard and White Star constituted a shipping cartel of imagination staggering financial dimensions, which would be even further increased by the completion of the two 80,000-ton vessels, later to be named the *Queen Mary* and the *Queen Elizabeth*.

In the meantime I was plugging along contentedly in the *Ascania* on the Canadian and New York trade. At the end of each voyage, docking in London River was always a fascinating experience for me. We would pick up a Channel pilot off Dungeness, and proceed by way of Dover Strait, the Downs, Edinburgh Channels and the Nore, to Gravesend, a distance of eighty-seven miles through channels lit by hundreds of flashing buoys and light vessels and crowded with traffic. We would time our arrival at Gravesend three hours before high tide.

This would enable us to go upriver with the tide. The distance from Gravesend to Surrey Commercial Dock is twenty-four miles. We would allow three hours for that passage, at a speed of eight knots. The river winds in many curves. The navigable channel for larger steamers varies from 1000 feet wide at Gravesend to slightly under 600 feet at Surrey Dock. The banks of the river are studded with numerous wharves, at which hundreds of steamers lie at their berths, and there are scores of vessels moored to buoys, besides thousands of Thames River barges. It is necessary for a steamer, such as the *Ascania*, displacing 20,000 tons of water, to proceed at moderate speed, to avoid raising a wash along the banks which might do damage to other vessels or break their moorings.

At Gravesend, after clearance by Customs Officials and the Port Medical Officer, we would embark a Thames River pilot and his own helmsman, known as the "Mud pilot."

Climbing to the bridge, the pilot would greet me as an old friend, and hand me a bundle of the latest newspapers. Then, taking his stand near the middle of the bridge, within easy speaking distance of the wheel, the engine room telegraphs, and the whistle lever, while his assistant ("Bert") took the wheel, the pilot would carry on a conversation with me and direct the ship's movements at the same time, with consummate skill, somewhat as follows:

"Half ahead. Steady as you go, Bert. Have you had a good voyage, Captain? Full ahead port. Starboard you may, Bert. The weather has not been too good lately. Had a lot of-Steady-y-y, Bert, half speed port — a lot of fog last week. There's a 'sailer' (barge) on your port bow, Bert. On the port tack. Go under his stern. Got hung up with a ship for seven — Slow both. One of them Dutchmen ahead — Starboard a bit. Yes, hung up for seven hours. Thick as a hedge. Steady. These little Dutchmen take up all the ruddy river. Plenty of water for 'em at the side but — Half ahead both — they must stick right in the — Port you may, Bert — middle."

So she moves slowly upriver, sometimes after midnight, amidst a maze of fixed and moving lights ashore and afloat, which, to the uninitiated, would be utterly confusing, and in two hours is in the upper reaches, near the King George Dock. Here two tugs, which have been steaming ahead of the ship, to lend a hand if required, come close under the bows and make their ropes fast, to assist her round the Isle of Dogs, which diverts the river into a great U-shaped bend.

When she arrives off Surrey Dock, four short blasts followed by two short blasts are blown on the steam whistle, to warn approaching ships that she is turning to port. Then, with her helm hard a-port and her engines churning furiously ahead and astern, and the tugs hanging on to her bows like snorting terriers, she is turned completely around till she is heading downstream and stemming the tide.

She drifts upstream on the tide until she is opposite the dock gates. Then, by skilful angling across the current, she drops slowly alongside the wooden pier (or "knuckle") at the entrance to the lock. Ropes are put ashore, and, under the supervision of the dockmaster, the ponderous gates swing open. She is warped into the lock, and the river gates are shut behind her.

Here the pilot goes ashore, and Bert, the "Mud pilot" takes over. He is a specialist in docking. The lock is pumped up to the level of the dock. The gates open. She forges ahead, and, twenty minutes later, she is moored in her discharging berth, and the voyage is over.

At 7 a.m., the stevedores swarm aboard. Hatches are thrown open, cranes and winches rattle, the cargo is rapidly lifted out of her holds and landed on the dock, or into barges that have crowded alongside. Flour, cheese, timber, bacon, grain, leather, copper, soap, apples, nails, paper — all the products of the great

Dominion of Canada, shipped at Montreal, come to light again. In a few days she will be unloaded, and her export cargo will begin to be loaded.

So ships are, as Kipling put it:

Swift shuttles of an Empire's loom,
That weave us main to main...

On 26th September 1934, when the *Ascania* was berthed at Montreal, I — like millions of other people throughout the world — heard and read of the launching and naming of the gigantic new Cunarder (until then known only as "Number 534") at John Brown's shipyard, Clydebank. The ceremony of launching and naming the vessel was performed by Her Majesty *Queen Mary* , wife of King George V, in the presence of a huge concourse of spectators, and the name of the ship was announced — *Queen Mary*.

There was much surprise, as well as loyal gratification, at this choice of a name, which set a new precedent. Almost all Cunarders have names ending in -ia. This had been a tradition for ninety-four years, since the pioneer Britannia of 1840. It had been widely rumoured that the huge new ship would be named Queen Victoria. According to a yarn that was afterwards circulated in shipping circles — and I must make it plain that it is only hearsay, and may probably not be true — the Board of Directors of the Cunard White Star Line had decided on the name Queen Victoria, and selected their Chairman to go up to London and ask the permission of King George V (grandson of Queen Victoria) to use the royal name.

According to this yarn, the Chairman was granted an audience at Buckingham Palace, and addressed the King as follows: "Your Majesty, the Cunard Line is building the best, biggest, and speediest ship in the world, and requests your gracious permission to name her after England's most illustrious Queen."

The King thought for a moment, and then replied, "My wife will be delighted!"

Two days after the *Queen Mary* was launched and named at Clydebank, I left Montreal in the *Ascania* at 11.30 p.m. on 28th September 1934. I was homeward bound, via the Strait of Belle Isle, with a full cargo and a full passenger list, on my twentieth voyage in command of her.

On our fifth day out from Montreal, in mid-ocean, we were in the thick of some of the heaviest weather that I have ever known in the North Atlantic. A full north-westerly gale was blowing, with very high following seas on our port quarter, and fierce squalls. The *Ascania* was shipping heavy water aft, and labouring and straining under the buffeting of the seas. The barometer stood at 29.68 (1005 mb) and was falling rapidly. All passenger decks had been cleared, and every precaution taken against damage.

As darkness closed in, I said to the Officer of the Watch, "A dirty night! God help the men in little old tramps in such weather as this. Keep a sharp lookout for lights ahead. Small steamers will be hove to and drifting."

At 6.30 p.m. (ship's time) on 2nd October, we were in Lat. 53 deg. 5 min. N., Long. 38 deg. 20 min. W. and labouring heavily, when the wireless operator on duty came running up to the bridge and handed me a message: **S O S S O S S.S. MILLPOOL TO ALL SHIPS. MILLPOOL 53.30 N. 37.10 W. AFTER HATCH STOVE IN MAIN TOPMAST GONE THREE MEN INJURED DRIVING HELPLESS BEFORE GALE USING TEMPORARY AERIAL.**

"Relay that signal to all ships," I ordered, and called out the watch below to stand by on deck for a rescue attempt. Soon all the officers were on the bridge. Pricking off the position on the chart, I saw that the *Ascania* was on a bearing S. 64 W., forty-six miles from the stricken *Millpool*'s position. It would have been useless to make directly for her given position, as she was drifting south-easterly before the gale. I therefore continued steering at full speed on the *Ascania*'s previous course of N. 85 E., which would bring us towards the *Millpool*'s line of drift.

Lloyd's Register of Shipping showed that the *S.S. Millpool* was a single screw coal burning, cargo steamer of 4222-tons gross, built in 1906. Subsequently it was ascertained that she was bound for Montreal from Danzig with a full cargo of rye. She had on board a Master, First, Second, and Third Mates, carpenter, boatswain, five seamen, Chief, Second, and Third Engineers, and nine stokers — a total of twenty-three men.

With her after hatch stove in, main topmast carried away, and three seamen injured, she was indeed in a desperate plight in that howling gale. Another steamer, the *S.S. Beaverhill*, was in the vicinity, S. 74 W. of the *Millpool*'s given position, seventy-four miles distant. Like the *Ascania*, she hastened to the rescue, and we maintained constant wireless touch.

At 7 p.m., I attempted to alter course to steer N. 70 E., to bring me more directly to the *Millpool*'s line of drift, but heavy squalls on the *Ascania*'s port quarter tended to bring her round to the wind. I was compelled to resume the 85 course, which I was able to maintain by going full speed (84 revolutions per minute) on the port engine and 70 revs. on the starboard engine.

At 7.45 p.m., the *Millpool* sent out a frantic signal: **"PLEASE STAND BY AND APPROACH NEAR."**

That was what we were desperately trying to do! Now hurricane squalls were sweeping over the *Ascania* at intervals of about fifteen minutes, reducing visibility to half a mile. Between the squalls, in driving spindrift, the visibility was not above three miles. The seas were forty feet high from trough to crest, and short between the crests, as though crowded together by the hurricane squalls. It seemed impossible that a little old steamer, such as the *Millpool*, with her hatch stove in, could live m the trough of such seas.

At 8.05 p.m., I sent a message: **ASCANIA TO MILLPOOL. GIVE ME YOUR POSITION AS NEAR AS POSSIBLE NOW. I AM TRYING TO GET D/F BEARINGS OF YOU BUT AT PRESENT YOUR SIGNALS ARE TOO WEAK ARE YOU STEAMING OR LYING IN. TROUGH OF SEA?**

Fifty minutes went by, the wind and seas still increasing, and no reply. I was fearing that she had foundered, when at 8.55 a message was received: **MILLPOOL TO ASCANIA. LAYING IN TROUGH OF SEA. POSITION AS NEAR AS POSSIBLE AS BEFORE.**

I visited the wireless room, to urge the necessity of getting wireless direction finder bearings of the *Millpool*, but the senior operator assured me that her signals were too weak, and that both he and the *Beaverhill* were making continual efforts.

At 9.30 p.m., the seas were still increasing, up to fifty feet in height, and the wind at hurricane force. I again tried to head up to the *Millpool*, and for forty-five minutes managed to steer a course between 55 and 65. I could do this only by going full ahead on the port engine and slow on the starboard engine; but this reduced my ship's speed so that she was unable to avoid the seas that now broke on her port beam. This buffeting caused very violent motion of the ship, which made furniture slide about, and alarmed our passengers, while dollops of water cascaded in through the exposed deck doors.

I had to go back onto an 85 course. It was my intention to run along till I judged that we were on the *Millpool*'s line of drift, then to heave to and stand directly towards her on a 290 course. I kept the *Beaverhill* informed of my courses and intentions.

At 10.5 p.m. the wireless reported a D/F bearing of the *Millpool* as 70, very approximate. I now steered between 70 and 85, my ship yawing badly, so that I had to use the engines during the squalls, as before, to prevent her from flying up into the wind.

At 10.30 p.m., the *Millpool* gave a bearing of which the relative was 60. Her wireless operator added: **THINGS ARE MUCH THE SAME HERE. DONT KNOW HOW THINGS ARE ON DECK NOW BUT THE WIRELESS ROOM IS FLOODED AND I AM WET AND COLD HOPE TO SEE YOU SOON.** He added: **MILLPOOL USING OIL NAVIGATION LIGHTS WHICH ARE NOT BURNING VERY BRIGHTLY.**

At 11 p.m., the *Beaverhill* requested the *Millpool* to fire rockets. No reply was received to this message.

At 12 midnight, ships' clocks were advanced forty minutes. No signals were now being received from the *Millpool*. At 1 a.m., both the *Ascania* and the *Beaverhill* heard faint sounds, which might have been signals from the *Millpool*, but they were extremely weak, and unreadable. After that, we heard no more wireless signals from her.

At 1.10 a.m., I judged that the *Ascania* was on the *Millpool*'s line of drift. Watching for a favourable chance, and using the helm and engines as required, I brought my ship round to a course of 290. She lay hove to on this course, making a speed of three knots into the head-on seas. At frequent intervals we burned blue lights. We kept a very sharp and anxious lookout.

At this time the master of the *Beaverhill* reported by wireless that he had reached the *Millpool*'s given position and could see nothing of her. He was then hove to and awaiting daylight.

The barometer stood at 29.55 (1000.7 mb), after which it began to rise — a good sign, but the seas were awesome. They rushed towards our bows, rearing their white crests higher than the tops of the forward Samson posts. We could now estimate accurately that they were between forty-five and fifty feet high, and, in isolated groups, sixty feet high. We were shipping large volumes of water over the bows. Our hearts were heavy at the absence of any sign of the *Millpool* or any further wireless signals from her. If she had foundered, her boats could not live in those precipitous seas.

At daylight, 7.40 a.m., I reached the *Millpool*'s last given position. I had heard nothing from her since 10.30 p.m. I had seen nothing of her, or of boats or wreckage.

The visibility was now four miles. I remained in constant touch by wireless with the *Beaverhill*, but we did not sight one another. Throughout that day, until 4 p.m., the *Ascania* and the *Beaverhill*, exchanging information on courses, continued the search in the vicinity of the *Millpool*'s given position and along her presumed line of drift. We searched in zigzags over a wide area of sea.

Four other vessels — the *S.S. Beaverford*, S.S. Hazelwood, *S.S. Wearpool*, and a German, *S.S. Bockenheim* — answered our wireless calls and joined in the search.

The storm gradually abated, and visibility increased to fifteen miles, but the *Millpool* had disappeared without trace. There were no boats to be seen — no wreckage — no bodies.

After having searched for twenty-one hours, the *Ascania* and *Beaverhill* resumed their voyages, knowing that the other four vessels were continuing the search.

No trace of the *Millpool* was ever found. She and her complement of twenty-three men had vanished.

An inquiry by the Board of Trade exonerated the owners from blame, and declared that the *Millpool*, though old, was seaworthy, and that all rules had been observed. But the Court suggested that, in future, "the age of ships should be taken particularly into account in standard surveys, so that risks of loss by perils of the sea may be more fully guarded against."

Often, I have pondered on the tragedy of the *Millpool*. The fact that her after hatch was stove in, and that her top mainmast was snapped off, indicates that she had broached to in a hurricane squall. Beam on to the precipitous seas, she had wallowed helpless in the trough, down by the stern, battered by sea after sea,

The S.S Millpool was a Trunk Deck Ship like the type shown here. (Public Domain)

which probably stove in her bridge or in some other way damaged her steering gear, and flooded her engine room.

Her cargo of rye would have swelled greatly when water entered her hold. This pressure may have sprung her rusty old hull plates. Then suddenly, I suppose, she filled and sank, and the chasms of the deep closed over her and all who were in her.

23

A Pioneer Trans-ocean Aviator — Charles Ulm my Passenger to Canada — His Fatal Last Flight — "Ascania" Hung up at Quebec — Eventful Winter Voyage — A Hurricane in the North Atlantic — " Usworth" in Distress in Mid-ocean — SOS at Midnight — "Jean Jadot" Stands By — "Ascania" Steams to the Rescue — Wireless Directions — The Scene at Dawn — Pouring Oil on Troubled Waters.

IN November, 1934, on my twenty-second voyage in command of the *Ascania*, I had an aeroplane as deck cargo, lashed down on the foredeck. Its crew of three were passengers in my ship, bound from London to Quebec. They were the famous Australian aviator Charles Ulm, with his assistants, G. M. Littlejohn and J. L. Skilling.

Their plan was to fly from Quebec across Canada to the West Coast, and then from Oakland, California, across the Pacific Ocean to Australia, via Honolulu and Fiji.

Charles Ulm had been copilot with Charles Kingsford Smith in the first crossing of the Pacific Ocean by air in 1928. In the same aircraft (the Southern Cross) he and Kingsford Smith had made the first flight from Australia to New Zealand, and return. In 1933, Ulm had made a record breaking flight from England to Australia in his monoplane, Faith in Australia. He had also carried the first passengers and airmail from Australia to New Zealand, and from Australia to New Guinea. His name must remain forever high in the Roll of Honour of pioneer ocean crossing aviators.

The aeroplane that he had with him in the *Ascania* was named Star of Australia. It was built in England. He showed me the interior arrangements. The space inside the fuselage was occupied chiefly by petrol tanks. The seats of the pilot, relief pilot and wireless operator had intercommunication by means of a speaking tube. "She's a flying petrol tank," Ulm explained.

I had many a talk to Charles Ulm, who had a seat at my table in the dining saloon during our passage to Quebec. He was a splendid type of Australian, then thirty-seven years of age. When I landed him, his companions, and the *Star of Australia* at Quebec, they had my heartfelt good wishes for success in the dangerous enterprise ahead of them.

I landed them at Quebec on 19th November 1934. Fifteen days later, on 4th December, they took off from Oakland, California. They were forced down in

The Southern Cross ws a Fokker F.VIIb/3m trimotor monoplane that was flown by Australian aviator Charles Ulm (Public Domain)

the Pacific Ocean, presumably through shortage of petrol. Radio contact with them was lost, and an extensive search was made for them by twenty-three ships, but in vain. Ulm had told me that, even if he were forced down, the buoyancy of the empty petrol tanks would keep his aircraft afloat indefinitely. This was known, and the search was continued for a long time. But, as no trace was ever found of them, the actual manner of their death may only be surmised.

That winter of 1934 was one of the worst on record for violent storms in the North Atlantic. On 23rd November, the *Ascania* left Montreal at 10 a.m., bound for London. She was one of the last vessels to clear out of Montreal that year before ice blocked the river. A few steamers were still loading cargo when we left among them the *S.S. Usworth*, a small British freighter of 3500 tons.

I had a river pilot, as usual, on the bridge. Our passage downstream in fog was very slow. Next morning, when we were proceeding at dead slow, in fog, in the narrow waters off the entrance to the port of Quebec, the *Ascania* fouled the anchor cable of a C.P.R. steamer, *S.S. Beaverbrae*, which was lying in the stream. My ship was "hung up" by her starboard propeller, with her engines stopped. While we were in this position, a cargo steamer of the Donaldson Line *S.S. Salaria*, loomed out of the fog, and scraped across the *Ascania*'s stern. It was a tangle. The air was blue with "language" on the bridges of the three ships concerned in the mix up.

The *Beaverbrae* unshackled her anchor cable, but it was still wrapped around the *Ascania*'s propeller. A tug then grappled up the *Beaverbrae*'s anchor. I decided to proceed into dock at Quebec for inspection. With the aid of five tugs, we manoeuvred into the dock, unable to use our own engines.

The anchor cable was freed without difficulty from our starboard propeller. Inspection revealed that no serious damage had been done. On the following day we cleared out from Quebec and reached London without further mishap. The ship was dry docked there, and it was found that she had been only slightly damaged, where the *Salaria* had scraped her stern. The repairs were effected in a few hours, and we got ready to leave on another voyage.

That voyage proved to be one of the most eventful that I have ever made. The *Ascania* left Surrey Dock in the Thames at 12 noon on 7th December 1934, with a light cargo and not many passengers. She was on her winter schedule, bound for Halifax and New York. We called at Southampton and Havre for more passengers and mails. On 11th December, at noon, when we were 738 miles to the westward of Havre, the ship ran into a moderate westerly gale, with a wind velocity of 30 knots and rough seas. The glass was falling, the wind and seas increasing. The gale freshened, and I reduced speed to 10 knots. On 12th December, the weather developed into a strong W.N.W. gale, with wind velocity of 44 knots, and high seas (up to twenty feet from trough to crest).

Next day the storm continued. The wind increased to a heavy gale (52 knots) and very high seas (up to forty feet). We were in the thick of a North Atlantic Snorter, with frequent squalls of rain, sleet, and hail. The ship was labouring, but "thrusting into it" well. On Thursday, 13th December, at noon, my, position by dead reckoning was in Lat. 49.41 N., Long. 32.41 W. We had had no sight of sun or stars for three days during the gale, and it was difficult to estimate drift and the scend[1] of the seas in their fury. We had run 1264 miles to the westward of Havre. The heavy gale continued. The wind hissed and tore at the seas, whipping their crests to spindrift, which obscured visibility and streamed in dense gusts of spray over the bridge.

At midnight on Thursday, our position by D.F. was in Lat. 49.20 N., Long. 34.34 W. I had had very little sleep during the three days that the storm had been raging. The log entry at midnight was "Fresh N.W. gale, high sea, frequent heavy rain squalls. The vessel is labouring and straining heavily, shipping water fore and aft. Course 257."

The *Ascania* had three wireless operators. A few minutes after midnight I was handed a radiogram: **JEAN JADOT TO ALL SHIPS. MIDNIGHT 13TH DECEMBER 1934. S.S. USWORTH SENDING OUT S O S IN LAT 48.36 N., LONG. 33.35 W. AM HERE PROCEEDING.**

From this it was apparent that the *S.S. Jean Jadot* (a Belgian freighter of 5,900 tons, Captain S. Gonthier bound from New York to Antwerp) was in the vicinity of the *Usworth*, and relaying the *Usworth'* s S O S.

Our operators could not hear the *Usworth*. We ascertained later that her wireless aerial had been carried away. She was transmitting on a temporary aerial, with short range, audible to the Jean Jadot. By good chance, Captain Gonthier of the *Jean Jadot* was able to speak and write English fluently and so keep us informed of events without need of using the international code language. All wireless messages between the ships were transmitted in Morse, in clear English.

The full details of the *Usworth*'s plight were at first not known to me but were subsequently established in evidence.

She was a single deck, three island, single screw, coal burning steamer of gross tonnage 3535, built in 1926, owned by the Dagleish Shipping Company, of Newcastle-upon-Tyne. She was 356 feet long and had five hatches and six watertight bulkheads. Her steering- gear was of the old fashioned rod-and-chain type, with the steering engine amidships. She was certified A.I at Lloyds. She had been bought by her owners for £51,000 and was insured for £27,800. Leaving Montreal at 7 a.m. on 3rd December, with a cargo of 5625 tons of wheat, the *Usworth* was the last ship to clear out of that port that year. She was loaded down to the Plimsoll mark, with a freeboard of 4 feet 6 inches. Calling at Sydney, Nova Scotia, for bunkers, she put to sea from that port at 11 p.m. on 6th December, eastbound to Queenstown for orders.

Under command of Captain J. J. Reed, a Northumberland man, forty years of age, the *Usworth* was a "two-watch ship," with a crew of twenty-six. She had a Chief Officer, Second Officer, eight deckhands, one wireless operator, one cook, one steward, a mess boy, three Engineer Officers, and eight firemen. All the crew were British, with the exception of the eight firemen, who were Afghans (from Peshawar, North-west India).

Of the eight deckhands, one was the carpenter, one the boatswain, two were apprentices, and the other four were A.B. seamen. She was not undermanned in accordance with the rules of the Board of Trade, but, as a two-watch ship, her crew worked twelve hours a day, as in sailing ships in olden times. If safety had been the dominant consideration, in excess of minimum legal requirements, she would have been better handled, especially in prolonged heavy weather, if she had had three Mates, and some additional A.B. seamen. This, however, was not the chief cause of her difficulties in the gale. She was, as the Court of Inquiry eventually found, "overwhelmed by the sea, during a hurricane."

The gale came up on her port quarter at midnight on 10th December, when she was four days out from Sydney, N.S. At 3 a.m. on the 11th, she shipped a heavy sea on the port side, which stove in the midships saloon door. The Captain put her about and hove to, but in the course of this manoeuvre the rod-and-chain steering gear parted. The port lead blocks were torn away from their fittings, and the bottle screws stripped.

The crew attempted to repair the steering gear, and to steer the vessel by means of wire tackles on the quadrant and poop winch, but at 8 a.m. the wire tackles carried away. The Captain then wirelessed for assistance and lashed the rudder. This signal was answered by the *Jean Jadot*, proceeding eastbound not many miles astern on the same track. The Belgian steamer arrived at 9 a.m., and stood by throughout that day and night, and next morning, while the storm continued to rage, and the crew of the *Usworth* worked desperately to rig a jury steering gear.

These efforts failed, and, at 12.30 p.m. on 12th December, the *Jean Jadot* took the *Usworth* in tow, making for the nearest port, Fayal in the Azores, 700 miles distant. This was a "stern tow." The course was in a south-easterly direction, running before the north-westerly gale. The *Usworth* remained headed into the wind and seas, with the tow rope over her stern, and her own engine going full astern: the correct procedure in the circumstances.

The gale was increasing. After three hours the towline parted, as darkness closed in on 12th December. Throughout that night, the crew continued rigging a jury steering gear, while the *Jean Jadot* stood by. Next morning this work was completed, and the *Usworth* proceeded under her own power on an easterly course, the *Jean Jadot* escorting her.

They had gone only twenty-five miles, when the wind increased to hurricane force, and both vessels hove to within sight of one another. In the fierce gale, the *Usworth*, with the wind and sea on her starboard bow, her rudder lashed five degrees to starboard, and her engines going slow, was riding the seas, as comfortably as could be expected, when darkness fell, and the gale increased phenomenally.

At 9.50 p.m., 13th December, three mountainous seas in succession struck her. She was thrown four or five points off her course and heeled over almost onto her beam ends. As she was recovering, she gave three jerks to port. Her grain cargo had shifted, and she lay wallowing in the trough of the seas with a list of twenty-five degrees to port.

The seas, crashing onto her deck, had carried away her wireless aerial, staved in a hatch aft, strained the coamings and hatch beams out of position, and carried away two derrick booms, the stokehold ventilators, and part of the bridge fittings.

Two of her three lifeboats had been washed overboard, and the third lay in its chocks smashed.

A temporary cover was rigged over the stove-in hatch. The Captain then ordered all hands available into the 'tween deck, to crawl into the after hold with shovels and try to trim the cargo, to bring the vessel back on an even keel. All except two Afghan stokers obeyed this order. These two remained in their quarters, reading the Koran. They were fatalists.

The effort to trim the ship was futile. A large amount of water had poured in through the stove-in hatch. More seas were breaking on board, and more water pouring down below. The vessel was gradually settling down. Ballast pumps were working on all hold bilges and in the engine room and stokehold. The *Usworth* was doomed, and her Master knew it. At 10.30 p.m., he ordered the wireless operator to send out the S O S. A temporary aerial was rigged, and the distress signal sent out.

In the darkness and terrible storm, the *Jean Jadot* and *Usworth* had become separated, and could not sight one another's lights. The three mountainous seas that had wrecked the *Usworth* had also caused part of the Belgian ship's cargo to shift. Her Captain had run off before the sea in order to secure it. But he was still in wireless contact, not more than twenty miles distant from the foundering steamer.

That was the situation, though its details were then unknown to me, when the Jean Jadot's relay of the *Usworth*'s S O S was first picked up by the *Ascania* at midnight.

The *Ascania* was approximately one hundred miles to the north-westward of the *Usworth*'s given position. The exact relative positions were difficult to compute in the gale that had lasted for three days and had now attained hurricane force.

My ship had been breasting the seas as comfortably as could be expected, hove to on her 257 course. At the first opportunity, in a relative smooth between the very high seas, I put my ship about at 0.20 a.m. on Friday, 14th December, and headed her on a 130 course, making for the *Usworth*'s given position, at full speed. On that course she was rolling heavily and shipping large volumes of water aft. I also sent a wireless message addressed to the Captain of the *Usworth*, giving him my position at 0.20 a.m., and stating that the *Ascania* was coming to his assistance, making about 14 knots.

At 1 a.m., our wireless operators heard and reported to me an exchange of messages:

JEAN JADOT TO USWORTH: HURRAH WE HAVE JUST SIGHTED YOU AGAIN, USWORTH TO JEAN JADOT: POSITION VERY SERIOUS. BADLY SETTLING DOWN, WILL HAVE TO ABANDON. AS LIFEBOATS HAVE BEEN WASHED AWAY, CAN YOU MANAGE TO TAKE CREW OFF?

JEAN JADOT TO USWORTH: CAN YOU POSSIBLY WAIT TILL DAYLIGHT?

USWORTH TO JEAN JADOT: CONDITION PRECARIOUS. WISH TO BE TAKEN OFF AS SOON AS POSSIBLE.

JEAN JADOT TO USWORTH: WHAT WOULD YOU SUGGEST BEST WAY? JUST NOW I CANNOT POSSIBLY SEND BOAT OVER TO YOU. CAN YOU MAKE SOME SORT OF RAFT? I WILL TRY AND SEND EMPTY BOAT ON YOUR LEE, BUT JUST NOW THE SEA IS WASHING OVER MY BOAT DECK.

USWORTH TO JEAN JADOT: TRYING TO THINK OF SOME WAY OF GETTING OFF. HAVE NOTHING TO MAKE RAFT WITH.

This exchange of wireless "talking" in Morse had occurred with intervals of up to fifteen minutes between messages. It enabled us to get direction finder bearings on the two ships, indicating that they were dead ahead on our 130 course.

At 2.40 a.m., I sent a message. **ASCANIA TO USWORTH AND JEAN JADOT: EXPECT TO SIGHT YOU ABOUT 5 A.M. IF YOU INTEND DRIFTING A BOAT OVER, I WILL SPREAD OIL TO WINDWARD, OR WHERE-EVER YOU SUGGEST. WHAT PLANS ARE YOU MAKING?**

The idea of "pouring oil on troubled waters" is very ancient, but it was only with the advent of many vessels burning oil fuel that it was used, especially during the 1914-18 war, extensively in rescue operations at sea. The spreading of an "oil slick" does not "calm" the sea. It has no effect on the height of the seas, but it stops them from breaking. It converts the surface from a series of curling, crashing wave crests into glassy undulating swells.

I had had experience of spreading oil, to make boat work easier when boarding neutral vessels in rough seas to inspect their cargoes, while I was serving in *H.M.S. Caronia* and in destroyers during the war.

By astonishing coincidence, I had written an article on that very subject, which was printed in the Daily Mail, London, on 6th December 1934, only eight days before I was called on to go to the rescue of the *Usworth*. In that article I had not only described the effects of spreading oil at sea, but had also given a description of the technique of rescue operations in heavy weather, as follows:

The rescue ship, after laying an "oil slick" in the line of drift of the distressed vessel, steams close up on the weather side of the distressed vessel and lowers her boat, taking great care to allow herself plenty of room to manoeuvre in order to avoid collision. She lies in this position, providing a lee, or shelter, till the boat pulls down to the wreck and takes off the crew. The boat then pulls down with the sea, using the wreck for shelter, while the rescue ship steams round into position to pick them up.

In extreme cases, instead of sending a crew in the boat, the rescue vessel may fire a line across the distressed vessel by means of a rocket or line firing gun. The distressed crew haul on this line and pull an empty boat over, which is also connected to the rescue ship by a long drift of line.

The crew contrive, as best they may, to jump into the boat, and she is then hauled back to the rescue ship. This method is known as "shuttling."

That article forecast the procedures that I would be adopting in mid-Atlantic a week after it was published. The idea had been fermenting in my mind during my search for the foundered *Millpool* two months previously, and in general while voyaging across the Atlantic in that stormy winter. The fact remains that my article in the Daily Mail was uncannily prophetic of the *Usworth* rescue operations.

My wireless message sent at 2.40 a.m. was the first suggestion of spreading an oil slick. I also asked the *Jean Jadot* to send out her Morse recognition signal at full strength, at frequent intervals, to enable us to get wireless direction finder bearings on her position with absolute accuracy, and this was done.

My signal sent at 2.40 a.m. was answered, ten minutes later, by the *Usworth*, which we now heard for the first time. Her aerial had been to some extent repaired. It was a desperate plea. **USWORTH TO CAPTAIN ASCANIA: WE HAVE NO BOATS. PLEASE DO YOUR UTMOST TO ASSIST IN PICKING UP CREW OF 26. MASTER.**

At 3 a.m. we heard, **JEAN JADOT TO USWORTH: I AM GOING TO LAY OIL TO LEEWARD OF YOU FOR YOU TO DRIFT INTO. ASCANIA IS COMING TO OUR ASSISTANCE AND IS ASKING FOR DIRECTION FINDER BEARINGS.**

At 3.18 a.m. we received, **JEAN JADOT TO CAPTAIN ASCANIA: WE HAVE JUST SPREAD OIL TO LEE OF USWORTH LYING SSW NNE DIRECTION. I WILL TRY FLOAT BOAT TO HIM AT DAWN. CAPTAIN JEAN JADOT.**

At 3.30 a.m., I asked the *Usworth* to fire rockets as a check on my D.F. bearings. She replied that her rockets were wet. The Jean Jadot then fired rockets for her at fifteen-minute intervals.

At 4.00 a.m., the log entry in the *Ascania* was: "Strong N.W. gale. Very high sea. Vessel labouring, straining, and rolling heavily. Engines racing. Hard squalls."

At 4.48 a.m., we sighted a rocket sent up by the Jean Jadot. It was right ahead on our course, at a distance of twenty-eight miles, as determined by later observations. She fired two more rockets at 5.02 a.m., which we sighted at the edge of the horizon. We knew then for certain that we were on a true course. At 6.02 a.m., we sighted the masthead lights of both vessels, on the horizon between nine and ten miles ahead. Wireless messages followed:

ASCANIA TO USWORTH, 6.05 A.M.: HAVE NOW SIGHTED YOU. JEAN JADOT TO CAPTAIN ASCANIA, 6.21 A.M.: HOVE TO NEAR USWORTH, BUT ACCOUNT SEA DEEM IT ADVISABLE WAIT A WHILE YET TO LAUNCH EVEN EMPTY BOAT WITH CHANCE OF SUCCESS. WOULD YOU MAKE US A LEE DURING OPERATIONS? MASTER.

S.S. USWORTH TO CAPTAIN ASCANIA AND CAPT JEAN JADOT.

6.39 A.M.: POSITION GETTING VERY PRECARIOUS. VESSEL GRADUALLY LISTING MORE. PLEASE DO YOUR UTMOST TO GET US OFF.

JEAN JADOT TO USWORTH: HAVE SPREAD OIL TO LEEWARD. WILL NOW DO SAME TO WINDWARD. DOING UTMOST TO SAVE YOU, BUT HAVE TO TAKE PRECAUTIONS, AS MY SHIP IS NOT VERY MANAGEABLE IN HEAVY SEA. AT FIRST STREAK OF DAWN, I WILL COME CLOSE TO YOU. HAVE ROCKET READY TO FIRE LINE OVER ME, AND I WILL TRY AND FLOAT EMPTY BOAT OVER TO YOU ON THE LINE.

ASCANIA TO JEAN JADOT, 6.40 A.M.: I AM GOING TO LAY OIL TO LEEWARD NOW. MUST DO SOMETHING QUICKLY.

Dawn was just breaking, at 6.45 a.m., as I slowed the *Ascania* to the leeward of the *Usworth*, hove to and began spreading oil. As the *Jean Jadot* was on the scene and engaged in rescue operations before I arrived, her Master had the initiative, and in that sense was in control of the situation. My duty was to ascertain his plan, and to stand by and assist him as required.

I estimated that the *Usworth* was drifting at the rate of two knots. She was in a serious plight, lying in the trough of the sea, down by the stern and with a heavy list to port. Heavy seas were crashing up her starboard side and breaking over her. She was lurching and wallowing violently and submerging her lee side up to the hatch coamings and the bridge deck. Four derricks, still attached to the goosenecks at the base of the foremast, were projecting over the side of the forward well deck and sawing violently to and fro on the top of the bulwarks, their ends dipping into the sea as she lurched. Abaft the funnel, a pair of davits were bent down double, their ends also dipping at intervals. Boats and ventilators were washed away, and her steering gear carried away. Her after hatch which had been stove in, was temporarily recovered. On her bridge and deck forward and aft we could see her crew, wearing life jackets, holding on to anything handy as she lurched.

Though the gale continued to rage, with squalls of rain and some hail, the weather was fortunately not icy cold. The temperature of the air and of the sea water, moderated here by the influence of the Gulf Stream, was 53 deg. F. That, and the rapidly increasing visibility, were almost the only favourable circumstances in the bad situation. There were patches of clear sky to the eastward, and a chance that some sunlight would struggle through later on.

The Jean Jadot, her grey painted hull standing high in the water, with her red boot topping showing (for she was lightly loaded, as also was the *Ascania*), steamed around to the *Usworth*'s weather quarter as dawn broke, and wirelessed to the *Usworth*: **WE ARE NOW COMING. FIRE ROCKET WHEN I BLOW WHISTLE.**

The great advantages of wireless signalling, even between ships in close visual range of one another, could scarcely have been more aptly demonstrated. The three ships could "talk" so that each was informed of what the two others were doing.

I had now spread an oil slick for two miles to the lee. The *Usworth* and the *Jean Jadot* had both drifted into it. Anxiously I watched for a puff of steam from the Belgian's whistle and then heard his signal. The two Mates and some seamen of the *Usworth* were grouped around a line firing gun on her poop deck with a big coil of line nearby.

At the signal they fired the line rocket which zoomed skywards towards the *Jean Jadot*, but, as they were shooting into a wind of heavy gale force (52 knots) the propulsion of the rocket was not sufficient to carry it to its mark, and it fell into the water thirty feet from the *Jean Jadot's* side. I could see the attitudes of dejection and weariness in the men of the *Usworth*, as they hauled in the wet and now oil soaked line and began to coil it for another attempt. Now the seas breaking on board the wreck had a coating of oil, which was no doubt making things very uncomfortable for the men on her decks.

She signalled, **USWORTH TO JEAN JADOT: CAN YOU SEND A MANNED LIFEBOAT? MY MEN ARE ALL IN.**

The Captain of the Belgian steamer quite correctly decided that the seas were too high to launch a manned boat at that stage. He therefore manoeuvred his ship again into position and attempted to fire a line with his line gun from his bows across the *Usworth*. Although he was firing downwind, that very fact meant that he dared not approach too close to the wreck. His rate of drift, being lightly loaded and higher in the water, was greater than that of the wreck, and his ship was not at all easy to manage in the very high seas and strong gale. He fired his rocket, but a gusty squall at that moment carried it astern of the *Usworth*. The two ships then drifted apart, and Captain Reed signalled, **PLEASE TRY TO MAN BOATS. IMPOSSIBLE TO THROW ANY MORE LINES AS COILS BEING WASHED AWAY AND CREW PLAYED OUT.**

It was then 8.53 a.m. I was continuing to spread oil in the lee. The sun broke through the clouds, making strange rainbow effects and marbling on the oily waters. Our passengers were lining the rails, intently watching the mid-ocean drama.

CHAPTER ENDNOTES

(1) "Scend of the sea" refers to the heaving or surging motion of a vessel as it rises and falls with the waves, particularly in a heavy sea. It can also describe the forward impulse or lift given to a vessel by the sea's motion. Essentially, it's the upward and forward movement a ship experiences as it interacts with the waves.

24

The "Usworth" Rescue — A Difficult Feat of Seamanship — Attempts to Fire a Line Across — Waiting for the Weather to Moderate — "Jean Jadot" Sends a Manned Boat — Heroic but Premature Decision — Disaster to the Belgian Boat — "Ascania" Sends a Boat — Third Officer Pollitt and His Gallant Crew — Manoeuvring into Position — The Risks of Collision — Getting the Boat Alongside — Survivors Rescued from the Wreck — Unexpected Publicity.

AT the change of the watch at 8 a.m., on that Friday, 14th December, 1934, the Chief Officer of the *Ascania* had entered the weather conditions in his log: "Strong gale with frequent heavy squalls. High steep sea and very heavy swell. Mainly cloudy and clear." It was in those conditions that Captain Gonthier in the *Jean Jadot* had manoeuvred his ship to windward of the *Usworth* at 8 a.m. and had attempted unsuccessfully to get a line across to her. He knew, as I did, that the glass was rising, and that the weather would probably moderate during the day. We would have eight hours of daylight in which to get the crew of the *Usworth* off — if she remained afloat! Every hour should bring conditions more favourable for launching a manned boat. On the other hand, there was the possibility that the *Usworth*, with her heavy list to port, might founder at any moment. Apart from that possibility, the men on her deck, utterly wearied as they were by their efforts during three sleepless days and nights, and wet through and covered in oil from the seas washing over the wreck, should be taken off as quickly as possible.

It was for this reason that the Belgian Captain, as soon as daylight broke, had attempted to drift a boat across to her. When his effort failed, his ship drifted past the stern of the *Usworth*, and in a few minutes was half a mile to leeward.

It was now my turn to attempt to send an unmanned boat to the distressed steamer. At 9.00 a.m., I steamed around to her windward side. For several hours previously I had been preparing for such an attempt. My boatswain, and some of our A.B. seamen, had been splicing boat falls to make a length of 5000 feet of 3½-inch Manila rope, which was coiled in readiness on deck. One end of this was secured to the thin rocket line. If the rocket line reached the *Usworth*, her crew would then haul in the 3½-inch Manila, by means of which a boat would be guided across to her.

S.S. Usworth founders in heavy seas (Public Domain)

One of our lifeboats was in readiness to be lowered for that purpose. It was protected against splintering, by mattresses lashed around the gunwales. All the gear in the boat was secured to the thwarts.

As I was steaming around to windward, Captain Reed sent me a wireless message. **USWORTH TO MASTER ASCANIA: POSITION GETTING VERY SERIOUS. CAN YOU NOT POSSIBLY MAN BOAT AND GET MY CREW OFF? MASTER.**

I could well understand his anxiety, but I had no right to hazard the lives of my crew, by calling for volunteers to man a boat in precipitous seas, while the *Usworth* was still afloat in weather that promised to moderate. But, if a line could he got across, and an unmanned boat sent over, then the *Usworth*'s crew could jump into that boat, and could be hauled to safety without need of further exertions on their part.

I therefore replied: **AM TRYING ROCKET NOW BUT IT SEEMS HOPELESS UNLESS THE WEATHER MODERATES. IF ROCKET MISSES WILL WAIT TO SEE IF WEATHER IMPROVES**. This was for the information also of the Master of the *Jean Jadot*.

When two ships are cruising around another one in a storm there is need for great care to avoid collision. The rate of drift of the *Ascania*, I estimated was four knots, and that of the *Usworth* two and a half knots. All three ships were forging ahead at varying rates, owing to wind pressure on their sides. That fact, combined with the violent motions of the vessels, and the difficulty of manoeuvring in the high wind and sea, made it extremely hazardous to approach too near the wreck, especially on her windward side.

I could not be unmindful of the fact that I had 800 souls on board the *Ascania*. A heavy collision with the *Usworth* could have put their lives in peril. As we steamed around to windward, the wreck, lying broadside in the trough, was at times obscured from our: view, except for her topmasts glimpsed above the crests of the seas, and even these were sometimes lost from sight in hail squalls.

I approached on her weather quarter. In that position, when the: wind and seas were astern, the *Ascania*'s propellers raced each time that the stern lifted; and when we were beam-on to the seas, my ship rolled and lurched violently.

We fired two rocket lines, but both missed. I now realized that it would be useless to make any further attempts of that kind. Even if we had succeeded in connecting with a line, the ships would have drifted too far apart before a boat could be hauled across. There was nothing to do but to wait until the weather moderated, and then to send a manned boat. But, despite the rapidly rising glass, heavy squalls of hail and sleet were sweeping over, and keeping the seas heaped up.

The *Ascania* and the *Jean Jadot* continued to steam around the *Usworth*, spreading oil both to windward and leeward of her, in the hope that this would diminish the force of the seas breaking over her. There was a blanket of oil on the seas, but, in weather of that severity, it could not be fully effective. The oil seemed to collect in patches. It subdued the spindrift to some extent, but not entirely.

During the forenoon, five other steamers, within 100 miles radius, having heard our exchange of wireless signals, wirelessed to me, asking if their assistance was required. I informed the two nearest, the *S.S. Manchester Commerce*, distant 35 miles, and the S.S. Kentucky, distant 60 miles, that I would be grateful for their assistance. They altered course accordingly and stood towards our position.

At 11 a.m., the Master of the *Jean Jadot* wirelessed to the *Usworth*: **I WILL TRY AND SEND MANNED BOAT NOW.**

That was what I also intended to do, but not until a little later. I had conferred with my officers, who were all of the opinion, as I was myself, that it would be folly to send a boat away in seas which were so confused and steep. We could admire the courage, but not so much the sound judgment, of the gallant Belgians, in their decision to lower a boat at that time.

My decision was to launch a manned boat from the *Ascania* at or near 2 p.m. That would allow a margin of two hours for rescue. operations, before darkness set in. The deciding factor was that the seas were moderating, if only slightly. If in the meantime the *Usworth* foundered, or looked like foundering immediately, we were ready to launch a boat or boats at any time; but, as far as could judge, she would keep afloat for several hours yet.

I wirelessed, at 11.5 a.m., **ASCANIA TO JEAN JADOT: I WILL LAY OIL TO LEEWARD FOR TEN MINUTES, THEN COME ROUND TO WINDWARD AND GIVE YOUR BOAT A LEE.**

While I was doing this, Captain Reed wirelessed at 11.13 a.m., **USWORTH TO MASTER ASCANIA: WHEN DO YOU THINK YOU WILL BE ABLE TO GET MANNED BOAT AWAY?**

ASCANIA TO USWORTH: SEA TOO BAD AT PRESENT BUT GLASS RISING. HAVE EVERY HOPE FOR THIS AFTERNOON.

USWORTH TO ASCANIA: SHIP'S LIST INCREASING EVERY HOUR. CREW BECOMING VERY ANXIOUS.

ASCANIA TO USWORTH: AM ALSO VERY ANXIOUS. WILL DO EVERYTHING POSSIBLE.

At this time the *Jean Jadot* was already proceeding to windward of the wreck and making preparations to lower a boat. I steamed around to windward of her and of the wreck. The purpose of this manoeuvre was to give the *Jean Jadot* a lee for her boat, by interposing the hulk of the *Ascania*, broadside on to the seas, to her windward side, to break the force of the seas and wind, to some extent.

The *Jean Jadot* approached the *Usworth* on the weather quarter. She would launch her boat there, which would then pull down, in her lee, to the lee side of the wreck. After taking men off from the wreck, the boat would then pull down to the lee of the wreck, while the *Jean Jadot* steamed around to pick the boat up.

At noon, the *Ascania* was in position to windward of the two other ships. At that time, in accordance with routine at the change of the watch, the Chief Officer of the *Ascania* entered in his log his observations of the weather: "Slight moderation in W.N.W. gale. Currently heavy squalls. High sea. Cloudy and clear. Vessel labouring and straining heavily."

A few minutes after noon, the Belgians lowered an empty lifeboat on their port side, in the lee, and we saw ten men climb down with difficulty on side ladders to man her. As I later ascertained, the names of these heroic men were: Second Officer J. Leblanc; Fourth Officer P. Lambert; Ahle Seamen Dobbelaere, Sprentels, De Plecker, Schrovens, De Jongh, Van Neste, Beeldens, and Hermans.

We saw the boat pulling away from the side of the Jean Jadot, rising and falling steeply in the oil covered swell and seas, frequently disappearing from sight in the trough, then reappearing, precariously perched on a crest. Her eight oars were pathetically inadequate as a means of propulsion against such tremendous and terrifying forces of heaving and swirling water; but she kept on, and at length disappeared from our sight close under the lee of the wreck. Getting ready also to launch a boat if required, I wirelessed at 1 p.m., **ASCANIA TO USWORTH: WHEN WE ARE ABLE TO SEND. BOAT, WHERE DO YOU SUGGEST BEST POSITION TO TAKE MEN OFF?**

The reply came immediately: **ABAFT FUNNEL**. After that, wireless communication with the *Usworth* ended. Her lone wireless operator had jumped into the Jean Jadot's boat, which at that moment was ranging alongside. He was entitled to do that, as Captain Reed •J had given the order to abandon ship, and it was "every man for, himself."

Though we could not see what was happening, I ascertained later that fourteen of the *Usworth*'s crew had jumped into the Belgian boat. They were: First Officer N. Storey; Second Officer W. Williamson; Second Engineer S. Carter; Wireless Operator D. Robertson; Able Seamen B. F. Murphy, B. J. Murphy, J. Chair, T. Breen; Apprentice J. Bray; Firemen Abdul Refus, Gulam Khan, Ahmed Ali, Waris Khan, and Makarab.

That left twelve men still on board the wreck, among them the Captain. These men had stood aside, so as not to overcrowd the Belgian boat. They perhaps reasoned also that the *Ascania* would presently be sending a bigger and better boat, but of that they had no certain knowledge.

Whatever their reasoning, they took a vital decision to remain on board the wreck. Two of the Afghans refused to jump into the Belgian boat. One of these said to his compatriots, "You go in the boat. I go to God!"

We glimpsed the Belgian boat pulling away to the lee of the wreck. As I could see that there were still some men in the *Usworth*, I decided that the time had come to launch the *Ascania*'s boat to go to their rescue.

Many hours previously, while steaming during the night in. response to the S O S, I had prepared for launching a boat. After conferring with my officers, I had decided to call for volunteers to man a boat. To begin with; every one of my six officers, volunteered to take charge of her.

It was then my responsibility to decide which of them should go. My choice was Third Officer E. J. R. Pollitt, a young and keen officer, who was a Lieutenant in the Royal Naval Reserve.

Next we called for volunteers for ten seamen to man the boat. Every seaman on board, and some of the stewards and firemen as well, volunteered.

That was in the best traditions of the sea. The *Ascania* carried twenty-six clincher built lifeboats, each thirty feet long, capable of carrying sixty-two persons. As the author of Lifeboat Efficiency — the standard textbook for the Lifeboat men's Certificate examination — I had certainly not neglected lifeboat drill in the *Ascania*. All my officers, and at least one hundred of the crew, were thoroughly trained in the handling of lifeboats.

Third Officer Pollitt, with my approval, selected ten Able Seamen to go with him in the boat. They were, like himself all younger men, with keen mentality and fine physique. Their names were: A.B. Seamen R. W. Beckett, G. Bowles, J. Brawn, D. Brodie, R. Brown, K. Campbell, J. W. Mortimer, W. Skinner, H. Ward, and A. Williams.

Our boat would be manned before it was lowered from the davits. This was the drill that my crew had often practised in harbour. It enabled the boat to be fended off and pulled away from the ship's side as soon as she hit the water.

As usual when she was at sea, the *Ascania* had two "sea boats," one on each side, in readiness for any emergency, such as the cry of "man overboard." The boat to be launched on this occasion was the portside sea boat. To prevent splintering, I had her starboard side well protected with mattresses. She carried two sets of oars, two axes, two sea anchors (canvas bags or drogues intended to keep the boat head-on to heavy seas), several tins of oil, spare red lights, and a coil of 2½-inch Manila rope, besides the usual lifeboat equipment.

The *Jean Jadot* steamed round to the lee of the *Usworth* to pick up her boat, but, at the rate of drift of the *Usworth*, it appeared likely that the Belgian boat, if lying to a sea anchor would soon pass under the bow of the wreck and lie to windward of her. I therefore spread more oil to windward and took a wide sweep to get into position on the *Usworth*'s weather quarter; As we did this, at 1.15 p.m., we sighted what appeared to be Jean Jadot's boat floating upside down, with several black objects, which might have been lifebelts, or bodies, or both, covered in oil, floating nearby.

This was only a momentary glimpse. It was impossible, because of the heavy sea and a blinding squall that was then passing over, to determine what had happened. I thought that perhaps the *Jean Jadot* had taken the men from the boat on board and had abandoned the boat.

Whatever had happened, Captain Gonthier was at that moment too preoccupied with the rescue operations and with handling his ship around the wreck to be able to send me a wireless message. I also was preoccupied with manoeuvring the *Ascania* into position for launching our boat. Suddenly in the squall we saw the Jean Jadot coming along on the opposite course to ours, apparently looking for his boat. I was forced to take a round turn out of the *Ascania* to avoid collision, and so lost position.

By 1.30 p.m., the *Jean Jadot* had drifted clear, and I was again approaching the *Usworth* on her starboard quarter, with the *Ascania*'s port sea boat manned and swung out, ready for lowering. With an officer in the stem keeping me informed by telephone of the distance off, I manoeuvred ship to a dead stop one hundred feet astern of the wreck, at 1.50 p.m., and gave the order, "Lower away!" which was instantly repeated by Pollitt in the stern sheets of the lifeboat.

It was an anxious moment. Heaving lines had been attached to the lower blocks of the boat falls, to haul them quickly out of the way as soon as they were unhooked. This was done as soon as the boat was waterborne, but, because of the great rate of drift, it was difficult to spring the boat away from the ship's side. I had the engines on the "stand by" to go astern, but, even at that, my proximity to the wreck was alarming. The two ships were plunging and rolling about in different directions. I had gone as close as was safe, without actually endangering my ship unduly.

To assist the boat in getting clear, she was pulled forward by a line from the forecastle head, which was passed aft in the boat in an effort to spring her off; but this manoeuvre was only partly successful. At the right moment Pollitt had given the orders, "Shove off. Out oars. Give way together," but, as the boat slithered forward under the *Ascania*'s bows, she was in imminent danger of being crushed by the ship's forefoot, which was rising clear out of the water.

I rang the engines to full astern both. At that instant also a heavy sea, sweeping around the bow, threw the boat clear, and off she went with the ten men bending their backs to the oars. Pulling was extremely difficult. The violent motion of the boat unshipped the oars from the thole pins. As weather oars missed stroke, the wind blew them across the boat. It was impossible for Pollitt as coxswain to use a steering oar, and he had to rely on the tiller and rudder.

At times the boat was hidden from our sight in the trough of the sea. Then we would sight her on a crest, the crew manfully toiling on. It seemed a miracle that they were able to propel her at all, across that wild intervening space and under the lee of the *Usworth*. I'll admit it now; as the saying goes, my heart was in my mouth all the time.

The *Ascania*'s boat had been launched at 1.50 p.m. As soon as she was clear, I wirelessed, **ASCANIA TO JEAN JADOT: PLEASE GIVE ME SOME INFORMATON ABOUT YOUR BOAT.**

The reply came ten minutes later, while my boat's crew were tossing on the seas, and that reply was appalling. **JEAN JADOT TO ASCANIA, 2 P.M.: HAVE ONLY TWO RESCUED ON BOARD, CADET BREY AND FIREMAN WARIS KHAN. TWELVE OTHERS WERE LOST THROUGH CAPSIZING OF BOAT. ALSO LOST TWO OF MY OWN BOAT'S CREW.**

So that was the situation — fourteen men drowned from the Belgian boat, including twelve who had been rescued by her from the *Usworth*!

This had occurred out of my sight. I ascertained later that the Belgian boat had capsized on the crest of an oily sea about 200 yards in the lee of the *Usworth*, in full view of the twelve men remaining in the wreck. The men who had been rescued from the *Usworth*, except for the two named in Captain Gonthier's message to me, had been too exhausted, by their previous long ordeals, to hold on to the upturned boat, or to swim in the oil covered water while the *Jean Jadot* rushed to pick them up.

In addition to the twelve men of the *Usworth* who had been drowned, two of the heroic Belgian crew had also given their lives— Fourth Officer Lambert and A.B. Seaman De Jongh.

The oil poured on troubled waters had not calmed the waters sufficiently to prevent the Belgian boat from capsizing. Worse than that, the blanket of oil had choked the men when they were flung into the sea from the boat, especially those who were too exhausted to struggle against its strangling effect. Of the twenty-three men who had been in the boat when she capsized, only nine had survived to be picked up by the *Jean Jadot*.

This grim news was not known in detail to the men in the *Ascania*'s boat when she was launched. They knew that some mishap had occurred to the Belgian boat; but, even if they had known the details, that would not have deterred them from going to the rescue of the twelve men still in the wreck. The time had come to make that effort. Only two hours remained before winter darkness would close in. It was certain that the *Usworth* would sink during the dark hours. She was already perilously awash.

From the bridge, I anxiously watched the progress of our boat. The *Ascania* had now drifted 200 yards to leeward. I moved her slowly up to leeward of the *Usworth* in order to keep our boat in sight.

In accordance with Captain Reed's directions, wirelessed at 1 p.m., Pollitt made for a position abaft the funnel, on the lee side of the wreck. It was extremely dangerous to get a boat alongside in that position. To have attempted to take the men off over the quarter of the *Usworth* would have been suicidal. Her stern and propeller were flinging out of the water at every moment. A position on the lee side forward was equally impracticable, as two derrick booms were laying across the bulwarks there, dipping into the water and sawing to and fro. On the after deck, also, .100 feet aft of the derrick booms, there were two bent boat davits projecting overside and dipping in the seas as she lurched.

Heavy seas were breaking over the wreck frequently. On the low side, she was now awash, with the sea surging inboard up to the hatch coamings and burying her to the level of the bridge deck. There, abaft the funnel, the twelve men waited on the bridge deck, drenched with oil and water.

Pollitt backed stern in, to about fifteen feet off, with oars out and ready to pull as the *Usworth* drifted down on the boat. At this, three of the men in the wreck decided to jump overboard and swim for it. They were the cook, T. Gibson; the steward, Hugh Hood; and the messroom boy, Lewis Jones — comprising, in fact, the entire commissariat department of the *Usworth*.

These three venturesome poor fellows had tragically failed to appreciate the difficulties of swimming in oil, and the force of the suction along the ship's side, due to drift. They struck out for the boat but were instantly swept along the ship's side towards the stern, their eyes, ears, mouth and nostrils filled with oil.

Despite efforts made by the boat's crew and the men on deck to throw lines and lifebuoys to them, they were carried under the stern, where two of them were mangled by the propeller, and the third was engulfed and carried out of sight in the steep seas.

After this, Pollitt decided that he must range alongside, and this he did with fine seamanship, courage, and skill. As the boat surged up level with the bridge deck, the nine men there, including the Captain, joined hands and jumped into her. They fell exhausted into the bottom of the lifeboat. One of them, an Afghan weighing eighteen stone, jumped onto the legs of A.B. Seaman K. Campbell of the lifeboat's crew, breaking Campbell's thigh.

Without a moment's delay, Pollitt shoved off from the side of the wreck. All but eight of his oars were now broken, and one of his men crippled, but, by great good fortune, the boat was flung clear of the wreck's side. The boat was pulled to leeward, and then aft clear of her stern. There, Pollitt streamed a sea anchor, to keep her head-on to the seas, but this proved ineffectual, and she lay broadside on, despite all their efforts.

The two lines from the second sea anchor that was in the lifeboat had been cut off to hold her alongside the *Usworth*, and the spare coil of 2½-inch Manila had been used also for that purpose.

The seaman with the broken leg was groaning in agony. The nine rescued men lay inert in the bottom of the boat, utterly done in. Their names were: Captain J. J. Reed; Chief Engineer J. Ellerington; Third Engineer K. Gray; Apprentice H. Bottomley; Able Seamen J. Rourke (carpenter) and F. Andrews; Firemen Said Rasul und Rizwan Ullah.

Fortunately the boat was still in the oil slick. The seas, though very high and steep, were only partly breaking; otherwise she would have capsized, as the Belgian boat had.

As the boat pulled clear, I steamed at full speed round the *Usworth*'s bow and came up under her stern. I stopped her about a hundred feet to windward of the boat, and drifted down broad- aide on, getting her into position amidships below the side door in B Deck, which was now opened.

Even on the lee side of the ship, the boat was lifting to within four feet of the sill of the door and then dropping vertically as much as twenty feet. Ladders were lowered. The big Afghan fireman, jumping for a ladder, missed his hold, and fell between the ship's side and the boat. With great difficulty, four of our seamen hoisted him into the boat again, all of them in imminent danger of being crushed. Bowlines were then lowered, and most of the men hoisted up in them. A few climbed up the ladders, and Pollitt was the last to leave the boat. He had accomplished a heroic and remarkable rescue.

The boat, being badly damaged, was cast adrift. To have attempted to hook her on, under davits, in such conditions would probably have been futile and could have been dangerous. I therefore abandoned her and turned my ship head-on to the seas. The boat had returned alongside at 3.10 p.m., after being away for one hour and twenty minutes.

The nine survivors and the boat's crew were given medical attention and comforts. They were soon in bed, having their first sleep for several days and nights.

As there was nothing more useful to be done there and then, I resumed my voyage at 3.30 p.m., and set course for Halifax. Seventeen seamen had lost their lives — fifteen from the *Usworth* and two from the *Jean Jadot*.

But eleven men had been rescued from the *Usworth*. Nine were now in the *Ascania* and two in the *Jean Jadot*. That was some consolation for the strenuous efforts that had been made in exceptionally difficult circumstances.

The Chief Engineer of the *Ascania* informed me later that, during the 81 hours that we had stood by, 119 tons of oil fuel had been pumped overboard. In that period also there had been more than 800 orders from the bridge to the engine room. I did not attempt to compute the number of steering orders that were given!

I was dog tired, but unwilling to admit it, as there were many' details still to attend to. At 3.30 p.m. I wirelessed, **ASCANIA TO ALL. SHIPS: ALL SURVIVORS RESCUED FROM USWORTH INCLUDING CAPTAIN, USWORTH REMAINS ABANDONED. DERELICT IN LAT. 48.10 N., LONG,· 31.50 w. HEAVY LIST TO PORT. DRIFTING SOUTH EAST. EXTREMELY DANGEROUS TO NAVIGATION.**

In the next few hours, many wireless messages were received from • various ships, congratulating the *Ascania* and the *Jean Jadot*,: on their efforts.

I sent a wireless message in code to the Cunard White Star offices in Liverpool and New York, giving details of the wreck and of the rescue, and names of the survivors and of the dead.

The news had been spread from ship to ship, and from ship to shore. I received not less than thirty marconigrams from leading newspapers and news agencies on both sides of the Atlantic, asking for "exclusive" stories. To all of these I replied, referring the inquirers to the Cunard White Star offices.

The owners released the facts to the press, and asked me for fuller details, to be published in the Sunday newspapers. I accordingly wirelessed a circumstantial report of the rescue operations, Wearied as I was, chiefly by lack of sleep for several days, I had not realized the intense excitement that my "plain unvarnished tale" — a matter-of-fact description of events would arouse on shore, and that millions of readers in America and Britain would be confronted on Sunday morning with huge headlines such as "HEROIC EPIC OF THE SEA," "DEATII DEFIED IN EFFORT TO SAVE LIVES," "THRILLING

MID-OCEAN RESCUE DRAMA," "GAMBLE WITH DEATII IN ATLANTIC EPIC," and suchlike.

As we steamed westward, now in easier weather, I was surprised to receive a wireless message in code from the Halifax Manager of Cunard White Star, informing me that arrangements had been made for a public welcome to the *Ascania* on her arrival at that port. I was to be met by pressmen, press photographers, and newsreel operators at the dock. Arrangements had been made for me to broadcast an account of the rescue, from Halifax radio station.

I replied, insisting that Third Officer Pollitt and his boat's crew were the actual heroes, and that they and Captain Reed and the '. survivors of the *Usworth* should certainly be included in any publicity.

As far as I was concerned, I did not feel that I had done anything heroic. I had not been in any personal danger. My ordeal had been one of anxiety, but not of risk. I believed then, as I still believe, that my part in what became known as "the *Usworth* rescue. "was a feat of practical seamanship which had fortunately, thanks to the good cooperation of my officers and crew, been carried through as well as could have been expected in the difficult circumstances, and with some luck on our side.

Pollitt and the men who had gone with him in the boat — as also the men who had gone in the Belgian boat had risked their lives to save life. They were heroes; no doubt about it; but as Pollitt himself put his point of view publicly on record, I cannot do better than quote it. "For my crew and myself," he said, "it was just a job that had to be done, and one which any others in the Merchant Service, irrespective of flag, would have been only too pleased to do in like circumstances."

That was true and sincere. We had to do something, and we had done our best to help brother seamen in peril. We had had no thought of the tremendous publicity that was to follow, and no thoughts of reward.

25

Sequels to the "Usworth" Rescue — Extensive Publicity — A Broadcast
from Halifax — "Dramatizing the News" — A Plain Unvarnished Tale
— New York Journalism — Awards and Honours — Civic Welcome at
Plymouth — Liverpool Shipwreck and Humane Society Awards —
Lloyd's Medals — "Salvage of Human Life" — New York Life Saving
Association's Medals — Shipwrecked Fishermen and Mariners' Society
Medals — Board of Trade Medals and Awards — Many Mementoes of
One Day's Work — Publicity and Seamanship

DURING the night of Friday, 14th December, 1934, the derelict *S.S.
Usworth* had sunk to the bottom of the Atlantic Ocean. So it was
surmised, for she was not sighted next day by ships on the lookout
for her, or ever again. And, as she sank, the fury of the seas that had overwhelmed
her subsided, as though Davy Jones were appeased by a gift of five thousand tons
of grain for his locker, and the sacrifice of the lives of seventeen seamen.

The *Ascania*, steaming westward, was in fine weather only 100 ' miles from the
scene of the wreck of the *Usworth*. We were due to arrive in Halifax on Tuesday
afternoon, 18th December, and in New York on 21st December. It was the
Christmas season, a time for sitting by cosy firesides and listening to stories. The
report of the *Usworth* tragedy and rescue, which I had wirelessed to Cunard head
office, was released to the press, together with dispatches from a French-
Canadian journalist, J. L. Dussault, who happened to be a passenger in the
Ascania. He had risen to the occasion of a world — "scoop" — in mid-ocean,

and had sent a vivid on-the-spot report, including interviews with Captain Reed and other survivors of the wreck.

These stories, being widely printed on both sides of the Atlantic, aroused such public interest that the Canadian Radio Commission sent me a marconigram, asking me to prepare the script of a talk of twenty minutes, to be given from Radio Station CHNS, Halifax, soon after the Ascania arrived at that port. The talk was to be relayed throughout the Canadian and U.S.A. national networks, and recorded for rebroadcasting by the B.B.C., London. Such "hook-ups" were a novelty in those days. The prospect of an audience of millions appalled me. I had no broadcasting experience.

Thinking to get out of it, I referred the matter to the Cunard Line for permission. I thought that Cunard were a little shy of publicity for "dramatic" events at sea; but I found out later that it was only adverse publicity that they were shy of.

A few hours later a message came through: **OWNERS ARE AGREEABLE. PLEASE PREPARE SCRIPT FOR TWENTY MINUTES TALK BY YOURSELF, LIEUTENANT POLLITT, AND CAPTAIN REED.**

This was a poser. In consultation with the other two, I prepared a script, which, after many alterations, we carefully rehearsed and timed. We were all green hands at the game and suffered in anticipation from "mike fright."I was to speak the introduction, describing events up to the launching of the *Ascania*'s lifeboat; then Pollitt would take over and describe the boat rescue; then I would chip in with a description of getting the men out of the boat and on board the *Ascania*, and a tribute to the work of the crews in my ship and in the *Jean Jadot*; then Captain Reed would conclude with a few remarks in his own words, expressing his feelings, and his heartfelt thanks for being alive.

We thought that our joint effort was pretty good for mariners out of their element, but we looked forward with trepidation. to the ordeal of speaking our pieces to a vast, invisible, and critical audience.

When the *Ascania* docked at Halifax, she was invaded by a swarm of reporters, photographers, and newsreel operators, who insisted on "getting the story" — and pictures — in detail. We were welcomed also by officials, including the Harbour Commissioners, who informed us that we were to be their guests at a banquet that evening, at the conclusion of which the broadcast was to be made at 11 p.m., Eastern American time, which would be correspondingly earlier in the evening in the four hourly time zones moving westwards throughout Canada and the United States.

Soon after we arrived at Halifax, at 5 p.m., I handed the script of the intended broadcast to the manager of Station CHNS, who came on board with various members of his staff, including trained scrip writers. They took my script into the ship's writing room and went into a huddle over it for an hour, while I was busy with the pressmen and photographers, and with routine matters of docking. At 6 p.m., the manager of the broadcasting studio saw me in my cabin, to discuss details of the broadcast. "Your script is very interesting," he said, "but I feel that it needs dramatizing. This is to be the most important broadcast ever put over from Halifax. It is the first time that a national hook up has originated from this station.

You will have millions of listeners."

"What do you mean by 'dramatizing'?" I asked him. "Dramatizing?" I roared. "I have put everything into that story. What more do you want?"

"Well," he said, soothingly, "we have several experienced radio actors and actresses in Halifax. I think that with their aid we might begin with a scene which would be described by our narrator, with appropriate background affects to imitate the howling of the wind and the crashing of seas."

"Oh," I asked, "and what words would the narrator speak?" "Something like this: 'It is a wild and stormy night in mid-Atlantic. The good ship *Ascania* is heaving up and down on the mighty waves, 100 feet high, sailing on a trip to Halifax. It is midnight, and most of the passengers have retired to their bedrooms for the night. But a few hardy souls are still in the smoke room, hanging on to their drinks, to prevent them from spilling onto the floor as she rolls and staggers about in a hurricane blowing at 200 miles an hour. Among them can be seen the stocky figure of Captain Bisset-'"

"-having a goodnight drink with a couple of blondes?" I interjected, sarcastically.

"Better not put that in," said the expert, hastily, and continue reading his script. " 'Suddenly the door opens, admitting a great squall of wind and an excited sailor, who holds on to the wall, and hands an urgent wireless message to the Captain.'"

"Stow it," I said. "Belay everything."

"What do you mean, sir?" asked the startled expert, who had probably never before heard a Cape Horn sailor really annoyed.

"Don't go any further," I said. "It's the most ridiculous tripe I've ever heard. Captains of ships don't carry on like that — not in bad weather anyhow. We'll read the script exactly as I wrote it, or there won't be any broadcast!"

With another pained look at me, he agreed, "Very well, Captain, as you say, of course."

"I'm sorry," I said, "to put your actors and actresses and script writers out of a job, but this story is too true, and tragic, to be 'dramatized'. The facts must speak for themselves."

So it happened. Pollitt and Captain Reed and I put the story over without a hitch, in our own words. Before midnight we were receiving telegrams from many parts of Canada and the U.S.A., from coast to coast, congratulating us on having told a story of the sea in a seamanlike way.

A recording of our talk was made by the "Blattnerphone" process at Ottawa, and transmitted across the Atlantic to London, where it was rebroadcast by the B.B.C. a few hours later.

This was only the beginning of the furore that the *Usworth* rescue aroused. Many Canadian newspapers printed the full text of our broadcast. The Halifax Mail commented that it was "the most impressive news event ever put over the air."

When the *Ascania* arrived at New York on Friday, 21st December, at 8 a.m., more reporters, photographers, and newsreel operators swarmed on board. The stories and pictures appeared in most of the New York newspapers that afternoon and next morning.

One of the feature writers, George Carroll, of the Sun, began his story with a bang:

The *Ascania* came into port today with a pink cheeked young Englishman who credited Providence with making him a hero when waves leaped high as housetops and 23 men faced death in mid-Atlantic.

"Only Providence could do it," said Lieut. E. J. R. Pollitt, thirty-two.

"Me — I was never so frightened in my life."

Captain J. G. P. Bisset, Master of the *Ascania*, supplemented his Third Officer's modest account.

"The *Jean Jadot* didn't get enough credit," he said. "She put down the first lifeboat."

Never before, according to the Captain, has he heard of men choking in an oiled sea. "Oil is a mixed blessing," he added. "It has to be used to smooth the waves, yet you can't swim in it. The cook, steward, and cabin boy who jumped from the *Usworth* into the sea were doomed."

The New York World Telegram headlined its story with a streamer across the page: THE OIL, LIKE A BLANKET OF POISON, KILLED THE SEAMEN ON THE USWORTH RESCUE, SAYS CAPT. BISSET.

Describing me as "a stocky, merry, ruddy Englishman with a tremendous grin and great pouches of laughter under his eyes," this paper quoted me as saying, "The oil blanket sliding over the towering seas smothered and choked those who fell into it. Oil smooths the waters but kills whoever gets into it."

The shipping columnist of the New York American, Harry Acton, whom I had met several times previously when I was in the *Berengaria* and in other Cunarders calling at New York, let himself go: '

Captain Bisset is the rarin' sailor man of the old days who likes things rough out there. When it's calm, and Neptune doesn't seem to want to fight, Cap'n Bisset is disgusted with this kind of sea life.

If it were not for the law which forbids the Captain to leave his bridge, we bet Bisset would have been in that lifeboat overside from his own *Ascania*.

Now I was really learning what is meant by "dramatizing" the news. Among scores of letters that I received from people who were complete strangers to me, there was one that rocked me. It was on monogrammed stationery, from a lady in Philadelphia:

> Dear Captain Bisset,
> I saw your picture in the paper and I think you are a Honey. I never knew Sea Captains were so young and handsome. I had an idea they were all old and ugly. Will you please send me your autograph and give me a thrill for Christmas? I never met any real hero in my life, so if you will I will be more than pleased. If you ever come to Philadelphia, call and see me.
> Sincerely,
> ETHEL F-

I thought it only right and proper to send this admirer a signed photograph, but I never had any opportunity of accepting her invitation to call and see her in her apartment, of which she so kindly gave me the number, in West Venango Street, Philadelphia.

The *Ascania* cleared out of New York at 5 p.m. on 21st December, having called there only for passengers. We then returned to Halifax for mails and passengers, and picked up the rescued men of the *Usworth*, who had been left there. On Christmas Day we were at sea, homeward bound. At this time the *Ascania* was regularly calling at Plymouth on eastbound passages, to land passengers and mails one day earlier than they could be landed in London.

On arrival at Plymouth, we found that our feat of seamanship had been given almost as much publicity in Britain as in Canada and the U.S.A. As the ship anchored, the Mayor of Plymouth, wearing his chains of office, came on board to give us a Civic Reception. This, in the home port of Sir Francis Drake and other great seamen and pirates, was really flattering. The Civic Reception was "news," and as such was cabled by Reuters all over the world. I believe that very few ships have been honoured in this way at Plymouth.

We landed the survivors of the *Usworth* at Plymouth, and next day, 1st January 1935, docked at London. So ended an eventful voyage; but, by this time, I may candidly admit, Pollitt and I were beginning to feel decidedly embarrassed by all the fuss that was being made over our having done what any other seamen would have done in the circumstances.

We would have to go through with it. The people who were pouring compliments and honours on us, we realized, were expressing their appreciation of the Merchant Service which we happened to represent. In that spirit the tributes we received were acceptable: not to us as individuals, but as members of the seafaring fraternity. Cinemas in London were showing the newsreels of our arrival in Halifax — strange to "see oorsel's as ithers see us"I I was invited to speak on the B.B.C. Saturday night feature programme, "In Town Tonight," and to my surprise was given two guineas as a fee.

The *Ascania* was laid up for a month for refit, which meant a holiday for her crew. The Cunard White Star Line awarded one month's extra pay (ten pounds) to each of the ten seamen who had gone in the lifeboat and made a cash presentation also to Third Officer Pollitt.

In the ensuing months, we had the ordeals and the gratifications of receiving many more awards and public compliments for our part in the *Usworth* rescue.

On 5th February 1935, in the Liverpool Town Hall, Pollitt and myself, and the ten seamen of the *Ascania*'s lifeboat crew, were each presented with the Silver Medal and Certificate of the Liverpool Shipwreck and Humane Society. The presentations were made by the Lord Mayor of Liverpool. Eulogistic speeches were made by the Chairman of the Shipwreck and Humane Society (T. H. Harper); a representative of the owners of the *Usworth* (S. S. W. Dagleish, of Newcastle-upon-Tyne); and Robert Crail, a director of the Cunard White Star Line, who declared fervently, "It was nothing but a sheer gamble with death, but it came off, thank God."

Two days later, 7th February, we attended Lloyd's Office, in London. It was an impressive scene. The library of the famous insurance office was crowded with spectators. The Chairman of Lloyd's (A. J. Aubrey), in the presence of Sir Percy Bates (Chairman of the Cunard Line) and other celebrities of the shipping world on the platform, presented me with a bronze tablet, recording the details of the rescue, "to be placed in a prominent position in the *Ascania*, so that all who travel in that ship may know of the glorious chapter which has been added by Captain Bisset and his officers and crew to the long and splendid history of the sea."

Pollitt was presented with Lloyd's Silver Medal for Saving Life at Sea, and the ten seamen of his lifeboat crew with Lloyd's Bronze Medal. (Similar awards were later made at Lloyd's Office in Antwerp, to the officers and crew of the *Jean Jadot*'s boat.)

After eloquent speeches, to which Pollitt and I briefly replied, the Chairman of Lloyd's called for "three cheers" which rocked the rafters, and also rocked us a little, especially when the cheers were repeated as we filed out after the ceremony through the crowded Underwriters' Room. A seaman could scarcely fail to be impressed by being cheered at Lloyd's. I wished that the Captain of the *Jean Jadot* had been there to share the honours.

We strolled along to the Baltic Exchange, for another ceremony in the offices of the Chamber of Shipping. There, the Lord Mayor of Newcastle-upon-Tyne (R. S. Dagleish), Chairman of Directors of the owners of the *Usworth*, presented me with a silver tea-and- coffee service, Pollitt with a silver salver, and the ten lifeboat seamen with ten pounds each in cash. In a supporting address, Sir Percy Bates made a penetrating remark. "No salvage is ever paid," he said, "for the saving of life at sea, but it is a noble custom that presentations should be made on occasions such as this."

That was not the end of the presentations, by any means. The *Ascania* cleared out of London on 8th February, bound for Halifax and New York. When we arrived at New York, the ship was boarded, on 20th February 1935, by the President of the Life Saving Benevolent Association of New York (Herbert L. Satterlee) a fine looking, white haired man with a "Yankee" beard, accompanied by shipping officials, and by press reporters and photographers. There, we were lined up on deck, while Pollitt and I were presented with the Gold Medals of the Life Saving Association, .and the ten life boatmen with bronze medals, and a cash gift of one hundred dollars each.

I thought that these handsome and generous awards would have closed the *Usworth* incident — but no, there were more to come. After three more voyages across the Atlantic, the *Ascania* docked at London on 10th June 1935.

Two days later we had to attend the office of the Shipwrecked Fishermen and Mariners' Royal Benevolent Society, in Carlton House, Regent Street, London, where Pollitt and the ten A.Bs who had manned the lifeboat were each presented with the Silver Life Saving Medal of that Society, while Chief Officer John Snow and I were given a cash award of twenty pounds (divided between us), under a bequest (the Emil Robin Life Saving Award) administered by the Society.

Nor was this yet the end of it. After another voyage, when we returned to London, Pollitt and his ten lifeboatmen were summoned to Buckingham Palace (10th July, 1935), and all decorated by King George V with the Board of Trade Silver Medal for Gallantry in Saving Life at Sea.

After another two voyages, Pollitt and I (on 4th September 1935) had to attend the Mansion House in London, where the Lord Mayor of London, Sir Phene Neal, on behalf of the Board of Trade, presented me with a silver rose bowl, and Pollitt with a silver cup. Similar presentations were later made in Brussels to Captain Gonthier and the officers of the *Jean Jadot*.

At all these impressive ceremonies, distinguished by eloquence on the part of the experienced speechmakers who made the presentation, Pollitt and I invariably replied briefly to the effect that we had only done our best in the traditions of the Merchant Service. We believed that and so could speak with sincerity; and I still believe it to this day. At no time, during the operations when we stood by the *Usworth*, had any of us any thoughts of rewards or honours for doing a job that had to be done.

Among the hundreds of letters that I received as the result of this publicity, the one that I valued most was from Captain Jack Reed: "I wish to congratulate you and your crew on your just awards for your exceptional gallantry... My worst ordeal since arriving home has been meeting the relatives of the lost ones... I have been pestered by the press with publicity... I enclose a photo they took of me, with the title SAFE AT HOME. It was due to your determination that this photo could be taken and published with that title."

To this the Captain's wife added a note: "Words seem futile to try to thank you. It was through your kindness and sympathy that my husband came home."

With this, at last, the various excitements of the *Usworth* rescue had ended. It was a minor, though tragic, incident in the saga of the sea. It would gradually be forgotten in the far more tragic events of a Second Great War that was looming up on the horizon.

I have recorded it here in some detail in these memoirs of my seafaring experiences, for its interest as a nautical operation that was typical of many such rescues that have been made at sea with much less publicity.

The *Usworth* was no *Titanic*. The men who died in her, and the men who were saved, were only the crew of a tramp steamer, but no less important as human beings for that The publicity that ensued was chiefly due to the extensive developments of radio communications which were occurring in the 1930s, enabling millions of people to hear news, and also to hear the voices of people "in the news," in a way never before known. Likewise, cinema newsreels and press photography were bringing pictures of people and events before the public gaze with rapidly increasing technical perfection. It happened that the *Usworth* rescue "made news" at that time, when these mediums of public ' information were being so remarkably improved.

But neither the great publicity, nor the handsome awards that were conferred on those of us who were lucky enough to have ' earned them, could alter the fact that what we had done was seamen's work, and that any pride we felt was in the way in which " that work had been done, rather than in the acclaim.

26

*Maiden Voyage of the "Normandie" — The First Eighty-
thousand ton Liner — She Takes the Blue Riband — The
"Mauretania" Retired from Service — A New Era Begins — My
Experiences in the "Ascania" on the Canadian Run Continued — A
Letter from Thornton Wilder — Some Other Letters — The Doyly
Carte Opera Company — A Cargo of Goldfish — A Pathetic
Stowaway — Threat of a New "Great" War.*

AFTER the *Usworth* rescue, I remained in command of the *Ascania*
for another two years, and in that time made twenty-five voyages
in her, from London to Canadian ports, and sometimes to New
York.

At the end of May 1935, there was news that thrilled the shipping world.
The mammoth French liner *Normandie*, on her maiden voyage westbound,
took the Blue Riband of the Atlantic, with a crossing from Bishop Rock
(Scilly Isles) to Ambrose Light Vessel (at the entrance to New York Bay), a
passage of 2971 miles, in 4 days 11 hours 14 minutes, at an average speed of
29.94 knots. On her return passage, eastbound, she attained an average speed
of 30.31 knots. She was thus the first passenger liner in history to maintain a
speed of thirty knots on an ocean crossing. It was a triumph for France and
marked a new era in shipping history. The age of the gigantic superliners had
gloriously arrived.

The *Normandie*, owned by the Compagnie Generale Trans-atlantique, was
built at the Penhoet shipyard at Saint-Nazaire, at the mouth of the Loire-in

Brittany, not in Normandy. She had been constructed in four years. Her keel was laid down in May 1931; she was launched in October 1932 and started on her maiden• voyage on 29th May 1935. She was of 82,000 tons gross, length 1029 • feet overall, beam 117 feet: the first liner in service of such gigantic dimensions, and built, it was said, at a cost equivalent to eight million pounds sterling, with subsidies from the French Government.

No one could, or would, deny this glory to France, a nation with so many glorious traditions. We could only hope that our *Queen Mary*, nearing completion (laid down in December 1930, launched in September 1934) would provide, as we were confident that she would, a worthy comparison with the superb French fait accompli.

At this time our old champion liner *Mauretania*, which had held the Blue Riband of the Atlantic for twenty-two years, was withdrawn from service. In twenty-seven years of ocean going service, she had steamed more than three million miles. She had made three hundred voyages to New York (600 ocean crossings) carrying, a total of 1¼ million passengers across the Atlantic, in addition to those carried on her wartime voyages to the Eastern Mediterranean. In the last few years of her ocean going life, she was a cruise ship, painted all white, taking thousands of holidaymakers on cruises to the Mediterranean and to the West Indies. She was by far the best-known and best-loved ship in her day. Now, about the time when the *Normandie* made her maiden voyage, the *Mauretania* went to the shipbreakers at Rosyth. An era had ended, and another had begun.

My voyages in the *Ascania*, on the Canadian run, in 1935 and 1936, were never monotonous. I was carrying, on an average, seven hundred passengers on each passage. Among distinguished people, who were seated at my table in the first-class dining room, from time to time, was Thornton Wilder, the greatly gifted and bestselling novelist; he bought a copy of *Ship Ahoy!* from the ship's barber, and — perhaps surprised to see that it was in its tenth edition — asked me to autograph it for him.

I could see the humour in that situation, as he was himself pursued everywhere by autograph hunters. Even on board ship, people were asking him to autograph copies of his bestselling and exquisitely written books, *The Bridge of San Luis Rey* and *The Woman of Andros*. He told me that he was going to Europe to get away from the blaze of publicity that followed him wherever he went in America. I thought that I might be able to learn from him some of the secrets of being a bestselling author. Instead, I found that I was being quizzed on some of the secrets of being a sea captain.

It soon appeared that Thornton Wilder was fascinated by the story of the *Usworth* rescue, which he had heard on the national broadcast six months previously. He was thinking of writing a book on it, which would certainly have been a masterpiece, but he eventually dropped that idea because he felt unsure of nautical details and terminology. A photograph of him was taken on the boat deck of the *Ascania*, with his back to the rail and the ocean and sky behind him. It was developed on board, and he gave me a print of it, inscribed with his signature and the date (July 5, 1935), to which he added, in his bold and clear calligraphy, an extract from *The Woman of Andros*. This, he explained, could be applied to some of the incidents of the *Usworth* rescue: "The mistakes we make through generosity are less terrible than the gains we acquire through caution."

It was his intention to return with me in the *Ascania* on a later voyage, after he had visited France. I sent him another print of the snapshot taken on board, and a few months later received a letter from him in his handwriting:

> 50 Deepwood Drive,
> New Haven, Conn.
> Nov. 21, 1935
> Dear Captain Bisset,
> I should have thanked you long ago for your thoughtfulness in sending me the snapshot. My family is very pleased with it, and so am I. I hoped to return on your boat, but sudden news of my father's illness made me rush to the next boat sailing from France, which was the *Britannic*. Davis and I were proud to see that you received still a further acknowledgment of your magnificent work at sea.
>
> I hope to cross with you again before long and become a true *Ascania* crew man.
>
> Sincerely yours,
> THORNTON WILDER.

The interest of this letter is that such a careful craftsman in words makes in it the common landsman's error, twice, of referring to a steamship as a "boat." He also uses the nonnautical expression "on your boat," instead of "in your boat" (or ship). So he would have a lot to learn before he could become an "*Ascania* crew man." No sailor ever voyages on a boat or ship, only in such vessels. But mistakes made through generosity are less terrible than gain acquired through caution.

I have received many letters from passengers, expressing thanks for conveying them across the ocean — thousands of such letter over the many years. One was from a French Canadian boy, who was photographed on the boat deck with me. I sent him a copy of the snapshot, and he replied:

> Mister the Captain,
> I thank you for the nice picture; you and the photo are well; but I am horrible. I beg your pardon for the bad English in which I write, but I translate my French sentence, word by, word.
> Now, I left you at the business of the ship.
>
> Yours truly,
> GIL LAQUIM.

Another letter was from a Japanese passenger, chatted affably a few times on deck:

> My dear captain,
> In order to express my hearty thankfulness for your kindness I want to have some drink in my room 114 at 15 Minute to Eight o'clock this evening. if you would come at that time I am Very Much appreciated.
>
> Yours truly,
> K. OGAWA.

Another, sinister and cryptic, was delivered on board at Mont- real an hour before the *Ascania* left the dock. It was entirely typewritten, with no clue to the sender:

> Confidential.
> See that 3d class passenger H. Dubois in room C 61 is buried at sea. Important documents. On return trip you will be rich.
>
> G. C. G. per S.

I did not take this opportunity of becoming rich. H. Dubois made it safely to his or her destination.

On one westbound passage, I had on board the entire Dayley Carte Light Opera Company, going on a tour of Canada with ' Gilbert and Sullivan operas. Each evening they would come down to dinner — about fifty of them — and, before sitting down at tables, would sing a spirited opening chorus from one of their operas, to the immense delight of the other passengers.

When we arrived at Montreal press photographers came, on board. By arrangement, the leading members of the cast were dressed in the costumes of The Pirates of Penzance. I allowed them to come up onto the bridge. There, a bevy of beautiful damsels and nasty looking pirates, armed with prop pistols and cutlasses, took me prisoner, and tied me, not very securely, with a 1-inch lanyard, to the engine telegraph, while the photographers shot the lot of us. These pictures were widely used for publicity; but I played a joke on the comedians, as I had borrowed the Chief Officer's uniform coat, with only three stripes on the sleeve, so that anyone with elementary nautical knowledge could see that they hadn't "captured the Captain" as descriptions on the press photos asserted. I insisted also on having another press photograph taken, in which, armed with a stage pistol, I stood over the "pirates" and made them scrub the decks!

Having completed a passage of 3203 miles from London to Montreal, the Company went immediately from the ship into a train, for a journey of 2900 miles further westward, overland to Vancouver, by the C.P.R. route — "from ocean to ocean. "They were to begin their Canadian tour at Vancouver and work back eastwards to Montreal.

When they arrived at Vancouver, the press reporters met the train and made a fuss of all the actors and actresses. One reporter, looking for a "new angle," buttonholed the stage carpenter, who was a Yorkshireman, and proud of it.

"Mr Barnsley," said the reporter, "having travelled right across Canada, what do you think of it?"

"Well," said Mr Barnsley, "if you must know, as far as I could see, it's all rocks and bloody Christmas trees!"

On one eastbound passage, we had as cargo 12,000 live goldfish, consigned from Montreal to London. They were in twenty-five tanks, and were placed in charge of the ship's butcher, who knew something about goldfish, having kept them as pets as a boy. The consignors of the fish supplied him with precise instructions for their care on the voyage. A certain amount of fresh water had to be added to the tanks each day, and the water in the tanks kept stirred up at intervals, to aerate it. If the fish seemed to be swimming too much with their snouts above water, they were in distress and wanted more air.

On our way downriver, before we reached Quebec, I sent for the butcher and asked him how the fish were travelling.

"They're O.K., sir," he said. "I've carried out the instructions as written down, but — " he handed me the paper that had been given to him " — there's no mention of feeding them!"

A little worried at the prospect of having 12,000 fish die of starvation, I asked, "What do they eat?"

"Ants' eggs," said the butcher.

"Ants' eggs! How many ants' eggs could twelve thousand goldfish eat in ten days — and where could we get the ants' eggs?"

"I reckon that it would take about three pounds weight of ants' eggs to keep 'em alive to London; but ants' eggs are very expensive," the butcher explained. "They are very light articles, sold by the ounce — probably a thousand ants' eggs to an ounce. If I put half an ounce of eggs into each tank a few times on the way over, that would keep the fish alive. We may be able to get ants' eggs at Quebec," he continued. "They are sold by chemists, what are called pharmacies or drugstores in this part o' the world, sir."

"Very well, then," I said. "Go ashore at Quebec and try to buy three pounds weight of ants' eggs — but it will be midnight when we arrive there. We'll be loading 300 tons of cargo, and clearing out again at 4 a.m."

The butcher went ashore at Quebec, accompanied by a French speaking shipping agents' clerk. Everything was shut up for the night, but, after awakening several apothecaries, who cursed them fluently for making such a ridiculous demand in the middle of the night, they found one who sold ants' eggs. They bought his whole stock. He served them with very bad grace and a long tirade about goldfish and crazy seamen who disturbed his night's rest.

Three days later, the bill for the eggs had apparently reached Montreal. In mid-ocean, I received a radio message from the consignors: **ON NO ACCOUNT FEED THE GOLDFISH.**

They had already enjoyed some of the ants' eggs, which did them no harm. During nine days passage to London, only six of the fish kicked the bucket.

On one winter voyage, we had a pathetic experience. Arrived at Halifax, after a stormy passage, in very cold weather, I gave orders for the usual lifeboat drill. In preparation for this exercise, the Chief Officer had the canvas covers taken off the lifeboats.

In one of the boats, he found a stowaway. She was a frail girl, thin and poorly dressed, and almost unconscious. She had been in the boat for eleven days. The ship's doctor sent her to a hospital on shore. She was gravely ill and had to have the toes of her left foot amputated through frostbite.

Before we left Halifax, three days later, our doctor saw her in hospital, and she told him what had happened. She was an English girl. She had heard about stowaways and their methods and was determined to go to Canada. She had come on board at Southampton in the guise of a visitor, carrying with her a rug, a thermos flask of tea, and some food to last her two or three days. Seeing one of the lifeboats partly uncovered, she crept into it and hid. Her intention was to give herself up after two or three days at sea.

Before the ship left Southampton, the seamen on deck went round as usual, and made everything secure against bad weather. They properly laced down the lifeboat covers. If these came adrift in a gale, they could be blown to shreds. The seamen did not look into the boat. The girl lay there, feeling snug, and relieved at not having been discovered.

Two days later, when the *Ascania* was plunging into a strong westerly gale, the stowaway girl decided to give herself up; but she was so cold, seasick, and weak that she could not loosen the cover. This was now stretched so bar tight by being wet with spray that it would have needed the skill and strength of a seaman to loosen it from outside. It was practically impossible to loosen it from inside, except by cutting it. She had no knife, and did not know that an axe was stowed in the lifeboat, with other gear, including emergency rations of drinking water, biscuits, chocolate, milk tablets, and meat extract.

Frequently she yelled for help, but her voice, muffled beneath the cover, was not heard in the fierce howling of the wind screeching through the funnel stays near nearby; or no one happened to be passing on deck as she yelled. In her dark hiding place, she did not know night from day. To knock on the boat's side with a tholepin or some other implement would have been more effective than singing out, but she did not think of doing that. As the days went by, she became weaker and weaker, from thirst, starvation and the intense cold.

It was lucky for her that I was a stickler for lifeboat drill. I had hesitated to turn the crew out at Halifax for this drill, with the temperature several degrees below freezing point, but had decided that the exercise must be carried out, regardless of weather. When the stowaway was found, our doctor believed she could not have lived more than another few hours.

She was returned to England in another Cunarder. When she was brought before "the Beak" (magistrate), at Southampton, charged with having been a stowaway, he decided that she had been punished enough, and let her go with a caution.

On 6th September 1935, I had on board the *Ascania*, for the short passage from Southampton to Havre, the veteran English Socialist Member of Parliament and editor, George Lansbury, who was going to France to attend an "Antiwar" meeting in Paris, I invited him onto the bridge, and into my cabin for a chat.

He told me that he was greatly disturbed at the prospect of a Second Great War, likely to arise from the Italian invasion of Abyssinia. It was about this time that I realized, as I suppose many other people did, that a new war had become inevitable. At a seaman, I did not look forward to that prospect with pleasurable anticipation. But politics was not my concern. Like all others of my profession, I had to leave politics to the politicians, and international affairs to those who thought that they understood them.

WHILE the *Ascania* was lying peacefully alongside the loading dock, at Montreal, on 16th October, 1935, during the midday dinner hour, I heard a commotion on deck. Stepping out of my cabin, I was in time to see a 6000-ton freighter, the *S.S. Norwegian*, of Liverpool, crash into the *Ascania*'s side amidships. She struck my ship with her stem, with a horrible impact, and there came to a dead stop, and backed away. A hole was torn in the Ascania's side, fortunately well above the waterline, and no one was hurt. The *Norwegian*'s bows were heavily dented by the impact.

I could not understand how such a thing could have happened, but an explanation was soon forthcoming. The *Norwegian* was being moved from one berth to another, with the aid of two tugs and her own engines. As she was turning, the engine room telegraph was rung to slow astern, but the engines went slow ahead! She was going the wrong way! That was an accident of a kind that very rarely happens.

Temporary repairs were made to the *Ascania*'s side by the Hall Engineering Company of Montreal, and we were able to clear out from that port on scheduled time. We arrived in London on 28th October, and made one more voyage to Montreal before the river froze, arriving back in London on 26th November.

There my Third Officer, E. J. Pollitt, received orders to proceed to Glasgow. He had been appointed as Third Officer in the *Queen Mary*. She was being manned in readiness for her trials in the Firth of Clyde! This coveted appointment was in part a recognition of Pollitt's gallantry and fine seamanship during the *Usworth* rescue. He had been advanced two years in promotion for his heroic work on that occasion and had thoroughly earned it.

On my next voyage, leaving London on 29th November, on the winter run to Halifax and New York, I took on board at Havre 110 boxes of gold, consigned to New York. This was on account of war debts and balance-of-trade payments, a common type of cargo in transatlantic liners on westbound passages in the 1920s and 1930s. The consignment that I carried was loaded at Havre, and later unloaded at New York, under heavy armed guard; but boxes of bullion are difficult to pilfer, and I never heard of any being lost in transit.

After my gold carrying voyage, I docked at London on 24th December 1935. Home for Christmas! The ship was then laid up for a month for her annual refit, and May and I went for a holiday to Looe, in Cornwall, early in January 1936.

We were in "rooms" across the harbour from the coastguard station. It was a gloomy holiday. Rain fell drearily every day; but, worst of all, there were daily news bulletins about the grave illness of King George V.

On 21st January, as usual, I was watching the hoisting of the ensign on the Looe coastguard station at 8 a.m. It fluttered up to the peak and then was slowly lowered to half-mast. I knew then that the King was dead. After breakfast, I went down to the village to buy a black tie; but there was none left. The stocks had been sold out in a few minutes after the shops had opened. We all felt that we had lost a personal friend.

May and I returned to London — a capital in mourning — black everywhere. In the drizzling rain, we joined a queue that was two miles long, to file past the catafalque, where the King's body was r: lying in State at Westminster Abbey. It was a most solemn occasion.

The new King, Edward VIII, who had been only a boy; of Prince of Wales, during the 1914-18 war, and was unmarried, still seemed too youthful for the responsibilities of Kingship; but everyone was ready to give him loyalty and devotion in those times of anxiety and international tension, when his reign began.

After two more voyages to Halifax and New York, I left London in the *Ascania* on Friday, 11th April 1936 (Good Friday) for my first voyage in that year bound for Montreal.

Calling at Southampton, I docked in the next berth to a new Cunarder — the *Queen Mary*!

She was there, in all her magnificence, after her trials in the Firth of Clyde, being got ready for her maiden voyage, under command of Sir Edgar Britten. I had been his Staff Captain in the *Berengaria* five years previously.

The *Queen Mary*! Britain's "wonder ship," ready to go into service at last, as flagship of the Cunard fleet, five years and five months after her keel was laid down at Brown's shipyard on the Clyde: in all that time we had been waiting for her to restore Britain's mercantile sea supremacy in response to the formidable challenges of the German, the Italian, and the French superliners; and now she was ready to do it!

No British ship, since the *Great Eastern* was launched on the Thames in 1858, had aroused such intense interest and pride of achievement in British hearts. The *Queen Mary* was six times bigger than the *Great Eastern*. That was the measure of maritime progress in seventy-six years since the *Great Eastern* had made her maiden voyage in 1860, crossing the Atlantic in eleven days, at an average speed of nine knots. And now, we knew, the *Queen Mary* on her trials had attained a speed of 30 knots, without being fully driven.

We were confident that she would compare favourably with the *Normandie*; but speed was not the only requisite. Steady reliability, with great carrying capacity, luxury and comfort for the passengers, and, above all, seaworthiness — in the sense of steadiness in heavy weather — and ease of handling, were the essentials of a gigantic liner.

Despite her immense bulk, the *Queen Mary*'s hull had the graceful lines of a yacht. She had been designed and built by men who thoroughly understood shipbuilding. She was Hull Number 534 built in Brown's shipyards. She was the 148th Cunard liner to be put into ocean going service in ninety-eight years (not counting the nine White Star vessels taken over at the merger in 1934).

So, the *Queen Mary* was the product of the long experience of a seafaring nation; great care had been put into her design, building, and equipment. She would be the "Queen of the Western Ocean," of that we had no doubt Unprecedented publicity had hailed her launching and commissioning. There was surely no one in the English speaking world — and few in European mainland countries — who did not know of her gigantic dimensions and luxurious appointments, even before her maiden voyage.

Thousands of sightseers were visiting her at Southampton, as she lay at her berth there at the Easter weekend. It was springtime, and hopes were high.

I was one of those visitors on that Saturday, Easter Eve, 11th April 1936 — a special case, as I was entitled to a slight hope that I might someday command her. I was then nearly fifty-three years of age, and had been going to sea for thirty-seven years, including twenty-nine years in the Cunard service; but I had been a Captain in the Cunard service for only five years. There were many Cunard Captains ahead of me in seniority; yet with ordinary luck, and the effluxion of time, if no serious mishaps intervened to mar my record, I could look ahead to some dim and remote future day when I might stand on her bridge as Master. There was no harm in wishful thinking.

Apart from Captain Britten, there were several of the *Queen Mary's* officers who had been former shipmates of mine, including Pollitt. They took me immediately up to the bridge, eager to astonish me, and I was astonished.

The *Queen Mary* was of 81,237 gross tonnage, more than five times greater than that of the *Ascania*, and seventy-five times greater than that of the barque *County of Pembroke*, in which I had first gone to sea. She was 1019 feet in length overall, 118 feet beam: an oil burning quadruple screw steamer with geared turbine engines; three huge, raked funnels (70 feet high), a raked stem, and a "cruiser" stern — an unusual feature in Cunard liners among her predecessors.

Her midships superstructure was exceptionally long in relation to her overall length, leaving relatively short foredeck and after deck: she had (unlike the later built *Queen Elizabeth*) a well deck forward.

She had twelve decks, communicating by means of companion ways and also electric elevators. She had passenger accommodation for 704 first-class, 751 cabin-class, and 583 tourist-class-total 2038 — and a crew of 1285. This meant that she would carry a total of 3323 souls when she was in normal service on the Atlantic passenger and mail run.

This number of souls was scarcely more than the old *Mauretania* had carried, but the amount of space per passenger, and consequently of comfort, was nearly three times greater in the *Queen Mary* than in the *Mauretania*. The comfort of passengers was the paramount consideration in the design of the *Queen Mary*. The number of troops that she would be able to carry in crowded conditions on wartime service was something that only time might reveal.

Among the "colossal" statistics, her four four-blade propellers, 19 feet 6 inches in diameter, each weighed thirty-five tons. Her two anchors, each weighing sixteen tons, each had 165 fathoms (990 feet) of chain cable attached. The chain cables, of forged steel, had links twenty-four inches long and four and a half inches thick. Each of the chain cables weighed seventy-two tons.

She had tanks for 7000 tons of oil fuel and 5000 tons of freshwater and would burn on an average 1000 tons of oil a day when at sea. She had twenty-four water tube boilers, with seven oil burners to each. Her engine power was 160,000 horsepower. She had cost five million pounds sterling to build.

It was her bridge that fascinated me. It was 120 feet across on inside measurements, including two overhangs eleven feet across, built in as "cabs." The wheelhouse — which had ten heavy plate glass windows forward, two of them being "clear view" screens — was thirty feet across, with sliding side doors. These, when opened, left a clear passage from wing to wing.

The outer bridge decks, or "wings," open to the air, were forty-five feet across on each side of the wheelhouse, including the over-hang cabs. They were protected by bulwarks 4 feet 6 inches high with slots to break the force of the wind and deflect it over the heads of anyone standing in the wings.

The bridge, measuring thirty feet fore and aft, curved slightly forward from the wings, with a more pronounced curve at the wheelhouse, presenting a sort of bow window appearance. The bridge was 230 feet from the stem, or approximately a quarter of the ship's length. Its deck was 89 feet above the waterline.

The cabs on the port and starboard wings were connected to one another and to the wheelhouse by voice pipes. In each cab, as also in the wheelhouse, was a panel holding pushbuttons for the steam whistles.

Strangely small were the steering wheels, of which there were two (one for emergency or alternative use) operating two entirely separate sets of telemotor steering gear. These wheels were of brass, and scarcely more than twenty-four inches in diameter. A child could have turned them with ease. They had scarcely any "resistance": how different from the old time manually operated steering wheels! I could have wished that they were of oak, not of brass. Mere sentiment!

A magnetic compass, and a gyrocompass, were handy to the wheels, which were connected also to a gyro repeater, used at sea, outside narrow waters.

Every modern navigational aid was installed — wireless direction finder, echo sounding fathometer, and so on, but no radar — then (in 1936). All the telegraphs engine room, docking, steering, and anchor telegraphs were electrically operated. The engine room telegraphs were duplicated, with provision for alternative use. They were in pairs, one for controlling the outer engines (propellers) and the other for the inner propellers. Revolution indicators, engine "tell tales" and helm indicators were placed handy to the telegraphs.

There were large lockers for flags and chart tables. On the after bulkhead were loud speaking telephones to forward, aft, crow's nest, engine room, and fire brigade stations. Emergency alarm bells were fitted to be sounded separately in the engineers', seamen's, firemen's, stewards' and passengers' quarters. A telephone was connected to three loudspeakers on each side of the boat deck, with switch enabling orders to be given either to the port or starboard boats, or both if desired.

A "Stone Lloyd" panel indicated forty-one bulkhead doors, hydraulically operated, that could be closed by pushbuttons, to make watertight compartments down below.

There were two chartrooms abaft the wheelhouse, the port chartroom for the Captain, and the starboard chartroom for the officers, each fitted with chart tables, chronometers, meteorological instruments, and other instruments and graphs. The Captain's chartroom had a settee, and windows looking out to the bridge and wheelhouse. Abaft the chartrooms was the "office," where the ship's books and papers of the deck department were kept.

A short companionway led down to the Captain's and officers' living quarters below the bridge.

There was nothing startlingly new in the bridge and its equipment, except the great dimensions of its deck space, commensurate with the ship's size; but everything was of the most modern style and finish, based on practical experience.

After taking in details of the bridge, I went below to look cursorily at the deck features. Nothing had been spared to make the *Queen Mary* perfect for her purpose as a passenger liner.

The highest deck for the use of passengers, known as the Sports Deck, was laid out for deck tennis, squash, and other games. Here too were dog kennels, and part of the deck was reserved for passengers who wished to exercise their pets.

On this deck also was the Wireless Shack — if it could be called a shack — for in this ship it was a splendid room with the most elabor-ate radio installations afloat, and ten operators. It provided, in addition to normal signalling, facilities for two-way radio telephone conversations from ship to shore, which could be put through ordinary telephones installed at five hundred different places in the ship, including most of the staterooms.

Next deck below, the Boat Deck, had twenty-four motor life- boats — twelve on each side — capable of carrying a total of 3300 persons. The boats sat snugly in davits well overhead, leaving a dear promenade right round the deck. They were patent gravity davits, enabling a boat to be swung out and lowered into the water by one man. At the after-end was a veranda cafe, and amidships a gymnasium, with a nonstop elevator running to the swimming pool, seven decks below.

Below the Boat Deck was the Promenade Deck, 750 feet long, enclosed with plate glass windows which could be opened if required. Inside on this deck were magnificent public rooms, including the Main Lounge, superbly furnished. The nine decks below this held the accommodation for passengers and crew, and the many and various services of the ship. Though the accommodation was on a scale of luxury and comfort that would have been undreamed of twenty-five years previously, that luxury had not been allowed to interfere with the basic requirements of strength, safety, and efficiency.

She was not a "floating hotel." She was a floating town, in which three thousand people would live in every comfort, as she sped on her way, linking the Old World and the New.

Returning to my dwarfed but still friendly *Ascania*, 1 continued my voyaging to Montreal. On 27th May 1936, when I was homeward bound in mid-Atlantic, I heard on the radio the thrilling news that the *Queen Mary* had begun her maiden voyage. I did not sight her, but I was in radio communication with her and knew of her progress.

She made the crossing from Cherbourg to Ambrose at 29.13 knots, and the return passage at 29.79 knots. On this voyage she was not being "driven" to beat the *Normandie*'s record of 30.31 knots. She was being thoroughly and finally tested under ocean going conditions. On her next voyage, eastbound, she took the Blue Riband from the *Normandie*, with a crossing from Ambrose to Cherbourg, steaming 2939 miles in 3 days 23 hours 57 minutes, at an average speed of 30.63 knots.

That was the first time that the Atlantic crossing was made, from shore to shore, in less than four days, but only three minutes less! Times on eastbound passages are usually less than on westbound passages, because of the influence of the Gulf Stream.

There was never more than a fractional difference in the speeds of the *Normandie* and the *Queen Mary*. They contended for the Blue Riband[1] and shared the honours; but it was never a "race" in the ordinary meaning of that word. No shipmaster would risk damaging his ship, especially a gigantic ship, by "pressing on regardless." Much depended on the weather.

The Blue Riband was won in 1935 by the *Normandie*, with a speed of 30.31 knots; in 1936 by the *Queen Mary*, 30.63 knots; in 1937 by the *Normandie*, 30.99 knots; in 1938 by the *Normandie*, 31.20 knots; and, a few weeks later, in 1938, it was wrested from her by the *Queen Mary*, 31.69 knots.

There was very little difference between them, either in size or speed. They shared the honours.

Throughout the year 1936, I plodded along in the *Ascania* at 14 knots in fine weather, and at dead slow in fogs or amid icebergs, but well content. She was neither a giantess nor a record breaker, but she did her work well.

On 16th July 1936, I cleared out of Montreal, in company with four other liners — the *Montcalm*, *Montrose*, *Antonia*, and *Sagunay* — all five vessels crowded with Canadians making a pilgrimage to the Canadian War Memorial at Vimy Ridge in Northern France, where, during the 1914-18 war, Canadian troops had suffered heavy casualties in battle and had won a victory and renown. In the *Ascania* I had 1125 "pilgrims" — most of them relatives of the fallen — and it was a sombre occasion. We landed the pilgrims at Havre on Saturday, 25th July, and next day heard the impressive service broadcast , at the unveiling of the Vimy Ridge Memorial.

We went on to London, and returned to Havre on 1st August, where most of the pilgrims reembarked, and they were landed at Montreal on 10th August. With such a solemn reminder of the high cost of war in human lives, it was depressing to read in the newspapers, and to hear on the radio, the continued accounts of increasing international tensions, pointing to the possibility of another "Great" War. If it had to come, we had better get ready for it.

Homeward bound, in mid-Atlantic, at 3 p.m. on Friday, 21st August (1936), we sighted the German "Zeppelin" airship, Hindenburg, on her Atlantic crossing. She gleamed in the sky, to the north of our track, and in a few minutes was gone again from sight.

At that time, many people thought that big gas filled dirigible airships might be developed to the point where they would replace surface vessels in the carriage of passengers and mails across oceans. The disaster to the Hindenburg, on her arrival in New York, put an end to that idea.

On my next voyage, leaving London on 27th August 1936, I had an unusual stowaway in the *Ascania*. On the morning of the third day out from Southampton, when the ship was 600 miles to the westward of Ireland, a large bird fluttered onto the boat deck, exhausted. One of the seamen ran to pick it up, and, unaware that it had a long neck, got the surprise of his life when its head shot up and gave him a jolt under the chin.

But he gamely held on to the bird. It was placed in a dog kennel which had bars in front and lots of headroom. No one on board knew what it was. We thought that it was a stork or a crane. It had long legs for wading but was obviously not a sea swimming bird. We christened it "George" despite the fact that its sex was unknown.

The stowaway refused to eat bread or meat but daintily swallowed some pieces of raw fish. We put a bucket of fresh water in George's cage. He dipped his long bill into this with obvious appreciation of our thoughtfulness.

When we arrived at Montreal, a Professor of Zoology from McGill University came on board and pronounced George to be a common European heron. The Professor advised that we should take him back to England. He kindly sent to the ship a can containing thirty live frogs. These were to be George's diet on the homeward passage — three a day.

George's method of eating frogs never varied. The frog was thrown into the kennel. After contemplating it for a few moments with his beady eyes, George would pick it up with a lightning stroke of his sharp beak and squeeze it until it stopped kicking. Then he would daintily dip it into the bucket of water, turn it over on its back, and swallow it whole.

On this diet George thrived. The ship was met on arrival at London by ornithologists, who "ringed" George, and liberated him near a heronry on the Upper Thames.

I never heard any satisfactory explanation of George's reason for venturing so far out to sea that he had become exhausted and had to alight on board a ship; nor did I ever hear of him again after he was liberated. He is probably the only heron who has ever crossed the Atlantic, and both ways at that.

On my next voyage, when I docked at Montreal on 5th October.; I received a letter there, which had been mailed in New Zealand — two months previously. It contained a warning of dire events to occur on 14th December. I thought it was from a "crank." In the sequel something did happen on 14th December:

> Takuti Street,
> Parnell,
> Auckland, New Zealand.
> Aug. 7th, 1936
>
> Master, "*Ascania*," Montreal.
>
> Dear Sir,
>
> Kindly be advised as follows: Beware navigation December First Quarter Moon over Merid. East Long. 35 deg. 14 min. 45 secs., after total eclipse on the 14th. Apply split second of that time to ship's local position.

Expect intense submarine disturbances with tidal waves. Intense electrical disturbances, and probably dislocation of the compass. Take more than ordinary precautions for the safety of the ship.

The disturbance will be worldwide, both on land and sea. Kindly pass the news around as much as possible. New York and most of Southern Europe will be in ruins.

Sincerely yours,
JOHN L. BRETT

I did not pay much heed to this warning. I did not expect to be in Russia, in the meridian of the calamity, on 14th December. According to my schedule, I would be docking in London on that date.

On 21st November, I began what was to be my last voyage in command of the *Ascania*, bound for Halifax and New York. On the fatal day of John L. Brett's prediction, I docked in the, Thames, with the agreeable prospect of being home again for Christmas. On arrival, I received news that I was to command a slightly bigger Cunarder, the *Lancastria*. I was to join her after taking a month's leave.

This was scarcely a world shaking calamity. Yet there was something happened that day. I cannot suppose that the eclipse of the moon had anything to do with it. All London was in a ferment; the whole British Empire and the wider world was in a ferment. King Edward the Eighth had abdicated! We lived in troubled times, modern times; times of "intense disturbances."

The New Zealand prophet had not been entirely wrong.

CHAPTER ENDNOTES

(1) The *SS United States* currently holds the Blue Riband, the record for the fastest crossing of the Atlantic Ocean by an ocean liner. It crossed the Atlantic in 3 days, 10 hours, and 40 minutes, beating the *RMS Queen Mary's* time by 10 hours.

28

*Accession of King George VI — Work Begun on Building the
"Queen Elizabeth" — Take Command of the "Lancastria" —
"Coronation Ceremonies" — Summer Cruises — In Command of
the "Scythia" — Launch of the New "Mauretania" and the Queen
Elizabeth — Luxury Cruising in the "Laconia" — Captain of the
"Franconia" — War Clouds Gathering- A Summer Cruise to Norway
and the Baltic — Days of Increasing Tension — Gasmasks for
Civilians — The Outbreak of War.*

WHEN King Edward VIII abdicated, in December, 1936, the succession passed to his brother, the Duke of York, who had married a Scot, the Lady Elizabeth Bowes-Lyons. The new King took the title of George VI, and his consort became *Queen Elizabeth*.

In that same eventful month, the keel of the second 80,000-ton Cunarder — to be named the *Queen Elizabeth* — was laid down at Brown's shipyards on the Clyde. The work of building her thus began six months after the *Queen Mary*'s maiden voyage. She was to be slightly bigger than the *Queen Mary*, with some minor improvements gained from experience in the earlier sister ship.

It appeared likely that the policy of building mammoth ships might eventually reduce the number of seagoing employees of the Cunard White Star Line. The bigger the fewer! No new medium sized liners had been built by Cunard since the *Franconia* and *Carinthia*, 1923 and 1925. The merger of the Cunard and White Star Lines in 1934 had brought additional vessels into the combined control, but those ships already had their officers and crews.

Now it was announced that a new *Mauretania* would be built, of 35,000 tons. She was laid down at Birkenhead on the Mersey, in May, 1937.

I took over command of the *Lancastria*, at Liverpool, on 20th January 1937. She was on passenger and mail service from Liverpool to Halifax and New York, voyaging on a route round the north of Ireland, with calls at Belfast and Greenock.

In service since 1922, the *Lancastria* was a twin screw, oil burning, steamer of 16,242 tons gross, with a speed of 17 knots. She had been one of the first vessels of the post-war building programme and was the first Cunarder with a "cruiser stern." She had originally been designed for the Anchor Line. Her name of *Tyrrhenia* had been changed to *Lancastria.*

During eleven months that I was in command of her, the *Lancastria* was

Postcard image of the R.M.S. Lancastria.
(Public Domain, but the original author is Odin Rosenving)

a maid-of-all-work. After one voyage to New York, she was converted to a cruise liner. In March and April, I took her on a "Scholars' cruise," with 900 passengers, nearly all schoolboys, visiting the Azores, Madeira, Santa Cruz, Casablanca, and Gibraltar. Then I took the ship to Montreal, and cleared out from there on 29th April 1937, with 650 passengers going to London to see the Coronation of King George VI and *Queen Elizabeth.* They saw the Coronation Procession on 14th May, had a look around the sights of the big city, and then rejoined the ship at Tilbury Dock on 19th May, and I took them around to Southampton, to see the Coronation Naval Review. This was sightseeing for me, too: the Naval Review was impressive, and the *Lancastria* was fully dressed for the occasion.

I landed my passengers at Southampton, to make their way back to Canada in other ships. Then I crossed to Boston, for a cruise from there to Plymouth, Ostend, Copenhagen and Helsinki in Finland, returning to London, via the Kiel Canal.

After that, between July and October, I took the *Lancastria* on eight different short cruises, averaging fourteen days on each cruise. Some were from London, some from Liverpool. The routes were varied, ranging from the Norwegian fjords and the Baltic to the Azores and the Mediterranean. At fares averaging fifteen pounds, these "summer cruises" offered a holiday at no great expense; but, with 650 passengers on each cruise, the venture was profitable to shipowners.

After these eight short cruises, I had had nearly enough of the constant excitement and changes of Pleasure Cruising. At the end of November 1937, I was given command of the *Scythia*, voyaging on regular schedules from Liverpool to Boston and New York, with calls at Belfast, Greenock, and sometimes at Galway in western Ireland.

The *Scythia*, 20,000 tons, speed 16 knots, was the biggest vessel that I had commanded until then. I had made one voyage in her in 1923 as Chief Officer and knew her well. She was a typical Cunarder, of the immediate post-war building programme (completed in 1920), but was ageing in 1938. On an average she carried 900 passengers and a crew of 400. I remained in command of her on routine voyages to Boston and New York, for fourteen months, from November 1937, until January 1939.

Throughout that period the European international tension was increasing alarmingly; Germany had arisen again in might. Despite attempts at "appeasement," it appeared that another Great War could not be avoided. Preparations for it were going on apace. The "War of Words" was already at boiling over point.

On 28th July, 1938, the new *Mauretania* was launched at Birkenhead, opposite Liverpool. She was the biggest vessel ever built on the Mersey, and being a few thousand tons greater in gross tonnage than her famous predecessor of that name, she was the biggest vessel ever built in England (which certainly does not include Scotland and Ulster). I had seen her taking shape at Gammell Laird's shipyard at Birkenhead every time that I passed in and out of the Mersey in the *Lancastria* and the *Scythia*.

On 27th September 1938, the *Queen Elizabeth* was launched and named at Clydebank. She could not be got ready for service for a year or more. War service or peace service — who could tell in those times of tension?

In mid-January 1939, I was transferred from command of the *Scythia*, and given command of the *Laconia*, then being fitted out for a luxury cruise.

Cruising was all the rage in those days. The *Laconia* was a twin screw 20,000-ton liner, built in 1922, sistership of the *Samaria*. This was my first voyage in her. We cleared out from Liverpool on 26th January with 120 passengers and picked up another 150 at Southampton. All the passengers were accommodated as first class, and the cruise arrangements were in the hands of Thomas Cook & Son. The procedures were similar to those in the world cruises that I had made as Chief Officer in the *Franconia* twelve years previously — the main difference being, as far as I was concerned, that I was now twelve years older, and had the responsibilities of command. This was to be a cruise of two months' duration to warm climates, chiefly to get away from the English winter.

Our first call was at Tenerife, Canary Isles. From there we went on to Dakar, in West Africa; then westwards across the Atlantic in the tropics, crossing the Line on 8th February, with the usual tomfool ceremony. In this I could now play only an advisory part: anything else would have been beneath the Captain's dignity. Alas! On 13th February, we arrived at Rio De Janeiro, and from there went on to Port of Spain, Trinidad; Curaçao; and Colon. I went ashore with the passengers for a Cook's Tour by train across the Isthmus to Panama. On 3rd March, we arrived at Kingston, Jamaica; and from there went on to Nassau in the Bahamas; and on to Miami, Florida; then to Madeira, and returned to Southampton on 21 March and to Liverpool on 23rd March.

In April and May, I made two routine scheduled voyages in command of the *Laconia*, from Liverpool to Boston and New York. On returning to England, early in June 1939, I was given command of the *Franconia*. She was booked for a cruise from New York to the lands of the Midnight Sun.

So — Captain of the *Franconia* — at last! I took her across to New York, arriving there on 26th June. At the Cunard Pier, I docked next to the new Mauretania, just arrived on her maiden voyage. I looked her over. She was a twin screw steamer of 35,000 tons, less than half the size of the *Queen Mary*, but built on somewhat similar lines, with a raked stem and a cruiser stern. She had neither the passenger carrying capacity nor the speed of her famous predecessor. Her speed was 23 knots — no record breaker — a comfortable and valuable addition to the Cunard fleet. She replaced the *Berengaria*, which had been withdrawn from service in 1938 and sent to the shipbreakers — chiefly because the costs of renewing electric installations would have been prohibitive. The original German plans were "lost."

The *Franconia* cleared out from New York on 1st July 1939, with 350 first-class passengers, a cruise staff of 29, and a crew of 461. The cruise was organized by the Raymond-Whitcomb Company of New York. All our passengers were wealthy Americans, who didn't have a care in the world.

We called at Reykjavik in Iceland, and went on to the North Cape of Norway, to see the Midnight Sun. There, on 15th July, I celebrated my fifty-sixth birthday. We cruised into and out of the Norwegian fjords, then to Oslo, Stockholm, Tallin, Leningrad — where some of our passengers went on a short "conducted tour" to Moscow. Then we went on to Helsinki, Danzig (the storm centre!), Copenhagen, Cherbourg and Southampton, where we arrived on 7th August. There our passengers disembarked, to return to New York in the· *Aquitania*. I took the *Franconia* to Liverpool, where she was laid, up for nine days, in preparation for returning to the ordinary mail and passenger transatlantic run, to Boston and New York.

I spent most of those nine days with shore leave, at our home in London. International tension was acute. Soon after I arrived home, May and I received a letter from the Marylebone Council (our municipality) to attend at the Marylebone Town Hall to be measured for gasmasks! We went there, and were duly measured, ; and were told that, if the situation worsened, our masks would be delivered to our homes.

A few days went by. The papers were full of rumours of war. Trenches were being dug in Hyde Park for antiaircraft gun crews. It was all very disturbing.

On the night of 17th August, as we were preparing for bed at 11 p.m., it was raining heavily. We heard the rumble of a motortruck outside our window. Then came a knock on the front door.

I went down and opened the door. A man in streaming oilskins handed me two gasmasks and hurried off without a word.

We took the gasmasks from their cases and tried them on. We looked like a pair of prehistoric monsters. This issue of gasmasks to the civilian population in London — seventeen days before the war actually began — seemed to us a sure sign that war was imminent.

Our hearts sank as we gazed at one another. The fact that I was to leave home next morning to join the *Franconia*, bound for Boston and New York, didn't raise our drooping spirits. May tried to cheer me up in her bright, optimistic way, but I hated having to leave her alone at such a critical time. During the twenty-six years that we had been married, we had grown accustomed to partings, but this was the most doleful that I had known.

Next day, 18th August, I left Liverpool in the *Franconia*, filled with gloomy forebodings. The ship was crowded with Americans who had cut short their vacations in Europe to hurry home.

While the *Franconia* was on her westbound passage, of nine days, from Liverpool to Boston, calling at Belfast and Galway, the weather in the Western Ocean was fine, but the war clouds were gathering ominously over Europe. Our passengers could hear the news bulletins broadcast from the

B.B.C. They could talk of nothing but war, war, war. Never before in history had the public mind been so fully prepared for a war as for this one.

On Sunday, 27th August, the *Franconia* docked at Boston at 7 a.m., and most of our passengers disembarked. A few hardy souls remained on board, to go on to New York. Among them was a Roman Catholic Priest, the Reverend Father Bradley, an Irishman with a broad brogue, who had embarked at Galway. I had become friendly with him on the passage over. He was the only person in the ship who thought that there would not be a war.

The *Franconia* cleared out from Boston at 12 noon. I had received coded instructions from the Admiralty to "darken ship" on the passage to New York. While we were outside U.S.A. territorial waters that night, all lights in the ship were covered, even the navigation lights. I had been used to that in the *Mauretania* during the 1914-18 war; and now I did not like it at all, especially in the busy traffic lanes at the approaches to New York; but all except British ships were brightly lit, and we could give the lit ships a wide berth.

On Monday, 28th August, the *Franconia* docked at New York at 1.30 p.m. Our passengers disembarked, and I was glad to see them landed. The Reverend Father Bradley said goodbye and went down the gangway; but a few moments later he returned and whispered to me, "There won't be any war. The Pope won't allow it!"

How wrong can one be?

The *Franconia* was due to leave New York at 5 p.m. on Friday, 1st September. On that day, the Germans invaded Poland at 5.30 a.m., Central European time, which is six hours ahead of New York time.

Early that morning, in New York, I received a coded message from the Cunard White Star Line head office, ordering me to prepare the ship for the possible outbreak of war. A few hours later, gangs of men swarmed on board and proceeded to paint everything from the top of the funnel to the waterline with "battleship grey." The *Franconia*'s departure, on her scheduled run to Liverpool with a call at Boston, was postponed until the following day. Passengers booked to embark at New York and at Boston were notified.

Some cancelled their bookings and could scarcely be blamed for doing that.

I mustered the crew and told them of the situation. They would be required to work all that day, and throughout the night, preparing the ship for wartime routines at sea. It was possible and likely — in fact almost certain — that war would be declared while we were at sea, homeward bound for Liverpool. We had to be prepared for that.

Not one of my crew of 400 deserted or showed any signs of funk. Tons of sand, and thousands of bags, were hoisted on board and stacked on deck at various places. The crew set to work with a will, filling the sandbags and placing them in positions on board to. protect vulnerable parts of the ship — such as the wheelhouse and chartrooms, the steering gear, the entrances to the engine room, crews' quarters and passengers' quarters, and deck gear — against, air attack or gunfire. These precautions were defensive only. We had no guns mounted in the ship. All glass portholes were painted black. All openings onto the deck were screened with curtains or doors. While all this was being done by the crew, the gangs of painters from on shore were slapping "battleship grey" over the *Franconia*'s formerly immaculate "cruise ship white" everywhere.

The painting and sandbagging of the *Franconia* were completed on Saturday morning, 2nd September. Our passengers from New York were then allowed on board. There were about one hundred of them prepared to take the risk of crossing the Atlantic in those circumstances. More were to come on board at Boston. I couldn't help admiring their pluck — or was it optimism?

At 1 p.m. on Saturday we unmoored and proceeded downriver, past the Statue of Liberty. When we dropped the pilot off Ambrose Light Vessel, his "Bon Voyage," with a handshake, was much more serious than usual.

The passage from Ambrose Light Vessel to Boston Light Vessel, 345 miles, was in the open ocean, to the southward of Long Island and round Nantucket Island. It would take a full twenty-four hours' steaming. Would the Germans dare to strike a blow so near to the American shore? We could take no chances of what the unpredictable Hitler might do.

Our lifeboats were swung out over the side, ready for immediate lowering. Extra lookouts were posted. Blackout conditions were strictly observed. Not the slightest glimmer of light — not even the lighting or smoking of a cigarette — was allowed on deck after dark.

At 6 a.m., Eastern American time, equivalent to 11 a.m. British time, on Sunday, 3rd September 1939, I heard the news of Britain's declaration of war. The *Franconia* was then off Nantucket Island, bearing up for Cape Cod, at the entrance to Massachusetts Bay.

Our passengers heard the news at breakfast time. We docked at Boston at 3.30 p.m. They could have left the ship there, but none of them did. On the contrary, the extra passengers booked to come on board at Boston did so. We then had 330 passengers on board for Liverpool. I received Admiralty orders to proceed to the nearest British port, Halifax, Nova Scotia, for further orders.

At 6 p.m. we headed out of Boston Harbour and set course in the gathering darkness across Massachusetts Bay and the Gulf of Maine, making for Halifax, a run of 370 miles.

It was "on" again. Another "Great" War, the future grim.

29

T HE "Six Years War" — as historians may eventually term it —
began with the German invasion of Poland on 1st September,
1939, and ended, almost exactly six years later, with the
unconditional surrender of Japan on 2nd September 1945.

The events of those years remain vividly in the memory of the millions
of people who endured them but will become "history" and legend to their
descendants of new generations maturing in the 1960s and afterwards.
Finally, only the printed records will remain. In the armed forces of the
British Commonwealth and Empire, during those six years, nearly 400,000
men were killed. In addition, 56,000 civilians were killed by enemy air raids.
The U.S.A. lost 325,000 men of the armed forces killed.

When the casualties of the other combatant nations, especially those of
Germany and the Soviet Union, are added, the total of the slain amounted
to millions. The numbers of the maimed and of the dispossessed, and the
value of the property destroyed and of the wealth expanded, were so

immense as to be beyond computation. In that perspective, my part in the gigantic conflict of the nations was that of only one individual among the millions engaged in war efforts of so many kinds. My duties were those of a merchant: seaman in command of troop transports. It happened that, in those six years, a total of over 500,000 troops, besides some wartime leaders rated as "Very Important Persons," were transported, in vessels under my command, on many voyages to and from zones of combat, ranging over six of the world's eight oceans, under hazards of abnormal navigation, and at times under enemy action.

My recollections of these voyages, based on my diaries, may be considered as a merchant seaman's contribution to the general history of the war, even though they record only the tasks which were entrusted to one shipmaster among the many who served in merchant ships great and small.

I therefore set down here a summary of my wartime voyages in no spirit of self-aggrandizement, but on the contrary in acknowledgment of the good fortune that allowed me to come through unscathed, and in gratitude to the officers and men of my crews who went through the war's ordeals with me. We of the Merchant Navy were not combatants in the ordinary meaning of that term. We were "the Navy of Supply" — conveying across the oceans and in narrow waters not only the men, equipment and supplies of the fighting services, but also food and other supplies for beleaguered civilians.

Of a total of 150,000 seamen who served in the British Merchant Navy during the war, 35,000 lost their lives by enemy action. A total of 3180 British merchant vessels was sunk. That was part of the cost of the victory ultimately attained. In the perspective of such stupendous events, how can I narrate my own more fortunate experiences, except in a spirit of humility? We who survived were the lucky ones, and that is the simple truth of the matter. But those who gave their lives made the sacrifice that cannot be surpassed.

On the outbreak of war on 3rd September 1939, I was in command of the *Franconia*, in service as a passenger liner, bound from New York, via Boston, to Liverpool. I expected that, when she arrived at Liverpool — or if she arrived there — she would be converted either into an armed merchant cruiser, a hospital ship, or a troop transport; or it was possible that she would continue as a passenger and mail liner. I did not know what plans had been made for her service in wartime. My immediate concern was to complete the voyage on which I was engaged.

When we left Boston at 6 p.m., local time, equivalent to 11 p.m. British time, on Sunday, 3rd September, Britain had already been at war for twelve hours. On that day the Donaldson liner, *S.S. Athenia*, was sunk off the north-west coast of Ireland. She was a vessel of 13,600 tons, carrying nearly 1000 passengers, many of whom were Americans. Most of her people took to the boats and were saved, but 125 lost their lives, including some Americans.

Germany had 200 submarines in commission at the outbreak of war. Some of them were already in the Atlantic when war was declared. Two days later, on 5th September, the small Cunard cargo vessel, *S.S. Bosnia* (2400 tons), engaged in the Mediterranean service was sunk off the coast of Portugal. She was torpedoed and also attacked by gunfire from a U-boat which surfaced.

After the war, all the facts about the sinking of the *Athenia* came to light. She was torpedoed without warning at 7.40 p.m. on 3rd September, by U-boat 30, commanded by Ober-Lieutenant Fritz Lemp of the German Navy. He had left the Port of Wilhelmshafen on 22nd August, with orders to proceed to a "waiting area" between 54 and 57 deg. N. Lat. and 12 to 19 deg.

The S.S. Athenia was the first merchant ship sunk in the opening hours of WW2. (Public Domain)

W. Long. Other U-boats were stationed in adjacent "boxes."So, in "Hitler's war," unrestricted U-boat warfare began from the very first day.

On leaving Boston in the *Franconia*, at dusk on 3rd September, with 330 passengers on board, I had orders to proceed to Halifax. I supposed that this meant that we would be joining a convoy, and my spirits rose accordingly.

But it doesn't do to suppose or guess too much, especially in wartime. No sooner had we let go the anchor in Halifax Harbour, at 7.10 p.m. on 4th September, than a naval launch ranged alongside. A naval officer came on board and handed me "the books." These were a bundle of confidential books and papers, containing wartime secret signal codes and other directions.

With these were my orders: to leave Halifax immediately and proceed to Liverpool alone and unescorted.

Those orders were handed to me thirty hours after the *Athenia* had been torpedoed. She had been westward bound, on a track very near that on which I would have to take the *Franconia* eastbound, making for Liverpool round the north of Ireland. It was not for me to question orders, so I proceeded to sea immediately. The ship was darkened under wartime routines and followed a track with zigzag courses as laid down in the books.

Next day the radio news bulletins, which my passengers could hear at frequent intervals, were giving frightening details of the sinking of the *Athenia*, presented as a German atrocity similar to the sinking of the *Lusitania* in the Kaiser's war.

I had extra lookouts posted, by day and by night, and kept the *Franconia* going at her full speed of 16 knots, with zigzag changes of course as prescribed, to put any submerged lurking U-boat off his aim. My ship was unarmed, and had no defence except her speed and zigzagging, and her drab grey paintwork. At night she was completely darkened — not a glimmer of light showing anywhere. Her boats were swung out over the side, ready for immediate lowering. I ordered boat stations daily, to ensure that every passenger would know what to do if we were hit. The lookout men were scanning not only the sea for enemy surface vessels, or periscopes of U-boats, but also the sky for the possible approach of enemy bombing aircraft.

At that early stage in the war, we did not know what striking power the German Air Force might have in long range bombing aircraft, or what measures, if any, could be taken by a ship to avoid air attack. We did not know what secret weapons Hitler might have up his sleeve. Would the Germans sow minefields from the air in the Atlantic shipping lanes? In such situations, it is no use having too much imagination or feeling jittery. The thing to do is to carry on, hoping for the best and being prepared for the worst at any minute. That first wartime passage of the Atlantic was one of the most anxious that I ever made, chiefly because the *Franconia* was unescorted and defenceless. A considerable number of my passengers were women and children and elderly civilians.

I stayed on the bridge throughout the passage of eight days, taking my meals and sleeping in the chartroom. It was not that I didn't trust the officers, but, in case of emergency, which could come without warning at any moment, I wanted to ensure that I would be where I should be — on the bridge and taking the full responsibility.

As we neared home, we were met by a light cruiser which steamed with us as an escort. Whether by this protection, or good luck, we made port without being attacked and entered the Mersey early in the afternoon of 12th September.

We made fast at the Liverpool Landing Stage at 3.30 p.m., to land our passengers. I received fifty-three letters from passengers, expressing their gratitude to me for having got them safely across the Atlantic in such hazardous conditions.

Dusk fell, and, as Liverpool was entirely blacked out, it was not possible to proceed into dock without lights. I therefore anchored my ship in the river overnight, and next morning docked her to begin discharging cargo.

By this time I had been given the information that the *Franconia* was to be used on war service as a troop transport.

So that was that! After the cargo was unloaded, I moved her next day to another dock, where she was to be stripped of her luxurious furniture and fittings which were designed to pamper millionaires and other luxury cruise passengers. Work began on converting her into a troop carrier, with the rough-and-ready accommodation that soldiers have to expect when they go to sea, enroute to battlefields.

In normal passenger service, the *Franconia* had accommodation for 253 first-class and 600 tourist-class passengers, total 853. As a transport she would be able to carry 3000 troops, and even a few more than that, with some crowding. I was given ten days' leave, and went with May for a quiet holiday in Somerset: perhaps the last we'd ever have — who could tell? The future was so uncertain.

Liverpool, like all other British cities, was totally blacked out at nighttime. There had been no German air raids yet. People were thinking that this war would follow the pattern of the previous one. The British Expeditionary Force had begun moving across to France on 10th September. In the meantime, the U.S.A. had made a proclamation of neutrality on 5th September. The French were manning their supposedly impregnable Maginot Line. Experts were saying that "defence is the best offence," "Hitler will soon run out of petrol," and "the war will be over by Christmas" — but the British Government, on 8th September, had announced preparations for a three years' war.

In expectation of German air raids on Britain, more than one million children, expectant mothers, and invalids had been evacuated from London and other large cities and billeted in rural districts. It looked like being a long and worrying war, that hadn't "warmed up" yet. Britain seemed almost alone. France was in the war, but hesitant. Italy, Japan, the U.S.A., Russia, Holland, Belgium, and the Scandinavian countries were all neutral. The Germans had quickly overrun Poland, with Russian approval and help. All was quiet on the Western Front. Some newspaper writers were calling it "a phoney war."

But in the Atlantic the war was real. Germany had instituted a counter blockade of Britain by sinking twenty British merchant vessels, by U-boat action, in the first fortnight. On 18th September, a U-boat torpedoed the big British aircraft carrier, *H.M.S. Courageous*, which sank with the loss of 518 lives. We who were seafarers knew that the war had already become a grim and bitter struggle in our field of operations, and that things would have to become worse before they could become better. Some were remembering the old satire:

In time of war, but not before,
God and the sailor you implore;
When the danger is past, and wrongs are righted,
God is forgotten, and the sailor slighted.

Even if that were true, it was also true that "sailors: don't care". We were used to a certain amount of danger, and the need for alert•. ness to avert it, at all times. War was, to us, another kind of storm.

On 24th September 1939, I returned from leave, to rejoin my ship at Liverpool. Every part of the passenger accommodation was now rigged with military bunks and hammocks. All the best furniture, curtains and carpets had been stripped out of her, and stored in warehouses, with the linen, best cutlery, glassware, crockery, and almost everything else valuable and portable.

Her crew had been reduced to 335, chiefly by paying off stewardesses, laundresses, and some men of the catering department. A 6-inch gun had been mounted on her stern, manned by a gun crew of the Honourable Artillery Company soldiers, not sailors. That was an important distinction. The gun was for defence, not offence. Troops on board a transport are entitled to defend themselves, but her crew are merchant seamen, unarmed, and, if taken prisoner, are to be treated as civilians. Not that there is much observance of the Rules of War nowadays, but it is always best, if possible, to conform with rules and regulations.

Just my luck, the *Franconia*'s sister ship, *Carinthia*, was being fitted out for service as an armed merchant cruiser, as also were the Cunarder *Andania* and the White Star liner *Laurentic*. Their fate could have been mine; but most of the Cunard and White Star vessels were to be used as troop transports.

The new *Mauretania*, after having made only one voyage to New York in peacetime, was now being fitted out at Liverpool as an armed merchant cruiser, with 6-inch guns mounted; but in the sequel she was not sent out on naval patrol.

On the day that war was declared, the *Queen Mary* had been at sea, bound for New York with 2000 passengers on ·board. She had made port safely, and was laid up there for the time being, as also was her rival, the *Normandie*.

While they were in a neutral port, they were under the protection of the neutral power, as also were some German merchant vessels, but, on this occasion, none of the German giant liners.

The *Queen Elizabeth*, nearing completion, lay in Brown's shipyard at Clydebank, a conspicuous target for enemy air raiders — even though no air raids had been made on Britain, as yet.

My orders were to proceed in the *Franconia* from Liverpool to Southampton for troops. At dead of night, 10.30 p.m. on 25th September we unmoored, moved out of the dock, and, with a Mersey pilot on board, and no passengers, felt our way downriver at dead slow in the total blackout. That kind of navigation is exasperating — but one gets used to it, as one gets used to all sorts of other exasperations, in wartime.

Outside the Mersey Bar, unknown and unseen dangers lurked. Destroyers were patrolling, as I had patrolled outside Plymouth so many times twenty years and more previously, but they were not much comfort to a 20,000-ton liner groping along on a zigzag course at midnight with no lights. I could only hope that one of them wouldn't get under my bows! Admiralty orders were that ships at sea were not to stop, for rescue work or anything else. Keep moving was the rule. A stopped ship is a sitting target for a sub. I was under the authority of the escorting destroyers as to speed and course. I remained on the bridge, in case a collision or other worse mishap — if a torpedo in the dark, or impact with an enemy mine should occur. It was a relief when daylight came, and we could clap on full speed with clear visibility. That, and zigzagging, were always the best defence against U-boat attack. Keep moving!

The passage from Liverpool to Southampton, 500 miles, took thirty-eight hours from berth to berth and then I could snatch a few hours' sleep.

We berthed at Southampton in the afternoon of 27th September. That was the day when Warsaw surrendered. The gallant Poles had been cracked like a nut between the pincers of Germany and Russia. Hitler thought that the war was over. Little did he know.

Next day, we took on board the *Franconia* 1301 troops, with their own mess kits, blankets, rifles, and other gear. We left Southampton at dusk, in company with three other passenger liners serving as troop transports. They were the *Alcantara* (20,000 tons, Royal Mail Line), the *Athlone Castle* (25,000 tons, Union Castle Line), and the *Empress of Australia* (22,000 tons, C.P.R. Line). We were in convoy, escorted by two destroyers. We were bound not for France, as we had expected, but for the Mediterranean.

Everything was blacked out in Southampton Water and in the Solent. This was my first experience of voyaging in convoy, and I did not like it. It is not an easy matter for a large vessel to keep station with other large vessels when zigzagging, even in broad daylight and on the open ocean. Constant watchfulness is necessary to maintain the set courses, speeds, and distances between the vessels. A sailor is happiest when he has plenty of sea room. He must be wide awake at all times, but especially when he is in convoy. In narrow waters at nighttime, with no shore lights, and no navigating lights either on his own or on the other vessels, and unlit destroyers darting hither and thither, then voyaging in convoy can be a nightmare.

Clear of the land, we began zigzagging on a south-westerly track, on predetermined courses and speeds, which had been handed to us with every precaution of secrecy. There was no doubt that U-boats were on the prowl in the Channel. The slightest gleam of light would have been an invitation to these lurking beasts of prey to close in for a kill. Yet I found myself worrying less about the chances of being torpedoed than of colliding with one of the other transports.

We were stationed half a mile apart, in two lines, forming a square, with the four big steamers at its corners — one destroyer ahead and one astern. At predetermined times, all six vessels altered course on the zigzag. Stationed ahead of me was the Alcantara, her bulk vaguely visible under the night sky, but her white wake could be discerned. This had to be kept sighted all the time. She towed a barrel astern, which made a slight disturbance in the water, easy for our lookout men on the bows to keep in sight. This was a help to us in maintaining our proper distance astern of her.

At nighttime in open water we steamed at nine knots, and in daylight hours increased speed to fourteen knots. We arrived without mishap in six days at Gibraltar, having covered a distance of 1550 miles by zigzag, at an average speed of 11 knots.

We anchored at Gibraltar at 2 p.m., on Tuesday, 3rd October 1939. Here the *Athlone Castle* left us. At 7 p.m., darkness setting in, the *Alcantara*, *Empress of Australia*, and *Franconia*, in company, with destroyer escort, put out into the Strait and headed eastwards for Malta — a distance of 1059 miles.

At dusk on 5th October, two days out from Gibraltar, the *Franconia* and the *Alcantara* collided. Whose fault it was, if anybody's, I need not say. Such things do happen in wartime, and nobody can be blamed. My ship was damaged, but, of the 1636 souls in her, I was the only person hurt. I was thrown to the deck by the impact, and a bone in my shoulder was fractured.

On the following day, 6th October, at 4 p.m., we limped into port at Malta. The troops were disembarked. The *Franconia* went into the floating dock, and I went into the Naval Hospital — both of us for repairs of damage, not caused by enemy action! It could have been worse.

Ten days later, I was discharged from hospital and rejoined my ship. She was now out of the floating dock, but there were more repairs to be made to her at her berth, and these were going on slowly — like the war.

Fighting had apparently ceased on land. There had been no German air raids on Britain or France. Hitler had put forward a "peace plan" for a conference based on his conquest of Poland and claim for colonies. Britain had rejected this proposal on 12th October. Two days later, on 14th October, a German U-boat had crept into the British naval base at Scapa Flow, on the north of Scotland, and had torpedoed and sunk the British battleship, *H.M.S. Royal Oak.*

At no time had the war at sea been phoney. In the first two months of the war, September and October 1939, a total of fifty-seven British merchant vessels had been sunk on trade routes converging to and from the British Islands. As in the previous "Great" War, Britain had declared a total sea blockade of Germany; and the Germans had declared a counter blockade of Britain. Each side hoped to starve the other into submission by blockade. That was a recognition of the vital part that seaborne trade plays in the life of nations.

The repairs to the *Franconia* were at last finished, one month after her arrival at Malta. Nobody seemed to be in a hurry. I was now waiting for orders, and on 9th November received them. A contingent of 709 Polish airmen, having escaped from the Germans and the Russians, had arrived at Malta in a Greek steamer, *S.S. Petris.* They wanted to fight on, under the flag of the Polish Government in exile, which had its headquarters in Paris.

These Poles were embarked in the *Franconia* on 9th November. I had orders to take them to Marseilles. But then I had to wait another week at Malta, to take on board three British naval motor torpedo boats, and their crews, numbering sixty in all, going to Liverpool. The boats were stowed on deck, and I was at last able to clear out of Malta on 16th November, after a stay there of six weeks of tedious inaction.

On the passage from Malta to Marseilles, 676 miles, the *Franconia* was unescorted. In the Gulf of Lyons, she met with heavy weather. Being under orders not to stop, I could not heave to, but had to press on. In consequence the ship received a buffeting, which caused damage down below and on deck.

We arrived at Marseilles on the morning of 19th November. The Polish airmen were disembarked and went on to Paris by train. I conferred with the Cunard agent and Lloyd's agent at Marseilles, and it was decided to put the repairs in hand then and there.

The French shipwrights made a good job of it. On 27th November, I cleared out from Marseilles, again unescorted, and zig-zagged to Gibraltar,

761 miles, arriving there at 7 a.m. on 30th November. I expected that I would have to wait there for a convoy. But no! Under Admiralty orders, I embarked eleven civilian passengers — one of them a woman, the only female in the ship — and cleared out an hour later, bound for Liverpool, unescorted!

Risks were being taken. The "phoney war" was livening up. An unsuccessful attempt had been made, on 8th November, to assassinate Hitler by a time bomb placed in his "beer cellar" at Munich. Then, on 18th October the Germans had introduced a new terror into the war at sea. They had begun sowing magnetic mines from the air. These things sank beneath the surface and exploded when the steel hull of a steamer passed over them.

What next? we wondered. But the Royal Navy also had some trump cards, including the Antisubmarine Direction Indicator Gear ("ASDIC"), to locate submerged U-boats, and Antisubmarine Bombs designed to be dropped on U-boats by the Fleet Air Arm. An answer would be found to every new weapon used by the enemy, including the magnetic mines. That answer was quickly found, in the "degaussing girdle" — a belt fixed around the hull of steel vessels, to counteract their magnetic influence on the mines. But for the time being the new German Secret Weapon was a terror.

The U-boat packs were ravening in the Atlantic, sinking merchant vessels in the war zone surrounding Britain, at the rate of one or two sinkings every day. Meanwhile, the German "pocket battleship," *Graf Spee*, attended by a supply ship, the *Altmark*, was raiding British commerce in the South Atlantic, at the approaches to Buenos Aires. Several British steamers had been sunk there, after their crews had been taken prisoner.

Two German cruisers, the *Gneisenau* and the *Scharnhorst*, were in the North Atlantic. On 23rd November, they encountered and sank the British armed merchant cruiser, *Rawalpindi*, S.E. of Iceland.

It would be only a matter of luck if the *Franconia* could run through these various hazards unscathed, on the passage from Gibraltar to Liverpool. On the fourth day out, we ran into a howling W.N.W. gale. Being forbidden to stop, or to deviate from the prescribed courses and speeds, I carried on, shipping high beam seas, which washed away one of the boats swung out in davits on the port side, and did some further damage to the ship, on deck and down below.

Yet that storm favoured me, for in such weather U-boat activity was curtailed. After running through the storm, I picked up the cruiser and destroyer patrols off the Scilly Isles, and passed safely into narrow waters, berthing without mishap in the Mersey, at dawn on 6th December.

My first voyage on war service had ended, with my ship and myself both slightly damaged. The *Franconia* was put into Gammel Laird's yards at Birkenhead for repairs, and I was given leave.

Home for Christmas! I went to our flat in London for Christmas and New Year. London was blacked out, but no air raids had occurred yet. The Russians had invaded Finland on 30th November, and Russia had been expelled from the League of Nations as an aggressor on 14th December. Britain and France had no way of sending military aid to the small nations of Eastern Europe, either by land or sea.

On 13th December, H.M. Cruisers *Ajax*, *Achilles*, and *Exeter* destroyed the *Graf Spee* in the South Atlantic. The war was still on in Finland, and at sea, but scarcely anywhere else. This was only an ominous calm, preceding the storm yet to break.

30

A Peaceful War — "Franconia" Laid Up for Repairs — Help for the Finns — "Too Little Too Late" — The Campaign in Norway — "Missing the Bus" — Troops for Narvik — "Franconia" at Harstad — The Dock Battalion — Air Raid in Bygden Fjord — Troops Reembarked — An Unescorted Passage — Attacked by a U-boat — Explosions in the Darkness — A Close Shave — Warned by a German Officer — Return to the Clyde — The End of the "Phoney War."

THAT first Christmas and New Year of the war were quiet — unhealthily so. Nothing much was happening, except that the Germans and Russians were digesting the loot of Poland, and the Russians were invading Finland. In severe winter conditions the Finns were putting up a heroic defence of their small country, a victim of crude aggression. On 5th January 1940, the Russians sent notes of protest to Sweden and Norway for supplying munitions to the Finns.

Britain and France could do little to help Finland, despite their obligations, under the League of Nations covenant, to aid any member nation which was a victim of aggression. The sea route to Finland, via the Baltic Sea, was blocked by the German Navy. The only way to send help to Finland would be by land transit across northern Norway from Tromsø, or across Norway and Sweden from Narvik. Both these Norwegian ports are north of the Arctic Circle but are navigable in all seasons of the year.

Germany was obtaining shipments of iron ore from the port of Lulea, on the Gulf of Bothnia, in northern Sweden, but this arm of the Baltic is frozen in winter. A railway runs from Lulea westwards to Narvik. There, German ships could load iron ore, and navigate southwards, within Norwegian territorial waters, to enter the Baltic through the Skagerrak and Kattegat Straits, without interference from the British Navy.

Repairs were going on very slowly to the *Franconia* at Liverpool. The shipyards had more work than they could handle, and each job had to take its turn. My leave was extended from time to time, and I remained in London, at a loose end.

On 14th February 1940, the British Government announced that all British merchant vessels in the North Sea would be armed. The Germans replied with an announcement that all British merchant vessels everywhere would be treated as warships. At this time (15th February 1940), it was announced that the British Government had authorized volunteers to join the Foreign Legion in Finland, in which Swedes, Danes, and Norwegians were already volunteering as individuals to help their Scandinavian kinfolk, the Finns.

The coast of Norway and its territorial waters facing the Atlantic had become strategically important. The neutrality of Norway was an advantage to the Germans, who could legitimately use Norwegian waters for the transit of their naval as well as their merchant ships. Both Britain and Germany wanted to gain possession of the Norwegian coast: the Germans to use its fjords as naval bases, and Britain to deny them that use. With this in mind, both sides were making plans to infringe Norway's neutrality — each hoping to do so with Norway's consent!

On 15th February, the German supply ship *Altmark*, which had been attending the *Graf Spee* in the South Atlantic, made her way through the British blockade in the North Atlantic, and reached Norwegian waters. She was a large vessel, with oil tanks and cargo holds, disguised as a Norwegian tanker. Below decks she had 300 British merchant seamen as prisoners, taken from ships captured by the *Graf Spee*.

A British destroyer, H.M.S. *Cossack*, commanded by Captain P. L. Vain, followed the Altmark into a Norwegian fjord, seized her, and released the prisoners. The Norwegian Government protested against this infringement of neutrality, in which both the Cossack and the Altmark were trespassers. From that time onwards, both Germany and Britain pushed ahead with plans to occupy had put to sea, the Commander-in-Chief of the British Home Fleet, lacking information that this was a German invasion of Norway, assumed that the Germans were trying to break out into the Atlantic, to attack a big convoy of merchant ships then enroute from America to Britain.

The British Home Fleet put to sea in overwhelming force from Scapa Flow, Rosyth and the Shetland Islands, trying to intercept the Germans fifty miles to the westward of the coast of Norway. In heavy gale conditions, the fleet failed to make effective contact with the Germans, who hugged the Norwegian shore, and made their military landings in Norway as planned. On 9th April, the Germans launched a full scale offensive, by sea, land, and air, against Denmark and Norway.

On that day I was enjoying a restful holiday with my wife at Seaton in Devonshire. We were staying at a guest house. In the afternoon we went for a walk and called at a farm cottage for a "Devonshire tea." There I heard on the radio that the Germans were invading Denmark and Norway. I hurried back to the guest house and hadn't been there a few minutes when a boy arrived with a telegram ordering me to rejoin my ship immediately. I took a taxi to Axminster, and the first train next morning from there, via London to Liverpool.

My orders were to take the *Franconia* from Liverpool to the Clyde, to embark troops for Norway. This was "it" at last — the end of the "phoney war." Like everyone else within a limited field of responsibility, I had no knowledge of what was really happening in Norway. I arrived in the *Franconia* at Gourock at 4 a.m. on 12th April, and berthed her in the King George V Dock at Glasgow at 1 p.m. Two days later, on 14th April, we embarked 1818 troops, and moved downriver to Gourock, to join a convoy.

On the preceding day, Admiral of the Fleet Lord Cork had left the Clyde in *H.M.S. Aurora*. He was to be Flag Officer in command of landing operations at Narvik. At the same time, the Military Commander, General Mackesy, had left Scapa Flow with an advance party of the Scots Guards, followed soon after by troopships carrying two military brigades.

At this time, German troops had already landed at their objectives in Norway. At Narvik, they had landed 2000 troops, supported by ten destroyers. A British destroyer flotilla had followed them into Narvik fjord and had engaged and sunk most of the German destroyers in a brilliant action within the narrow waters of the fjord.

As German troops were in possession of the town of Narvik, in a strong position for defence against a landing from seaward, it was decided that the British assault troops should be landed at the small port of Harstad, on Vaagsfjord, thirty-five miles from Narvik. There, a base would be built up, and contact made with Norwegian army units, to attack Narvik overland.

British advance forces landed at Harstad on 15th April, and reinforcements soon after. Other British and some French forces had been landed at Namsos, Aadalsnes, and other points in central and southern Norway, but all these expeditions had been organized in expectation of meeting with only a "token" resistance from Norwegians, and not in any expectation of finding the Germans already in occupation and heavily counter attacking.

On 15th April, I anchored the *Franconia* at Gourock, with orders to join there a convoy of four French troopships, escorted by four French destroyers. The British troops that I had on board were chiefly Army Service Corps, including a "Dock Battalion" of stevedores and other specialists required for unloading munitions and army supplies for the military base at Harstad. They had with them a great quantity of gear, such as blocks, gins, rope and wire falls, nets, mats, hooks, and other apparatus of their calling. They were an Army Unit, in uniform, and carrying rifles and machine guns for self-defence, but they were workmen, not field troops.

With the French convoy, the *Franconia* put to sea from Gourock at 5 a.m. on 16th April. We made up the western coast of Scotland in a strong gale, with rain, and, in Pentland Firth (the strait between the north of Scotland and the Orkney Islands), were taken under escort by *H.M.S. Repulse* with four British destroyers.

We headed northwards. Next morning early, the French ships left that convoy and proceeded into Namsos, their destination.

H.M.S. Repulse signalled to me, "Follow my zigzag and keep close astern." I was very glad of this powerful escort, the more so as I had not yet been ordered to a definite destination, and my charts of the Norwegian coast were rather small scale. I was congratulating myself on all this, when, on Saturday afternoon, 20th April, we sighted the northern cape of Ando Island — the most northerly of the Lofoten Islands. This is in 69 deg. N. Lat., well inside the Arctic Circle. There was a blizzard, with gusts of gale force, and darkness was setting in. Without any preliminaries my battleship escort signalled, "Proceed to Harstad, and with that turned and made off to seaward.

Fortunately, I had experience of the Norwegian fjords, on various pleasure cruises that I had made there, in the *Franconia* and other liners — but this was no pleasure cruise!

For four hours, I felt my way anxiously across Andfjord and into Vaagsfjord, between flurries of snow that cut visibility to nil.

I was forbidden to use radio, except to receive messages, and there were no lights showing anywhere. At 7 p.m., I thankfully anchored among the dark shapes of many other ships lying off Harstad. The snow was now continuous, but the signalman managed to get a brief message through to the shore by Morse lamp, announcing our arrival. After half an hour or so, a reply came from the shore, "What are you doing here?"

I made no reply, thinking that they should know. Apart from that, I did not like to use the lamp too much, in case a U-boat might be hanging around.

After a further delay, an order came from the shore, "Proceed to Bygden Fjord." I saw from my chart that this was a small fjord twelve miles from Harstad. To take a 20,000-ton liner into it in broad daylight would need care. In pitch darkness and a snowstorm it would be a decidedly hazardous passage. By wonderful good luck, the snowstorm ceased at that moment, and the snow covered shoreline was visible against the dark water. I made my way cautiously along the shore, found Bygden Fjord, entered, and anchored at midnight. No sooner was the anchor let go than the snowstorm began again and smothered everything. The ship's run from the Clyde to Bygden had been 1360 miles, by zigzag.

Next morning, at six o'clock, I heard the faint sound of a steam whistle. Very slowly it came nearer, and then, out of the snow, to my amazement, loomed the shape of a Mersey ferry! These small steamers, plying normally across the Mersey between Liverpool and the Cheshire shore, in smooth waters, were certainly never designed for ocean going. This one had been commandeered at Liverpool and ordered to Harstad. How she had made that ocean passage during the gales that had been continuous throughout the first weeks of the operations in Norway was beyond my understanding; but there she was and had been there for a few days before the *Franconia* arrived. She was serving as a tender to disembark troops and stores from ships at anchor.

She ranged alongside and made fast. A military officer was first up the accommodation ladder. To my further surprise, he was an old friend of mine, named Roberts, Passenger Manager at the Cunard Office in London, now an Army Captain serving as Military Movement Officer. "Can I have some breakfast?" he asked. "We're in camp near Harstad, and the grub is terrible!" I soon arranged this, and he explained, "I've come to take the Dock Battalion ashore."

The troops began filing down the accommodation ladder to the ferry. They were so laden with gear that they could hardly walk. Each man wore a long fleece lined leather coat, Balaclava cap, "tin hat," gas cape, woollen mittens, and fur lined boots. In that climate, they needed it all, for sure. Each man carried his kit bag and a rifle — and some had machine guns — and whatever he could carry of the gear for unloading ships. They had to go very carefully and slowly down the ladder. Some of the gear, such as coils of wire and rope, being too heavy to handle, had to be put on board the tender with our derricks.

The weather cleared somewhat during the forenoon, and I saw that a battleship, *H.M.S. Warspite*, and four destroyers were anchored in the fjord. They would be safer there from U-boat or air bombing attack than in the open roads off Harstad, where a dozen or more transports and supply ships lay at anchor, scattered at intervals in the bay.

Thousands of troops were camped on shore at Harstad in extremely difficult conditions. Snow lay on the ground from twelve inches to three feet deep. It appeared unlikely that the troops could march overland thirty or forty miles, across mountains, to attack Narvik, until the thaw began, in another month or so.

At 2 p.m. Captain Roberts informed me that the troops of the Dock Battalion were all embarked in the ferry. They numbered 904 men. Other tenders, known as "puffers" (small Norwegian coastal steamers) were

A German Heinkel He-111 high level bomber.
(Public Domain, German Federated Archives)

coming to take off the remaining 914 troops of various army units that remained in the *Franconia*, and the army stores that were in her holds.

Even after a good breakfast and lunch, Captain Roberts still looked hungry, so I had a hamper made up for him, containing a couple of hams and rounds of beef, and a few bottles of rum and Scotch whisky. He went off feeling happier but not looking forward to his snowbound camp on shore. The ferry shoved off into a blizzard, and in a few minutes was out of sight. I felt sad as those men went, thinking that probably I would never see any of them again.

Another tender came alongside, and disembarkation of the troops continued. The weather cleared, and at 4 p.m. two Heinkel bombers came over at 5000 feet altitude. Bombs fell 300 yards from the *Franconia* without doing any damage, while the *Warspite* and destroyers opened up a lively A.A. fire. The bombers disappeared in the clouds, and tried again a few minutes later, but again missed their mark. It was lucky for us that the German "Stuka" dive bombers, at that stage in the campaign, did not have airfields enabling them to operate in northern Norway. A ship is not an easy mark for high level bombers such as the Heinkel's.

Disembarkation of the troops was completed before dark, and unloading of the cargo continued, without lights, throughout the night. It was all discharged next morning, Monday, 22nd April, at six o'clock. I was anxious to remove my ship from that uncomfortable and dangerous place as soon as possible, but I had no orders. As there was no other means of communication with the Commander-in-Chief at Harstad, I broke wireless silence and asked for instructions. The reply came a few hours later, "Remain at anchor with steam up until further notice."

Throughout that day I was fretting and fuming, scanning the sky for bombers, but fortunately a blizzard raged most of the day, giving us some protection from that kind of attack. At 6 p.m., it was still snowing hard, and darkness had set in, when I heard the faint hooting of a steam whistle. Out of the murk came the Mersey ferry, full of men, and moored alongside. Captain Roberts came up the ladder and informed me, "I have brought the Dock Battalion back again, to be returned to the Clyde. The C.-in-C. Harstad does not want them!"

The men streamed up the accommodation ladder, all smiles. I have never seen men so happy to be anywhere as those men were to be back on board the good ship *Franconia*, which they had left only thirty hours previously.

Such muddle! There was no need for them at Harstad. They brought with them their rations and gear. Every man of the 904 was back on board. My orders now were to put to sea at 8 p.m., but I had to inform the C.-in-C. that this was impossible in the weather conditions prevailing. I could not have got out of the narrow fjord in pitch blackness in snowsqualls so heavy that snow now lay on the boat deck twelve inches deep. A strong wind was blowing, and in the darkness, it was impracticable to swing out our derricks and hoist the heavier gear of the Dock Battalion on board. It was left in the ferry tender, which cast off at midnight and returned to Harstad. My amended orders now were to put out of the fjord at daybreak and make for Harstad. During the night the squalls increased, and at 3 a.m. I had to let go the second anchor to hold her.

At 7 a.m. (Tuesday 23rd April 1940), the anchors were hove up. The weather had moderated. I got out of the fjord safely and proceeded to an anchorage off Harstad. Here the Mersey ferry came out from the shore, and this time she had on board to be embarked in the *Franconia* a party of 278 naval officers and ratings. They were survivors of the British destroyers *Cossack*, *Hardy*, *Eskimo*, and others which had been sunk or damaged in the naval battle at Narvik a fortnight previously. With them were 28 naval wounded, and 9 German naval prisoners. These, with the 904 soldiers of the Dock Battalion and my crew of 374, made a total of 1588 souls on board. My orders were to return to the Clyde.

Two destroyers escorted me from Harstad to the northern end of Ando Island, and there left me alone in the open ocean, to make my way unescorted on a passage of 1350 miles or so through waters infested with U-boats and probably German naval surface units as well. Fortunately it was bad weather with poor visibility. I headed westwards at full speed, to get as far away from the land as quickly as possible.

The German prisoners were locked in cabins, with a guard under orders to release them in case of our being torpedoed. One of the officer prisoners asked to see me on a very urgent matter. I had him brought to my cabin. In English with a strong German accent, he said, "Be extra careful, Captain. The U-boats are out to get you. They will be waiting off the north coast of Scotland. I have warned you!"

He was going on in an excitable manner when I stopped him, and said, "We know all about it. Half your U-boats are already destroyed, and our Navy will get the rest of them."

I could see that he imagined that he and his companions would get scant consideration if we were torpedoed. "I'll take every possible precaution," I assured him.

At 5 p.m., on that first day out, we sighted a surfaced submarine, and in the half-darkness did not know if it was German or British. Nor did I wait to inquire. Turning stern-on to it, at full speed, with our stern gun manned, I got away, and in a few minutes, it was out of sight. Most of the people in the *Franconia*, quite understandably, had "the wind up," on realizing that we were unescorted, and not in convoy.

Setting course, on a zigzag southward, between the Shetland and Faroe Islands, we were nearing the north coast of Scotland at midnight on Thursday, 25th April, making for the entrance to the Minch Channel (between the west coast of Scotland and the outer Hebrides). Having had very little sleep for three days on the passage from Harstad, I lay down on my settee in the chartroom for a nap. At 4 a.m., two heavy explosions, in quick succession, shook the ship. The shock threw me off the settee onto the deck, as the ship heeled over. In two jumps I was on the bridge, ordering boat stations, thinking that we had been torpedoed, or that we had struck a mine. Not only my own crew, but the naval party that we had on board were on the boat deck in a few seconds, ready to man the lifeboats.

In a few seconds more, on reports from the engine room, I could see that we had not been hit, and that we were making full speed on an even keel. On analysing the probabilities, I was of the opinion, supported by my officers and the naval officers on board, that a U-boat had fired two torpedoes at us, at an extreme range. These had destroyed themselves and had exploded very near our stern — a close shave, the difference between life and death in a split second! At 9 a.m., we entered the Minch. Twelve hours later, rounding Sanda Island, at the entrance to the Firth of Clyde, we ran into thick fog. I was up all night, as we proceeded at dead slow, in the fog and without lights, in that busy traffic lane in narrow waters. At 8 a.m., on Saturday 27th April, having made a passage of 1355 miles from Harstad in four days, we anchored off Gourock. I made a signal to the Naval Office, announcing our arrival. The reply came, "What are you doing here?" They were evidently as much in the dark about the *Franconia's* movements as the C.-in-C. at Harstad had been.

Having been almost without sleep or rest for a week, I made no reply, and went to bed for the day, with orders "NOT to be disturbed": The naval party went ashore in launches at Gourock. Two days later, the Dock Battalion was disembarked at the King George V Dock in Glasgow, after their interesting tourist voyage to the Norwegian fjords. When they had all gone ashore, we found two machine guns, and a number of rifles, under the bunks in several of the cabins. Well, they were not really soldiers, and I'm sure that, if they had been called upon, they would have done a good job unloading ships!

On Thursday, 2nd May 1940, I moved the *Franconia* downriver, to anchor, in company with a number of other transports, at "the Tail of the Bank," near the river mouth, on the northern side, opposite Gourock.

There we lay for a week, wondering what was coming next. On 10th May, I was ordered to proceed upriver to the King George V Dock at Glasgow, and moored my ship there at 4 p.m.

That was the day when the Germans invaded Holland and Belgium. On that day, too, the Right Honourable Neville Chamberlain resigned as Britain's Prime Minister, and the Right Honourable Winston Churchill became, in his own words, "His Majesty's First Minister."

No more "phoney war"! The Blitzkrieg was on.

31

*"Queen Elizabeth" Goes to New York — "Queen Mary" Goes to
Sydney — "Franconia" Lands Troops in Iceland — Churchill Prime
Minister — German Blitzkrieg — Allies Evacuate Norway —
Disaster of Dunkirk — "Franconia" Takes Troops from Norway —
Heavy Risks — Transports and Escorts — " Carinthia" Sunk off
Ireland — German Battle — Cruisers sink H.M.S. "Glorious" —
25,000 Troops Safely Brought Home — Italy Enters the War.*

ONE thing was noticeable on the Clyde — the world's biggest
ship — *Queen Elizabeth*, was no longer there. She had vanished
like a grey ghost.

On the outbreak of war, in September 1939, she was in the fitting out
basin at Brown's yards, Clydebank, being made ready for the Atlantic
passenger service. All the intended luxurious inner fittings were discarded,
for the time being, but there was much electrical, plumbing, joinery, and
other essential fitting still to be done. This was completed in five months.
Towards the end of February 1940, she was placed under command of
Captain J. C. Townley, and a crew of 500 were signed on for a coastal voyage.
No secret was made of the intention to move her to Southampton for final
fitting out in the big graving dock there.

Painted grey all over, she moved down the Clyde to the Tail of the Bank,
where some tests were made of her steering gear and engines, and her
compasses were adjusted. Then, without the usual thorough seagoing trials,

she was formally handed over by the ship builders to the Cunard White Star Line. If there were any German spies in Glasgow, they had plenty of opportunity to report that she was going to Southampton. She even had a Southampton pilot on board.

She anchored at Gourock. There her crew were informed that she was not going to Southampton, but on an ocean voyage, requiring them to sign new articles. Anyone wishing not to go would be taken ashore. Only a few asked to be released. On 2nd March, 1940, the *Queen Elizabeth* put to sea, steamed down the Firth of Clyde, rounded the Mull of Kintyre, and headed out into the Western Ocean. Five days later, she docked in New York, alongside the *Queen Mary* and the Normandie, safe in that friendly neutral port.

On 20th March, the *Queen Mary* put to sea from New York, and made for Australia, via Trinidad and Cape Town. She anchored in Sydney Harbour on 16th April, and there was stripped of all her luxurious fittings, and converted for use as a troop transport.

On the outbreak of war, the 35,000-ton *Mauretania* had been converted, at Liverpool, to an armed merchant cruiser, but was not used for that service, for which she was too big and bulky. Instead, she was reconverted to her ordinary mercantile status, and, on 10th December 1939, cleared out from Liverpool, and was laid up in New York until March 1940. She then left New York, and went via the Panama Canal to Australia, to join the *Queen Mary* and other big liners there, as a troop transport.

On the day that the Germans' invaded Holland and Belgium, 10th May 1940, a British naval expedition occupied Reykjavik, in Iceland, meeting with no opposition. Iceland was a Dominion of Denmark, but fully self-governing, under the Agreement of Union of 1918, by which the King of Denmark was recognized as King of Iceland also. Though this was only a formality, the occupation of Denmark by the Germans, in April 1940, had created a situation in which Britain was justified, under international law, in taking Iceland under armed protection, to deny its use to the Germans. British forces had likewise occupied the Faroe Islands, a Danish possession, on 16th April, meeting with no resistance.

In King George V Dock at Glasgow, on 10th May, I had orders to embark troops and load military supplies in the *Franconia* for an expedition to Iceland, to be made in company with the 16,000-ton Cunarder, *Lancastria*. These troops would relieve the Royal Marines, who on that day had landed in Iceland. The soldiers would establish a military base at Reykjavik, in sufficient strength to deter the Germans from making any attempt to occupy Iceland. The Master of the *Lancastria*, Captain Rudolph Sharp, and his Chief Officer, Harry Grattidge, were old cronies of mine, and I knew the ship herself very well, having commanded her for ten months in 1937 as a "cruise liner." She had a speed of 17 knots, slightly better than the *Franconia*'s 16 knots, but for all practical purposes the two vessels could keep together very well in company as transports.

In the *Franconia*, I embarked 1875 troops, mostly of the 5th Yorkshire Regiment, and 22 Army Nurses, and loaded 500 tons of Army stores. With a crew of 367, I had a total of 2264 souls on board. Sharp in the *Lancastria* had some 1500 troops and a crew of 300, and a cargo of military stores. The arrangements for this expedition had been made before the German Blitzkrieg on the Western Front had begun, and no one thought of cancelling it on that account. On 13th May, Prime Minister Churchill announced, "I have nothing to offer but blood and toil and tears and sweat" — and how right he was!

On 14th May, the *Franconia* and *Lancastria* moved downriver, and out of the Clyde at dusk, escorted by two destroyers, *Havant* and *Foxhound*. We were well clear of the land next morning, on course for Iceland, in fine weather, zigzagging at 16 knots. On this passage, we were not molested by the enemy. We anchored in the bay at Reykjavik at 1 p.m. on Friday, 17th May 1940.

For four days we remained there, disembarking the troops and unloading the stores. At this time the war news from the Western front, and also from Norway, was extremely serious. The Germans had overrun Holland in five days and had thrust with tremendous force and mobility into Belgium and Flanders. Their mechanized armies had made all old fashioned ideas of "trench warfare" obsolete. The Maginot Line mentality of static defence was useless against the new tactics and weapons of mechanized mobility and rapid movement of armoured vehicles supported by bombing and machine gunning from the air, and the dropping of parachute troops.

In Norway also, German thoroughness in planning their combined operations by sea, land, and air, and their use of new tactical weapons, had won successes against the Allied forces, consisting of Norwegian, British, French, and Polish naval, military, and air units operating without a strong central direction. The Allies had been driven out of Southern Norway (Andalsnes) and Central Norway (Namsos) on 2nd May, and the King and Government of Norway had moved to Tromsø in the Far North (100 miles north of Narvik).

The Allied military forces based on Harstad had increased to some 20,000 troops, but, because of difficulties of weather and terrain, had not yet been able to advance to attack the German garrison of 2000 troops holding Narvik town. In the meantime, German reinforcements were moving northwards overland from Namsos, and it appeared that the Allied force at Harstad might soon have to contend against an enemy overwhelmingly superior in numbers and weapons, including Stuka dive bombers.

On 12th May, a combined naval and military attack was launched by the Allied forces against Narvik but not pressed through to the capture of the town. In this operation, the British battleship, *H.M.S. Resolution*, was damaged by German dive bombers, and, on 21st May, the British cruiser *Effingham* was sunk by dive bombers. It appeared unlikely that Northern Norway could be held by the Allied forces available there.

That was the serious situation, in Norway and also in Holland, Belgium, and Flanders, while the *Franconia* and *Lancastria* were landing a British garrison in faraway Iceland; yet in view of the strategic importance of Iceland in relation to sea communications in the North Atlantic, the military occupation and defence of that country by British forces was an essential precaution, of great value, not only to Britain, but also to Canada and the U.S.A., in the long run.

On 21st May, the *Franconia* and *Lancastria* left Reykjavik, with escort as before, to return to the Clyde, but, on this passage, we had a "lame duck" in company — the naval net laying vessel, *Guardian*, with a speed of only 12 knots. This was frustrating but could not be helped. The speed of a convoy is that of its slowest unit. This meant that the two liners would be more vulnerable to U-boat attack at their reduced speeds and also would be one day more on the passage than was necessary. It seemed a pity to risk the loss of two big transports as a slight insurance of a small net layer, but orders were orders, and, then as ever, we had to grin and bear them.

In the *Lancastria*, 600 Royal Marines were embarked at Reykjavik to be returned to Britain. Thirty of these were transferred to the *Franconia* as an A.A. guard. We made the return to the Clyde in four days, meeting with no enemy, and anchored off Gourock at 6 a.m. on Saturday, 25th May.

The military situation on the Western Front on that day was extremely grave. The Germans had reached Boulogne on 23rd May and thereby had surrounded most of the British Expeditionary Force, together with some French forces, which had advanced into Belgium. These, and the Belgium Army, now had their backs to the sea, and were being compressed towards Dunkirk.

No sooner had the *Franconia* and *Lancastria* anchored at Gourock than we were ordered to proceed immediately to Liverpool. Before the anchors could be hove up, that order was cancelled. Though we did not then know it, we were required, under the first of these orders, to be available to assist in the impending evacuation of the British Expeditionary Force from France. On the second thoughts of someone in authority, we were required to remain in the Clyde, in readiness to assist in the evacuation of the Allied Expeditionary

Force from Northern Norway! The decision to withdraw from Norway had been taken on 24th May, the day before the *Franconia* and *Lancastria* had arrived in the Clyde from Iceland.

Under the first order, the White Star liner *Georgie* (27,000 tons, Captain Gregg) had been sent from the Clyde to Liverpool on 24th May. Under the second order, she arrived back in the Clyde on 26th May. Conflicting instructions of this kind were only to be expected in the extreme state of emergency that had developed.

Anchored with us also at Gourock, in readiness for the impending operation in Norway, was the *Furness Withy* luxury liner, *Monarch of Bermuda* (22,000 tons, Captain Francis), a stylish quadruple screw vessel with a speed of 19 knots.

That Sunday, 26th May 1940, was proclaimed as a day of National Prayer in Britain. That was the day when the British Expeditionary Force, of ten divisions, fell back to Dunkirk, and the decision was taken to attempt to evacuate them by sea.

"God and the sailor you implore!" The "miracle" of Dunkirk followed, when, between 28th May and 2nd June, nearly one thousand small vessels, including destroyers, trawlers, yachts and even open boats — in calm weather — transferred 220,000 British and 112,000 French and Belgian troops across Dover Strait to England, to fight another day.

On that same day, the Allied Naval Military and Air Forces in Northern Norway succeeded in capturing the town of Narvik! That operation, so long prepared, was carried through three days after the directive had reached the C.-in-C., Admiral Lord Cork, to withdraw from Norway. The purpose of the operation was only to destroy the harbour facilities at Narvik as a farewell gesture. This was done, and the 25,000 troops of all services under Lord Cork's command were then hurriedly withdrawn to Harstad and other points, in readiness for evacuation by sea.

At 10.30 p.m. on that fateful day, Tuesday, 28th May, when Narvik was captured and the evacuation of Dunkirk had begun, the *Franconia*, in company with the *Lancastria*, *Georgie*, and *Monarch of Bermuda*, put to sea from the Clyde, bound for Norway, with destroyer escort. At sea we were joined by two liners of the Polish Gydnia-Amerika Line — the *Batory* (14,000 tons) and *Sobieski* (11,000 tons), stylish and speedy motor vessels of 20 knots.

These six transports comprised Group One in the evacuation operation. They were intended to go inshore first, to embark as many troops as possible, and to hasten back to Britain at full speed. Group Two comprised four liners — *Oronsay*, *Orama*, *Ormonde* and *Arandora Star* — and three Irish Channel packet steamers, *Royal Ulsterman*, *Ulster Monarch*, and *Ulster Prince*, together with a dozen or more naval storeships and small auxiliary vessels, intended to embark the remainder of the troops and as much military stores and equipment as time might permit.

The rendezvous for both groups was at sea, 180 miles to the westward of Harstad. There the Evacuation Fleet assembled, on 2nd and 3rd June, under the protection of a cruiser, *H.M.S. Coventry*, and ten destroyers.

Somewhere within that war zone, unknown to us at that time, but only to be expected, were numerous and powerful units of the British Home Fleet, as many as could be spared from the even more urgent and important tasks of protecting the operations at Dunkirk from German naval attack.

The British naval forces in the Norwegian zone of operations included the battleships *Renown* and *Repulse* and two aircraft. carriers, *Ark Royal* and *Glorious*, besides several cruisers and flotillas of destroyers.

Unknown to us, also, German Naval Intelligence had "cracked the code," and discovered that there was a rendezvous of British ships off the coast of Northern Norway.

Not realizing that the evacuation of our military forces was intended, but assuming that the transports were bringing reinforcements and supplies to Harstad, a powerful German squadron of surface fighting ships, comprising the battlecruisers *Scharnhorst, Gneisenau,* and *Hipper*, with four destroyers, put to sea from Kiel on 4th June, and headed northwards to do whatever damage it could. This squadron was under the command of Admiral Marschall. That was the day (4th June, 1940), when Prime Minister Churchill reported in the House of Commons on the evacuation from Dunkirk, and uttered his resounding declaration of British defiance: "We shall go on to the end. We shall fight in France. We shall fight on the seas and the oceans. We shall fight in the air. We shall defend our shores, whatever the cost may be. We shall fight on the beaches. We shall fight in the fields and on the streets. We shall fight in the hills. We shall never surrender!"

On three successive afternoons, 4th, 5th, and 6th June, the six transports of Group One left the convoy at the rendezvous, in pairs, under destroyer escort, and stood in towards the coast. We were to arrive and embark troops at nighttime, but in fact there was not much cover of darkness in that season, north of the Arctic Circle!

The *Georgie* and *Franconia* went in together, and anchored in Andfjord at 4.30 a.m. on Thursday, 6th June. With good timing, destroyers crowded with troops met us. In the *Franconia*, at anchor for seven hours, I embarked a total of 2617 troops. They comprised 2497 British and 69 French soldiers, and 51 Air Force men.

Altogether, the six transports of Group One embarked a total of 15,000 troops and reassembled without mishap at the rendezvous. Even with all that movement, German reconnaissance had failed to detect that evacuation operations were in progress. This was indeed remarkable, as they had daylight for almost twenty-four hours a day, for scouting, but our movements had been protected from air observation to some extent, by naval fighter aircraft from the aircraft carriers, and by A.A. guns on shore and mounted in all vessels engaged in the operations.

On Friday, 7th June, Group One headed southwards from the rendezvous, bound for the Clyde on a hazardous passage of 1300 miles with our precious human freight of some 18,000 souls, including the crews and the troops.

Zigzagging at 16 knots, we were escorted for part of the passage by H.M.S. *Vindictive* (an antiaircraft cruiser) and three destroyers. We were unaware that our course took us within 150 miles of Admiral Marschall's powerful squadron, which could easily have caught up with us and sent every ship in the convoy and its escort to Davy Jones's locker.

A few hours after Group One had left the rendezvous, we sighted a lone German aircraft, and all ships in the Group and escort opened fire on it with all they had. It turned tail, without dropping any bombs. Weather conditions were hazy. This incident was explained when German naval documents were published after the war. The aircraft that we had sighted was on reconnaissance from Admiral Marschall's squadron.

Its observer reported "Four large ships and three escorts steaming southwards."

The German Admiral, incorrectly supposing that we were transports returning empty after delivering troops, decided not to give chase, but to press on northwards in search of bigger game. Some hours later, he changed his mind and detached the heavy cruiser *Hipper* to chase us. This cruiser came across the *Orama* (of Group Two) which was returning unescorted, and sank her with a few 8-inch shells. Luckily the *Orama* had no troops on board. She had been sent back empty because of her fuel shortage. Perhaps because of this distraction, the Hipper failed to catch up with Group One, which was steaming away from him in hazy conditions at 17 knots, a high speed for a convoy.

The strong British squadron, including the *Renown* and *Repulse*, was also led astray, as the Germans were, by faulty deductions from incomplete Intelligence. Instead of covering the evacuation operations, or getting to grips with the German squadron, our powerful fighting ships had gone off on a wild goose chase to the westward, misled by an incorrect report that the *Scharnhorst* and *Gneisenau* had been sighted far out at sea, making for Iceland.

So the six transports of Group One continued making speedy headway to the southward, unmolested. At 1 a.m. on 8th June, we passed the Faroes, and were taken under escort by a battleship, H.M.S. *Valiant*, and four destroyers. These stayed with us for ten hours, and then left us, but five more destroyers then took over the escort. The Royal Navy, despite its many other tasks at that time, did not leave Group One unprotected.

On that day, 8th June, I heard that the *Franconia*'s sister-ship, *Carinthia*, on patrol as an armed merchant cruiser off the west coast of Ireland, was torpedoed and sunk by a U-boat.

On that same tragic day, the *Scharnhorst* and *Gneisenau*, off the Norwegian coast, sighted and sank the British aircraft carrier, *H.M.S. Glorious*, and also her two supporting destroyers, *Acasta* and *Ardent*, with the loss of 1474 lives. But these men had not died in vain. A torpedo from the *Acasta* struck the *Scharnhorst*, killing forty-eight of her crew and flooding her engine rooms, so that she had to limp into Trondheim, taking with her the *Gneisenau*, Hipper and the four destroyers of the squadron as an escort. The German striking force was thereby immobilized for the time being. This gave a reprieve to the many vessels of Group Two, engaged in completing the evacuation of the Narvik-Harstad area.

While all this excitement was going on, Group One got clear away. The six transports arrived without mishap at Gourock on Monday, 10th June, 1940, at 6 a.m.

Group Two also completed its tasks, transporting 10,000 troops and a large quantity of stores safely back to Britain. The King of Norway, refusing to surrender to the Germans, went into exile. He left Tromsø on 7th June in *H.M.S. Devonshire* (a cruiser) and found sanctuary in Britain, as the Queen of the Netherlands had done on 13th May.

Hostilities in Norway ceased. The Germans had won that round. We were "taking it on the chin," and there was more of that to come. A few hours after the transports of Group One from Norway had anchored at Gourock, on 10th June 1940, the "big news" of that day came through. Italy had declared war on Britain and France!

The Mediterranean and North Africa would be combat zones!

France was collapsing under the German hammer blows. Mussolini's declaration of war was the action of a jackal. Britain's fortunes were at zero, but we had not the slightest doubt that we would win in the end.

Undated and uncredited photo of James Bisset that
appears on the back cover of the 1st edition. (Bisset)

32

The Fall of France — Evacuating B.E.F. — Remnants from Brittany — Loss of the "Andania" — "The Queen Mary" Brings Anzacs to Britain — Chaos in France — "Franconia" Damaged by a Dive bomber — Conflicting Naval Orders — The Loss of the "Lancastria" — Worst Sea disaster of the War — "Our Finest Hour" — "Franconia" in Dry-Dock for Repairs — The "Battle of Britain."

O N 11th June, 1940, after landing at Gourock the troops that I had brought from Norway in the *Franconia*, I was instructed to take my ship to her home port at Liverpool.

Arrived in the Mersey at 9 a.m. on 12th June, I "tied up" in Gladstone Dock, then went ashore, and was given a fortnight's leave. I was told that my ship would be laid up until 29th June.

It suited me well to have leave at that time. On arrival at Gourock, I had received a letter from my wife, informing me that we had a new home. Under the Government's policy of getting as many people as possible to leave London and live in the country, she had found a small house for us at Cheltenham, in Gloucestershire. This would be our home, I supposed, for the duration of the war. I wanted to see it!

Taking an early morning train from Liverpool on 13th June, I travelled via Chester, Crewe, and Birmingham, to arrive at Cheltenham at 3 p.m., a journey of six hours.

At 4,.15 p.m., May and I were having afternoon tea in the garden of our new abode, when a boy arrived on a bicycle with a telegram for me: Rejoin your ship immediately.

I had been at home exactly one hour when my leave was cancelled. Taking the train from Cheltenham at 6 p.m., I was on board the *Franconia* again at midnight, after an absence of sixteen hours. Everything at Liverpool was in pitch darkness.

Chaos! My orders were to proceed to Plymouth urgently. The crew had been recalled by telegrams and messengers, but only a few were as yet on board. More kept arriving. At crack of dawn, 5 a.m. on 14th June, I backed the *Franconia* out into the river and anchored. She needed oil fuel, fresh water, and stores. I went ashore to the Naval Control Office, and was instructed to proceed to Plymouth that day, in company with the *Lancastria*. "You'll be under naval orders there," the officer told me, "To assist in evacuating British and French troops and civilians from France. Dozens of ships are being called up for that purpose," he added.

"What! Another Dunkirk?" "Looks like it!"

It was on that day that the Germans entered Paris. They had gone through the supposedly impregnable Maginot Line like a hot knife through butter. Their panzers and airborne troops were sweeping through northern and western France, making for the seaports on the Atlantic coast, occupying town after town, meeting with only pockets of resistance from disorganized French troops and a remnant of British forces stubbornly fighting rearguard actions. All roads to the South of France and to the Biscayan ports and the Spanish frontier were choked with fleeing civilians.

The *Franconia* and *Lancastria* left the Mersey in company that afternoon on the tide. Next day, 15th June, at 4.30 p.m., we anchored at Plymouth. Many other transports were there. I thought that perhaps we might be taking the B.E.F. back to France. But no! We were ordered to go to Brest — empty — and departed from Plymouth at 11.30 p.m.

The passage from Plymouth to Brest, at nighttime and by zigzags, took us ten hours. We arrived off Brest at 9.30 a.m., on Sunday, 16th June.

On that day, as I learned later, the Cunarder Andania, in service as an armed merchant cruiser, was torpedoed and sunk by a U-boat off Reykjavik, Iceland. This indicated that the Germans now had long range U-boats, probably based on the Norwegian coast, capable of destroying our shipping in mid-ocean on the North Atlantic route, and not only in the near approaches to Britain.

Something else had happened on that day, of intense interest to shipping people. The *Queen Mary* had returned to the Clyde! After being converted to a troopship at Sydney, Australia, she had joined a convoy consisting of the veteran Cunarder *Aquitania* and the new Cunarder *Mauretania*, the C.P.R. liners *Empress of Britain* and *Empress of Japan*, and the Royal Mail liner *Andes* — all big and speedy vessels — and had left Sydney on 5th May, with Australian and New Zealand troops, bound for the Middle East. When this convoy was at sea in the Indian Ocean, on 15th May, the Admiralty had diverted it to Cape Town, and from there it was sent on to the Clyde, with the idea that the Anzacs might be more urgently required to assist in the defence of Britain or France than in the Middle East.

So, during the stress and strain of the German military Blitzkrieg in Western Europe, the *Queen Mary* was exposed to the hazards of war in the Atlantic and in the narrow waters off the west coast of Britain, and to the risks of air attack in the Clyde. The idea that she was "too big" and costly to be risked on war service had been discarded under the pressure of events.

On this, her first voyage as a transport, her full troop carrying capacity was not used, and probably not realized. The Aussies travelled in her in style, with passenger cabin accommodation. She had only 3000 of them on board. A time would come when she would carry five times that number of troops, packed like sardines, as experience would teach. In all, some 8000 Australians and 6000 New Zealanders were landed in Britain from that convoy.

On that day (16th May 1940), the political and military situation in France was almost as bad as it could be, from the Allies' point of view. The French Government, headed by M. Reynaud, resigned. The veteran Marshal Petain formed a government and asked the Germans for an armistice. Britain was left, to fight on, alone.

The destination of the *Franconia* and *Lancastria* — the port of Brest, 250 miles by rail from Paris, and the most westerly point on the French coast — had been chosen, a week or more previously, as a suitable evacuation port for some remnants of the British Expeditionary Force which had not got away at Dunkirk. These remnants were of many different units. They had been retreating for three weeks from Flanders, and some from Rheims, Paris, and Orleans. The decision to evacuate them from Brest had been taken without allowing for the speed and mobility of the German advance, the disruption of rail and road transport by air bombing, and the disorganization and collapse of the French armies.

When we arrived off Brest, we could not see the town for a pall of black smoke. This came from oil tanks that had been set alight, presumably by the French to deny the use of the oil to the rapidly approaching Germans.

We now received naval orders not to go into the port of Brest, but to proceed to Quiberon, a small fishing port 100 miles to the south-eastward, on the shore of the Bay of Biscay. From this we assumed that the troops we were to embark had bypassed Brest and had gone to Quiberon. In fact, the demoralization of the Allied Land Forces had turned their retreat into a rout, to such an extent that Naval Intelligence could not keep up with what was happening on shore. The troops were waiting for transports not at Quiberon, but at Saint Nazaire, another thirty miles farther to the southward, at the mouth of the Loire.

The *Franconia* and *Lancastria* steamed in company along the coast, in fine weather and sunshine, on that peaceful looking Sunday afternoon, and arrived off Quiberon at 5 p.m. Several other transports were already in the harbour. The entrance to the port was protected by a boom. The gateway in the boom was opened for us, and we made for it in line ahead, the *Franconia* leading.

R.M.S. Fraconia under attack. (AI)

When I was almost in the gateway, a German dive bomber swooped down, out of the blue. Our A.A. guns opened fire, as he released a stick of three bombs, and, flattening out from his dive, let go a burst of machine gun bullets.

The bombs fell under the stern of the *Franconia*, exploding as they hit the seabed. Her stern was lifted clean out of the water, and the ship shuddered. I ordered the helm hard down, and sheered off from the boom, to manoeuvre better in open water if the enemy returned to the attack. He was then climbing away rapidly and soon disappeared from sight. In a few minutes I received a report from the engine room that we were damaged down below.

Plates had been sprung in her hull aft, causing a leak. More serious, one of her engines had been jarred out of alignment. I took her slowly out to seaward, but she was crippled. There was nothing to do but to anchor, and to attempt to effect repairs under cover of darkness. At 6.45 p.m., I let go the anchor, four miles offshore, and at that moment another German aircraft came over, on reconnaissance. He kept high, and did not attack us.

In the meantime, the *Lancastria*, undamaged, had proceeded through the boom gate and anchored in Quiberon Harbour. There Sharp learned that there were no British troops waiting to be evacuated from that port. He asked for naval instructions, and in company with the other transports at Quiberon, was ordered to proceed to Saint Nazaire.

In the dusk the *Lancastria* passed the anchored *Franconia*. My engineers were working desperately to seal the leaks in the *Franconia's* sprung plates and to realign her engines. At midnight she was in going order again. I reported the situation by radio, in code, to the appropriate naval authorities, expecting to be ordered to Saint Nazaire. After some delay the surprising reply came: Proceed to Brest!

At 1 a.m. on 17th June, I hove up the anchor, and shaped course to return to Brest, unescorted. At dawn I was off that port, but there were no destroyers, tugs, pilot vessels, or any other vessels in sight. The thick pall of smoke from the burning oil lay over the town and the harbour. I put out to sea, and stood on and off throughout the day, keeping way on, to have a chance of manoeuvring if another air attack should come.

During that day, my consort, the *Lancastria*, was lying at anchor, three miles off Saint Nazaire. She embarked 4000 troops and some civilians, brought out to her from that port in destroyers and tugs. She then remained at anchor, waiting for further orders, or for escort in convoy. In the early afternoon, she was attacked by dive bombers and struck by three bombs. She sank, with an appalling loss of life. Some 2000 men were drowned in the oily water that surrounded her when her deep fuel tanks were burst open by the bombs. This was the heaviest death toll in any ship sunk during the war. But 2000 survived, among them Captain Sharp and Chief Officer Grattidge. They were picked up out of the water by rescuing boats, of which many were launched from other ships or put out from the shore. Captain Sharp had been four hours in the water when he was picked up.

Late in the afternoon, off Brest, 130 miles from the scene of that disaster, and unaware of it, I received a naval W/T signal[1]: DO NOT GO INTO FRENCH PORTS. This I took to mean that I should wait offshore during the night, for evacuees to be brought out to me from Brest in tugs, or other small craft. I therefore cruised around slowly in the darkness, but no vessels came out from the shore. At 10.15 p.m., I sent a W/T request for instructions.

The reply to this was sent apparently by someone who had no idea of what was happening. It rocked me: Proceed to Brest!

Ours not to reason why. I'd have to do it, whatever my own opinion might be. I therefore bore up at midnight for the entrance to the port, looking for a tug or a pilot boat to take me in. Half an hour later, at 0.30 a.m. (18th June), a naval tug ranged alongside, and the tugmaster told me: Do not go into Brest!

With so many contradictory orders, I had to rely on my own judgment. The tugmaster informed me that the Germans were already in Brest, and that consequently no troops or other evacuees could possibly be brought out to me from there.

Only four hours of darkness then remained. If I waited off Brest until daylight, I would simply be inviting another bomb attack. As no useful purpose could be served by waiting, I proceeded out to sea. At dawn I was fifty miles offshore. I shaped course for Liverpool for repairs, informing Naval Control by W/T of my intention. No countermanding orders came, so I continued on my course at full speed, unescorted. In the sequel I was told that I had taken the correct decision, having a duty to preserve my ship and the lives of my crew.

That evening (18th June 1940), steaming homewards in the Irish Sea, I heard Prime Minister Churchill's broadcast, announcing that a German invasion of Britain was imminent, and his dramatic words, "Let us so bear ourselves that men will say, 'This was their finest hour!'"

On 19th June, at noon, the *Franconia* docked at Liverpool. The loss of the *Lancastria* had been announced on the German radio, but the news was not officially released in Britain until five weeks later. It was, however, known at the Cunard office. Our hearts were heavy with sorrow for the victims of this horrifying disaster, which was obscured from public notice at the time by the general consternation caused by the fall of France.

On 20th June, Winston Churchill again sounded a warning of an imminent German invasion of Britain, and said, "All depends on winning this battle, here in Britain, now, this summer!"

If that was so, the situation was indeed grave, but nobody had the slightest idea that Britain should give in.

A survey was made of the *Franconia*, and she was put into dry dock for repairs. These were estimated to take five weeks. The crew were given leave, and I went to Cheltenham for a needed holiday. It seemed unlikely that a German military invasion of Britain could succeed. The English Channel was a moat that panzers could not cross. The Royal Navy and the Royal Air

Force, and our military shore defences, would see to that. As in Napoleon's day, so now, the sea was our surest shield.

Britain would be exposed to air raids; but hit-and-run raids are not an invasion. The Germans did not have the naval power, or enough shipping, to transport their armies to Britain, or to succeed against heavy opposition "on the beaches." They could have sent light forces of airborne troops for parachute landings in remote places, but everywhere throughout Britain they would have ·met with resistance from "Home Guard" local units: some of these were armed only with sporting guns, and even pitchforks, if they had no better weapons.

Despite this feeling of tension, I enjoyed my holiday in the West Country. The trees were in full leaf, and the war seemed unreal and far away. Then suddenly the "Battle of Britain" began.

This was not an invasion, but a series of air bombing raids that would continue for nearly four years. The first bombs dropped on Britain by the German Air Force fell on docks in South Wales on 10th July 1940. That was ten months after the declaration of war. It set the precedent for air raids on cities, in which civilians on both sides would suffer as in no previous war in history. It was significant that the first German air raids were launched against dockyards at our western sea approaches.

That was an indication of the German strategy of counter blockade. Being now in control of the entire European mainland shore, from Norway to the Bay of Biscay, they could establish naval and air bases from which short range attacks could be made against our shipping in the North Atlantic, the North Sea, the Strait of Dover, and the English Channel. The air attacks constituted a serious new menace to shipping, which might have the effect of closing all ports on our eastern and southern shores, including the ports of London and Southampton, until the Coastal Command of the R.A.F. could provide protection.

Immediately after the fall of France, many merchant vessels were sunk by German bombers in the Channel. Only our western sea approaches could be considered relatively remote from air- bombing attacks. The ports of South Wales, the Mersey, and the Clyde had become Britain's chief sea gateways and would remain so throughout the war. It was for that reason that German air raids on Britain began with an attempt to destroy the docks in South Wales.

Hitler hoped to win the war against Britain, not by armed invasion, but by sea blockade and air raids. In the face of this threat, the people of Britain accepted industrial conscription and food rationing, tightened their belts, and went on with their work, prepared for a long struggle.

After the fall of France, and the entry of Italy into the war, new military fronts were opened in North Africa, to tackle Hitler's jackal ally, and to create large scale diversions in the Mediterranean, the Balkans, and the Middle East, which would draw off some of the weight of the German military threat to the British Isles.

On 1st August 1940, I was recalled from leave and rejoined the *Franconia* at Liverpool. There I was informed that I was to embark troops on the Clyde, to join a convoy to Suez, with reinforcements and supplies for the British Army in Egypt.

The entry of Italy into the war had temporarily closed the Mediterranean to British mercantile shipping and troop transports. This made it necessary to send military reinforcements and supplies from Britain to Egypt on a long haul via the Cape of Good Hope, the Indian Ocean, and the Red Sea, to Suez. That passage, of 12,000 miles, would take at least forty days at the average speed of convoys, 12 knots, allowing for calls enroute for fuel and fresh water.

That was the kind of trouble that Mussolini had caused us.

The convoy of seventeen ships that I was to join would take out 25,000 British troops and an immense quantity of military supplies for General Wavell's Army in the Middle East, which at that time already numbered 85,000 men, comprising British and Anzac brigades. The Italians had 250,000 troops in Libya, and 200,000 in Ethiopia.

The horizons of the war were widening.

CHAPTER ENDNOTES

(1) Wireless/Telegraphy – an older term for radio transmissions. In this case to probably indicate a coded transmission.

33

A Convoy to the Middle East — The Long Haul Around South Africa — Seventeen Transports in Company — Calls at Freetown, Cape Town, and Durban — Our Arrival at Suez — The Serious Situation at Home — Air Blitz Increases — Epic of the "Jervis Bay" — My Return from Suez — "Empress of Britain" Torpedoed — A Hush-hush Mission to Gibraltar — Reinforcements for "The Rock" — War in the Mediterranean — Home for Christmas but Only Just.

ON Sunday, 4th August, 1940, after a passage from Liverpool, unescorted, I brought the *Franconia* to anchor at Gourock at noon. Five other transports were lying in the bay. They were the passenger liners *Empress of Canada* (C.P.R. Line, 21,500 tons), and *Andes* (Royal Mail Line, 25,000 tons); and three freighters, *Suffolk* (Federal Line, 11,000 tons), *Lanarkshire* (Clan Line, 10,000 tons), and *Memnon* (Egyptian Line, 3000 tons).

Tenders and barges were clustered around the transports, embarking troops and loading stores and army supplies. An hour after the *Franconia* had anchored, tenders came out from the shore, and we also began embarking troops and loading stores. This work went on all afternoon, and throughout the night.

I went ashore to the Naval Control Office, for a conference, at which the masters of the ships in the convoy were given instructions on the route and the procedures to be followed. To my great pleasure, I met Captain John

Kinley, a Manxman, who was in command of the *Empress of Canada*. I had not seen him for thirty-six years, since we had been shipmates in the full rigged sailing ship, *County of Cardigan*, when he was First Mate, and I Second Mate, on a voyage round Cape Horn in 1904.

On Tuesday, 6th August 1940, at break of day, the six transports got under way. On board the *Franconia*, I had 2765, soldiers, 87 army nurses, 106 civilians, and a crew of 352: total 3310 souls. We proceeded down the Firth of Clyde, to round the Mull of Kintyre and head westward into the Atlantic. Here we had a rendezvous with eleven transports, which had embarked. troops and loaded stores at Liverpool.

These vessels were: the *Stratheden* (P. & 0., 23,000 tons), *Strathaird* (P. & 0., 22,000 tons); *Empress of Britain* (C.P.R., 42,000 tons), *Orion* (Orient Line, 23,000 tons), *Otranto* (Orient Line, 20,000 tons), *Ormonde* (Orient Line, 15,000 tons), *Monarch of Bermuda* (Furness Withy Line, 22,000 tons), *Batory* (Polish Line, 14,000 tons), and three freighters, *Waiwera* (Shaw Savill Line, 12,000 tons), *Clan Macaulay* (Clan Line, 11,000 tons), and *Aska* (British India Line, 8000 tons).

It was an impressive display of Britain's reserve of sea carrying power. There were thirty thousand souls and twenty-five million pounds worth of ships and stores afloat in that convoy, embarked on an ocean passage of 12,000 miles to the Middle East, at a time when our own homeland was believed to be in imminent danger of invasion!

Britain could spare those men, those ships, and those military supplies, risking their destruction at sea, in terms of a strategy not of passive defence, but of counter offensive.

This convoy was typical. It was escorted at the outset by two cruisers, H.M.S. *Kent* and H.M.S. *Shropshire*, and six destroyers. Land based aircraft of the Fleet Air Arm and of the newly established Coastal Command of the R.A.F. patrolled overhead, on the lookout for enemy aircraft, U-boats, surface raiders, or mine fields. Occasionally we sighted other naval vessels, including minesweepers, patrolling the north-western approaches to Britain's Atlantic portals.

Before we were out of the North Channel, the *Ormonde* had to turn back, with engine trouble. The convoy could not wait for a laggard in that dangerous place. Our course would take us far out into the Atlantic, to the westward of Ireland, beyond the reach of German bombers based on the coast of France.

On our third day out, Wednesday, 9th August 1940, when we were well to the westward and free of the land, the destroyers left us, having reached the limit of their effective fuel range. At this point the convoy headed southwards. Seven of the passenger liners — *Strathaird, Stratheden, Empress of*

Britain, Empress of Canada, Monarch of Bermuda, Andes, and *Batory* — all capable of a speed of 20 knots — were detached and sent ahead as a "fast convoy," under escort of *H.M.S. Kent.*

The remaining nine vessels — *Orion, Otranto, Franconia,* and the six freighters — under escort of *H.M.S. Shropshire,* plugged along at 14 knots. On 10th August we passed east of the Azores. On 16th August, after a passage of 3701 miles, by detour and zigzag, eleven days out from the Clyde, we put into port at Freetown, on the West Coast of Africa, in the British colony of Sierra Leone.

This port, sweltering hot, 8 degrees N. of the Equator, offers few attractions as a tourist resort, but was of the utmost value for British sea communications in wartime. It was a fuelling and watering point for steamers, especially necessary for passenger liners converted to war service. Many passenger liners are designed on their normal peacetime service, to go not more than 4000 miles without refuelling and watering.

As we came to anchor, near a British cruiser, troops lining the rail of the *Franconia* were making humorous and sarcastic comments about the Navy. A naval rating, who was wearing white shorts and a black beard, stood it for a while, and then sang out, "Where are you evacuating from now?"

The troops were not allowed ashore at Freetown. After a stay of two days there, in sweltering steamy heat, the convoy put to sea. Ten days later, on 28th August, we docked at Cape Town in Table Bay, a passage of 3233 miles from Freetown.

Shore leave was granted at Cape Town, and the troops made the most of it, glad to stretch their legs after being in crowded quarters on board for three weeks.

Next day, the *Franconia* was detached from the convoy, and proceeded to Durban, as a matter of convenience in refuelling and taking in fresh water. I was escorted on the passage of 961 miles by *H.M.S. Dragon,* and berthed at Durban at 8 a.m. on 1st September. The troops went ashore for a route march, and afterwards had short leave in the town, being required to return on board by 6 p.m.

At 10.30 p.m., the *Franconia* put to sea, in company now with *S.S. Llangibby* Castle (Union Castle Line, 10,000 tons), a smart vessel normally in service in East African waters. We were escorted by the armed merchant cruiser *Kanimbla,* of the Royal Australian Navy, a twin screw motor vessel of 11,000 tons, owned by the Australian firm of McIlwraith McEacharn, and employed in peacetime in the Australian interstate coastal passenger and cargo trade. She was commanded by Captain F. E. Getting, R.A.N., and had been refuelled at Durban after patrolling in the Indian Ocean.

Off Durban we joined up with the original convoy, which had now come on from Cape Town, and proceeded in company north- wards along the East Coast of Africa, under escort of *H.M.S. Shropshire* and *H.M.A.S. Kanimbla.*

On 10th September we rounded Cape Gardafui, passed Aden two days later, and, after an exhausting passage of the Red Sea, in extremely hot weather, anchored at Suez on 16th September, six weeks out from the Clyde. We could have arrived there in ten days, if Mussolini had not blocked the Mediterranean temporarily. Here, one of the *Franconia*'s engineers died of heat stroke, and was buried ashore. The town of Suez, if it could be called a town, was a place of torment, with heat, flies, and dust. Tens of thousands of troops, and vast dumps of war material, were in the vicinity.

The war news was grim. While we had been at sea, there had been heavy German air raids on British ports. The Luftwaffe had bombed docks at Dover, Weymouth, Portland, Portsmouth, Southampton, and Newcastle-upon-Tyne, and, on 16th August, had dropped the first bombs on London. On 25th August, the R.A.F. had raided Berlin, and the pattern of modern warfare had taken its shape of terror attacks against noncombatant civilians, bringing home, for the first time in centuries, the real meaning of war to people who, until then, had been accustomed to cheering their heroes from safe distances, far from the scenes of combat.

On 7th September, the "London Blitz" had begun with full scale day raids on the London docks and Central London, which were continued for several successive days. A bomb had damaged Buckingham Palace, and one had fallen near St. Paul's Cathedral, without exploding. A bomb had been dropped on Madame Tussaud's Waxworks Exhibition, very near the flat in Baker Street which was my London home, containing the furniture, household effects, and personal possessions which my wife and I had accumulated there. Things were getting really serious!

It was officially announced that 258 civilians in the U.K. had been killed by air raids in July, 1075 in August, and 6954 in September. On 17th September, there had been an air raid on Glasgow, and H.M. cruiser *Sussex* was severely damaged in the Clyde. Even the western ports of Britain were not beyond the enemy's reach. Yet the losses of German aircraft on these raids had been heavy. The Royal Air Force was increasing its strength greatly, and carrying the war to the enemy, with ever increasing hitting power. Britain could "take it" — and also could "dish it out."

The *Franconia* remained at Suez for eight days, loaded a cargo of 1000 tons of baled cotton, and embarked 207 British women and children from Egypt and Palestine, to be taken to South Africa for safety. On 24th September, we left Suez in convoy, with the *Empress of Britain*, *Empress of Canada*, *Otranto*, *Andes*, *Strathaird*, and *Suffolk*, escorted by the Australian cruiser, *H.M.A.S. Hobart*, and four destroyers. There was a risk of air attacks in the Red Sea, and in the narrow Strait of Bab el Mandeb, from the adjacent Italian held territories of Ethiopia and Eritrea, if Mussolini's airmen had the nerve to press home the tactical advantage that they held.

The escorting warships bristled with A.A. guns, as did also the transports. In the *Franconia* we had an A.A. guard of twenty-five men, with half a dozen guns pointed to the sky; but no attack came, and, on 28th September, we were through the strait and out into the Gulf of Aden. Here *H.M.A.S. Hobart* left us, and *H.M.A.S. Kanimbla* took over the escort. We now headed southwards, along the coast of East Africa.

On 8th October, as directed, I left the convoy, and proceeded alone into Durban, to disembark my women and children passengers, and to embark 130 troops and naval ratings for passage to the U.K. I also loaded 970 tons of sugar and 407 tons of meal, then went on, alone and unescorted, to Cape Town.

There I loaded more cargo and embarked another sixty troops. As the convoy had gone on ahead, several days previously, I left Cape Town, on 15th October, alone and unescorted, having on board 190 troops, 21 A.A. guard, and a crew of 352, with 2550 tons of cargo (all foodstuffs) and 20 bags of mail.

On 24th October, I anchored at Freetown, refuelled and watered, and on the following day put to sea from that port, alone and unescorted, and feeling anything but optimistic. News had come through that the biggest liner in the convoy ahead of me, the *Empress of Britain*, had been torpedoed and sunk by a U-boat 150 miles west of the Irish coast.

That was in the track that I would have to take. There was nothing to do but proceed at full speed, zigzagging, and keeping a sharp lookout. Luck was with me. On 4th November, I anchored, the *Franconia* at Gourock in the Clyde, safe home after a voyage of three months, on which she had steamed 25,397 miles.

That was a fair average specimen of service in the convoys of troop transports that took out reinforcements and supplies from Britain to the Middle East by that long haul around the Cape of Good Hope. Usually there was one such convoy leaving Britain each month, in addition to convoys from Australia across the Indian Ocean to Suez. The haul around the Cape would have to continue until Italy could be knocked out of the war, and the Mediterranean again opened to traffic.

On 6th November 1940, I docked my ship in Glasgow, and next day was given four days' leave — not much time for the special job I now had to do. This was to move the furniture, carpets and other household effects from our flat in Baker Street, to storage at Cheltenham! We managed to do this, with much travelling by rail and road, and expenditure of cash and energy, obtaining a van, loading our goods and chattels into it at Baker Street, and storing them in two horseboxes on a farm near Cheltenham — then I got back to my ship on 11th November, tired out, and heartily cursing the war's alarms and excursions.

I had seen many signs of bomb damage in London. The "Blitz" was in full swing. London was a target that couldn't be missed. Officially announced civilian casualties in the U.K. in October were 6334 killed and 8695 injured. That was what Goering had meant by saying, "There are no more islands!" Yet more than 2000 German aircraft had been shot down over Britain, and

Smoke rising from the London Docks
(credit US Government Archives, Public Domain)

into the water, in the first three months of the big Blitz.

Likewise, the war at sea was being waged with unprecedented ferocity. In October, 250 Allied merchant vessels had been sunk, with heavy loss of life and cargoes; but also a large number of U-boats had been destroyed.

On 5th November 1940, there was one of the most thrilling incidents of the war at sea. The German surface raider, *Admiral Scheer*, a "pocket battleship," had got out into the Atlantic. She attacked a convoy of thirty-eight ships in mid-ocean, mostly cargo vessels carrying foodstuffs to Britain from the U.S.A. and Canada. The only escort of the convoy was the armed merchant cruiser *Jervis Bay* an elderly liner of 14,000 tons, commanded by

Captain Fogarty Fegan, R.N., and manned chiefly by merchant seamen of the Royal Naval Reserve.

Five ships of the convoy were sunk, but the Jervis Bay, though armed only with 6-inch guns, and far outranged by the enemy's 11-inch guns, engaged him in a hopeless battle, while thirty ships of the convoy scattered and got safely away. The *Jervis Bay* was sunk, with heavy loss of life. Captain Fegan was posthumously awarded the Victoria Cross for this gallant action.

Now it was clear that convoys were liable to be attacked even in mid-ocean. There was no complete safety anywhere, but the convoy system remained effective, for there is always some safety in numbers.

At Glasgow, on 12th November 1940, I was informed that the *Franconia's* next task would be to take reinforcements and supplies to Gibraltar. This operation was cloaked in secrecy and rightly regarded as requiring special protection. The western sea approaches to Gibraltar were now within easy range of enemy U-boats, surface raiders, and aircraft based on Brest, Saint Nazaire, and Bordeaux. The enemy would make every effort to prevent reinforcements and supplies from reaching Gibraltar. Nevertheless, our garrison there had to be strengthened.

Four transports were assigned to this task. They were the *Franconia* and three freighters — *Clan Forbes* (Clan Line, 7500 tons), *Clan Fraser*, (Clan Line, 7500 tons), and *New Zealand Star*, (Blue Star Line, 10,700 tons) — all having a speed of 16 knots.

In the *Franconia* I embarked 89 naval ratings, 637 soldiers, 1244 air force men, and a crew of 324 — total 2234 souls — and loaded 1000 tons of naval and military supplies. My ship would be the biggest and most attractive target in the convoy, but the three freighters also carried large quantities of war material, including munitions and aircraft, of high priority from our point of view, and from the point of view of the enemy.

On 15th November, in winter dusk and slight fog, I weighed anchor at Gourock and put to sea, in company with the two "Clan" freighters, escorted by *H.M.S. Dido* and four destroyers. Off the Mull of Kintyre we were joined by the *New Zealand Star*, which had been loaded at Liverpool, and a powerful naval escort of *H.M.S. Furious* (aircraft carrier), *H.M.S. Manchester* (cruiser), and four more destroyers.

The Royal Navy was leaving nothing to chance on this expedition! Setting course to the westward at 16 knots, zigzagging, in line ahead, with the destroyers patrolling on both sides, we met with no enemy attack, and next day ran into a heavy north-westerly. gale. This provided further protection against U-boats, which are at a disadvantage in heavy weather, and usually submerge deep during a storm.

The destroyers hove to, and we proceeded without them. On the third day, 700 miles offshore, we headed southwards, on a detour that took us almost to Madeira before we headed eastwards for the Strait of Gibraltar. On 21st November, at 6 p.m., six days out from the Clyde, we moored to the detached Mole at Gibraltar, after a passage of 2188 miles.

Our arrival was greeted with much satisfaction, but in an atmosphere of "hush-hush," as there was something big in the wind. I was soon informed what this was. The 1244 Royal Air Force men that I had brought in the *Franconia* were to be transferred from her at Gibraltar into warships, to be taken on to Malta and Alexandria, by the short route to the Middle East. At no time had the British Navy conceded control of the Mediterranean to Mussolini. The fall of France had seriously affected the balance of naval power in the Mediterranean. Before that, French power in that sea had been a match for Italian power, with the British Mediterranean Fleet ensuring preponderance; but now the whole task of dealing with Mussolini's navy fell on Britain. It was a task eagerly accepted.

All units of the French Navy that had happened to be in British ports, or at Alexandria, when France capitulated, had been taken over by Britain. On 3rd July, a British squadron from Gibraltar, under command of Admiral Sir James Somerville, had demanded surrender of a powerful French squadron then lying at anchor at Oran, in French Morocco. When this was refused by the French Admiral Gensoul, the British ships had opened fire, sinking or heavily damaging three French battleships and a destroyer. One French battleship, the *Strasbourg*, and five destroyers, had escaped to Toulon. Another French battleship, the *Richelieu*, was attacked and crippled by the British Fleet Air Arm, at Dakar, in French West Africa.

Regrettable though these actions were, they were a necessity of war, to prevent the French Fleet from being taken over by Germany and Italy. But the French were indignant, and in reprisal made two air raids on British ships at Gibraltar.

As for the Italian Navy, it was sheltering in its ports, capable only of sneak raids. When one of its squadrons had emerged, the Australian cruiser, H.M.A.S. *Sydney*, had engaged and sunk the crack Italian cruiser, *Bartolomeo Colleoni*, off Crete, on 19th July. The Fleet Air Arm had heavily attacked the Italian Naval Base at Taranto, on 11th November, crippling three battleships and two cruisers.

Italy had declared war on Greece on 28th October, and had begun a military invasion of Greece, across the Adriatic, but the Italian Army was making very slow headway against resolute Greek defence. British troops had been landed in Greece on 3rd November.

Yet the Italian Navy was still potentially a menace. At the outbreak of the war it consisted of six battleships, nineteen cruisers, fifty destroyers, and 120 submarines. The Italian Air Force was reported to have 2000 aircraft capable of ranging over the Mediterranean from bases in Southern Italy and Sicily, or from Libya.

Powerful British naval and military forces were stationed at Gibraltar and Malta. It was thought that Spain, with aid from Germany, might attempt to recapture the Rock Fortress of "Gib.," which the British had captured in 1704, and had held firmly ever since then. General Franco had repeatedly claimed the return of Gibraltar to Spain.

On the naval station at Gibraltar were the battleship *H.M.S. Renown*, the aircraft carrier *H.M.S. Ark Royal*, and a large number of heavy and light cruisers and destroyers, and other naval units. I had the privilege of meeting Admiral Somerville, Admiral Holland, Admiral North, Captain Steele, R.N. (Captain of the Port), Captain Packer, R.N., General Macfarland (O.C. troops), and other naval and military officers, who in various ways expressed gratification at the safe arrival of our convoy, with such substantial reinforcements and supplies.

The "hush-hush" operation got under way at 4.30 a.m. on 25th November, when the R.A.F. men left the *Franconia* and went on board the cruisers *Manchester* and *Southampton*. At 7.5 a.m., the cruisers put to sea, in company with *H.M.S Renown*, *Ark Royal*, *Sheffield*, and seven destroyers. The Italian Navy was unlikely to challenge a British squadron of that strength. In due course the heavily escorted airmen arrived safely at Malta.

At Gibraltar, the *Franconia* and the three freighters unloaded the naval and military supplies that we had brought, and loaded an assortment of cargo, which included unwanted stores and even bicycles and a large number of empty beer barrels!

The news from home was of an increase in the air blitz. In November there were raids by the R.A.F. on Essen, Munich, Danzig, Dresden, Hamburg, and Cologne (damaging the cathedral); and by the Luftwaffe on Coventry (destroying the cathedral), Birmingham, Southampton, and Liverpool.

The first air raid on Liverpool was on 28th November, while I was at Gibraltar. I wondered if it would affect future docking arrangements in my home port. No detailed information was given on the radio, for obvious reasons; but it was announced that 4588 civilians were killed and 6202 injured by air raids in the U.K. in November.

On 30th November, I embarked 126 merchant seamen at Gibraltar as passengers in the *Franconia*. These were the crews of two British freighters, *Hermes* (Captain Beale) and *Temple Comb* (Captain Phillips), who had been taken as prisoners by the French in Moroccan ports after the "incident" at Oran. They had spent several months in prisons and concentration camps in Morocco, before being released and sent to Gibraltar. They had harrowing tales to tell of their experiences.

Another 284 passengers came on board, including naval ratings, soldiers, and some civilians. On 7th December the convoy put to sea, to return home, after a stay of sixteen days at Gib. In the *Franconia* I had 409 passengers, 323 crew, a cargo chiefly of empty beer barrels, and 350 bags of mail. Christmas mail! We would be home for Christmas!

Our naval escort, as before, was very strong. We left Gibraltar escorted by two battleships, *H.M.S. Argus* and *H.M.S. Ramillies*, and six destroyers. At sea we were joined by *H.M.S. Furious* and *H.M.S. Dido*, and later by an armed merchant cruiser, *H.M.S. California* (of the Anchor Line). On 12th December, off the west coast of Ireland, we were joined by *H.M.S. Cairo* (A.A. cruiser) and four destroyers.

All that escort for one liner and three almost empty freighters made us feel very safe. It was bitter winter weather, with southerly gales, when we made our landfall at Islay Island (off the west coast of Scotland) on 13th December, and hauled across to Rathlin Island. The gale continued next day as we entered the Firth of Clyde, and anchored, with some difficulty, in Gourock Bay, among a large number of other ships lying there, on 14th December, at 4p.m.

Next morning, though storm and rain continued, my passengers were landed by tender. That night the wind was stronger than before, and I let go the second anchor. On the following afternoon (16th December), a steamer riding at anchor near by, *S.S. Ettrick* (11,000 tons), dragged her anchor and fell across the *Franconia's* stem, but caused only slight damage to our paravane fairlead. Such was our stormy homecoming.

A big new convoy for the Middle East was being got ready at Gourock. I wondered if I would be home for Christmas, after all. But on 20th December the storm subsided, and I was able to take the *Franconia* upriver to King George V Dock in Glasgow, and berthed her there at 5 p.m., to begin unloading the empty beer barrels.

Next day I was given leave, and, after a slow and trying rail- journey, arrived at Cheltenham on 22nd December.

So, I had made it!

The war news was as gloomy as the weather. There was not much "peace on earth, goodwill to all men," on that second Christmas of the war. Air raids continued, and, on three successive nights — 20th, 21st, and 22nd December — Liverpool was again heavily bombed.

But, far away in the Western Desert of Egypt, the British Army, including the Anzacs, had opened an offensive into Libya on 9th December, and, in one week, had captured Sidi Barrani, Sollum, and Fort Capuzzo, taking 35,000 Italian prisoners.

This was the first successful Allied military offensive of the war — the first indication of the beginning of a turn of the tide. It would be necessary for Hitler to go to the aid of his braggart ally, in North Africa, and also in Greece. That would draw off some of the German armed might from Western Europe — a comforting thought, which, as far as I was concerned, showed that my two trooping voyages in six months — one to Suez and one to Gibraltar — had been a contribution to help in building up that new front on which our enemies had met with their first serious military reverses.

Arrived home three days before Christmas, I was feeling seedy, suffering from lumbago[1] , probably due to long hours on the bridge during the winter gales on the passage from Gibraltar to the Clyde, and the sudden change from a warm to a cold clime. But many other people were going down — with 'flu.

I spent Christmas Eve in bed, while my wife went off to do whatever Christmas shopping was possible with our food ration tickets. During that day, the telephone rang, and I got out of bed to answer it. The call was from Glasgow, ordering me to return immediately to my ship!

At 9.30 a.m. on Christmas Day, I left Cheltenham by train, and, after twelve hours' cold and miserable travelling, was on board the *Franconia* that evening at 10 p.m. She was in darkness. There was no steward — nothing! So ended a not very merry Christmas at home.

CHAPTER ENDNOTES

(1) Lumbago is an outdated medical term that describes pain in the lower back region. This region centres around the lumbar area of the spine, which reaches from the lowest rib down to the buttocks. Today, most medical professionals will use the term "lower back pain." Pain from lumbago ranges from mild to severe.

34

*Big Convoy to the Middle East — Australian Troops in the
"Franconia" — German Raiders in the Indian Ocean — Safe Arrival
at Suez — Embarking Italian Prisoners — Cargoes of Foodstuffs —
German Invasion of Russia — Britain Gains an Ally — Japanese
Attack on Pearl Harbour — U.S.A. Enters the War — The
"Franconia" at Trinidad — I am Ordered to Leave Her — Rumours
of the Galley Gazette — A Hearty Send-off — On the Beach at Port
of Spain — A Captain Without a Ship*

THE reason for my recall from Christmas leave was that a sudden
decision had been taken to include the *Franconia* in the big convoy
that was being got ready to go to the Middle East. More
reinforcements and supplies were urgently required for the military offensive
in the Western Desert.

All the *Franconia*'s crew had been given home leave on 21st December
1940, and they were recalled by telegrams three days later. Most of them had
gone to their homes in Liverpool, or elsewhere in England. When I arrived
on board the ship, in dock at Glasgow, at 10 p.m. on Christmas Day, I found
only the caretakers there. Soon afterwards, the Staff Captain, "Bert"
Birtenshaw, arrived. He had been with me in the *Franconia* on all her wartime
wanderings. He was always reliable, efficient, a sterling old friend, and a good
shipmate.

Throughout Boxing Day, the crew kept on arriving. On 27th December,
at 11 a.m., we moved the ship out of the dock, and proceeded downriver, to

come to anchor off Gourock at 3 p.m. There we lay idle for a week. The haste in recalling the crew from their Christmas leave had been unnecessary. We did not begin embarking troops until 3rd January 1941 — that was ten days after the urgent recall of the crew — but it was no use growling, as such fits and starts are typical in wartime. The embarkation of troops requires preparations to receive them, which are usually begun too soon and completed belatedly, with frustrating delays while everything is checked, to ensure that nothing is left behind.

The troops who were embarked in the *Franconia* were 2600 Australians. They came aboard in tenders, as Happy as Larry[1] at the prospect of getting away from Britain's cold and wet winter to the hot and dry climate of the Middle East, and of joining their mates who had already gone into action there with brilliant success. These troops, originally part of the 6th Australian Division, had arrived in Britain in June 1940 — some of them in the *Queen Mary* on her maiden voyage as a transport — and had been stationed at first on Salisbury Plain, and later at Colchester, in readiness for the German invasion which did not happen. They now formed the 25th Australian Brigade. Together with the 18th Australian Brigade, which had been embarked at Glasgow for the Middle East on 15th November 1940, they were the nucleus of the Australian 9th Division, under command of Major General Wynter. They were being transferred from Britain to the Middle East to join with the Australian 6th and 7th Divisions, already there, under General Blarney as C.-in-C.

Although the Aussies were embarked in the *Franconia* on 3rd January, they had a tedious and cold wait on board, as the convoy was not ready to put to sea until eight days after that. Troops were being embarked and stores loaded in eleven transports on the Clyde, and in ten more on the Mersey. The two portions of the convoy were to be conjoined at sea, off the Mull of Kintyre.

In addition to the Aussies, I embarked 103 naval ratings and 20 army nurses. With a crew of 319, I had 3042 souls on board, in crowded conditions. The 'flu epidemic was raging. There were 300 cases of it on board the *Franconia*, and I was one of them. Fortunately, we had several army doctors, besides the nurses, and plenty of drugs on board. On 8th January, I had to stay in bed, with a temperature of 102. I kept on getting up and collapsing again.

Staff Captain Birtenshaw, Chief Officer Boston, First Officer Patchett, Second Officers Bridgewater and Smith, and Third Officers Skinner and Hewitt all rose to the occasion, as their profession required, and I had no need to worry.

At last all was ready, and, on 11th January 1941, at 11.30 p.m., a bleak and dark night, the Glasgow portion of the convoy got under way. We anchored two hours later in Rothsay Bay, in the Firth of Clyde, and proceeded again at 4.30 a.m. The Liverpool portion had been delayed. We joined up with it at daylight, off the Mull of Kintyre, and proceeded westwards, headed for the open Atlantic.

The twenty-one transports in this convoy were all passenger liners, which in peacetime were rated among the smartest, speediest, and best appointed ships in the world. This was the biggest movement of troops, over a long distance by sea, in one operation, that had yet been attempted. There were approximately 55,000 British, Australian, and New Zealand troops, and 6000 crew members, in the twenty-one liners, besides some 40,000 tons of stores. No wonder it had taken time to get started!

The vessels in the convoy had been commandeered, or, more politely,

COMPANY / Ship Name	TONNAGE	COMPANY / Ship Name	TONNAGE
ANCHOR LINE		**CANADIAN PACIFIC RAILWAY**	
Nea Belles	17,000	Empress of Japan	22,000
Cameronia	16,000	Empress of Australia	22,000
TOTAL	33,000	Duchess of York	20,000
CUNARD WHITE STAR LINE		Duchess of Richmond	20,000
Britannic	27,000	Duchess of Bedford	20,000
Franconia	20,000	TOTAL	104,000
Samaria	19,000	**ORIENT LINE**	
TOTAL	66,000	Ormonde	15,000
UNION CASTLE LINE		TOTAL	15,000
Cape Town Castle	27,000	**DUTCH N.A.S.M. LINE**	
Athlone Castle	25,000	Pennland	16,000
Windsor Castle	19,000	TOTAL	16,000
Arundel Castle	19,000	**ROYAL MAIL LINE**	
Durban Castle	17,000	Highland Princess	14,000
Winchester Castle	17,000	Highland Chieftain	14,000
TOTAL	124,000	TOTAL	28,000
FURNESS WITHY LINE			
Monarch of Bermuda	22,000		
TOTAL	22,000		

"requisitioned" from eight different shipping companies. These were:

The Spanish Armada of the year 1588 was a tinpot show com- pared with this; but we who were engaged in it were not concerned with romantic ideas. Each man had his job to do and did it to the best of his ability. That was all.

On the bridge the principal worry was to keep station precisely, and to alter course on zigzag at the prescribed times. The ships steamed in three lines ahead, of seven in each line, averaging 15 knots. Powerful naval escort was provided by *H.M.S. Ramillies*, with some heavy and light cruisers and a flotilla of destroyers at the outset. The Commodore of the convoy was Admiral Sir Richard Hall, R.N., in the *Athlone Castle*.

All went well, and in a week, we were in fine and warm weather. On 25th January 1941, the convoy arrived at Freetown, having made a wide sweep westward into the Atlantic, on a passage of 4413 miles from the Clyde. The arrival of twenty-one liners and two cruisers, requiring fuel and fresh water, would be a sensational event in any port in the world; but at that remote port and small town the Naval Control Office had everything well organized. In four days all the ships were refuelled and watered. The convoy put to sea again on 29th January. The troops had not been allowed ashore at Freetown.

Our supplies of draught beer were running low. One of the transports, the Anchor liner *Nea Bellas*, was commanded by Captain Sir David Bone, author of one of the best books of sailing ship reminiscences ever written, *The Brassbounder*. When his ship ran out of beer in the sweltering heat of Freetown, the troops renamed her "Near Hell as Possible!" She had been originally built for the Anchor Line as the *Tuscania*, then sold to a Greek firm, who named her *Nea Bellas*. On the outbreak of war, she was taken over by the British Ministry of Transport in her Greek name.

On 1st February we crossed the Equator. That evening, the *Franconia*'s supply of draught beer was finished! A week later, we were off Cape Town. Half of the convoy put in there for fuel and refreshments, while the *Franconia* and the others went on to Durban. When we docked at Durban on 11th February, the beer drought was broken. The troops went ashore, after having been on board in cramped quarters since 3rd January. They had three days on shore. They were made welcome by a Committee headed by Miss Ethel Campbell. This lady, a resident of Durban, was always informed by the authorities when Australian troops were expected. She was their "mother" at Durban and had first become interested in them during the 1914-18 war. They called her "the Angel of Durban." When the ship was due to leave, she was the only civilian allowed on the long mole, and didn't the Aussies give her a big cheer? In Durban we heard the secret news that almost everyone in South Africa knew. The gigantic Cunarder, *Queen Elizabeth*, had put into Cape Town for fuel! She had left New York in November (1940), to go to the naval docks at Singapore. There she was converted to a troop transport. She then proceeded to Sydney, where she arrived in February 1941, and soon after went into service, with the *Queen Mary* and *Mauretania*, transporting Australian reinforcements to Suez.

Meanwhile, on 16th February, off Durban, the convoy in which the *Franconia* was voyaging joined up with the ships that had come on from Cape Town, and proceeded northwards in the Indian Ocean, escorted now by the Australian cruiser, *H.M.A.S. Australia*, and the British cruiser, *H.M.S. Emerald*.

At this time two German commerce raiders were in the Indian Ocean. One was the auxiliary cruiser, *Atlantis*; the other was the formidable "pocket battleship," *Admiral Scheer*, which had six 11-inch and eight 5.9-inch guns. These raiders, refuelled from three supply ships in mid-ocean, were on the lookout for our convoy. The Scheer, on 21st and 22nd February, sank three ships off Zanzibar, directly in our track, ahead of us, and not fifty miles from our position. As her speed was 26 knots, she could easily have come up with us had she known our movements.

On that day, 21st February, four transports left the convoy, under escort of *H.M.S. Emerald*, to land troops and supplies at Mombasa, the port of Kenya. British military forces in Kenya had begun advancing into Ethiopia and Italian Somaliland. *H.M.A.S. Australia* went off in search of the Scheer, and the main convoy proceeded northwards under escort of *H.M.S. Hawkins*.

On 25th February we passed through Socotra Straits, and on 3rd March anchored off Suez, after a passage of sixteen days from Durban. It was not practicable to disembark all troops immediately. On 8th March, the troops being still on board, there was warning of an air raid, and the transports were ordered to scatter. I took the *Franconia* twenty miles out to sea, and returned to Suez next day, 9th March, at 7 p.m. That same night, disembarkation began and was completed on 11th March. Some of the Aussies who had made that long outward passage with me were soon to be flung into battle in the Western Desert, and to distinguish themselves by their heroic and long sustained defence of Tobruk against German armoured counterattacks.

The main problem in a long distance troop transport operation is to find some economic use for transports on the return passage, after the troops are disembarked at a war zone. This problem was easily solved in the present instance. Instead of returning empty, the transports were to embark Italian prisoners of war! Tens of thousands of these miserable specimens had surrendered already in the Western Desert campaign. To provide them with quarters and food in Egypt would have put an added strain on army supplies. It was therefore decided to ship them off to South Africa, to get them out of the way as quickly as possible.

Nothing could have been more convenient for this purpose than the presence at Suez of large and empty passenger liners! On 15th March, I embarked in the *Franconia* 2514 prisoners and a guard of 181 Cape Town Highlanders — in kilts! The prisoners were a poor looking lot, and quite docile.

That was the day when President Roosevelt of the U.S.A. declared that the time had come for "an end of compromise with tyranny." In a broadcast he announced that the U.S.A. would "lend-lease" ships, planes, food, and munitions to Britain and her allies, "until victory is won."

On 18th March, in convoy with ten other transports, the *Franconia* left Suez, and on 4th April arrived at Durban. Here the prisoners were disembarked, and the ship was fumigated. It was now decided that this was the time and place to put her into dry dock, for her annual overhaul and painting, and afterwards to load cargo.

After a fortnight at Durban, I proceeded to Cape Town, and there joined a convoy of five ships, homeward bound. We left Cape Town on 27th April. In the *Franconia* I had 3865 tons of cargo, mostly foodstuffs, and 118 passengers, all service personnel. We called at Freetown, and on 21st May docked in Glasgow. That voyage to Suez had lasted four months, during which the *Franconia* had steamed 27,607 miles.

The war was now livening up extensively. At the end of March 1941, the Germans had gone to the aid of the Italians in North Africa, and soon afterwards in Greece. They made powerful military thrusts, with Blitzkrieg success at the outset. Then, on 10th May, Hitler's deputy, Rudolf Hess, piloted a plane from Augsburg to Scotland, landed by parachute, and declared that he had come on "a private peace mission!" Whatever his mission might have been, it did not succeed. He was held as a military prisoner.

While the *Franconia*'s cargo was being unloaded at Glasgow, I had a week's holiday at Cheltenham. It was in that week that the German battleship, *Bismarck*, raiding in the North Atlantic, on 24th May 1941, sank Britain's biggest battleship, *H.M.S. Hood*, with the loss of 2000 lives. The *Bismarck* was herself damaged in this action. She was pursued and sunk by other units of the British Navy, on 27th May.

On 29th May, I went to Liverpool for instructions at the head office of the Cunard White Star Line. The bomb damage at Liverpool was extensive and saddening. I was told that I was to continue in command of the *Franconia*, on another voyage in convoy to the Middle East.

At Glasgow on 2nd June 1941, I embarked 3052 troops, and next day put to sea in convoy with fourteen other transports, including liners and freighters, under naval escort of *H.M.S. Birmingham* and the armed merchant cruiser, *H.M.S. Dunnottar Castle*, and destroyers.

Arrived at Durban on 5th July, I received instructions to disembark the troops, which were then taken on to Suez in other transports. The *Franconia* loaded a cargo of foodstuffs at Durban and at Cape Town. On 20th July she left Cape Town, alone, with a cargo of 3670 tons and 300 passengers, homeward bound for Liverpool.

I was directed to proceed, not to Freetown, but across the South Atlantic to Port of Spain in Trinidad Island, at the south-eastern edge of the Caribbean Sea. That region was under the protection of the United States

Navy. Ten months previously, in September 1940, Britain had given the U.S. a ninety-nine year lease of bases in Jamaica, St Lucia, Trinidad, Antigua, and British Guiana, in exchange for fifty destroyers. The American policy of "lend-lease" implied the American protection of British and other Allied shipping in American waters, including the Caribbean region.

The whole direction of war on land in Europe had drastically changed with the German invasion of Russia on 22nd June 1941. Britain now had an ally. On 12th July, the Anglo-Soviet Agreement was signed in Moscow, for mutual assistance against "Hitlerite Germany," with no separate peace. Britain's war against Germany had then been in progress for nearly two years, during which Russia had given assistance to Germany, but none to Britain. Now it was different, even though, at the outset, the German Blitzkrieg offensive into Russia had met with successes on the pattern that had already become familiar elsewhere.

German strategy was now irrevocably committed to military action in Eastern Europe and North Africa, with naval and air attacks against Britain in the west. There was no respite in the Battle of the Atlantic, but gradually the ferocity of the German counter blockade of Britain would diminish as measures were taken to meet it. The actively friendly attitude of the U.S.A. foreshadowed eventual American participation in the war on our side. In the meantime, facilities for refuelling British ships at Trinidad enabled vessels going home from Cape Town to put in there, instead of at Freetown, taking a track less liable to U-boat attack than on the route along the West Coast of Africa, and across the Bay of Biscay.

The *Franconia* made the passage from Cape Town to Trinidad, 5628 miles, in fifteen days, at an average speed of 15 knots, and anchored at Port of Spain on 4th August.

After taking in 2300 tons of oil and 945 tons of fresh water, we put to sea on 5th August. Twelve days later, we let go the anchor in the Mersey. The passage from Trinidad to the Mersey was 4499 miles by zigzag.

It was a pleasant summer, even though the news was that the Germans were hammering at the gates of Moscow and Leningrad, and a new menace was looming up. The Japanese, though neutral in the European war, began to expand their military activities in China and Southeast Asia, and now took French Indochina under their "protection." There was already a Tripartite Pact of mutual assistance between Germany, Italy, and Japan. It had become clearer that the U.S.A. would eventually have to intervene in the war, if only to counterbalance Japanese aggression in the Pacific. The question was: When?

I had five weeks' holiday at Cheltenham and rejoined the *Franconia* at Liverpool on 23rd September 1941. She was being got ready for another convoy to the Middle East. On 30th September, she put to sea from the Mersey, in a convoy of nine transports, and next day we joined up with thirteen more transports from the Clyde. In the *Franconia* I had 3114 troops and twelve nurses. With a crew of 335, I had 3461 souls on board — a crowd!

After calls at Freetown and Durban, we arrived at Suez on 2nd December 1941 — nine weeks out from Liverpool.

The *Franconia* remained only two days at Suez, embarked 296 troops, loaded 732 bags of mail, and left for Aden.

While we were in the Red Sea, on 8th December 1941, the news came through of the Japanese attack on the American Fleet at Pearl Harbour in the Hawaiian Islands.

Britain now had another ally.

The U.S.A. had entered the war. The Great Powers were now all in it, on one side or the other, committed to a struggle that would decide the course of history for centuries.

My instructions were to proceed from Aden to Berbera, the port of British Somaliland. There we arrived on 10th December 1941, and embarked 1435 Italian prisoners of war and a guard of 95 of the Royal African Rifles. Five days later we berthed at Mombasa in Kenya, landed the prisoners and their guard, and loaded 1500 tons of cargo, chiefly bags of coffee. On 23rd December we berthed at Durban, for the third Christmas of the war — this time far from home — and with no sign of "peace on earth," yet.

The Japanese Air Force had proved itself to be a formidable striking force. In the attack on Pearl Harbour, entirely airborne, the Japanese, with heavy bombs and torpedoes, had sunk four U.S. battleships, one auxiliary battleship, and one destroyer, and had heavily damaged ten other U.S.N. vessels, including four battleships and two cruisers. Then, three days later, on 10th December 1941, two British battleships, *H.M.S. Prince of Wales* and *H.M.S. Repulse*, were sunk by Japanese air attack off the Malayan coast.

If it was not known before, it was now proved for all time that ships are extremely vulnerable to air attack. When aircraft could sink great armoured ships, grim prospects opened for thin hulled troop transports!

My orders now were to put the *Franconia* into dry dock at Durban, for overhaul and painting, and afterwards to load cargo at Durban and Cape Town, for Liverpool.

On 15th January 1942, we left Cape Town, carrying 3542 tons of cargo, 3914 bags of mail, and 459 passengers, with directions to make for Freetown. There we arrived on 24th January and refuelled. My orders then were to proceed to Trinidad, to avoid air attacks which were being made off the Bay of Biscay.

On 26th January, alone and unescorted, the *Franconia* put to sea from Freetown, and, proceeding almost due westerly across the Atlantic in the vicinity of 10 deg. N. Lat., anchored on 5th February in the harbour of Port of Spain, Trinidad, after a passage of 3720 miles by zigzag.

There were a large number of oil tankers in the port, also American warships and merchant vessels. This was considered a safe refuelling and watering depot, believed to be beyond the reach of U-boats.

As my Chief Engineer reported that the electric generator required repairs, we lay at anchor a few days after refuelling, while parts of the generator were sent to repair shops on shore. Our anchorage was a mile from the wharves.

On 9th February a launch came off from the shore, with the Cunard agent, who had received a cable message in code from the Company's head office in Liverpool. He asked to see me in my cabin, alone, and there, in secrecy, handed the message to me. It read: "Land at Trinidad with all your gear and await further orders. Staff Captain Birtenshaw will take the ship home to Liverpool." This could only mean that I was to be given command of another ship due to arrive at Trinidad soon. I had not expected a transfer to occur in a port which seemed a long way from anywhere.

Such changes were usually made in home ports, after the completion of a voyage. I was sorry indeed to leave the *Franconia*, after having been in command of her for two years and eight months, most of that time on war service. As a transport she had made ten voyages, had steamed 120,000 miles, and had carried a total of 29,800 military passengers. That was one British liner's contribution to the war effort, and not exceptional, for many others had similar records of service.

The news soon got around that I was leaving. My steward, Williams — the "Captain's Tiger," who had been with me also, before the war, in the *Berengaria* — helped me to pack my gear, in two trunks, which together weighed 320 pounds. I had various uniforms, besides tropical whites, also greatcoats, woollens and cottons for all climes, instruments, books, papers, and all the personal paraphernalia that one accumulates with ample living space in a Captain's cabin and chartroom. The Cunard agent informed me that he had arranged accommodation for me on shore.

I was sorry that I could not take my steward with me, but he had signed on in the *Franconia* for the voyage. As we packed, he said to me, confidentially, "According to the Galley Gazette, sir, you're going to be given command of the *Queen Mary*!"

"Rubbish!" I said, with a smile. The Galley Gazette was the name of an imaginary newspaper, spreading rumours which were rife on shipboard at all times, but especially so in wartime. "Guess again!" I told him. "There are plenty of other Cunarders."

I scarcely gave the matter another thought. It was no use guessing what ship I would be joining next, but the *Queen Mary* was not among my surmises. As far as I knew, she and the *Queen Elizabeth* were transporting troops from Australia to Suez, beyond the reach of the U-boats infesting the Atlantic.

What the future might hold was so unpredictable that it would be a waste of time to guess at it. At this time the Japanese were driving south in Malaya, threatening Singapore, and had landed in the East Indies and in New Guinea. It was possible that an invasion of Australia might be attempted. In that case there would be ample work for the two Queens and other transports in the Indian and Pacific Oceans.

During the day, while I was packing, several deputations of seamen, firemen, and stewards came to bid me farewell. Among them I noticed men who at various times had been brought up before me for punishment for leave breaking and other minor offences. As they shook hands with me, they grinned happily, probably thinking, "Well, you won't have the pleasure of logging us any more!" I thought it showed a good spirit that they came to bid me a friendly farewell; but seafarers are like that. If they do wrong and the Captain gives them a fair hearing and a square deal, they bear no malice.

Next day, 10th February 1942, before lunch, the ship's officers of the navigating, engineer, and catering departments, and the gunners and military staff, asked me to come to a farewell party in the lounge. After a couple of rounds of drinks, the Chief Engineer (Claude Shore) made a little speech, and presented me with a clock. "It isn't much of a clock, as clocks go — and we hope this one goes — but it is the best that we could get on shore, in this port, at this time, at such short notice," he said, "and our hearts are in it, and we hope that it will tick a long time for you, and that it will go with you, wherever you go!"

The warmth of these sentiments, in such unusual circumstances, overwhelmed me. How could I know that I would ever see any of those men again? I couldn't think of any corny jokes to cheer the occasion. "Seamen are used to partings," I said, "but this is different. I thank you for all that you have done while we have been shipmates. I wish you all, and the old *Franconia*, the best of luck... " Then I had to stop speaking, or I would have dissolved in tears...". and a good voyage home," I concluded, "on this voyage and every other."

After lunch it was time for me to go. The launch was alongside, with my baggage on board. After a handshake all round, I was just stepping on to the side ladder, when my steward, Williams — he would be Bert Birtenshaw's steward now stepped up to me and said, "Wouldn't you like to take Ginger with you, sir, to keep you company?"

Ginger was a tiny golden kitten that he had picked up a few weeks previously in a Cape Town cafe and had brought on board hidden in his pocket. She had lived in my cabin, a playful waif, and every chair cover had her claw marks and hairs on it. But she demanded too much attention. At night, sometimes, when I would try to relax by playing a game of "patience," she would watch every move of my hands intently for a few minutes, then spring on the table and scatter all the cards. To part from her now meant that I was really leaving my ship. Would it be saving her life if I took her ashore and then into my new ship? After a few moments' hesitation, I said to the steward, "She'll be better where she is! You keep her, and look, after her for me."

At the moment when I stepped into the launch, Birtenshaw became Master of the *Franconia*. She was his ship now. He followed me down the ladder, and boarded the launch, to accompany me to the shore. He ordered the coxswain to take a turn slowly round the ship, while the crew manned the rails and gave three cheers. Then we made for the shore. It was the first time I had ever left a ship in that way, handing over command in mid-voyage, and with a "send off." Such occasions are rare in the Merchant Navy, and this one was almost more than I could bear.

As she faded into the distance, my heart went down into my boots. Bert tried to cheer me up, but he wasn't feeling too happy either. A big responsibility had suddenly devolved upon him, and he was well able to take it, but neither of us looked forward to parting as shipmates. At the landing steps we said a glassy eyed goodbye, and Bert shoved off to return to his *Franconia*, leaving me alone on the quay, a stranger, a Captain without a ship.

CHAPTER ENDNOTES

(1) "Happy as Larry" is an informal idiom that means to be extremely happy or carefree. The idiom is believed to have originated in Australia and New Zealand in the 1870s. One theory is that it comes from the name of a successful Australian boxer named Larry Foley. Another theory is that the word "Larry" comes from the Australian slang word "larrikin," which means a hooligan or a happy-go-lucky teen.

35

The Zenith of Ambition — Appointed to Command the "Queen Mary" — A Delay at Trinidad — Waiting for a "Monster" — U-boats in the Caribbean Sea — My Hurried Departure by Flying-boat — I Nearly Miss My Ship — Alighting at Miami — A Night Drive to Key West — A Tug Voyage in a Choppy Sea — Steak and Chips for Breakfast — An Anchorage far Offshore — Going Aboard Under Difficulties — Captain Townley Hands Over to Me — Meeting the Officers — First American Troops for Australia — The Anchor's Weighed — No Use Worrying Too Much.

ASHORE at Port of Spain, Trinidad, at 4 p.m. on 10th February 1942, I was met by the Cunard agents, in an atmosphere of hush-hush. They professed not to know why I was in Trinidad, and they wouldn't even venture an opinion. All hotels in the town being full, they found a comfortable apartment for me in "Kent House" on the outskirts of the town. I had a flat with lounge, bedroom, kitchen, bathroom and veranda, amidst lovely tropical gardens, and a black married couple to look after me.

Next day I visited the Naval Control Office. There I was told, as a profound secret, that the *Queen Mary* was due in ten or twelve days, and that I was to take command of her when she arrived!

The Naval Control Officer said, "She'll be calling here, outward bound from Boston to Australia. You are to relieve Captain Townley. That's all I know, and it's hush-hush. Not a word to be spoken to anybody. I'll send word to you in your diggings when she's nearing port. You'll have about ten days to wait."

I went out into the street with my mind in a whirl. So, the Galley Gazette rumour had been a good guess! I was then fifty-eight years of age, and had been going to sea for forty-three years, including thirty-five years in the Cunard service. I had been a Captain in Cunarders for eleven years. I was now one of the Senior Cunard Captains, and as such I was eligible to be given command of the *Queen Mary*; yet I had not been expecting that promotion there and then!

I went to the Cunard agents' office, to see if any further information would be forthcoming. They knew quite well that I was to take over the *Queen Mary*, and they knew that I knew, but we fenced along with one another, and her name was not mentioned. The nearest was a hint, "Very confidentially, not to be mentioned at all, one of the Monsters may be putting into this port soon!"

"The Monsters" was an American waterfront term, used in New York to describe the *Queen Mary, Queen Elizabeth*, and *Normandie*. By a sad coincidence, news reached Trinidad that day that the gigantic French liner *Normandie* had caught fire at her berth in New York on the preceding day, 9th February 1942. Sabotage was suspected but never proved. The fire raged down below. In the course of firefighting operations, she had filled with water on one side, broken her moorings and rolled over, to sink and lie submerged on her side at the pier — a total loss, as far as any plan to put her into war service was concerned.

Now there were only two "Monsters" in service. That term was one which no one who ever served in either of the two Queens would use to describe them. It implied that they were ungainly or monstrous, which was quite wrong! It was only a joke, arising from the secrecy that avoided mentioning their names and so attempted to conceal their movements.

The *Queen Mary* and *Queen Elizabeth* had called at Trinidad on their first voyages outwards from New York to Australia. Being designed for peacetime service in the North Atlantic, their steaming range was normally limited to 4000 miles, as they took in oil and fresh water at the end of each crossing. In an emergency they had an extreme range of not more than 6000 miles.

This made it necessary for them to put into an intermediate port between New York and Cape Town. Replenishments of fresh water were as essential as oil fuel, and more so when large numbers of troops were carried, increasing the amount of water required for cooking, washing, and other essential needs, besides that used in the boilers.

It was difficult to preserve secrecy when one of the Queens was expected at a port such as Port of Spain. She would require 6000 tons of oil fuel and 4000 tons of fresh water, besides a few hundred tons of locally procured foodstuffs to replenish her stores. Time was required to get all this in readiness. The huge amounts required caused everyone concerned to make surmises based on previous experience. Also, extra navigational aids, such as buoys or landmarks, were installed in the harbour approaches. The local folk soon learned to connect these with the arrival of a "Monster."

But the motto was, "Sealed lips save ships," and no one would dream of spreading gossip which might come to the notice of German Naval Intelligence. It was thought that the Caribbean Sea and the American shore were beyond the range of U-boats. In this mistaken belief a large number of vessels, including tankers, navigated in those waters unescorted, and even with their lights showing.

A rude awakening was s0on to come. At that very time (as revealed in the post-war memoirs of Admiral Doenitz) a number of long- range U-boats were making their way westward across the Atlantic. They were refuelled in mid-ocean from large submarine tankers which were known as "milch cows." Some of these U-boats, in February 1942, were making for Trinidad, and others for Oruba and Curacao in Dutch Guiana, where oil tankers congregated:

I took things quietly for a week at Kent House, but, as the day of the *Queen Mary* 's expected arrival drew near, I was tense in anticipation of taking command of one of the two biggest ships in the world, and that under wartime risks. In the early months of the war, it had been officially decided that the *Queen Mary* was too big to be risked on war service. It had been said then that to fill her with troops would be "putting too many eggs in one basket," and that she would present such a big target to U-boats and aircraft that they couldn't miss.

But Lord Nelson's dictum, "You must leave something to chance," had been remembered and applied in the decision to risk her, and the *Queen Elizabeth*, in service as transports, and rightly so, for no war at sea could ever be won by ships rotting in harbours.

On the night of Thursday, 19th February 1942, I went to bed early at Kent House, wondering, "Will tomorrow be the day?"

Just as I was dozing off, at 11 p.m., I heard two muffled explosions from the direction of the harbour, four miles away. These were followed by the sounds of aircraft roaring overhead at a low level, and then I fell asleep.

At 6 a.m. I was awakened by the servant with a cup of tea. "Terble tings happen last night, terble tings!" she exclaimed. "Ships sunk in de harbour. Everybody all excited!"

Vaguely remembering the muffled explosions that I had heard, I sprang out of bed in dismay. Had the *Queen Mary* arrived and been sunk? I wondered. "Was it a big ship?" I asked, anxiously.

"Ah doant know, massa. I heerd it was two oil tankers sunk!"

This was somewhat reassuring, but my thoughts were racing. If a U-boat had entered the harbour of Port of Spain, it and possibly others would still be in the vicinity. The *Queen Mary* would be diverted from Trinidad! I would miss my ship!

While I was considering this miserable possibility, the telephone bell rang. "Naval Control speaking. All plans are changed. We want you to go to Miami in Florida, U.S.A., by the flying boat service, leaving Trinidad flying boat port today at twelve noon. You will require a passport and a visa to enter the U.S.A. You will be allowed to take only forty-five pounds of baggage. The Cunard agents will provide you with a ticket to Miami. If I may say so, sir, you will need to hustle to get a British passport and a U.S. visa in the time available. Kindly call at this office for orders before you go out to the airport."

It is not my habit to argue with the Navy, but on this occasion I did so. "You said that I can take only forty-five pounds weight of baggage?" I asked.

"That's right. This is a civilian airline, and that is their limit for each passenger."

"I have all my uniforms, tropical clothing, books and instruments, weighing 320 pounds, and I'm bound for a country a great distance from here, and God only knows where after that. I must have my baggage. Please see what you can do about it!"

"We'll let you know!" said the bored voice at the other end of the line.

Ten minutes later, the phone rang again, and the same bored voice said, "All right, Captain. We've spoken to the airways company, and you can take all your baggage. See you later. 'Bye." Before I had finished breakfast, the Cunard agent was at my door with a utility truck. "I've booked your airline ticket," he said, "and as a special favour they'll take all your baggage — but we'll have to hustle to get your passport and visa through. Officials in (the)Port of Spain aren't used to hustle!"

After I had said hasty goodbyes to my Kent House friends, we pushed off, loaded with baggage, and made for the Passport Office. The agent explained matters there, as far as was necessary, to a sleepy looking clerk, emphasizing the need for urgency. "Waal," said the clerk, scratching his ear, "I opine that I will have to give you an Emergency Passport. I've never issued one of these before, but we have forms somewhere here-if I can find them. You will need three photographs of yourself," he told me. "They are essential I am positive of that!"

We dashed off to a local ten-cent store. Here we found a miraculous slot machine that took photos "while you wait." I dropped a coin into the slot, grinned, pulled a lever. After three minutes whirring and clanking, a photo dropped out. I did this three times, and we hurried back to the Passport Office with the results.

There the clerk proudly produced three faded and frayed Emergency Passport forms, which looked as though they had been lying in the bottom of a drawer for fifty years. Writing laboriously with a pen that had a crossed nib, he took half an hour to fill up the forms, then affixed wax seals and the photos, collected a fee, and advised us to go to the U.S. Consulate for a visa.

After more delay there, we had the documents complete, and arrived at

The Sikorsky S-42 Pan Am Flying Boat "Brazilian Clipper" was used to connect Miami and Brazil, with stops that included Trinidad, during WW2. (Public Domain, Library of Congress)

the Naval Control Office' at 11 a.m. There I was given my orders — to disembark from the plane at Miami and proceed by bus to Key West, where a U.S-naval officer would meet me with further instructions.

We hastened to the Cunard agent's office, collected my baggage, and dashed out to the airport, arriving there with only three minutes to spare. I was feeling acutely aware of another dictum of Lord Nelson: "Lose not an hour!"

This was the first time that I had ever been in an aeroplane. I had the usual qualms of first voyagers. The "Sikorsky" flying boat was a civil aviation aircraft on a regular scheduled run from Buenos Aires to New York, with many intermediate stops, some of them overnight. The distance by her route from Port of Spain to Miami would be 1600 miles, taking most of two days, with an overnight stop at Porto Rico — slow travelling in comparison with airline schedules afterwards to be developed, but wonderfully speedy, to my way of thinking in 1942, in comparison with surface transits by sea.

The Sikorsky was, literally, a flying boat — a hull with wings — and that made her all the more wonderful to me. She was loaded with twenty-two passengers, four crew, and ten tons of mail and baggage, including my bulky 320 pounds weight of trunks. With a deafening roar and a huge bow wave she tore across the bay at noon, and was airborne — I felt helpless and useless, and resigned to that situation. If a ship's engine stops in mid-ocean, there you are; but if a plane's engine stops in mid-air, where are you?

Our course to the northward skirted the island chain of the Lesser Antilles. Presently, over the mountainous island of Tobago, we encountered air pockets and the flying boat bounced up and down. I began to feel squeamish and visualized the rather humiliating spectacle of the Captain to-be of the *Queen Mary* being sick into a brown paper bag. But before this dreadful thing could happen we were out of the air pockets and into plain sailing, or plain flying.

At 4 p.m. we alighted at San Juan, Puerto Rico, and went ashore in a launch to spend the night at the Condado Hotel.

Next morning, Saturday, 21st February 1942, we took off again at 9 a.m., and, with two ports of call, in Haiti and Cuba, alighted at Miami at 6.15 p.m.

Ashore by launch with the other passengers, I found that my Emergency Passport and large quantity of luggage made me an object of suspicion to the U.S. Customs and Immigration officials. They were on the lookout for smugglers, and possibly also for German spies. I could not explain to them exactly why I was arriving in that way, wearing a British merchant sea captain's uniform, and with a smudgy British passport of a kind that they had never seen before, adorned with photos taken in a slot machine, and with such a great amount of luggage.

These officials had not been told to clear me through. They insisted on examining my luggage and found more uniforms there! Very suspicious! I told them that I was under orders to proceed to the Naval Office at Key West without delay. That was as much as I could properly say. I believe that they detained me while they phoned through to Key West to verify my story. Cleared at last, I got a taxi truck to take me and my luggage to the bus station-only to find that the bus for Key West (130 miles away) had left ten minutes previously.

The next bus would be leaving in three hours' time Porto Rico at 1 a.m., the "owl express," filled with revellers. Would I be in time, or would I miss my ship after all? "Waste not an hour!" I put a phone call through to the

Naval Control Office at Key West and reported my situation. I was told to take the 1 a.m. bus.

Beginning to feel bedraggled, I went to an hotel in Miami, had a hot bath and a late supper, and boarded the bus in good time. The bus route was southwards along the shore from Miami for thirty miles, and then for nearly 100 miles along the embankment of Florida Keys. I dozed fitfully, and was dumped out at Key West at 5.30 a.m.

A young naval officer met me. He took me to the U.S. Naval Club. In a few minutes I was turned in and sleeping soundly. He called me with a cup of coffee at 7.30 a.m., and then escorted me to the Naval Control Office.

There I was informed that the *Queen Mary* was being refuelled at an anchorage twenty-three miles offshore. A naval tug was in readiness to take me out to her. The reason why she was being refuelled off Key West instead of at Trinidad was the presence of U-boats at and near Trinidad and elsewhere in the Caribbean. Apart from the ships which the U-boats had sunk in Port of Spain, they had played merry hell at Curacao and Oruba, sinking a number of tankers which were riding at anchor in those ports, fully lit. The Naval Control Officer gave me my "route orders" to take the *Queen Mary* on from Key West to Rio de Janeiro; "You'll have escort," he said, grimly, " — and you'll need it!"

At 8.30 a.m., I boarded the naval tug, in which my baggage was already stowed. Just as we were leaving, two very young Ensigns asked if they might come along to have a look at the *Queen Mary* ! Not much secrecy, then, as to her presence off Key West! "If the tugmaster agrees, and promises to bring you back, I have no objection," I said. "But don't try to stow away!" They jumped aboard and we shoved off.

The tugmaster, a hard bitten old Chief Petty Officer, made us comfortable on the settee of the pilot house, which was also the galley. We cleared the breakwaters, and, with a fresh south-westerly wind and a choppy sea, the tug began cutting capers. We stood on, doing a steady six knots, with heavy sprays breaking over her blunt bows. She was shuddering in every rivet as she plunged and bucketed about. The cook now came into the pilothouse, to begin preparing breakfast.

"Sir," he said to me, "I've been a sea cook for forty years, and it will be the greatest honour of my life to blow that I've cooked a meal for the Captain of the biggest ship in the world!"

"He usually cooks meals only for me," remarked the tugmaster, sarcastically.

"And this tug is the smallest ship in the world, or damn near it," said the cook. "And what will you have for breakfast, sir? Steak and fried potatoes? I hope so, because that's all we have!"

"Steak and fried potatoes will be just the thing," I assured him. Tying on his apron, and grinning broadly, the cook switched on the electric hot plate in the corner of the pilothouse and began slicing potatoes. In a few minutes a beautiful aroma of sizzling fat filled the pilothouse, and a light blue haze eddied out through the lee door.

As the tug was now rolling and pitching heavily, I glanced at the two young Ensigns, who were sitting very silently beside me on the settee. They were green round the gills. "Want breakfast?" the cook asked them.

"No, we've had it," they gasped, and they both went hurriedly out on deck, for a breath of fresh air. I could sympathize with them. My thoughts went back to the day, forty-three years previously, when I had first put to sea as an apprentice in the barque *County of Pembroke*, and I had been very seasick as soon as we had crossed the Mersey Bar. The Mate had made me drink a pint of sea water. That had cured me, and I had never been seasick since then! But I hesitated to recommend this cure to the two young Ensigns.

Despite some difficulty in controlling the tray and the dishes, I enjoyed my breakfast, complimented the cook on his culinary prowess, then settled down to help the tugmaster find the *Queen Mary*. There was a light mist, cutting visibility down to five miles, but, after three hours' steaming, steering by compass, we sighted her dead ahead. Her blurred outline gave her the appearance of a great rock set in the middle of the sea. I went aft to look for the two Ensigns but found them collapsed in the middle of a coil of towing-hawser, beyond caring if the *Queen Mary* was in sight or not.

Two U.S. destroyers were patrolling around the anchored ship, on the lookout for U-boats. As we drew nearer, I could make out two tankers, one moored on each side of her, amidships, feeding her with oil fuel and fresh water. Though the tankers were vessels of 6000 tons, they were dwarfed by her tremendous bulk. Gazing up at her, almost from sea level on the tug's deck, I felt overawed at the responsibility soon to be mine and realized then that this was the supreme moment of my nautical career. From the half-deck of a Cape Horn barque to the bridge of the *Queen Mary* had been a long climb.

With such a sea running, it was going to be a difficult job to get the tug alongside, but the tugmaster had a staunch heart, and knew his work. The *Queen Mary* was lying to one anchor, head-on to the wind, with seventy-five fathoms of cable out, and yawing through fifty degrees. Watching his chance when she yawed to starboard and made a temporary lee, he ran up alongside the star- board tanker. The tanker's crew threw a heaving line, which was deftly caught, and a bow rope was passed up to the tanker's deck. With his men tending this skilfully, the tugmaster let the tug fall back slowly until the rope took the strain, and then she gradually got alongside and was made fast forward and aft.

The tug was jumping heavily — sometimes level with the tanker's deck, and, a few seconds later, lying ten feet below with seas sloshing up between the two vessels and drenching everybody. I looked up beyond the tanker to the bridge of the *Queen Mary* , 100 feet above the deck of the tug on which I stood. On the wing of the bridge several officers were leaning over the rail of the starboard "cab,″ peering down at the proceedings. Among them I could recognize Captain John Townley and Staff Captain Harry Grattidge. The rails of the upper passenger decks were crowded with thousands of American troops, singing out comments intended to be funny, in the manner of troops in transports the world over.

I had an audience! "Don't get wet!" the troops yelled.

Sound advice, as we were already dripping wet. A Jacob's ladder was thrown over from the tanker. A rope was lowered with a bowline passed under my armpits, the other end held by willing hands above. Waiting for a lull, I made a jump for it, and landed on the tanker's deck safely, but wet to the skin. Next, my baggage was slung on board. As the last box reached the tanker's deck, the tug's bow rope carried away with a crack like a rifle shot, and she sheered off. "Bon voyage!" I heard the tugmaster sing out. His mission accomplished, he pointed in the general direction of Key West and was soon lost to view in the murk astern. The two Ensigns were now in his pilothouse. They had seen the *Queen Mary.*

Stepping from the heaving tanker through a side door, I was met by some of the officers and took an elevator up six decks to the Captain's cabin under the bridge. Captain John Townley welcomed me there. He had reached the Cunard Company's retiring age of sixty- three years and was not happy at having to retire from the sea, but the rules were inflexible.

He told me that the *Queen Mary* had left Boston two days previously. She had on board 8398 U.S. troops and 905 crew — total 9303 souls. This was the biggest number of troops ever embarked in one transport until that time, and the first contingent of U.S. troops to be sent to Australia. Because of her speed (30 knots), she voyaged alone and not in convoy but was escorted in coastal waters by relays of U.S. cruisers and destroyers, with air patrols.

Captain Townley told me that he had been ordered to proceed to Trinidad, but because of U-boat activity had been diverted to Key West. I knew something about this and could tell him what had happened at Trinidad; but he really surprised me when he informed me that, on the previous night, ten ships — most of them tankers — had been torpedoed near the *Queen Mary* 's track. "I consider that I'm mighty lucky to have arrived here!" he added.

The ship was anchored twenty-three miles out because, with her great draught (approximately 40 feet) and the choppy seas, it was not prudent to anchor in anything less than ten fathoms (60 feet). He would hand over command to me on the following morning and would then go ashore to Key West by a naval tug.

After I had changed into dry clothes, Townley and I spent two hours at paperwork, as he handed over to me all manner of information about the ship and her crew. Attached to the ship was a Military Permanent Staff of 157, British and American, including the quartering officers and provosts, and 100 gunners.

The next formality and necessary procedure was to invite the Heads of Departments into the Captain's cabin to meet me. These included the Staff Captain and Chief Officer; the Chief Engineer and Staff Chief Engineer; the Surgeon, the Purser, the Chief Steward; and the Commandant and Deputy Commandant of the Military Permanent Staff. Only the military men were strangers to me. All the others had been shipmates with me on various voyages, in Cunard ships, during the preceding thirty-five years when they and I had been climbing the long ladder of promotion. We had those memories in common.

That night, while Townley was finishing his packing, I was accommodated temporarily in a spare cabin next to his, under the bridge. It was a restless night for me. I could scarcely sleep a wink. Next morning, 23rd February 1942, at 9 a.m., after we had visited the bridge and chartroom together, Captain Townley formally handed over command of the *Queen Mary* to me. The weather had moderated, and a tug ranged alongside without difficulty to embark him. The crew and troops gave him a rousing cheer. I could well imagine his feelings, as I had been through a somewhat similar ordeal on leaving the *Franconia* thirteen days previously.

He was to go by train from Key West to New York and then home — as a passenger.

My first action as Captain was to step onto the bridge. My old shipmate Harry Grattidge, Staff Captain, called up the junior officers to the bridge to meet me. There were many of them, of the various departments, and some I had not previously known. I felt it essential to know and sum up each officer personally. They came up to the bridge in relays throughout the morning, and I spoke to each one for a few minutes.

The tankers remained alongside, and the destroyers were in the offing, patrolling on the lookout for U-boats. The tankers would act as a buffer against torpedoes if a U-boat sneaked up to within firing range. I doubt if their captains appreciated that situation as much as we did!

I could not leave the anchorage without naval orders. These were slow in coming. A thorough naval and air patrol was being made of the route that we would take. I made an inspection of the ship in all her departments, as far as this was possible in one day. The troops, though crowded, seemed to have settled down well. Large numbers of games of dice were in progress.

This was the first time that American troops had ever been embarked in the *Queen Mary* . They were "draftees" (conscripts) only partly trained, and most of them had never been to sea before: Some of them whiled away the time by carving their names on the teakwood rails. After conferring with the Military Commandant, I decided not to make a fuss about this. These men might soon be going into battle, and some of them would never return to their homes and loved ones. Let them amuse themselves!

Hard to take, especially for an old sailing ship man, such as myself, were the blobs of chewing gum spattering the decks. The seamen bitterly complained that they had to use scrapers to get it off. As there were miles of decks to clean, this was no joke. Yet we had to take that, too. After all, there was a war on. We had to grin and bear more than chewing gum stuck to the decks and bulkheads. She wasn't a luxury liner now. She was only a troop transport! On Wednesday, 25th February, 1942, I received naval orders to put to sea and continue the voyage. We then had in the tanks 8300 tons of oil fuel and 6500 tons of fresh water, besides 1000 tons of consumable stores on board.

At 4 p.m., I gave the order to heave up the anchor. I went out to the starboard wing of the bridge, to watch the immense mud- hook come out of the water. Then I ordered "Full speed ahead," and set the course.

She was under way! I believe that I am a modest person, but at that moment, I admit, I had a feeling of pride at being in command of such a magnificent vessel.

Such a moment can come to a seaman only once in his life, when he attains what he knows is the zenith of his ambition. After that, there is little further time for thinking about himself. He must think of his ship. His duty is to bring her into port.

That requires attention to details. In big ships or little, sea routines are the same. The principles of seamanship and navigation apply in all ships. In bigger ships, there are more specialists to attend to details than in small ships, but finally the executive responsibility is the Captain's. Whether he lets that worry him too much, too little, or not at all, depends on his temperament, and on his previous experience.

I was not worrying too much.

*My Voyages in the "Queen Mary" — The First American Troops
Taken to Australia — U-boats in the Caribbean Sea — A fire in Mid-
ocean — Invasion Scare at Sydney — Heavy Weather South of
Tasmania — Taking Ameri- can Troops to Britain — British
Reinforcements for the Middle East — The Battle of El Alamein —
Turning Point in the War — German Prisoners in the "Queen Mary"
— I am Awarded the C.B.E. — Fifteen Thousand Troops in one
Transport — "Standee" Beds and Two Meals a Day — An Acoustic
Mine Explodes — More Grey Hairs for the Captain.*

S O began my voyaging, in command of the *Queen Mary*, and later of
the *Queen Elizabeth*, which, for five years, during the war and the
war's aftermath, were extensive and hazardous.

Most of my wartime service, from 1942 to 1945 was in the *Queen Mary*.
Her record as a troop transport, in the total number of troops carried and
mileages steamed, has never been surpassed, though it was almost equalled
by that of the *Queen Elizabeth*. My notes of these voyages will indicate the
massive movements of troops in these two vessels, which in wartime were
veiled in secrecy.

For narrative convenience, I set down the dates of these voyages in
numbered sequence, but referring only to those on which I was in command
(i.e., not including voyages which the ships made under other commanders
while I was occasionally on leave); but the Queens continued in service while

Voyage 1	Key West - Sydney, Australia			
(Troops 8,398, Crew 905. Total 9303 souls)				
Location	Status	Date	Miles	Km
Key West	depart	25-Feb-42		
Rio de Janerio	arrive	6-Mar-42	5,787	9,313
	depart	8-Mar-42		
Cape Town	arrive	14-Mar-42	3,401	5,473
	depart	15-Mar-42		
Freemantle	arrive	23-Mar-42	4,801	7,726
	depart	24-Mar-42		
Sydney	arrive	28-Mar-42	2,377	3,825
Ship: R.M.S. *Queen Mary*		TOTAL	16,366	26,338

their captains and crews had leave ashore in relays, and their full story is much greater than any one man's recollection of it.

On leaving the anchorage off Key West, I set course as directed on a western sweep around Cuba, then easterly into the Caribbean Sea, where we belted along at 30 knots, on a circuitous course, avoiding the usual steamer tracks, and zigzagging. The destroyers had left us, being unable to keep up that cracking pace for long, but U.S. air patrols kept us in sight.

To get out of the Caribbean Sea eastwards to the Atlantic Ocean, I was directed to use the Anegada Passage, off the Virgin Islands. I did not like the look of it on the chart, knowing that U-boats would probably be lurking in the channels between the islands. I liked it still less when we approached the passage in bright daylight with calm weather and perfect visibility. Speed and zigzag were our chief defence against U-boat attack. At 30 knots the *Queen Mary* could outrun a submerged U-boat and could perhaps even outrun torpedoes unless they were fired from very short range, for their speed also is not much more than thirty knots.

The Anegada Passage is too narrow for a good zigzag at 30 knots, but we pressed on, zigzagging, and swerved through without mishap. We sighted only a tramp steamer, which was doing ten knots. Half an hour later, we picked up an S O S call. That tramp steamer had been torpedoed ten miles astern of the *Queen Mary*. The U-boat commander had missed his big chance and must have been a very disappointed man.

One of the cruel necessities of the war at sea was the order not to answer S O S calls. These were sometimes sent out as a ruse of war by the enemy, to attract vessels to his vicinity. Even if the call were genuine, it would be answered only by naval vessels equipped with ASDIC and depth charges. The *Queen Mary*, like all other troop transports, was under naval orders to stand on, at the prescribed courses and speeds, and never to stop at sea for rescue work or to answer distress calls — or even if a man fell overboard!

At Rio we anchored in the Roads, to be refuelled and watered from tankers which came alongside. Seldom except at New York did the *Queen Mary* go alongside wharves. It was safer to lie in mid-stream. With her great length, she needed three-quarters of a mile of swinging room at anchor, with a depth of at least forty-five feet all round. Few harbours have such anchorage room in their inner basins.

In peacetime her anchors were seldom used. In wartime they were put to a full test. It was always a thrill to see the 16-ton anchor let go, to plunge into the water on its cable of steel links, each link weighing 224 pounds. What a splash and rattle that made!

While we lay at Rio, the German radio announced our arrival there and threatened that we would be sunk on leaving.

This may have been "war of nerves," but in such cases who can tell who's bluffing? We hove up the anchor at 5 p.m., and cleared out of Rio in the dusk, driving on at full speed, with not a light showing. A few days later we heard on the Japanese radio that the *Queen Mary* had been sunk. When this was reported to me by the Senior Wireless Officer, I said to him, "Keep it under your hat. Don't let the troops know that we've been sunk. It might worry them."

When we were in the South Atlantic, 1500 miles from land, and unescorted, I had a real fright. Soon after midnight, when all seemed serene, the fire alarm sounded on the bridge. I sprang from my settee in the chartroom, and almost instantly smelled smoke! Such an emergency was well provided for in the ship's design. There was a fire station, with men always on duty, and others instantly at call, under control of the Master-at-Arms. In the fire station are large scale plans of the ship, fitted with automatic indicators showing exactly where a fire has broken out. This is done not only by electric alarm bells, but also by an automatic device which draws air through tubes from every part of the ship to the fire station. Smoke drawn with the air through one of these tubes activates a photo-electric cell, which shows the firewatcher where the fire is. On the bridge is an indicator panel, showing the seat of the fire.

I knew immediately that fire had broken out in the deckhead of a compartment on B Deck, below the bridge. This was due to a fault in the insulation of electric wiring. In a few seconds the fire brigade was in action. That part of the ship was sealed off.

The troops, of whom one hundred were quartered in the compartment that had caught fire, showed perfect discipline, and there was no panic — most of the men in other parts of the ship were not aware of the fire alarm.

Smoke and fumes rose to the bridge, but at short intervals reports came through by telephone from the fire station, and from the officers at the seat of the fire, indicating that it was being got under control.

After two hours the danger was ended; but they were anxious hours for me. Having so recently heard of the destruction of the *Normandie* by fire and having been in a fire in the old *Mauretania*, I knew how quickly a fire can spread down below in a big liner. The designers of the Queen ships had equipped them with every device to meet this menace. Troops in crowded transports were given not only boat drill, but also fire drill, and being men under discipline, were not as prone to panic as civilian passengers might be.

At Cape Town we lay at anchor under the majestic bluff of Table Mountain. This anchorage is open from S.W. to N.W., but the sea was calm, and tankers were able to come alongside. The troops were not allowed ashore in this or any other port of call, in which our stay was limited to the amount of time required for refuelling and watering.

Here we embarked General Sir Thomas Blarney, Commander-in-Chief of the Australian Army. With him was his wife. They had flown from Cairo to Cape Town, to join the *Queen Mary*, as General Blarney's services were urgently required to organize the military defences of Australia.

Lady Blarney was the only woman on board the *Queen Mary*, in company with 9304 men! This fact caused some consternation. The Concert Party on board decided that they might have to eliminate jokes from their repertoire which were intended for male audiences only. However, Lady Blarney appreciated the situation, and thoughtfully did not attend the concerts.

Leaving Cape Town, we rounded the Cape of Good Hope and ran the easting down for 4800 miles to Fremantle, in eight days, with no escort and very little zigzagging, averaging 25 knots, mostly with following seas which made it advisable not to drive her too hard. When travelling at speed, she has an additional draught of five feet aft (known as "squat"), but it is better to avoid "racing" her propellers at full speed when the stern lifts to following seas. How different from my passage on this same track in the full rigged ship *County of Cardigan* thirty-nine years previously!

Nearing Fremantle we were met by two U.S.N. cruisers, *Barker* and *Bulwer*. We anchored for eighteen hours in Gage Roads, one mile off the North Mole, and took 6000 tons of oil and 2000 tons of fresh water. General Blarney and his wife left us here and went on by air to Melbourne.

Two days after leaving Fremantle, we entered Bass Strait, in a south-westerly gale, and were met by two U.S. destroyers. They had to give up, but next day, by cutting off a corner as we took a wide detour into the Tasman Sea, rejoined us and escorted us into Sydney. It was 5 p.m. on Saturday, 28th March 1942, when we made Sydney Heads, got a pilot, and anchored inside the harbour in Athol Bight, near the Zoo, at 6.30 p.m., as darkness was setting in. The arrival of this first contingent of American troops in Australia (while a big Australian Expeditionary Force was in the Middle East and Malaya) was a profound "security" secret.

Tenders (Sydney ferry steamers) ranged alongside, and the troops disembarked into them by gangplanks from side doors in the *Queen Mary*'s lower decks. All the troops were landed by 1 a.m. and were taken in buses to camps outside the city. The troops had been on board for thirty-four days since leaving Boston on 23rd February.

Australia was expecting a Japanese invasion, as Britain had been expecting a German invasion twenty-one months previously. Singapore had fallen on 15th February, the Japanese had landed in Java, Timor, and New Guinea, and the entire Australian nation was being mobilized for a desperate defence, with most of their best trained fighting men and equipment far away from home.

I went ashore next day, a sunny Sunday afternoon, and found Sydney looking very different from its happy-go-lucky appearance on my visit there, in the cruise liner *Franconia* fifteen years previously. Time was marching on! Now the beaches had barbed wire entanglements, there were air raid shelters in the parks, fortifications of sandbags lined the public buildings, and, as a supreme defence precaution, the clock tower at the General Post Office had been dismantled and carted away. The streets were thronged with Australian soldiers, mainly militiamen, partly trained.

As the *Queen Mary* was to remain in this port for nine days, the crew were put to work cleaning and painting ship, and were given shore leave in relays. I visited my brother Douglas and his family. It was Eastertime. I was hospitably entertained ashore by Australian and American naval officers, and at the New South Wales Club, the Royal Sydney Yacht Squadron, and the Imperial Services Club, and enjoyed the relaxation.

Voyage 2	Sydney, Australia - New York City			
(Passengers 58, Crew 832. Total 890 souls)				
Location	Status	Date	Miles	Km
Sydney	depart	6-Apr-42		
Freemantle	arrive	11-Apr-42	2,891	4,653
	depart	12-Apr-42		
Cape Town	arrive	21-Apr-42	5,167	8,315
	depart	22-Apr-42		
Rio de Janerio	arrive	27-Apr-42	3,311	5,329
	depart	28-Apr-42		
New York City	arrive	7-May-42	5,540	8,916
Ship: R.M.S. Queen Mary		TOTAL	16,909	27,212

The news that "the Yanks" had arrived in the *Queen Mary* created a sensation in Sydney. Soon the men in American uniforms became a familiar sight in the streets, and a new chapter in Australian history was being written.

As we put to sea, one mile outside Sydney Heads, at 12 noon on Monday, 6th April 1942, we met the *Queen Elizabeth* coming in, under command of Captain Fall, with the second contingent of American troops for Australia. This was the first time that I had seen the *Queen Elizabeth* in commission, and it was the first time that the two sisters had met at sea.

There was a rumour (false) that Japanese submarines were in Bass Strait. Taking no chances, the Naval Control Office sent me to Fremantle on a route passing wide to the south of Tasmania. There in Lat. 45 deg. S. the westerly winds and high seas made it necessary to reduce speed to 9 knots for several hours, to avoid damage. Despite that, we made Fremantle in five days, averaging 24 knots.

At dawn on 6th May 1942, in the North Atlantic, 600 miles from New York, we sighted five lifeboats in company, under sail, headed for the Bermuda Islands. The weather was fine, and the breeze fair for them. It was a hard decision not to stop and pick up brother seamen in distress, but the U-boat which had torpedoed their ship was probably keeping them in sight, waiting to strike at a rescuing vessel.

I had to give the lifeboats a wide berth, and continued zigzagging at full speed, but I made a signal to them, slowly, with a powerful Morse lamp, stating that I would report their position and course by radio to the Navy. This I did, and they were picked up by a U.S.N. ship next day and taken on to Bermuda.

These lifeboats were from a passenger and cargo liner, *S.S. Lady Drake*, 8000 tons of the Canadian National Line, bound from Halifax to Bermuda.

Voyage 3	New York City - Gourock, Scotland			
(Troops 9,880, Crew 875. Total 10,755 souls)				
Location	Status	Date	Miles	Km
New York City	depart	11-May-42		
Gourock	arrive	16-May-42	3,345	5,383
Ship: R.M.S. Queen Mary		TOTAL	3,345	5,383

She had been torpedoed on 5th May, and the survivors had been in the boats overnight when we sighted them.

In one of the boats was the son of the *Queen Mary*'s Chief Purser, Charles Johnson, whose feelings were harrowed, as were those of the son, when we sped by. But the son had a sense of humour. When he reached Bermuda, he cabled to his father at New York: "Dad useless as usual. Passed us by. But we made it."

This was the first time in history that ten thousand souls had voyaged in one ship. We had three U.S. destroyers as escort for the first day out. I was then routed eastwards through the iceberg region, at a season when icebergs were plentiful. To my consternation, I saw that my given route would bring me exactly over the spot where the *Titanic* had struck a berg on 14th April, 1912. That was thirty years and one month previously, but I knew that spot only too well. I sent a radio signal to Naval Control, asking permission to divert a little, but giving no reasons. I did not care to put my superstitious feelings into a naval code message. The reply came from some unfeeling naval person, "Keep to your route unless otherwise directed."

At dead of night, the *Queen Mary*, with more than 10,000 souls on board, steamed over the very spot believed by seamen to be haunted by the *Titanic's* ghost. I was one of the few on board who knew it. It was a trying moment, but at that spot we sighted neither bergs nor ghosts, though we sighted many bergs a few miles farther on. We were in the iceberg region two nights, and they were anxious hours for me.

As we closed in towards the land, we were met by two U.S.N. cruisers and two destroyers. The troops we disembarked at Gourock were the first big contingent of American soldiers to land in Britain in that war.

I had short leave of three days and went by train from Glasgow to Cheltenham for a visit of only one day. My arrival was a complete surprise to May, as was also the news that I was in command of the *Queen Mary*. Perhaps she was more worried than pleased at my promotion. She had heard rumours that the *Queen Mary* had been sunk with all hands. "Just as well you didn't let me know that you were in her then!" she said. "Now I won't know what to believe if I hear it again."

Voyage 4	Sydney, Australia - New York City			
(Passengers 58, Crew 832. Total 890 souls)				
Location	Status	Date	Miles	Km
Glascow	depart	22-May-42		
Freetown	arrive	30-May-42	4,536	7,300
	depart	31-May-42		
Cape Town	arrive	6-Jun-42	3,534	5,687
	depart	8-Jun-42		
Simon's Town	arrive	8-Jun-42	85	137
	depart	10-Jun-42		
Suez	arrive	22-Jun-42	6,167	9,925
Ship: R.M.S. *Queen Mary*		**TOTAL**	**14,322**	**23,049**

There was no way in which I could have let my wife know that I had been given command of the *Queen Mary*. It was absolutely forbidden to mention the names of ships, or ship's movements, in telegrams and letters, or in newspaper reports.

Returned to my ship, on 21st May, I found that I was under orders to embark troops urgently for a voyage to the Middle East.

This voyage was one of the most anxious that I had to make during the war. The troops on board (British and some Americans) were urgently required in the Middle East, where Rommel had begun a heavy drive from Libya towards Egypt on 26th May. Intelligence that this German counterattack in the Western Desert was impending had caused our hurried departure from the Clyde. There was no time to assemble a convoy. The *Queen Mary* would have to "go it alone," and this was the first time that troops from Britain were embarked in her for the Middle East. She carried four times as many troops as I had formerly carried to Suez in the Franconia. As a transport she was equivalent to four 20,000-ton liners, but, even more important, she could get to her destination in half the time that would be taken by a normal convoy. From this point of view she was the equivalent in long term service of eight ordinary transports voyaging in convoy.

In addition to the troops, she was loaded in her two holds and lower decks with 1000 tons of military stores. Among other things, she had 11 tons of currency notes in the cargo pay for the Eighth Army!

Escorted for a few hundred miles at the outset by destroyers, we soon left them behind, and in eight days reached Freetown. This is no place for such a big ship — a bad approach, strong currents, shoal water on the bar, and the river congested with tankers, naval vessels, and other ships — but we had to go somewhere for oil, and in wartime extraordinary risks have to be taken. We got in and out without any mishaps except a few more grey hairs on my head.

While we lay at anchor off Cape Town, with oil and water tankers alongside, heavy weather came up from the westward, and I had to take my ship around to the sheltered bay of Simon's Town (in the lee of the Cape of Good Hope) to complete refuelling, watering, and loading stores. There was much "cag" (conferring) with Naval Control here on my route to Suez, to avoid Japanese sub- marines reported in the Indian Ocean. The track laid down from Simon's Town to Suez, 6167 miles without intermediate ports of call, would strain her fuel endurance to the utmost. She would be at sea for twelve days. The amount of food required for 10,409 people for twelve days is in itself a nice calculation. That passage was the longest that the *Queen Mary* ever made from port to port. It was her absolute limit of endurance, without replenishments. Only the extreme urgency of the military situation in the Middle East could have justified the decision to attempt it.

We were escorted from Simon's Town by a cruiser, *H.M.S. Mauritius*. She stayed with us to 15 deg. S. Lat. (off Mozambique) then was relieved by *H.M.S. Devonshire*, which left us in 5 deg. N. Lat. The escort was then taken over by various British and Australian naval vessels in the Gulf of Aden, the Red Sea, and the Gulf of Suez. The month of June is in the hottest season of the year in that evaporating basin, twelve hundred miles long, landlocked within desert wastes. The heat and humidity were almost unbearable, especially down below at nighttime, when everything had to be kept closed to maintain the blackout. To add to our difficulties, a sandstorm developed, and the atmosphere was filled with dust like a dense, yellow, but hot and dry fog, in which navigation became a nightmare.

Hundreds of improvised sea water showers were rigged below decks for the sweltering troops, and these were in constant use. As many men as possible were allowed to sleep on deck at night. Despite these arrangements, there were many cases of heat prostration. The barber's shop, which was air conditioned, was used as a temporary hospital. After a few hours in its cooled atmosphere, most of the sufferers recovered, but three men died and were buried at sea. The engine room crew and kitchen staff suffered the torments of the damned, but they are a hardy race and accustomed to high temperatures.

The harbour at Suez is a poor place for a gigantic ship, being shallow and cramped. We anchored three miles from the quay and landed the troops in Nile ferryboats and barges. There were plenty of these craft, all manned by Arabs — good boatmen, but noisy and stubborn. It was curious to see them, amid the turmoil, spread a prayer mat on the deck and say their prayers with troops clambering all around them.

In twelve hours, from 6 a.m. to 6 p.m. on 22nd June 1942, all the troops were disembarked, and the stores unloaded. On the preceding day, the Germans had captured Tobruk, and were driving on towards Mersa Matruh and El Alamein, knocking at the gates of Egypt. The reinforcements brought in the *Queen Mary* were flung into the battle of El Alamein a week after they were disembarked. They helped to turn the tide in one of the most decisive battles of the war on land. This was the first big defeat of German panzer forces in the war. The German plan was to drive on through Egypt and the Middle East in a gigantic "pincers movement," to link eventually with their armies then driving through southern Russia to the Caucasus.

They were halted and driven back at El Alamein, nearly five months before the Russian counter offensive at Stalingrad began on 22nd November 1942. The Allied counter offensives in North Africa, and heavy bombing of German cities, took pressure off the Russians, who, until then, had been

Voyage 5		Suez - New York City		
(Troops 2,565, Crew 871. Total 3,436 souls)				
Location	Status	Date	Miles	Km
Suez	depart	23-Jun-42		
Simon's Town	arrive	5-Jul-42	6,123	9,854
	depart	7-Jul-42		
Rio de Janerio	arrive	12-Jul-42	3,290	5,295
	depart	13-Jul-42		
New York City	arrive	21-Jul-42	4,801	7,726
Ship: R.M.S. *Queen Mary*		TOTAL	14,214	22,875

heavily defeated by the German armies. It is for that reason that the first battle of El Alamein, which checked the German thrust into Egypt on 2nd July, 1942, should rightly be considered as the turning point of the war.

The passengers were a mixed bag, including 1398 German prisoners of war and 300 Polish guards; also naval, military, air force troops and some women of the auxiliary services, and women and children civilians. The Germans, mostly blond and very young, had been in the desert for many months, and their uniforms were bedraggled. The men were sullen, but kept their quarters clean, and gave little trouble beyond scrawling a few anti-British slogans on the bulkheads of their cabins. When these were found, the occupants had to clean them off and were then put into the "brig" on a bread-and-water diet for a few days. Next, six men in one of the cabins decided to be sarcastic and wrote the words "Rule Britannia" in large letters on the bulkhead. They too were punished, just to show that we played no favourites!

In those parts of the ship where the prisoners ate, slept, or took exercise, barbed wire barricades were erected, with machine gun nests at tactical points, to prevent any attempt at a concerted rush. The men of the Polish guard were mostly young. They were armed with small Italian rifles, with bayonets like meat skewers. These rifles were hair trigger weapons. On the first day several rifles were accidentally discharged, usually by the guard dropping the butt too sharply on the deck. No one was hurt, but I did not like the idea of random bullets whistling in my ship and asked the military commandant to intervene. He gave orders that the rifles should be carried unloaded, with ammunition in a belt pouch.

At Simon's Town, 610 of our "transit passengers" were landed, including all the women and children. We then went on to Rio. While we lay at anchor overnight there on 12th July, two of the German prisoners succeeded in prising off the iron cover riveted over the porthole of their cabin. They got through the porthole and dropped to the deck of a tanker alongside. One of them was seen and caught, but the other dived into the water and tried to reach the shore by swimming. When he was halfway to the shore, he was attacked by a shark and had part of his left arm torn off. He was picked up by a ferry which happened to be passing and was handed over to the police. After hospital treatment, he was brought back on board the *Queen Mary* next day. The prisoners were landed at New York.

The ship was docked at Pier 90 in New York for twelve days. There, I heard that, in the King's Birthday Honours List of 11th June — while I was en route to Suez — I had been appointed a Commander of the Order of the British Empire (C.B.E.) Civil Division — a decoration sometimes conferred on shipmasters of the Merchant Navy in recognition of wartime services, and highly esteemed. I did not know of this award until seven weeks after it had been conferred on me. I was required, if possible, to attend an Investiture ceremony at Buckingham Palace in London, to receive the award in person from King George VI.

Voyage 6	New York City - Gourock, Scotland			
(Troops 15,125, Crew 863. Total 15,988 souls)				
Location	Status	Date	Miles	Km
New York City	depart	2-Aug-42		
Gourock	arrive	7-Aug-42	3,410	5,488
Ship: R.M.S. *Queen Mary*		TOTAL	3,410	5,488

This was the greatest number of human beings that had ever been embarked in one vessel for an ocean crossing passage. The total, only twelve less than sixteen thousand souls, was later to be exceeded on a few, but only a few Atlantic crossings, in the *Queen Mary*, and in the *Queen Elizabeth*, but for practical purposes, sixteen thousand (a few more or less) was the extreme limit of the carrying capacity of each of these two gigantic transports. I cannot imagine that in any future war such huge vessels will ever again be in service as transports, or that such risks will ever again be taken as to embark the equivalent of one complete Army Division in one ship, to cross an ocean under hazard of enemy attack.

I would not admit it or show it, but I was inwardly deeply perturbed at the responsibility thrust upon me. Yet I had already become accustomed to it, to some extent. The difference between transporting 10,000 and 16,000 souls within one hull is a matter of mathematics rather than of quality. In either case, there would be appalling loss of life if the ship were sunk. The American military authorities evidently had confidence in the *Queen Mary*'s ability to "deliver the goods." In peacetime she was fitted out to carry 2038 passengers and 1285 crew: total 3323 souls. Now as a troop transport, she was asked to carry five times that number.

The overcrowding was met by installing 12,500 Standee bunks in every available space, including the cabins and most of the public rooms; but even with that, on this voyage, nearly 3500 troops had no bunks and had to sleep on reserved parts of the decks. These were described as the "overload," carried only during summer months, when no great hardship was suffered by the troops who had to sleep for four or five nights on planks.

"Standee" beds, an American invention, were made of tubular metal uprights, with hinged tubular frames attached to which strips of canvas were stretched with rope lacings. There would be three or more beds in one tier, according to the height of the deckhead in any compartment. In the daytime, the beds could be hinged upwards and secured to the bulkhead or deckhead with a small chain and hook. They were light in weight, easily cleaned, and had no crevices to harbour vermin.

Only two meals a day were served, each in six "sittings." Breakfast was "on" from 6.30 a.m. to 11. a.m., and dinner from 3 p.m. to 7.30 p.m.

The officers' dining room — which in peacetime was the tourist lounge — seated 350. The troops' mess hall — which was the first-class dining room seated 2000. The mess tables, of metal, with wooden benches, seated on an average eighteen men, with two mess orderlies to each table. The orderlies formed in queues to the kitchen, and drew the food in large metal containers ("mess kids"), then carried it into the mess hall and dished it out at the tables.

Each sitting lasted forty-five minutes. Every soldier carried his own knife, fork, plate, and spoon. The men entered the mess hall at one end, and left it at the other end, to avoid clashing with the queue waiting for the next sitting. The utensils, known as "eating irons," were designed to be hooked together and held by a wire handle. Each man, on filing out of the mess hall, swizzled his gear in a battery of four tanks in succession, holding soapy water, boiling fresh water, boiling disinfectant, and finally, boiling sea water, then took it to his quarters to drain dry.

Each day there was Emergency Drill, in case it were necessary to abandon ship. The *Queen Mary* had thirty lifeboats, capable of accommodating three thousand men, and enough life rafts to support seventeen thousand men. The Military Commandant remarked to me fervently, "I hope it won't be necessary to abandon ship!"

"Not as fervently as I hope it!" I said, and explained further, "The Captain must be the last to leave• a sinking ship. I can't see myself having much chance at the end of a queue of 15,987 men on the boat deck!"

On this record breaking passage (not of speed, but of carrying capacity), I had one scare when we were 200 miles north-west of the Irish coast. Soon after we had altered course on zigzag, a tremendous explosion occurred in the sea, 400 yards off our port quarter. A geyser of water rose 300 feet into the air, and the engine room crew reported feeling a heavy concussion. But no damage was done, and we sped on, without sighting a U-boat. The probability is that this explosion had been caused by an "acoustic mine," which had been set off by the vibration of the ship's four propellers. It was merely the mercy of Providence that we had altered course when we did. Otherwise we would have passed right over the mine. The troops were landed at Gourock on 7th August 1942, and I was given a month's shore leave, being relieved by Captain Illingworth. During the five months that I had been in command of the *Queen Mary*, my hair had gone grey. I wasn't aware that I was worrying too much, but the settee in the chartroom of the *Queen Mary* was never a comfortable bed.

In Command of the "*Queen Elizabeth*" — My First Atlantic
Crossings in Her — The "*Queen Mary*" cuts a Cruiser in Halves —
Her Remarkable Collision with the "Curacao" — The Loss of the
"Laconia" off Freetown — An Investiture at Buckingham Palace —
The Fourth Christmas of the War — British Troops from the Clyde
to Suez — Return of Australian Troops from the Middle East to
Their Homeland — Commodore of Five Big Transports — A
Massive Movement by Sea — Historic Homecoming of the
Australian Imperial Force

A MONTH'S leave at Cheltenham, in August 1942, was a pleasant
relaxation. I spent most of the time gardening, far from the sights,
sounds, and excitements of the sea. On 3rd September, we had
been at war for three years; and now the tide was turning in our favour.

On 7th September, I went to Glasgow, and there I was given command
of the *Queen Elizabeth*, for one "round voyage" to New York, to relieve
Captain Fall, who was due for a spell ashore. Both the Queens were bringing
large numbers of American troops to Britain, on frequent eastbound
passages, and taking civilian refugees and various special passengers to
America on the west bound passages.

Transports in wartime could not operate on fixed schedules. Each
wartime ocean passage could therefore be viewed as a voyage, terminating at
the port of disembarkation, wherever that might be.

We left the anchorage at the Tail of the ·Bank (opposite Gourock) at
10.45 p.m., in darkness, without naval escort, and were far out to sea before

Voyage 7	New York City - Gourock, Scotland			
(Troops 1,708, Crew 860. Total 2,568 souls)				
Location	Status	Date	Miles	Km
The Clyde	depart	8-Sep-42		
New York City	arrive	14-Sep-42	3,574	5,752
Ship: R.M.S. *Queen Elizabeth*		**TOTAL**	**3,574**	**5,752**

dawn. I found that the *Queen Elizabeth* was very similar to the *Queen Mary* in handling. There was no difference in their speed, and their arrangements were practically identical. The chief difference in their appearance was that the *Queen Mary* had three funnels, and a forward welldeck; whereas the *Queen Elizabeth* had two funnels, and a flush planked deck forward, with the cargo hatches and winches and the anchor gear set into the flush deck. This gave a large and pleasing view of the foredeck, as seen from the bridge, extending from below the bridgehouse to the bows in an unbroken sweep, with consequent increased "legroom" for passengers promenading.

As the biggest vessel in the Cunard White Star fleet (in fact the biggest vessel in the world), the *Queen Elizabeth* was the flagship and usually flew the swallow tail pennant of the Commodore, who at that time was R. S. Irving.

On arrival at New York on 14th September, I found that the Q.E. would be laid up there for three weeks, waiting for another contingent of American troops. My old love, the *Queen Mary*, was already there, under command of Captain Illingworth, waiting to embark Canadian troops. She left New York, bound for the Clyde, on 27th September.

What happened to her on that passage is a matter of history, and I know of it only from hearsay. I considered myself lucky not to have been in her at that time, when one of the most remarkable mishaps in the history of the sea occurred: A mishap for which no one in the *Queen Mary* was to blame in the slightest, for it was an effect of the abnormal conditions of navigation in wartime.

Off the northwest of Ireland, on 2nd October 1942, the *Queen Mary* was met by an antiaircraft cruiser, *H.M.S. Curacao*, and four destroyers, which were to escort her to the Clyde. The weather was squally, with fresh north-westerly wind, rough seas, and good visibility.

The Curacao proceeded ahead at 28 knots, doing her own zigzags, while the *Queen Mary* made the predetermined zigzags, also at 28 knots. The destroyers formed a screen three miles ahead. At times the Curacao came so close under the bows of the *Queen Mary* that the officers on the bridge would lose sight of her.

According to what I was told later — and I believe it — the *Queen Mary* performed her zigzags punctually and strictly according to orders, but it appeared that the Officer of the Watch in the cruiser may have misjudged, by a few seconds only, the amount of time required to get clear of her bows as the big ship altered course. No one will ever know exactly how it happened, but suddenly there was a dreadful impact as the *Queen Mary*'s bows struck the Curacao amidships, broadside on.

The tremendous weight of the gigantic liner, thrusting on at a speed of 28 knots, was such that her hardened steel bows tore through the 3-inch armour plated sides of the cruiser, and cut the cruiser almost exactly in halves!

It was a horrifying moment for those on the bridge and decks of the *Queen Mary* when they saw the halves of the Curacao rolling over and over, one along each side of the giant ship, to disappear into the turbulence of the wake.

Rafts and lifebuoys were thrown overboard from the *Queen Mary*, but beyond that she could take no part in rescue operations, as it was forbidden absolutely to stop. The destroyers raced back to the rescue immediately, but, of the Curacao's complement of 410, only seventy-two survived.

That was a heavy loss of life, but relatively small in relation to what might have happened, if the cruiser's ammunition had exploded under the bows of the *Queen Mary*.

As it was, the *Queen Mary* suffered damage to her stem on the waterline. She had to reduce speed to 20 knots until she reached the Clyde. There, emergency repairs were made by John Brown & Co. Ltd, which enabled her to cross the Atlantic to Boston for dry docking and final repairs.

Even though the Curacao was a light cruiser (of 4000 tons displacement), her destruction in that manner remains unique in the annals of the sea. The explanation of such a phenomenal happening was not only in the immense weight and speed of the *Queen Mary*, but also in the design and special strengthening of her bows, intended to avert damage to her from collisions at high speed with other vessels, derelicts, wreckage or icebergs in mid-ocean. On seeing her in dry dock, one realized that, despite her immense bulk, her bows were shaped almost to a knife edge at the stem. The streamlining of her hull is as graceful as that of a racing yacht, but of huge dimensions. It was that streamlining which enabled her to plough through an armoured cruiser, almost life a knife through cheese. Never before had a merchant vessel sunk an armoured cruiser by ramming her and cutting her in halves — and let us hope that such a thing will never happen again!

Bearing in mind what had just happened to the *Queen Mary*, I was more wary than usual of naval escorts when the Q.E. closed in towards the land; but the Navy had already been warned to give the Queens plenty of sea room. The track was patrolled, ahead, and to both sides, by relays of

Voyage 8	New York City - Gourock, Scotland			
(Troops 10,890, Crew 856. Total 11,746 souls)				
Location	Status	Date	Miles	Km
New York City	depart	5-Oct-42		
Gourock	arrive	11-Oct-42	3,690	5,938
Ship: R.M.S. *Queen Elizabeth*		TOTAL	3,690	5,938

destroyers and minesweepers, and aircraft patrolled the skies; but the idea of an individual close escort, for either of the Queens, had been discarded.

Arrived at Gourock, I left the Q.E., to rejoin the Q.M., but, as she was still under repairs, I was given a fortnight's leave. I went to Liverpool, to see the General Manager of Cunard White Star Limited, Mr S. J. Lister. He and his staff had the great responsibility of shore organization, not only of the movements of the two Queens, but of a dozen or more other Cunard and White Star vessels, on war service.

Among the many details managed at the Company's head office were the arrangements for shore leave for the masters, officers, and crews of all Cunard White Star vessels when they reached home ports. This leave had to be arranged in rotation, so that the ships could be kept in service. Even when ships lay at anchor, they had to be kept manned, in case of gales in open roadstead's, or air attacks, with steam up ready to get under way at short notice.

Because so many docks in Britain were damaged, ships were usually cleaned, reprovisioned, refuelled and rewatered while they lay at anchor — all this requiring working crews to be kept on board. Despite such problems, the Cunard White Star management arranged for approximately one-sixth of the crew to be relieved at the end of each long voyage, on returning to a British port. They were given rail warrants to travel from the Clyde to their homes in Liverpool, London, or Southampton, and to rejoin their ship on her next outward voyage, or to join some other ship. This management of a seagoing staff which totalled 10,000 or more, in very difficult circumstances, was smoothly conducted, thanks chiefly to S. J. Lister's brilliant organizing ability. Shipmasters going on leave or returning from leave usually went to Liverpool to report to the General Manager, and to receive instructions of future postings and movements.

I heard now of the loss of the *Laconia*, the vessel of 20,000 tons which I had commanded on a luxury cruise in the early months of 1939. She was torpedoed off Freetown, on 12th September 1942, in service as a transport, having on board 1500 Italian prisoners of war, besides troops and others from the Middle East. The loss of life was heavy, but strange to relate, the U-boat which had sunk her, in company with other U-boats forming a "pack" waiting off Freetown, took part in rescue work, picking up people from the water and from boats. While they were doing this, Allied land based aircraft came over and began bombing the U-boats. To complete the strange sequence of events, some of the *Laconia*'s survivors were rescued by a Vichy-French cruiser and taken on to Casablanca.

I went to Cheltenham for my leave. Ten days later, I received a notice from Head Office, extending my leave, so that I could attend an Investiture at Buckingham Palace on 3rd November, to receive the decoration of C.B.E. from the King.

The official notice stated that service uniforms or morning dress should be worn. This put me in a spot of bother, as I had gone on leave in civilian garb. My uniforms with my other gear were in the "Left Luggage" at the Cunard office in Glasgow!

There was not time to go there, so I hurried to London for an interview with Moss Brothers. They had no difficulty in fitting me out, from collar to boots, and brass hat as well, in the uniform of a Captain of the Royal Naval Reserve — hired for twenty-six shillings a day. Mr Moss cheerfully remarked, "It fits you perfectly, sir. Others will be in the same boat. All that glisters is not gold!"

"Are you quoting that correctly?" I asked.

"Yes, sir. Merchant of Venice. Act 2, Scene 7," said the learned outfitter. Comfortable enough in my hired plumage, I proceeded to Buckingham Palace at the appointed time, 10 a.m. on Tuesday, • 3rd November 1942, and showed my letter of admission at the gates. I found that I was one of a crowd of 300 summoned to the Investiture — to receive decorations of various kinds for war services or civilian service.

We were briefed by a Court Chamberlain as to procedures. "Listen for your name to be called. Advance. Bow to the King. After receiving the decoration, go to the back of the room. Please do not talk more loudly than the string orchestra is playing! Stand erect for decorations to be hooked on to the breast. Bow the head for neck decorations."

It was all efficient. I realized that the organization of Buckingham Palace is as careful as the organization of a ship.

While we were waiting for the King to enter, I wandered round the anteroom, looking at the vases, paintings, and sculptures. I became aware that a small man in morning dress was following me and watching me closely.

I turned on him. "You here for decoration?"

"No, I'm in the Diplomatic Corps!" Then he added, "I've been in Turkey for two years with a diplomatic mission. I got back to London yesterday with only the clothes I stood up in and found an order to attend this Investiture. So I went to Moss Brothers and got outfitted with a morning dress, from collar to boots, and a topper as well, for twenty-six shillings a day. 'All that glisters is not gold.' Merchant of Venice, Act 2, Scene 7. I was in the cubicle next to you!"

The Chamberlains formed us into queues. The King entered, attired in Admiral's uniform, and stood on the dais. When my name was called, I stepped up the ramp to the dais, as others had done before me, and bowed. Hats and caps were not worn, at this indoor ceremony. Therefore, there was no saluting. As I bowed, the King placed the pink ribbon of the C.B.E. around my neck. Attached to it was the blue and gold enamel Maltese Cross of the Order.

"How long have you been at sea?" "Forty-four years, Your Majesty." "Good luck!"

I stepped back, turned right, went down the ramp. At the foot of the ramp was a table covered with small white boxes. An attendant in livery stood by the table. Before I could say "Knife" he had whipped my C.B.E. off my neck, wound the ribbon round his fingers, put it all neatly into a box, and handed it back to me.

And I was through! Even allowing half a minute per man, the King would have to be on the dais for 2½ hours conferring the decorations. Seldom have I seen such efficiency of organization in high places.

Returned to Glasgow on 5th November 1942, I found that the *Queen Mary* had been temporarily repaired and had been taken to Boston, under command of Captain Illingworth. I was ordered to proceed to New York in the *Queen Elizabeth* — as a passenger! — for she was now under command of Captain Fall. At New York I was to resume command of the *Queen Mary*, relieving Illingworth.

It was a novel experience to me to be a passenger, especially in a ship that I had so recently commanded.

I was given a first-class cabin to myself on A Deck and soon found that in the neighbouring cabins were celebrities of the theatrical and film world — Basil Dean, Alexander Korda, Douglas Fairbanks, and G. S. Robinson. They had priority passages, since entertainment in wartime is highly important for sustaining the morale of troops and civilians.

The ship carried 7300 passengers, including civilian evacuees (women and children), naval, military and air force people, and all sorts of political, diplomatic, and businesspeople going on special missions. She had a crew of 870.

I remained in mufti, had my meals in the dining room at the Staff Captain's table, went for walks around the decks, attended entertainments in the lounge, visited friends in their cabins, played deck games, enjoyed a few drinks, and did all those things that I never did as Captain in wartime.

Voyage 9	New York City - Gourock, Scotland			
(Troops 10,389, Crew 950. Total 11,339 souls)				
Location	Status	Date	Miles	Km
New York City	depart	8-Dec-42		
Gourock	arrive	14-Dec-42	3,685	5,930
Ship: R.M.S. *Queen Mary*		TOTAL	3,685	5,930

Arrived in New York on 13th November, I relieved Illingworth in command of the *Queen Mary* a few days later. She was lying at. Pier 90, preparing to embark troops.

This was a passage in severe winter weather, with north-westerly gales, which made the ship roll heavily for four days. My route, given to me by the Naval Control Office, was far to the northwards of the usual winter tracks, and took me to the vicinity of Greenland and Iceland. I had no rest, but at least I was thinking that I might be home for Christmas!

On arrival in the Clyde, I found that the *Queen Mary* was to embark troops for the Middle East. At this time the threat of a German military invasion of Britain had passed. The "theatres of war" were deep in Russia, and in North Africa and the Pacific.

I was now under orders to take British and American troops from Britain to Suez, to replace Australian troops which were to be withdrawn from the Middle East and thrown into battle against the Japanese in the war in the Pacific. Not a day could be wasted. The troops were embarked, and we sailed from the Clyde two days before Christmas — and that was the fourth Christmas of the War!

Among the troops on this passage I had 2000 Royal Air Force men, and 160 women. On Christmas Day we were 600 miles to the westward of Ireland, and headed southwards in a north-westerly gale, with mountainous seas. Most of the troops were seasick, or at least decidedly uncomfortable. The Chief Steward and his staff worked hard to prepare a slap-up Christmas Dinner of turkey and plum pudding, but most of it went to waste.

On this voyage my officers were: Staff Captain Thompson; Chief Officer Harrison; First Officers Wright and Milloy; other navigating officers Davis, Aldridge, Hewitt, Lamb, and Gates; Chief Engineer Botting; Staff Chief Engineer Harding; Senior Second Engineer Bailey. On various voyages, changes were made as officers were relieved or transferred to other ships. I regret that I have not preserved notes of all these changes, but for this voyage I happened to keep a list of those who served with me and shared the worries. We called at Aden for replenishments of oil to take us on to Suez.

Voyage 10	Gourock, Scotland to Suez			
(Passengers 10,669, Crew 880. Total 11,579 souls)				
Location	Status	Date	Miles	Km
Gourock	depart	23-Dec-42		
Freetown	arrive	29-Dec-42	4,067	6,545
	depart	30-Dec-42		
Cape Town	arrive	5-Jan-43	3,650	5,874
	depart	7-Jan-43		
Aden	arrive	15-Jan-43	5,175	8,328
	depart	15-Jan-43		
Suez	arrive	18-Jan-43	1,335	2,148
Ship: R.M.S. *Queen Mary*		TOTAL	14,227	22,896

After disembarking the troops at Suez, I went ashore to see Admiral Halifax, the Senior British Naval Officer at that port.

I thought that I was beyond being surprised at anything that might happen in wartime, but what the Admiral told me surprised me. On instructions of the Australian Government, the whole of the Australian forces in the Middle East, in total 31,451 troops, were to be returned to their homeland, to be engaged in the defence of Australia, and in the counter offensive that had already been launched against the Japanese in the Pacific Islands. These troops were to be embarked from Suez, in a convoy of only five transports, under naval escort.

The transports were the *Queen Mary* (Cunard White Star Line, 81,237 tons); *Aquitania* (Cunard White Star Line, 45,646 tons); *Ile de France* (Compagnie Generale Transatlantique, but at that time under P. & O. management, 43,450 tons); *Nieuw Amsterdam* (Holland Amerika Line, 36,667 tons); and *Queen of Bermuda* (Furness Withy Line, 22,500 tons).

I was to be Commodore of this convoy: an honour, certainly, but one which I would rather have been excused, as it meant that the *Queen Mary*'s speed — her best defence — would have to be curbed to that of the slowest of the five vessels, which happened to be the *Queen of Bermuda* (18 knots).

"I suppose," the Admiral said, "that you would prefer to go it alone, but on this occasion, it has been decided that naval protection must be provided for all the transports on the entire route across the Indian Ocean. Therefore, the *Queen Mary* will be included in the convoy. The enemy is in possession of Singapore, and it is possible that their heavy surface units, as well as submarines, may venture out to intercept you. The distance, even from Aden to Fremantle, would be too great, by diversions and zigzags, to be covered without refuelling and watering. It is not advisable to call at Colombo, which may be within range of enemy air attack. You will refuel at a mid-ocean rendezvous, Addu Atoll, at the southern end of the Maldive Islands, where there is a large and safe anchorage."

I kept my thoughts to myself. A Merchant Captain does not argue with the Navy, least of all with an Admiral, but I was not relishing the prospect of a lengthened voyage in convoy. The *Queen Mary* by herself could have made the passage from Suez to Fremantle, refuelling at Aden, in ten or twelve days. To dawdle in company with four other liners, at the speed of the slowest of them, and to wait for the convoy to be assembled, would be a waste of time! Nor did I relish the prospect of being Commodore, required to engage in manoeuvres under naval direction, with four other big steamers — two of them British, one French, and one Dutch — requiring much flag signalling by day and difficult watchkeeping by night under blackout conditions.

The Admiral could surmise my suppressed thoughts. He said, "You will embark troops in the *Queen Mary* at Suez, but, because of the danger of air raids, we do not want you to lie at anchor here a moment longer than necessary. As soon as your troops are embarked, you will proceed to Massawa. There you will be joined after a few days by the *Aquitania* and *Ile de France*. You will then proceed in company with these two, on orders from the Naval Officer in Command at Massawa, to a rendezvous with *Nieuw Amsterdam* and *Queen of Bermuda* in the Gulf of Aden, then proceed under escort to be provided. Complete route instructions will be given to you in the morning. Goodbye and good luck!"

Inwardly fuming at the waste of time implied in these arrangements, as far as the *Queen Mary* was concerned, and not looking forward with any pleasure to taking such a big ship into the little known port of Massawa in the Red Sea, and into a coral atoll in the Indian Ocean, I controlled my feelings, murmured, "Very good, sir. Thank you!" and hurried back to my ship.

The Aussies were already being embarked.

Voyage 11	Suez - Sydney			
(Troops 9,995, Crew 877. Total 10,872 souls)				
Location	Status	Date	Miles	Km
Suez	depart	25-Jan-43		
Massawa	arrive	28-Jan-43	960	1,545
	depart	3-Feb-43		
Addu Atoll	arrive	9-Feb-43	2,615	4,208
	depart	10-Feb-43		
Freemantle	arrive	18-Feb-43	3,327	5,354
	depart	20-Feb-43		
Sydney	arrive	27-Feb-43	3,006	4,838
Ship: R.M.S. *Queen Mary*		TOTAL	9,908	15,945

That passage of thirty-three days and 9908 miles steaming in convoy, which could have been accomplished by the *Queen Mary* within eighteen days, if she had been allowed to proceed alone, was the most anxious voyage that I made in her, and the biggest responsibility that I have ever had thrust upon me. But I was not the only one who worried. It was said that the Australian Prime Minister, John Curtin, suffered intense anxiety while the convoy was in transit, and that his hair turned grey and his health almost broke down under the strain of waiting for coded naval messages reporting the convoy's progress across an ocean to which the Japanese Fleet at Singapore and Java had access.

Had the convoy been attacked, the *Queen Mary* would have been the main target. With nearly 10,000 Australian troops on board (including 132 army nurses), she was taking back to their homeland approximately one-third of the total number of troops embarked in the convoy. These men had been seasoned and proved in battle for three years in the Middle East. They were veterans of renown.

It was probably not a naval decision alone to include the *Queen Mary* in a convoy steaming at only 18 knots. Political directives were involved. That decision having been taken, the Navy handled the arrangements with efficiency.

The *Queen Mary* left Suez at 8 p.m., in darkness, and made slow progress in the Red Sea throughout that night, next day and night, and the following day and night, in order to arrive at the entrance to Massawa in daylight. This port, in Eritrea (formerly an Italian colony) had been captured by a British expedition a year or so previously.

Its approach is studded with islands and shoals for some seventy miles. I had never been there before, and it looked uninviting on the chart, but I had been ordered to take the *Queen Mary* in, so I had to do it. I was old enough to know that the mere fact that a thing looks difficult doesn't mean that it can't be done.

Fine clear weather favoured us, and there were plenty of landmarks available for cross bearings. At an easy speed, we meandered along the channels and anchored a mile off the entrance to the inner basin. The Italians had blocked the entrance by sinking some steamers in it.

In sweltering heat and impatience, we lay at anchor off Massawa for a week. First the *Aquitania*, then the *Ile de France* arrived from Suez, both crowded with troops. Then we were ordered to sea and met the *Nieuw Amsterdam* and *Queen of Bermuda* off Perim.

The sizes and complements of the five transports were:

Ship	Tonnage	Troops	Crew	Total
Queen Mary	81,237	9,995	877	10,872
Aquitania	45,646	6,953	606	7,559
Ile de France	43,450	6,531	675	7,206
Nieuw Amsterdam	36,667	6,241	465	6,706
Queen of Bermuda	22,500	1,731	253	1,984
TOTALS	229,500	31,451	2,876	34,327

The *Queen Mary* steamed in the middle, with two of the other ships in line ahead on each side of her. Each of the transports mounted two 6-inch guns, one forward and one aft-and a battery of A.A. guns. The Q.M. had sixty-six A.A. guns, and a hundred or more gunners on the Permanent Staff. In the Gulf of Aden we were escorted by destroyers. Off Cape Gardafui, the escort was taken over by two cruisers, *H.M.S. Gambia* and *H.M.S. Devonshire*. The Senior Officer of the escorts was Admiral Tennant, R.N., Flag Officer of the 4th Cruiser Squadron. He was helpful, and did not ask me to indulge in fancy manoeuvres or insist on unnecessary flag-signalling, so my work as Commodore was not as arduous as it might have been.

Captain Manser of *H.M.S. Gambia* sent me a signal: "Here we are again!" Then I remembered. He had been a midshipman with me in *H.M.T.B.D. Alarm*, away back in 1916, during the Kaiser's war. When the convoy and escorting cruisers arrived at Addu Atoll, I had a pleasant surprise. This remote spot, almost on the Equator and 600 miles south-westerly from Colombo, is normally uninhabited and off the track of shipping; but in wartime it had become transformed into a secret refuelling and watering base and anchorage for the British Eastern Fleet in the Indian Ocean. The atoll is formed by a ring of coral reefs and islands, enclosing a perfectly sheltered lagoon of three miles in diameter, with a sandy bottom and soundings of from thirty to sixty feet all over.

It has an easy deepwater entrance through a gap in the reef, and perfectly calm water inside, big enough for a large number of vessels to ride securely at anchor. The water was so still and crystal clear that, when the *Queen Mary*'s anchor plunged to the bottom, in ten fathoms (60 feet), we could see the anchor resting on the bottom. Naval oil tankers and water tankers were waiting for us there.

Other vessels at anchor included naval store ships, a hospital ship, fighting units of the Eastern Fleet, and flying boats. On one of the islands was an airstrip, and there were sheds, repair shops, and a radio station on shore. This secret base, a wartime alternative to Trincomalee in Ceylon, was of utmost value in British naval strategy in the Indian Ocean. It is doubtful if the enemy knew of its existence as a base at that time.

The convoy left Addu at 2 p.m. on 10th February, under escort of Gambia and Devonshire. Our route would now bring us within striking range of any Japanese sortie from Malacca Strait or Sunda Strait; but the Navy was on guard. Soon after we put to sea, we sighted the British Eastern Fleet, with the battleships *H.M.S. Resolution* and *H.M.S. Warspite*, and several cruisers and destroyers, patrolling to the northwards. They closed in and remained with us until darkness set in. Next day they were out of sight, but not out of mind or radio contact. This was a comforting thought.

The Australian troops were in fine fettle, and happy at the prospect of soon being home. They were orderly, clean, well behaved, and keen to keep out of any trouble, as they were to be given a month's leave when they arrived. On board the *Queen Mary* they had a regimental brass band, and plenty of organized entertainments. They kept fit by long daily sessions of callisthenics. Although their favourite gambling game of "Two Up" was forbidden, it went on in many quiet corners. The O.C. Troops told me that his only reason for trying to stop gambling was that he did not want some of his men to arrive home "broke," with no money to spend on their home leave.

On 16th February, 800 miles off Fremantle, *Gambia* and *Devonshire* left us. The escort was then taken over by the Dutch cruiser *Van Tromp* and three Dutch destroyers, *Van Galen, Tjerk Hiddes*, and *Heemskerck*. A great cheer went up from the troops when at last the shores of Australia hove in sight.

Leaving Fremantle, we were escorted by *H.M.A.S. Adelaide* and the Dutch destroyers. In Bass Strait they left us, to proceed into Melbourne, with the *Nieuw Amsterdam*, while *H.M.A.S. Australia* and two U.S.N. destroyers, *Henley* and *Battery*, escorted the other four transports to Sydney.

As we steamed through Sydney Heads and up the harbour on that fine sunny Saturday afternoon, 27th February, 1943, the troops lined the rails and cheered, ferry steamers and tugs tooted "cock-a- doodle-do," and crowds on the headlands waved hats, handkerchiefs and flags, blew whistles and sent "Coo-ee" calls across the water. Despite "security" precautions, the word had gone round that the "boys" of the Second Australian Imperial Force had come home.

Disembarkation began immediately, and that Saturday night in Sydney was one of those Saturday nights that will be long remembered.

Prime Minister John Curtin could relax, and so could we all. I have seen some homecomings, but seldom one more joyous than this.

A story went the rounds, and I do not altogether believe it. It was said that when the *Queen Mary* came to anchor in Athol Bight, a tug ranged alongside her under her bridge. As Sydney tugs so often do, the tug engineer chose this moment to stoke his furnaces too heavily with coal. Great clouds of black smoke belched from the tug's funnel and billowed upwards into the *Queen Mary*'s wheelhouse and chartroom.

According to the story, I stood this for a while and then went out to the wing of the bridge with a megaphone, leaned over the rail and sang out to the tugmaster eighty feet below, "Hey, skipper, if you don't stop making black smoke, I'll spit down your funnel and put your bloody fires out!"

Now, would I have said a thing like that?

38

Troop-carrying in the North Atlantic — The Shuttle-service of the "Queen" Ships — Victory in North Africa — The Invasion of Italy — Organization on Board the Mammoth Transports — Procedures of Embarkation- — Emergency Drills and Discipline of the Troops — Keeping the Ship Clean — Recreations on Board — The Captain's Responsibilities — Sleeping with One Eye Open — My Sixtieth Birthday — The Greatest Number of Souls Ever Carried in One Vessel.

THAT visit of the *Queen Mary* to Sydney, in February-March, 1943, was the last voyage of either of the Queen ships to Australia. For the remaining duration of the war, and afterwards, they operated only on the North Atlantic express service, for which they were originally designed.

On leaving Sydney, we had only 180 passengers, but when we arrived at Cape Town the plot thickened! We embarked 4050 Italian prisoners of war, who had been captured in North Africa, brought to South Africa, and now were to be taken to Britain to work for their keep — they were seeing the world.

Here we embarked also a mixed bag of 4276 other passengers, who included British, Free French, Dutch, Polish, Norwegian, and New Zealand naval, military, and air-force personnel, and merchant seamen, besides civilians of various degrees of importance, who had to go to Britain.

Voyage 12		Sydney - Gourock		
(Troops 8,326, Crew 874. Total 9,200 souls)				
Location	Status	Date	Miles	Km
Sydney	depart	22-Mar-43		
Freemantle	arrive	26-Mar-43	2,770	4,458
	depart	29-Mar-43		
Cape Town	arrive	6-Apr-43	4,945	7,958
	depart	9-Apr-43		
Freetown	arrive	15-Apr-43	3,685	5,930
	depart	16-Apr-43		
Gourock	arrive	22-Apr-43	4,060	6,534
Ship: R.M.S. Queen Mary		TOTAL	15,460	24,880

The Italian prisoners were docile. When allowed on deck for exercise, they would form themselves into choirs and sing for hours.

The tide of war was running in our favour. No naval escorts were provided for the *Queen Mary* in the Atlantic. We crept into the Clyde in a fog

Voyage 13	Gourock, Scotland - New York City			
(Troops 6,235, Crew 922. Total 7,157 souls)				
Location	Status	Date	Miles	Km
New York City	depart	10-Jun-43		
Gourock	arrive	16-Jun-43	3,585	5,769
Ship: R.M.S. Queen Mary		TOTAL	3,585	5,769

on Thursday before Easter (Good Friday Eve). So ended the *Queen Mary*'s globetrotting. She was never again seen at Rio de Janeiro, Freetown, Cape Town, Suez, Fremantle, or Sydney. Her next task, with the *Queen Elizabeth*, was to maintain a shuttle service across the North Atlantic, bringing American and Canadian troops to Britain, in preparation for an Allied invasion of Western Europe. These included great numbers of air force men, for the bombing of Germany.

I was relieved by Captain Illingworth and had a month's leave at Cheltenham.

The passengers included 4350 German prisoners of war, who were being cleared out of camps in Britain and sent to the U.S.A. We left Gourock at 10.30 p.m., in darkness, and proceeded unescorted, as had now become usual. We anchored off Quarantine in New York and landed the prisoners in tenders. •

At this time, Allied Forces had completely won the battle of North Africa and were massing in Tunisia for the invasion of Italy. This began on 11th June with the capture of Pantelleria Island by airborne troops-the stepping-

Voyage 14	New York City - Gourock			
(Troops 15,281, Crew 927. Total 16,208 souls)				
Location	Status	Date	Miles	Km
New York City	depart	24-Jun-43		
Gourock	arrive	30-Jun-43	3,473	5,589
Ship: R.M.S. Queen Mary		TOTAL	3,473	5,589

stone to Sicily. Huge numbers of U.S. troops were being brought across the Atlantic to West and North African ports and to Britain. Many transports, in addition to the Queens, were employed in these movements.

U-boats were still active in the Atlantic, but ninety-seven per cent of freighters in convoy were reaching their destinations.

This was one of the "record" passages in "overload," an example of what the Queen ships could do as transports, when they were crowded to the limit. The passage was made at an average speed of 29.11 knots. Thus was sea-power demonstrated, and the Germans could find no answer to it. Their counter-blockade of Britain had failed. The land forces and air forces which would overwhelm them were seaborne to the theatres of war.

The fact that neither of the Queen ships came under direct enemy attack was little less than wonderful. They came and went like great grey ghosts, and never followed the same tracks twice, except at the near approaches to the Clyde and to New York. There, they would have been vulnerable, but naval protection made U-boat attacks too difficult, and minesweepers cleared the tracks. The Queens usually approached and left port in the hours of darkness.

They would have been vulnerable to air-attacks when they were at anchor in the Clyde, but they never loitered there long enough for German Intelligence to organize such attacks: in fact, no air-attack on them was ever made. The Luftwaffe let Hitler down seriously in that respect. In the open ocean, there was little danger. Their speed and zigzag tactics would baffle any U-boat, unless by blind mischance they passed within less than half a mile of a U-boat that was already in a set firing position. The odds against that happening were so great that it didn't happen. The tracks were widely varied. Sometimes we went near Iceland; at other times near the Azores.

A few hours before leaving port, the Captain went ashore to the Naval Control Office, accompanied by his Chief Navigating Officer, Radio Officer, and Cypher Officer, and was given the route in exact detail, showing courses, speeds, and zigzags to be followed at precise times throughout the passage, with the latest information on positions of U-boats, derelicts, icebergs, and the positions and courses of convoys or independent ships which would be near the route at any time, and of arrangements for providing air and surface naval escorts. He was also given the latest signal code books (which were frequently changed), and the instructions for breaking wireless silence, if this should become necessary.

If, after the ship left port, the Navy had further intelligence of dangers near her track they would send out secret coded messages giving precise orders for avoiding the dangerous area. These were called "diversions." Sometimes as many as six of them would be received on a trans-Atlantic passage, adding to the distances by several hundred miles.

On a typical passage-for example, that of the *Queen Mary* leaving New York on 24th June 1943, her crew consisted of 120 in the Deck Department; 258 in the Engine Department; 430 in the Catering Department; and 119 Permanent Staff. Total, 927.

The Deck Department consisted of the Captain, Staff Captain, navigating officers, radio officers (10), carpenters, boatswains, quartermasters, able seamen, ordinary seamen ("deck-boys"), ship's police and fire brigade. Besides navigating the ship, this department was responsible for the cleanliness of decks, painting of the superstructure, and the efficiency of lifeboats and other lifesaving apparatus.

The Engine Department consisted of the Chief Engineer, Staff Chief Engineer, and 256 others, of whom 105 rated as Engineer Officers. That high proportion of qualified technicians indicated the difference between oil burning liners and the old fashioned coal burning liners. There was very little heavy drudgery in the boiler rooms of an oil burner, but a great deal of technical skill required.

When steaming at normal full speed, the *Queen Mary* burned 1000 tons of oil every twenty-four hours. Though she would make the Atlantic crossing in approximately five days, she usually had 8000 tons of oil in her tanks when leaving port. She had 6500 tons of fresh water and used between 700 and 800 tons a day for all purposes. The use of fresh water for drinking and ablutions was necessarily rationed when 16,000 people were on board. The drinking water, carried in special tanks, was chlorinated and filtered before going through the taps. Sea water was laid on, in both hot and cold supply, to bathrooms, and used for toilet flushing, washing decks, and in every other possible way to conserve the freshwater supply.

The Catering Department, with which may be included the Purser's Department of some thirty clerks, was under control of the Purser, the Chief Steward, and the Second Steward. It included Chef, cooks, butchers, bakers, confectioners, pantrymen, waiters, storekeepers, stewards and kitchen porters. In addition to preparing and serving meals, the Catering Department

Ship Provision for 16,000 Passengers

Pounds	Kilograms	Description
4,600	2,087	of cheese
18,000	8,165	of jams
21,500	9,752	of bacon and hams
29,000	13,154	of fresh fruit
31,000	14,061	of canned fruit
31,000	14,061	of sugar, tea, and coffee
53,600	24,313	of butter, eggs, and milk powder
76,000	34,473	of flour and cereals
124,300	56,381	of potatoes
155,000	70,307	of meat and poultry

was responsible for the cleanliness of passenger quarters inside the ship. In both these tasks they received full assistance from the troops.

The amount of provisions required for 16,000 people for five or six days made a formidable shopping list. A typical list was:

There were nine canteens in the ship, selling soft drinks, cigarettes, toilet articles, and candy, but no chewing gum!

The Catering Department had the assistance of about 300 of the troops (apart from the mess orderlies), helping the butchers and bakers, preparing vegetables for the cooks, and getting stores up from the refrigerators and storerooms.

The Permanent Staff included gunners, and the officers of the various fighting services, British, American, and other Allies, who served as liaison between the ship's people and the troops embarked on any passage. The Permanent Staff was so called because its members remained in the ship. Besides the Officer Commanding Troops, it included Security Officers, Provost Marshal, Red Cross officials, Padres, Medical Officers and others whose duties were to assist in the embarkation and disembarkation of troops, quartering, messing, emergency drills, and in general to maintain good order and discipline, acting in conjunction with the officers of the various units embarked.

To attempt to embark 15,000 troops in one vessel, usually at nighttime, without careful preliminary planning, would have resulted in chaos. Most of the troops had never previously set foot in a ship. It was the work of the Permanent Staff to plan the details. Though they were soldiers ·and not sailors, they were under the jurisdiction of the ship's Captain and Staff Captain, and "belonged" to the ship as she voyaged to and fro.

Voyage 15	Gourock - New York City			
(Troops 4,427, Crew 908. Total 5,335 souls)				
Location	Status	Date	Miles	Km
Gourock	depart	4-Jul-43		
New York City	arrive	10-Jul-43	3,330	5,359
Ship: R.M.S. *Queen Mary*		TOTAL	3,330	5,359

When the ship arrived in New York, a conference was held to decide the date of embarkation and to settle details. Three days before she was due to leave port, an advance party of 2000 came on board to make themselves familiar with the ship and the special duties that they would perform on the passage. They included military police, sentries, guides, kitchen porters, mess orderlies, anti-submarine lookouts, and extra gunners. For administrative purposes, the ship was divided into three areas — "red," "white," and "blue."

The main embarkation began at 7 p.m. The troops were brought in ferries from their camps upriver. They were landed on the pier, formed up, and marched on board. As each man crossed the gangway, he was given a coloured card showing where he would sleep, when and where he would eat, and where he would muster for emergency drills. Guides directed the men to their sleeping quarters, and there they had to remain until the embarkation was completed. Any necessary orders were given from the Orderly Room by loudspeakers. Usually embarkation was completed by 1 a.m. By that time most of the men had turned in to their Standee beds. The order was then "Lights out" until 6 a.m.

Usually the *Queen Mary* undocked from New York at noon, and proceeded down the harbour slowly, with naval and air escort until she was well out to sea before darkness set in, and she could then make her way at full speed during the night.

Before the ship left the pier, the military officers of all the units on board were mustered in the main lounge and addressed by the Staff Captain and the O.C. Troops, on the details of ship's routine, emergency drills, air raid drills, blackout, and procedures to abandon ship if that should become necessary. The officers of the various units were then responsible for seeing that their men were similarly informed.

While the ship was proceeding down harbour, all the troops were exercised, firstly in air raid drill — when every man had to take cover in his sleeping quarters below decks — and secondly in the emergency drill, when everyone mustered on the upper decks in readiness to abandon ship if that signal should be given. The drills were repeated daily throughout the voyage, and occasionally at night to accustom the men to moving about in darkness.

Every man was shown how to wear his lifebelt, properly adjusted. He carried it with him wherever he went in the ship, hugging it to him like a bosom friend, until he was disembarked on the "other side" of the ocean.

The only troops exempted from the drills were the gun crews, anti-submarine lookouts, mess orderlies and kitchen helpers, and the "Sweeping Parties." It was surprising how much litter 15,000 soldiers could spread in a ship in five days. The Sweeping Parties were organized to keep all the troop accommodation swept, on all decks and in all alleyways and compartments. They were constantly on the go during daylight hours, but it was during the drills that they were able to make a good job of it.

There were hundreds of litter bins, but the troops seemed to avoid them. Tons of cigarette butts and candy wrappings were dropped here, there, and everywhere. It was the work of seamen to wash and scrub the decks with sea water and sand. This was done during the night, except for the part of the decks occupied in summer by the "overload," which were scrubbed when the troops moved off from there at 6 a.m.

Although the ship was only five days at sea, arrangements were made for recreation, amusements and religion, observances under control of the padres and Red Cross officers. Two movie shows were held daily on the promenade deck, which was enclosed and could be darkened. Concerts were held in the lounge, and at times in the large mess hall in the evenings. Portable gramophones and records were on loan. All kinds of books, games, and puzzles could be had for the asking.

I spent most of my time on the bridge and in the chartroom and left arrangements below decks to the Staff Captain and the Commandant of the Permanent Staff. The troops who came under my notice were mostly those who strolled around on the upper decks. I could see them there when they were mustered for emergency drills, a packed mass of men in uniform, wearing their lifebelts. At such times I had the feeling that my responsibility for the safety of so many human beings was almost more than would bear thinking about. Every precaution was taken, but who knew when a torpedo or mine might strike?

That could come at any moment, and it was for that reason that I took my only rest at sea in the chartroom. There I had a comfortable enough settee, reading lamp, heaters, ventilation, and a window looking out onto the bridge. I was on the spot if anything unusual should happen. Knowing that I was in the chartroom, the officers and men on the bridge preserved silence. I had every confidence in my officers, but the responsibility was mine. It was their duty, in case of doubt or difficulty, to call me in time to shoulder it. They knew that, if I were wanted, I could be on the bridge in a flash.

Voyage 16	New York City - Gourock			
(Troops 15,740, Crew 943. Total 16,683 souls)				
Location	Status	Date	Miles	Km
New York City	depart	25-Jul-43		
Gourock	arrive	30-Jul-43	3,353	5,396
Ship: R.M.S. *Queen Mary*		TOTAL	3,353	5,396

Before attempting to sleep, I took every possible precaution for the safety of the ship and then had the comfortable feeling that there was nothing more to be done. I slept in old uniforms, to be ready for the jump — if I had to be the last man of sixteen thousand to leave a sinking ship — but I never slept deeply; always, like a horse under a tree, with one eye and one ear open.

When not at drill, meals, or recreation, large numbers of soldiers and airmen wandered around on the upper decks. They just sat or stood around, gazing out to sea with a faraway look in their eyes, and probably thinking of home. Some of them would never return, and they knew it. I did not begrudge them the pleasure of carving their initials on the teakwood rails.

When the ship was entering port, most of the troops congregated on the upper decks, to see whatever was to be seen on their first sight of land. Precautions had to be taken to prevent them from crowding suddenly to one side. The underwater section of the Queen ships is almost box-shaped and flatbottomed amidships. When the *Queen Mary* listed ten degrees, her draught on the low side was increased by four feet. In narrow and relatively shallow waters, she had to be kept on an even trim. Fifteen thousand troops on the upper decks represent one thousand tons of mobile humanity

Among the passengers were 1925 German prisoners of war from North Africa, and their guards. We anchored at Quarantine in New York Harbour and disembarked them into tenders.

The ship then lay at the Cunard dock (Pier 90) in New York for a fortnight, awaiting her next "cargo" of fighting men.

On Thursday, 15th July 1943, in New York, I was overtaken by my sixtieth birthday. I did not like it at all. It meant that I would have only three more years at sea before reaching the retiring age. I had been going to sea for nearly forty-five years, and I could account for them; but they seemed to have gone by too quickly. I thought that I had never felt fitter in my life than on my sixtieth birthday.

But Time is the one enemy that no man can defeat. I had to face the fact — retire in three years!

Well, if my luck held, I would surely see the end of the war, and the victory of the forces of freedom, for which so many men, millions of them, were willing to risk their lives.

This was the greatest number of human beings ever embarked in one vessel on an ocean crossing [1]. It was a "record" that will probably never be surpassed. The time of the passage was 4 days 20 hours 42 minutes, at an average speed of 28.73 knots.

CHAPTER ENDNOTES

(1) The record still stands in 2025. The largest number of passengers ever recorded on a ship crossing the Atlantic Ocean was 7,604 people, carried by the Royal Caribbean's "Symphony of the Seas" cruise ship, including 5,350 passengers and 2,224 crew members; setting a new record for the most people on a single ship during a transatlantic crossing in peacetime

39

Germans on the Defensive — Western Allies Invade Italy — Prime Minister Churchill in the "Queen Mary" — Crossing for the Quebec Conference — Accommodation of the Special Party — No Code Word for "Pray" — Large Numbers of Troops Transported in the "Queen" Ships — Fifth Christmas of the War — Britain an Armed Camp — "D" Day — Western Allies Invade Normandy — Heavy Air-Bombing of Germany — The "Flying Bombs" in Britain — A Message from the Queen Mother — Victory in Sight.

ON arrival at Gourock on 30th July, 1943, I was informed with profound secrecy that a Very Important Person was to be embarked in the *Queen Mary* for the next westbound crossing in a few days' time-none other than the Right Hon. Winston Churchill, P.C., Prime Minister of Great Britain, going to Canada, with a party of naval, military, air-force and political advisers, to confer with President Roosevelt and U.S. service chiefs. I was to land the party at Halifax. The conference would be held at Quebec.

At this time the war news was tremendous. The United States 7th Army and British 8th Army (including Canadian divisions) had landed in Sicily on 9th July. Rome had been bombed by 700 U.S. planes on 19th July. Then, on 25th July, Mussolini had resigned, and was arrested by a government in which Marshal Badoglio was Prime Minister. It was clear enough that the Allied strategy of attacking the "soft underbelly" of the Axis in Italy would pay a full dividend.

In the meantime, the R.A.F. had heavily raided Hamburg on 24th July, dropping 2300 tons of bombs on that city in one night. This raid had been followed on three successive nights by equally heavy "thousand-bomber" raids by the U.S.A.A.F. and R.A.F. It was said that 20,000 people were killed in Hamburg, and 60,000 injured in these raids. The great German seaport was smashed to rubble.

On the Eastern Front, the Germans were retreating before a slow Russian counteroffensive. In the Pacific, Australian and American naval, military, and air-forces had inflicted heavy defeats on the Japanese in the Solomon Islands and New Guinea.

The Prime Minister's Special Party consisted of himself, Mrs Churchill, Miss Mary Churchill, the First Lord of the Admiralty (Admiral Sir Dudley Pounds), the British Minister of War Trans- port (Lord Leathers), and Chiefs of Staff, Lord Louis Mountbatten, Sir Charles Portal, General Sir Alan Brooke, Sir Ralph Metcalf, General Ismay, and their staffs, including Mr Churchill's Private Detective, Thompson, and a special guard of the Royal

Voyage 17	Gourock - Halifax			
(Troops 2,305, Crew 1,036. Total 3,341 souls)				
Location	Status	Date	Miles	Km
Gourock	depart	5-Aug-42		
Halifax	arrive	9-Aug-43	2,686	4,323
Ship: R.M.S. Queen Mary		TOTAL	2,686	4,323

Marines, besides secretaries, clerks, typists, cipher officers, and personal servants — 150 all told.

The whole party was accommodated on the main deck. The Prime Minister and his family occupied a suite amidships on the port side, with a private dining room for fourteen persons, and near by a large conference room and a secret map room. Stretched fore and aft of this were typing rooms, coding offices, sleeping cabins and sitting rooms, a rest room for the ladies, and a lounge. Marine sentries guarded all this part of the ship.

The map room had a chart of the North Atlantic, and maps of all the fighting fronts pinned to the bulkheads, with electric lights over them. The Prime Minister spent an hour here each day, studying the situation in conjunction with all the latest reports. He and Mrs Churchill and Mary, and some of the Staff Chiefs, came up by my invitation each day to the bridge, and were keenly interested in the working of the ship.

As usual when he went to sea, the Prime Minister wore a reefer jacket and a yachtsman's cap. This was the first time that I had seen this famous man at close quarters.

One day on the bridge he remarked to me, "Ah, I see that the wind's coming from dead ahead, Captain."

This was too much for me to take. "No, sir," I said. "It's coming from dead astern!"

"Huh!" said the Prime Minister. But he took it well enough, and shortly afterwards went below. I have never believed in flattery, at the expense of nautical truth, even though tact is a requisite for Cunard officers.

Throughout this passage, the *Queen Mary* was escorted by cruisers. It was said that the German Government had offered a reward equivalent to fifty thousand pounds to any U-boat commander who would sink the *Queen Mary* or the *Queen Elizabeth*. I doubt whether the U-boat captains would have needed such a cash incentive.

It was against the rules for the *Queen Mary* to break wireless silence, except in extreme emergency. She could receive but not" send radio signals. The lengthy cipher messages sent out by the Prime Minister and his party were flashed by Morse lamp to an escorting cruiser, which then dashed away for a hundred miles or so off the course and transmitted the signals by radio. This prevented CT-boats[1] from getting radio-direction-finder bearings on the *Queen Mary's* position and track.

Having these V.I.Ps on board increased my anxieties, but I could not take more precautions for the ship's safety than I was already taking on passages with fifteen thousand troops on board, most of whom were unknown to fame — the American G.ls, who thronged the *Queen Mary*'s decks on the eastbound crossings, bound for the battlefields of Europe.

I could even forgive that G.I. who said loudly in my hearing, "I bet the British wish they could build a ship like this!"

No bite.

Winston Churchill's habit of using the word "pray" instead of "please" in his dispatches caused the coding staff a slight headache. Many of his messages began "Pray inform ... " and there was no word for "pray" in the four-letter codes, which were changed every twenty-four hours. A special block of letters had to be devised for it.

When we arrived at Halifax, we berthed alongside Ocean Quay, which had been enlarged and its approaches specially dredged to accommodate the Queen ships. The Port Authorities at Halifax felt it keenly that Canadian troops had to go to New York to be embarked in the Queens. Despite their efforts, I had some anxiety in getting her alongside on this, her first and very special visit to that port. But, with the aid of six tugs, it was accomplished.

The arrival of the Great Man was supposed to be a profound secret, but all Halifax seemed to know of it. Thousands of citizens surrounded the high railings of the Dock Estate, to see the ship come slowly to her berth. A railroad train was waiting alongside the dock. The Northwest Mounted Police formed a Guard of Honour on the dock and along the train siding.

The Prime Minister, now wearing his billycock hat, and smoking a big cigar, walked down the gangway, followed by his retinue, and boarded the waiting train. He went along the train to the observation platform at the after end, and from there espied the big crowd of citizens peering at him through the wrought-iron gates and railings of the dock. He asked the officer of the guard to open the gates and let the crowd in. They rushed through and surrounded the platform on which the P.M. stood. He made a speech to them. "Keep your hearts up and all will be well!"

The train pulled out, amid rousing cheers. For eighteen days the *Queen Mary* lay at Halifax, while the Quebec Conference was held, attended by President Roosevelt and Prime Minister Churchill, with their retinues, to

Voyage 18	Halifax - Gourock			
(Troops 15,116, Crew 937. Total 16,053 souls)				
Location	Status	Date	Miles	Km
Halifax	depart	27-Aug-43		
Gourock	arrive	31-Aug-43	2,734	4,400
Ship: R.M.S. *Queen Mary*		TOTAL	2,734	4,400

draw up the plans for an invasion of Western Europe across the English Channel. After this conference, the Prime Minister and some of his staff returned to Britain in a cruiser, but most of his staff reembarked in the *Queen Mary*, in company with a big contingent of Canadian troops.

The troops consisted of 14,989 Canadians, and the Special Party 127. This was the biggest number of people ever embarked from a Canadian port in one vessel, and rates among the record trooping passages of all time. Any passage on which 16,000 souls were embarked could fairly be considered as remarkable in maritime records.

On arriving at the Clyde, I was relieved by Captain Illingworth and given home leave, which was subsequently extended to nearly two months. I spent most of the time at Cheltenham, with visits to Liverpool for conferences on technical matters with the Cunard General Manager, S. T. Lister, and his assistant, Robert Crail.

During this time, Captain Illingworth made three round voyages in the *Queen Mary* from the Clyde to New York and brought over another 40,000

Voyage 19	Gourock - New York City			
(Troops 1,475, Crew 903. Total 2,378 souls)				
Location	Status	Date	Miles	Km
Gourock	depart	5-Nov-43		
New York City	arrive	11-Nov-43	3,868	6,225
Ship: R.M.S. *Queen Mary*		TOTAL	3,868	6,225

U.S. Troops. The *Queen Elizabeth* was likewise busy on the shuttle service. On an average, each ship was bringing not less than 20,000 troops a month to Britain.

The two vessels combined brought a total of 320,500 U.S. and Canadian troops to Britain during the calendar year 1943. On this shuttle service, each of the Queens was doing work equivalent to that of ten normal troop transports. Together, they were equal to a fleet of twenty normal transports. That calculation takes into account their high speed, which enabled them to make more round voyages in a given time than ordinary liners could make.

Gone was the peacetime idea that the Queen ships were "white elephants," and that they would be "too big" for wartime service. But, despite the fact that they went through the war without mishap, there was a terrible risk and an element of luck in their survival. Speedier but not bigger ships have since been built, for passenger services, but I believe that 50,000 tons will be considered by ship designers in future as the practical limit of size for convenient handling of passenger liners and troop transports into and out of harbours. If that is so, the records of troop-carrying capacity, established by the *Queen Mary* and the *Queen Elizabeth* during the 1939-45 war, and especially during the "peak" year, 1943, may never be equalled or surpassed, and will be considered phenomenal in the history of the sea and ships.

While I was on leave, in September and October, Italy collapsed under the Allied offensive and was knocked out of the war. The Russians were slowly advancing in the Crimean region and had reached the Dnieper River. The Japanese were being forced back in New Guinea and the Solomon

Voyage 20	New York City - Gourock			
(Troops 2,305, Crew 1,036. Total 3,341 souls)				
Location	Status	Date	Miles	Km
New York City	depart	15-Nov-43		
Gourock	arrive	20-Nov-43	3,241	5,216
Ship: R.M.S. *Queen Mary*		TOTAL	3,241	5,216

Voyage 21	Gourock - New York City			
(Troops 1,203, Crew 910. Total 2,113 souls)				
Location	Status	Date	Miles	Km
Gourock	depart	24-Nov-43		
New York City	arrive	30-Nov-43	3,399	5,470
Ship: R.M.S. Queen Mary		TOTAL	3,399	5,470

Islands. German cities were being relentlessly bombed by immense air-raids from Britain.

Early in November, I rejoined the *Queen Mary* at Gourock.

It was now winter weather, with gales and fog, but the shuttle service went on. At New York we embarked U.S. troops, and a contingent of Australian airmen, who had been brought across the Pacific from Australia to San Francisco, and from there across the U.S.A. by train.

On this passage we undocked at New York in fog and proceeded dead

Voyage 22	New York City - Gourock			
(Troops 11,907, Crew 1080. Total 12,987 souls)				
Location	Status	Date	Miles	Km
New York City	depart	3-Dec-43		
Gourock	arrive	9-Dec-43	3,743	6,024
Ship: R.M.S. Queen Mary		TOTAL	3,743	6,024

slow down harbour. Outside, we met with a southerly gale, and had a long passage, with diversions that took us near Greenland and Iceland. I had very little rest and was wondering if I would be home for Christmas. But no! We had a quick turnaround.

It seemed that we would have Christmas in New York. But no!

Another quick turnaround.

We had Christmas Day at sea, in very heavy weather, which continued throughout the passage. A splendid Christmas Dinner was served, but many of the troops could not stomach it.

That was the fifth Christmas of the war, but peace and goodwill were at last in sight. Her Majesty *Queen Mary* (the Queen Mother) sent her Christmas greetings to the "Captain, Officers and Ship's company, and all on board the ship which bears her name."

King George VI sent Christmas greetings addressed "to all the seamen of the Merchant Navy and the Fishing Fleets, and especially to those who must spend Christmas Day away from home."

Voyage 23	Gourock - New York City			
(Troops 2,847, Crew 1,087. Total 3,914 souls)				
Location	Status	Date	Miles	Km
Gourock	depart	14-Dec-43		
New York City	arrive	20-Dec-43	3,774	6,074
Ship: R.M.S. Queen Mary		TOTAL	3,774	6,074

The King's message was heartening: "The thoughts of all of us turn with gratitude to the men who stood steadfast throughout the darkest days, who never faltered even when the enemy's attacks on our ships were at their fiercest.

"You, seamen of the Merchant Navy, have played a great part in the success achieved by our fighting forces in all their overseas theatres of war. Without your devoted service there could be no victory for our arms.

"From the master in command to the boy on his first voyage, you have worked together, with the steady discipline of free men who know what is at stake. Your reward is the consciousness of duty done, and the affection and respect of all your countrymen. On New Year's Day of 1944, I was at home at Cheltenham. While I was on leave for six weeks, Captain Illingworth took the *Queen Mary* on two round voyages to New York and brought over another 24,000 U.S. troops to Britain.

At this time the Germans had flung large forces into Northern Italy, in an attempt to bolster their collapsed ally. They had to withdraw forces from the Russian front and the "West Wall" defences for that purpose, but they were being pressed back in Italy by the British and American armies. Despite the fact that the Western Allies had opened this great "Second Front" in Southern Europe, the Russians were clamouring for them to open yet another front in Western Europe.

The heavy air bombardment of Germany by British and American air forces was continuing, and most of the cities of Western Germany were already in ruins. It was clear that Germany was beaten but intended to go down fighting.

Voyage 24	New York City - Gourock			
(Troops 11,990, Crew 1087. Total 12,077 souls)				
Location	Status	Date	Miles	Km
New York City	depart	23-Dec-43		
Gourock	arrive	29-Dec-43	3,690	5,938
Ship: R.M.S. Queen Mary		TOTAL	3,690	5,938

Voyage 25	Gourock - New York City			
(Troops 1,332, Crew 940. Total 2,272 souls)				
Location	Status	Date	Miles	Km
Gourock	depart	21-Feb-44		
New York City	arrive	27-Feb-44	3,632	5,845
Ship: R.M.S. Queen Mary		TOTAL	3,632	5,845

Voyage 26	New York City - Gourock			
(Troops 11,950, Crew 1,109. Total 13,059 souls)				
Location	Status	Date	Miles	Km
New York City	depart	1-Mar-44		
Gourock	arrive	7-Mar-44	3,632	5,845
Ship: R.M.S. Queen Mary		TOTAL	3,632	5,845

Voyage 27	Gourock - New York City			
(Troops 2,042, Crew 1,123. Total 3,165 souls)				
Location	Status	Date	Miles	Km
Gourock	depart	14-Dec-43		
New York City	arrive	20-Dec-43	3,685	5,930
Ship: R.M.S. Queen Mary		TOTAL	3,685	5,930

Voyage 28	New York City - Gourock			
(Troops 12,072, Crew 1,099. Total 13,171 souls)				
Location	Status	Date	Miles	Km
New York City	depart	21-Mar-44		
Gourock	arrive	27-Mar-44	3,785	6,091
Ship: R.M.S. Queen Mary		TOTAL	3,785	6,091

It was in preparation for the invasion of Western Europe — which would open a Third Front against Germany — that U.S. and Canadian troops were being rushed across the Atlantic to camps in Britain, to reinforce the large numbers of British soldiers and airmen already in training and in action.

Voyage 29	Gourock - New York City			
(Troops 1,246, Crew 1,091. Total 2,337 souls)				
Location	Status	Date	Miles	Km
Gourock	depart	1-Apr-44		
New York City	arrive	6-Apr-44	3,803	6,120
Ship: R.M.S. Queen Mary		TOTAL	3,803	6,120

Voyage 30	New York City - Gourock			
(Troops 11,979, Crew 935. Total 13,065 souls)				
Location	Status	Date	Miles	Km
New York City	depart	10-Apr-44		
Gourock	arrive	16-Apr-44	4,069	6,548
Ship: R.M.S. Queen Mary		TOTAL	4,069	6,548

Voyage 31	Gourock - New York City			
(Troops 968, Crew 935. Total 1,903 souls)				
Location	Status	Date	Miles	Km
Gourock	depart	20-Apr-44		
New York City	arrive	26-Apr-44	3,844	6,186
Ship: R.M.S. Queen Mary		TOTAL	3,844	6,186

The *Queen Mary* was now due for an overhaul and bottom painting. She was put into the Bayonne Dry Dock at New York for eight days and then was moved to Pier 90 and lay there for nearly a month for mechanical overhaul, and painting of the superstructure and interior.

Then came the inspiring news on 6th and 7th June of "D" Day- the invasion of Normandy by Allied Forces based on Britain.

Voyage 32	New York City - Gourock			
(Troops 11,993, Crew 1,112. Total 13,105 souls)				
Location	Status	Date	Miles	Km
New York City	depart	7-Jun-44		
Gourock	arrive	13-Jun-44	3,777	6,078
Ship: R.M.S. Queen Mary		TOTAL	3,777	6,078

On this passage, we heard the daily news bulletins broadcasting details of the invasion of Normandy. On the day of our arrival at Gourock, we heard the grim news of the first "Flying Bomb" landing in southern England. These were jet propelled and were at first described as "pilotless aircraft." They caused the consternation that any new weapon causes in warfare until the answer to it is found. The most effective answer would be to capture the bases from which they were being launched near Calais. This was the task of the armies which had breached the German "West Wall" in Normandy.

More and more troops were needed!

Among the passengers were 2987 German prisoners of war and 313 British and Canadian guards. There were also 920 troops of various units in transit, and 678 civilians. Among the civilians were Lord and Lady Keynes, and Doctor Wellington Koo.

We carried, as usual, a large amount of mail on this trip 2654 bags. That was typical. Almost the whole of the mail to and from the American and Canadian forces in Britain, besides civilian mail, was being conveyed across

Voyage 33	Gourock - New York City			
(Troops 4,898 Crew 1,103. Total 6,001 souls)				
Location	Status	Date	Miles	Km
Gourock	depart	17-Jun-44		
New York City	arrive	23-Jun-44	3,608	5,806
Ship: R.M.S. *Queen Mary*		TOTAL	3,608	5,806

the Atlantic in the two Queen ships. That was an aspect of their wartime service. On their eastbound passages, they also usually carried 1000 tons of cargo, including foodstuffs and military stores.

On this passage I exhibited on all notice boards throughout the ship a message received from Her Majesty *Queen Mary*: "Since I launched the *Queen Mary* nearly ten years ago, almost half her life has been spent on active war service. Now, as the war enters upon this decisive phase, I send my warm

Voyage 34	New York City - Gourock			
(Troops 14,533, Crew 1,105. Total 15,638 souls)				
Location	Status	Date	Miles	Km
New York City	depart	1-Jul-44		
Gourock	arrive	7-Jul-44	3,611	5,811
Ship: R.M.S. *Queen Mary*		TOTAL	3,611	5,811

greetings to the Captain, the Officers and the Ship's Company, and to all those who sail in the ship that bears my name.

"It is always a source of pride and of pleasure to me to receive news of the magnificent work the *Queen Mary* is doing in the transport of troops from every quarter of the Empire and Commonwealth, and from the United States of America, to the theatres of war. I pray that before very long it may be her joyful duty to carry the victorious soldiers of the United Nations back to their homes and families in many parts of the world.

"My earnest hope is that the many friendships born on board the *Queen Mary* during the years of war will continue into the happier years of peace to come, and that she will always prove herself a strong link, and a messenger of goodwill, between the great English-speaking Nations."

On the passenger-list were 3988 German prisoners of war, and their guard of 468. We had 5395 bags of mail on board, and 69 boxes of gold!

Voyage 35	Gourock - New York City			
(Troops 5,060, Crew 1,102. Total 6,162 souls)				
Location	Status	Date	Miles	Km
Gourock	depart	11-Jul-44		
New York City	arrive	17-Jul-44	3,664	5,897
Ship: R.M.S. *Queen Mary*		TOTAL	3,664	5,897

In mid-Atlantic on this westbound passage, I attained my 61st birthday. Included in the total of troops on this passage were 464 U.S. army nurses, going to join military hospitals in Britain, which were now receiving wounded from Normandy.

In five months, February-July 1944, I had made twelve crossings of the Atlantic in the *Queen Mary*, bringing a total of 74,504 troops to Britain on the six eastbound passages.

Voyage 36	New York City - Gourock			
(Troops 12,009, Crew 1,130. Total 13,139 souls)				
Location	Status	Date	Miles	Km
New York City	depart	23-Jul-44		
Gourock	arrive	28-Jul-44	3,403	5,477
Ship: R.M.S. *Queen Mary*		TOTAL	3,403	5,477

I was due for leave, and enjoyed a quiet month at Cheltenham, gardening and resting, and trying to forget about the war. As far as I could judge from the news of the day, Germany was as good as beaten.

It was a lovely summer. We had come through, and victory was in sight.

CHAPTER ENDNOTES
(1) Specially equipped German ships/shore stations that had direction finding equipment and target plotting capabilities.

40

O N Monday, 28th August, 1944, after a month's leave at Cheltenham, I went to Liverpool to see the General Manager of the Cunard White Star Line (S. T. Lister). I was on my way to Glasgow to rejoin the *Queen Mary.* "I have important news for you," he said.

He was smiling. My heart stood still.

"You have been appointed Commodore, in succession to Sir Robert Irving, who has reached the retiring age!" He shook my hand warmly. "Congratulations, Commodore Bisset!"

After forty-six years at sea, and thirty-seven years in the Cunard service, I had attained what could fairly be considered the zenith of ambition of a merchant seaman. My thoughts went back to my boyhood in Liverpool, when I had peered wistfully through the railings at the Landing Stage, watching what were then considered the big and stylish Cunard and White

Star liners arriving and departing, visions of magnificence so far beyond my wildest dreams and hopes.

And now — Commodore of the Cunard White Star Line! Yet it had all happened gradually, one step at a time in the long climb up the ladder of promotion and increased responsibility; so that, when this day came, I was, to some extent, prepared for it. I knew "Bob" Irving well. I had served under his command as his Chief Officer in the Carmania in 1919. He had been the first Captain of the *Queen Mary*, on her maiden voyage in 1936, and had been Commodore throughout the war years. I had met him at many conferences. And now I was to step into his shoes, for the final two years of my own seagoing career.

Lister interrupted my reverie. "You'll be flying your pennant in the *Queen Mary* for the time being," he said. "She's in the Clyde now. She'll be ready to leave next week-and this is very hush-hush — she will take a certain Very Important Person and his Special Party to America. That's all. we know at present. Mr Crail will be going up with you to Glasgow, and there will be a conference on board. In the meantime, I suppose you'll be getting your uniforms altered," he added, in a matter-of-fact tone, "and you won't have very much time to have that done."

"I'll see Paisleys in Glasgow about that," I told him. For nearly ten years I had been wearing the four gold rings of a Captain on the sleeve of my uniforms. Now there would be the insignia of Commodore in the Merchant Navy — one broad band of gold braid, the width of four rings conjoined, and no merchant seamen could expect more than that.

That afternoon, Robert Crail and I caught the train to Glasgow, arriving at midnight. Within a few days, my uniforms were ready. The "hush-hush" conference was held, and we were told that the Special Party to be embarked would consist of the Prime Minister and Chiefs of Staff, going to Halifax for another conference at Quebec.

The Special Party, numbering 195, included the Prime Minister and Mrs Churchill; the Minister of War Transport, Lord Leathers; First Sea Lord,

Voyage 37	Gourock - Halifax - New York City			
(Troops 3,594, Crew 1,107. Total 4,701 souls)				
Location	Status	Date	Miles	Km
Gourock	depart	5-Sep-44		
Halifax	arrive	10-Sep-44	3,210	5,166
	depart	10-Sep-44		
New York City	arrive	11-Sep-44	670	1,078
Ship: R.M.S. *Queen Mary*		TOTAL	3,880	6,244

Admiral Cunningham; Chiefs of Staff, Sir Ralph Metcalf, Sir Alan Brooke, Sir Charles Portal, General Ismay, and their staffs and retinues. They were quartered, as previously, in special accommodation on the main deck.

Among the 3399 other passengers were some U.S. and Canadian sick and wounded soldiers, who were accommodated in wards from which Standee beds had been removed and in which hospital cots were installed. The *Queen Mary* and *Queen Elizabeth* were now in service partly as hospital carriers on the westbound crossings but continued as troop transports on the eastbound crossings.

On this passage, the *Queen Mary* left Gourock in darkness at 8.30 p.m., and, for the first time since the war had begun, made her route, under naval orders, southwards through the Irish Sea, and then westerly to the south of Ireland.

That was an indication of the Navy's confidence that the U-boats were beaten. Until then, these horrible things had infested the Irish Sea and the waters off the south of Ireland. We were escorted by cruisers and destroyers, in relays. There was always a chance that a German surface raider — the *Tirpitz* or the *Admiral Scheer* — might sneak out from Norway into mid-Atlantic, in a last desperate stroke of the German Navy. The *Queen Mary* was diverted to the southwards, continued zigzagging, and made Halifax safely in 4 days 19 hours 12 minutes, at an average speed of 27.86 knots.

The Special Party and some other passengers disembarked at Halifax Quay at 2.15 p.m. on Sunday, 10th September. The ship left two hours later for New York, making a good run there at an average speed of 28.76 knots, much of it in the hours of darkness and blacked out.

But now we had radar installed — the "magic binoculars" of the sailors' dream for centuries-the eye that pierces fog and darkness — the greatest miracle of the twentieth century, in its use at sea.

With radar, safety at sea, or at least immunity from the hazards of collision in fog and darkness, seemed to be at last assured. I felt humbly grateful that I had been spared to use this marvellous development of science before my time came to retire from seafaring, and while I needed its help in the responsibilities that I had to bear.

On arriving at New York, we heard the news of Germany's "last resort" secret weapon. The first rocket bomb in history had landed at Chiswick, in London, on 8th September, fired from a base in Holland.

So the Modern Age had arrived with a bang. London was the target, and the Londoners did not whimper. They could "take it." The *Queen Mary* lay at New York for eleven days, then embarked 8888 troops and re-embarked the Special Party of 196.

Voyage 38	New York City - Gourock			
(Troops 9,084, Crew 1,110. Total 10,194 souls)				
Location	Status	Date	Miles	Km
New York City	depart	20-Sep-44		
Gourock	arrive	25-Sep-44	3,505	5,641
Ship: R.M.S. Queen Mary		**TOTAL**	**3,505**	**5,641**

For "security" reasons, the Prime Minister himself did not board the ship at Pier 90 but joined her from a tender at the Quarantine Station. Then we put to sea under U.S. naval escort, which was relieved by British cruiser escort in mid-ocean.

As previously, the "Grand Old Man" came up to the bridge each day, for a chat about the weather and the navigation of the ship. He was intensely interested in the new radar installation. At the end of the voyage, when we came to anchor in the Clyde, he addressed the troops over the loudspeaker system, wishing them the best of luck and a speedy victory.

When leaving the ship, he gave me a signed photograph of him- self, and a letter:

My Dear Commodore,

Mrs Churchill and I wish to thank you and through you all those who have been concerned in making this voyage so comfortable for ourselves and the members of the Mission.

All the arrangements were quite admirable, and the facilities provided enabled the Staffs to continue their duties and get through a great amount of essential work.

We hope that, at some future date, we may again travel in your fine ship.

Yours sincerely,
WINSTON S. CHURCHILL

It was a cheerful homecoming for the Architect of Victory, who would soon, perhaps, be an Architect of Peace. At this time, Allied Forces in the West had liberated the whole of France and Belgium, had reached the Lower Rhine, and were invading Holland. General Eisenhower issued, on 28th September, a proclamation to the German people: "The Allies come as conquerors, but not as oppressors."

Voyage 39	Gourock - New York City			
(Troops 5,047, Crew 1,086. Total 6,133 souls)				
Location	Status	Date	Miles	Km
Gourock	depart	2-Oct-44		
New York City	arrive	8-Oct-44	3,718	5,984
Ship: R.M.S. Queen Mary		TOTAL	3,718	5,984

Among the passengers were sick and wounded U.S. soldiers, with nurses and doctors; also a party of U.S. Congressmen; and Bing Crosby and Fred Astaire, entertainers.

We were still following zigzag courses and diversion routes and taking full wartime precautions. U-boats were still at sea, but now we were using the Irish Sea approach to the Clyde, enabling the ocean crossing to be made in warmer latitudes, under the influence of the Gulf Stream.

The passengers included 2888 troops (many of them wounded), and 128

Voyage 40	New York City - Gourock			
(Troops 11,891, Crew 1,061. Total 12,960 souls)				
Location	Status	Date	Miles	Km
New York City	depart	12-Oct-44		
Gourock	arrive	18-Oct-44	3,611	5,811
Ship: R.M.S. Queen Mary		TOTAL	3,611	5,811

civilians. It was a great inconvenience that the Queen ships could not be brought alongside any wharf in the Clyde. The docks had been damaged by air-raids, but also the river channel was too narrow and shallow to permit safe handling of the ships upstream. That situation required the use of a very large number of tenders at Gourock, to disembark the troops, embark passengers, and to refuel, water, and reprovision the ships. All this had to be done as quickly as possible for the sake of a quick turnaround, and to enable the ships to get away as quickly as possible from an anchorage where they might have been exposed to air-raids.

Voyage 41	Gourock - New York City			
(Troops 3,016, Crew 1,059. Total 4,075 souls)				
Location	Status	Date	Miles	Km
Gourock	depart	22-Oct-44		
New York City	arrive	28-Oct-44	3,839	6,178
Ship: R.M.S. Queen Mary		TOTAL	3,839	6,178

On an average they remained only four or five days at Gourock. As one-sixth of the crew were relieved at the end of each round voyage, having one round voyage off, and another one-sixth of the crew, in rotation, had forty-eight hours' local leave, to attend to their affairs and communicate with their homes, these arrangements meant that approximately one-third of the crew were allowed ashore while the ship was at anchor at Gourock. A special tender service was maintained for them, and for conveying temporary workers from and to the shore to replace them in shipboard work.

A further complication now was the need to transform part of the troop accommodation to hospital accommodation for the westbound passages, and to change it again to troop accommodation at New York. All this, done under pressures of urgency, required much detailed organization while the vessels were in port.

The only port in Britain in which the Queen ships could go alongside the quay was Southampton, but that port had been so heavily damaged by German air raids, and its approaches were so vulnerable to U-boat and air-

Voyage 42	New York City - Gourock			
(Troops 11,968, Crew 1,065. Total 13,033 souls)				
Location	Status	Date	Miles	Km
New York City	depart	3-Nov-44		
Gourock	arrive	9-Nov-44	3,777	6,078
Ship: R.M.S. Queen Mary		TOTAL	3,777	6,078

attack after the fall of France, that the Queens had to be based on Gourock.

But now we were hoping that Southampton would again become serviceable as a port: the sooner the better!

The troops had been embarked at Pier 90 during the night of 1st November, but next morning the fog was so thick that we couldn't risk undocking. It continued dense all that day, 2nd Nov- ember, and next morning was almost as bad. The Port Director, Commodore Runicke, asked me if I would be willing to proceed at high water, 1.15 p.m. on 3rd November. There was a great "schemozzle" about this, but I said that I would try, as the troops who were crowded on board had become restless and had already used up two days' provisions. With the aid of ten tugs, I backed the ship out into the river at high tide, and, by great luck, the fog began to lift at that moment, and we got free of the land by nightfall.

Voyage 43	Gourock - New York City			
(Troops 2,477 Crew 1,076. Total 3,553 souls)				
Location	Status	Date	Miles	Km
Gourock	depart	13-Nov-44		
New York City	arrive	19-Nov-44	3,596	5,787
Ship: R.M.S. *Queen Mary*		TOTAL	3,596	5,787

Voyaging with the troops on this passage were Micky Rooney, entertainer, and Walter Lippmann, journalist-both of them boosters of war morale.

This was my fortieth voyage, or more precisely, ocean passage, in the *Queen Mary* in wartime, and I had grown to love her. How marvellously she answered her helm on the zigzags-like the old champion *Mauretania* — and how splendidly she breasted the seas in all weathers and responded to every demand put on her! She was, like the *Mauretania* of yore, a happy ship, a lucky ship. She had become a personality, majestic but friendly. That feeling of being "alive" had come from the confidence placed in her, not only by those who had built her, and by those who served in her at sea, but also by troops and other passengers in their tens of thousands who were entrusted to her safekeeping in their transits from shore to shore.

The teeming life of the thousands of troops, below decks and at their emergency drills, is something that may never be exactly repeated in nautical history; for, though they were only five days at sea, every moment of that passage was lived on the alert for disaster that could come without warning, and they knew it. But always came the landfall, and the rattling of the anchor cable in the hawsepipe at Gourock, or the fussy tugs nosing alongside off the Statue of Liberty, ready to ease her into the dock and the ring off of the engines.

It was on this passage, in mid-November, 1944, that the *Queen Mary* ran into some of the heaviest weather that I have ever seen in the North Atlantic. It was a north-easterly gale, which, on our prescribed zigzag course, had to be taken abeam from time to time. I reduced speed to 22 knots, but, even at that, she rolled through 23 degrees.

This was uncomfortable, but not dangerous, but some of the people on board — not sailors — thought that their end was nigh. Under strict censorship, nothing was published in wartime, either in Britain or the U.S.A., on the movements of ships, but millions of people had seen the unheralded comings and goings of the Queen transports, and hundreds of thousands had voyaged in them. A rumour was spread that the *Queen Mary* had "nearly

Voyage 44	New York City - Gourock			
(Troops 11,996, Crew 1,084. Total 13,080 souls)				
Location	Status	Date	Miles	Km
New York City	depart	10-Dec-44		
Gourock	arrive	16-Dec-44	3,695	5,947
Ship: R.M.S. Queen Mary		TOTAL	3,695	5,947

rolled over in a storm"; but, like many another rumour spread in wartime, it was more than a little exaggerated.

She was what is known as "a good sea-boat" — if a steamer of 80,000 tons, with twelve decks, can be called "a boat"!

On arriving at New York, we put her into dry dock, and had three weeks to enjoy the rest and recreation that New York can offer to sailors with some time and money to spend ashore.

Being now due for leave, and also required for conferences arising from my duties as Commodore-including discussions on the intention to use Southampton again as the home port of the Queens — I had the pleasure of spending that sixth Christmas of the war at home.

41

O N 1st February, 1945, after six weeks' home leave, I went to the Clyde, and took over command of the Queen Mary again, from Captain Illingworth. In two winter voyages under his command she had brought another 25,000 U.S. troops to Britain.

Reinforcements were urgently needed for the Allied Armies invading Germany in the West. In December the Germans had launched a determined counterattack in the Ardennes. This offensive, under Field-Marshal van Runstedt, was a bold but hopeless last fling by the German Army. It succeeded for the time being in checking the Allied advance to the Rhine but was made possible only by weakening the German forces. on their Eastern Front

Among the civilians on this passage were Catherine Cornell, and the British orchestral conductors, Sir Thomas Beecham (with Lady Beecham, herself a concert pianist), and Sir Malcolm Sargent. I invited them to the

Voyage 45	Gourock - New York City			
(Troops 3,293, Crew 1,140. Total 4,433 souls)				
Location	Status	Date	Miles	Km
Gourock	depart	5-Feb-45		
New York City	arrive	11-Feb-45	3,439	5,535
Ship: R.M.S. Queen Mary		TOTAL	3,439	5,535

Voyage 46	New York City - Gourock			
(Troops 11,226, Crew 1,382. Total 12,608 souls)				
Location	Status	Date	Miles	Km
New York City	depart	18-Feb-45		
Gourock	arrive	25-Feb-45	3,539	5,695
Ship: R.M.S. Queen Mary		TOTAL	3,539	5,695

Voyage 47	New York City - Gourock			
(Troops 4,111, Crew 1,366. Total 5,477 souls)				
Location	Status	Date	Miles	Km
New York City	depart	5-Mar-45		
Gourock	arrive	11-Mar-45	3,774	6,074
Ship: R.M.S. Queen Mary		TOTAL	3,774	6,074

Voyage 48	New York City - Gourock			
(Troops 10,905, Crew 1,385. Total 12,290 souls)				
Location	Status	Date	Miles	Km
New York City	depart	17-Mar-45		
Gourock	arrive	23-Mar-45	3,523	5,670
Ship: R.M.S. Queen Mary		TOTAL	3,523	5,670

bridge, and Sir Thomas remarked that conducting the *Queen Mary* seemed more difficult than conducting a symphony orchestra. Despite that, I would not have cared to exchange jobs with him.

When we arrived in New York, the atmosphere of imminent victory in Europe prevailed. The Allied Armies in the West had crossed the German frontier in January and had penetrated deeply into Germany in February and March, while the Soviet Armies on the East were swarming into Poland, Austria, Czechoslovakia and East Prussia.

It appeared that further American reinforcements of the Allied forces in Europe would not be necessary. The *Queen Mary* was laid in waiting at New York until that point was decided. She was put into dry dock for overhaul, then week after week went by, as the war news made it more and more clear that her further services as a troop transport on eastbound passages would be no longer required.

President Roosevelt fell seriously ill on his return from the Yalta Conference. On 12th April, the American nation in particular, and the world in general, was stunned by the news of his death. He had died on the eve of victory. New York was in deep mourning, and American emotion at its strongest.

Sixteen days later (28th April 1945), Mussolini was captured by Communist guerrilla forces in northern Italy, and was killed as a prisoner there and then. Two days after that, on the eve of May Day, Adolf Hitler committed suicide in Berlin.

On 7th May, the remnant of German resistance collapsed with Germany's

Voyage 50	New York City - Gourock			
(Passengers 1,207, Crew 1,026. Total 2,233 souls)				
Location	Status	Date	Miles	Km
New York City	depart	5-Jun-45		
Gourock	arrive	10-Jun-45	3,264	5,253
Ship: R.M.S. *Queen Mary*		TOTAL	3,264	5,253

unconditional surrender. At this news of final victory in Europe, "V.E. Day" was celebrated, in New York as elsewhere, with wild rejoicings.

The U.S. War Department announced that 400,000 American troops would stay in Europe, to occupy Germany, and that two million would be repatriated as soon as possible. The announcement added that six million Americans would be sent to fight against Japan.

American casualties in the European war numbered 150,000 men killed, and 650,000 wounded or invalided.

In all this atmosphere of victory and excitement, it became clear that the *Queen Mary* and the *Queen Elizabeth*, together with a large number of other transports, would now be required to bring U.S. and Canadian troops back home.

No blackout! No zigzags! No U-boats! No surface raiders! No enemy aircraft! No manning of guns! No extra lookouts!

It seemed incredible that we were steaming with full navigation lights on. Victory! Peace again, after five years and ten months of groping in the dark!

Most of our passengers on this crossing were British women and children, who had been sent to the U.S.A. or Canada for safety during the war. They were going home!

The British Government announced that 56,000 civilians had been killed and 160,000 wounded by enemy air attacks in Britain during the war.

The Admiralty announced that, from September 1939 to V.E. Day, a total of 4280 Allied merchant ships and 490 ships of neutral countries had been lost by enemy action.

The war was continuing in the Pacific, where the Japanese were being compressed to their last stand. They had no naval forces in the Atlantic and were unlikely to send any there. The only menace to shipping in the Atlantic now might be from moored or floating mines not yet swept up, or not yet made harmless by their automatic devices. That menace was so slight that it was no cause for serious worry.

When I arrived at Gourock, I received a letter that was waiting for me there, from the secretary to the Prime Minister:

10 Downing Street, Whitehall.
30th May, 1945.
Sir,
I am desired by the Prime Minister to inform you that it is his intention, on the occasion of the forthcoming list of Birth- day Honours, to submit your name to the King with a recommendation that he may be graciously pleased to approve that the honour of Knighthood be conferred upon you.

Before doing so, the Prime Minister would be glad to be assured that this mark of His Majesty's favour would be agree- able to you, and I am to ask that you will be so good as to communicate with me accordingly at your earliest convenience.

Yours faithfully,
J.M. MARTIN

As only three days then remained before the King's Birthday, I telephoned to Mr Martin from Glasgow, formally accepting the honour, and confirmed this by letter. The *Queen Mary* was lying at Gourock, under orders to embark a full load of American troops for repatriation without delay.

My knighthood was announced in the King's Birthday List published on Thursday, 14th June. On that day I was aboard the *Queen Mary* at Gourock, embarking the American troops, and next day put to sea.

Voyage 51	Gourock - New York City			
(Passengers 14,477 Crew 893. Total 15,670 souls)				
Location	Status	Date	Miles	Km
Gourock	depart	15-Jun-45		
New York City	arrive	20-Jun-45	3,203	5,155
Ship: R.M.S. *Queen Mary*		TOTAL	3,203	5,155

These were the first U.S. troops to be returned as brigaded units to their

With Bisset in command, R.M.S. Queen Mary arriving in New York at the end of Voyage #51 on June 20, 1945
(Public Domain, U.S. Navy photo 80-GK-5645; U.S. Defense Visual Information Photo HD-SN-99-03026)

homeland at the end of the war in Europe. Some of them had been on service in Europe for three years. Many of them had been brought over in the *Queen Mary* or *Queen Elizabeth*, including some who had voyaged with me on the *Queen Mary*'s first crossing to Britain with U.S. troops, in August 1942.

As the wartime dangers, at least in the Atlantic, had ended, the veil of censorship, which had concealed all movements of shipping, could now be lifted. I did some addition sums, from my private memoranda. In thirty-nine months, from 25th February 1942 to 10th June 1945, I had made forty-eight voyages in command of the *Queen Mary*, and two in command of the *Queen Elizabeth*.

On the forty-eight voyages that I had made in command of the *Queen Mary*, she had steamed a total of 247,825 miles. She had carried a total of 297,809 brigaded troops to theatres of war, and 71,627 other passengers, including transit troops, sick and wounded troops, prisoners of war, and civilians, away from theatres of war. On the two voyages on which I had commanded the *Queen Elizabeth*, she had steamed 7164 miles and had carried 10,890 brigaded troops and 1708 others.

Adding to these the details of my previous service in the *Franconia*, I found that in 5¾ years of war service the three transports while under my command had steamed a total of 375,089 miles and had carried a total of 338,499 brigaded troops and 73,335 other wartime passengers. That made a grand total of 411,834 who had voyaged with me, under wartime conditions, as passengers, to and from various theatres of war.

This total does not include the crews and permanent staffs, who were viewed as "ships' people."

Though my wartime service had been performed only as a duty to which I was called in the practice of my profession, as all other merchant seamen were called in their various spheres of service, in ships great and small, the fact that I had been entrusted with command on the *Queen Mary* on so many of her wartime voyages was considered meritorious, and had earned the honours which had been conferred on me.

I wished that I could have shared those honours with all my shipmates, who had shared the work and the risks, not only in war time, but during the forty-seven years of seagoing in which I had learned seamanship.

Now, on 16th June 1945, in mid-ocean, westward bound across the Atlantic with the first contingent of American troops returning victorious to their homeland, I received a radio signal from the Admiralty: "Following from the Prime Minister to Commodore Bisset: Please accept my warm congratulations on your knighthood.

It well becomes the Commander of such a proud vessel which has played no inconspicuous part in our victory."

This was indeed gratifying from such a source, but in fact the *Queen Mary*, despite her huge bulk, had always tried not to be too conspicuous! I replied, thinking not only of the war against Japan, but also of the British General Elections, which were to be held on 5th July: "Following from Commodore Bisset to Prime Minister: Warmest thanks for your message of congratulations, and best wishes to you for further victory in the near future."

I had not anticipated the tremendous reception that New York was preparing for the *Queen Mary* on this occasion.

As we steamed up the harbour at noon, on 20th June, the 14,777 G.I.s on board swarmed onto the upper decks, excitedly cheering at their first view for many a day of the Statue of Liberty and of "Little Old New York." Blimps and helicopters flew low overhead, with loudspeakers blaring out the latest songs and messages of "Welcome home!" Harbour craft steamed alongside, with flags flying, bands playing, and crowded with thousands of cheering people. Every ship in the harbour blew three long blasts of welcome as we passed, and the *Queen Mary*'s deep toned booming steam whistle — which could be heard at a distance of twenty miles — responded with an almost continuous series of blasts that made a deafening roar. The ship was gaily decorated with flags, as also was the Cunard White Star Pier, and flags flew everywhere on the masts of the skyscrapers, from the windows of which people were leaning out, waving flags, and throwing down showers of paper.

We docked at 3.10 p.m., and the troops began disembarking immediately, while bands played and the crowds cheered, laughed, and wept with joy at the heroes' homecoming.

Reporters and photographers swarmed on board but were fobbed off until a formal press conference next day. Then I found myself facing 130 reporters in the lounge and had to answer hundreds of questions.

Censorship had been lifted, after all the years of silence and mystery. Hundreds of questions were fired at me.

"Is it true that the *Queen Mary* ran through a pack of twenty- five U-boats?"

My answer, though not intended to be so, was sensational in its effect on the hardened newsman!" never sighted an enemy submarine!"

I had to explain this further: "U-boats are heard, not seen. I didn't want to sight them. They wanted to sight me!"

"Does the *Queen Mary* carry any underwater device for detecting submarines?"

"No. Her propellers and bow wave create so much noise that any outside noises would be drowned out."

"What guns did the *Queen Mary* carry?"

"Two six-inch and sixty A.A. guns, but she never sighted any enemy vessel or aircraft and never fired a gun in anger!"

"Is it true that she was struck by a wave, and rolled over to within five inches of the point where they don't come back?"

"That is the first I've heard of it!"

"Is it true that the *Queen Mary*'s engines have been run to death during the war, and are of no further use?"

"Our engineers know better than to allow such a thing to happen. She's running as well as ever and has a long life ahead of her!"

"Did any soldiers fall overboard?"

"Nobody has ever fallen overboard from the *Queen Mary*!"

So it went on, until all rumours were disposed of, and then the pressmen got the real story, when I revealed, for the first time since censorship was lifted, exactly what the *Queen Mary* and *Queen Elizabeth* had done during the war; what ports they had visited; and the huge total number of troops that they had carried.

All this was reported widely in the American press, and summaries of it cabled to Britain and elsewhere.

George Horne in the New York Times described the *Queen Mary* as "a ship with a charmed life." He added: "Her most important passengers were the legions of dogfaces, airmen, corpsmen and nurses of the American armed forces.... No matter what happens in the future to the big Queen, there will be something of America with her to the end. . . . She roamed without convoy, streaking across the Atlantic alone, cleaving the deep blue water of the Pacific alone, running whole divisions on urgent deliveries that undoubtedly helped turn the recurring tides of war."

Paul Gallico (who had made a wartime crossing in the *Queen Mary*) wrote: "I remember her for her dazzling speed through the submarine zones, and the graceful and easy way she would lean over into the zigzags designed to frustrate the undersea wolf- packs.... I remember her for the way she swallowed up 15,000 G.Is at a clip, housed and fed and transported them with never a slip and for the wonderful, teeming life that filled her during those war crossings, the ceaseless barking of the loudspeakers. Wherever she goes, may fair winds, calm seas, and good luck go with her."

After the press conference, I had to face the photographers, and newsreel operators. On the following day, I was invited to give three broadcasts — "Headline Edition" (WJZ), "Report to the Nation" (WABC) and "Washington Story" {WJZ). The first two were in studios with no spectators. The third nearly scared the daylights out of me. It was in a theatre full of people. Verily, a sea captain has to be able to turn his hand to anything.

In the meantime, the *Queen Mary*'s crew, and shore-gangs, were at work, dismantling the A.A. gun mountings and the lookout posts erected above the bridge, and taking away the bomb splinter shields from hatchways and entrances, beginning to get her ready for return to peacetime service; but it was obvious that for many a voyage yet she would be packed like a sardine can — on the westbound crossings.

We remained only six days in New York. It was strange to be embarking only a few passengers, mainly civilians, including women and children.

Among the passengers on this, my fiftieth voyage in the *Queen Mary*, were Bob Hope, the comedian, and his party, going to entertain the troops in

Voyage 52	New York City - Gourock			
(Passengers 1,040, Crew 903. Total 1,943 souls)				
Location	Status	Date	Miles	Km
New York City	depart	26-Jun-45		
Gourock	arrive	1-Jul-45	3,200	5,150
Ship: R.M.S. Queen Mary		TOTAL	3,200	5,150

Occupied Germany. I chatted to him a lot, and every time I made a joke, out came his notebook and he jotted it down . . . so I learned one of the secrets of being a successful comedian ... I nearly teamed up with him.

That was my last voyage in the *Queen Mary*. I was to leave her and transfer my pennant to the *Queen Elizabeth*. It was also the last time that the *Queen Mary* anchored in the Clyde. That river, where both the Queens were born, had been their home port in Britain during the war, but now they were to operate from Southampton, where they could go alongside the quay, and also into dry dock for overhaul. The damaged docks there were being reconstructed and were almost ready.

I handed the *Queen Mary* over to Illingworth and left her with a pang of regret; but for me now it was a case of "Off with the old love, and on with the new."

The *Queen Elizabeth*, biggest ship in the world, was to be the flagship of the Cunard White Star Line in the days of post-war reconstruction, and my duty was to take command of her, in the last year of my seagoing career.

42

The Accolade of Knighthood — Choosing My Name — Ceremony at Buckingham Palace — The Atomic Bomb — The "Queen Elizabeth" — Repatriating U.S. and Canadian Troops — War's Aftermaths — A Difficulty at Halifax — Reading the "Lesson" at Saint Paul's Cathedral — An Ordeal and a Privilege — Canadians in Bulk Quantities — Celebrities in the Tourist Class — Thirteen Thousand Christmas Dinners — A Christmas Broadcast-Dawn of a Peaceful New Year.

AFTER leaving the *Queen Mary* at Gourock, on 2nd July, 1945, I had eight weeks ashore, partly for a rest at home at Cheltenham, and partly to attend conferences on arrangements for using Southampton as terminal port for Cunard White Star transatlantic services. But there was another matter. I had received a letter from the private secretary of the Home Secretary:

Home Office,
Whitehall,
18th June 1945.

Sir,

With reference to the arrangements for conferring upon you the dignity of knighthood, I am desired by the Home Secretary to say that he has the honour to convey to you the King's Commands to attend at Buckingham Palace on Tuesday, 10th July, at 10.15 a.m., in order that you may receive the accolade at the hands of His Majesty.

Dress Service Dress, Morning Dress, or Civil Defence Uniform.

I shall be glad if you will inform me at your very earliest convenience whether you are able to attend, and by which of your first names you desire in future to be known.

I am, sir,

Your obedient servant,

R. J. HEWISON.

The final sentence in this letter caused me some bother. My fond parents, without consulting me in the slightest, had conferred upon me the three Christian names of "James Gordon Partridge." The third of these was a family surname on my mother's side of the family. It could be ruled out as an appellation for a nautical knight!

I would have to be either "Sir James" or "Sir Gordon."

In my boyhood, my family had ignored "James" and always called me "Gordon." When I went to sea as an apprentice, at the age of fifteen, the Captain of the County of Pembroke, a Welshman, said to me on the first day, "Indeed to goodness, 'Gordon' won't do for a sailor's name. It's too fancy! Haven't you another name?"

"James," I told him.

"Very well, we'll call you 'Jimmy' on board this barque!" he said. And so it was in all my sailing-ship days.

Years later, when I had become an officer in the Cunard service, my brother officers appeared to think that "Jimmy" was not suitable, and they took to calling me "Bill" Bisset, probably for the sake of alliteration. And so I was known to my cronies for many years.

But now that it had to be either "Sir James" or "Sir Gordon," I remembered the Welsh Captain's opinion that "Gordon" was too fancy for a sailor. So I settled for "Sir James," and notified the Home Secretary's secretary accordingly.

On the day before the appointed day, my wife and I went up to London, and stayed overnight at the Cumberland Hotel. After breakfast next morning, I put on my Number One uniform. It was made of thick wool. I had also a heavy raincoat, for, although this was the midsummer season, a drizzle of rain was falling. Intending to take a taxi to the Palace, I went out from the hotel at the right time but couldn't find a taxi!

So we took the tube to Green Park, and walked, hurrying along. We arrived at the Palace with only a few minutes to spare, and I was admitted to the anteroom, sweating and feeling very anxious. There was no handkerchief in any of my pockets!

Twenty or more knights were there, looking cool, calm, and collected. One of them, Sir Harold Stanford Cooper, Managing Director of the Ford Motor Company, noticed my predicament. He produced handkerchiefs from several of his pockets, like a conjuror producing rabbits from a hat. "Here y'are. Help yourself!" A Court Chamberlain led us into the audience room and told us what to do. When each knight's name would be called, he would be required to advance and kneel bare headed before the King to receive the accolade. There was a cushion to kneel on, and alongside it a handrail for the use of elderly or otherwise stiff jointed or wheezy knights, who might find difficulty in kneeling or rising.

One knight insisted on rehearsing his kneel, to see if he could do it with the aid of the handrail.

Other honours besides knighthoods were being conferred, and each person to receive an honour was allowed to have three guests to attend the Investiture. The guests sat in the audience chamber, and May was among them, looking very smart in a new dress for the occasion.

The King entered, and took his place, sword in hand. As I had noticed on a previous occasion, everything at Buckingham Palace is well organized. All the knights summoned on this occasion were to receive the accolade of Knight Bachelor. Our names were called in alphabetical order.

Two As and one B were ahead of me. The procedure is to kneel on one knee. I had no need of the handrail. The King touched me lightly on each shoulder with his sword.

"Rise, Sir James!"

All the knights and other recipients of honours waited until the ceremony was over, and the King withdrew. Then we were courteously shown out into the rain, and that was that.

My wife and relatives still called me "Gordon," and my old cronies still called me "Bill."

I returned to Cheltenham, and, five days later, on 15th July 1945, celebrated my 62nd birthday.

At that time the public sensation was the result of the British General Elections held on 5th July. The Conservatives had been heavily defeated, and Winston Churchill would no longer be Prime Minister!

The war against Japan continued. A large part of the British Navy was in Far Eastern waters, to cooperate with the U.S. and Australian Navies in the final overthrow of Japanese expansionist ambitions.

In the Atlantic, every available transport, including the two Queens, was continuing the massive repatriation of U.S. and Canadian troops from Europe. I was required to take part in several conferences on the reopening of Southampton as terminal port for the Queens and other Cunard White

Voyage 53	South Hampton - New York City			
(Passengers 14,996, Crew 854. Total 15,850 souls)				
Location	Status	Date	Miles	Km
South Hampton	depart	26-Aug-45		
Gourock	arrive	31-Aug-45	3,209	5,164
Ship: R.M.S. *Queen Elizabeth*		**TOTAL**	**3,209**	**5,164**

Star transports. Were there floating mines in the Channel? We consulted the experts at the Admiralty and decided that the *Queen Mary* should make for Southampton on her next homeward passage, arriving 12th August, to be followed by the *Queen Elizabeth* a week later. I would then take over command of the *Queen Elizabeth*. Both ships were to remain in the troop-transport service for another six months or so, before being reconverted to peacetime passenger and mail service. On 7th August, news came through that the terrible weapon of the "atomic bomb" had been dropped on the

Voyage 54	New York City - South Hampton			
(Passengers 1,558 Crew 906. Total 2,464 souls)				
Location	Status	Date	Miles	Km
New York City	depart	4-Sep-45		
Gourock	arrive	10-Sep-45	3,164	5,092
Ship: R.M.S. *Queen Elizabeth*		**TOTAL**	**3,164**	**5,092**

Japanese city of Hiroshima. A week later, Japan surrendered unconditionally. This was ratified on 2nd September, and the Six Years' War was over! It was in that atmosphere of final victory that I took over command of the *Queen Elizabeth*, at Southampton, on 23rd August 1945.

Among the passengers were the U.S. Secretary of State Byrnes and his party of twenty-eight, including John Foster Dulles. The time taken on the passage was 4 days 21 hours, at an average speed of 27 knots. This speed, which was improved on some passages to an average of 28 knots, was typical in the service of both Queen transports at this period. We were aiming to run a regular schedule, making the crossing each way in a few hours under five days, without trying for any "records" of speed.

Not a minute was being wasted during the turnarounds, either at Southampton or New York. It was very much more convenient to refuel,

Voyage 55	South Hampton - New York City			
(Passengers 14,979 Crew 851. Total 15,830 souls)				
Location	Status	Date	Miles	Km
Gourock	depart	14-Sep-45		
New York City	arrive	19-Sep-45	3,149	5,068
Ship: R.M.S. Queen Elizabeth		TOTAL	3,149	5,068

water, take in stores, and embark troops from the quayside at Southampton than it had been at the anchorage at Gourock during the war!

The ships were still painted battleship grey, but, when we arrived in New York on 24th September, I had the *Queen Elizabeth's* funnels painted in Cunard contrasting red and black, which seemed wonderfully gay and triumphant, after the years of drabness.

At this time the eastbound passengers included parties of officials of the United Nations Relief and Rehabilitation Administration ("UNRRA"), and

Voyage 56	New York City - South Hampton			
(Passengers 1,207, Crew 1,026. Total 2,233 souls)				
Location	Status	Date	Miles	Km
New York City	depart	24-Sep-45		
Gourock	arrive	29-Sep-45	3,175	5,110
Ship: R.M.S. Queen Elizabeth		TOTAL	3,175	5,110

others on official business, but very few civilian tourists. The food and accommodation were not luxurious. The *Queen Elizabeth* had never been anything else than a troop transport. She had never been properly fitted out for civilian passenger traffic.

This was, I believe, the biggest number of troops ever carried in the *Queen Elizabeth* — certainly the greatest number she carried under my command. The troops were in festive mood, with no blackouts, and plenty of entertainment.

Voyage 57	South Hampton - New York City			
(Passengers 15,077, Crew 855. Total 15,932 souls)				
Location	Status	Date	Miles	Km
South Hampton	depart	4-Oct-45		
Gourock	arrive	9-Oct-45	3,141	5,055
Ship: R.M.S. Queen Elizabeth		TOTAL	3,141	5,055

Voyage 58	New York City - South Hampton			
(Passengers 986, Crew 859. Total 1,845 souls)				
Location	Status	Date	Miles	Km
New York City	depart	12-Oct-45		
Gourock	arrive	18-Oct-45	3,174	5,108
Ship: R.M.S. Queen Elizabeth		TOTAL	3,174	5,108

The U.S. officers of the Permanent Staff had now left the ship, as she was to be used for transporting Canadians to Halifax.

This was the first big contingent of Canadians repatriated in a Queen transport, and their homecoming was welcomed with joy. Despite drizzling rain, big crowds were waiting at the quay and on the foreshores. The Canadian Government had requested that homecoming Canadians should be landed at Halifax during the winter months.

Voyage 59	South Hampton - Halifax			
(Passengers 12,517 Crew 864. Total 15,381 souls)				
Location	Status	Date	Miles	Km
South Hampton	depart	22-Oct-45		
Halifax	arrive	26-Oct-45	2,556	4,113
Ship: R.M.S. Queen Elizabeth		TOTAL	2,556	4,113

The *Queen Mary* and the *Queen Elizabeth* had both been at that part several times during the war. The passage from Britain to Halifax is shorter than to New York, the ocean track is free of drifting icebergs in winter, and the approaches to the quay are easy. Unfortunately, the quay was not an enclosed dock, but a wharf open to swell from the south-eastward. In the event of a south-easterly gale, a giant ship might be likely to range back and forth and break her moorings.

That was my opinion, shared by other Captains who handled Queen ships into and out of Halifax. The local port authorities were indignant when I expressed the opinion that it would be wiser to disembark Canadian troops from the Queens at New York or Boston than at Halifax. They pointed out that Halifax was the birthplace of Samuel Cunard in 1787, and also that Canadians, for patriotic reasons, should step ashore on their own soil when returning victorious. These were strong arguments, but not strong enough to prevent the ship from breaking her moorings, and possibly suffering damage, if a south-easterly gale should blow up!

Voyage 60	Halifax - South Hampton			
(Passengers 1,820 Crew 861. Total 2,681 souls)				
Location	Status	Date	Miles	Km
Halifax	depart	31-Oct-45		
South Hampton	arrive	5-Nov-45	2,563	4,125
Ship: R.M.S. Queen Elizabeth		TOTAL	2,563	4,125

Despite the urgings of the "Haligonians," I decided to recommend to the British and Canadian Governments, and to the Admiralty and the Cunard White Star Management, that future disembarkations of Canadian troops from the Queens should be at Boston or New York. This raised a storm, as the truth sometimes does, but the first duty of a shipmaster is to ensure the safety of his vessel at all times, whether at sea or in harbour.

A party of Canadian parliamentarians, including the Hon. Vincent Massey (Prime Minister) and his wife, and officials and high-ranking officers Manager) on the question of using Halifax for disembarking Canadian troops from the Queen transports.

I had met Sir Percy Bates several times previously; and every time I met him, I respected him more. He was a baronet, and, in the true meaning of that term, a gentleman. He was a man of wide knowledge and culture, a greatly experienced businessman, but, above all, a lovable and kindly personality. He it was who, as Chairman of the Cunard White Star Line, had been mainly responsible for the decision to build the Queen ships, beginning with the Queen Mary, during the "Great Depression" of the early 1930s, and he had raised the finance to do it, at a time when most men of business were scared to invest their capital in anything.

On my recommendation, it was decided that New York would be the terminal for disembarking Canadian troops. That paint settled, I went to St. Paul's Cathedral, at 11 a.m. on the morning of the National Service for Seafarers, which was to be held at 5 p.m. I wanted to "look over the ground."

On entering the cathedral, I asked one of the vergers, "Where will Captain Bisset stand when he reads the Lesson this evening?" He looked at me keenly. "You are Captain Bisset," he said. "I recognize you from having seen your photo in the papers. I'm glad you've come, because the electrician would like to make a voice test. The Cathedral has been wired for a loud-speaker system!" The electrician was soon found, and I ascended into the reading- pulpit, recited the days of the week, and counted one to ten. "O.K.," said the electrician, "if you pitch your voice like that, and speak in the direction of the mike, all will be well."

I examined the Bible on the lectern — the biggest Bible I had ever seen. It was already opened at the 61st Chapter of Isaiah. Much to my surprise, I found that the page was torn right across. It had been mended with transparent sticky tape, but this would not interfere with my reading. A young clergyman went through the text with me and gave me advice on which words to emphasize. That afternoon, I put on my Number One uniform, and arrived with my wife at the West Door of the Cathedral at 4.15 p.m. The doors were not yet opened, but a great crowd was assembling in the churchyard, and on the steps. The blue cloth and gold braid of naval and mercantile uniforms predominated. There were Admirals and other high-ranking officers in plenty, and parties from naval establishments, including the nursing services, Women's Royal Naval Service, and Sea Cadets, besides veterans from the Greenwich Hospital for Aged Seamen, boys from the School of Navigation at Southampton, and officers and men of the Merchant Navy, foreign ambassadors, political and civic dignitaries, and the general public. When the doors were opened, and we entered, the Head Verger showed us to our pew, which was behind the pew of the parliamentary party. He said to me sombrely, "When it is time for you to read the Lesson, I shall come for you and stand in the aisle by the pew. I shall be carrying my silver wand. When I bow to you, please rise and follow me. I shall conduct you to the bottom of the pulpit steps. You will bow to me and ascend the steps." Then he added, "The rest will be up to you! When you have finished reading the Lesson, I shall conduct you back to your pew in a like manner."

Sir Percy Bates, who was seated nearby, said to me, "Read slowly and distinctly, and we all feel sure that you will make a good job of it!"

That was heartening, and I needed some heartening, as the great Cathedral was now packed to the doors with many thousands of people. At 5 p.m. precisely, there was a hush, as King George VI and *Queen Elizabeth* entered, with their attendants, and took their seats in a pew across the aisle from the parliamentary party.

In a few moments the service was under way, with the singing of the hymn, "Lead us, Heavenly Father, lead us o'er the world's tempestuous sea."

After the Lord's Prayer and other prayers, my time had come. The verger stood by my wife whispered, "Good luck!" and I undocked. My escort went ahead dead slow, past the King and Queen on the right and the Cabinet on the left, and then across the stone paving of the transept (227 feet wide). I was more used to full speed ahead than dead slow. My friends told me afterwards that I was doing a slight zigzag to keep astern of the verger and following him with a Western Ocean roll.

In the pulpit I took a good look at the congregation, which was a sea of faces. After a few seconds, I announced the Lesson, and began, "The spirit of the Lord God is upon me."

Those were the words of the Prophet Isaiah, not mine.

I did not feel nervous, as I read on.... "And they shall build the old wastes, they shall raise up the former desolations, and they shall repair the waste cities.... Ye shall be named the Priests of the Lord ... ye shall eat the riches of the Gentiles, and in their glory shall ye boast yourselves "

But I was glad when I got through to the end "For as the earth bringeth forth her bud, and as the garden causeth the things that are sown in it to spring forth; so the Lord God will cause righteous- ness and praise to spring forth before all the nations."

Under escort as previously, I returned to my pew without mishap. My wife whispered, "Excellent!" and I was satisfied. The service continued with psalms, hymns, prayers, and sermon, to its conclusion with the favourite old hymn:

were on board. On arrival at Southampton, the ship was put into dry dock for routine overhaul, and I had six weeks on shore.

A big occasion was now looming up for me. While the ship was at Halifax, I received a radiogram, inviting me to "read the Lesson" (from the Bible) at the annual National Service for Seafarers, to be held in St. Paul's Cathedral, London, on 8th November 1945. The service this year, at the end of a war in which so many seamen of the Royal Navy and the Merchant Navy had lost their lives, would have special significance, and would be attended by the King and Queen, the Prime Minister (Mr Attlee) and the Cabinet, and a very big congregation of seamen and civilians.

I replied, accepting the responsibility, and appreciating the privilege. I also inquired what "lesson" I would have to read, and was informed that it would be from the Old Testament, the 61st Chapter of the Book of Isaiah, consisting of eleven verses, beginning, "The Spirit of the Lord God is upon me; because the Lord hath anointed me to preach good tidings unto the meek."

Reaching for my Bible, I read the chapter through with some bewilderment. I am ashamed to confess that I couldn't make head or tail of it. I could not see that it had anything to do with seafaring; but I am no theologian.

However, I typed it out and pasted it on my shaving mirror. During the homeward voyage from Halifax, I learned it off by heart, and was still not much wiser as to what it meant. On leaving the *Queen Elizabeth* in dry dock at Southampton I went up to London to report to Sir Percy Bates (Chairman of the Cunard White Star Line) and to Mr Robert Crail (now General

Eternal Father, strong to save,
Whose arm hath bound the restless wave,
Who bidd'st the mighty ocean deep
Its own appointed limits keep;
O hear us when we cry to Thee
For those in peril on the sea.

Then "God Save the King," and slowly the great church emptied. I was told that 5000 people had attended the service.

Christmas at sea, the first Christmas of peace — after many a year — if not altogether of goodwill on earth, yet The *Queen Elizabeth* was still on war service as a transport, crowded to her winter-time capacity, with every Standee bed occupied. On Christmas morning, she was thrusting through a south-westerly gale, with hurricane squalls and mountainous seas. I spoke

Voyage 61	South Hampton - New York City			
(Canadian Troops 12,404, Crew 870. Total 13,272 souls)				
Location	Status	Date	Miles	Km
South Hampton	depart	22-Dec-45		
New York City	arrive	28-Dec-45	3,136	5,047
Ship: R.M.S. *Queen Elizabeth*		TOTAL	3,136	5,047

Christmas greetings over the loudspeaker system to the crew and the troops. Then the Catering Department began serving 13,272 Christmas dinners — no small order, even if a considerable number of the troops chose to go without. At 11.20 a.m., I spoke on the B.B.C. "Christmas broadcast." This was an authentic hook up (not tape-recorded), from many people, in many places. My greetings were introduced as "from the Captain of the biggest ship in the world, the *Queen Elizabeth*, now in mid-ocean, taking twelve thousand Canadian troops home."

When we docked at New York it was snowing. Canadian-owned troop trains were lined up at the pier. The troops marched down the gangways and boarded the trains in the blizzard.

Voyage 62	New York City - South Hampton			
(Passengers 1,091, Crew 869. Total 1,960 souls)				
Location	Status	Date	Miles	Km
New York City	depart	30-Dec-45		
Gourock	arrive	5-Jan-46	3,174	5,108
Ship: R.M.S. Queen Elizabeth		TOTAL	3,174	5,108

New Year's Day at sea, and the passengers at my table were Mrs Eleanor Roosevelt, Senator and Mrs Connolly, and Senator and Mrs Vandenburg. They were members of a U.S. delegation going to a conference of the United Nations Organization to be held in London.

So the year 1946 arrived. Great numbers of U.S. and Canadian troops had been shipped home during the preceding six months, but there were many yet waiting their turn.

But now the end of the war service of the Queens could be foreseen, and then they could be refitted for their normal peacetime work, which had for so long been interrupted. The *Queen Elizabeth* had steamed nearly half a million miles and had carried a total of 700,000 troops and other wartime passengers, without having been finally fitted up by her builders, undergoing the regular trials, or making what is usually viewed as the "Maiden Voyage" of an ocean-going liner.

When trooping was ended, she and the *Queen Mary* would have to be refitted for a new lease of life, much less secretive, less dangerous and less crowded than the extraordinary life that had been theirs during the war.

Repatriating Canadians — Winston Churchill Takes a Holiday — His Farewell to Politics — A Speech at Sea — Magna Carta as Cargo — I Am Honoured at Cambridge University — Doctor of Laws — An Oration in Latin — "Scorner of Danger" — The "Queen Elizabeth" Ends her Wartime Service — A Troopship Captain's Retrospect-Stupendous War- time Achievement of the "Queen" Transports — All in the Day's Work.

DURING the first three months of the year 1946, the *Queen Elizabeth* and the *Queen Mary* continued in troop transport service, from Southampton to New York. Many other transports were also engaged in that service. The huge operation of repatriating nearly two million U.S. and Canadian troops was accomplished within nine months after Germany's surrender. Even that seemed a long time to those who had to wait their turn. But the end of it was in sight!

Voyage 63	South Hampton - New York City			
(Canadian Troops 12,314, Crew 883. Total 13,197 souls)				
Location	Status	Date	Miles	Km
South Hampton	depart	9-Jan-46		
New York City	arrive	14-Jan-46	3,144	5,060
Ship: R.M.S. *Queen Elizabeth*		**TOTAL**	**3,144**	**5,060**

Included statistically among the troops on these westbound passages were usually a few civilians of V.I.P. or official status, who were accommodated on a reserved part of A Deck, with its own small dining-room and lounge, and a few stateroom suites.

On this occasion, one hour before the *Queen Elizabeth* was to leave Southampton, my special passengers strolled on board-Ex- Prime Minister Winston Churchill and Mrs Churchill, going to the U.S.A. for a three months' holiday at Miami, Florida. That was the first time they had been in the *Queen Elizabeth.*

As on previous occasions, "the Man who had Won the War and Lost the Peace" wore his yachting uniform and cap, and I invited him up to the bridge daily. On the day before we made port, he spoke to the troops over the loud-speaker system.

This speech, which was his farewell to politics, or at least to the leading role that he had played in politics for so long, at such a crucial time in history, was not reported in the press, but was so typical of his style of oratory that I feel it should be reported here:

> My friends and shipmates in the *Queen Elizabeth*!
>
> For most of you it is homeward bound. It has been a good voyage in a great ship, with a fine Captain-or indeed Commodore. We have not got there yet, but I am quite sure he will find the way all right. At any rate, he has been over the track before, and, as I can testify myself, having been several times with him, in those days there used to be U-boats and things like that. They all seem to have dropped off now and we don't have to worry about them at all. Something has happened. The seas are clear, the old flag flies, and those who have done the work, or some of it-because the British did some-turn home again, their task accomplished, and their duty done.
>
> What a strange, fearful, yet glittering chapter this war has been! What changes it has wrought throughout the world and in the fortunes of so many families! What an interruption in all the plans each of us had made! What a surrender of the liberties we prized! What a casting away of comfort and safety! What a pride in peril! What a glory shines on the brave and true! The good cause has not been overthrown. Tyrants have been hurled from their place of power, and those who sought to enslave the future of mankind have paid, or will pay, the final penalty.
>
> You Canadians, many of whom served in the Canadian Fifth Division, no doubt have your minds filled with the victorious war

scenes of Italy and the Rhine. But we Englishmen always think of the days of 1940, when the Canadian Army Corps stood almost alone in Kent and Sussex, and the Germans had twenty-five divisions ready to leap across the Channel and wipe Great Britain out of life and history. I think about those days, too, sometimes, and how fine it was to see everyone, at home and throughout the Empire, moved by the same impulse, so simple, so sublime-"Conquer or die!"

Victory in arms, or in any walk of life, is only the opportunity of doing better on a larger scale and at a higher level. Do not be anxious about the future! Be vigilant, be strong, be clear-sighted, but do not be worried. Our future is in our hands. Our lives are what we choose to make them. The great British Commonwealth and Empire, emerging from the fire once again, glorious and free, will form a structure and an organization within which there will be room for all, and a fair chance for all.

Yesterday I was on the bridge, watching the mountainous waves, and this ship-which is no pup-cutting through them and mocking their anger. I asked myself, why is it the ship beats the waves, when they are so many and the ship is one? The reason is that the ship has a purpose, and the waves have none. They just flop around, innumerable, tireless, but ineffective. The ship with the purpose takes us where we want to go.

Let us therefore have purpose, both in our national and Imperial policy, and in our own private lives. Thus the future will be fruitful for each and for all, and the reward of the warriors will not be unworthy of the deeds they have done.

As these words resounded in the gigantic ship, with her engines throbbing as she pounded through the seas at thirty knots, and thirteen thousand souls in her, listening, I felt, as many of the others on board must have felt, that the power of eloquent, persuasive words has always been, and perhaps always will be, the strongest influence on human lives. We had heard Winston Chur- chill's political swansong, and the occasion was memorable. He had the last word in the "War of Words," and it was fitting that this final message was delivered at sea.

Voyage 64	New York City - South Hampton			
(Passengers 899, Crew 885. Total 1,784 souls)				
Location	Status	Date	Miles	Km
New York City	depart	16-Jan-46		
Gourock	arrive	23-Jan-46	3,174	5,108
Ship: R.M.S. Queen Elizabeth		TOTAL	3,174	5,108

On this eastbound passage I had a valuable piece of cargo-Magna Carta in a tin box! This was the "Lincoln Copy" — one of only four copies of the famous document extant since it was signed by King John at Runnymede in the year 1215 A.D. It had been preserved in Lincoln Cathedral, and was sent in the *Queen Mary* to New York, in August 1939, for exhibition at the World's Fair, at Flushing Meadows (near New York City). It was there exhibited in the British pavilion and seen by ten million people. After the outbreak of war, it was taken for safekeeping to the Library of Congress, Washington, D.C., and, when the United States entered the war, it was placed with other precious documents in the vaults at Fort Knox, Kentucky.

Now, in 1946, after seven years in the U.S.A., it was to be returned to Lincoln Cathedral. The British Consul-General in New York, Sir Francis Evans, brought it on board, and handed it over to me in a short ceremony in the lounge of the *Queen Elizabeth*, in the presence of a crowd of officials, reporters, and press photographers.

The document was packed in a metal box that was lined with copper and sealed with lead. The Consul General told me that the box had been sealed six days previously, in the Library of Congress, at Washington, D.C. The box measured 26½ inches square by 4½ inches wide on the outside. It had two stout leather straps and a handle for carrying it. The weight of the package was sixty pounds. It was labelled: "On His Britannic Majesty's Service-His Majesty's Principal Secretary of State for Foreign Affairs, &c., &c., &c.,-Foreign Office-London."

I was given a form of receipt to sign for "One Tin Box containing the Magna Carta."

I had no doubt of the contents, but how could I be sure? I had the receipt altered to "One Tin Box alleged to contain the Magna Carta" and signed it in that form. My amendment was only a technicality, but the press reporters seized upon it as a good story. The Magna Carta was literally priceless, uninsurable, irreplaceable, and non-vendible. I said to the reporters, "It's the most precious cargo ever carried in the *Queen Elizabeth*," and then added "

— except the 750,000 troops who have voyaged to and fro in her!" That was also a story.

After signing the receipt, I handed the package to the ship's Master-at-arms and went down below with him and two of his men to the strong-room on D Deck. I held the keys of this room, in which were tiers of steel safes of various sizes, where passengers could place jewellery and other valuables by arrangements made through the Purser. On opening the biggest of the safes, I found to my consternation that the Tin Box was half an inch too big to fit into it!

That being so, I decided that the most secure place in the ship, in which to keep the priceless package, would be in my cabin under the bridge. I had the box taken there, keeping my eye on it all the time, and put it under my bed! The war being over, I was no longer sleeping in the chartroom on the bridge, but in my cabin, to which no one except myself had a door key, and no one had access except my steward, or others by my special invitation.

For four nights on the passage, I slept on Magna Carta-and duly delivered the sealed box safely to the Foreign Office and Lincoln Cathedral officials who met the ship at Southampton. English press reporters somehow got this story and headlined it. — "Commodore Sleeps with Magna Carta under his Bed-First Man in History to do so."

A doubtful distinction, but probably true.

Having got rid of that weight on my mind, I handed over command of the *Queen Elizabeth* for one round voyage to Captain Ford, as I had an engagement on shore.

I had received an invitation from the Senate of the University of Cambridge, asking if I would accept from that University the Honorary Degree of Doctor of Law!

The others to be honoured in that way at the same time were Monsieur Rene Massigli (French Ambassador), Field-Marshal iord Alanbrooke, Field-Marshal Alexander, Air-Marshal Tedder, and Lord Keynes.

I was astonished at this invitation. It would be the first time that a seaman of the Merchant Navy had ever been honoured in that way by any British university. I was well aware that the honour was not for my academic attainments, since I had left school at the age of fourteen, and had written no learned works except Lifeboat Efficiency, a manual of practical instruction, and Ship Ahoy! ("Nautical Notes for Ocean Travellers"). It was the Merchant Navy that was to be honoured through me. For that reason I accepted the honour. It would be a precedent and a reminder to future generations that merchant seamen, rough seadogs as we were supposed to be, played our part in making life secure for those on shore, even for those who lived placidly in academic cloisters, "far from the maddening crowd's ignoble strife."

On the day before the ceremony, my wife and I went up to Cambridge. We were taken in tow hospitably by the Master of Pembroke College, Sir Montague Butler, and Lady Butler. That evening we dined with the Dons and students in Pembroke Hall, in surroundings of Gothic splendour and serenity. I was thinking of my own young days, learning navigation the hard way in a Cape Horn barque, on a diet of "salt horse" and pantiles. These students had it easier than I had, but I did not envy them for that. Next day, at 11.30 a.m., I went to Clare College, to meet the Chancellor, Earl Baldwin (former Prime Minister), Vice-Chancellor Thirkell (Master of Clare College), and the five others who were to receive Honorary Degrees at that day's "Congregation." We proceeded to the Robing Room at the "Old Schools," and there each of the candidates was fitted out with a Doctor's fl.at black cap and black gown with scarlet facings.

A procession was then formed to walk a short distance to the Senate House. Bedells, wearing shiny top hats and carrying silver wands, cleared the way, if it needed clearing, followed by the Chancellor in his robes-then the six fledgeling Honorary Doctors, in pairs, in our scarlet, followed by a long file of Professors and Doctors, and University Officials, all in their academic robes. I felt like a peacock on parade.

Crowds of undergraduates in academical caps and black gowns lined the route. The Senate House was filled with Senior Members of the University and their friends-admission by ticket only. My wife was there, with Lady Butler. Everything was organized to the last detail.

The Chancellor and Vice-Chancellor took their seats centrally on the dais, while the six candidates were seated in front of them, below the dais. Each was to be "presented" individually. The Orator (W. K. C. Guthrie) stood on the dais. A Bedell led the French Ambassador forward, and the Orator began a eulogy of him-in Latin.

This lasted five minutes. When it ended, thunderous applause broke out, as the Chancellor took the new Doctor by the hand, said something to him in Latin, and seated him on the dais.

Then came the turns of the two Field Marshals and of the Air Marshal in succession. Then I stood and listened to the Orator praising me in Latin. He began:

Nautas undique diligunt puellae.
Nautis nescio quid videmus esse
Blandi. Quid valeat genus patescit.

This, I later discovered, means:

Every nice girl loves a sailor.
Every nice girl loves a tar.
For there's something about a sailor-
Well, you know what sailors are!

Not one word of the ceremony was spoken in English; but the Latin texts were printed. The recipients of the. Honorary Degrees were afterwards supplied with a translation into English. The translation of my encomium was as follows:

You know the song, though I confess that it does not lend itself easily to a rendering into Latin. Indeed, it is particularly difficult to sing a sailor's praises in that language, for the ancients — though hope of gain or the fear of their enemies might lure them into ships — had no love of the sea. They would have been quite incapable of understanding that "sea fever" of which our Poet-Laureate loves to write; their epithets for sailors are "timid" and "fearful," but we, on the contrary, think of sailors as "jolly" and we say that "sailors don't care"; and we are right, for that is in fact the character of British seamen.

These men (and it is now my privilege to present one of the foremost of them to you) do not look for their protection to "triple bronze," as Horace suggested, but rather to a heart that, whatever dangers it may have to face, knows how to joke and be merry.

Let us, then, after honouring the luminaries of the military firmament, give a hearty welcome to the man to whose un- wearied courage and outstanding skill the generals themselves owe the successful issue of their plans. We have praised our armies spread over the globe from Burma to the Atlantic, from Iceland's snows to the heat of Africa. We have extolled the courage of the soldiers, the wisdom of their leaders, the trained discipline of the Navy which was a broom to sweep the seas of our enemies. But what could Military, or even Naval skill have availed without the heroes of the Merchant Navy, always on the spot, always ready to transport, wherever the necessities of the conflict might demand, men, vehicles, guns, supplies-all the infinite apparatus of modern war?

Most of these men have neither sought nor obtained great glory. But we ourselves are their monument; for, had they not been willing to risk their lives daily in the cause of liberty, we should assuredly not be sitting here in safety and comfort.

All honour, then, to our friend. He has served forty-six years at sea, commanded a warship in the previous war, and in this one has been Master of our greatest merchant vessels, in which he has carried countless thousands of our brave men safe and sound across the oceans. Several times our leader Churchill himself, with whose safety our fortunes were bound up, entrusted himself to his care.

Now, as Captain of the ship which bears the name of our *Queen Elizabeth*, he has begun to put his talents at the service of peace, bringing to our shores the delegates of a number of American countries to the First Assembly of the United Nations.

So, I ask your applause for a prince of navigators and a scorner of danger, be it from storm or foe.

As the concluding phrases of this, to me, almost meaningless encomium rang out — *Plausui vestro commendo navigatorum prin- cipem, tempestatum hostium irrisorem* — I was beckoned onto the dais, welcomed there by the Chancellor, and I had become a Doctor of Law, duly signed, sealed, and delivered, Honoris Causa.

I may add that I have never been a "scorner of danger." Like all other seamen, I have a profound respect for danger and avoid it as much as possible.

Lord Keynes followed-as a Doctor of Science-praised by the Orator, not only as an economist, but also as a patron of the theatre and ballet.

Then the procession was reformed and returned to the Robing Room. From there we went to Clare College, where a scrumptious lunch was served in the Great Hall.

My wife and I caught the 5. p.m. train to London, after a day that was so different from any other that I had ever experienced or expected, that at times since I have wondered if it was all a dream.

Voyage 65	South Hampton - New York City			
(Canadian Troops 12,114, Crew 879. Total 13,093 souls)				
Location	Status	Date	Miles	Km
South Hampton	depart	15-Feb-46		
New York City	arrive	20-Feb-46	3,140	5,053
Ship: R.M.S. *Queen Elizabeth*		TOTAL	3,140	5,053

Voyage 66	New York City - South Hampton			
(Passengers 1,709, crew 814. Total 2,523 souls),				
Location	Status	Date	Miles	Km
New York City	depart	28-Feb-46		
Gourock	arrive	6-Mar-46	3,172	5,105
Ship: R.M.S. *Queen Elizabeth*		TOTAL	3,172	5,105

That was the last voyage of the *Queen Elizabeth* under wartime conditions, fitted up as a troop transport. She was now to be released from troop-transport service and equipped in the manner originally intended by her designers, as a passenger-and-mail liner, for peacetime service. The conversion would be a work of many months. The *Queen Mary* was to make a few more westbound crossings with troops, then she too was to be converted to peacetime service.

In nearly nine months, since "V.E." Day, from 15th June 1945, to 6th March, 1946, I had made sixteen crossings of the Atlantic- two in the *Queen Mary* and fourteen in the *Queen Elizabeth*. On the eight westbound crossings I had transported a total of 59,829 United States troops and 49,000 Canadian troops for repatriation; and on the eastbound crossings a total of 10,097 other passengers; and had steamed a total of 49,474 miles.

Adding these to the statistics of my previous voyages under belligerent conditions in the *Franconia, Queen Mary* and *Queen Elizabeth*, I reckoned that these three vessels, in transport service under my command, had steamed a total of 424,563 miles, and had carried a total of 447,777 brigaded troops, and 83,432 other military and wartime passengers, to and from the various theatres of war, making a final total of 531,209 who had voyaged under wartime conditions with me, without counting the crews and Permanent Staffs.

Other Cunard Captains-Townley, Irving, Illingworth, Fall, and Ford-had commanded the Queens on many wartime voyages. In total, the two "grey giantesses" had transported approximately one and a half million troops during the war and the subsequent shuttle-service of repatriation.

Not only those other Captains, but all the members of the crews of the two Queens, had applied their skills and had shared in the hazards and hard work of an achievement that was now generally recognized as stupendous and unprecedented, and probably never likely to be repeated.

As I had commanded the Queens on sixty-six voyages under wartime conditions, and held the rank of Commodore, I had come under the notice of those who wished to recognize the work of the Merchant Navy with the award of public honours; but at no time, then or since, have I felt that I had earned those honours unaided. Far from it!

I had been brought up as a boy never to have an exaggerated opinion of myself; to take successes or reverses as they come, as all in the day's work. From that point of view I considered that my war service, like that of millions of others, had been done in the way of duty. I had accepted responsibilities that were placed upon me, because I had been trained in years of service in subordinate positions, and I was therefore qualified to accept the bigger responsibilities when they came my way.

Good health, good digestion, and a cheerful spirit had seen me through; a good wife and a home to go to; good shipmates on board; tolerant and thoughtful employers, generous in their appreciation of efforts: and great ships, yes, great ships that had answered every call that had been made on them, "scorners of danger, be it from storm or foe."

44

*The "Queen Elizabeth" Fitted out for Peacetime Service — A
Fire Breaks Out on Board — Serious Danger — Lifeboats for the
Fire Brigade — She Returns to the Clyde for Refitting — A Huge
Operation-Reborn in Her True Colours — Work Completed at
Southampton — The "Wonder" Ship-Winning the Peace — The
Vision of Sir Percy Bates — Gala Trials over the Measured Miles —
Her Majesty the Queen Takes the Wheel-A Royal Party in a Royal
Ship — The Men Who Built Her and Refitted Her — Preparations
For Her Maiden Voyage of Peacetime.*

THE work of reconditioning the *Queen Elizabeth* for her peacetime service, and of repairing the wear and tear of six years of war service, was one of the biggest operations of its kind ever attempted. She had never undergone the "speed trials" and other tests usual before a ship is handed over by her builders to her owners. Her voyage from the Clyde to New York, in March 1940, had not been a "maiden voyage," but the movement of an uncompleted vessel from one berth to another!

At Singapore and at Sydney, she had been gutted of most of the peacetime equipment that had been fitted into her, and equipped with the rough-and-ready fittings of a troop transport; but, because she had never been completed by her builders, John Brown & Co. Ltd, of Clydebank — even though she had steamed 600,000 miles and had carried 750,000 troops and others in six years — she was a "hull without a soul."

Now she was to be fitted, furnished, and furbished in all her glory, according to the original specifications, with some additions. She was to be overhauled and reconditioned from stem to stern, and from truck to keelson, cleaned and painted all over, inside and out, in her true colours, and got ready to take her trials and make her maiden voyage!

When she docked at Berth 101, Southampton, on 6th March 1946, she was laid up, and half her crew were paid off, to take a long holiday on shore, or to join other vessels. A nucleus crew of between 300 and 400 were retained, for maintenance of the ship in port, and to move her, as would be required, from Southampton to the Clyde, where most of the refitting was to be done. I remained in command of her, and lived on board, during these operations. It was not feasible to put her into dry dock at Brown's shipyards on the Clyde, because of the difficulties of navigating her immense bulk up the narrow, winding, and comparatively shallow stream. As much work as possible would therefore have to be done while she would lie at anchor at the Tail of the Bank, near the mouth of the Clyde, and the completion in dry dock at Southampton.

Two days after her arrival at Southampton from New York, as she lay alongside the quay on 8th March 1946, while the Heads and technicians were beginning their systematic survey of her condition and needs, I had one of the biggest frights of my life.

Just as I was finishing breakfast in my cabin, at 8.50 a.m., the fire-alarm sounded!

I hurried to the bridge and saw that the seat of the fire was in a compartment on the promenade deck, on the port side, abaft and below the bridge. This compartment had been set aside as a temporary "isolation hospital" for sufferers from contagious diseases, such as mumps, diphtheria, and the like. It had not been used for that purpose for some time, but was a storeroom for drugs, bandages, and other medical equipment, which included ether, methylated spirits, and other highly inflammable material.

Apparently, a bottle of medical alcohol or some other spirit had broken, and filled the closed compartment with fumes. A workman from on shore had entered this compartment, contrary to rules, to enjoy a cigarette, and had set the ship on fire!

This happened to be the only enclosed place in the whole ship that had not been fitted with automatic sprinklers. The fire spread rapidly as the woodwork, bedding, and medical stores caught alight, with dense white smoke.

Under routine when the ship was in port, her fire-brigade had a watchman always on duty in the fire-station, but some of the men of the brigade had been paid off, and others were on shore with short leave. Before the ship's ventilating fans could be stopped, they had drawn smoke down below from the inlets on deck near the seat of the fire. This smoke was dense on every deck. The exposed position of the seat of the fire made it impossible to seal it off with fireproof bulkheads such as were installed on all the lower decks. I ran to the seat of the fire, and found several stewards and other members of the crew playing hoses on the flames, but the thick smoke and chemical fumes were keeping them too far away to be of much use.

Was this to be the end of my nautical career-the biggest ship in the world, under my command, to be destroyed by fire while she lay, after all the risks of wartime, peacefully in port? At such times one thinks quickly.

The Southampton Fire Brigade arrived alongside in a few minutes, but they were hampered by the great height of the promen-ade deck above the dockside. I gave orders for several of the ship's lifeboats to be lowered down to the wharf. This was done without a moment's delay. The firemen got into them, with their shore hoses. They were then hoisted up to the level of the seat of the fire, and directed jets of water, from their stance in the boats, through portholes in the side of the hospital-probably the only time that such a thing had been done.

Other firemen, from the ship and the shore, played hoses in the first-class compartments adjoining the seat of the fire and on the deck below it. The fire was a stubborn one, but after three hours of hard work and anxiety, it was got under control and put out. By that time, apart from direct damage by fire and water, the heat had warped several massive steel beams supporting the boat- deck, above the seat of the fire, and had pushed the deck up with them into a huge blister.

After all her war perils, that was the nearest that the *Queen Elizabeth* had come to being destroyed.

She lay at Southampton for three weeks, and then I took her to the Clyde, and anchored her at Gourock on 31st March.

Her renovations began. I lived on board, with a sufficient crew of seamen and engineers to cope with any nautical emergency that might arise, such as a gale causing her to drag her anchors, and also to be available for the many conferences that were necessary on the details of refitting her.

For two and a half months she lay there, while Brown's technicians, craftsmen, and other workmen swarmed all over her, with a continuous service of tenders from and to the shore, giving her the greatest "spring-cleaning" that has ever been attempted in any ship at anchor. Two thousand of "Brown's people" were engaged in this work. The transformation of her appearance, both outside and inside, was wonderful to behold.

The heavy degaussing cables fitted around the hull were taken away. Hundreds of painters were put overside in stages, to chip off her grey wartime paint, down to the waterline. They then applied a coat of anti-corrosive paint, and, after that, painted her for the first time in the Cunard colours — black hull, white superstructure, and red funnels with black top and two thin black rings. The smell of paint was everywhere, and no wonder, since thirty tons of it were used on the exterior alone.

Down below, engineers were overhauling, and, where necessary, replacing working parts of her propulsion machinery; electricians examined, tested, and repaired her 4000 miles of wiring and all the electrical installations, including lighting, heating, power-motors of many uses, her intercommunication system, cargo and baggage winches, and kitchen equipment; plumbers examined and repaired her plumbing; carpenters, joiners, furnishers, and interior decorators carried on with the work of fitting her out, from where it had been interrupted six years previously. With this grand renovation she was at last becoming herself and being almost reborn.

Throughout this period, I had the help of Staff Captain John Wood, who remained on board with me. A heavy burden was borne by Chief Engineer J. Swanson, who had served on many wartime voyages in both the Queens, and had been awarded the C.B.E., in recognition of those services. He was assisted during the renovations by Staff Chief Engineer W. Harding. They were the men who knew the "innards" of the ship better than anyone else, and they were in almost daily consultations with Brown's people on the work in progress.

Sir Percy Bates, Chairman of Cunard White Star Limited, came up from Liverpool to see how the work was progressing. He was well content to see his vision at last materializing, as the world's biggest and proudest ship put on her finery, after being a drab for so long. "You'll command her on her maiden voyage," he told me, and added, wistfully, "I hope to be with you on that passage!"

Early in June, most of the heavy work to be done on her at the Clyde was completed. I would have to take her to Southampton to be dry docked for bottom-painting and overhaul of rudder and propellers. There, too, her interior decorations and furnishings would be completed, making use, as much as possible, of the fitments brought from storage at Singapore and Sydney.

On 15th June, we put to sea from Gourock, and next day berthed at Southampton. I moved her into dry dock and then went for a month's holiday to Cheltenham. On 15th July, I glumly celebrated my 63rd birthday- I had reached the retiring age!

However, as I was in good health and fine fettle, the Directors of Cunard White Star had decided to stretch a point, and to retain my services a little longer, so that I could command the *Queen Elizabeth* on her maiden voyage, and until she "settled in" to her work as a passenger-liner.

On 6th August (1946), I returned on board and continued in command of that beautiful big ship during the final stages of her fitting-up and furbishing. As the work neared completion, an atmosphere of excitement was developing, not only at Southampton, but far and wide, in shipping circles and among the general public, as reports of her wonders spread.

The *Queen Mary* was at this time maintaining, in conjunction with the Aquitania and the second *Mauretania*, the schedule of a regular weekly passenger-and-mail service between Southampton and New York, but all these three were still in their wartime garb and fittings, only slightly modified, as were also the *Franconia*, the *Britannic*, the *Ascania* and the other survivors of the war, owned by Cunard White Star and other lines.

The *Queen Elizabeth* was the first big British ship to be reconditioned, and the decision to do that quickly had been a demonstration to the world in general, and to the British people in particular, that

Britain was not sitting down to mourn in the ashes of post-war desolation, but was determined to rise again, in a great effort of post-war reconstruction. It was for this reason that the *Queen Elizabeth* was now acclaimed in her new and bright garb as a "wonder ship" and a symbol of British determination to "win the peace."

There, at Southampton — one of the heaviest bombed of British cities, where weeds grew lush in "bombed lots" amid the rubble — she lay at the quay in glory, a promise of the better days soon to come. Over seven thousand applications had been received to book passages in her for her maiden voyage. Some of these had been on the books since she was launched and named in September 1938. Many applicants would have to be disappointed. Her normal passenger capacity now was 790 first-class, 680 cabin-class, and 790 tourist-class: total, 2260. They would have plenty of space per person! The huge public rooms which, during the war, had been crowded with Standee beds, were now opulently fitted out as drawing-rooms, lounges, writing rooms, smoking-rooms, restaurants, cinemas, swimming pools, gymnasiums, wintergardens, cocktail bars, lobbies, a library, shops, and a children's play-room-all superbly panelled, decorated, fitted and furnished. She. had everything. She was a "floating city."

In August and September, press photographers and reporters, from the popular and technical papers and magazines, both British and foreign, came on board, and wide publicity was given to her impending trials and maiden voyage.

On 6th September, Sir Percy Bates visited the ship and stayed on board overnight. He now told me that arrangements were being made for a visit by

Her Majesty *Queen Elizabeth* (wife of King George VI), to the ship which was named for her. The Queen would come on board for the official trial runs, to be held in Loch Fyne on the Firth of Clyde, over the "measured mile," on 8th October. After that, the ship would make her maiden voyage, from Southampton to New York, leaving Southampton on 16th October. "We do not expect you to attempt to make speed records," he said, "either on the trials or on the maiden voyage. The *Queen Mary* still holds the Blue Riband with her eastbound crossing in 1938 at 31.69 knots, and that is quite good enough! We shall be satisfied with crossings in four and a half days, more or less, according to the weather, at average speeds of from 27 to 29 knots, without driving the ships at their utmost speeds. The original idea in building these vessels," he explained further, "was to establish a weekly service from both sides of the Atlantic with the two ships only, each taking a fortnight for the round voyage, that is, five days on the passage each way, and two days in port at each end. That may take some time to organize, as the *Queen Mary* has yet to be refitted, but it will come eventually, and for that purpose an average of 28 knots will be enough!"

Apart from the fact that these were orders from the owners, I agreed completely with the reasoning. I knew well enough that each of the Queens was capable of speeds of up to 33 knots, as I had driven them at that speed in short bursts on occasions during wartime when danger was near or thought to be near; but no sensible man drives a ship or a wheeled vehicle at the utmost speed of which it is mechanically capable, except in emergency. Full speed means "comfortable full speed," without undue vibration or strain, at sea as on land.

On 5th October, the refitting of the *Queen Elizabeth* was completed to its last detail, and she was ready for her trials in the Firth of Clyde. I took her out of Southampton early next morning for calibration of the direction-finding gear and compass adjustment off the "Nab" — a light-tower marking the eastern approaches to the Solent-and then I took her on to the Clyde.

In the Firth of Clyde, where we arrived early in the morning of 7th October, I made two unofficial runs over the "measured mile" in Loch Fyne (actually a measured two miles marked by posts on shore), and satisfied myself that she could do thirty knots without straining. (Loch Fyne is an "arm" of the Firth of Clyde.)

I then took her into the river, and let go the anchor off Gourock at 11 a.m. Her return to that "hole" that had been so familiar to her in wartime was a triumph. All was now in readiness for the official trials next day.

A large party of V.1.Ps came on board and spent the night. They included nine directors of the Cunard White Star Line-Sir Percy Bates (Chairman), and Lady Bates; Sir Thomas Brocklebank, Deputy Chairman; Lord Royden;

Mr F. A. Bates, and Mrs Bates; Mr S. J. Lister; Mr A. B. Cauty; Mr R. Crail (General Manager) and Mrs Crail; Mr F. Charlton, and Mrs Charlton; Mr W. Donald, and Mrs Donald.

Their guests included the Rt Hon. Alfred Barnes, Minister of Transport, and Mrs Barnes; Lord Aberconway, Chairman of John Brown Ltd., and Lady Aberconway; Vice-Admiral Hamilton, Flag Officer at Rosyth, and Miss Hamilton.

Senior officials of the Cunard White Star Line were also on board, including Messrs P. Furness, Assistant Manager; H. J. Flewitt, Secretary; B. H. Russell, London Manager; G. M. Paterson, Naval Architect; J. Austin, Superintendent Engineer; Captain B. H. Davies, Chief Marine Superintendent, and others who had contributed, in their various fields, of work and worry, to the triumphant occasion.

There were many "Ahs" and "Ohs" of delight as the visitors toured the "wonder ship" and found her beyond their expectations. Next day dawned fair. Sir Percy Bates went ashore by tender to welcome the Royal Party, who arrived by railroad at Greenock Pier at 10.30 a.m. There they embarked in the small Clyde steamer, which was whimsically named the *Queen Mary II*, and were brought out to the *Queen Elizabeth*.

The Royal Party consisted of *Queen Elizabeth* and her two teenage daughters, H.R.H. Princess Elizabeth and H.R.H. Princess Margaret Rose, accompanied by their Ladies-in-Waiting, and personal attendants. Everything had been organized to the last detail and went like clockwork.

The Royal Party came on board the ship precisely at 11.0 a.m., by a gangway to the first-class entrance on the main deck. The Queen's Standard was then broken at the mainmast head. As planned, I was waiting at the head of the gangway with the Senior Officers-Staff Captain Wood; Chief Engineer Swanson; Staff Chief Engineer Harding; Surgeon Maguire; Purser Carine; Chief Steward Jones; and Chief Radio Officer Farman.

Sir Percy Bates presented me to the Queen, and I then presented the Senior Officers to her. The party then went up in the elevators to the promenade deck, where I excused myself and proceeded to the bridge to weigh anchor.

The ship was under way and turning at 11.15 a.m. In the mean- time the Directors and the other high officials on board, and their wives, were presented to the Queen by Sir Percy Bates, in the lounge. The Royal Party then, escorted by some of the Directors and Staff Captain Wood, went on a tour of inspection of the ship. A large party of newspaper reporters and press photographers were also on board.

Lunch was served at 1.00 p.m. I remained on the bridge, while the ship was proceeding quietly at 20 knots, to the starting point of the "measured miles."

The Queen and the Princesses came up to the bridge at 2.50 p.m., as the ship was turning into position for the first (northward) run over the measured miles. I explained to them that we were not out to establish a speed record, but only to ascertain what speed would be developed with the engines working at 175,000 h.p.

The young Princesses had stopwatches. The ship on her north- ward run covered the first measured mile in 2 min. 1.3 sec., at a speed of 29.71 knots, and the second mile in 2 min. I sec., at 29.75 knots.

The sun was shining brilliantly as she turned in a wide circle at speed, and bore up for the southward run over the measured miles. *Queen Elizabeth* then took the wheel of the *Queen Elizabeth,* and, with some advice from myself, kept the ship on course. The first mile was covered in 2 minutes precisely, at 30 knots, and the second mile at the same speed. The Queen then handed over the wheel to the quartermaster and was obviously highly pleased with an experience which was unique in nautical history.

The Royal Party remained on the bridge for forty minutes, and went below at 3.30 p.m. for a further inspection of the ship, until tea was served at 4.30 p.m. In the meantime speed had been reduced, and the ship was on course to return to the anchorage at Gourock. The anchor was let go there at 5.00 p.m. Two tenders ranged along- side to take off the Royal Party and other visitors, while I stood at the head of the gangway to bid them farewell. They were all away by 5.30 p.m., and a memorable day had ended without the slightest hitch in any of the arrangements.

Next day, 400 guests were embarked for the short run to Southampton. There had been immense publicity in the press and on the radio for the Queen's visit to her name-ship.

As we steamed southwards in the Irish Sea, a British submarine surfaced half a mile abeam and signalled, "What a beautiful target!" I replied, "I have been thinking that too, ever since I sighted you!" A few miles farther on, we passed a coastal steamer, a collier of some 2000 tons, plugging along at all of six knots. Her Master hoisted the flag-signal, "What ship is that?"

I made my numbers, as required by law, and hoisted the *Queen Elizabeth*'s recognition flags GBSS.

Our passengers were enjoying themselves, celebrating the completion of a great work with sustained cordiality in the bar. Sir Percy Bates was delighted with the ship's behaviour, and in his quiet and distinguished way enjoyed this triumph of so many years of hopes and plans. He was looking forward keenly to being on board during her maiden voyage to New York.

We docked at Southampton at 11 p.m. on 10th October. The passengers from the Clyde were safely landed, except one man, who was too ill to be moved from his cabin. I asked Surgeon Maguire to examine him. He reported, "He'll be all right tomorrow. He's suffering from blood in his alcohol stream!"

Next day, a party of Members of Parliament-including the Lord Chancellor, the Speaker of the House of Commons, and the witty author, Sir A. P. Herbert-came on board to inspect the ship and were entertained at lunch by Sir Percy Bates and myself. With them came yet another party of pressmen.

By this time the press publicity for the maiden voyage of the *Queen Elizabeth* was intense on both sides of the Atlantic, reflecting a genuine public interest in this spectacular demonstration of Britain's determination to win the victories of peace, and to turn the energies of wartime into the tasks of post-war rebuilding. Here was visible proof that Britain would rise again, and quickly! The great ship had become a symbol of the renewal of hope.

One writer among the many enthusiasts described her in glowing words as "gleaming like a yacht, vast like a city, towering over the dockside in her enormous grace.... Where once she was grey and secret, now she is carnival with lights. Where once she was stark and stripped, now she is gay and opulent with the warm extravagance of luxury.... She is the ultimate in liners, the greatest ship in the world!"

45

"Maiden Voyage" of the "Queen Elizabeth" — Death of Sir Percy
Bates — Festivity and Sadness — Bolsheviks on Board — A
Memorial Service in Mid-ocean — "Post-war Reconstruction" —
Peace and Goodwill at Last — Inauguration of the Weekly Schedule
of the "Queen" Liners — A Duke and Duchess Cross the Atlantic —
Tact and Publicity — A Christening at Sea — My Last Voyage in
Command — "Time to Leave Her" — My Career From the
Half-deck to the Bridge — Looking Ahead

THEN came the day, Wednesday, 16th October, 1946, when the
Queen Elizabeth was to put to sea from Southampton on her
maiden voyage.
A poem was written by Sir A. P. Herbert for the occasion.

BON VOYAGE
At last, young giant, infant of the fleet,
Your medals on, you sail down Civvy Street:
And may you serve the peaceful folk you bring
As well, as nobly, as you served the King!
Here come your passengers; but who will check
The ghosts of soldiers crowding on your deck?

The civilian passengers came on board, a total of 2288 of them, who had
been lucky enough to have their bookings confirmed — her fullest carrying
capacity, now. They arrived from London in four boat trains.

Among them, as a well-kept secret, were the Soviet Russian leaders, Molotov and Vyshinsky, with a party of twelve tough-looking guards, secretaries and interpreters, bound for a United Nations meeting in New York! They were accommodated in a first-class suite on B Deck. A large force of British police and detectives escorted them on board and patrolled and cordoned the ship. The ship's Master-at-Arms and his staff also took precautions for the safety of the Russian party throughout the voyage.

Many celebrated people were among the passengers, and there was the feeling of a great occasion. The ship was dressed with flags from early morning, but in mid-morning sad news came through- Sir Percy Bates had died during the preceding night. His brother, Fred Bates, who was to succeed him as Chairman of the Cunard White Star Line, sent me a message, requesting that the flag of the *Queen Elizabeth* should not be lowered to half-mast. I realized that Sir Percy would have wished it that way. Nothing should mar the festivity of the departure of the liner; but I decided to pay a tribute to the memory of Sir Percy after we had put to sea.

At 2 p.m., we cast off moorings, and proceeded down harbour, with great "to-do," as tens of thousands of people lined the shores to cheer and wave, and every ship, big and small, in Southampton Water and the Solent, sounded its steam-whistle in farewell blasts, to which we responded again and again with our basso profundo resonance.

The Nab Tower was abeam at 4.24 p.m. There the pilot left us. The ships were not calling at Cherbourg, so I set course from the Nab to Ambrose Channel Light Vessel, by the regular Winter Track, a distance of 3143 miles, gave the order "Off stations," and rang the engines to full ahead. Chief Engineer Swanson had conferred with me, and we had decided to keep the speed to an average of 28 knots, weather permitting.

Among the passengers, in addition to the grim-looking Russians, were Jan Masaryk, Foreign Minister of Czechoslovakia; U.S. Senator Connolly; two famous humourists — A. P. Herbert of Punch and Ludwig Bemelmans of The New Yorker; Mrs Helena Rubinstein, the "Beauty Queen"; and many leaders of business and "society" on both sides of the Atlantic.

Yes, we had got back to normal. As before the war, so now again the great Cunarders would carry "everybody who was anybody" across the Atlantic. The *Queen Elizabeth* was booked up for months ahead on crossings both ways. Her maiden voyage would be the first of two thousand, perhaps more, crossings of the Atlantic that she would make before her time came to retire. In her useful life- time, she would earn a total of perhaps 300 million pounds in fares, to set off against her heavy capital cost and working expenses in service-and that was "big business" in the spirit of the modern Merchant Adventurers who had built her.

Before nightfall, we were well out to sea, doing 28 knots in fine weather. The passengers were astounded at the luxury of the meals served. All kinds of food, drink, cigarettes — and nothing rationed — after years of austerity! These things had been brought over from New York in the Aquitania specially for the *Queen Elizabeth*'s maiden voyage.

I sent an invitation to the two leaders of the Russian Party to come to my cabin. They accepted, and arrived in a procession, in single file. Ahead strode a huge military officer in uniform, with a revolver in holster on his hip. Behind him walked Molotov, then Vyshinsky, then two more guards, and an interpreter brought up the rear. The guards remained outside my cabin, but the interpreter entered, while greetings were exchanged, and then left. The occasion was only sociable, and my two terribly famous or notorious guests spoke or understood enough English to get along.

I asked Molotov, "Will you have some vodka?"

He exercised his veto, and replied ·with his famous "No." "Whiskey?" I asked.

"Da! Da! (Yes, Yes). Veesky! Veesky very good!"

Vyshinsky was of the same opinion. We charged our glasses and drank health's and to the good ship *Queen Elizabeth*. Then I invited them onto the bridge. They brought their guards and the interpreter with them and were keenly interested in the equipment and methods of navigation. After a while Molotov indicated that he would like to take the wheel!

I had a look around the North Atlantic, and agreed to let him steer for a few minutes. He did so without mishap. An American newspaper man on board heard of this, and radioed to his paper, "Molotov took the wheel, but veered to the Left!"

After the party had returned to their suite, my cabin steward asked me, "What did you think of them, sir?"

"Quite jolly and pleasant fellows!" I said.

"Don't you believe it, sir," said the steward, earnestly. "That there Vyshinsky bloke has murdered thousands!"

In mid-ocean I lowered the flag to half-mast and held a memorial service in the lounge for Sir Percy Bates. This was attended by officers and men from all the departments in the ship, and by as many of the passengers as wished to attend. After the Lord's Prayer, I read a short, prepared address:

Shipmates and fellow voyagers, we are gathered to pay our respects to the memory of Sir Percy Bates, late Chairman of the Cunard White Star Line, who died early in the morning of our departure from Southampton.

Sir Percy Bates was mainly responsible for the building of these two great vessels, *Queen Mary* and *Queen Elizabeth*. He watched them grow, from masses of steel girders and plates, into the magnificent structures that they are today. They were the children of his brain. He lived for them, he worked for them, he wore himself out with anxieties for them, and he has died for them.

We who knew him, admired him, and loved him, have felt a shock of intense sorrow at his untimely passing-untimely, for he was to have been with us on this maiden voyage, and, like all of us in any way connected with this ship, he had looked forward with high hopes to its accomplishment.

He was a man of great integrity, strong purpose, and, withal, of sympathetic understanding. All of us who have worked with him, or for him, both ashore and afloat, feel that we have lost a firm and valued friend. He loved the sea, he loved the ships, and he loved those who do business in the great waters. Here, in this ship, in mid-ocean, we remember him, with grief in our hearts, and profound sympathy in our thoughts for Lady Bates and his sorrowing family and all the loved ones he has left behind.

He was not only a shipowner and man of business. He loved books and was a man of wide reading and culture.

There is a poem by Tennyson, "Crossing the Bar," well known but not less beautiful for that, which I feel that I may appropriately read to you on this occasion, for it expresses our thoughts, and I believe that the man who has gone from us would have liked this to be done:

> Sunset and evening star,
> And one clear call for me!
> And may there be no moaning of the Bar,
> When I put out to sea,
>
> But such a tide, as, moving, seems asleep,
> Too full for sound and foam,
> When that which drew from out the boundless deep
> Turns again home.
>
> Twilight and evening bell,
> And after that the dark!
> And may there be no sadness of farewell
> When I embark;
>
> For though from out our borne of Time and Place
> The flood may bear me far,
> I hope to see my Pilot face to face
> When I have crossed the bar.

While reading these lines, as clearly and firmly as I was able, as the audience stood silent in the huge lounge of the great ship, so sumptuously furnished, and the ship sped on, I felt such a surge of emotion that I could scarcely read on to the end. The lines on the page from which I was reading became blurred, and a lump rose in my throat, but I continued and finished without faltering, then announced what I knew had been Sir Percy's favourite hymn, "Praise my soul, the King of Heaven," with which the service concluded.

Some years previously, I had heard Tennyson's "Crossing the Bar" recited by the Bishop of Winchester, at the funeral of Captain Sir James Charles; in Netley cemetery, on the shores of Southampton Water. Sir James Charles, under whom I had served as a Junior Officer, had died at sea, when in command of the Aquitania, be- tween Cherbourg and Southampton, homeward bound from New York. He held the rank of Commodore of the Cunard White Star Line and was due to retire at the end of the voyage on which he died. His emotions on making his last voyage in command had been too much for him to bear, and he had died of a broken heart, as his ship was entering port. His death in that way had been profoundly moving to all who knew him. His funeral was attended by hundreds of ships' people and others from Southampton. When the Bishop of Winchester, at the open grave, had read "Crossing the Bar," many of the hardened seamen there were very near to tears.

It was this memory, added to the pathos of Sir Percy Bates's answering the "clear call" to embark into eternity on the very morning of the *Queen Elizabeth's* putting to sea — and my own impending retirement from command — which had caused me almost to break down when I read the requiem verses.

A duty had been done, and a heavy one. I went immediately onto the bridge, cast an eye on the weather, course, and speed, and saw that all was well.

The arrival of the *Queen Elizabeth* at New York, on Monday, 21st October 1946, was another of those big occasions which were crowding in upon me in the last phases of my seafaring career. As on a previous occasion, when I had brought the first American troops home in the *Queen Mary*, so now, again, New York was agog with excitement and curiosity at the arrival of the first great liner from Europe in her peacetime garb of splendour. For years she had been a familiar sight in her grim grey bulk, proceeding up or down harbour with her boats swung out, and her upper decks crowded, and more than crowded, with masses of troops. Now, in America, as in England, she was a symbol of the rebuilding of peace, and of the return of the worried world to the promise of better times. We arrived off Ambrose Channel Light

Vessel at 3.42 a.m., having made the crossing from the Nab Tower, 3143 nautical miles, in 4 days 16 hours, 18 minutes, at an average speed of 27.99 knots, exactly as planned, without driving her too hard.

Pilot Mason was embarked, and we anchored at Quarantine at 5 a.m. for the usual inspections by U.S. Health and Immigration officials. At 7 a.m. we were under way again, proceeding up harbour. As the first beams of wintry sunlight struggled through the morning haze, twelve tugs came out to escort us, while blimps and helicopters with photographers hovered overhead, and two fire- fighting floats of the Port of New York Authority came to meet us, spraying out white plumes of festive foam.

The symphony of steam-whistles blared, the ship was gaily dressed in flags, bands played, and a waiting crowd cheered as we docked at Pier 90 at 8 a.m. Officials and pressmen swarmed on board. Fifty New York Police and Federal officers came to guard the Russian party, who refused to hold a press conference, and hurried off in bullet-proof automobiles. The Mayor of New York, and many other official and semi-official personages came on board, and stayed for lunch, to which the pressmen were also invited.

Our passengers had disembarked. The voyage had been "uneventful." Nothing sensational had happened. The only sensation was in the transformation of the ship herself from a troop carrier to a beautiful, big, safe passenger-liner; and that was a big enough "story." In the following three days, the general public were allowed on board for sightseeing tours. Ten thousand persons paid one dollar each for admission tickets, the proceeds going to seamen's charities.

Among the sightseers were many former G.Is, who had voyaged in the *Queen Elizabeth* in wartime. They hardly knew her now, except for the fact that some of them found their names carved on the teak rails. These names had not been planed off during the renovations, but were varnished, and allowed to stand .as a war memorial.

I was asked to take part in a broadcast show from a studio in the city and agreed to do so. The manager of the studio said, "It will take only a few minutes, and we'll have the script already written out for you." When I arrived, I found that half a dozen other people who were "in the news" had been invited likewise.

We were seated at desks on a stage, in a sort of theatre in which there was an audience of five hundred or more. I studied my script and found that it was chiefly about the teakwood rails and the brave boys who had carved their names on it, and that many of them would never return. Just before the show started, the producer of the show-a large flamboyant man with the energy of a bull moose-came to my desk and said, "How do you feel, Captain? I hope you like your script, because I wrote it myself!"

"I feel fine," I told him. "The script is in places very moving." "O.K., then," the producer said, briskly. "Now, this is what you do. When you come to that bit at the end, about the brave boys who will never come back, but tears into your voice, and we'll give you a musical build-up."

"I'm no actor," I said. "Is there any way that I can get out of this gracefully?"

"Hell, Cap.," he asked, pained, "don't you feel sad about the brave fellas who won't come back?"

"More than you feel, probably," I said, "but I'm not used to musical build-ups, that's all."

"But you're on stage, and surely you won't back out now!" he argued.

"All right, I'll go through with it," I told him.

I was third on the list of performers. The Bull Moose led me to the front of the stage, and told the audience, seen and unseen, what a wonderful man I was, with such exaggeration that for a moment I thought that he was talking about somebody else. Then I went back to my desk to read my script. As I came to the final paragraph about the boys who would never return, the orchestra, with an electric organ and drums, provided a sobbing tremolo accompani-ment that began softly and worked up to a crescendo which nearly drowned out what I was saying.

The act brought thunderous applause, and I bowed myself off stage. In the wings a delectable blonde gave me a dazzling smile and handed me a cheque for 100 dollars "with many thanks from our sponsors!" This hadn't been mentioned previously, and was as much a surprise to me as everything else in the show had been. The ship was in port for only four days and put to sea again a 6 p.m. on the fifth day, with 2444 passengers. They were the first big contingent of dollar-spending tourists to go to Europe after the war had ended. We docked at Southampton at 2 a.m. on Thursday, 31st October, and left again for New York at 8.15 a.m. on the following Wednesday, 6th November.

She had not yet settled into a regular quick turnaround in ports, but now the *Queen Mary* was laid up for refit, and it was intended that the two liners would begin their regular weekly service, one leaving from each side of the ocean every Wednesday, in the Spring of 1947.

I would have retired before then.

It was arranged that I would remain in command of the *Queen Elizabeth* during the winter months and make my last voyage in command early in January.

On my westbound passage, leaving Southampton on 6th Nov- ember, 1946, I had many celebrities on board, but none quite as celebrated as the two who came quietly up the gangway, accompanied by a guard of detectives, at 10 p.m. on the evening before we were due to leave — the Duke and Duchess of Windsor!

I met them at the head of the gangway and accompanied them to their reserved suite. I found them very easy people to talk to- natural and unaffected. The Duchess said to me, "Americans call my husband the DOOK, but they don't call me the DOOKESS!" A steward and stewardess attended them in their suite through- out the voyage. I asked the Duke, "Would you like the ship's police to be stationed on duty outside your suite?"

"No need," he said. "A few days ago thieves broke into our apartment in London and stole most of our jewellery. There isn't much left!"

As I spoke to the ex-King, and the lady for whom he had renounced his kingdom, I saw them as a handsome and happy couple- much better-looking, both of them, then would have been expected from photographs that had been published in some newspapers. They accepted an invitation to my cabin, with a small party of others, and afterwards visited the bridge-but they did not ask to steer the ship!

We were at sea on Sunday, 10th November. As a ship is "the Captain's parish," I held Divine Service in the main lounge at 11 a.m. The Duke and Duchess of Windsor attended. As usual, I conducted a shortened form of the Order of Morning Prayer, as laid down in the Book of Common Prayer of the Church of England.

The service we used at sea always began with "God Save the King," and then followed the order of service, prepared and typed out by the Purser, including three hymns, a Bible reading, prayers, and one of the Psalms. We did not "sing" the Psalm but read it aloud-the Captain reading the first verse, the congregation in unison the second, the Captain the third, and so on.

Usually I conned over the Psalm in my cabin before taking the service, but on this occasion, I was busy with other work, and did not look at the Psalm for that day until it was my turn to begin reading it from the typewritten sheet.

I began: "Psalm 146. Praise the Lord, 0 my soul: while I live I will praise the Lord."

The congregation responded: "Yea, as long as I have any being, I will sing praises unto my God."

I began reading the next verse, with a sudden feeling that some- one present might be offended, but I had to go on with it: "O put not your trust in princes, nor in any child of man: for there is no help in them!"

I glanced at the Duke and Duchess, but they joined in the responses of the next verses as though they hadn't noticed anything. The service being over, I walked out of the lounge and was immediately tackled by some U.S.

press reporters who were on board: "Say, Captain, did you read that Psalm on purpose?"

"NO!" I told them. "It was an absolute coincidence. It is a Psalm that we often read. For heaven's sake don't go and make a song and dance about it. It would be altogether the wrong sort of story to greet the Duke and Duchess on their arrival in America. I would hate to do anything to offend them in the slightest."

To give those newsmen their full due, they refrained from using that story!

The day before we arrived in New York, I had a radio-telephone call from the Cunard office, asking if I could arrange for the Duke and Duchess of Windsor to hold a press conference on board when we arrived. I saw the Duke, who agreed, "It's no use trying to avoid the press!" I made arrangements accordingly for the interview to take place in the ship's cinema, half an hour after we docked.

About seventy pressmen and presswomen were assembled there when I escorted the celebrated pair to the conference. The Duke and Duchess were seated on easy chairs on a small, raised platform, and answered questions freely for twenty minutes. Some of the questions were cheeky and unanswerable, but the man who was born to be King, and trained to be King, and had actually been King and Emperor of the greatest Empire in the world, was imper-turbable, as was also the wife of his choice, and good humour prevailed. At the end, the Duke thanked them for attending.

I escorted the Duke and Duchess to their suite, where they invited me in. The Duke surprised me by saying, "I am sorry to hear that you will soon be retiring from the sea."

"That is true, but it is supposed to be a secret," I said, and explained that, since the death of Commodore Charles on what had been announced as his last voyage, there was a tradition that no publicity should be given to any Cunard Captain's impending retirement. "But it's a secret hard to keep," I added. 'I'm not looking forward to being unemployed!"

"I can sympathize with you," said the Duke. "I know what it feels like to be unemployed!"

He presented me with a pair of gold cufflinks. "We wish you the best of luck, and many happy years of retirement."

A few minutes later, I escorted them to the head of the gangway, and they stepped ashore in America.

I was to make a few more voyages, but not many, before retiring. I was determined not to become miserable, but to accept the inevitable in good heart.

The *Queen Elizabeth* left New York on 14th November 1946 and berthed at Southampton on 19th November. We made a quicker turnaround this time, leaving Southampton again on 22nd Nov- ember, and docked in New York on 27th November.

After a stay of only two days, we left New York on 29th November. This was the quick turnaround aimed at, but it required hustle to accomplish the disembarking and embarking of passengers, unloading and loading cargo and mails, refuelling, watering, and storing the ship, all within forty-eight hours, together with the paperwork of entering the ship and clearing her outwards. It was done, and that was the first time that it was proved that it could be done; From the Company's point of view, this was the precedent which showed that a weekly service could be maintained by the two Queen liners, unaided by a third vessel. From that point of view it was history making.

A writer from the smart weekly, The New Yorker, came on board, at the height of the hustle, and asked to see me. His impressions were only partly flattering to me:

We went to the Captain's cabin, and introduced ourselves to Sir James, whom we found in his shirtsleeves. He has brambly grey eyebrows, out of which we half expected to see birds fly, a paunch as round and tight as a medicine ball, and a pleasant Victorian air.

When we asked if it wasn't something of a letdown to command. the Elizabeth on a peacetime run, he said, "Oh aye, but not too bad. We've no bombs and torpedoes, but we do have the passengers!"

Then he threw back his head and laughed, to show he was only pulling our leg. The Elizabeth was concluding a record forty-three-hour turnaround, which did not give him much time...

On that eastbound passage, when the ship was off Bishop's Rock, at 6.45 p.m. on 3rd December (1946), a baby was born on board, the daughter of Mr and Mrs Foley. Two hours later, at the request of the parents, I christened her Elizabeth Dawn. That was the second time that I had christened a baby in the "Captain's Parish." We docked at Southampton next morning, and Captain Ford relieved me for one month (two round voyages), so that I could have Christmas at home.

Then, on 27th December 1946, I rejoined the *Queen Elizabeth*, for my last voyage in command. We met with heavy weather on the westbound crossing, and docked at New York on 1st January 1947, at noon.

New Year's Day-another year turned over on the calendar!

We were due to leave on 3rd January, but a heavy blanket of fog came down, and we were unable to move out of the dock until 2.30 a.m. on 4th January-fourteen and a half hour late. We would make up the lost time with an extra effort from the engines during the crossing.

It was impossible to keep the secret that this was my last voyage in command. Among the passengers I had John G. Winant, war- time U.S. Ambassador to Britain, now crossing to London to receive the highest decoration that Britain can confer, the Order of Merit. I had also on board some unofficial ambassadors of goodwill- Madeleine Carroll, Myra Hess, and Marlene Dietrich!

On 8th January, at sea, I was asked to attend a gathering of representatives of all the Departments in the ship. On behalf of the crew, Staff Captain Sorrell presented me with an Illuminated Address and Token Gift. He made a short speech, appropriate to the occasion, referring to "the spirit of comradeship and good cheer that has pervaded this vessel, and every other vessel under Commodore Bisset's command."

I replied, attributing that spirit of comradeship to all in the crew. "Whether in the days of war or peace," I said, "I always had the feeling that you were with me. That lightened my burden of responsibility. I could always feel that the crew were my good friends. In saying farewell, I wish each one of the crew God's Speed, and may all your days at sea be as happy as you have made them for me!"

We docked at Southampton at midnight on 8th January. The moorings were made fast. She was to leave again in the afternoon of 10th January, under command of Captain Ford.

That gave me two days to pack all my gear and leave her. My wife came from Cheltenham and helped me with my packing and fare- wells. It was the rule in the Cunard White Star Line, as in other big shipping companies, that the wives of Captains-as of all others in the crew-never voyaged in the ship with their husbands. A sailor's domestic life must be lived on shore.

Those were two busy days, with pressmen and photographers in plenty, and a continual stream of crew members calling at my cabin to say farewell in person. Meanwhile, the packing of my gear continued. I discarded several uniform suits, but kept my Number One Uniform and cap-just in case...

I never had occasion to wear them again.

All my gear was put ashore to be consigned by rail to Chelten- ham. My wife left the ship to attend to this. I remained to hand over command formally to Captain Ford, who joined his ship at 2 p.m. on 10th January.

At 3 p.m., in a civilian suit, overcoat, and hat, I walked down the gangway, feeling lonely, and stepped ashore.

I was sixty-three years and six months of age and had been going to sea for forty-eight years and four months, since I signed indentures as an apprentice in sail.

I had served in thirty-seven vessels — a barque, a ship, twenty-five steamers of the Merchant Navy, and ten of the Royal Navy. In my progress from the half-deck of the County of Pembroke to the bridge of the *Queen Elizabeth*, I had seen the development of navigation and seamanship from sail to coal-burning steamers, and then to oil-burning steamers, including the biggest. I had been at sea during two great wars, and in the years of peace.

Now, I was "unemployed at last," but I had no intention of rusting. I intended to look for something to do on shore. I was active in mind and body. I had memories, but I was not looking astern at my life's wake. I was looking ahead and shaping my course to a destination beyond the horizon.

Epilogue

LOOKING back, I feel that I have led an active life, and that I have nothing to regret in my boyhood decision to adopt seafaring as a career. More than one million people have made ocean voyages as my shipmates, and that term includes passengers, in vessels under my command or in which I was serving as a watchkeeping officer. I have had responsibilities for bringing them safely to their destinations, and in all humility, I may say now that I have done so without any serious mishap, as much by good luck as by good judgment, or by a combination of both, especially in wartime.

I have had the opportunity of observing and experiencing the tremendous developments in nautical techniques which occurred throughout the first half of the Twentieth Century, in times of peace, and during two wars at sea of unprecedented ferocity and magnitude. My experiences, in one way and another, have been typical of those of tens of thousands of merchant seamen of my generation. This story of my life has been compiled in detail, not to emphasize the unusual, but rather to put on record the normal routines and disciplines of the mercantile marine, during the period of transition from wind driven vessels to screw driven vessels of the largest size. That half-century was a turning point not only in nautical history, but in the history of civilization. It brought changes, some for the better and some for the worse, not only at sea but on land. Those changes are what my memoirs have described, within the limits of my personal view of them.

When I retired from command at sea in 1947, I did not feel that I was finished with active life at the age of sixty-three. I was taking ashore an accumulated experience so extensive that it was a pity to let it rust; but I knew, too, that younger men in any service can rise only when their seniors retire. There is no easy way to pass on to others a store of practical knowledge. The spoken or printed word may be helpful, to some extent, but the only way of learning how to do anything is to do it. That applies in seafaring as much as, or more than, in other professions, arts, and trades.

My success as a seaman had been due to good health, good fortune, and a cheerful and sociable temperament. The nearest that I can find to an expression of my practical philosophy is in a poem by Thomas Henry Basil Webb, a young military officer (in the Welsh Guards) who was killed in action during the 1914-18 War:

A PRAYER

Give me a good digestion, Lord,
And also something to digest;
But when or how that something comes I leave to Thee,
Who knowest best.

Give me a healthy body, Lord;
Give me the sense to keep it so;
Also a heart that is not bored,
Whatever work I have to do.

Give me a healthy mind, good Lord,
That finds the good that dodges sight,
And, seeing sin, is not appalled,
But seeks a way to put it right.

Give me a point of view, good Lord,
Let me know what it is, and why;
Don't let me worry overmuch
About the thing that's known as "I."

Give me a sense of humour, Lord,
Give me the power to see a joke;
To get some happiness from life
And pass it on to other folk.

After stepping ashore from the *Queen Elizabeth* at Southampton on 10th January 1947, I went with May to our home at Cheltenham, feeling like a duck out of water. A few days later, I went to Liverpool, at the invitation of the Board of Directors of Cunard White Star Limited, for a paying-off ceremony. The Chairman (Fred Bates) and the other directors expressed thanks to me for what they described as my long and faithful services to the Company. They gave me six months leave on full pay, after which I would be retired on a pension.

Further, one of the directors, who was Chairman of the Port Line (a newly formed subsidiary of Cunard, operating cargo and passenger motor vessels of medium size from London and from New York to Australia and New Zealand), offered a trip round the world for my wife and myself as passengers in a Port Line vessel! This would be "busman's holiday" — a long sea voyage for a man who had been nearly fifty years at sea — but to me it was a wonderful prospect: to be voyaging as a passenger with my wife on board, for the first time in my life.

In the meantime, John Gordon, editor of the London Sunday Express, had offered me £1000 for my memoirs to be published in serial form. When I returned to Cheltenham, a representative of that newspaper, Mr Rodin, spent several days interviewing me. The result was published in six instalments in the Sunday Express in August-September 1947.

On 25th September 1947, May and I embarked at London as passengers in the twin-screw Motor Vessel *Port Napier*, 11,879 tons, average speed 14 knots, built by Swan Hunter & Wigham Richardson at Wallsend-on-Tyne. This was her maiden voyage. She was under command of Captain G. Hazlewood and had a general cargo and twenty-four passengers.

Having nothing to do but relax — a passenger at last — while other people had all the worries and responsibilities, I enjoyed that ex-perience greatly. We called at Las Palmas, Durban, Adelaide, and Melbourne, and arrived at Sydney on 24th November 1947, after a passage of 13,100 miles.

Our intention was to have a holiday ashore in Australia for a few months, and then to return to England in another Port Line vessel. After staying for a couple of weeks with my brother, O. D. Bisset, at his home at Warrawee, near Sydney, we moved to the Pacific Hotel at Manly Beach, one of the most beautiful surfing beaches in the world. We found life so free and easy, and the Australians so friendly and good-natured, that we decided we would settle in Australia.

Among the many people we met at Sydney was William Gaston Walkley. He was Managing Director of Australian Motorists Petrol Company Limited (later to be named Ampol Petroleum Ltd.), and he lived near us at Manly. A New Zealander, he had migrated to Sydney and in 1936 had formed the first Australian owned petrol distributing firm. Despite the opposition of pessimists, he had raised the necessary finance to import oil from the U.S.A.

and the Persian Gulf, and to distribute it to dealers under the trade name of "Am- pol." The venture had prospered greatly, and by 1948 "Ampol" had become one of the biggest oil distributing companies in Australia.

"Bill" Walkley and I became good friends. He was interested in the sea and ships. His company had several oil tankers under long term charter and was planning to build its own tanker fleet — an ambition that has since been achieved. One evening "Bill" Walkley surprised me by inviting me to join the "Ampol" organization as Chief Public Relations Officer. This would not be a nine-to-five office job, he explained. I would be expected to give radio talks, and to travel around Australia, giving talks sponsored by "Ampol," to tell of the work of the Merchant Navy and of my service in Cunard ships.

So that would be my new career on shore-a professional Old Salt, spinning yarns! Nothing could be easier. I doubt whether any Ancient Mariner has ever had such audiences organized for him, as he were now to be readymade for me. I had been called "Lucky Bisset" when I was at sea, and now my luck still held good on shore. I accepted the generous offer with alacrity.

My wife remained in Australia, while I returned to England to dispose of our home and effects there. My passage was in the Port Line *M.V. Port Quebec,* a single-screw cargo vessel of 9000 tons, Captain Fuller. As she carried no passengers, it was necessary to sign me on as a member of the crew. I suggested that I should be signed on as cabin-boy, so that I could write my reminiscences under the arresting title of From Commodore to Cabin Boy, but instead I was signed on as a supernumerary engineer, which was fair enough.

After calling at New Zealand ports, we went on through the Panama Canal, and to New York. There I transferred to *R.M.S. Queen Elizabeth* — as a passenger and I received a cordial welcome on board from Commodore Ford and the crew. We docked at Southampton on 6th July 1948, nine days before my 65th birthday.

After disposing of our home at Cheltenham and packing some of our furniture and effects for shipment to Australia, I reembarked at London on 1st September 1948, in the *Port Napier,* and arrived at Sydney on 22nd October 1948, to begin my new career. May and I found a nice little house at Manly Cove and settled in there in January 1949. We fell in love with this place, and its small garden, and its view out through Sydney Heads to the Pacific Ocean, where I j could see the ships going and coming.

Sometimes I "went to sea" again — in a hired skiff for exercise at ,. Manly Cove, or on passages from Manly to Sydney Cove in the ferry steamers, half an hour's run. The ferry masters, knowing me, usually invited me to the bridge, and even asked me if I'd like to take a trick at the wheel. I had also learned to drive a motor car, and how to make it go ahead or astern, to port or starboard.

In November 1948, I was notified that I had been awarded the decoration of Commander of the Legion of Merit (U.S.A.). The citation was as follows:

Commodore Sir James G. P. Bisset, Royal Naval Reserve, Retired, performed exceptionally meritorious services as Master of *H.M.T. Queen Elizabeth* and *H.M.T. Queen Mary* from February 1942 to December 1945. He contributed immeasurably to the successful prosecution of World War II by the United States, in transporting under hazardous conditions nearly one half million American troops to and from the theatres of war. Commodore Bisset's navigating skill, his tireless energy and unflagging devotion to duty over long periods of time made possible the safe and swift transportation of unprecedented concentrations of human lives at sea.

(Signed) HARRY TRUMAN,
President of the United States of America.

My work as a professional spinner of Old Salt's yarns began in earnest with a series of broadcasts from a Sydney radio station, followed by tours to all parts of Australia, arranged chiefly by the proficient and genial General Manager of "Ampol," W. M. Leonardo. On the average I gave four talks a week, and travelled many thousands of miles by road, sea, and air, convivially meeting thousands of people, many of whom were ex-servicemen who had voyaged with me in the *Franconia* or the Queens during the war. "Do you remember ... ?" they'd ask, and of course I remembered.

According to a log which I kept, in ten years, 1949-59, I gave 1828 talks to audiences in Australia, and certainly more than 200,000 people heard and saw me in person at these talks, which were given at meetings of Returned Servicemen's Clubs, Rotary Clubs, and other social clubs and societies of many kinds, Including church social clubs. On several occasions I distributed prizes at Speech Days at High Schools. Further, I was honoured by 44 Civic Receptions in Australian cities and towns. In most cases this was done at the instigation of local ex-servicemen, as their way of showing appreciation of the merchant navy's work in wartime.

Among posts of honour accorded to me in Sydney were those of President of the Shiplovers' Society, President of the English Speaking Union, and Councillor of the Royal Empire Society. I also be- came Chairman of Directors of a company, Fire Fighting Equipment Ltd. I was made an honorary member of the Royal Sydney Yacht Squadron, the Royal Motor Yacht Club, the Millions Club, and the League of Ancient Mariners.

So my life in Australia was filled with interest, and the years went by happily, in intense activity.

Early in 1957, when I was seventy-three years of age, my friend Harold Woodward, a member of the Shiplovers' Society at Sydney, suggested that I should make an arrangement with an experienced Australian literary man, P. R. Stephensen, to collaborate with me in compiling my memoirs for publication in book form. Harold Wood- ward, a native of Liverpool, had voyaged with me in the Franconia from the Clyde to Suez in 1941, when he was in the Australian Army. He was a veteran of the siege of Tobruk, and a collector of sea books, having more than 2000 volumes of nautical interest in his library.

I knew of P. R. Stephensen, as literary collaborator with Captain W. H. S. Jones, of Melbourne, in one of the finest books of sailing ship life ever written, The Cape Horn Breed, published in 1956. Harold Woodward introduced us, and for three years thereafter P.R. Stephensen and I worked in close and happy collaboration at our literary task. I had kept full diaries and had a vast mass of documentary material. It was P.R.S. who arranged this material in chronological order and insisted that the routine details of sea-life are more important for the purposes of historical record than "sensational" or exceptional incidents in a seaman's life. I was guided by his advice that my story should be told in three volumes, entitled Sail Ho! (published 1958), Tramps and Ladies (1959), and the present volume (1961). The cover designs of these volumes are by John Allcot, the famous marine artist, of Sydney, a Cape Horn sailor and Liverpool man, like myself.

In March 1960, the manuscript being completed, May and I returned to England as passengers in the S.S. Ixion. As I read these proofs in March 1961, I am expecting publication of this final volume in time for my 78th birthday, 15th July, 1961. Whether my life story sinks or swims, I send it on its way with the Sailor's Farewell, three long blasts, and to my readers I wish Bon Voyage and good digestion — and something to digest.

Second Edition Endnotes

Bisset remains the most decorated of Cunard Commodores. Bisset died on 28 March 1967, aged 83 years, and was interred at Bournemouth, UK.

In 1998 the Cunard Line was sold to Carnival Corporation.